Prescient Visions

Prescient Visions

*/ˈpreSH(ē)ənt/ having
or showing knowledge of events
before they take place*

Eric Pepin

Higher Balance Publishing
Santa Rosa, California

This book has been transcribed and compiled
from live lectures given by Eric Pepin.
Some elements of the live format have been preserved.

Published by Higher Balance Institute,
5213 El Mercado Pkwy, Ste. C,
Santa Rosa, CA 95403
www.higherbalance.com

ISBN: 978-1-939410-17-7

Library of Congress Control Number: 2015953950
Prescient Visions: /'preSH(ē)ənt/ Having or Showing
Knowledge of Events Before They Take Place / Eric Pepin

Published 2015.

Other Books by Eric Pepin

The Handbook of the Navigator:
What is God, the Psychic Connection to Spiritual
Awakening, and the Conscious Universe

Meditation Within Eternity:
The Modern Mystics Guide to Gaining Unlimited
Spiritual Energy, Accessing Higher Consciousness,
and Meditation Techniques for Spiritual Growth

Igniting the Sixth Sense:
The Lost Human Sensory that Holds the Key to Spiritual
Awakening and Unlocking the Power of the Universe

Silent Awakening:
True Telepathy, Effective Energy Healing
and the Journey to Infinite Awareness

Waking the Immortal Within:
Develop Your Spiritual Presence,
Awaken the Inner Master and Explore Hidden Realities

Guild of PSI:
Psychic Abilities –
the Link Between Paranormal and Spiritual Realities

Books by Higher Balance

Bending God: *A Memoir*

"The intuitive mind is a sacred gift
And the rational mind is a faithful servant.
We have created a society that honors the servant
And has forgotten the gift."

—Albert Einstein

Acknowledgements

I am nothing in this world without you. You who have become more than my voice, but rather the unseen presence of my spirit. It is you that have made immortally, a gift that is bestowed by love, devotion and gratitude of the tireless endeavors of your essence. I try to find reason enough to deserve such beauty, such goodness and devotion. It struggles within me to know that, that thank you will never be enough. My fear is failure in your eyes. My eternal gratitude is that you believe in me and each day it makes me want to be better than the last, for it is you that is the example of what I hope to be. I will remember you and all that you have done when we hold each other once again on the edge of eternity, once again.

My everlasting gratefulness for your tireless hours of sorting and making sense of my mumblings, profanities, and repetitive cognitions. Defining the course upon the mass to safe harbor. Thank you for seeing through it and finding my voice.

Loretta Huinker
Ray Ross
Eric Robison

To those who toiled with compass adjustments, for all to find true north. For those who climb the masses heights and faced its galling winds.

Diane Pfaff
Katherine Malone

The steadying of the helm when I grew tired or unsteady.

Steve Pfaff

To the masses that held the strength to move this ship. That would be *you* dear friend, thank you for this wondrous voyage.

Eric J. Pepin

CONTENTS

INTRODUCTION

The incredible miracles performed by ancient mystics and spiritual masters throughout history have captured the imaginations of our present culture, especially those of us whose thoughts inhabit the realm of spirituality and mysticism.

Spiritual people like you and I differ from the majority of people in a very distinct way. When they hear or read stories of miracles that defy the laws of physics, they're simply amazed; they perceive the miracle as a mere performance, nothing more than pure entertainment. On the other hand, spiritual people will see it from the perspective of wonder and curiosity. To us, it's much more than entertainment, it's a learning experience.

We are curious to know how it was accomplished and how we can accomplish the same feat. What thoughts were passing through the mind of that mystic at the moment of truth; when the very fabric of reality was cut and stitched back together to suit the needs and desires of the mystic? What role do emotions play in this process of editing reality? Do feelings override thoughts? Is there a limit to what can be done and are there consequences for pushing these boundaries? And, most importantly, how does one's spirituality tie into this?

I invite you to explore the how's and why's of bending reality in the pages that follow. Search the depths of your mind for the unsolved riddles of the spiritual masters, travel to an unknown place yet to be discovered, then uncover the secrets once known only by the most advanced mystics of the past.

Between the covers of this book you'll find the answers your inner truth, your higher consciousness, your Navigator has been searching for since the moment of your incarnation into this life. It's now time for you to reveal the truths of your Navigator.

Let us begin ...

Chapter 1

Mɪɴᴅ Sᴛᴏʀᴍ

Ancient tales and stories are passed down from generation to generation. Whether they are biblical, fairytales, or folklore from ancient tribes, every culture has them. Do you ever wonder how much of these stories are really true or if they have been fabricated by some very imaginative people? Well, there is a great amount of truth in those mythical stories; however, the facts are usually embellished. I get a kick out of those religious people who laugh at the mystical stories of other cultures, but they believe that Jesus walked on water or that God spoke to Moses from a burning bush. It's obvious they believe in some things, yet clearly not others. So it's okay for their particular belief system but that is where they draw the line.

I'm going to focus on weather manipulation in all its forms: what took place in ancient times, how it was achieved, and how you can achieve it too. Do I believe it's possible to affect and manipulate the weather? Absolutely. Do I think it's a task that can be performed randomly or easily? No, and I'll tell you why. Hopefully it will make a lot of sense to you. On that same token, I'm going to teach you to how to manipulate weather yourself. I'm pretty confident that with trial and error, you will be able to achieve it.

Is there a spiritual benefit
associated with manipulating the weather?

You should ask yourself if everything must have a spiritual asso-
ciation. There are a lot of people who aren't interested in *just* the
spiritual aspect of manipulating the weather. Living life is about
spirituality; likewise, existing and being a part of this world is
about spirituality. So any other interaction that's above normal
would definitely be an aspect of spirituality. If you looked at a
tree in great depth and truly understood it, you would find God.
That's an idiom, but there's also a truth to it. How deeply can you
perceive? I've often said to you that, at certain points, there are
frequencies that are dispersed, and if you catch them at the right
time, you will feel like you've been *fed*.

You wondered, "How was this spiritual?" I think this addresses
the fact that all aspects of life and how we integrate with it can
be spiritual, as long as you're not suppressing, harming, or doing
anything wrong to someone. You can find a form of beauty in
everything. All forms of beauty are a form of finding your spirituality, in my opinion.

If you affect the weather to some degree, what are your limits
and possibilities? More so, what does that say about the communion you're having with reality, with life, the Gaia consciousness,
and the elements around you? To me, that is a very spiritual state
of mind.

Jesus, a great Master whom everyone recognizes, was in
a boat on the Sea of Galilee in the middle of a storm when he
affected the weather. He didn't just snap his fingers and watch the
storm dissipate. He was sleeping through a lot of it when his disciples, panicking, woke him up. He told them, "Calm down. Don't
be afraid." He went to the side of the boat; the rain was coming
down extremely hard and there were big gusts of wind, lightning,
and black clouds. He became very still, studied the storm, and
used mind over matter while working with the elements. It didn't
happen immediately with a snap of his fingers, but something
obviously happened. The real question is what?

You need to keep something in mind that Jesus said. Even though many people think that way, Jesus wasn't the only one who could do these things. Jesus told us, "You can do as I do and even greater." He didn't say this in order to reach out to the people who uphold other belief systems so he could convert them to his way of thinking. His intention was to teach his disciples to heal and do other things that he believed in with great conviction. My point is, what one person can do, another can do also. The important thing to remember is that if you want to rise to that occasion, you absolutely can.

As far as communion with the weather goes, you're talking about what Jesus did, rather than what was written about the way it stopped.

Jesus is a spiritual icon to millions of the world's people. His ability to control the storm is an act that we all hold in great esteem. We want to be like him; we want to be like Buddha; we want to be like Krishna. Isn't that the point?

Jesus communed with this giant storm to quell and calm it. I don't think Jesus looked up to the storm and the sky ripped open like a giant zipper and the sun popped out. A calming effect slowly happened. There was a sense of progression. The first effect was that something was happening within him. And then something was happening with the storm, and the third effect was the byproduct of it all; again coming back to my favorite number - three.

You mentioned Jesus, but I also heard other stories about ancient tribes that do rain dances.

Yes, the American Indians performed rain dances. I believe you can find a variation of this in almost any culture. The ancient tales contain stories about how some wizards brought down the fog so they could go into battle and not be seen. The same thing goes for the tales of King Arthur of England.

So, if there is a measure of truth to the story of Jesus in the boat, what is it? How was it done, and how can someone else achieve the same result? That is my point for this discussion. There are plenty of people who have seen me manipulate the weather in various ways from cloud bursting to stopping and starting rain. You could literally consider these to be modern day miracles. I am not the only one who can do these things. I've taught many students to do them, too.

The biggest thing to keep in mind when you go out to work with the weather is that you should do it by yourself. If there is more than one person with you and they know what you're going to do, this will create a conflict of interest because they will also try to manipulate the weather. You will cancel each other out. It's like two people throwing one stick: you want to throw it in one direction but the other person wants to throw it in the opposite direction. It creates a big problem since there is only one stick. Let me give you a better example. What if both people decide to throw the stick in the same direction? Doesn't common sense tell you that it's not as easy as it sounds? Think about two people picking up a stick and throwing it. Isn't it possible that one person could throw it a lot better than two people at the same time? You might think that it will go further if two people threw it, but both people have to be synchronized for it to work at all.

So, when you have other people trying to do these things with you, it's not that they're intentionally trying to do it wrong; it's just that the Universe, or Gaia, has to choose which one to respond to first. It's like having a pet and both people are clapping their hands saying, "Here doggy, here doggy." The dog becomes confused with which one to respond to.

When you do this kind of work, go off and try to do it on your own first. If you bring people with you, they don't need to know what you're doing. Let them witness the act. Let them experience what happens. You can tell them what you're going to do, like I do. Somebody might ask me to do something and I'll do it, but I don't like to perform for people. I have a big pet peeve about that. When I feel close enough to students, I will do certain things for them, as well as teach them things so they can witness and experience it. You'll find that some people will put you under pressure if you make certain claims. You're going to discover that when you're under pressure, their expectations will limit your success.

So again, you don't want to succumb to those circumstances where you have a lot of pressure because then you get into a collective-mind-consciousness of being doubted or challenged. All these uncontrollable fears start popping into your head like, *what if I can't do it? What if I'm not going to be able to do it? What if they don't believe me or they call me a fraud because I couldn't do it right?* This, in itself, is going to erode your effectiveness.

Now, you might wonder why you are able to do it when you're by yourself but not with other people around. It's all about the technique. It comes from a place that is not created by the organic brain. It is such a clear state of consciousness that it takes practice to hold your mind there. So, when you have something very demanding on your brain, like the thoughts and doubts of other people, your Babbler fires up the engine until it takes over, and that makes it very difficult for you to hold your thoughts in a steady place.

Now, believers are a different story. They have a sense of anticipation and belief in the power of your success. Of course, the non-believers think the believers are brainwashed and don't know what they're talking about. The believers can act as a catalyst because their minds are clear and they're working with you, not against you. They fully expect this to happen. You're the operator, you create it and, therefore, you get a better result.

Most psychics have difficulty doing anything while under observation because their mind is babbling too much or they are afraid of making a mistake. It's as if it would be better to secretly observe and record the results than let the other person know that they're going to be observed and recorded. In the back of their mind, there is that Babbler preventing them from going into a *slipstream state of mind*, or the *In-Between state of mind*. It would be very difficult if you were under that kind of pressure.

Does that dynamic have anything to do with the behavior of particles?

I believe there is a correlation, yes. I believe you're referring to quantum physics. For example, a circuit board in a computer usually works perfectly well, but when investigated to see how it works, it stops working. There is no reason for that to happen.

Or a particle split in half with one part going in one direction and the other part going in the opposite direction. If one part is stopped, for whatever reason, the other part will stop instantaneously. In quantum physics this is all very quirky, but I do believe that there's a correlation between the two. When people who have a doubting state of mind are producing this kind of energy, I think it manipulates reality and it holds things in a certain way.

It seems like it's easier to control a gray sky than a clear sky. What makes storm weather easier to control? The ionization in water. Blessing water creates beautiful designs and structures and you don't have to be a priest to do that. You just have to believe you're going to have an effect. Maybe you can't go against the bigger program, the Doe, but you can manipulate a little tiny one by your will. This is why water, on the lowest level, can be structured into beautiful designs from people blessing it. They believe when it is blessed that something good happens, no matter their religious background.

Regardless of belief or religious affiliation, when water is blessed something very beautiful is created by the water crystals. People can connect with this water; maybe it's because the human body consists of fifty to seventy-five percent water. It might be because seventy-one percent of our planet's surface is made up of water. Whatever the reason, there seems to be a very good connection. So when you look at cloudy weather and wonder if you can influence it, it is a lot easier than affecting earthier, organic matter. In a lot of a ways, matter is very hard to manipulate because of its lower density energy. Water appears to be on the threshold of energy and matter. It is perceived as being something much finer. Maybe this is why you can affect it. At any rate, it is easiest to affect clouds and smaller weather patterns when you first begin to work with it.

So, when I'm outside and there is cloud cover and I want the sun to come through, this is the technique that I use: first, I acknowledge what I am, but I don't use words. I look at the clouds and, rather than concentrating on their size, I feel oneness with them. It's as if I breathe them in; I accept them. There's a certain calmness that comes over me. It's not a dreariness of the rain; it's just a communion with it all, and I allow myself to flow with it. I have an expectation that the clouds will open because I can conceive the effect that I'm looking for.

When I look at the sky, acknowledge who I am, and feel this moment with the weather, there's a part of me that is conscious of the moisture in the air, the smell of the air, and the temperature or the air moving against me. I don't think of it as being undesirable. I feel it as being very desirable, like I want it to rain on me. I want to feel the rain on my skin. I want to enjoy the experience of this weather, this temperature. So, I become conscious of things I don't normally pay attention to.

You think of sunshine as being a desirable thing, so again you have to work with those emotions and be conscientious of what you feel and what you think. I'm not feeling anything negative for the rain, but I'm not necessarily thinking anything positive either. I'm just being. For a moment, I feel like I'm a tree and the water is on me. It's good, it's purifying, and it's clean. There is a point when my mind is clear. It's an in between branch off where I'm feeling the air. I'm feeling and becoming one with the moisture. I'm becoming one with the moment.

There's a part of me that feels the rhythm of the air when it's windy. When it blows, it's almost as if I'm pulling the wind into my body like I want it to push me. When it eases, there's a part of me that eases with it. Then it comes back in and there's a part of me that almost begins to know or sense when it's going to begin and when it's going to stop. *There's a knowing.* Being that aware of yourself allows you to become totally conscious of it. You have to know what to pay attention to.

There is a pattern to every single thing. Follow that pattern for a little while. It's like pushing somebody on a swing: they already have momentum, but you're going to give them a push to help them with that momentum. They would lose it if you didn't push; maybe not a lot, but after a while the swing will stop. You also have to believe that you're moving the wind. That's when it blows again; you're pulling it, you're not just letting it push you, but you're pulling it towards you. When it calms, you already know the rhythm, so you pretend that you're helping to calm it. Now you're feeling that you're part of it, this wind, and you're helping it. You are a helper now. You have some control over this.

What happens when the person on the swing goes upward and you decide to give her a push that takes her a little bit higher? What is your first fear? That you're going to push her too high and something bad is going to happen. Put that expectation away and push harder. Low and behold, that gust of wind is a lot stronger now!

You may convince yourself that the gust of wind is a mere coincidence. Fine. Continue to work with that. It's going to calm down, so just flow with it. Let it pull in and pull out. Then you're going to work on it again, but this time be aware of the movement of your hands. Everything your hands do is another form of communication. Your hands will make this rolling motion as you're trying to explain something because you're saying, "It's longer," or you'll make a waving motion with your hands to get someone to come over to you. Most people never think about this.

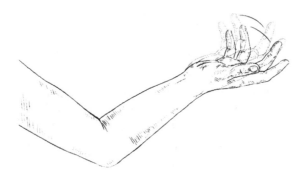

If you pay attention to yourself when you say "stop" or when you talk, you're going to find that your hands won't know what to do with themselves. But if you can automate this and just talk and roll your hands around to help explain what you're talking about, you'll find there's a certain feeling that comes with it. You're talking through an emotion inside of you that's also rolling, so be aware of what your hands are doing.

When you have your hands straight out, you're almost feeling the wind on your body and on your hands at the same time. It's like touching or caressing the wind. You're using your tactile senses to gauge the weight of the wind like it has volume. You're moving in and out with it now and it's very calm. Then, when you want the wind to become stronger, you roll your hands: palms up, outstretched slightly from your left to the right. You're reaching out to pull the wind on you like a big wave coming in from the ocean.

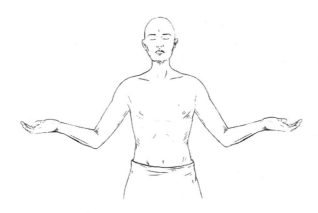

You will get a huge gust of wind. Usually it starts off slow and then it gets very strong. It's much stronger than anything you've been experiencing up to that point. The real question now is: are you manipulating the weather or is this just a coincidence? Can you now make the wind stop? What do you do? You tell it to calm down; you *feel* calm. Use your hands and pat the air with your palms facing down, both hands out, and you feel calm.

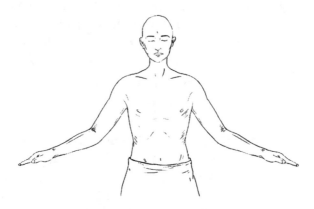

The wind is like a rowdy child. So don't expect it to calm down right away. You're trying to help it to get its bearings. So you're saying in a way, "Calm down. It's all right to relax." And you're feeling calm and feeling that it's one with you. You can feel it internally in your chest area; it's a very subtle feeling. It's like you're talking to the wind. It may get a little rowdy again before settling down, but it will stop. It may take fifteen seconds or it may take longer, but when it stops there's nothing. Not so much as a speck of dust moves and it's dead quiet.

You must remember that you cannot expect instantaneous results. So if you move your hand, it's not going to happen right away. There's always a delay of several minutes because you're dealing with a big atmosphere and different wind currents. There has to be time for the wind to travel, but you shouldn't think about that too much. Otherwise you will overthink the process and make it more complicated than it really is. In most cases, you need to wait anywhere from two to ten seconds to see a result.

Never feel that if something doesn't instantly happen for you that you're doing something wrong. You just need to under-stand how things work. Sometimes things take a little bit longer depending on where you are, and what phase the weather is in. It takes a little while for things to react.

Now rain is a little bit different, yet in many other ways it's very much the same. With rain, it takes energy to move energy.

So, you have to remember there is Prana everywhere. Somewhere in the back of your mind, you have to understand that you're just working with the natural energies that are already making these molecules do what they're doing. It's important that it makes some sense to you. With rain, it's an anticipation of the inner feeling of rain.

It's easier if it's already raining. If there's no rain, it's very hard to get the rain to start; however, once you're really good at this you can do it. If you do make it rain when there are no clouds in the sky, remember that the Indian rain dancers were out there for at least twenty-four hours before anything happened. Don't think you're going to go outside and the clouds are just going to open. You have to work with the potential of there being rain; there's just nothing coming down yet. The potential has to be already there and you're going to shake it up a little bit to get it to come down. You have to work within reason.

You have an unknown inner sense of what's going on in your environment. The problem is, you never pay attention to it, but primitive people do. If you pay attention to that inner sense, you become in tune with that awareness.

I start feeling the weather just like I do with the wind. I'm aware of the moisture, the wind temperature, the air movement. That's all very important, and feeling it on my face is particularly important. Right away I go for my hands, and in this particular case, I try to get familiar with feeling rain drops hitting my face or my hands. I don't hold my hands out flat but just keep them at my sides. When I feel the drops, I begin to get this anticipation of the rain drops falling. If they're big drops, a big rain could potentially happen. If they're little drops, I know it's just going to sprinkle. It's just common sense.

When I am challenged to make it rain heavily, I don't think about their request in the sense of forcing something to happen because that isn't necessarily the way it works. I'm thinking about my intent, my desire for it to rain harder. I have a communion of being aware of the weather, a feeling of the weather and a knowing that there is moisture there. I evoke a feeling of a hard rain. There's a difference between the way a light rain feels and the way heavy rain feels. Heavy rain feels really wet and thumpy like lots of little bumps. I anticipate that's what I'm already beginning to feel, even though that's not the case. I project it like I'm feeling it.

It's like I'm talking to it and it responds by forming the condensation and it just starts coming down faster. All of a sudden, there's a rain shower going on. If somebody asks me to make it stop, immediately I go back to the feeling with that kind of intent. I recreate the same feeling in my chest center, in the area of my heart and project it.

I don't expect immediate results. There are certain organic processes that have to take place in order to produce the intended result. I just make this connection with the environment by thinking about my little moment in this one particular spot.

Let's say that you have a solid cloud covering with no ripple or break anywhere and you want to make the clouds dissipate. Follow this format: feel the air, feel the moisture, become conscious of your environment. Quiet your thoughts, relax your breathing, and feel your environment. Become aware, become conscious, and become loving to it. Feel it in your chest, not in words or reaching out and touching something but with an emotional communion.

Be in the moment, look at the sky, and scan for any weak spots, not holes, but where a hole could potentially be. Start there and create that same expectation when you look up at the sky and think it's going to clear because you see it getting brighter. Then the clearing gets wider and, all of a sudden, it falls apart. There's a feeling associated with that.

Evoke that expectation as if you know it's already bright and ten steps ahead of what it should be. Have a sense that the sun is already peeking through the clouds a little bit. Just a little bit, though, because if it's too much, too fast, it won't work.

Don't think about how big this storm is, or how many clouds there are, or how much water there is. Just think about this one spot. If there are no dimples, no sense of any openings anywhere, just stare at the spot and desire that dimple, that break where you want it to soften up a little bit, just a break in the clouds. It will give you that softness. Everywhere else will be dark but that softness will suddenly start to open.

Now someone might argue that it's naturally going to happen based on where you're standing and the way the clouds are moving. That's fine. As you keep working with this dimple to get it to open, have the expectation of where you want it to go and it's going to get bigger and wider. There's going to be more softening in other spots and it's just going to open.

It's like a locomotive in motion; you cannot stop the movement even if you stop doing it. It has its own momentum. If you work with it, it will stay unless there are so many clouds that you know eventually it's going to close. Now, when you move away and start talking, or you try to forget about it, it will begin to close and build again. If you remain conscientious, it's almost as if it doesn't know what to do and it will either take one direction or continue spreading, and then you'll see more spots opening.

So, now you've naturally started it, it's working for you, and its actually moving with you and you are pushing it at the same time, like the swing; you're working with it. Your expectation now matches what's actually happening. The more you work it with your mind, the bigger the opening is going to get. It becomes like a flow. It becomes natural and you just know what's going to happen. It's all about this feeling of knowing in your chest that you're manipulating ahead of the game.

Can you explain what weather is to the Gaia organism?

For the most part, it's what science says it is. It's the ground heating up, the air pressure rising, temperatures dropping and creating vacuums of air. We feel them going over land masses. Storms are an accumulation of moisture due to heat and pressure, so science is relatively accurate. Sometimes though, the weather is almost a manifestation of the lower vibration of the consciousness of the planet moving across the surface of the planet. Whether it is a storm or whatever, it's like hemispheres of the brain.

Humans also act as a nervous system, being the nerve endings: we are all independent yet we're clustered. Say you're trying to sell something and one end of town is avidly buying it but the other end isn't buying anything at all. That's an example of this cluster consciousness. Different areas feel differently, and if you pay attention you will notice it.

Wind movement often has its own kind of semi-intelligence. In large part, it is natural, but it's fair to say that you're in control of all your thoughts. Would you say then, that your environment has a big effect on your thoughts? Think about it. Would you say that you're in a better mood on a sunny day than on a rainy day? Would you say that you feel differently in a warmer room versus a colder room? Would you feel different in a hot room versus a warm room? Would it affect how you think, how you react, and what you're doing?

Just as you react to your environment, the planet does the same thing; it is partly conscious and partly being manipulated by the environment. When I connect with the weather, I don't necessarily connect with the weather. I feel like I'm connecting with an intelligence. I feel like I'm talking to something rather than making it do something. I don't look at the weather as just being weather; I look at the weather as an intelligence.

I don't look at weather as being a thing or a reaction or just *a something*. I see it as being individual in its own way, but not like a person or a pet. It's an intelligence. By reciprocating to that intelligence, being non-threatening and in communion with it, it wants to work with me. So I choose to work with it.

I think about the globe as a whole. On one side it's sunny, over here it's cloudy, and there's a hurricane over there. It's almost like how a person has one mood and one feeling. On the globe it's like there's a variety of things happening all at once.

What do you think is happening in your brain? Your motor gears in one area are about the size of a dime and your taste sensory in another area is about the size of a pencil tip. Don't you feel the chair underneath you right now as you are sitting? Aren't you doing many things simultaneously? Isn't it possible to be mad at somebody and also be laughing at something at the same time? It's no different than that. It's just your perception. Try to think *bigger picture.* That's the secret.

There is one step when you are manipulating weather where you really exist in the weather and it feels like there's a momentum that's very weak. But sometimes it's very strong; it affects your ability to do whatever you would like to do.

Remember what I said about working with the weather initially? When you work with the weather, you're dancing with it, and there's a point when you take the lead and work with it. You've already done the first step. You let *it* move *you.* You're becoming one with it because it's moving you, but at some point you take the lead. You lead the dance.

It's just a point in your mind. When you know you're ready, you just do it but you can't force it. That's the big thing. You can't just say you're going to do this; I want this. You can feel the anticipation for it but you can't say you *have* to. When you want something in life, don't pray for it. Prayers are like demanding something. I *need* this. I *need* that. No, *you wish for it.* A wish is like a desire. You're not demanding anything. It's not even that you're really asking. You're just putting this desire out and you're willfully hoping for a response.

There's a difference between wishing and hoping. Every word for everything there is in life, whether it's a wall, a candle, a plastic box, whatever, holds a certain feeling. Feel and manifest what you wish for and project it out as a wish. There's something very specific about the feeling of a wish. You can't quite put your finger on it. If I say snow cone, you've already got it. You can feel the crunchy, bristled cold of it. You become aware of the cone, maybe feel the paper. Everything has a feeling: a cell phone has a feeling; keys have a feeling.

When I say joy, joy has a feeling that you can immediately relate to. It's the same with sadness. When I say *wish*, you were all over the board trying to peg that one down. That's because it's an "in" word. *It's a glitch word.* It's something you're hoping for, yet not necessarily hoping for at the same time because hope holds a different kind of feeling. Hope immediately has a sense to it. You can feel hope.

When you wish for something, there's almost part of you that has an anticipation of something that will be. It's different. It's a very special word and that's why people say *make three wishes* or *wish for this to happen*. Who came up with that? Who came up with wish? Why don't you just hope for it? Why not just ask for it? Why wish for it? There's something very special about wishing. It's not asking and it's not hoping. It's not demanding. *It's the most polite way to put something out there, saying you need help with something but you're not asking for help ... but you sure would like it.* I have never known the Universe, not once, to refuse when asked correctly. It's always very willing to step in. It's all about how you ask.

Chapter 2

Cloud Busting

Cloud busting is probably the easiest technique in weather manipulation. Choose a day that has puffy clouds in between patches of blue sky. When you first practice this, you want to start off with small, tiny clouds. It's best to begin with slow moving clouds that are just floating around. Select a very small one and just stare at it. Your mind will become relaxed and calm and have the same kind of expectation: the expectation that you know the cloud is getting smaller. It's shrinking, it's evaporating, and it's turning back into a minor form of moisture.

Visualize it getting smaller and smaller. If you project the emotion from your chest center and you have confidence that it's getting smaller, it will literally begin to shrink in size as you observe it. Be sure to keep your eyes on it; if you take your eyes off of it for a moment, it's going to stop shrinking. You can move your head, you can talk and slowly move around and it will stay the way you left it. If you go back to staring *directly* at it and continue working with it, it will evaporate. It will completely vanish in front of your eyes.

You can even tell people which cloud you're working on, but the more people that are concentrating on the same cloud; the more likely they will cancel each other out. You have to selectively choose a cloud that works for you. You can point it out and the best way to do that is to describe where it is in the sky and then tell your companions that you don't want them to look at your cloud until it's over a certain spot of your choosing. Then ask them to tell you what they see when your cloud reaches said spot. Their response will be, "Well, I don't see it. It's gone."

Some people will dismiss it as atmospheric conditions, but there is absolutely a connection between the mind consciousness and what's happening out there. Cloud busting is just taking clouds and breaking them down. You concentrate, look at it, have non-thought, get into that zone, and see it getting smaller and smaller. It's literally very reactive.

What is it about that technique that will feed your other techniques or other exercises?

When you start off with cloud busting and you find that you can do it, it helps you to psychologically beat the Governor that's holding you in the Doe and also the design that says you can't do it. The more you build your confidence up, the more you'll begin to change. Every day there are people telling you what you can't do, yet there's a million stories out there about people who apply themselves and do whatever they were told they couldn't do. They achieved their goals against all odds. *Reality is what you choose to make it.* If you say it's impossible to affect the weather, then it's going to be impossible to affect it. But if you *know* that you can, then you will.

Cloud busting allows you to see immediate results and that encourages your will to become even stronger and trust it more. You will be in awe of yourself. You will test yourself, and your confidence will grow. Cloud busting is an encouraging thing. Sometimes you need these little successes that the Babbler cannot deny. Once you beat the Babbler, the door just gets bigger and bigger and bigger because you're saying, "If I can do this then I should be able to do that." But be careful not to take huge steps. Don't say, "By the end of the week I should be able to create a storm." Be reasonable with yourself. Some things you will excel at while some things will take a little longer. You'll do fantastic things if you don't set unrealistic expectations on yourself. Work with that and then move on to other things; you'll get bigger and better at it. There's nothing you can't do. There's nothing I do that you can't learn to do.

Chapter 3

The Arena of the Mind

S ome of my students have wondered if the In-Between is connected with controlling the weather. In the In-Between state of consciousness you are residing in a dimensional state of being. In the In-Between state, your dimensional bodies become clearer and more pronounced, as does the dimensionality of our reality. You are able to interact with several dimensions at once. The properties and "laws" that once governed you and held you in this place are loosened as you are able to free yourself and shed the conventional knowledge of the world. I discuss the In-Between state in more detail in Chapter Twelve.

The In-Between is a very intense area and you can't control the weather when you're In-Between because it is so different. At the same time, there are different facets of that state of mind. It's just like a tree with different branches bearing different fruits. Instead of just one side having fruit, each limb might give something different, like lemons. When you're In-Between, you're at all the outer branches. You're at the utmost rather than just dealing with the fruit. It's from the same place, yet something very different. When you experience it, you'll understand what I mean.

In controlling the weather, you're in that space within your mind but not nearly as deep. You're more in this everyday state of mind, but you're operating everything from a different place. You're not operating it from your mind or your brain; you're operating it from a different intelligence, and that intelligence emanates from your chest center, and I mean that literally.

It's like a different dimensional body and its brain, its center of conceiving, of contemplation, is in your chest. You use it all the time; you just don't recognize it in a conscious way. When you think it's going to rain and you go outside, you know it's going to rain, so where do you feel it? Ask yourself, where do you feel the knowing? You're going to feel it in your upper chest area. There's a certain kind of intelligence there just like the other types of intelligence in different parts of your body, but this particular one is very rooted to dimensional things.

I know that if I have to deal with something, I don't deal with it in my brain. I rationalize and work it all out right in my chest as a kind of intelligence. In this dimension, we think all of our thoughts are in the brain because we're here and so is the brain. That's one of the most limiting beliefs there is. You have to think outside the box. There are other kinds of intelligences.

When you get hungry you know you're hungry, but where does this thought come from? You're told *by science* that your brain's telling you. You're told *biologically* that your brain knows. Do you know how you *really* know this? An intelligence communicates with you and your brain simply interprets it. It tells you that you're supposed to use this intelligence. Well, you don't need to use it, even though you already understand it. You are just not paying attention to it because you're automating yourself.

It is what you're trained to do. The stomach communicates this information to the brain and the brain reacts. The stomach knows what's going on, but it will wait for the food to be digested. That is your consciousness, your normal consciousness. That's what you're doing with everything in your life. You're putting the brain in charge. You know everything already so if you could just bypass the brain, things would be a lot faster. You would suddenly become a genius.

The intelligence in your upper chest knows all things dimensional. It knows when there's an entity in the room. It knows how to communicate with it. It knows how to do all sorts of things.

You just have to pay attention to it; and when you pay attention, you'll be amazed at what you discover.

Can using your chest intelligence allow you to maintain in the In-Between longer?

Not necessarily, but if you don't use your chest intelligence, you're going to be forced to use your other intelligences, or the brain, which is much slower. How long you are able to stay In-Between depends on using your chest intelligence, your skills, and knowledge that you have obtained.

Does this intelligence have a connection with your chakras?

No, the chakras are another dimensional body. This is just another way of understanding how to work with all of them. Your chest intelligence is very independent, yet it is very real. I accept it like my hands, my taste buds, or any part of my body. It's just part of me. So, by telling you not to think with your brain, or to meditate, I'm really trying to get you to realize that you can think from your chest center. Much of everything spiritual, dimensional, and multi-dimensional, is all in there. It's this intelligence that's there.

Is that the sixth sense?

The sixth sense is not any one particular thing. The sixth sense is in your brain but it's the part that communicates with the dimensional intelligence. One part of your brain is motor gears, another part is smell, and sight might be in the back of your head. There is also the pineal gland, or the seat of the soul, or the seat of your sixth sense. It is the interpreter for other forms of data.

The sixth sense goes into many areas. When you go In-Between, you're not really using the dimensional intelligence. In-Between is part of the sixth sense; it's just another facet of an amazing amount of abilities you have. But, the human race has lost touch with it. People are unconscious of it; they're asleep.

Would the groin be a significant type of intelligence?

Ironically, that's a yes and a no answer. You've heard the expression, "He thinks with his genitals." That isn't the case. You're actually thinking with your organic brain. You desire, but you're having the pleasure through the penis. It's different. There is not really an intelligence there. It's a source that releases chemicals biologically in your brain from what it senses, and that's very pleasing. That's the guarantee that you're going to pro-create, and it's one of the most gratifying feelings you can have. But it's not what makes you think. Your brain is making you think because it's wired that way so that you will spread your genetics, so that procreation happens, so that cells can move through the evolutionary process and propagate.

When you think about sex, you're thinking in your brain. You are creating all these scenarios in the brain, and then you're associating it with your body. A male is thinking of conquering, and a female is thinking about nurturing. She wants your emotions and she wants to draw you in. Men and women are designed a little bit differently, and this is all from the organic brain. The genitals are just mechanisms to achieve the process. It is very important that you study this within you because this mechanism is very subtle.

When I point to my chest, I don't even think heart. I'm not thinking lungs, muscles, or flesh. When I think of my chest intelligence, it's just as real to me as pointing to my head. When you point to your head, what do you feel or what do you think? You just know this is where it's all happening, or so you think. Can you feel it happening in there? No, but if you're thinking about sex and you are planning on doing something about it, where are you thinking from? You're going to point to your head. It's an inner knowing, the greater Middle Pillar which is your true self.

Is the brain in your upper chest different than the stomach intelligence?

Yes, your stomach intelligence is different. Your stomach intelligence is more rooted in this dimension than the chest intelligence. It's funny because when you think about sex, you'd think the idea would come from the genitals. It doesn't, but the gratifying part does. However, if you were to ask yourself where it's really coming from, you would point to your head. When you ask yourself where your hunger is coming from you don't say from your head. You say it's from your stomach. That's how you know it's an intelligence.

What about that intuitive gut feeling, when you feel something bad?

It's a different kind of intelligence because there are two of them. There's an intelligence that's visual when you think there's something wrong. Then there's the intuitive one that comes from your stomach. There is intelligence there and it's using a different level of vibration to communicate and gather information. The brain is really a fancy translator. All of these different brains are just fancy translators calculating complex information and spitting it out to your inner self. Any of these other intelligences will take over based on the primary dimension you're residing in. They will become the dominant one. That's how you survive when you go into other dimensions or other frequencies. You adapt and you take on that function.

What about when something feels very strange or very dimensional like the weather? Could you talk about the significance of that?

Where do you feel it? You feel it in your chest; that's the first tipoff. Pay attention to where you feel it. What's telling you something weird is going on? Not your brain, it's in your chest. It's being translated in your brain because this is the frequency you're in. Follow the source and that will tell you something because your 'weird meter' is there in your chest. That is your dimensional intelligence, so anything that comes from there comes from a very specific source of information.

It's a very specific sensory; it has its own methods of gathering information. Your brain uses your five senses. Your chest area uses at least eight different senses that are just as functional as your physical body sensory. So your chest area discerns that for you. Unfortunately, your organic brain filters out ninety percent of it.

A lot of these vibrations and feelings come from the chest area. If you can learn to pay more attention to your chest area and discern what it's saying, you'll force the organic brain to tell you more of the truth. But it will always lie to you to some degree. You just have to work at it. It will tell you about people, and you can pose questions to it like, "Can I trust this person?" I use my brain. But then I feel it. Then I feel, "Can I trust this person?" I search for the answer in my chest.

You do the same thing but you choose not to listen to it. You *feel* it. You know when you're being scanned, if you listen to that sensory. How do you know? Well, to that sensory, there might as well be hands on your physical body. Most people react to it; they just don't know why they're reacting that way. Women, intuitively, deal with it a lot more often than men because men mentally scan others and it projects a certain kind of energy. If a male looked at another male in the same way, they feel violated. It's about being conscientious of what's going on in that sensory. Pay attention to what you're feeling, and giving it a bona fide reason. If you can learn to do that well, you bypass the middle man, the brain.

That reminds me of an exercise where salt crystals are put under a microscope and you project energy to see how it affects the formation of the crystals. Sometimes they say it actually formulates the crystals in a certain shape that matches a thought projection.

Thought is a very powerful thing. In Dr. Masaru Emoto's book, *The Hidden Messages in Water, he* conducted a study with frozen water crystals. The pictures show how the water crystals reacted to both positive and negative words. In this study, when the water was prayed over or positive words were used, the pictures had beautiful patterns that looked like snowflakes. But when shouting or negative words were used, the water took on chaotic patterns. When the water was not subjected to any particular thought at all, the water created random patterns. This study was panned as pseudoscience and was very controversial, but there is also some truth to it.

On the smallest level of particles, string theory scientists are proving it reacts like energy.

Right, I think it reacts to will.

If that's the case and it responds to will, then what prevents a person from affecting their reality?

I would say it's the greater will which is the global consciousness of the planet and the global consciousness of the Universe. All living things have a set blueprint of what's going to happen. It's like saying your computer has a blueprint of how it's supposed to operate. The computer has a BIOS – a small inerasable program that contains the instructions needed to begin operation. It controls the data flow between the operating system, the application programs, and the hardware devices. But sometimes the programs don't do exactly what they are supposed to do. Whether or not it's a glitch or a programming error, something isn't working quite right so you get a weird response. When it starts to glitch too much, what do most people do? They reboot the computer in the hopes that the original settings will clear the problem and the computer will re-correct itself. That is a very simple analogy; hopefully it makes sense to you.

I believe that the Universe has a diagram of where it wants to go. It's like a blueprint that reality is based upon for this particular frequency, for this dimension. And I believe that, on occasion, some people are able to bend the rules of that blueprint. They include spiritual masters, the people who have developed their psychic abilities and can work with it. Sometimes they do things but later realize that they shouldn't have done it because it resulted in some other consequence.

I believe that the main programming has a rebooting process that's faster than a millisecond and it's constantly happening. It is what stabilizes reality within a certain framework; otherwise, reality would be dramatically affected and nothing could exist. The master frequency, the most powerful, is what we call the *Doe*. It holds things in a steady process and allows the vast majority of people to work together as a collective.

Imagine that you have a hundred people together in a field, all holding hands to create a great big circle. Then you tell them they have to run across the field as a group. What do you think is going to happen? Do you think this big ball of humans is going to be able to run across that field very well? Absolutely not! It will all be jumbled like a knot. They're going to have to move slowly, and as they do, they'll find their groove. But there is always that one person who trips or steps on someone else's foot. That would be the glitch, and the other people may be affected but they stabilize it, so it's just an isolated incident. That person can probably regroup without anybody on the other side ever knowing it happened.

This is a crude way of describing this, but it is what I understand in my mind's-eye. Reality is running on a base process and if the collective all starts to move in a certain direction, everybody goes that way. We can change reality but it has to be changed *as a whole*. If we don't work as a whole, then there's a bit of a problem. So that is what holds reality together. As people progressively become more spiritual, they affect one another which progresses this kind of thinking.

Originally, we were talking about people who could do miracles during a time period when extraordinary things supposedly happened. The people back then may have been less educated, perhaps more gullible. But I wonder if people were able to do more miraculous things because the collective hadn't yet formulated as much doubt as it has today. There obviously were formulations of consciousness going on then, but I don't think it was as developed as it is now. I do think there's a very strong interweaving of all that, but one person cannot permanently affect something. When Moses parted the sea, the water collapsed afterwards. Maybe that was to drown the people who were following closely behind, but Moses also knew they had to move quickly.

So, reality has the master program and we are only able to affect it in certain ways. There's a remnant or an echo by reflecting on the thought, "What just happened was amazing!" But I think that people have the tendency to fall asleep into the *Doe* again, and then they forget about the miracle they just experienced. It's not that they literally forget it, but there's not a sense of deep reflection that holds them there.

A while ago, we did some classes where some pretty amazing things happened and the students were in awe of it, yet just ten minutes later they were talking about tying their shoes. One of the students said to the others, "What is the matter with you guys? Didn't you see what just happened?" And they replied, "Well, yeah." So, there is an effect, but only certain individuals can retain that knowledge for any length of time.

In terms of the collective consciousness, if 75% of the planet believes there is a hell, why doesn't hell manifest into reality?

Personally, I don't think that most people believe in hell. You could say that people have a very different version of the concept of hell, so they negate it themselves. Nobody has a very good idea of what hell is and that is what keeps it from manifesting. You can talk to a religious person about hell, but all you will get from them is a basic idea of what hell is supposed to be because nobody can specifically describe it.

The other thing is that the master program is so refined in certain ways that it prevents hell from manifesting because, for the Universe, it would be the same as for you to stop breathing. You could consciously hold your breath, but eventually your body is going to force you to breathe again. The Universe has a plan for the movement of human consciousness. The Universe is not going to say, "Hell has now been created for all of the people because they want to believe in it now." It has a much greater program than that. If you want to cut your finger, you could, but it would go against every instinct of protecting yourself that you have. It's the same thing.

When people have a strong belief in something, like "God resides on a throne up in the sky," is that the reason they can't manifest that because it's a higher level concept or something that's hard-coded into the truth of the Universe?

That's a double-edged sword because, in some ways, people do manifest their own truth. There are people who've had near-death experiences where they went through a tunnel of light and saw Jesus at the end of the tunnel, or even family members. Then they think, "This is proof of life after death." People can be culturally ignorant. They say, "This is proof that my religion is the only true religion." So, I'll ask them, "What about the people who live in India? People there talk about going through the tunnel and seeing Krishna at the end? What about when they see Buddha?

Or Milarepa? Or an aboriginal elder? What makes their experience less valid than yours? Their stories are true and have been documented. They just aren't as well-known in cultures where that isn't the dominant belief system."

As you know, I don't believe that people are brain dead when they're having these near-death experiences. I think that their heart and their organs have stopped, but I do believe that the brain is still functioning electrically, and then they are resuscitated. This is why in some studies, guys are able to go under in high G-force, and when they do, they see the same tunnel effect with their family at the end of the tunnel. Or you can wear helmets that throw off magnetic rays that distort how the brain works, creating all these unusual paranormal feelings and sensing people around them. But that doesn't mean it's not true. Maybe that's what's opening up other dimensions to them and they're now figuring that out.

So, in some ways I think people create their own realities, but I think they're short lived. I hate to say this because people don't want to have their bubble burst. They want to believe in certain things because it gives them some level of comfort. Well, I'm not necessarily interested in comfort. I'm interested in the truth, and I believe that the truth will be more beautiful than anything humanity can imagine.

Having said that, even if they manifest certain things, it is the way their consciousness creates a departure scenario for them to separate better. If you could see what happens after they go through those experiences, perhaps it would fade away and they would merge into the Gaia consciousness without even realizing it. For them, it's like going into a very deep, happy, blissful sleep but they're actually moving into this other consciousness. Or, the speed of their consciousness will ramp up, moving faster and faster with data expanding in their mind. It's like waking from a dream and taking a few minutes to orient yourself to where you are after you've been sleeping.

If you're an older soul, when you pass on there's this moment of disarray because you're still hanging onto that limited consciousness you felt you always were in this life. So when you cross over, instead of dissipating into the Gaia consciousness you have this flooding of awareness. It's like you're coming out of a dream, or you're waking up because when you wake up, there's times when you're groggy and you forget where you are or what you are doing. It takes you some time to get your bearings and then you're on top of your game. If somebody rushed in and said, "Hey, name ten flavors of pizza pies," you might be a little confused and disoriented. However, if somebody came in and did that to you when you were on your A game, you would quickly say, "Pepperoni, cheese, Hawaiian." It's the same effect.

So, the master program is going to override your brain. You just have to trust it and remember that you did the work on yourself so you can feel comfortable with that. I think that you can create hell in the same way. As I have explained before, a lot of these scenarios are biologically-based in the brain and they speed up so fast that time feels slow outside of you.

I don't like it when people bunch all of these things into just one paranormal event and say, "It's all about the death experience." No, a lot of near-death experiences are not really physical death. A lot of it is still your brain working with you as your body shuts down. At that point, your brain is saying, "Well, the body shut down. We're dying. What is your expectation for dying?" And you think, "Well, I'm a Christian," or "I'm a Buddhist," or "I'm an American Indian." And so, if you're American Indian you see an eagle and, all of a sudden, you see the sky, and maybe you're doing a dance with some snakes around you that you don't think are poisonous. So it's a positive thing. You're going to see whatever you were exposed to in your belief system. It is what the brain is going to interpret to be alright with leaving your body.

I remember reading a story once about a man in Africa who was attacked by a lion and lived through it. He said, "At first, there's the shock. Then there's this feeling of knowing you're going to die, and then there's some other part of you that doesn't feel any pain. You're like a rag doll being tossed around but there's no more awareness of the suffering. There's a very peaceful, blissful point that you feel."

Most likely, your body is releasing so many endorphins that it would be more intense than taking heroin. On the same token, your body is helping you cope with the trauma. It doesn't have to. Why does it do that? Why doesn't it just let you suffer to the bitter end? Well, there is a reason for that. It's the same reason that when you're dying, your brain takes you into a near-death experience of your guilt or your shame, or if you're looking forward to meeting a religious figure, or a member of your family. Your brain is going to show you those things in order to create whatever you need to experience so you can accept or find comfort in what is happening. And it's going to be blissful and wonderful. If you really believe that you're going to hell for something you did, then you're going to create a very negative scenario.

I remember another story that I read where this guy was saying, "I went to hell." When he was asked what hell was he said, "Well, it wasn't fiery or anything, but I knew it was hell." And they asked how he knew that. He explained, "As I was floating above the planet, I was handed this puzzle with lots of pieces but the pieces never quite fit. And the piece that I had just placed changed shape every time that I looked away for the next one. I had a sense of dread and eternal frustration, an anxiety to put it all together. But I also felt, in that moment, that it was possible, so I could never give up."

You have this dread of it not working and you want to escape that place, knowing that you're going to be there forever. It was this feeling of an inner-loop that just never ended, like a snake biting its own tail. And then the person was resuscitated and brought back. Well, this is something he perceived. It was his sense of fear or what he projected, but it was his brain experiencing that.

Doctors really never talk about how many people have this type of experience. They always say these people are clinically dead, but can they say that they had no brain activity at all? In the vast majority of cases, I believe there will still be some level of brain activity. You do not leave your body until all the energy is released. It's like two magnets being sucked together. Your soul or your consciousness resides in the organic body, and they are electrically woven together. Only when the body fully shuts down will the soul be released. If the body is not 100% shut down, it still locks your consciousness there.

I think it's extremely difficult to have a true clinical death. There are examples of people who have been frozen and were later resuscitated. I was just reading about a case where this person was frozen for 20 minutes or so, but there is no mention that the person was clinically dead. Their body temperature went down to 68 degrees. Well, 98.6 is ideal, but 68 degrees isn't necessarily frozen either. It means, electrically, the brain still could be functioning at some level while all the organs are shut down.

I read an article where scientists have come up with something that can be put into the body system to put into a stasis where all the cells shut down. They're experimenting with mice but they're looking at using this procedure for people who are going to die but just need a couple more hours to have an organ transplant. They're going to use this to shut the body down until they receive the organ. This procedure will give them the extra few hours they need. Eventually, they're hoping that maybe they can extend this period of stasis into weeks, months, or even years. It's still in the experimental stages right now.

They've found a way to apply this to mammals, and they're saying there's no reason why it shouldn't be applied to human beings to put us into a form of hibernation where, literally, all our cells are hardly functioning at all. Scientists say this has great possibilities for cancer patients because they will be able to shut the body down so the cancer can't take root or grow. There are a lot of uses for this procedure, but is it brain death? Is there still electricity moving through the brain? And, if so, what is it doing, what is it thinking, what is it relaying? Will that person relate to people when they come out of it?

So the Universe will reset them but they will go back to doing whatever they believed before?

Well, let's put it this way. I have done some pretty amazing things in the past, and people have watched in awe, teary-eyed, and in shock. Sometimes within 24 hours, they're back to functioning as if nothing extraordinary happened. If you went back 500 years ago, or even 2000 years ago and witnessed a miracle, you would probably pitch a tent out in front of the person's house. Then you would dedicate the rest of your life to better living. You wouldn't care about material things anymore. You would just say, "This is it!"

In this day and age, the collective consciousness is so intense. People have been over-stimulated and reprogrammed by movies, radio, and TV that it is now interwoven with the vibration of the Doe. I think that people fall asleep a lot easier now. They absolutely can see amazing miracles and then act as if they never happened. But there is a good reason for that; there are a lot of charlatans and a lot of bunk out there.

I know someone who has seen things that would truly defy logic; absolutely and positively there's no way smoke and mirrors could do that miracle, but then he'd go into denial by saying, "There's just no way that this happened." Or he'd say, "It could have been this," or, "It might have been a freak meteor shower," or whatever.

I don't blame him for that, but I've learned that no matter what I do, no matter how amazing it is, there is always something in the back of every human's brain that causes people to say, "No, that had to be fake because it can't be done that way. It just isn't possible!" No matter how much they want to believe it! In ancient days, maybe people would be blown away by smoke and mirrors, and I'm sure in lot of cases they were. But when they saw the real deal, they also believed it. And maybe that's what inspired those people to reach the higher levels and experience their gifts.

I think the only way to truly convince people to believe something is to teach them to do it themselves. That is really why I started Higher Balance all of those years ago. In this day and age, no matter what I do, people will be in awe for about 24 hours, but then it's back to the same old routine of asking me to do another 'parlor trick.' You could say it's this resetting effect, or you could say it is being a cynic and we've learned in our society to be that way.

You've got to teach the individual to awaken. You've got to snap them out of this sleep state. It is why Higher Balance put out *The Handbook of the Navigator*. We're trying to get people to recognize that they're asleep. If they realize that, they will awaken from the dream. But first, they've got to be able to realize it and then practice staying awake.

I've seen you do some amazing miracles, but if I try to recall them now, my brain will fragment them into different days. Why does that happen?

It's your psychological and sociological programming. It's the same reason you can't count the F's in the paragraph from *Handbook of the Navigator* when they're right in front of you. You are designed to be an organism on this planet whose purpose is to procreate. You must never, ever forget that. It's not really your enemy. I don't want anybody to think of it that way. But you have to always remember the real purpose of the organic part of you, which is the mechanism that's constantly battling with your mind. It's always trying to make you fall asleep and it's always trying to stay in control.

Remember what I taught you: *If you can't control your thoughts and tell yourself to be quiet, who's really in charge? Is it the brain that's pretending to be you or the core of who you really are?*

So this is why it's a battle; it's a fight; it's a dedication to truly awaken. The highest ideal that we instinctively feel in the core of our being is that there's something more to life than what we organically perceive. So we fight and struggle to attain it to stay awake long enough. So, the brain fragments these things and it breaks them all down over time, making you fall back into automation. The brain knows how to isolate the experience like the body knows how to isolate a virus.

If you were to use the movie, *The Matrix*, as an example you could say that Neo was the virus to the computer even though he was searching for something greater. It's all about semantics and how you want to look at it, because I don't want to say "virus" and have people think this is negative thing. It is like a good virus, because there's some program inside of you still left that is fighting to awaken. The brain tries to shut it down by suppressing and controlling it. This is what's going on biologically; it's just another computer. And if you let it, it will eradicate everything. I think there are people that totally can erase everything from their mind and they can't even remember what happened.

If you can remember parts of a movie, why do you forget an amazing experience? It happens because it is a problem for the organic part of you and the programming knows this. It eradicates an experience which could potentially lead to something greater. In earlier times, these were 'seeds' for you to fight for a higher consciousness, but just like anything else, the program gets smarter as it evolves. It is also evolving. Everything strives to control the system so it doesn't get out of hand. Remember, White Cells will always be fewer in number.

The bottom line is that the organism is the bigger plan. It's bigger than all of us. The whole Universe is going somewhere; there's a reason for that, but there is an additional purpose for some of us to be here. We are to help guide the planet. We're the ones in this large mass of people who are moving. There are always people who are working with everybody else, guiding them to walk this way, concentrate, focus, and not to rush. They're stabilizing the other group around them to function better. They are sprinkled everywhere throughout the Earth, each one able to work with the few.

I certainly believe that White Cells have a divine purpose, and they always have. They're a necessity; if the world didn't have them, then this world would not be here. There must be co-creators. There must be people that are in tune with the Universe.

We act as conduits to experience this reality; we internalize it and we release that data back to a higher consciousness.

In a sense, we are what I call nodes - different kinds of neural synapses that translate what is going on in this dimension to a higher dimension. In the same way, your hands are an extension outward and your nerves give you information and transfer it into electrical data. We're just a more complex version of the same thing, in singular units, but very differently designed. We are scattered across the planet or the Universe, if you will, and we *internalize* reality from a spiritual perspective rather than just *functioning* in reality and not having that connection.

You mentioned before that miracles are the one thing that inspired White Cells to fight for their spirituality. What is the main source of inspiration in this modern era?

Awakening people in this day and age has become a problem; it's getting more difficult now. On one hand, technology is a good thing for society and humanity, but on the other hand, it's also helped train the organic brain which, in a lot of ways, can be your enemy. You have to master the brain. Don't allow it to just run on its own. You're in the arena of the mind and everything matters.

The brain gains its fuel and its strength from the data it collects. It then mimics what it learned by incorporating that data into your life. The more data you give the brain, the broader the spectrum of situations and experiences it's able to mimic. The data you accumulate through movies, the internet, magazines and communication with other people is so progressively pushed forward that the brain looks at one thing as its basis of operation. It wants to contain you as much as it can so that you function only as a biological organism. That's the only agenda of the brain.

If you look at any type of bio-organic life with a scientific perspective, you'll see that organism has a goal. Scientists say the reason we developed intelligence was in order for the cells to survive. It's what our species developed as a survival mechanism.

Every species takes a direction and it creates its own design for survival.

Our design, as humans, is intelligence. Our intelligence continues to grow in order for our species to survive and progress. Whether it's right or wrong, it doesn't matter. In my opinion, your brain is designed to keep you asleep.

What would it mean to you if you were to awaken right now? Think about it. If you were to awaken right now without even being able to define the meaning of awakening, you probably would have the inclination that you'd become separated from your organic body. You'll still be in it. You just instinctively gain greater control over everything.

That's what the brain fears. It knows what you fear because it's within you. It fears your awakening so it prevents you from separating from it. This is really a very good thing because every living thing in life has a sense of survival, a sense of self-preservation. If you put a plant in a dark room with a single light source, it will start to grow towards the light. It seeks out what gives it life. You never hear about an animal willingly committing suicide. If human beings commit suicide, it's from great levels of despair or their brain's chemistry is a little off.

Your brain uses the data that you collect through your senses to enrich you. It enriches you because your brain sees most of that data as means of self-preservation. It's saying, "Absorb this knowledge. Absorb this data. Let's utilize it. Let's create better clothing. Let's create better shelter. You can procreate better. It's good for your existence. Let's make medicine. Let's live longer. Let's live better." All these things are good for self-preservation.

But there's a wire crisscross when you say, "I want to separate from the body," or, "I want to gain something that makes me move beyond the body." Nobody ever really thinks about it that way. Nobody ever thinks about death. The desire for separation really says to your inner instinct, or your brain, or your cells that you're ready to move on. The body says, "What do you mean you want to move on? What do you mean you want to separate? You can't do that."

At that point, conflict sets in, and the brain steps in to maintain your existence here. It removes certain factors from your consciousness. It does all of this because it now sees separation as a threat. Organically and spiritually, the brain and the spirit don't necessarily mix. Your spirit is supposed to leave your body when you're dead, not while you're alive. The brain says, "Well, you can't leave. I'm going to keep you here. And if you're going to willingly do this, I need to fix this and prevent the separation from happening."

Psychologically, what do the vast majority of people who have suffered traumas do? They forget the experience. They block it out. Well, it's the same for people who experience miracles. They block it out. There's a connection there. You've got to understand how to *'think without thinking.'*

In other words, don't think with your brain. You're aware of everything already. Get used to that without the contemplation of separation. *Don't think about reaching enlightenment.* Do everything else, but don't contemplate it because then the brain will prevent it from happening and it will be a challenge. If it's too soon for you to learn this then the challenge is even more daunting because you are thinking, "What if I can't do it? What if I'm not able to do it? I'm doomed forever!" There's a time and a place for everything.

By learning to create miracles instead of witnessing them, will it be harder for your brain to block the experience and create fuel for your enlightenment?

Yes, and for one reason only. If you perform miracles, it's almost as if you teach your consciousness and your brain that there's nothing to fear. You're able to perform the miracle and still exist. The brain no longer sees these actions as a threat anymore.

When somebody witnesses a miracle, they often think, "I want to be just like them." Well, what do they mean by "be just like them?" They believe the person is detached and connected to something higher. That's a problem because detachment isn't the only factor in the formula. Rather than focusing on what you're going to become, focus on what you're doing.

These miracles are more about taking little steps instead of huge leaps. But you must realize the little steps rapidly add up. Ultimately, they accelerate your progression. That's what I'm trying to teach you, but you need to communicate with yourself and say, "I have no intentions of dying," when you attempt these acts.

I think a lot of spiritual organizations create more of a problem when they teach you not to be concerned about life. "Forget and just detach from everything in life. Have detachment and you'll find spirituality." I think there might have been a truth to that about 2000 years ago, but in this day and age, the vast majority can't do that. We're too integrated with life. Even if you are out in the middle of a field doing nothing, or sitting in a cave, you'd still hear a plane flying over your head. You will still hear the traffic around you. You would still call out internally for all the comforts that you knew you were familiar with at one time.

I know someone who is very much into tribal spiritual stuff. He absolutely believed in extracting himself from the world. He went to Hawaii in order to pursue this "natural" lifestyle. He was very dedicated, hardcore, opinionated, and adamant about going back to simplicity and isolating himself from everything. He believed that we, as people, could go there in our mind if we could get away from all this constant stimulation.

I wondered about him for a while, but I knew what was going to happen. He was going to go stir crazy after a very short time. Low and behold, I spoke to another friend that also knows him and asked what happened to him. The friend said, "Oh, he came back about two or three weeks later and is working this job now." He just couldn't do it.

It's like I've said before, "you can't unlearn what you already know." Everything is integrated in our lives now. We've become too accustomed to 'things.' Just as a tree grows towards the light, we've shaped ourselves to the design in which our civilization currently exists. It's very hard for us to work out of that. I believe it's biologically ingrained into our design.

When you experience the In-Between states, you're thinking almost nothing. Your thinking is absolutely limited, yet you're in a higher state of consciousness. That's one way of achieving detachment. A lot of spiritual schools teach you that you should just detach, detach, detach and you will find what you want. I don't think that's the way to go. I think a lot of people are trying to find enlightenment but not necessarily *seeking enlightenment*. I think they're seeking peacefulness. They're becoming more simplistic in their way of living. Clearly, their day to day lives are less stressful than what most people are used to, but when they come across a situation that tempts them to go back to their old way of life, they go nuts.

I think about the Buddhist monks that came over to America and made a home in California. While they were meditating and they were in a deep state of consciousness, some kids came up to them and cut their throats. It was a horrible, horrible situation but the investigation gave us insight into the monk's lives. When the investigators arrived at this isolated place where the monks lived, they went through their rooms and all their stuff, and what did they find in their rooms? Pornography. It tells you that these monks were just as vulnerable as everybody else in spite of their spirituality. They were just as interested as other males in certain things, but lacked discipline.

We're very naïve in our personal belief system as to what reality is. No matter how much some spiritual schools tell us to discipline ourselves better by not thinking about this or engaging in that, we are too hardwired into this reality to simply detach from it. In my opinion, my approach is much better because it's the truth.

The Universe was created for us to experience it. That's the purpose of life. You're not here just to find enlightenment. That's not your purpose. Something was created for you; something beautiful, something amazing, something astonishing. Don't think about all of the other wondrous places you can go to or all these other universes just because you don't think this one is stimulating enough. This Universe is amazing! There are so many levels to it. You have to find a happy medium. That's when you're going to attain enlightenment.

Don't separate yourself from people or love. Don't separate yourself from money, but don't engross yourself in it either. Take the middle path. Keep one foot in this world and *want* to be here. Enjoy what's here. Reflect on what *here* is. Reflect on the beauty of what is here and enjoy all of those things, but *seek your spirituality at the same time.*

Red Cells choose to go in one direction which, ironically, is the opposite of spirituality. And these other schools teach their students to go to the opposite extreme by forgetting all about reality in an attempt to become more spiritual. Well, to me, there's a big problem because now you're detaching from the beauty of this world.

Some schools teach, "You shouldn't eat spicy food and certain other types of food. You shouldn't have anything that stimulates you." I agree that you shouldn't harm your body – the body is your temple. It is the mechanism that's going to allow you to attain enlightenment on any level. If you start polluting your body with chemicals and drugs, then you're not going to discover a higher state of consciousness through that body. You're going to find a false level of consciousness, and then you've ruined all the machinery you had to get you there. But, on the same token, I think you need to experience the flavors of life, the healthier ones, the more robust ones that some religions say you shouldn't explore.

As my mother used to say, "It's okay to eat everything that you want to try. Just exercise some moderation." Don't gorge yourself with food. You can have your cheesecake, but do you have to eat the whole thing? That's the type of philosophy that we have to go by. Enjoy life; enjoy the people in your life. Appreciate what you have in your life. But if you sit here and you're miserable because you think by escaping all of this that you're going to be happier, you're really preventing yourself from being able to achieve that happiness.

If you're a matador, you cannot take the bull by the horns. If you do that, you're going to get gored and you'll lose. You've got to put the cape up and let the bull run around a little so it tires out first. Then you can do whatever you want. In the same way, you've got to work with the brain a little bit. Be smarter and say, "I'm not trying to escape from you. I'm trying to improve you. This higher level is still another part of this level. It's all one thing." When you can work in that level and make it non-threatening, you'll want to be here. You'll want to live forever. You'll want to work with the brain, but you'll want a broader spectrum of opportunities. This is when you're going to have better breakthroughs.

The reason why people cannot move into higher states of enlightenment or into enlightenment cycles is because of a particular fear they are holding onto. What is it?

It's fear of Death.

Exactly, it's the fear of death that prevents you from moving into the higher levels. I've said numerous times that your body will still breathe when you are there. It's the same thing that happens if you get hit in the head and go into a coma; your body keeps functioning. The only people who do not survive a coma are those who are severely damaged. You're not damaged. Your brain can do a million things at the same time. Don't worry about your breathing. You're going to open your eyes when you're done. You'd be lucky to meditate for an hour without distraction.

Let yourself go. Learn to just tell your body, "Hey it's cool. Automate. Go on autopilot." You don't have to think about breathing. Are you thinking about breathing right now? Probably not, yet you're doing it. Why do you worry when you're meditating that you're going to stop breathing. You're not. It's always the same fear. Fear controls the mind. The big problem is that you don't even recognize it as fear. You have to be able to recognize something in order to move beyond it.

On the same token, I think if you destroy your body by committing suicide, you're doing the opposite thing. You're not going to release yourself and get there sooner. You're going to be all jacked up because you were supposed to get data from this dimension. This is part of the big picture. There's a reason behind it all.

If you detach from reality, are you still able to affect the collective consciousness?

If you choose to detach, the challenge becomes detaching from the fact that you're trying to detach in the first place. Think about it. You can achieve it, but it's like holding your breath until you turn blue. It doesn't necessarily mean you're going to pass out, but what are you doing to your body at the same time? You're destroying a lot of cells. I think if you push yourself hard enough, you are going to detach from reality. You are going to go out there, but there's a big problem with all of that.

There's a much easier way to achieve the very same thing that detachment offers, if not more so. Most people don't have the stamina to commit to complete detachment anyway. For this reason, they say, "Well, there's no reason for me to pursue this path because I can't be like an isolated Buddhist monk. There's no hope for me." Rubbish! There's plenty of hope for you. *You just have to learn to dance with the bull while waving a cape instead of trying to grab the bull by the horns.* You're going to lose if you try to force this. If you try to go hardcore, you're likely going to lose. If you think you're going to detach from everything by going to Hawaii or some other place where you can isolate yourself, you're going to get a big reality shock. You're going to come back with a bad taste in your mouth thinking you can't do anything right. If you beat yourself up enough, you're going to give up on your spirituality. The brain is going to win and you're just going to say, "I can't do this."

Don't set any expectations. They're your worst enemy. If you don't achieve it because it turns out to be harder than you thought, you're programming yourself to think you'll probably never be able to do it. You're telling yourself that you're a loser and not a winner. I'm saying to you, "You are a guaranteed winner, but you've just got to work with the flow." You've got to realize that there's a different strategy you can utilize, and that strategy doesn't have to go against the grain.

I'm always saying, "Harness the wind. Harness the flow. Feel the flow." I'm always talking about moving with something. What is it that I'm referring to? Do not try to force something like this. Don't paddle up the stream. Flow with it. There's always a different method if you just use your brain in a positive way. There is a way.

You must communicate with your organic self. You've got to talk to the cells of your body in a way that your organic self can comprehend like, "This is good for the both of us." Then you've got to convince yourself. When you can convince yourself, that's when you're going to have even bigger breakthroughs.

You must be at peace with your inner universe and say, "I have your best interests in mind," and internally feel that. Don't just say the words. Your cells don't understand words. They *feel* what you feel emotionally. You create the connection that your spirituality is what is making you feel wholesome and happy, and everything is good because of it. You must prove to your body that these positive changes come from this thing that you're doing. Show yourself that it's making you stronger, better, and more improved! It's going to consciously work on some other level.

The body's intelligences, all grouped together, have a big say in what you're doing. You may think you're in control, but on a micro level they're collectively in control. That's the autopilot instinct. For example, can you tell yourself not to be hungry? If so, how long do you think you could do that? The answer is until that intelligence has had enough. What exactly is telling you that you are hungry? What is setting off those receptors? If you're uncomfortable sitting in a chair, how long do you think you could sit there? Well, if you think you don't have to convince your body to let you move to these higher levels and that it's a good place for you, you're wrong.

You've got to recognize what things are. When you can do that, you're dancing with the bull. You're working with the flow. You're harnessing this thing. Talk to the cells in your body and say, "Look, we're going to take this to the highest level. We're going to propagate life everywhere." What do you think goes through my mind? Why do you think I'm able to do the things that I'm able to do? What is spiritually going through Eric Pepin's head and his body?

I love every sensation of this dimension. I love every aspect of life. In my head, I tell the cells of my body that I am proliferating life. I'm helping other living beings to expand. This is in agreement with my cells; therefore, I have less conflict from them. I'm not saying they don't have their moments. But I have a greater harmony because of my perception of life; enjoying life, and enjoying my spirituality and these other dimensions.

I've made this agreement with my body that works very well for me, and I think this is what most spiritual people do. Even Buddha said when he reached enlightenment, "It's not this path and that path. It's the middle path." People interpret that however they want to, and when they share their interpretation you are getting their opinion.

That is what Buddha figured out himself, but it is nothing new. It is just a matter of trying to communicate it in a better way, to get the message across to you. The message helps no one if it can't be understood.

I'm trying to get back to the harmony that I have with life. I feel people; I feel what it's like to be a human. I'm not the kind of teacher that only preaches. I'm alive! Be alive! Enjoy life. Enjoy who you are. Be charismatic. Be fun. You can be spiritual at the same time. I think it's a better, faster way to attain what you need to do. Your goal is to help life. Internalize that and say, "This is my goal. Help me to reach these higher states of consciousness and I will proliferate life."

Everything is a living organism. The planet is a living organism. I've convinced my body, on one particularly important level, to think like I think. I've come to a certain agreement and this is what allows me to work with these higher dimensions, to come and go, to connect, and to do these things. There's no threat.

I see it as a dance; as an embrace. I see it as being important to my life because I say, *"Look cells. If you guys take this away from me, we're not going to live. I'm going to be down and out. Spirituality is my sunshine. It's my water. I eat food for you, but if you want me to grow, you've got to give me this too and we're all going to be happy."*

In a simple way, I'm trying to say what I internally feel. Obviously it's much more complex than this, but I'm trying to explain to you that, somehow, in some way, you have to love life. You have to be a lover of life. Somehow you've got to have that communication with the cells of your body. Be aware they are very limited in what they understand, but there's programming in them also. If you find a way to work with the programming, you can beat the program. Then you can harness that potential.

Don't fight old age. You're going to grow old. Embrace it. I hate it, too. But there are perks that come with aging, and that's what you have to look for. You have to find the positive in everything, harness it, and see where it's going to take you. If you never grew old, you would never become wiser. Not at least in this reality.

There's a way to preserve age but there will also come a point when you're going to want to die. You're going to want to move on because there's only so much you can take in this world. But for right now, live! Be alive! Dance, sing, have a good time. Live life. Enjoy it, but pursue your spirituality too and know that it's your sunshine. It's like breathing! It's another form of giving yourself life, and that's what you have to understand. Most people never contemplate that. They never get that connection. And if they do, they don't think about it enough.

Your body is made of billions of living cells. Within it, there are sources of information that I call *originators* that work with the other cells of your body. Together they communicate something to you or react to something. The reaction starts with one single cell, but there's always an originator.

Knowing that the world is a living organism, convince yourself that you're the cell that will make the difference. Convince yourself that you are needed to the planet as an extra sensory cell. Convince yourself and communicate to the greater cell, which you exist within, that you are required to be of a greater importance.

It's ironic that humans turn to science to try to convince themselves when, "Science says so and so, therefore, it must be true." It erodes the doubt so that you can have a successful breakthrough. This is why I talk in the manner that I do.

Science has found that not only are there white cells, but there are also super white cells. White cells are, ironically, asleep in hibernation. These cells have ancient knowledge. It turns out this is useful against ancient, powerful viruses that the cells had previously battled. So when you contract one of these viruses and it starts to wipe out all the other white cells and destroys the body; somehow, something awakens from your inner universe.

Perhaps super cells are awakened by the inner desire to survive. With their ancient knowledge, they start to fiercely battle against this powerful virus. Sometimes they're awakened too late, but if they're awakened in time, they almost always win the battle. They're that fierce. They're that powerful. They're that determined.

So be that Super White Cell. Be that. Do not *try* to be. *Know that you are.* Send out to this planet, this organism, through emotion that you are useful in that way. Acknowledge all the other living cells, but stand out in a sense. You are amongst them, you're functioning, but you're a Super White Cell and you're waiting to be awakened if you're needed.

The planet has a consciousness and it's everywhere. Let it know what you acknowledge yourself to be. When it chooses to put you to use, it's another form of enlightenment. It is enlightenment. It's a part of that awakening process.

You're no longer held to the basic rules of the Doe. You've now been granted permission to bend the rules because of what you were designed to do. Acknowledge that you serve it. There's not a reason or a need to keep you in a certain alignment or a certain place. Since it knows that you're going to serve it, there must be a reason why you're concerned. There must be a reason why you want to awaken. You have to let the planet know that you're ready when it's ready. *You have to internalize that.* That is part of the great awakening.

If you were to ask me what I feel, or what Christ felt, or Buddha felt, or any great being? They felt exactly what I'm talking about now. They knew and accepted, without any ego. That was their role. That was their purpose.

Now, maybe they thought of it as the Gaia Mind. Maybe they had other words for the same thing. It was the same thing, just different semantics to describe it. Internally, the universal knowing within them understood what it was: they served this higher purpose to affect something greater.

That's what you have to come to terms with. You have to awaken. You have to say, "I don't have to be awakened this minute, but I'm ready. That's what I prepared for. That's why I am here and what I was born to do. That's what I know as truth."

A Red Cell won't feel anything. They don't even comprehend what I'm saying; they can't even conceive it. But the older White Cell is thinking, "That's it! That's it! That's what I'm feeling. That's what's calling me." If you don't know what's calling you, how do you know how to respond to it? You feel it, but what is it you feel? You're searching.

You are part of an organism. It's hard to understand the planet as an organism because then it begs the question, "How is that spiritual?" It's all the same in the end! The planet is also a part of this thing that wants to live: God – The Universe! You're here now, in this world, in this dimension to serve the Universe. You're here to serve God. Call it whatever you want, but you cannot serve It unless you are willing to accept that as what you're here to do. You need to come to terms with that.

Now, it doesn't mean you're going to go around healing people and fighting demons. Do not have anticipation. This is what grounds you. Just practice what you have learned. Meditate. Breathe. Enjoy life. Practice the exercises that I have taught you.

Your consciousness will unfold just like a rose will start from a bud and then bloom; that is what you have to understand. It will open on its own. Do not set expectations. Do not set demands. If you set demands on the Universe and you set expectations, you won't get anything. It doesn't understand that.

It doesn't matter to me what other people think about me because I already know who and what I am. Remember not to become arrogant about who you are. Don't become overconfident. Spiritual people have an inner beauty. That's what you feel from them. They are what they are. They know who and what they are.

You don't have to be as intelligent as they are to be bright. You can be a 500 watt light bulb in the dark or you can be a candle; I guarantee you that both of them are going to be seen. Maybe you'll be outshined by somebody. Well, if they're shining brighter, then they must be doing something better than you. No ego. Just flow. If it's dark, it's dark. Any light will shine. Be any kind of light the Universe wants you to be, but let it know that you understand that's what you were designed for. Internalize that.

Chapter 4

THE HIDDEN KEY

I want to tell you about a key that I personally use in my spiritual practices. Everybody wonders how I do what I do, so I'm constantly thinking of ways to communicate and show you what I do.

I want to create a level of enlightenment within people. You have to work, study, and become very spiritual to reach enlightenment. Most people think that you're either enlightened or you're not. I don't see it as just an on or off switch.

There are a series of thoughts that have to occur. These thoughts are what evolve the dimensional being enabling them to harness the consciousness of the Universe. By harnessing the consciousness of the Universe, you have God-like consciousness. How do I show you how to do that? I'll begin by telling you how to use a 'key.'

What is a 'key'?

There many kinds of keys. In this case, a key is not a physical metal key. Rather, it's a frequency that you carry within you. It is how you feel. A key is a thing of beauty. It is an emotion that you feel and emanate but don't verbalize internally. You must maintain non-thought but still think without words. It's a place with a very specific feeling that you are aware of in your chest or your heart area.

It's this other intelligence that I often speak about, and you feel a certain emotion with that intelligence. It is a level of calmness, or inner peace without anything clinging to it. That feeling is married with happiness, or the feeling of whatever effect you are creating. You use a key to affect another being, create a dimensional portal, or make a plant grow. Of course, there's a lot more to the complexity of all this, but they are all frequencies – like recipes.

So I find this indifferent place inside of me. It's a place of non-motivated physical intention, but there's definitely an intention involved. I then feel a level of bliss which is kindness, love, and passion, like you just want to hug and love something. It's not the act of hugging; I'm not thinking about physically touching someone. The hug you imagine depends on your true heart. There are fake hugs, fake expressions, like gestures of just meeting somebody and hugging them or saying hello to the family and hugging them.

There are a deep moments within people who genuinely love another person and genuinely emote from this heart-place of absolute love. It's like broadcasting. It's almost like you're speaking and saying, "I want to bathe you in this feeling. I want to protect you. I want to nourish you. I want to heal you." You are emoting a certain feeling out; it's a real thing. That's what I feel as part of this key that I create.

Reality is based on the fabric of God. As sure as your flesh is a collection of individual organisms, reality in this dimension is the flesh of God. In order to approach God, you must resonate with Its truest form, or at least attempt to try the best you can to create that form within yourself. If I'm going to ask the Universe to do something for me, I can't say it in words. I have to talk in a different universal language. This is what I'm trying to teach you.

What's the process for creating a key?

I create a feeling of clarity, or calmness within my chest center. Then I fill it with the emotion of absolute love. It's like I want to reach out and hold or caress something, but I'm not searching for a physical acknowledgement. So, there is an acknowledgment there. Let's use the concept of filling a jelly doughnut. Placing the filling inside of the doughnut is my intention, but the substance of my intention creates the key.

Here's another example. Let's say I have a plant and I want to make it grow. I approach the plant without intent. Otherwise the plant would feel the intent. My intent is like a barrier to it since the projection is coming from a human. The human feels alien to the plant, yet at the same time, it's also familiar. The plant is going to react a certain way. There's a certain guaranteed reaction for every action. So I approach it without emotion: no feeling, no vibe, no intention, no love, nothing.

Then I muster within me this absolute feeling of deep love that I would have for God. I feel it in my chest area and I emote it out onto the plant. In some cases, I project it out with my breath because I believe moisture can hold data. So I breathe this intention of love and the plant is just going, "Aahhhhh, this is wonderful!" This feeling is what tells it to grow, expand, and flourish. It's a communication that's not in words. It's a feeling. *What does it feel like?* That's what everybody's missing. What does something feel like? That's what you've got to broadcast. *That is code.*

Do you visualize the whole plant growing?

I don't see the plant growing as a whole plant. I am feeling what it's like to see the molecular structure of the plant bursting and spreading. I feel what it's like to see the micro-organisms - the cells - working very rapidly, faster than usual, creating and building. Then I see the harnessing and outstretching of the plant like a vine, but it's really a curled leaf. I see the curling and I see moisture moving through the leaf like blood through veins, and I project this by breathing outward. That's what I encourage the plant to do.

Here is the greatest secret – I did not choose to affect it on a *macro* level. I chose to affect it on a *micro* level. I went to the micro-organism level and communicated with that. Not seeing it as a whole but seeing it as micro-verse and it's most intimate level of singular beings.

The ones you really need to communicate with are the individual micro components. You need to communicate your intent directly to the most finite level in order to create an effect on the macro - as a whole - so that, collectively, each individual does what you need them to do. The intent is presented in a very good-spirited state of consciousness. This God-like consciousness is familiar to them as the universal command. It's where the code comes from that instructs them to exist the way they do.

In the end, it's God. You can call upon this beauty of God; it doesn't have to be so perfect for a plant so just do the best you can. It's like God saying, "Well, this is what I want you to do." I encode that feeling and project it. As I'm maintaining the outer core of love, the inner core is simultaneously sending out my whole intention, or will, to the micro-organisms, the molecular life living within that plant. I don't see the leaf unrolling; I see the micro life growing.

You create the key within your heart area and you project it outwards. The projection, the beaming out, the moving outward, is what I call *the key*. It's extended outside of me as if I reach out to unlock something. I reach out in my interpretation mentally with something other than my hand. This reaching out is a tool because it's coded with data. It has a certain dressing of intentions in there, but they're not the same intentions you physically understand. So, you've got to throw out your human thinking. The dressing of the intention is the notches on the side of the key. It's what unlocks the tumblers inside the lock.

The projection reaches out to create an effect, and I'm absolutely confident it will have an effect. It doesn't dawn on me to question whether the plant will react or not. I simply *know* it will. The fact that I believe it and know it will happen is what maintains the structure of the key. Doubt deteriorates the quality of the key; then the micro life won't react to it.

Like all things, this takes practice. All the classes I've ever taught are like keys, if you know how to apply them. If you understand *Ties That Bind*, which is the class on energy, you can combine the skills you need to create and project these keys. *Ties That Bind* is one of the chapters in my previous book, *Meditation Within Eternity*.

Do you have to be at a certain skill level to project the key?

You have to be at a certain level of purity so that you have the consistency to be able to hold a frequency that is close to that of God. You can throw yourself down in front of a truck and say you're doing it for God, but in truth, are you? Are you not being a martyr? You have to refine yourself as a spiritual being by the choice of your existence; the choice of the level at which you exist.

Even I fluctuate from a spiritual state of being to a normal state of being. It's just easier for me to return to this spiritual place than it is for most people. You cannot perform miracles so easily if you're in a normal state of mind because you exist in the reality of the Doe which holds you there. You must create a new state of mind or an environment around you that evokes a spiritual state of being; something that makes you feel spiritual and connected. You have to inspire yourself to be spiritual. You have to actively choose to seek out the spiritual in everyday life when you decide you want to go to that place in order to do the work.

Can keys be found in nature?

Yes. Go for a walk in nature and find a tree that's emanating a key twenty-four/seven. That will emote back to you like a reflection so that you are in that spiritual zone. Then you can choose to operate from there and harness that vibration - that key. The classes I teach and the knowledge I give are also keys to be harnessed; these are your tools.

Certain things have the code and certain things do not. Getting up out of bed and sitting at the edge of my bed feeling whatever I feel in the morning does not hold the code. It holds a certain feeling, but it doesn't hold the code. Going down stairs and sitting in my chair relaxing does not hold the code.

When I'm in the shower and the water temperature is ever so right, I just stare or lean into the wall of the shower. The water is beating rhythmically and there is a certain moment that comes, a micro moment. If you feel it, you can leap into it because you recognize it. It's as if time stops and you feel a certain inner peace. Part of you is pulled into that place. It's very calming, very beautiful, and after a few moments, you're pulled back into the shower. *That is a moment.*

Imagine walking through a park. The wind is blowing and the kids are playing but, for some reason, something speaks to you. You feel the gentle warm breeze on your body and there's a part of you that slows. You don't realize you're slowing, but you recognize that something is happening. To somebody like me, time stops. Even though in your world I'm still moving, there's a sense of serenity for me in that moment. There's a savoring.

There's something to be said about that moment. That moment is a key. It's data. It's a very important place.

Do all trees hold these keys?

No, you can look at a dozen trees and they all look beautiful, but then there's that one tree that holds your attention. In that moment, it reflects a key. That key is not the tree itself. The key is what you are feeling in your chest area when you observe it. Most human beings project out and say, "This is the cause." It is a cause but it's not what you're really after. You're looking for the *feeling* that tree evokes inside yourself. It's a certain kind of peacefulness, and it's distinctly different than the breezes or the shower. These are the specific words to a language you have to learn to decode. It is at least as difficult as learning to speak another language. There is no translation software program for this. And this language is more alien than a spoken language.

There are times when I will sit down in the corner of the bathroom, in the dark, and just be still. I'm not after the darkness in an evil way. It doesn't even occur to me in that sense. There is a peaceful moment that comes from the echoing of the structure of the bathroom. There's a certain *'deafening quietness'* with its small little ticks here and there; that's what I savor. It is a moment of peace of a certain kind of language. There's a certain vibration about it that I'm after. It's like a restful moment, yet it's none of those things. It's what it makes me *feel like*; that's what I'm really after.

I put myself in a position that projects the feeling into me, but if I don't acknowledge the feeling inside, then I'm just functioning (on a physical level). It's like eating a piece of gourmet chocolate – rather than just chewing and swallowing it, I savor it. I savor the feels-like. I put forth the effort to contemplate this. It's not about thinking. It's an inner savoring that comes from your inner being.

Moments like these come and go. Sometimes you lose them because of the intruding sounds in the environment, but it's still there. You might think these moments come when it's quiet, yet it's a different kind of savoring. There are plenty of other moments in loud environments, too.

How do you feel these moments?

I take a deep breath, draw it in and feel. There's an inner peace to the moment, although it will leave soon. I call it a *shift*. Sometimes you walk into your room and there will be a shift. I can feel a shift happen in a whole restaurant. The next minute everybody's clanging dishes and talking. I can create the emotion I want, project it outward, and then everybody will suddenly get quiet.

Can Red Cells feel it too? Why do they all get quiet?

Because, unconsciously, they're reacting to some kind of communication they don't understand. It's like a wave comes over them and they suddenly feel like they have less to talk about. Someone like me sees it happen like a big wave.

What if I took you through a situation I know you can relate to and create the emotions I've been explaining. You understand the example I gave of the shower, the feeling, the moment. You understand the moment of sitting out on a grassy hill and feeling each blade of grass underneath your hands; there's a moment that you're savoring. There's a feeling. If I can create a series of very specific emotions and you can hold them within you, I suspect, theoretically, you will shift to a very high state of consciousness. This is a live frequency that has no other choice but turning and opening a key inside of you in the end.

You were talking about windows that capture the mind and take you to a faraway place, and you were talking about its purpose. On one level, it's to contemplate, to get used to it, to understand it better. Was there another use you had in mind for that? Did you have anything else to add to that?

A window is a moment in which you experience something on the other side of it. I use the word window because, as a human being, I understand there's something to see through that window.

To me, a window is an opportunity, an opening, a hole in a wall, but you could also climb through it. When I say "window," you automatically think of it as being something you could climb through. I don't call it a doorway because a window has glass, and glass has clarity. If I call it a doorway, you will perceive it differently. If I call it a window, you really shouldn't climb through it, but it is a window of opportunity. If you really need to get out, it's still a way to get out. It's just a matter of perception. Will you allow yourself to do it? Most people won't because they're told by their Governor it's a window, not a door. So, it makes more sense to call it a window rather than a doorway.

You might not recognize the feeling as being a language; hence, the reason it's on the other side. It's something you can view but can't touch. You can't necessarily get to it because you're told you're not supposed to. You're told you're not supposed to because you're not in the physical realms of how you identify with reality by touch, smell, taste, hearing, and sight. So, you have to recognize that it is something real. It does something more than what you may perceive it to do. Music can sometimes create those things, but the problem is the music is so tailor made for evoking very standardized emotions that you can relate to very easily.

This is a lot more intricate. That's why you have to recognize that it takes great skill. You cannot allow a secondary thought to come in if you're going to follow the process of creating this state of consciousness. The instant you do, you've polluted it.

This is where skill and training come in. You can sit there and say, 'Well, I'm spiritual. I did this and I do that, so it should work. You must learn to hold the note perfectly. If you can't hold the note perfectly, then you do not gain entrance. Work on your art. Work on your perfection.

So, I'm going to create a series of feelings in you based on what's going through my mind right now. You must use your imagination as I talk you through it. It may even help to record these words and listen to them as if it were a meditation. Capture the feels-like of the words as I speak them.

You're now in the moment. You're standing in the shower. Feel the wall of the shower. Feel the water moving. The water's moving in a rhythm. You're watching the water. The water is now turning into molecular lights, sparkling, moving.

You're now sitting in a field. You can feel the grass. The grass on your hands. The thickness of the grass and the blades between your fingers. You can feel a soft summer breeze moving across you. The warmth of the sun on your face and on your back.

As you look up, you see a tree to your left side. The tree to your left side is a giant, mighty oak tree with big wide girthing branches. It has a certain tone, a certain thickness, a certain calmness it is projecting to you.

If you can internalize each one of those words, those expressions as an emotion that is a communication that I am giving you. *Feel how it makes you feel.* It's a way to get around the Babbler.

If I say to you, "You're sitting at the kitchen table flipping through the newspaper. You're now putting on your shoes." You can't hit those higher states of consciousness by listening to this kind of communication.

Does it happen sporadically, or can you evoke it?

You can evoke it. I suspect that if I can formulate for you a series of evocations of thought, you can evoke the feelings you need. If you can follow that specific pattern, there's going to be a result. The only way it won't work is if you mess it all up with secondary thoughts and emotions. You can't un-know something you already know. The question is, do you deserve it?

Well, I trust in the Universe and I know how complex it is. If it doesn't work, then you weren't able to hold all your tones well enough so you need to go back and study your other classes. If you've studied your classes and learned your skills, you'll understand when to jump, when to hop, and when to bend a certain way. If you bend too hard, you'll break. If you bend too little, it won't be enough.

You'll know how to bend because you've studied your other classes. Your mental reactions should be perfected art from reflecting and working with them. If you use your skills of wax-on/wax-off, it should work. So, if you don't have a good enough resonance, you won't get in. If you've got negative energy, you won't get in. Now does that mean everybody who doesn't get in is a jerk and has terrible energy? No, it means maybe your rhythm hasn't been perfected yet.

An ordinary fisherman doesn't have it when casting a line out, but a fly-fisher does. It's the rhythm. It's not the fishing pole. It's not the fly. It's not the casting of the line. It's the dance. It's the feeling it evokes when I see this movement, this dance. There's a certain conscious zone that I feel. I don't know anything about fly-fishing, but it's a language and I can feel it. I know that's what fly-fishers feel if they are really into the zone, but they probably don't know many other languages.

It's the rhythm. How does the rhythm feel? There is no rhythm of sound; there is a rhythm of movement. What does the movement feel like? I'm trying to give you the secret to understanding the Universe right now. I'm trying to teach you what I'm feeling as an enlightened being.

There is obviously something distinctly different that I'm doing that other people aren't doing. I feel that emotion and I gravitate towards it. It's pleasing to my inner being. It's talking to me. The fisherman isn't talking to me. The fishing pole isn't talking to me. The line curling in the air as it touches the water and lifts again is not exactly talking to me, but there is something in that action that is visually bringing me into the zone. There's something very familiar about that act. What could it mean? Why does it feel so good? Is it because it's calm, because it's perfection? Is it movement without thought? Whatever it is, there is information there that can't be summarized in any specific way; it's a feeling. You already know it. You have this ability.

I believe the hemispheres of the brain plays a huge role in all this and helps you to become more fluidic. You must have an inner balance of masculine and feminine energy. *Just find that inner balance.* That's what triggers your brain to turn on certain centers. You have to use the organic brain to help you to get through this organic dimension first, and like the fly fisherman, it will help you to get into the zone, to become more fluidic.

You were talking about these keys, or windows that you can move into. I know what you're talking about. I've looked at sunsets and I felt this before. What do I do with that feeling, that key?

Take a plant and project that feeling of a sunset into that plant through a key. How will the plant respond to that sunset? Maybe it won't respond at all. Maybe it will make the plant grow like crazy, or maybe it'll kill it altogether. If you learn how to internalize these languages, then you can emote them out to people, objects, and to the Universe to talk to God. God doesn't understand words. Sometimes you've got to come up with the next best level of communication. All these keys need to be memorized so that you can put together a galactic sentence to see what the response is going to be from the Universe. It might change night to day. And that's how I do miracles!

Something inside of me has to say that *I want it to rain.* I don't verbally say, "I want it to rain." There is a different kind of communication that says, "I want it to rain," but it certainly isn't in vocal words. It's like playing an instrument perfectly; if one note is out of tune, nothing will happen because my key is missing a notch. I could have all the other notches right, but there's one too long or too short. The difference between a master and a novice is how good can they master and hold these things.

In one of my other books, *Meditation Within Eternity,* I taught you everything you need to know about energy. This is a big key. This is the *missing link* that nobody understands and most people don't have the aptitude to learn. If you really want to do what I can do, then you're going to have to work on it and master it. As sure as a fish will swim in water, once you get through certain states of mind, it will come to you.

I have a bonsai tree. Should I simply project a feeling of love to that tree?

You've got to create that feeling in your heart center. Feel that bonsai inside yourself. Feel it. Love it. Nourish it and desire to give that love as if it's an act from your inner self, projecting it all into that plant.

See the water within the veins of the tree. *See* each cellular being of it growing. That's what you've got to talk to, not the whole bonsai. If somebody talked to the planet as a whole, would they get an answer? If you were in a UFO and said, "Hey planet, how's it going," what is the planet going to do? But if you went down and talked to several people who live on this planet, that information would spread in a micro-organism level until you've got a big response from the planet because we are the cells of the planet. *You have to talk to the micro level.* Visualize it, and feel what it is to be that micro level. If you use your assimilation skills to assimilate that micro level, you've got a hell of a key being created.

So you create that key?

Yes, and you have to do it all without any force.

What about love or intent?

Love it. If you will it, it won't work. Shower it with what you desire of it and what you expect it to do. You want it to reciprocate that love. How does it give you love? It doesn't communicate the way you do, so it gives it to you visually. What does a plant give that's beautiful to us? Flowers, growth, lushness and all you're saying is, "Return what I've just given you. Show me love back." It'll want to reciprocate. It will want to give it back to you.

So, as I bring my love, I bring it to the One, The Force?

I recommend that you work with plants rather than trying to commune with the Universe right away because it's so vast. It is vast but in a way it's molecular, it's tiny, and it's everywhere. So, I don't perceive it as being that vast. When I think like a human, I see the vastness of it. Its vastness is a key that I can't hold onto – it's so massive. It's a limitation of human thought.

By mastering the smaller things, eventually, just like with any other skill, you will get better at it. You will work up to the bigger things. Just practice on stuff that you can reap rewards from. I could say to you "hello" from here and you would respond back "hello." Or I could say "hello" from the Swiss Alps and there would be a long pause before I heard a response from you. In that amount of time, I might have left, thinking there was no response.

We all have certain expectations of how we think things should work, but they don't always work the way we expect them to. Wait until the next day and see what the result is. Don't sit there feeling disappointed that the plant didn't react instantly. You've got to understand you're asking an awful lot of that micro universe. It needs to gather its energy, but it *will* react. So you have to look the next day and see if there's a difference.

At other times you can make it happen even faster but there has to be outside resources to make it happen that fast. Use other techniques, like manifestation, to make molecules formulate into matter to build into the plant at a faster-than-natural rate.

Having an expectation can be very dangerous also. Most people would say, "Oh I was hoping to see something." You are now degrading the key that you set in motion because that plant is feeling the failure that you feel for it. That's going to be easily projected because it is more natural to think negatively. I would suggest walking away when you're done. There's no doubt in my mind there's going to be an effect. It's doesn't occur to me to doubt.

Is meditating for world peace effective?

When I see groups of people all mediating on world peace, I see good intention coupled with an ineffective method. Think about their methods, how they're meditating for world peace and compare it to what I've just taught you. They feel it and they project love. They project a sense of happiness to the people, but they just see the planet in a happy space. It'll have some effect but it's not going to have the effect it was meant to have.

What would be a better way?

You want to look at life on a molecular level and see the human race like bacteria. You want to start on individuals and see them as being small pieces of bacteria. See them emanating out with a vibration to other people and see it spreading out more like bacteria in a Petri dish. It creates a different feeling in you. In fact, it's so odd to think that way that it's actually uniquely refreshing.

Don't think of bacteria as a bad thing; you've got to be careful how you perceive things. Perceive positively rather than negatively. See the planet as a living organism but not as a whole. Think about it like you would the bonsai. You want to see the molecular level of human life. You want to perceive human beings in their bodies. The cells of their bodies communicate to the cells of all human life. Let it start there and work its way out.

Good music is banging on a guitar. Fantastic music is an art that takes skill and perfection. In the end, fantastic music is a masterpiece and lasts a lifetime. So the approach must be done with precision.

Who are you talking to when you want to create peace on earth? Are you talking to the right thing or should you be talking to much smaller things? You might think, "Well, that seems overwhelming because there are trillions of cells in just one person." If we started a long time ago with thousands of years of spiritual people doing their thing, I think we would have things pretty well covered by now.

You think in terms of how long it's going to take and, ultimately, you think failure. Without even saying it, there's a subconscious acknowledgement of size. So right away, you are programmed with certain thoughts that you are not even acknowledging on the surface. You should stop and check what you just felt. You don't want to entertain those subconscious thoughts. When you do find them, you're trained not to acknowledge them. If you acknowledge them, you start thinking that it is overwhelming.

I'll give you a new way to think about this whole thing. Imagine a little speck of bacteria is placed in a Petri dish. What happens in twenty four hours? It reproduces. Sometimes starting smaller is faster.

Some of my students ask, "What can I do?" Well, some of you will become healers. Some of you will become warriors. Some of you will become communicators to transcend time and space to other worlds. If you can learn to talk the way I'm teaching you to talk, and you can learn to communicate on a micro-verse level, you can project your skills.

If you are a healer, project a healing for the world on a micro level. Don't try to heal the people from AIDS. For example, *attack the virus*; think molecularly. See the virus in your mind. You know it already through the collective consciousness; you simply have to choose to move into the collective consciousness and not think in words but *feel it* in your mind. I want to say visualize, but it's not a visualization, it's a knowing. You can feel it now if you think about the virus, the organism. What does it feel like? It has a feeling and that is what you have to heal or destroy. Then broadcast that frequency out to a living organism as the secret to destroy this.

As a communicator, you can transcend time and space to other worlds if you can learn to communicate in this sense. Warriors will fight other beings that are projecting damage to the micro-level of this organism. The planet is a micro-organism. It is a living thing made out of billions of smaller living organisms. It's a matter of how you perceive life. You cannot look at life as human life; you've got to look at it as an organism made of smaller living organisms. Then you start working your way back and forth. My mind has never stopped seeing the world as living organisms. It's never thought of it in an individual format.

I see people moving in waves. I see streets as blood vessels. I see Gaia. I see the micro-organism all the time. People spend too much time thinking on this one dimension they're in. This is why they cannot bend or fold time and space. It's a perception they lock themselves into. It doesn't occur to me to think in that way. When I think of peoples' thoughts, I think of them as a wave of consciousness that was created from a few cells which manipulated other cells. It's like a bacteria consciousness. This thought wave, which can be positive or negative, is broadcast to the organic level where it manifests as a reaction.

That's how I perceive everything. I see continents as hemispheres. To me it's all like bacteria communicating. I see everything as electrical energy, communicating like a bacteria spreading. The closest thing to God is not a human, nor is it a plant. *The closest thing to God is the smallest thing that's a breath away from being energy that just crossed over to being matter.* Talk to the bridge between energy and matter. The bridge is the molecular level.

The bridge is the potential to connect.

Yes, if you want to call it that. That is where you've got to go. It's how you talk to that micro level. What does it understand? You can find micro life so finite that if you were to will it dead, it would die. That's how receptive it is to your energy field, and if you will life into it, it will flourish. It's all within us.

When you say "all within us,"
is that because of the Prana within us.

Yes. All is one. You just simply need to figure out how to release it. Thinking in human terms will confuse you.

So this is what you're talking about when you say,
"Turn your inward outward?"

Yes.

That's the key you're explaining?

Yes, I've been referring to it all the time; it's just a matter of explaining it in different ways. Some people will wonder why I didn't explain it this way at the very beginning. It wouldn't have made sense at the beginning. You had to go through all that to get to this understanding. You're always working from the macro to the micro because you're already in the macro. I can't expect you to be in the micro if you're just not there. I have to take you from where you are and bring you to here.

So, on a micro level you can use your abilities to help other people; heal somebody that's ill, clear the negative energy in a house, and defend yourself from another person who has very dark energy and evil intentions. Collectively, globally, you can work with others on a macro level. It's all a matter of how you focus that energy or how you connect into the grid. Macro or micro doesn't matter in the end. It's just a matter of perceiving where it is, and that's the hard part. The final agenda is basically global influence, but this is just one part of it.

I do see things much grander and larger than that. When groups attempt to meditate on a subject, they bomb it with thought. In my opinion, this creates little or no effect. The secret is in the preparation of focused consciousness and the ability to imagine or envision the micro level of the subject. It's the micro level that effectively masses outwards to create an effect on a global level. By applying the technique of focused attention, non-thought, mind projection, empathy, and so forth, on a micro level, that is what may create an effect on a macro level. Earth and its inhabitants are a micro life. It is a perception. By having this perception, a certain frequency is permitted to exist. Operating or functioning in this frequency allows the total effect.

When working on a micro level you cannot expect instantaneous visual results. Micro life works on a different schedule. Not having a visual experience may cause an outward emotion that can cancel the micro level effect. Sending negative emotion after projecting is not recommended. After finishing your projection, you should enter a non-thought state, physically remove yourself from the location of the target and not think about it for at least 20 to 30 minutes.

**I need to get to the other side of the rabbit hole.
I'm partially through, but not all the way.
I'm still working on getting to the other side.**

Well, I think you're going to get there just fine. It's like sitting out in the rain: just keep listening, keep thinking about it, and keep absorbing the material. As sure as you're going to get wet sitting out in the rain, as long as you keep listening to it, it's going to click. You'll enter an enlightenment cycle and one day it'll just hit you. I was very young when I entered my first two enlighten-ment cycles. You won't see it coming. You may be thinking about something completely off topic when it hits you.

It all makes sense. I'm so glad that you're sharing, teaching, and bringing out the truth.

I'm frustrated at many of the other teachers in the world. Yet, I feel like I have no right to say that. Who would say such a thing? Who would be so arrogant and cocky? There are a lot of teachers who don't teach any of this, and the ones that do aren't really releasing the information out there. There are a lot of people who I'm not reaching yet. Maybe somebody else on the other side of planet is saying in Chinese, "Damn all the other spiritual teachers for not saying anything about all of this!"

There are a lot of different variations of my teachings. They're all one course but I see them as categories of areas I want to enter. In other words, you could be an artist using your paints and palettes, yet that world is different than the part of you that's a professional mountain biker. You could blend two areas together but, for the most part, these realities are very separate functions. Your nine to five job would be a whole different reality from the others. I see these as micro bubbles of different things.

In another class, you talked about going In-Between and you tried to explain this vampire-like state where you see things differently and have different abilities. When you're in that state, do you have different abilities or "gifts?"

So, seeing energy is more of a dimensional effect. You could also factor in the micro level, but for me that's a different place. I see the physical dimension as a place of power because that's where we reside right now. Beings like vampires see the world differ-ently. No matter what your skill, every single White Cell has the ability to go to that place that you are talking about. So that's not a moment of learning your skill. Every single White Cell will have the ability to go into that hyper dimensional state and see those things.

So there's not a certain skill you'll have when you're there that others will not have?

Well, you can develop skills that others don't have, but it doesn't mean that they can't do the same thing. The ability to go into that place where you can see and experience phenomena is not unique to certain individuals. You don't need a special skill to go there. But in that place, you may choose to work on healing, or some other skill, but that's not what defines you by being in there.

It's something else that defines your skills. It's like saying that you go to the desert and decide you want to ride a mountain bike. It's just a matter of choosing to ride your mountain bike in the desert. So, the place itself does not decide your skills.

In your heart, you know your skill. Your desire to do it makes it your skill. You don't need just one skill. You could have dozens of skills and they can also change. If I wanted to be an expert healer, all I'd have to do is just feel the desire to heal, and over a short period of time I will manifest those skills that I once had. Everything I teach is something I once mastered and moved past; hence, the teacher that I've become.

The things you're interested in as well as your skill level in those things will change over time. You're constantly changing and the Universe is ever growing. You will meet the needs that your environment requires of you. That is evolution. This is hyper dimensional evolution. You are here for a reason. You have a specific purpose that you are here to serve. Every White Cell feels it, knows it. It's ingrained in us.

The biggest obstacle to figuring out your purpose is the fear of ending up doing just one thing and being stuck with that. It's like saying you're a healer and that's all you are; that's all you're always going to be. You might be fine with that, but deep down inside, there's a sense of knowing that you need to adapt to other things. There are other great explorations you want to experience. So this is always the fear. You have all these things you want to do, but because you can't choose just one, you constantly end up lost.

I chose to master one skill and then move on. I think most people want to have their hand in every pot; they want it all. I think that's good; it's how I teach. You sample this, you sample that, but sooner or later you need to ask yourself what you need to perfect at this point of your life to serve the Universe. You can convert to being anything you need to be. You just have to let yourself go there and know that you're not limited to that one place. You are a warrior. Every White Cell knows they're a warrior. Every White Cell feels a desire within them to heal. Every White Cell has a telepathic-empathetic sensory in them. But there comes a point where you have to decide what you must do. You must become the molecule that reaches to the other molecule to build the organ.

Your frequency and energy can adapt very quickly when you decide to move on and master something else, but you have to tell the Universe that you're willing to be whatever It needs you to be. That is the beauty and magnificence of being a powerful White Cell. You can be used by the Universe to adapt to the situation where you're most needed. *Sometimes when you win, you really lose. Sometimes when you lose, you really win.* This ability to become a super weapon, a super gift, a super whatever is within you; and that makes you deadly to the Darkside.

There's a part of you that just wants to be consumed by this love for God and desire to serve, but you're eventually going to get bored because God is going to get bored. There's a project going on; it's called the Universe. You have to be receptive to whatever It needs you to do. You have to think of yourself as an expression of God and be willing to be that expression for any moment God chooses.

Sometimes I feel like a dog and God is my owner and I live to make God happy; just like my dog. My dog's happy and thrilled to see me when I come home. His tail is wagging. He loves me to death even though I left him all day out on the porch with the door locked. He's not thinking, "Hey where the hell have you been all day? I've been stuck here all day, you jerk!" Sure as the sun is going to rise, my dog is going to be happy to see me.

I'm a dog to God and I'll love and be obedient to God in every sense, but I also know that I have different roles to serve and I can't just sit there and stare into space. I know I have to go out and help God to achieve Its purpose. There is a game plan in all of this and I want to participate.

Chapter 5

DIMENSIONS: WALK WITH ME

Dimension walking is the ability to physically move in an altered state of consciousness. This allows you to experience the second, third, or fourth levels of dimensions around you.

When you walk in a normal state of consciousness, you see and experience the physical environment around you, like trees, houses, and streets. When you walk dimensionally in an altered state of consciousness, you can see things like electrical storms with sparks forming everywhere, objects moving through the air, and entities. You can see dimensional things of various types. Every environment you put yourself in offers a very different experience. Dimension walking is largely what you experience within yourself by observation. Nothing's going to leap out and grab you. Nothing's going to shock you.

**So, you experience what's already there
if you just remove your fear?**

Under normal circumstances, you wouldn't see these things. The idea is to train yourself to become aware of the things that are there. In other words, you want to see them in greater detail and also see things you never thought were there before.

Is it part of raising your sensory, so to speak?

Yes, it's raising your sensory. Let's say your senses are operating at a lower frequency, so what you see is what you're capable of seeing at that level, yet there are a million different things going on around you. For me, everything has an illumination. Everything has a molecular structure. What I see is like switching through cable channels, so to speak. I can just mentally flip through and see different things.

There are all sorts of things going on but the idea is to slowly become more aware of them. The number one thing that I want to stress to you is *consistency*. If you do not work on something consistently, you will never evolve to a level where you can experience it fully.

Consistency is the number one secret to learning and developing anything. You're not going to practice one or two times and master a technique right away. Most people enjoy the knowledge as they grow with it, but they don't take it to the next level by consistently practicing. So remember, if you want to develop this skill to its full potential, practice makes perfect. You must be persistent in practicing what you're learning.

Dimension walking can be compared with using drugs, which I strongly oppose doing. It's like walking down the road in the middle of the night on about ten hits of acid, and I do mean a very large dose. You suddenly become aware of the things that were always there but you didn't notice before. By going into this state of consciousness, you can experience things without ever taking any drugs.

The information you gain from the experience of dimension walking is actually very useful, but when you are on a hallucinogen, your mind is so scattered that you can't even begin to fully process what you're experiencing. You may think you can, but you lose most of the complexity of the information when you come back down from that drug-induced state. With dimension walking, you retain an immense amount of information. So this is one of the benefits, but don't expect to have an intense experience immediately.

Will the experiences from dimension walking be more intense if you practice with another person or a group of people?

No, dimension walking with others won't be as successful as doing it by yourself. If you're walking down a very quiet road, just knowing you have a friend somewhere nearby is enough to distract you. Have you ever been out in nature with no one else around, totally by yourself? When you have that perfect sense of isolation, isn't there a feeling of contentment? That's the first step in dimension walking.

The idea is to consciously move through an environment in a heightened state of consciousness and let it take you to the higher levels. That's what you're trying to achieve. When you're with other people, you may become easily distracted and it becomes a competition. They might see things that you think you should be seeing. They might start pointing things out or make too much noise. In the beginning, you must do this on your own to truly develop your own skills. It's best to begin in an area away from the city, especially in nature where it's darker with less lighting, but later on you can do this in the city.

With practice, you will be able to see all kinds of things. I can spot other beings and aliens amongst us. I can physically see them; they look totally different than how they would appear if they were human. I'll see their energy fields differently, or I'll sense them through a crowd and specifically be able to tell you what kind of entity it is.

So, this state of consciousness heightens your senses. Your sense of sight increases because you start to see energy fields without really having to use your will constantly. You just look around and see them. Your sense of hearing increases to such a level where the slightest sound is like four times louder to you. Of course, it's going to take time for you to develop your skill at this level. So, certain things are going to happen while dimension walking besides just being able to see things. If you're looking at an open field at night, you might see dimensional squares. You might wonder why they'd be such a perfect square if it's dimensional. It looks man-made. All things seem to take on a geometric shape, whether it is a diamond shape, square, or triangular. The Universe has a standard of structuralization. So, you'll see black squares on the land masses. Those are literally dimensional doors.

Can you go through those doors?

You could under the right circumstances. They're basically a miniaturization of the Bermuda Triangle or the Devil's Triangle. There are miniature versions all over the world. Some of them are usually higher in the air while others are at ground level, but you have to be in the right state of mind, have the right set of circumstances, and the right temperature. There are so many things that must be perfect for that to happen.

I remember one story I'd heard of a little girl and boy who disappeared when walking around a corner.

Where did they go?

Probably to another dimension.

Were they happy there?

Well, they might be dead. There are dimensions that you cannot physically exist in as a human being.

So you immediately die when you go through the doors that lead to certain dimensions?

Yes, not everything is like the cartoons and works out perfectly all of the time. Dimensional doors are somehow connected like dotted lines to other planets. Let's say you walk through a dimensional door and it automatically puts you on Jupiter. How are you physically going to exist on Jupiter? You'd be dead in a matter of seconds.

So don't go through the doors?

I don't recommend it. You could go through a dimensional door and end up in some other world that's completely uninhabitable. How many planets in the Universe do you think are identical to the Earth?

How do you know whether or not to go through these doors?

If you have years of experience and have developed projection, you would send your probe before stepping through it physically. You'll eventually reach a point when you will know whether or not you should go through it. You will no longer need to project, but you have to start somewhere. In any case, don't be consumed with all the visuals of the experience. Be more concerned with taking in the overall picture.

Are there any visual clues that might alert us of a dimension that isn't able to support human life?

If you look over a darkened area and go into the right state of mind, you'll see balls of light. You'll also see a bright electrical flash of light. Those are energy dimensions. Nobody else will see it except those people who are in the right state of mind. These are all pitches; they're frequencies. Your mind is energy; your body is energy; so your tonal is the frequency at which that energy vibrates.

Do the balls of light cross through the doors?

No, these are not the same kind of dimensional doors. There are dimensional doors that travel from point A to point B within the same physical plane. Then there are dimensions of time and space which pass through and coexist with this physical dimension.

So, there are two different kinds of dimensional doors: those that take you through space and time between two points in the same plane, and those that take you to completely different planes - different frequencies.

Is the Bermuda Triangle a dimensional door?

Yes, the Bermuda Triangle is a dimensional vortex of types. Just for the record, I don't necessarily believe that the Bermuda Triangle always sends objects from point A to point B. I highly suspect that there is a lot of stuff at the bottom of the ocean within the area of the Bermuda triangle. I also strongly believe that there are times when objects physically disappear from this dimension and are physically reconstructed in another.

For instance, I remember reading about a huge barge that was being pulled by a tugboat, and as they were crossing through the Triangle the barge suddenly disappeared. It was completely invisible, yet the rope was still tied to the barge and there was strong tension there. The rope went out the distance from the tugboat to the barge and stopped in midair. It was probably about 50 feet. Then the barge must have moved further out of that dimensional area and just reappeared.

What are the balls of light and what causes them?

The balls of light could be a rippling effect of this dimension clashing with another. The rippling effect produces a ball of light or a flash or something. A lot of times, energy isn't as well-illuminated as it is with a light bulb. You'll see a purple flash, but it's a dark flash. You'll know it's an illumination, but it's not really a light. It's like a splash of the color purple. The same goes for other colors. They're faded and darker lights; nonetheless, they're there.

So the balls are a clash of energy?

Yes, you're seeing another dimension clashing with ours. It's like taking a translucent piece of glass and putting it up against this reality. You're going to see what's here, but you're also going to see the other piece of glass on top of it. So, what appears to be here is really not here. It's just an image of another place coexisting with this place.

Things like poltergeists, spirits, and demons all use dimensional vortices; both major and minor ones. Some phenomena you'll experience when you are in a vortex are physical, like significant temperature drops and unexplained wind. You'll feel a vacuum because the temperature and pressure in the other dimension is different. It's like opening the doors to a cold building on a hot day; the sheer temperature difference creates the vacuum of air and this is what happens with dimensional doors. Wind currents will develop out of nowhere.

A lot of times, when you're in dimensional areas, just your presence and your consciousness is enough to create the effect. You'll suddenly feel a gust of wind coming out of nowhere, or from an unusual angle. This is very important because standard wind movements usually follow a pattern and when you get the pattern to break, you can be sure it's something dimensional. If your energy is high enough, it'll create just enough agitation to trigger the effect. It only takes one simple grain of sand to make the pearl.

In other words, you are at the right place at the right time. Everybody else might walk through without an unusual effect; however, since you decide to dimensionally walk or go into an altered state of consciousness, you are agitating the energy. Each thought is a specific frequency of energy, like a tone that you're broadcasting. Even though it can't necessarily be heard, it can interact with energy fields, which may be even more sensitive to the thought than you are.

Magnetism is the secret of the universe. It is the secret of the dimensions, and it is the secret of everything. I'm not talking about your standard refrigerator magnet. It's a different kind of magnetism which maintains the structure of this giant hologram of reality. Change, or alter the frequency or magnetism and you will create a ripple in time and space. There will be an opening, a tear, and you'll see stars and planets.

Everything has an A polarity and a B polarity; there is always a movement that creates this - North Pole, South Pole, dimension, time, space. Everything has two polarities except for one thing: The Universe itself has an A polarity but there is no B that can be detected. Everything else can be weighed or measured. Everything has a numerical value, which is really the reason why it exists.

So, if everything has a certain value as a form of magnetism, you can change this field of magnetism even if it's in a small portion of an area. It's like creating an illumination of a certain space. By creating this illuminated space, you create a magnetism that cancels the effect of the A-B and makes it only one.

You don't have to be a scientist to grasp this concept; we'd have to go into a lot more detail to be scientifically accurate. The point is to have a basic understanding of how this works.

There is a frequency created by these two magnetic polarities that holds this whole dimension together, theoretically speaking. If you could create a device that changes the polarity in a given amount of space, you could create a doorway to another universe. The door is pushed open by this device which is a pulsating frequency that interferes with the A-B polarity for a moment. This means that some other dimension, or some other frequency, is randomly going to open on the other side.

Is that how a black hole works?

No, I'll use the Bermuda Triangle for an example to try to explain this better. We know the Bermuda Triangle creates these different effects during the colder months of the year, which is usually December, January, and February. There is also the axis of the planet to consider, which is proportionally different during that timeframe. That probably changes the magnetism of the whole planet.

Now, there's likely to be a massive deposit of iron or some other element that creates a significant amount of magnetism somewhere underneath the ocean floor. With all of the other circumstances, such as the atmospheric pressure and the temperature being just right, a chain reaction is triggered that creates a dimensional vortex for a few moments.

There's a possibility we might never see the Bermuda Triangle active again because of changes to the atmosphere from chemicals and other pollutants in the last fifty years or so. Substances in the ground or the air open those natural dimensional doorways. Also, your body weight, what you ate that day, the minerals in your body, the direction of the sunlight, the type of elements in the earth, and the air temperature are all factors that have to perfectly align with each other to open a dimensional vortex.

So a dimensional vortex could be artificially created?

Yes, it could be artificially stimulated. This is probably the best kept secret to date because it really is the secret of space travel and the potential for time travel. There are several films that were made on this subject, like *The Philadelphia Experiment*.

Is that the one about the ship?

Yes, they supposedly built generators into four trucks. The generators could emit an A or B polarity magnetism. They bombarded the ship with these magnetic frequencies and created a vortex. Therefore, the ship disappeared for a long period of time. A great wealth of information was obtained but we may never know that information.

Things like this do happen, but they're rarely recorded. The ones that are recorded don't get the attention they deserve. A few years ago, I read about a group of mountain climbers in California who climbed to an area well-known for geodes. That's a stone that is lined with crystals, but you only discover that when you cut it open. They found a geode on the mountain and brought it back with them. They decided to cut the geode open to see what was inside of it. Although this should have been an easy task, the geode kept breaking the saws as they tried to cut through it. They ended up bringing it to a machine shop that had a special diamond plated saw blade to cut it open. When they finally did that, there wasn't a quartz crystal inside as there should have been. They actually found a spark plug from a 1920's farm tractor inside of the geode. The spark plugs were huge in size at that time. A geologist confirmed that the stone turned out to be 500,000 years old. The dates were based on how long geodes take to form; however the date could have been off by a factor of 10 either way. It is remarkable, nevertheless. How did that spark plug become encased in the stone hundreds of thousands of years ago?

Anything could have happened. It could have come from a tractor that was near a volcanic eruption and the masses of energy somehow warped time and space and put the tractor somewhere else. Or maybe a UFO picked it up, dissected it, and then travelled to a prehistoric time and dumped everything after studying it. The UFO threw it out at the right place but the wrong time and it got encased in stone. And then we found it millions of years later. The possibilities are endless. I would highly suspect that this has something to do with dimensional travel.

So, back to dimensional walking again. Under the right circumstances, you will become more aware of or be able to experience certain beings. By "experience," I mean feel, know, hear, smell, taste, or see something to confirm their existence.

It's very important to control your thoughts and maintain a state of non-thought. Thought is everything. If your mind wanders or you walk too fast, you won't be able to reach the necessary state of consciousness to experience these things. If you want to achieve this state of mind consistently, you have to first reach this state of consciousness so you can recognize it. Then you can gradually build up to something much bigger and better. If you rush, you're not going to achieve it, and you'll never learn how to evoke it in the future.

I'm going to explain precisely what I go through in order to help you achieve this state to experience dimension walking. When dimension walking, or practicing any other paranormal technique, *never put your hands in your pockets*. Your hands are your sensory; you can experience energy with them. Your hands have a very complex nerve structure. They are designed to be very sensitive, very data oriented.

Your body can be utilized to experience energies as one whole device. For example, you don't just have to hear or see something in order to experience it; you literally can feel with your entire body. When I dimension walk, I'm always aware of how my entire body feels and what it's experiencing. For instance, if your body feels coolness, you might actually feel something beyond that if you pay close attention. It might not be just cool air. You might be aware of certain dimensional information embedded in the cool air. So, your hands and fingers should always be out at your side or moving around.

Relaxing and keeping your mind clear is a very important part of dimension walking. You should do your best to maintain non-thought. It's almost like you're calmly waiting for something to happen without being anxious. When I dimension walk, my breathing is extremely shallow and slow through my nose. In fact, I'm not even thinking about my breath. Breathing faster causes your mind to think faster. Slowing your breathing causes your thoughts to slow down. Breathing is directly connected to your mental thought; there's no doubt about it. Just relax into your breathing; let everything go and take in the environment.

Think about your childhood. When you were a child, you were more sensitive. In fact, you probably heard more noises, saw strange shapes, and were generally more afraid at night. You were told it's your imagination, but I don't think it was your imagination at all. You saw things that you couldn't explain and you were afraid. Your senses were so polished, so intense from being afraid, you became more aware. You lost those senses over time.

When you were a child, there may have been a time when you were out by yourself, maybe in a field or a forest, and you hit a peak moment of awareness of your environment. For some reason, your senses intensified and there was a sort of communion between you and nature. You should try to feel this as you attempt to dimension walk. It's almost like going into a trance. That's what you want to experience. For me, the smell of sweet grass or dried hay would trigger this feeling. That smell has a very soothing effect that allows you to begin to go into the right state of mind. But you can't do it if you're with other people. Other people's consciousness will distract you from reaching this state, so I suggest you dimension walk by yourself. Think about when you were in that state as a child. You did it when you were alone.

The biggest secret to walking dimensionally is actually the act of walking; hence, where its name derived from. Non-thought, relaxing, thinking of the childhood state of mind, and taking in the environment are all critical. *Walking is the key.* When you start to walk, focus on the rhythm of your footsteps. It's the sound of your foot hitting the ground that connects you with that state of mind.

It is the rhythm of your feet scraping on the ground that sends you into an altered state of consciousness. It won't work if you only move your feet in rhythm without doing all the other things that I just mentioned. It's a recipe which invokes a whole intricate state of mind. By putting yourself into a relaxed state, breathing

a certain way, evoking thought in a certain way, feeling the temperature of the air and the sun on your face, and experiencing the environment, you reach the proper tonal to dimension walk. Take your time. Spend a half hour working your way up to this. *Don't rush it. Allow it to happen.*

It's going to be hard to reach that childhood state of consciousness, especially when you're challenged because you've already begun to forget about it. It's like a secret place in your mind. Once you start to move and listen to the rhythms of your feet hitting the ground, it starts to come back to you.

It's like a metronome. A metronome is a device used by musicians because of its steady beat, but it is also used for hypnosis, or inducing relaxation, and is conducive to putting you into a deeper state of consciousness.

Imagine the audible ticking sound of a grandfather clock. That's about the tempo you want for walking. So, you allow your feet to create the same pattern. That particular rhythm is very effective on the human brain. Too fast or too slow won't work. As you are moving to this rhythm you will, all of a sudden, shift your consciousness.

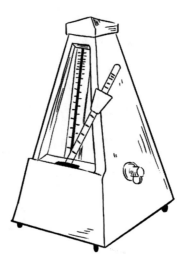

Now, the problem is that your brain is going to start to say, "Hey, it's working!" And the moment you start thinking about whether or not it's working, you'll have to start all over again. If it was so easy, everybody on the planet would be doing it. That's why only certain human beings are capable of doing these things.

You cannot think about what you're doing. Do not analyze yourself; do your analyzing when you're done. Just move and observe. If you see a dimensional door, don't say, "Oh my god! There's a dimensional door!" It'll collapse. Do not give anything specific awareness. The moment you give it specific awareness, you fall right back down into a normal train of thought. It's the machine, the organic brain, that has to say what it is. You see a dog, your brain says "dog." You see a human being, you say, "Oh, there's a person over there." It's like it can't shut up. It has to identify everything to you. Ignore all of that. Just move and experience.

Imagine you're driving a car going 85 miles per hour, along with everyone else on the highway. You can see the trees and the mountains. After twelve hours of driving you pull over and get out of the car. It's like time has slowed down. All of a sudden, you can experience the smell of the fresh air. You can hear the birds chirping. You can see the water in the river up close, even its color. You can see the shore. You can see the insects moving around. You can see everything in immense detail. Then you get back in the car and get back on the road again. This is what you're doing every day in your life.

Teach yourself to slow down. When you slow down, what was once a blur solidifies and, all of a sudden, you see things you've never seen before. You slow time and space down to a point where you can observe this entire crystallization of a giant monument in details you could never experience before.

So you're basically saying to slow down from the speed of our everyday lives, which is 85 miles per hour?

Yes, slowing down is part of awareness. If you force yourself, by willfully turning inwards, and if you choose to take control of your awareness then you are truly reaching awareness. You are truly on a path of enlightenment. When you do not think of these things, you don't move forwards. It is the not easiest thing to do because the world is constantly distracting you, *the idea is to turn inwards*. When you turn inwards, you become aware of things that you were never aware of before. This is all about slowing down. Slowness is actually faster than fast, because you experience knowledge in greater detail. So if you experience more knowledge because you're going slow, don't you learn more? This is why I often say, *"You have to slow down to move faster."*

So, the idea is to not let time and space, this frequency, push you along. Slow it with your mind so that you can experience things you weren't aware of before. This is part of the teachings.

So, would it be advantageous to dimension walk at night since there aren't as many distractions?

Yes, you will probably have more success at night. You can even dimension walk on a street at night. More than likely, you've naturally stumbled across some of it already while walking at night and feeling at peace with yourself. Not really scared, but just looking at the street lights, seeing the dark trees and other shadowy objects.

To me, the dark is just like a cloak. It's like something warm hiding you. You can look out and nobody knows you're there. You can move stealthily. There's surrealness to it that I revel in. When I walk down the street and there are no cars, there's a yellowish glow illuminating the street and there's absolute silence. There's a certain feeling of expectation, like something could happen. Maybe there's a vampire. Maybe there's a person hiding or something dangerous unseen by the naked eye.

As a result of this expectation, your awareness is heightened. It's basically saying, "There's a lot happening, be aware of it! You just have to turn that knob a little bit more to tune in to it." And that's what you have to do. But expect nothing when you do it. When you expect to see something, or you're anticipating something, you will see nothing. You have to be sincere in your heart. Just by experiencing the environment, you will see or experience something.

Recently, a student of mine was walking home very late at night and he was in a certain state of mind, walking dimensionally as I taught him. He sensed something to his right and he saw a tentacle-like appendage on the top of a wall as it was retracting. It was very solidified, very physical, not like a shadow or energy type thing.

He'd also told me that he saw what looked like a man with wings or a gryphon type being in the distance. Then the gryphon realized that this human, my student, could see him, which was abnormal. So the gryphon quickly got scared and left.

If these things are already there and they're going to mess with you, they're going to do it whether or not you see them. So, what if they realize they're seen?

If they become aware that they've been observed, it doesn't necessarily mean they're going to mess with you. Sometimes dimensional beings can't see human beings. In fact, they can't see much of this reality at all. They can see some parts of it, but the moment you can see them, it's like you suddenly materialized and they see you because you've connected on the same frequency. Maybe that's why they panic.

In the movie *Interview with the Vampire*, the vampire Lestat was telling the human Louis that vampires don't see reality the way humans do. Louis couldn't understand that, so Lestat finally turned him into a vampire. After Louis was bitten, he opened his eyes and everything had life force surrounding it. The leaves all had a shimmering array of dark colors, like a dim illumination. The stone of the statues became like skin and he realized how differently a vampire sees this reality.

It's the same as the dimensional level you experience when dimension walking. Everything is structurally the same but it takes on a whole different feeling. Look at your environment when the lighting changes. The whole environment starts to change yet it's all the same. It takes on a whole different feeling and the structural integrity has changed. Then you begin to see what looks like static electricity in the air. It's actually energy. It's the same dimension, just dark. That's the the way that I see. Everything becomes more dimensional and the walls become energy.

Exercise

Stand up and look at a blank wall. Get closer to the wall and just stare at it. I want to point something out to you. If you stare at the wall, you're going to notice something. You're going to see a dimension. It's almost going to look like static electricity on the wall, or a wave of energy, or like there is something in between your eyes and the wall. The wall takes on a grainier type of energy. It's like there's a blue hue that's optically invisible.

If you stare into it long enough, you'll start to see more complexities of the energy because your mind is switching between two frequencies, like switching TV channels. You'll start to see different things and after a while you won't even see the hue. You'll switch to seeing billions of little scattery dots, or the wall might start to look three dimensional. Or you'll see two or three walls at a time.

Why does the visual stop and restart when I blink my eyes?

Blinking signifies resetting; this is Nature's way of preventing you from perpetulating into this state of consciousness. Maybe you've never noticed it, but if you stare, you go into a trance. You start to feel different. When you blink it's like nature's way of resetting the computer, your mind, right back to the standard setting. If your tonal starts to move upward from 35 to 40, 45, 50, 55, 60 and you blink, you're reset to 35 again. But you can get past this with practice.

When I stare at myself in the mirror, I'll suddenly see color patterns, like molecules, contours and lines between my arms and my hair.

This is all dimensional structure.

So, I'm seeing myself dimensionally?

Yes. A lot of times, you'll be told, "It's your eyes playing optical tricks." Well, what's an optical trick in the first place? It's something that you're observing that is tangibly observable. So, if it's observable, it's a given effect. I don't believe in illusions, whether it is inward or outward. When I look at the carpet, I see shades of tan, brown, and white. Somebody else could look at the same carpet and see black and shades of gray. So, the experience you get from it is what matters.

An illusion is something that your mind is projecting that's supposedly not real, but the simple fact that you're seeing it makes it a tangible experience. You give thought to it. So how can anything be an illusion? There's a purpose or a logic behind it. In this dimension, nothing should exist in the first place. Something came from nothing. Once you've pondered the universe and how it came into existence in the first place, you realize that something has to come from something. So where did it all come from? At this point, this whole universe could be an illusion.

You can get nauseated looking at the wall. You can go out to an environment and experience the same thing as what you're seeing while looking at the wall. The more often that you set yourself in that state of consciousness, the more you will see dimensionally. You'll see this energy in an entire valley, or other incredible things.

When you were talking about "Interview with the Vampire," you described how a vampire sees reality. Is that how animals see things because they have a different relationship with nature?

Yes. You will often see cats and dogs looking at, chasing, or even playing with things that are not accessible to our senses. They'll bark at the wall and stare at it. There's no insect, strings, or anything hanging. There's just nothing there, yet they see something.

Sight is basically light. You're not seeing out; rather you're seeing something coming at you. The reality you see is projected. It's like a giant film right now. Just because you can see distance, that doesn't mean your eye is going there, taking it and coming back. Everything is moving here. It's just a matter of how the brain interprets it. This reality is really being projected at you from light bouncing off of it. The light turns shades of color which create structure in the brain. It puts the dots together very quickly. If there's no light to bounce off of the structures, they disappear. So, you are seeing at the speed of light.

Because the human eye is curved, it sees at a certain frequency, which is light. Light is energy and energy is a frequency. Let's say you're able to see a frequency of 35 when you look directly out of the front of your eye. As you shift your gaze and use your peripheral vision, you see higher and higher frequencies. In other words, the frequency you see is dependent on the angle at which you direct your vision.

So, looking straight in front of you, you see a frequency of 35, not literally but you get the idea. As your gaze moves to the left or right, you start to see frequencies of 36, 37, 38, 39, 40, 41, 42, 43, 44, 45, 50. When you look out of the corner of your eye, it gets up to 100. Now, you can barely see the objects in front of you, but you can still see them.

An entity, for instance, or a dimensional structure is usually moving at a frequency of 200, but at certain points the energy starts to slow from 200 down to 100 or to 65. So, you might be sitting down and all of a sudden you see something move in the corner of your eye. When you turn your head to look, there's nothing there because you're looking at a lower frequency now.

So, if you see something, just keep it at the side of your head.

Yes, don't look directly at it until you start training yourself to see correctly, which means you can control the pupil of your eye. You can control the muscles in your eye and this will narrow and bend the optic frequencies. This is how you see auras. When you look directly at something, you don't see the aura. But when you look with your peripheral vision, you see the energy. Well, that energy is of the same frequency of 100 or higher. So, if you can see that energy, you can teach yourself to see even higher frequencies because the brain will adapt for you and raise your level of 35 up to whatever you want.

So, dogs and cats see directly at a level of 100. That's how they are able to see dimensional objects and entities. I've seen dogs stand still and growl with hair standing up like they're looking at a human being. They're looking at a being that's resonating at 100, which is totally imperceptible to most human beings.

So basically, you can increase the spectrum of all your senses.

You don't have to raise all your senses right away, but yes. When meditating, you can do it easily; it's an accumulating effect. If you can acquire energy and you can project it forth to do something, then you can achieve all these things very quickly. This is why you have to meditate. It isn't just for relaxing. Meditation trains you to keep your mind silent and breathe slowly. It trains you to control your energy, and most of all, meditation collects energy for you. You collect Prana when you meditate. This is the reason why the particular meditation taught in *Meditation Within Eternity* is universally the best meditation. It does everything.

Are you sure it's the only meditation I need to do?

Yes, that's why you're already having experiences. Most people never have those kinds of experiences in their entire life; even those who've meditated for years.

When I meditate, should I focus on the energy coming in or not think at all and just sit there?

It doesn't matter if you think about the energy or not, as long as you're aware of it. *Aware* means you don't have to think about it. Your goal is to achieve and maintain non-thought. You can be aware of something without having to give it thought.

Is that because I already know that when I sit down and meditate I'm gathering Prana energy?

Right, you already know that you're absorbing Prana as a result of sitting down to meditate. You'll feel it. You'll just know what's happening. That's all you need to know.

I like silence better than music when I meditate.

If you meditate in silence, your mind gets accustomed to that. So, every time there's a loud noise, or somebody is talking, or anything else is breaking your focus, your mind becomes distracted.

By having constant irritation (music), eventually you're so immune to it that you no longer even think about it. Your mind is just so willful, so powerful, so focused that you can be in psychic combat and nobody's going to distract you, or screw with your awareness because you're just so trained to be right on target. It's like running with ten pound weights on your arms and legs. You can run without them and get a great cardiovascular workout, but you build more strength by running with them.

You can meditate with or without music. When you meditate without music, it's like running with ten pound weights. You're going to get to a point where you forget that you have the music on. When you go to do something, you're going to have this added ability that you weren't aware you had. The brain is a machine, so if you have the operational manual, you understand how it works.

This meditation was based on the fundamental understanding of why the brain does what it does, and what prevents long-time meditators from achieving even higher levels faster. The goal is not to just make somebody feel spiritual. You're training the mind to develop all of these psychic abilities. That's part of the gameplay. So, it should never be perceived as standard meditation. Standard meditation is great if you just want to relax and find peace and balance within you. You want all those things, but you also want to discipline your mind so that you can do psychic things, leave your body and go places, move energy out from your body, sense or analyze somebody, or open up a dimensional door. So this is part of the "Iron Man" workout, rather than just doing one set of something.

This way we'll be able to train the mind to put up with distraction.

That's right, and it's very important to train your mind in that way. Imagine you're walking in your everyday state of consciousness and you go into non-thought. Now you can see dimensional objects and entities moving. All of a sudden, you see this guy riding his bike and playing a radio. Against your will, your mind is going to automatically focus on that guy and the song he's playing. You'll start thinking about that song and then you'll realize that everything just collapsed.

This is why we do what we do. I could go over the entire meditation. Every single specific part has been very well thought out. But it's there for a reason.

Does the tone of the music increase your emotions?

Absolutely. What happens when you listen to rock and roll all the time? You get tired of it. You get immune to it, right? Sometimes we do meditations specifically to pump people up but eventually you build up an immunity to it. Then, after a while, the music isn't necessary anymore and you can shut it off, but not yet. It's a tool.

Can I experiment by dimension walking with two other people?

You can do whatever you want to do, but there's a reason for my instructions. My experience tells me it doesn't work as well when you're with other people. Initially, it's a very personal thing. You're trying to fool your brain. So why guarantee failure? Failure means discouragement. Discouragement means you'll give up eventually because you can't do it. Failure is the number one reason why people don't reach enlightenment. Failure leads to discouragement. You could become so discouraged that you just give up. You will stop developing even though you are doing so well because you decided what is successful and what is not. You are not supposed to move mountains within a few months.

It's sad, but that's how karma weeds out the weak from the strong. If I had been undisciplined and easily discouraged when I was younger, I would never have achieved the things that I have achieved. But discouragement is there for a reason.

What technique should we practice to prepare for dimension walking?

Doing Aums before you dimension walk will help you get into the ideal state of mind faster. Aums are more than just a sound that you create; they're a tonal. Aums are a very specific pitch that creates a certain state of consciousness very similar to meditating for long periods of time, so it works very quickly. This state of consciousness allows your mind to do things.

Everything we do is an exercise to assist us in our spiritual growth, our psychic abilities, or to enhance these abilities. We do Aums to supplement our abilities just like an athlete would use protein or amino acid supplements to boost their performance.

Does that boost come from the pitch of the Aum?

The Aums create a certain feeling that puts you into a state of non-thought.

Is an Aum similar to an Om?

We call them Aums, but it's the same thing. The second byproduct of doing Aums is the creation of a dimensional vortex. Under the right circumstances at the right moment, you are likely to attract spiritual beings who will do the Aums with you. You will hear a very defined, singular voice coming from a physical place joining in on the Aum.

It's not so much the sound. Aums create the perfect tonal, making you resonate in an excellent state of mind. When you're all done, you'll feel relaxed. You'll feel like you just meditated. Aums can be used to remove entities and negative forces. The sound raises your tonal, but your tonal is energy and your energy starts to expand and fill the room.

Sometimes when doing Aums in a very cold room, within 10 minutes or so, the room temperature will raise 5 to 10 degrees. People will be sweating and the room will just feel hot.

Aums are a good way to purify energy. You can use them for places that have really bad energy that's been impacted into the furniture and the walls. When you walk in, if you do about ten really good Aums, they will permeate everything by intensifying the vibrations of the place. They cleanse everything giving it a higher vibration.

When they are done perfectly, Aums create a ringing sound, much like running your finger on the edge of a wine glass. That is a perfect Aum. That is what you are striving to achieve. You need a minimum of two people, but it's best with four. It's that ringing sound that you are trying to achieve. So, Aums are very powerful in their own way.

So it helps to have somebody else join in
when you're doing Aums?

Right, it's good, because the other person or being vibrates at the same tonal. They're going to reach the same level that you're at. They're helping you cleanse energy. Why would they want to do that if they're negative? So, generally positive forces come out.

Does this also help to raise the tonal of the other people that
are doing the Aums with you?

Yes, it helps their tonal also.

Should we sit in the half-lotus position?

Only if you're comfortable in the half-lotus. If you're not comfortable, go into an Indian-leg style. When you're with others, sit in a circle facing slightly to your left so that your right knee is just in front of the left knee of the person to your right. So, you'll face just slightly to the left of the center of the circle. Place your hands in your lap and think of projecting your sound to the middle of the circle.

Now, let your breath out slowly. Don't rush yourself. A loud Aum doesn't necessarily mean a fast Aum. When somebody is done, wait for everybody to finish before you restart. Always breathe in through your nose. Keep your eyes shut. Remember that good tonal is healthy tonal. Think of it as healing you of diseases like cancer, tumors, or viruses in your body. It's resetting the life force of your body.

There's an ancient story that tells of a very, very, dark, dark place. Hell, if you want to call it that. It's basically a true story. There were several enlightened beings that had gotten into a dark battle. At the end of the battle, the darkness still remained and only three enlightened beings existed. As a last resort, they sat down in a circle in the middle of this place and they started doing Aums. The Aum is so powerful because of the virtue of their consciousness and their total commitment to it that it created a force of energy that wiped out everything negative.

Isn't the word "amen" actually derived from a bell vibration?

Oh, yes. Absolutely.

**You mentioned good Aums and bad Aums.
How do you do a good Aum?**

A good, strong Aum feels like it's being pulled from your chi chakra. If you truly go into a good Aum, you won't even realize you're doing it. You'll be so entranced that it'll just keep coming out and you won't even know you have air coming out of your mouth. You're just totally devoid of consciousness, but you still know what's happening. It's like you're using the lower parts of your lungs. Just take your time, but get a good amount of energy into it. Let your mind drift, and don't think about anything. Just do it!

Chapter 6

CYCLES OF THE SOUL

I f you truly desire to know and understand God, then you must realize that you are in a learning process, and your goal is to evolve. In order to move forward or evolve, it requires a process of many incarnations. You reincarnate in order to progress intellectually, spiritually, and consciously.

One lifetime is simply not enough time to experience everything that life has to offer. Ten lifetimes may not be enough. In order to express a deeper understanding of the Universe, the age of it, the content within it, the vastness of it, you have to be able to reflect and comprehend a knowledge base that's built upon the complexity of compounded experiences. You learn to appreciate and experience more because of the richness of your experiences in the past.

At thirty years old, if you looked back at yourself when you were twenty, you would see a vast difference in your consciousness, your perception of things, and your emotional openness to things because you have changed and evolved. You can see this progression when you're forty, fifty, or sixty but you do not live long enough to experience *everything* in just one lifetime. It would take lifetimes to savor the finer moments of something so vast and so incredible. You reincarnate to improve, to become more than who you were before, and you do this so that God can experience through you.

When someone actually incarnates,
how does a soul enter the body?

A spirit, a soul, or a being who wishes to incarnate enters a body at the moment of birth. When the baby's head crowns during birth, a spirit, or a soul incarnates into the baby. In some ways, that's why there's a soft spot on the skull; it's an area that allows the spirit to come into the body.

Possession by a spirit or entity is not possible; therefore, it is extremely unlikely that an entity is going to go through a human being's energy field to get to the baby that is developing within the mother's body. The only opportunity is when the baby's actually crowning and leaving the mother's body; otherwise, the mother's energy field is too strong to allow that entrance.

Can two souls interfere with each other
or try to move into one body?

There are certainly situations where this has been known to occur, but it is extremely difficult and not something that can easily happen. Think of it like two magnets pushing against each other. The magnets try to repel each other. When the baby is presented and there is an opportunity for a soul to move in, the energy moves into that field and instantly starts to create a reaction that pushes other energy fields away.

What causes a soul to incarnate
into a particular family or place?

It depends on the soul. Many people who created a soul and then died are able to hold their dimensional body together. If they are not evolved or developed enough, they are pushed and moved randomly through various energy fields of the earth and space until an opportunity arises and they find the right place to go.

It's an instinct. It's like a salmon finding its way up a river, only much stronger and, of course, we're talking frequencies of light, speeds of light or energy, so time is very different.

A baby's birth is like a beacon of light. A soul can sense these windows of opportunity and seize the best one. It's a fallacy to say that people always incarnate into the same family. People don't want to let go of loved ones who have passed on so they create the concept that they'll be incarnated back into their family again. Unfortunately, when you let your emotions become too involved, it creates a loss in spiritual knowledge. Sometimes you have to remove some of the untruths to get to the truth.

As a soul becomes trained and more advanced, this knowledge becomes part of their consciousness. They develop higher levels of abilities to exist outside of the physical body; therefore, they do not have as much of a need to search for the appropriate body to work with. They may find other things to do.

As they become more advanced, they can become more selective. They can choose to be born on a different continent, or maybe follow a person that is pregnant. Everything is very appealing at that point. There's not a sense of one kind of person being better than another. When you leave your body, you have a higher level of understanding things. You want to explore different possibilities other than those you've already experienced before. That's why a different culture might be very appealing to you as a more advanced being.

Does everyone reincarnate?

No. There are more people than there are prospective souls in each generation. A soul is created by pondering on one's identity, one's self, and the majority of human beings are biochemical, biological beings who think, feel, and have emotions. But as science dictates, they are, more or less, creations of nature in the sense that they have chemicals and reactions and trained thought.

They create a sense of identity; they are real; they are beautiful; they are beings. But when they die, if they did not pursue the creation of a soul, they surrender all of their experiences to the Gaia consciousness. If the planet is a living organism, it must also utilize some source to attain its knowledge. It's the same way that the cells of your body die, giving you their electrical impulse, their soul, and become part of your consciousness. The large majority of people have not developed a soul in the sense that it's going to individually progress.

I understand that may seem harsh to some of you. A soul is created when a person is at a point where she has evolved intellectually, emotionally, and spiritually. It's not really a matter of intelligence but more of a sensory within you, or a moment that God speaks to you and you realize there's something more than what you perceived. There is a moment of realization where you begin to reflect on the idea that you are something more than what you thought you were.

It is the moment of the second conception, meaning that you were conceived biologically within the womb as a biological creation with some forces of energy, and now you have matured to a point where you've now created your dimensional body. You are now building a dimensional body to go beyond this physical life. Much like your physical body, it's going to require a kind of food or energy to build it. That creation is based upon how you reflect on things, how you think, or how you evolve over time.

When you die, at what point does your soul actually leave your body?

There's a variety of situations in which you can die. Many near-death experiences aren't really instances of the soul leaving the body, although this is something you would like to believe. A near-death experience is often described as traveling down a tunnel and in this tunnel, the person having the near-death experience may see their loved ones, or a religious being. Many cultures see a representative of their religion in the tunnel. It's not always Jesus; it could be Buddha, Krishna, or even a family member.

A near-death experience can be created under circumstances with magnetic waves. Various institutions have been able to create the same tunnel effect in their test subjects with similar results. They believe the near-death experience is an actual brain event. Just because the heart has stopped beating and the body has stopped breathing, brain death does not necessarily set in. Even if there is a significant decrease in the functioning of the brain, there may be deep regions of the brain that are still functioning on a minimal level of energy. So that person has not departed their physical body at that point.

The physical body is like an engine that is turned on: this is birth. Electricity is created and moving, the body fluids are moving, the metrics of a body is alive; it's functioning. The body is like a generator that creates an electrical magnetic field to hold the soul in place. As long as this energy field exists, it holds a frequency that ties the physical body into the dimensional one like Velcro.

When you die, or when the heart stops and the body begins to shut down, this energy field begins to fail. It begins to decrease and the power of it to hold your soul diminishes to the point where the soul can depart. Now, what's interesting is that people who undergo a near-death experience describe floating above their bodies as they start to pass on. When they're brought back to life, they feel as if they are pulled back in, and there's a truth to that.

When doctors shock the body to get it to start creating that energy field again, it is like a magnetic force that literally pulls that frequency right back into it. The reason for this is, your soul energy is so aligned to your body from being within it for such a long period of time that there's a significant relationship. Even if the body is physically dead, there may not be a complete death in the brain yet. When the brain has completely collapsed, then the soul is free to go, but it will linger until that absolute death is there. It's almost as if something's holding it close until those final moments.

This explains many of the stories of people floating above the surgery room reading labels of things in the room, describing something they couldn't possibly have seen from their bed while under anesthesia, or telling of conversations they couldn't possibly have heard under the circumstances. The moment the soul leaves is when the majority of the energy field that exists within the body that gives it biological life completely collapses.

When you die and your soul is free, do you float around? What happens after physical death?

The soul will linger until the body completely dies. True brain death must occur before you can actually move away. It also depends on whether you have created a soul or not. If you haven't created a soul, there is a deep sense of peace. There is a feeling of release. It is a very beautiful state and you surrender yourself to the Gaia mind frequency. You merge with this very nurturing and loving energy that you came from biologically. It's a very loving thing.

If you have created a soul, you linger and feel the Gaia energy all around you. Depending on the degree of your development, you will decide how enticing that energy truly is. If you have evolved enough, you will immediately recognize it and as soon as the body collapses, you will move on. But you're in a stasis. There is a period of time where you are trying to figure out what's going on. It feels very different; it's unusual. It's comparable to the dream state. You're no longer thinking with your normal mental faculties. You're no longer using the neuro-synapses, or the limitations of the brain. The mind is thinking faster, but it's also trying to understand what is happening to its consciousness. There's no longer a body, so there's a part of you that's looking for that body and trying to come to terms with the fact that it's not there, or that you've left it. It's very alien. It's during this process that the *hovering*, so to speak, takes place, and others may feel your presence.

In some cases, you may not feel anything at all. Keep in mind that energy moves much quicker than you can blink an eye, but to energy, time is very different. Thought moves so much faster in comparison to the organic brain, so everything appears to be in stillness. It's like everything is in extremely slow motion. It is very hard to relate to the physical reality anymore.

As energy, you don't think anything of dying. There are no lights, there's no reaction, there's nothing. The moment this process happens, it's as if everybody is there but they're not there. It's almost like stepping into a whole other dimension because it's a different vibration. Reality also changes. For a moment, you can sense or see everybody around you, and then it just vanishes. There are different scenarios, not just one situation that fits everybody.

There's a moment where this energy is reflecting at a hyper dimensional God speed and it gets its bearings. When this happens, it's like the Universe is communicating to you. It's as if you've tuned into God and you are adjusting to the way It is communicating what you need to do. God/The Universe is going to guide you to what you need to do. That's really what's happening at the moment of death.

When you're in that stasis and you're trying to tune in, is that something you need to know how to do or is it instinctual?

It's as instinctual as a baby knowing how to suckle at its mother's breast.

Are there other souls or guides that help you at all?

There are other beings who may have known you in other lifetimes that are in this in-between place. Time is different and movement is much faster as energy beings, so they can be present because they sense this happening. They sense it because there's a grid of awareness. When you're energy, you're part of a massive matrix. This is very different than what you perceive right now. They will be drawn to your death moment.

It's not just about easing you; it's more about the excitement of your arrival. It's more about the joy of you returning. To these souls, it's the opposite of what it is to your family and friends in this dimension. To these other souls, your physical death is like birth. It's very exciting and very beautiful, so they will come from many places if they're available. If they're not already reincarnated, they will want to be present. You may have known them as family at one time and you're going to remember it. You're also going to understand that they are more than just one thing and so there's a deep sense of family, a deep sense of love.

Many cultures have gleaned a little bit of this fascinating world and twisted it to fit their own perception of things in this reality. It's where a lot of their religious concepts and beliefs were drawn from. Some people who sense and feel these beings in a near-death experience may bring the experience back. They may say, "My brother was there," or "my sister was there," or "my mother was there." That's only what the organic brain can understand or interpret. There is a lot more information there but when it goes back into the collective of the organic brain, the organic brain uses its own filters and says, "This is how we're going to allow this to be perceived. This is how we're going to let you interpret it." There's a coping mechanism within the biological brain and this comes from primitive times.

Essentially, everybody has a different interpretation of what happens based on their religious beliefs. The organic brain is amazing, but it's nothing compared to your hyper dimensional consciousness.

When people use hallucinogens and have profound experiences, they often come back and say, "I remember those experiences and believe they happened but I don't remember how I did the things that I did." The brain edits and limits the information. Unfortunately, you're describing your hyper dimensional experience with your organic brain and there are no words that can do that effectively. It could be that the experience is so beyond your comprehension now that the brain literally has to gut a lot of that information. It leaves you with the best interpretation that you can handle. You have to try to evolve to get the substance of it later. This goes right back to the purpose of reincarnation: to learn, to experience, to grow, because how much you're actually going to hold from that experience will be based upon your current intellect.

When someone's dying, and their life is flashing before their eyes, and they leave the body and enter into this stasis, is it possible to get stuck there?

To better explain the *"life flashing before your eyes"* experience, I'll refer back to the story of my car accident. I was driving and there was an accident ahead of me. It was raining out and it was hard to tell what was going on. My car hit some cars that were blocking the road and flipped over and upside down. It landed on the roof and evidently went a great distance down the hill and into the guardrails.

I remember being upside down inside the car with the windshield shattered and water coming in from the road. I remember thinking about all the people I loved and all the things I would miss, knowing I was more than likely going to die. I recall thinking about things I wished I had said to the people that I loved. I thought about so many different things. I remember pausing and saying to myself, "When the heck am I going to hit the guardrails?" Then I went back to thinking, all the while my biological body was pumped full of adrenaline.

I stopped again and thought, "This is really taking a long time." Eventually the car hit the railings and it came to a full stop. The point is, the brain thinks at a certain speed. Your consciousness also thinks at a certain speed. Everybody can attest to the fact that at some point, there is a time where your thought process speeds up, a point where your mind works a little bit faster.

When people say they saw their life flash before their eyes, it's because the brain suddenly jumped the rails of its limitations. It actually experiences much higher expectations than what it normally does. The brain goes through a moment of shock and it jumps into hyper speed. In hyper speed, it processes what would normally take twenty minutes, in just two seconds. While you're in that state of mind, everything seems like real time, but if you were to perceive your outer reality, everything would be in slow motion.

Many people will go through a hyper dimensional state, very fast thinking, and this could happen beyond the first level of seeing your life flash before you. You're reflecting on all of the deeds in your life at hyper speed. You're reflecting on all the people you've done wrong, all the people you've done right, all the things you wish you had not done, all the things you have done. The brain is really weighing you, in a sense. It's establishing your experiences. It's sorting them super-fast so that you create a frequency. That frequency is going to determine how and if the Universe is going to respond to you.

Most people just say you die and then you're reincarnated, but there's a myriad of different things that can happen to you depending on how you die. Whether you die traumatically, or in your sleep, the state of your brain in your final moments is a factor. No matter what, one of two things will happen. Either you're going to surrender your energy into the Gaia consciousness or you're going to be spinning. Your energy will be all over the place, but it'll immediately begin to put itself together very rapidly no matter how you die. In some cases, you die so quickly that you don't even know you're dead. This leads into ghosts and spirits.

The way that you die can have a big effect on your perception. There are rare cases in which a person ends up haunting, or becoming a ghost or a spirit and doesn't feel that communication from the Universe directing them where they need to go next. Usually these are beings that have developed a soul to some extent, but they did not have a lot of time to develop it in their physical life. They must have been developed in a previous life;

however, the circumstances of this life were very limiting in the aspect of their spiritual development.

When they died, they either believed they weren't dead, or they died suddenly, or traumatically, and didn't have time to realize they died. If you look at haunting stories, you'll see that there's always a story with some emotional conflict. Either the emotional conflict of their death is very strong, or the impact of how they died is very intense, or they didn't believe they were going to live after death. If they have some kind of consciousness at all, the first conclusion they will make is that they must be dreaming. When that happens, they imprint or freeze the last moments of their consciousness.

In other words, their physical consciousness becomes a mold for them to become a dimensional being; a being made of energy that strongly believes it is still in the physical state and its faculties are not working correctly. In some cases, they form an energy body that looks like their physical body. It's holographic in a sense. Or they might remain as energy, as orbs of light. There are no limitations to what you are as a spirit or a soul. It's just a perception of what the person creates in their mind.

They are in a dream state. It's like running in your dream and knowing that someone's chasing you. In your dream your saying, "I've got to get away but why can't I run any faster?" You're almost in slow motion and then, two seconds later, you forget that you were even running and your mind has already jumped to something else. Later on in the dream, you're back running again and thinking someone's chasing you, and you can't run fast enough. You don't always have a sense of time in your dream state of consciousness. This gets into beings or souls who get stuck in this process of crossing over so they can't connect with the higher energy to direct their next path.

Can you move on and reincarnate after you've been stuck?

Yes, as soon as the consciousness can accept that you're no longer physical and in this dimension. It's the same thing that happens when you dream and, all of a sudden, you realize you're dreaming. What an epiphany; what an awakening. It's possible, and the dream mind is not so different than what you're moving into. There's a reason why dreams happen and that's a whole other discussion, but it is still an energy vibration that's very similar to the real thing.

When you can have that realization, or somebody from this reality convinces you to reflect and possibly wake you out of your dream state of consciousness, if it can occur at that moment, you then have a higher consciousness kick in. You relax and then, all of a sudden, you realize you've been in a bad dream.

Whether it's for a day, a year, a hundred years, time is irrelevant to you as an energy being. There's no decay, there's no decomposition, there's no understanding of time having an effect of creation or deterioration. If you can't remember that you are only energy, you are not going to remember what you did twenty minutes ago, or a hundred years ago. Every moment feels like the now just like it does in your dream. You don't recall how long you have been dreaming while in the dream. You can only sense and experience the very moment you're in without fully being able to reflect.

Almost every culture that believes in ghosts or spirits has a means of trying to get a hold of the spirit to inform them that they're dead: "Go to the light." "This is who you really are." "You're not part of the living anymore." They're really trying to wake the spirit out of its dream. In a dream, somebody could be telling you you're dreaming but until you get it you're stuck there. This is where you get these concepts of people trying to convince spirits to move on.

When they say, "Move on to the light," the light represents a doorway. When most people think about the light, they usually see a doorway. The light is bright, like blue white light. What's on the other side? The other side is reality. If you go through the light from reality, you can call it heaven. You can call it whatever you want, but if you internally ask yourself what it means, you'll realize that it means to wake up.

Every culture has a degree of understanding this, especially from their spiritual guides and such, so it's a matter of interpretation. If you ask me to distill all these different interpretations down to the bottom line, the bottom line is to wake a being out of its dream.

When you wake up, you resume your physical incarnation from the moment of your death. It just picks up from there and the Universe progresses you to wherever you need to go, which will be based upon your consciousness. What you know, what you've learned, and what you've experienced becomes like a frequency, it is a weight of volume but without volume or weight. It's a frequency.

If you're a ghost and then awaken and move on how will that affect you in your next life?

Let's say you die and you end up in a glitch where you become a ghost. You do this for three hundred years and then one day somebody comes along and helps you to awaken. You awaken and pick up where you should have gone three hundred years ago. You incarnate and then as a matured adult, at some point you're put under hypnosis and you're asked about your past lives. Is this your question?

Yes.

You'd remember being a ghost because you'd finally be able to formulate all those fragmented memories that you weren't able to as an entity. You would remember what it was like to be an entity.

The purpose of reincarnation is to expand your consciousness. This conversation helps you expand your consciousness so that you have a broader spectrum of possibilities when you use a form of hypnosis or some other form to awaken your memories. Your understanding of what I am saying expands the possibilities, or opens up the doorways in the deeper recesses of your mind where all these memories are compressed and packed away, making them more accessible.

You may possibly recall being a ghost at some point. Any soul is a ghost. It's really about defining what is a haunting. A haunting often sounds like a bad thing to you, but it's a repetition of where the entity is stuck in very frustrating circumstances. Entities are constantly coming and going, but they're not ghosts who are stuck in this grid; they are two different things. Entities are more conscious of their efforts whereas a ghost is not.

What is karma and does it determine how you reincarnate?

Karma is very misunderstood in the West. In some cases, it is also misunderstood in the East. The traditional concept of karma to most Westerners is that you do something bad and it comes back to you ten-fold. You do something good and it comes back to you so much greater. That's not really how karma works. A lot of people think of it as some outside force. Karma is a process.

Your frequency will determine the possibilities of where the Universe is going to move you or push you. In essence, if you were a tyrant or you were destructive and hateful, the Gaia mind certainly would look at everything you did, absorb it, and recognize it as negative aspects of human life. But let's say you did develop as a soul; therefore, you were not moved into the Gaia mind. It does happen; negative people do progress and this is how you get bad entities and beings. Karma is going to be your weight, your volume. This is what I was trying to describe as your frequency. It is what permits you and determines where you may move on to. *Karma is your frequency.*

It's not necessarily a boomeranging effect. Karma is really something that is evaluating you. It is a process to decide what will happen for you. A person could say, "Well this person has good karma. Wonderful things happen to them; they're very good. But I see very bad people that have great luck and it doesn't make any sense."

The person with good karma also has a good vibration, and that good vibration is what allows positive things to happen to them because it is reciprocated. It's what they put out. People receive it and reciprocate it back to them. This makes greater and better opportunities and a more prosperous life, in many ways. The Universe is more receptive to people who have positive energy, but karma is misinterpreted because people tend to be affected by their acts.

If you're a really negative person, you usually have more negative things happen to you. The sad part is, that person intentionally stays negative because they're constantly feeling kicked aside, or beat up, or they are tired of the opportunities in life always passing them by. This perpetuates itself. This could be perceived as karma, or that bad forces are affecting them because they are so negative. Once again it's about taking a closer look at what karma really is.

Karma is not some force that acts as a repayment of your deeds. Karma is really the representation of your deeds. It's a name to call your deeding process, your vibration. Your karma is your vibration. It's what you have become through your existence, through your actions, through your decisions, through what you have evolved to.

When a ghost is disembodied and it needs to wake up before it can continue on its process, doesn't it have a brain to utilize in order to wake up? Or does it then have to sit there and wait until someone alive comes along and wakes it up?

The Universe isn't that cruel. The Universe doesn't see time in the same way that we do. It doesn't see a thousand years as being a thousand years; so it seems cruel to us that you could be haunting the same place for a thousand years. It's just a non-issue to energy. When you ask if an entity has a brain to wake up like we do, that's not exactly the case. An entity is still stuck in the last state of consciousness that it came from. It hasn't moved on to a higher level yet.

In other words, it thinks it's still human and by doing so, it has limited itself to a human way of thinking. It has all the faculties it would have if it had a brain. It does not know its own possibilities, so it limits itself or governs itself to work within that human way of thinking. But it's still more than enough to do the job. It can wake itself out of its own dream, and that does happen.

This is a natural mechanism that even you have so that you can wake yourself out of a dream. You wake up out of a dream because you have a biological body deeply rooted with this brain. That mechanism is going to wake you up when you have to go to the bathroom. You're either going to relieve yourself and wake up, or your organs are going to shout until your consciousness wakes you up. You don't have that as a spirit or ghost. This is why it can go on forever.

Imagine if you didn't have any biological needs and you were immortal. You didn't have anything connecting with you to feel the demands of your body. How long do you think you might be able to stay in the dream world? If you didn't have a physical body and didn't have to ever wake up, it would be infinite. You'd have to have some very unusual circumstances to wake you up out of it. Hence, the process possibly lasting a hundred or a thousand years.

Why can't we automatically remember our past lives?

The human mind can only handle so much. The language of the Universe is emotion. *There is not necessarily a word for every single emotion, but there's an emotion for every single word.* You can say that you know what the table feels-like; its coolness, its smoothness, and the feels-like of the softness of the couch, and its fabric. The touch of a light bulb even has an emotion to it, a feeling, and a memory of what it contains for its "is-ness."

When there are tragedies in your life or people that you love die, there's a pain that you eventually overcome but it never leaves you. Imagine you departed and moved beyond this life, but carry with you the memories of the tragedies. Imagine you have lived many lives with many tragedies. Think what it would be like if you brought all those memories back into a biological body when you reincarnated. How much death, how much love, how much despair, and how much separation do you think you would feel? How much would your physical body be able to handle? How many people in your life do you love right at this moment? Can you imagine living the rest of your life without them? Now imagine a lifetime of that.

Your brain guards you from traumatic experiences, whether they are violent or psychologically traumatizing. There are things that you just don't remember. The brain puts them back into the recesses of your mind. This is also where your memories of all your past lives are held. It's maybe even deeper, but they are there in the same place. There are memories that your brain protects you from.

In this particular case, those memories would be surfacing in a newborn. They're deeply recessed because, in the very beginning, the brain isn't biologically designed to connect the neurological pathways with the structure of your brain to even begin to process basic things like sight and sound. It's very limited.

The brain is still building and developing its sensory to handle reality while you're young, so it's definitely shoving all the past life data into a very deep place because it can't process it yet. It can't even begin to conceive to process that information.

You grow up developing your brain as a biological being, but some of this information begins to rise to the top. It begins to surface and it comes out in small phobias or interests, or likes and desires. But, in some cases, deep-seated memories will pop up.

You don't remember because a baby's brain cannot handle it. It's designed to shove it all into a deep place in the same way as handling a traumatic experience, and it's probably for the best. Only when you leave your body, or your biological process do you remember everything, and the main reason for that is because you are biological.

No matter how developed you are, you still have chemicals reacting in your body to create emotions, anxieties, and depressions. Your body is a big chemistry lab. When you actually move outside of that chemistry lab, you will then absorb all of your memories and thoughts without becoming overwhelmed by them. You will still feel, but you have a better sense, an inner wisdom, a comfort of being able to look at it in a more compassionate and understanding way.

As an organic body, these chemicals would be responding like crazy and would overwhelm you. You'd be suicidal and depressed, just coping emotionally with what you were feeling. It's a natural process to repress that information.

Can you remember past lives while you're alive? If so, why would you want to?

You can remember your past life memories while you're alive, but you're never going to remember them one hundred percent. Think about who you are now, all the things you've done and how much of that you can actually recall. If you really think about it, what you do recall is the most impactful emotions you've ever felt. You've probably forgotten a lot of people's names; you've probably forgotten a lot of the details, and you'd really have to start sifting and sorting to remember it all. It's the same with past lives.

As you begin to bring back past life memories there's a sense of knowing, but there are going to be peaks and valleys in the clarity just like there are peaks and valleys in this life. You're going to remember big moments in those other lives. You can remember them, but it's not like it suddenly and completely changes who you are. It simply adds to who you are. It enriches you as a being *in the now*, as far as wisdom and insight goes.

You'll find that a person who has past life information most likely doesn't even know they do. They just seem very wise. They seem to be wise beyond their years. They seem to have a natural wisdom about them, and in many cases, that wisdom is coming from past lives. It's that building of consciousness that I told you about earlier on.

Can remembering past lives contribute to the awakening process?

Absolutely. There are people who have greater purposes. They feel that information within them and the need to access it, but it can be chaotic because they do not take the brain into consideration, or how it's going to cope and deal with that information.

If it's done appropriately, it can be integrated with your current consciousness and it will give you a greater sense of completion, or wholeness. You're also going to have a clearer thought process in how to apply yourself. You will know what you need to do. You're going to have a sense of, "Oh, this makes sense," or "That makes sense," or "Why didn't that occur to me before?"

Can past lives have an influence on your present life?

Not always, but sometimes the careers and partners that you may choose have a lot to do with past lives. In many cases, people from other past lives find that they were married to similar people, have similar careers, or are somehow interconnected. So, there's definitely a strong connection there.

Is reincarnation specific to humans on this planet?

When you are regressed into a past life and see yourself as an animal, such as a hawk, a bird, or a horse, it is really you connecting into the Gaia mind rather than a past life experience. Because you are open to this type of concept, you are misinterpreting the experiences you may be having.

Let's experience this now.

Lie back and imagine yourself as a hawk. Imagine feeling your wing span with the feathers pushed and tightened into your flesh. Feel your chest and the lightness of your chest cage, the air pushing up in the warm thermals of your body. See out of your eyes. Notice it's more of a wider expansive view, maybe a slightly different coloration than what you are used to. You might feel the speed and the momentum of flight.

You can experience these things on profound levels when you get clarity of mind and rightfully assume that this was an incarnation of a past life. How would you know otherwise?

You can do this with any living thing. It's an innate ability within you. It's part of feeling the matrix. It's just a matter of how much you're willing to let yourself go to feel these things. Your inner Governor tries to hold you back from these experiences and limits what you believe are possibilities so that you don't even begin to try them. When you experience these things, you think they're absolutely unique, and so you jump to conclusions.

Animals are unable to store memories that would contribute to an incarnation. They certainly have emotions, and they are undoubtedly more intelligent than we give them credit for. But their concept of time and their ability to retain information makes them unlikely candidates for reincarnation.

In other words, a bird in the wild may live a life expectancy of three to fifteen years, depending on the bird. The processes of that bird are capturing, feeding and mating. There might be a few challenges with predators and different weather circumstances, but it will be a repetitive existence. How much can you really learn in the end? If you take the population of the animal kingdom into consideration, you're dealing with an exponentially larger number of possibilities than with the human population.

You cannot incarnate from animals or into animals. It does not make sense if you understand the process of attaining knowledge and consciousness and the expansion of that. There are, however, certain animals that could figure into this. Whales, dolphins, and elephants have the potential to experience reincarnation. They show a different level of intelligence than other animals. You need a certain level of organic capability in order to begin building a soul. You have to be able to reflect. The majority of animals are unable to do that to any great degree. There are a great many people who feel a very strong affinity to animals, and they feel that they've been an animal in the past, but it's more of the Gaia mind.

So to be clear, you think it is possible for a whale, or a dolphin, or an elephant to reincarnate?

A dolphin would be a little bit questionable, but I certainly believe that about elephants and whales. It depends on what type of whales, of course.

If most people don't reflect enough to reincarnate, then how then can these animals?

I would put them in the same category as alien intelligences. Are you going to say that because an alien being doesn't think or look like a human being, it can't incarnate or have a soul? There are certain things that are beyond the limits of how we think. It doesn't mean that your thinking is wrong. If you can contemplate and reflect, you can potentially build a soul. I think certain whales reflect. When I've studied them and have been near them, I have communicated with them. There's a symbiotic energy going on and there's certain information that I'm privy to.

I've observed the same thing when I've been around elephants. As human beings, we've had to evolve and create things outside of our intelligence. We've created and produced physical objects through our imagination. Elephants have created a different kind of intelligence; an intelligence and a reality within their minds. They communicate in a different way compared with the speech patterns that humans' use. There's a very strong telepathic mode there and their reality is an alien way of thinking.

They have one foot in our reality and one foot out of our reality, but it is just as real. Their two becomes one; two creates a process of a third birth. Their reality is absolutely alien for us to conceive, so we observe through what we've learned to understand. That's the beauty of those who've been incarnated a lot and those who are incarnating. This is the purpose of it. It's to have the understanding that there's so much more for you to understand, experience, and see. It's just profound and wondrous.

How does a new soul or someone without any past lives awaken?

The majority of people who actually do this program will have great results. If they're looking for this kind of material, they are already well beyond the first soul phase. There's a reason why they are looking for this. They want to learn from it because there's something inside of them that's built up and they are trying to free it.

Let's say there is someone who has had only one past life and now they are getting a lot of information. I would say that this information is more from the Gaia mind. They've managed to slip into that and they're going to get assorted pieces of information.

The difference is that when you have past life memories you often can get smells and tastes. There's a very personal feeling that's attached to it. It's like the way you recognize your mother. Would you recognize your mother if you hadn't seen her for ten years? Would you recognize your mother in twenty years, thirty years, forty or fifty years? If you hadn't seen her for sixty years and she was standing right in front of you, do you believe that you would recognize her? Maybe she would need to talk a little bit, but you would feel her. That's the trick. When you go into the Gaia mind everything is amazing, but it's a different kind of connection altogether. A new White Cell would not necessarily see that or make that connection right away.

So an experience of tapping into the Gaia mind definitely feels different than a past life memory?

Yes, it's different. It's not as personable. It's real, it's profound, but it's different.

Let's say you're very spiritual in one life and in another you're not, what happens then?

The good work you've done will hold you over for a few lives if you are not really stimulated to awaken a few times around. There is a very strong Navigator in people to wake up, so it's unlikely that you would be born into a life where you wouldn't reawaken at some point. You would know that you want to awaken as early as ten years old, even earlier in some cases. For some it doesn't hit them until they are twenty or thirty. Usually this is because of the environment that your brain is subjected to. You may have religious parents, anti-religious parents, scientific parents, musically oriented parents, or art oriented parents.

In any case, the product of your parent's thinking is super-imposed on you. This will determine how long it's going to take you to march to the beat of your own drum. If you are constantly programmed from a very young age that all of this spiritual teaching is rubbish, that none of it is real, and this is all foolishness, you may not come around until you're forty or fifty.

You're going to have to work out all of that programming, but rest assured, your Navigator isn't going to give up. Your Navigator now is going to be constantly fighting with your rational mind. You are going to want to believe these types of teachings, but you will struggle with internalizing the truth because you've been convinced all your life that the world and reality abides by a certain set of rules.

In most cases with Red Cell parents, a person creates a duality where their brain is just regurgitating what it was fed in childhood, but their Navigator struggles to follow what they feel is true. If you had parents or a social structure that encouraged finding your inner self, it would have been a definite advantage.

That being said, I know many people who have had atheist or religious family members but they knew at a very young age they disagreed with what their parents had to say. They didn't know how they knew; they just knew. It was the Navigator. Having a strong Navigator is wonderful, but what was shown to you in life, what you were exposed to is what really determines whether or not you have that extra advantage.

Does the ability to awaken increase with the number of incarnations?

You can become enlightened in your first life. It's an interpretation of what is enlightenment. *Enlightenment is when you finally plug in completely. If* you fully plug in, it doesn't mean you've made it to the top and it's time to kick back now. It doesn't work that way. You want to investigate more richness of life. It just never ends.

What if that person hasn't developed their dimensional consciousness through past lives?

You can be a pretty simple person and still be enlightened. Some shamans are enlightened and aren't necessarily the most brilliant person intellectually, like compared to a biophysicist. There are a lot of enlightened beings and while they may have different perspectives, you'll find that they have a lot of fundamental similarities of what they understand.

There can be a level of enlightenment within a person, but the knowledge they possess and the expression of that knowledge through language is something that's human. Everybody looks at it this way: "Can you prove to me how enlightened you are?" It's more about whether or not you can communicate what you know well enough to convince others that you are brilliant. If you can't do that, then they make the assumption that you are probably not enlightened and won't give you the time of day.

If you can sit down and reflect so deeply on your soul, so deeply on what reality is, so deeply that you shift and move into the Gaia mind and into a greater consciousness, then you can find enlightenment in your first life. It's rare, but you're not asking me whether I think it's rare or not. You're asking me if it's possible. I'll say to you go back a few thousand years and you'll see there was less education, less possibility of understanding knowledge. There were only simple things in life, and yet there were still a few enlightened beings.

Can there be repercussions for not awakening in a lifetime?

If you do not awaken; if you do not realize that you can have a soul, if you do not build a soul, or if you simply do not reflect on something other than just physical life, you will be absorbed into the Gaia mind. You might consider that a repercussion. In a sense, you've decided this one lifetime was it. You've lived your life and truly it's the end of it all. Just like many scientists believe: you're dead, you're buried in the ground, and that's it. Nothing more after that. Is that a bad thing? No, it can be a very beautiful thing.

When you're ready to throw in the towel and die, you think very differently. But for those who've never worked on building their spiritual body, then it's like a surrender. It's like lying down into some very warm arms and dissipating, but you are forever alive because you are constantly in the memory. When human beings say, "I'll never be forgotten as long as you think of me," it is really a truth. What is life? Life is just a bunch of memories. And if you think of things you've done or people you've loved or pets you've had, that memory exists as if it were happening now. Well, imagine the Gaia mind; everything is constantly existing in its memory.

One consequence of not awakening is losing your ability to move on to a next life. Other repercussions lie on the vibration and density of your soul, and the qualities of what you perceived in your life. If you want to ask, "Can there be consequences for that?" Well, yes. If you've had extremely negative energy and very suppressive energy, if you suppressed others, likely you will end up in a suppressive existence. This can become very complicated. For example, there are people in certain countries that live in horrible, horrible conditions. Some forms of Hinduism believe in a hierarchy, that if you are born into a bad life it's because you did very bad things and that's why you have this hardship. Conversely, if you've been very good, well, that's why you're wealthy and you should be considered wonderful and great. I don't necessarily buy into that, but there's a certain level of truth to some of it.

The vibration of your energy will be instinctually attracted to similar situations, if you're not too evolved. If you oppressed others, your karma, your frequency, is going to draw you toward oppressive energies, which could mean that you're born into a country in complete turmoil. There are so many levels that weigh it all out; it's beyond us to figure it out completely. It's like finite mathematics on a super conscious level for the Universe to weigh and figure it all out. In the end, you're going to be attracted or cycle into circumstances that would best match your previous frequency.

Is the attraction a form of choice? Is there a level of choice involved in reincarnation?

It's not really choice until you've evolved your consciousness enough so you can actually feel these energies and choose to follow them or pick a direction. It eventually becomes a choice, but the repercussions of not developing a soul or not developing it well enough in the beginning is going to mean you're pushed and shoved in certain directions. Like a bottle in the ocean, you're going to follow the current and it's going to lead you to where you will end up. There is, and is not, a duality there if you listen carefully to what I'm saying.

Can a soul die?

Technically, no. Reflect on the definition of what you consider dying. A soul can never die. It can choose its moment of surrender, absolute surrender, and generally that surrender is always surrendering to God. Surrender comes when one says, "Okay, I've lived the fullest, richest life that a being could live. I just want to become one with you." If you internally ask yourself what you're really looking for in that moment, you'll find you're asking yourself to return to that from whence you came. You want the highest level of completion. You yearn to be returned to that from which you've been separated. You yearn to become one with God.

In the end, after you've explored all the wonders of this universe and other universes and have fulfilled the amount of experiences you should have in your journey, you yearn to return to the place that you came from. You return to the consciousness of God, and that is a different level of the concept of a sugar cube dissolving into water. Instead of surrendering to the level of Gaia, or a galaxy, or this universe, you've really returned to full completion and you choose that moment when you want to return. At that point, everything you've ever experienced becomes one for God.

Can a soul be reabsorbed into the Gaia consciousness after it has evolved to a certain point?

I would say that it can happen in very rare cases. Sometimes, and I know this may sound bizarre, certain souls that are advanced will choose to give themselves to the Gaia consciousness as a way to accelerate its growth. It's rare, but it does happen. There are souls who have stopped their development. If you spend several lifetimes not really progressing, you're either stagnating or you're digressing. The universe and the planet are constantly progressing. If you are not going to move forward, you're resigning yourself to become the 'sugar cube' again.

All the intelligences of the Earth are growing in tonal and energy. Inevitably, all human beings are forced to evolve. If you're not evolving yourself spiritually as all beings are, the level of the Gaia mind is going to reach a tonal that matches the place where you have stopped progressing. So, yes, you could end up getting ahead but then just surrender and become part of Gaia, even though at one time you were more advanced than others.

Is it possible to break free of the reincarnation process and just be an energy being?

Absolutely.

Are you then part of some higher reincarnation process?

Reincarnation, in the terms we are referencing for this conversation, is incarnating back into a physical body. Let's dissect this here a little bit more. You're thinking like a human being when you assume that if you're not in a physical body, then you're not incarnating. You can incarnate into other kinds of bodies that aren't necessarily physical as our bodies are right here, right now. They would just be different kinds of energy frequencies that suit your energy and allow you to explore the dimension in which the vessel exists. These physical bodies interpret this dimension.

There is always an incarnation process because you are really a finite level of energy. At the higher level of reincarnation, you sample other dimensions and collect new experiences through those samplings so that you can attain consciousness and information. To subject yourself to these experiences, you have to allow yourself to transmute into some other lower form of energy to convey its experiences to you. In human bodies, whenever you touch something, it turns into electricity and becomes part of your energy. Whenever you smell something, it becomes energy; whenever you hear something, it becomes energy. Your body is a giant machine that's designed to convert data into energy for you because that's what you are. The brain is the bigger conductor in this process. It is the final converter that changes it into the purest level of energy for the mind.

In essence, you need different vessels designed specifically to explore all of the different realities. Therefore, the incarnation process is infinite. It's just a matter of where, when, how, and what you choose, or what is chosen for you.

When you say that you incarnate to sample, who are you? What is the identity between incarnations?

It's not really you as you think of yourself right now. It is the process of becoming enlightened. The brain is your frame, but it's also your enemy because it is designed to be part of this dimension. Your brain is doing its job when it wraps you into this dimension. At some point, you have to realize that's what's happening. This is where your whole spiritual path is going now. There's an acceptance and there's a conflict. You're beginning to realize that this brain and body aren't who you really are. You're trying to begin that separation while you're still physically here rather than out of your body.

What are some of the things you can do to trigger past life memories?

Reflect on what you're interested in now. Past lives tend to surface in old things; that doesn't necessarily mean antique things. It could be something from twenty years ago, if you're twenty years old. If you're drawn to castles, find the next best thing near you, like old churches with cobblestones. Travel to a city that's older, like Boston, which might be more practical than traveling to England. Touch, smell, listen, sit still, feel a place. Any way that you can absorb information through your sensory is the best way to begin to shift yourself.

Clear yourself like you've learned to do in meditation. Center yourself and then go into this environment without any intentions. Simply experience the environment. If you let the smells, textures, and the feelings come in, even though it may not be from the original place where your memories come from it will potentially jolt something from the deeper recesses of your mind. Sometimes it's water or the smell of the ocean, the feel of the beach, the sand on your feet, or the heat from the sand. Sometimes it's a pine forest and feeling the pine cones or pine needles, or hearing the wind through the trees. For others it's the sound of a motor, or a car, or a train. You have already connected with these things; you just never realized that you are drawn towards them.

There are times in your life when you start to zone in on a certain thing. It could be a moment in the park, a moment in your car, or it could be just looking at someone, but there's a moment when something's talking to you. Something feels odd and strangely familiar to you, but because you can't place it with your present memories, your brain overrides it and says, "Move on." You have to ask yourself what things are attractive to you, what, things are unconsciously talking to you? When you can figure those things out, then you need to explore them.

Sometimes it's art, but not actually creating the art. It's putting yourself in an art museum and walking through the different exhibitions; maybe finding some pieces of art that you're absolutely drawn to. You never would have found it had you not exposed yourself to a vast variety of sculptures and paintings, but you would know it's something you needed to do. Why would you know that you needed to do it? It's that inner knowing, it's that inner Navigator. It's about listening and putting yourself in circumstances in order to have it jump out at you.

Listen rather than function. Functioning would be like entering the gallery and thinking with your brain, "I'm going to do this; I'm going to do that. Here's my list of things to look at." You've got to put that all aside and let your mind be silent, like a walking meditation. Just see where it takes you; see where the Universe moves you to instead of the rational brain pointing out a whole game plan. Let yourself flow.

You already know what you need to look at; your Navigator's already talking to you. You're just not listening. That is the problem. You need to listen. When you listen, you will find things that are going to jolt your memory. Smells can do it, sounds can do it. In some cases, it is like the surreal sound at a drive-in movie theater. When you park your car and the movie's running and you walk out in the dark to go get popcorn, it's the crunching sound of your feet on the dirt, the echoing in people's cars, it's surreal. But if you stay too grounded and tag those sounds as the movie, or your footsteps, or the cars, you will miss what's going on. Don't think about all that. Enjoy what's going on. There's something trying to speak to you and you can feel it. You just have to let yourself go with it.

If you don't get it completely, don't get frustrated. There will be another time and another time after that. The experiences will get more intense. Don't program your brain to have resistance by saying, "I'm frustrated because it's not coming through." That is just a reinforcement preventing it from happening.

You have to realize when you're sensing your Navigator instead of focusing on the physical things your body is doing. When you can pay more attention, you begin to exploit those experiences by putting yourself in those situations. If you are out with your family and you sense something at an old church building, for example, make a mental note that you felt something interesting and then, when you have the opportunity, or you have time by yourself, take a little drive and do your investigation. Spend that time walking through there and listen to your footsteps against the wood echoing through the church. Feel the textures of things. Open yourself up without any preconceived ideas of what you should expect. As soon as you have expectations, you're limiting the information you're going to get.

Does this tie into your suggestion that we should try to eat the food from a lot of different countries?

Yes. Let's look at all the cultures that have integrated into America. First you see them change their clothing, then their hair style, their jewelry, their cars, their houses. Eventually everything changes, but there's usually one particular thing that people can never let go of. The food from their culture is something they always hang onto. Food is something you hang on to from your childhood. Even if you grew up as an American, whatever you ate from your youth, no matter the quality, you will crave it. This is something that's built into us biologically.

Survival is based upon food. Nine times out of ten if you see an animal, wild or domestic, they are looking for food; that's all they have on the brain. Human beings aren't that much different. We have an abundance of food. We've learned to be selective with food that has made an imprint on our brain. It carries over in your mind when you move on to another life. If you've spent a significant amount of time in a past life in a certain culture, when you eat the food from that culture and open yourself to the experience, you're going to have flashbacks. You're going to reflect on it, and you're going to have profound breakthroughs if you have any connection to that food.

Let's say you do a reincarnation session and have good results. Go out and have Russian food. Go out and have Indian food; experience as many different types of food as possible. When you're done with each type, take in all the tastes, textures, and feelings in a very tactile way and experience it. Don't set any expectations, like you're going to suddenly wake up from a past life. Take that time that you spent there in the restaurant, go back home, and listen to your reincarnation recording. You will have a better success rate if you ate Indian food and ultimately had past lives in India. You're going to see it come through much clearer. It's a crafty way of assisting yourself to help your consciousness move.

All of these memories carry with you and can be accessed. People who eat a variety of food usually have better regression sessions and get better results than people who have a very limited diet. There is definitely a connection with food, and it's something that carries over spiritually from life to life.

Are certain souls more prone to choosing or incarnating into one sex versus the other?

For the majority of souls or spirits there is not a gender choice at the moment of conception simply because the Universe just moves you as the opportunity arises. You don't necessarily know a baby's gender before it's born, unless there is an ultrasound, because you can't pick up on the sex of the baby just from the energy field. Some very powerful spiritual beings have been both female and male in a balanced nature. In your physical life, you'll find that most spiritual people who are rather advanced are going to have very feminine energy and very masculine energy at the same time. Sometimes you don't quite know how to judge them because they're very balanced internally. They haven't really chosen either sex.

If there is a preference by an advanced being, it will most likely be male oriented because of the sociological structure of societies. The world is still dominated by males and there is still more opportunity for a male to communicate and teach. However, you will see more female spiritual masters rising up now because cultures are rapidly changing, particularly with the progression of women's rights. Before all of this, it was unusual to find enlightened spiritual teachers that were female.

There are certainly both advantages and disadvantages in how the biological brain is designed for a male versus a female. The regions utilized by each are very different. Women have a much higher level of psychic abilities than males, meaning that they have a sensory or ability telepathically and empathically to do certain things. Whereas males tend to have a more analytical mind.

In a psychological study of men and women, they were asked to draw a bicycle. The females drew a triangle with two circles while the males drew a very detail oriented bicycle. It's how the mind works; it visualizes so it can structuralize things better. That's not to say that all women and men perform this way. It is just a choice of what direction the brain is plugging into. This is why you have spiritual teachers who have masculine-feminine energy. They are uniting both parts of the brain so that they're able to launch on a better spiritual level and work through their brain to communicate outward.

If you're a woman during your incarnation but you don't feel feminine, what can that mean?

It could mean several different things. It could be that in your past lives, you were male more often than female. Let's say for the past ten lives you've been men, and not just a man but very dominant, aggressive, and outspoken. That type of energy is going to carry over. If that's the case, and you're a female this time around, you and your body are going to be at odds because you're not adapting well to this particular biological role. The same thing goes for femininity with frequent female past lives bleeding over into the physical.

This brings forth the issue of sexuality, which is genetic in part; that's how the brain is designed. As science progresses they will understand these things. People are born a certain way and that genetic predisposition partly accounts for who you will become. However, what you are exposed to, what you accept in your life, and your perspective of things is what shapes you. Other cultures have a completely different perspective than Americans on mates, multiple mates, genders, and what's considered acceptable and what's not. What you're exposed to during your formative years becomes what you are, and who's to say whether it's natural or unnatural?

Look at nature. The animals on this planet are instinctual. There's no real decision making done as far as societal behavior goes. However, there are numerous examples in science journals of animals who exhibit gay and bisexual behavior. This is real "birds and bees" stuff, so to speak. This is nature. Is it a mistake on God's part, or does God not make mistakes as many religions proclaim?

Neurobiologists are finding slight differences in the brain and they think it's sociological. The missing factor is a spiritual aspect. What gender you were in your past life is going to be a factor. If you're an advanced soul that's been around for a while, you will have a very strong balance of masculine-feminine energy. There's a certain balance in that it could be one of three factors: genetic, sociological, or spiritual, or perhaps all three.

Can a soul only reincarnate into one body at a time?

There have been cases where people have claimed that they've been more than one person or they have been in multiple places at the same time. In this physical dimension, it's fair to say that there are many possibilities, especially when you consider quantum physics. This is getting into an area now that is easy to explain and simultaneously not so easy to explain.

Is it possible, as a soul, to exist in two separate places at the same time? Yes, because you are infinitely energy. Possibilities can be separate. Can one hand feel the carpet and the other feel the hair on your head at the same time? You are one being taking in two sources of data. Everything that you perceive, you see individually because that's how you see yourself as a human being. You need to see yourself split in half or just look at your two hands. They work together for one unit, but they also work independently.

One soul in two different places could be a possibility in this physical dimension, but it's very unlikely. This isn't something that would occur often or in every lifetime. In rare cases, a soul is required to be in more places at one time; there is no other choice. In a situation such as that it divides itself, but when both bodies pass on it will unite itself and become whole again. In other words, you leap from life to life accumulating your consciousness. The time period is the same, but you've split into two data pools collecting experiences that will eventually merge back to one. It's rare and it's really a mind bender for you because you perceive yourselves as individuals.

Is there a way to tell if someone is an old soul?

That is one of those inner knowing's. You know where a person's been and you know what they're about when you meet them. You can look at a person and know that they're fake. You see them dressed a certain way, combing their hair a certain way, acting a certain way and you know that it's a camouflage. It's all a shell and underneath there isn't much going on intellectually. Then there are other people that you meet and know there's a rich source of information there, that the person is very complex; you just know this. How do you know this? Because your inner knowing tells you so. In many cases, this is a result of how many lives they've lived.

How does the creation of a soul affect the Universe?

The creation of a soul is a necessity. God created the universe; the universe is the body of God or a portion of God's body. The planets, the moons, the stars, all of these things are the flesh, and the spirit of God. The consciousness is intertwined, just like your body is the flesh and your soul is the consciousness of it – the Universe is also intertwined, it's all one.

When you reach out and touch something, there is a form of information that's exchanged. Cells may die to pass on their electrical bit of information, along with thousands of others that move their way through your inner universe to become part of your consciousness. After they give their information to the brain, the brain is able to disperse that data into a different kind of consciousness. Life throughout the Universe, on all levels, whether it's planets or intelligent beings, in some way serves a greater or lesser level of this exchange of information.

A human being is energy, has energy, everything is converted into energy, and when they die that energy moves to the next level, to the planet. The planet might live billions of years, but that's just a blink of an eye to the Universe. It's just a different size portion or existence in time. The planet, in turn, releases all of the data it's received from its micro level, which would be living beings, to the solar system. A solar system might die in trillions of years and be given to the galaxy, and the galaxy might disappear in trillions and trillions of years, but it'll give its complete evolution to the next level up.

A soul is really a higher level of that process. In your body you have your standard level of information exchange and then you have other living organisms in your body that have different roles or different levels of importance. All of it is important in the end, but sometimes there are certain cells that have different purposes; longer life expectancies, or a different array of abilities or sensory in order to conduct what they need to contribute to the bigger picture, which is your entire universe.

In the same way, souls serve a higher purpose for the planet than other organisms do. Souls are extremely important to the Universe, to God. They're one of the most important things to the Universe because they act as ambassadors when they surrender themselves to the Universe rather than just the planet like other living organisms do. They actually move to a higher frequency and back again, life after life in a different level of contribution instead of living a micro life.

When a really advanced soul incarnates into specific circumstances, is it by their choice or can they be directed by other soul collectives?

Again, using the human body as a reference, you can have an infection in your toe and the white cells throughout your entire body somehow know they must fight this infection in your toe. They will journey an infinite amount of space, infinite because they are micro, to get to this place to assist, to fight this battle. For whom are they fighting this battle? For themselves, or is there a greater cause? The greater cause is the whole, it's you. They sacrifice their lives in this process. Interestingly enough white cells reincarnate in a sense; you never catch the same cold twice. Red cells, on the other hand, have a different purpose to serve the whole in their micro life. They live out their existence and that's the end of it.

Science has now discovered what are called super white cells. They have ancient memory and ancient knowledge. So when a virus comes into the body and the regular white cells can't handle it, it's as if there's a certain knowing that these super white cells possess. These super cells then react in order to battle these viruses of which they seem to have this greater knowledge. Sometimes it's too late for them to react and the body can't respond because these cells weren't able to get into the action fast enough. The destruction was too vast. Obviously, there is a delegation of some sort going on through our inner universe.

We are made in the image of God, not as flesh, but in spirit. It may be in an alien way, it may be different but it's also very similar. Instead of cells in a body, there are beings that intervene to help with the propagation of life. While there are viruses or negative beings who try to bring about destruction of life, there are more advanced beings willing to intervene at times to help.

If you die on one planet and reincarnate into a different world or dimension, can you then reincarnate back into that first world?

It depends on what level you are and the circumstances of your choices. The endurance of the soul is unbelievable. It's made of the fabric of God. A soul is indestructible, but it has to serve some form of purpose.

Can you program something into your next incarnation?

Yes, you absolutely can. Most of the time people do this without even knowing it. Again, this goes back to food and the little things you enjoyed from other lives. You can deliberately attempt to send a message in your psyche to come forward in a certain future life. Spiritual masters will use this as a device to help in their awakening process in the next life, if they know they're going to come back immediately.

People ask about trying to wake up inside their dreams as a way to help you wake up in this reality. To them I say look at your hand before you go to bed; study it. See the fingers but don't move around. Don't follow your hand up and down or look around, just look at the palm. As you're looking at the palm, become aware of the flesh around it, the meatier muscles. Then as you're looking at the center, become aware of the bluer veins inside versus the pigment. Look at the creases in the palm of your hand. Become aware of your fingers that are sticking out and the space in between and the notches and the folds in between, and then absorb that into you. Open your hand and close it several times. Just think of yourself as a machine. Be aware of yourself opening and closing your hand.

While you are sleeping, if you are dreaming, there will come a point when your hand will appear and you will look at it. Look at your hand in the dream. The same visual conditions that exist in our waking life exist in your dream state. What I mean is, you don't see yourself in the dream as a separate person. You are looking out of your own eyes just as in real life. In your dream, you're doing the same thing, but it's a whole different reality around you, and helps to wake you up in your dream.

Now, let's take this a step further. You could say at this moment, "As I look at my hand, I will awaken to who and what I am. As I look at my hand, I will awaken to who and what I am." In your next life, there might come a moment one day when you're sitting down and you look at your hand and you awaken. You just have this huge memory that floods your mind. This could be done unknowingly.

You could be a person who had a home on a mountainside in a past life and you watched the sun rise every morning. You might think, "What has that got to do with anything?" Well, maybe there were two pine trees, one to the left, one to the right and the sun would rise in the middle every day; and you reflected on your life in that moment. That was the time of day that you did certain reflective activities or spiritual things. Perhaps if you go out to a forest one morning and by chance you sit down and watch a sunrise with the two trees, one on the left and one on the right, it may profoundly awaken you. Or, if you use this material we're discussing consistently enough, it's going to jolt certain things in your memory. You're going to go out in life and you may just have a serious flash of information surface. It happens all the time.

The answer to the question is yes, you can program certain things to assist your awakening process. But most people lack consistency. You could do it to affect your next life, but the question is, will you be consistent enough this week, this month, this year, the next five years? Very unlikely. It's the same thing that you would have experienced in any other life. It's very unlikely unless you're highly disciplined.

Can you tap into another person's past lives?

Absolutely. Sometimes it's easier to pick up on somebody else's past lives than it is for you to remember your own past lives. It sounds a little quirky, but the reasoning is, if you are already psychically developed and you can sense things and feel things, you simply apply those skills to trying to feel who the person was in a past life. It's as if there's a better flow in the brain to somehow accept information from the back of that person's mind or their frequency. That information is more accessible to you because your brain isn't filtering it and because the laws of perception say this: everything that you experience is from an external place brought internally. Your hearing is from the outside world, your sight is from the outside world, and your smell is from the outside world.

When you look at someone and impose your telepathic abilities on them, it's almost as if that information follows the same principle and the brain accepts it easier than trying to retrieve information from an internal source and trying to bring it forward. It's not that you just look at everybody and the information runs through you, you have to go into a deeper state and, in a spiritual way, and you link. Your intent is know what this person was in a past life, just like if you were to predict their future because you have the ability to also pick up on information. It's not going to be a play by play of their life. It's not complete information; it's going to be bits and pieces just like anything else.

How does a human reincarnate on a totally alien planet?

Again, it's a choice. At a certain point you evolve enough spiritually to move on. You will not find an alien being who's lived only one life on their world, suddenly have the ability to move across the solar system, the galaxy, or the universe and incarnate their second lifetime as a human. There is a progression of what you must contribute to your own planet, meaning your data collected through reflection and an evolutionary process of consciousness. Before you even have the ability to migrate dimensionally, or to the other side of the universe, you must be aware that you need to move past the planet's magnetism that holds you in place. This is the same type of magnetism that your body has to hold your soul in place.

The planets are designed to hold you here. The planet has its own mechanism for developing its consciousness to grow. If souls who were contributing to its growth were able to release so easily, the planet would never be able to evolve. Life is like the planet's neural system; it contributes to the planet's consciousness. A planet wants to give life. A planet wants to do this because it's building a neural system. All the mechanisms of life on that planet are dying and giving its collective energy to the consciousness of that planet. This process is a form of inner procreation in a sense, but different. It's the same reason the cells in your body adapt, grow, become bigger, better and faster from the moment you are born. The planet is doing the same thing. It's designed not to let you escape. You have to evolve and only the few that truly do are then able to move on to different places.

Are you suggesting that most people who've had only a few lives are not likely to have had lives in alien worlds or dimensions?

If you think about how most people interpret reincarnation, it's very rare that you come across somebody who claims to be only aliens in their past life.

So, it is more likely that, if someone had an alien memory, they're probably tapping into some sort of galactic grid?

Not necessarily, they could be tapping into Gaia. The Gaia mind isn't exclusive to the knowledge of the Earth. The Gaia mind is very connected to the rest of the galactic mind. It's just a different hierarchy. Its neighbor is another solar system or another galaxy and there could be an exchange of information going on constantly, and it is possible to tap into that. This information exchange creates a whole daisy chain throughout the entire galaxy, or the universe, if you think about it; the possibilities are infinite.

If a person claims to have memories of past alien lives, it's also possible they have evolved intensely in another world and this is their first life here on Earth. Because of this, they're very limited in a way. Maybe because they were alien, they have not lived any physical lives, but they are probably super evolved, spiritually. The problem is, the soul is foreign in a world that is completely strange. And so they're almost as limited as a person who incarnates for the first time. They don't understand the textures, the colors, the structures, the technology, the communication, and the verbiage. It's all extremely alien to them, but they usually mature much faster because there is an enriched background behind them. In fact, I would say that's the path I've taken.

What would happen if the population suddenly shrank due to a catastrophic event?

What happens when people use drugs? What happens when something traumatic happens, or chemicals get into your body system and make it to your brain? Brain damage. Your brain will attempt to heal itself and rebuild. During that process you are limited or less capable. Take a stroke, for instance. A stroke will usually kill certain portions of your brain and you have to practice to regain skills that were lost. You either get back a one hundred percent functionality, or you don't.

According to archeological evidence, the planet's been on the brink of total destruction on several occasions but there's always a turnaround. The planet is still very young when you consider the age of the galaxy or universe. With that in mind, if you look at a young human as an analogy, you could say that a baby shows remarkable resiliency from brain damage whereas an older adult does not. In this case, the planet would have a downtime and it would rebuild from there. But more importantly, there is a large amount of data that's released during those time periods and usually that contributes to refining and learning from one's mistakes in a very unusual way.

What happens to a soul when there are no bodies to reincarnate into?

A large majority of souls are just going to be a contribution to the Gaia mind. The few that escape certainly can find bodies throughout the world because there will always be a larger portion of the population not developing a soul.

Would there ever be a case of massive soul migration?

Yes, it has happened on many occasions.

What would the circumstances be in order for that to take place?

A world dying, such as a sun going supernova before the populous of the planet can actually leave through mechanical means or scientific means. They would either disperse and that energy would then proliferate the other surrounding solar system much like how an individual gives to a planet. The souls from the dying world would scatter in millions of directions. They would become like grains of sands for souls in other worlds. It wouldn't be like a huge flood of those souls for one planet. It doesn't work that way. The universe is so vast at this point, it just would be thinned out so that maybe only two or three would even end up incarnating on our world.

You also have to keep in mind that, on some planets, the process for its inhabitants evolving souls is a much more difficult challenge than it would be on other worlds. Again, it's the opportunities that are there in combination with what the vessel can offer. Man has created and developed our planet because we have fingers and toes and hands. Perhaps a planet that has a large population may not have as many intelligent souls developing on it, while other planets may have an abundant amount. There are many factors to consider. The most challenging point is realizing those factors.

People look at and consider everything from a very human perspective. We assume the rest of the universe works the same way as it does here, and that's a big mistake. It is difficult to escape that mindset, however, because our conversations are built around that human perspective. It is simply the easiest way to really teach you.

How do you tell the difference between a true past life memory, psychic impression, or genetic recall?

Science has recently had to acknowledge reincarnation from a scientific perspective. Now, they don't want to believe that it's from a soul dying and moving on to another life. Instead, they are willing to consider the possibility that it is a genetic memory. For instance, they now believe it is possible that the "past life memories" people may be having are legitimate. However, it is theorized that these memories are not from a past life but are the result of memories from your mother, father, or family members stored into your sensory; your vision, or your sense of smell. It is believed that somehow that information was recorded and imposed genetically on your DNA, like micro information. Think of how much information can be stored on a computer chip, and then just think of the possibilities that can be achieved with the brain, which is infinitely more advanced.

According to this theory, you should not and would not have memories from your mother that occurred after you were born, because there's no way to transfer that data. There are different theories explaining how memory of past lives has come into the big picture and that's one of them.

When first attempting to retrieve past life memories, it's very difficult because the brain just sees everything as imagery. Let me propose a question to you. You have a memory of going to Hawaii and a memory of watching something about Hawaii on television. How do you know which is real in your memory? It feels different right? This may not be the answer anybody wants to hear, because it certainly leaves a lot of room for error. However, in the beginning, you have to accept that. It is going to take time to discern these nuances. You can have memory within your own mind that you can discern whether it was real or not. You feel it, you know it.

This gets back to that knowing that I keep talking about. It's very clear and defined; you are unable to doubt it. When you start to have memories of past lives you're going to know the difference between a memory and your imagination. If you don't feel that knowing then very likely it is imagination. Some people may argue that you could concoct almost anything and buy into it. But that is not true, you would know the difference; you're just lying to everybody else.

Does reincarnation occur within the constraints of time as we know it?

It's in accordance with time because the universe is expanding. Everything is making a forward progression. The forward motion is based upon the wave of previous knowledge that's building. The Universe is moving forward, attempting to return back to energy. The Universe started off as energy, solidified into lower frequencies of energy, which created matter. Matter then produced different organic levels of life to microscopically integrate with this reality through means of both organic matter and energy. The organic matter could then collect enough information to become energy and energy progressively returns to the source of where the experience was designated to begin. It's the return of that process.

You would not be able to incarnate into past lives from the future. You can't incarnate into the future and you can't incarnate in the past. You can review the past through the Gaia mind or the collective consciousness of the universe. It is recorded memory just like you can review your own memory. Under hypnosis, what little you can remember now usually gets a lot sharper and a lot better because it's recorded in your mind. Anything that goes into the future is really just speculative future; it's not written future. The Gaia mind can predict very far into the future, but it is still only a prediction. For example, if I picked up an object and motioned to throw it to you, before the object left my hand you'd be calculating the necessary motions to catch it. You would already be sensing and calculating what it is that I'm doing and where the object is going to be thrown.

Consider a supercomputer predicting the landing location of a rubber ball after being thrown in a room. Imagine you're in a huge room and you take a super ball and slam it on the ground. Before you even throw it, I say to you, "Put your finger on the spot that it's going to land." You couldn't possibly do that. However, with a supercomputer you can measure the room, the density of the air, the ball diameter, the density of the ball, and you measure the direction it's thrown in. You put in a certain amount of information and that computer is able to calculate those variables and give you an exact location the ball will end up landing.

Now the question is, is the future predictable? Yes, it's just a matter of perception but to what degree? If you look at it as human beings, you are limited to how far you can push those calculations, but you do it all the time. You judge people by it, you judge actions by it, and you judge your day based upon the calculations you're expecting to have happen or how a person will react to certain circumstances. The better you know them, or the more information you have about them, the better and more accurately you can predict. The future is also predictable to God, to the ultimate level, the Universe. As humans, the future looks pre-written if we tap into this greater consciousness for that information.

What is your take on the popular New Age ideology that time and the future has not already taken place? Other people say that all things that are going to happen have already happened, that it's all happening in one moment, and that time doesn't really exist. Time is an illusion.

We are in the *now*, we are making judgment calls, and we are co-creators with God. We are the cutting edge of God's greatest exploration. The *now* is very real. We are like a wave; we are the crest, but there is what's behind us and there is what's ahead of us. We can only surmise or judge a certain distance and God can certainly judge a distance far ahead of that. But still the *now* is critical because anything can change at any given moment, within a split second, depending on the consensus of what's going on.

Can you die and reincarnate into the same time period? Can I die and reincarnate into the child of my pregnant friend tomorrow?

If she gives birth, sure. If you're advanced enough and you've been around, yes.

It can be that specific?

Absolutely. I chose my birth.

How about a group of people? Can they collectively incarnate?

Think of it as a school of fish jumping out of the water and into a bucket. It's more likely one is going to jump into the bucket than a whole school. Realistically, you have to weigh this all out to a certain degree. It's more likely that a bunch of fish can jump out into a bunch of different pans while some can jump in a little sooner and some jump in a little later. But as long as they're within a reasonable time space, they can all find each other. Then once they're in reality on this grid, like homing pigeons, they can tie their lives together.

People sometimes talk about spanning several lives with the same people or having soul mates.

There was a story once about a criminal who did something illegal and then disappeared. Ten years later, another man was in

Rome in a tourist area. Looking around, he recognized this other guy that he knew from a decade ago who looked just like the criminal. So, he got on the phone to the police and said, "Hey, you won't believe who I just saw." The authorities came and picked up the suspected criminal and sure enough, it was the same person.

There are only so many equations, and that's just one life. Now, imagine the people who have lived several lives. The world is not as big as it seems. There is also this whole natural attraction idea that you are drawn to similar souls. You have an inner sensory within you and it's going to attract other people who you may have known in your past lives because you're still familiar with their frequency. You, unknowingly, move towards them, or they move to you, or you both happen to end up in the same city even though you came from two different directions. It's completely feasible.

You've said that when a women is about to give birth, there is a special moment where the soul is allowed to come in.

Yes. It's not really a moment, there's a fair length of time. When the baby is born, the energy field is minimal. You can gauge it by the soft spots, or fontanels of the skull. Ironically, the spot at the front of the skull begins to close at the same time the energy field starts to strengthen, around two to four months while the back soft spot is fused shut by nineteen months. You are then prevented from moving into that frequency. Some may be different, but I would not say how much time you have. It really depends.

In that place before you incarnate, can you communicate with others that have not incarnated yet?

You can absolutely communicate with anybody that is not in an incarnated body. It is like a connective consciousness in that place. As an energy being, it is very difficult to communicate with somebody who has already incarnated. It is comparable to an entity or "ghost" trying to speak to you. It is a matter of trying to match up two completely different dimensional structures (bodies) and communication mechanisms. It's flesh versus pure energy. And if it is done, it is done emotionally or telepathically. Even then, it is very hard because you are not certain if you are on the other end of real communication. Then, when the person or being tries to communicate with you, you are interpreting it through your organic awareness, an awareness that you have developed of who you think you are.

Does the frequency of your soul have any effect on your physical characteristics? Does it have anything to do with more dominant awakened chakras?

Yes, physically to a certain degree but not completely. People's faces are defined by the muscle structure in their face. Identical twins, for example, can look completely different depending on their mind set. One is not going to have a bigger nose or shorter nose, or bigger eyes and smaller eyes, or bigger teeth and smaller teeth. You certainly can affect the structure of your face and that can be very impactful. It is based on how your mind is working through your face. Your eyes say an awful lot.

Do chakras play a role in the reincarnation process and if so, how can you use this knowledge to enhance your meditation? Are your chakras a middle man to lock into the soul?

They are absolutely a middle man; it is not a matter of locking into the soul, as much as it is a means to assist and work directly with your soul through your physical body. Chakra points are the happy medium of your physical body and your spiritual energies. In essence, a chakra point is a doorway, micro doorway if you will, or a means to manipulate the stimulation of your energy frequencies and what is going on with them. If you think of your chakra points, you go right back to emotion, the Universal language.

What are your chakra points? They are associated very much with emotion. Each one of them has an emotional connection. It is just a very complex emotion, but if you really think about it, it is definitely an emotional complex. It is your tuning fork that has a two way effect. It is very physical, this tuning fork, but the results of banging it create an effect that is vibratory. You are manipulating your other energies that are partially physical and partially dimensional. It has an effect on every level. Both in a physical aspect of how it is going to come back out of you and how it is going to be represented because it is affecting your consciousness, your mind and your brain.

The more balanced your energy is, the more your consciousness is going to be able to convey what it wants to convey to you. You are controlling the brain better, you are empowering your consciousness, and you are feeding energy to your dimensional self. The very source of this information is able to materialize bio-chemically through the neurons in your brain so that you can have these memories and it can find its place in you. By manipulating chakra points, you are working with that same happy medium: physical and dimensional. There is going to be an after effect just by tuning them. You are training your brain to be more stable, less jittery and shaky. You are creating a better platform so this very vast and complex information can express itself to your current consciousness.

Since chakras work on specific frequencies, do they tie into your `I`s at all?

Yes, they tie into the `I`s in one aspect. The `I`s are from your deepest rooted physical self. The I's imitate consciousness; they imitate your true mind but the experiences they provide are fake. They are from the organic world. Your chakra points should be seen as dials. They are not just buttons; they are dials that can be utilized to manipulate how high you are going to turn up the volume, so to speak. You can experiment with the intensity and the effects as you intensify them. They have the ability to control the `I`s.

If you think of your lower chakra, you are really thinking about base needs: your physical comfort, maybe the desire for food and such, sexual drive. You can tone that chakra down and shut off those desires so that you have clarity. Your heart chakra is going to be very emotional, picking up other people's emotions, your feelings, whether you're hurt, happy, or depressed. You can tune your mind to cut down on too much rationalization, too much thought, too many demands, too many expectations of the way you think your life should be. The chakras are connected, in a sense that you can use them to shut down those mechanisms. And if you could shut them all down, you are left with one thing: the purity of what is left – your Middle Pillar, your true `I`. So there is a connection.

You cannot look at the chakra points as being one function. There are a lot of functions within each one. Most people believe these things can only have one function that one chakra must be able to do only one thing, and that is not the truth at all. You need to move beyond that type of limited thinking. You have to think multi-dimensionally.

When you reincarnate, is your totality reincarnating, or is some part of you staying somewhere else?

No, the whole totality is moving with you. Let me present it in a different way. It is a 'yes' and 'no' answer. Yes, your totality is moving with you but there are always fragments of you that are also dispersed in other words. How many people have you affected in your life? Would you say that all of them have a piece of you? Isn't there a part of you within the people that you have touched in your life? Perhaps not in energy terms, but in terms of consciousness. They have experienced your frequency and there is a part of it in them. Think of your friends, or your family, your mom and your dad, or a lover; you have this frequency that is exclusively theirs. In a sense you have already inter-threaded with other people, but your true self is the core of who you are. It is just a matter of perspective.

Do planets reincarnate or go through a similar process?

Yes, but instead of incarnating as planets they incarnate into solar systems or galaxies. A planet's incarnation is going to be extremely different than a human incarnation. The hope is that the planet will reach an elevated level of its own consciousness as the consciousness on it, meaning the people, evolve.

When the planet finally becomes more conscious because of organic life giving their experiences back to it, it will go through a whole different process. At that point, it will be more energy than solid and will remain that way rather than return to the physical. A planet goes through micro lives; it is almost incarnating within itself. It does not really maintain its self-identity. And let's not forget that time is very different for a planet than it would be for a human.

When a planet goes through a whole cycle, does it still hold all its experiences in the Gaia mind?

It simply transfers it. The clarity is lost; it is not as clear or as refined. It is compacting and compressing the experiences. If you understand how computers work, you can compare this concept to a hard drive that has a compression ratio. In order to look at that compressed information, it takes longer for the computer to individually decompress it, expand it, and then utilize it, and then it recompresses it. It is like that.

Is there a similar process for the Universe
when it finally moves into energy?

It's hard to look at the Universe in that way because the physical universe is like the tip of God's finger in a glass of water and we are the part that is in the water. We cannot look at this as a whole and finished process. It is just because we are physical and organic, that is how we choose to perceive it.

Is reincarnation actually a metaphor to explain
something very difficult to understand?

Of course it is. Again, you can look at this on many different levels. Looking at it individually, you can say it is a progression for your consciousness. On another level, you can think of it as being a microorganism with billions of organisms within it, which is really data building up a higher frequency. And there are also many levels as to what it is doing all at the same time. It is a metaphor to explain one thing, but behind it all, there is a much bigger purpose. That is what I said at the very beginning: *It is really the bigger process of the collective consciousness of God experiencing.* It is just the mechanism of how that data percolates up to the top and each individual layer processes what is going on in their own micro level.

The biggest problem is interpretation because, as humans, we want to interpret everything. We gravitate to and get stuck in the concept of the physical aspect of how we perceive. It is the hardest thing for us to escape that paradigm. Therefore, sometimes you just have to surrender to the situation and it will surface on its own. Just accept that there are possibilities that are beyond what you can conceive. In that complexity, you may not be able to find that understanding, however, you do not *need* to fully understand it. What is more important is that you get the gist of what is going on.

What role does the Darkside play in reincarnation?

The Darkside does not want you to reincarnate. It does not want you to progress. The Darkside is the totality of anti-life, anti-matter, anti-existence; therefore, it wants the proliferation of life to stop. What is the proliferation of life? It is experience. If you can stop experiencing, you can stop the process of God's journey through this dimension. God is only interested in the cause and effect of its presence in this dimension. What is happening and how it perceives, due to the effects of this dimension, is what intrigues God. And it is a journey. It is a thing of interest. Why bother doing it if it is not. Life is about experiencing.

There is a resistance of energy in this dimension; *for every action there is an equal and opposite reaction.* Let us say, on the crudest level, that the opposite reaction to the actual formation of reality is the process of returning back to energy. At any point that process can happen, and that is what the Darkside desires. It does not want you to incarnate. It does not want the planet to evolve. It does not want the Universe to expand. It does not want proliferation of life. It wants it all to stop, and if that did happen, we all would cease to exist.

If you die, and then later your body is cloned from your DNA, what happens to the soul?

The soul moves on. There is no problem with cloning. Cloning only biologically recreates you. It does not copy your memories; your memories are your frequency, it is who you are. If science could copy your memories, it would just create a twin of you. The energy would have to be re-manifested, re-built, and re-shaped. It is impossible for there to be an exact copy of you because in one millisecond of just moving your head, you are now someone different because your experience has changed. You have just collected a different experience than what you originally had from your original body.

Who you are is based upon what you have seen in your life. It is based upon the people you touched, that you loved, that you fought with, that you argued with; it is all of these things that create your identity from these experiences. A clone will never be able to have the same argument that you had with someone. Even if they had the same argument, they will never be able to clone the same person who made that argument, their nationality, their personality, their *feel*. They would have to identically create your entire life from beginning to end in order to create that identical structure of consciousness.

Now, they may get a similar trace of memories that were genetically stored, and maybe certain personality traits that were genetically handed over to you, but the bottom line is – a clone is not going to be you. It cannot be you. It cannot be a copy of you. It would simply have the same physical body with a lot of similarities, but for the most part, you would be completely unique.

What about cryogenics and its effects on your soul?

Cryogenics has been built up to be more than what it actually is. I would love to think they can bring you back physically with all your memories intact, but with the whole deep freezing process, I do not believe it works as well as people say it does. The real science behind it basically states that all the brain cells are absolutely destroyed. Even if the frozen person had the memories, their soul is going to be based upon what they know and it will just react. That person might have to take some time and build it, and sort it, and put it all together. By that time, they would be just like a typical Red Cell. It might take days or weeks for them to rebuild the energy to even build that second soul, which could take years for it to get there no matter how gifted they were. And then, in that process, they are still seeing and experiencing new things, which are already altering the totality of what they are.

What is the most someone could hope to gain by recalling a past life?

Advancement. By obtaining past life information, you tend to accelerate the *now*. You tend to be able to refine and advance yourself more rapidly before you leave this world. In other words, you are doing work on yourself now to build your soul, to strengthen your energy field, but to also expand your consciousness so that you can understand more. By accessing past life memory, you also obtain the wisdom that comes behind it; that is most valuable. Remove your bigotry and ignorance, remove all those things and you will become a more refined being. Your frequency would be higher. If you could obtain a higher frequency in this life, the things you perceive and understand would become so much greater than before.

For instance, let us say that you are a racist and you are asked to read a book on the lives of certain people. You read this book and it moves you in such a way that it changes your opinions on things. It shows you perspectives of other races that you had never considered before. And so when you are done with that book, you can no longer lead your life exactly the same way you used to. Your opinions have changed. The core of who you are is very much the same, but your perspective has grown and you no longer react to things in the same manner.

Remembering past lives is like reading volumes of books. It helps to accelerate this life, the person you are at this moment, to help achieve the ultimate goal that you have been looking for life after life. Strive for the highest state of consciousness you can attain so you can make decisions as to where you go after this life rather than being placed into the next process. If you reach a certain level of enlightenment in this life, you can make that choice because you have reached your ultimate goals. Remembering past lives is helping you to grow, in this moment, instead of being limited. You are not allowed to remember certain things in this life due to natural laws of nature.

No one said you are not allowed to have these memories. It is just the way it worked out biologically. That is how the brain works to prevent certain states of psyche. It is how the cards fell. If the Universe was a little bit gentler on us, it would have said, "Okay, at 20 years old you can have all your memories back," but it does not work that way.

Again, the planet does not necessarily want everybody to reincarnate because then it means everybody would escape from its consciousness. What if all the cells in your body decided that they did not want to report to you? All of a sudden, you would lose your ability to hear, to see, to taste, to smell, as well as your ability to touch. All of a sudden, you have no data because your cells are all saying, "We are independent." You would cease to progress.

In essence, the planet is designed to limit you. This is what this whole battle with the Doe is about. The Doe is designed to keep you functioning as an organism on this planet. You evolve to a certain level, but it is designed to keep you down. Reincarnation and experiencing those memories is a tool in the process of you moving beyond the Doe because it is making you stronger as a vibration. You have a greater surplus of information added to you.

I am now going to share with you a technique that I have been utilizing for the past twenty years. It's very unique, it's very different and it can be quite shocking. You're going to learn to look at a friend or yourself in the mirror and actually see them physically change before your eyes. Literally, their facial structure will morph, and their clothing will change to what they wore in a past life as well. Now there is some debate on this method of whether or not it's a hallucination or your brain seeing fractal images because of the lighting. I have no interest in the finer details on whether it's an illusion or not an illusion. I believe this technique is a doorway and a tool that will help you to understand certain emotions or feelings that are deep within you. It's going to be profound.

You can expect to see significant facial structure changes. You may look at the person and their appearance could change to that of an American Indian, an African American, or somebody from England or Ireland. In some cases, you may see a person look like a Neanderthal or a primitive man because the forehead becomes elongated and the eyes become very shadowed. You may even see something that resembles an insect or someone with alien like features. Do not become fearful. Do not allow your emotions to overwhelm you or control you. There are other worlds in the Universe. There are other creatures besides human beings, and it's very likely that you or the other person you are studying may appear very alien or different then what you expect. Also, there is a morphing period as the face begins to take on structure that makes things very difficult to distinguish, and your brain naturally wants to put a structure to it. There is a part of you that is fighting the process and trying to analyze it. When it comes forward then it will represent itself correctly.

While using this technique, one person reported they had a very bad scar on their throat area from a previous motorcycle accident, and it actually disappeared before his eyes. He appeared as if he was the age he had been before the accident had happened. Other people have done this exercise and seen their mother, their brother, their sister, or their best friend morph into a past life as an American Indian, a female or a male, in full garb, the feathers, the jewelry, everything. Some people argue that you are only going to see facial changes or slight differences. I assure you that is not the case. The more that you allow yourself to flow with this, the greater the experiences become, and they are just absolutely phenomenal. Try to control your fear because it can be very shocking and very surprising. And, of course, when you are looking at somebody and they are not familiar, there is another part of your psyche that wants to react in fear because it's as if you are in the room with a stranger all of a sudden.

Lighting is the key here. For a beginner, start off with dim lighting. Use two candles in the room and shut off the rest of the lights. That's the kind of illumination you want. You could also let the lighting from an outside room flow into a darker room, but you ultimately want a darker room. Light tends to break the frequency that allows this to happen easily. You need to use the dark as a tool to break that barrier in your brain.

Some people have asked, "How is this possible?" I do not believe that you are travelling in the past. The Gaia mind, or the mind of the planet, has memories of every living creature, every living being. You are tuning in to another person's frequency, much like psychic work is done, as I have taught in other classes. You are tuning into their frequency or your frequency in a mirror, and you are able to see overlaps, the memory of the Gaia mind creating an image, or the presence of past impressions.

Morphing Exercise

To prepare to go through a step by step process, you must first choose a partner or a mirror if you don't have a partner to work with. The person should be no more than a foot away from your knee caps. I recommend that you sit on the floor Indian style, or half lotus, or you can sit in a chair so that you are a little bit more relaxed. Have a distance of about one foot between you and your partner. You can also have your knee caps touching the other person. If you are using a mirror, you want the mirror to be maybe two to three feet away. Maybe not even that far; however, you'll find your own level of comfort. Again, the lighting in the room should be extremely dim, only one or two candles in brightness. You don't want to be disturbed and you don't want any distractions.

Look at the other person. If you're using a mirror, think of your reflection as another person. Set your eyes on the facial area, maybe rest your eyes on the bridge of the nose or the forehead area, and just stare. Don't blink a lot. Once you get better with this, much like seeing auras, you won't have to be so dramatic in this exercise. You will be able to blink; you will be able to do it much quicker. But in the beginning, you do have to train yourself and get past the barriers of the brain that filter the success of this exercise. As you stare at the other person, very calmly, you want to have a relaxed face. You don't want to be smiling, you don't want to move around a lot, and you don't want to make a lot of changes, you want to keep your face in this still position, very relaxed.

If you can relax yourself and allow yourself to let go, the face will begin to fade out. There is a fading process where it gets blurred, and then the blurring progresses to a darker, blacking out period. And very rapidly it will begin to restructure as if another face comes forward. You may only be able to see half the face or the eyes at first. You will notice that there will be either a smoothness to the skin or more wrinkles. The eyes will be seated differently; the bridge of the nose will be shaped differently. Either bangs of hair will be falling over the forehead, or the forehead extended and larger. But you will begin to see distinguishable differences in the facial structure. As you get better, you will be able to see the color, the jewelry being worn scars, and other parts of the body. The other person, who is changing, will be doing the same to you, so they will need you to also remain very still.

The face will begin to change and continue to morph from one face to the other. Or if it remains the same, that person may not have many past lives or they may only have a few past lives. With people who have experienced many past lives, in some cases, you may only see one or two faces but the next time you do this, you will see a lot more. From young children to adults to elderly people to different cultures; there seems to be no end to the possibilities of facial morphing. It is absolutely fascinating to see the features and the structures of their face.

Always have a pen and a notepad handy, and immediately take notes and draw some sketches so that you can recall your memory better. You are going to be captivated and you will want to continue with your observations of the other person, or your image in the mirror. Again, I stress to you not to overreact; do not panic. Not just for you, but for the other person who may also be observing some changes. They might reach up to touch their nose to scratch it and you might be seeing something that you find a bit intimidating, maybe a primitive man or something looking back at you. And you might take that as this person is reaching for you. As with any of my teachings, they are very potent. You must come into it with a mind of study rather than a mind of fearfulness. There's nothing to fear, it's just information.

When you are finished, simply turn the lights on brighter and relax for a little bit. The other person is going to have great interest in what you have to say so just share what you've seen, what you got out of it, and the impressions of that information.

You can combine your telepathy training and the reincarnation visual effects to receive better details of past lives. There is a very intriguing amount of information that can be exchanged or received from this process. You would be able to do forms of reincarnation readings then. It's perfectly acceptable to communicate while you are observing, but stay still, stay calm, keep the tone of your voice down, and don't get too excited and cause fear in the other person. You can also communicate with a voice recorder while using a mirror, observing what you're seeing and noting these observations.

It is very interesting to use the other format (below) for past life memory regression. You can take the notes of what you've seen in the person, and then later without giving them that information, see if there is a connection between what you've seen with past life information, what you've gathered, and what they say they have experienced during their reincarnation memory process through this program. If you wear glasses, you may want to try it with your glasses, and you may want to try it without your glasses at different times. If you are having trouble seeing the person, adjust the lighting to either darker or brighter. Another tip is to also create more distance between you and the other person, or bring them closer. Sometimes different people need different amounts of space between them to get better results. You can achieve the best results by adjusting the lighting level.

This technique will take you through a hypnosis session, through reincarnation memories, and help you remember some of the past lives that you have forgotten. Be sure that your phone is off and you don't have any worries to disturb you. You should place a sign on your door or in your hallway saying that nobody is to disturb you in any way. And you might want to record this exercise to make it easier for you.

Now stretch, and take some time stretching your body, your arms, and your legs just to make sure you feel good and you've relieved most of the tension in your body. Next, find a place to lie down. Be sure that your legs and arms aren't crossed; they should be lying at your sides. Your legs shouldn't be crossed and should be an inch or two apart.

Past Life Regression

Take a nice deep breath through your nose and exhale through your mouth. Do this three times. Now look up towards the ceiling, or whatever is above you, and find a spot to place your eyes. Just stare at that spot as if you are drifting off into it. Let your mind flow, let it relax as if you are allowing yourself to go into a trance. Just stare at that spot, as if every moment and every thought was fixated on that one spot. And everything feels at peace, everything feels relaxed within you. You are comfortable, drifting away, just staring at that one spot.

Imagine that a metronome begins ticking in the background and it is going to help take you to that place. The sound of the metronome is a deep sleep. Deep sleep. It takes you away as you stare at the spot on the ceiling. Feel your mind relaxing. It helps ease your mind. This is making you tired and sleepy. Your eyes now are beginning to close. You feel tired. It's as if you have been busy all day long and you haven't had much rest. Your eyes just want to close; they just want to relax. You just want to drift away. Like magnets, you can feel them pulling from one end to the other to shut. Allow them to collapse and tell yourself that it is time to rest. Your eyes are closed.

In your mind, you are to say the following: My arms are heavy. My arms are heavy. My arms are heavy. My arms are as heavy as lead. My arms are as heavy as lead. My arms are as heavy as lead. I cannot move my right arm, It's as heavy as lead. I cannot move my right arm, it's as heavy as lead. I cannot move my left arm, it's heavy as lead. I cannot move my left arm, it's heavy as lead. My arms are as heavy as lead. My legs are heavy. My legs are heavy. My right leg is as heavy as lead. My right leg is heavy as lead. I cannot move my right leg it is so heavy. My left leg is heavy as lead. My left leg is as heavy as lead. I cannot move my left leg. My legs are as heavy as lead.

Starting with your toes, feel soothing, healing, warm light going through your toes, through the muscles of each toe, through the toenails, through the dips and curves. Soothing, healing, warm light. Working its way now through the ball and the arch of your feet, to the curves and the roundness and the smoothness of your feet. Through the tough strong muscles, the soothing, healing, warm light working its way back and forth, back and forth. Through your feet. Through the muscles and the tendons. It's working its way through your ankle and back down through the top part of your feet, through the muscles and the joints and the tendons, back to your ankles and down to your toes. Soothing, healing, warm light.

This light now is moving up your legs, from your feet, to your kneecaps, back and forth. Through the bone, the marrow, the muscle, the nerves, the blood vessels, soothing, healing, warm light. Working its way through your kneecap, through the joints, through the tendons, working its way up to your hips, through the larger muscles in your thighs, back down to the knee caps, through the bone and the muscle and the tissue and the blood cells. Soothing, healing, warm light. Working its way now through your lower abdominal area. Between your legs, your thighs, the bottom of your spine, soothing, healing, warm light. Working its way now through the lower intestines, throughout your body, almost as if you were slowly slipping into a nice warm bath. With your feet and your legs first, just sliding into it. Soothing, healing, warm light. Working its way through your stomach region, heading up towards your chest, over your armpits, soothing, healing, warm light. Working its way now through your back, soaking through the muscles, through the bones, through the tendons, soothing, healing, warm light.

It's working its way through your shoulders now, through your neck, and back down to your shoulders through the shoulder blades, underneath them, through your heart and your intestines, your kidneys and your liver, and your lungs. Soothing, healing, warm light. Working its way down both your arms, from your shoulders down to your elbows. Soothing, healing, warm light. Visualizing all of this, seeing all of this, experiencing all of this, soothing, healing, warm light. Working its way now from your elbows to your wrists, back and forth, back and forth. Through the muscles and the tendons, soothing, healing, warm light. Working its way now into the palm of your hand, through the muscle of the lower part of your thumb to the tip of your thumb nail. Through the arches of the fingertips and the knuckles, to the joints, muscles and the tendons, fingertips. Soothing, healing, warm light now penetrating your whole body from the neck down. Like sliding into a nice hot bath.

This light now is working its way through your throat area, through your tongue, through the back of your neck, through the muscles, through the glands. Through the back of your scalp, through each individual hair, as many as there may be. Soothing, healing, warm light. Working its way now through the front of the muscles of your cheeks, your lips, your nose, your eyes, soothing, healing, warm light. As it becomes part of your mind, part of your brain, soothing, healing, warm light.

You are sinking. You are sinking. You feel yourself sinking into the floor. You are sinking. Relaxed and comfortable, you are going deeper now. Deeper into your mind, deeper into your consciousness, deeper into your brain. Feeling relaxed and comfortable.

As I count down from 10 to zero, you are going to go into a deep, deep trance. Deep within to the resources of your mind, and I am going to take you through there, and you are going to follow me and it's going to be safe.

I'm going to go now deep into your mind, ten. Going down, down, down, deeper, deeper, deeper, nine. Going down, down, down, eight. Deeper, deeper, deeper, feeling relaxed and comfortable. Sinking, going further into your mind like a journey. You are falling down a river on a summer's day, you are going deep within your mind, seven. Down, down, down, deeper, deeper, deeper, six. Down, down, down, deeper, deeper, deeper, five. You are going into a deep, deep trance, relaxed and comfortable. I will guide you through this journey, safe and relaxed. Going down, down, down, four. Deep sleep, deep sleep. The metronome takes you deeper, and deeper, and deeper, three. You're almost there now. You're almost to the furthest regions of your mind, within the realms of memories forgotten. Two. Deep sleep.

You're going to stop before you come to the last level, and you now are going to remember your bathroom, the bathroom that you use each and every day. You're going to remember it now in your mind, as a clear vivid picture, what it is to see the bathroom sink, the mirrors, the medicine cabinet. What it is to see the toilet, perhaps the things that you use each and every day in the bathroom. See the shower curtain, whatever color it may be. See whatever may be on the floor. See everything as vivid as your memory. Now it fades away, it fades away to black. You are feeling relaxed and comfortable.

You now see something round. As you look closer you know it is orange. It is a fruit. You see that fruit and you can see each contour of its structure up close. You begin to open that orange, and as it opens you see the fluids that come from it dripping from it. As you look closer your nose can smell the citrus from it, the essence of the orange. You experience it. It fades away; it all fades away into black.

Soothing and relaxed, you now approach one. Down, down, down, deeper, deeper, deeper. You are now in a relaxed and deep trance. You go to the past, to your childhood. You now see a small bit of light, and it approaches. It is a memory. This memory that approaches you is from a childhood birthday. It becomes your reality now that you see it in your mind's eye. You see the things that look familiar. Perhaps the family members, perhaps your mother's or your father's haircut. The table, the walls, the pictures, the furniture, even the smells that remind you of home from your childhood are clear and vivid within your mind. For all things are possible in this state of consciousness; you are in a trance and you can remember these things clearly. It all fades now. Fades away to black.

Soothing and relaxed. You are now going to do deeper. Below zero, far, far within your mind's memories. You are going there now, down, down, down, deeper, deeper, deeper. You see a bit of light in the distance. It comes closer to you. It becomes brighter and larger. It is a memory of the past. It is vivid and clear to you. You are now seeing your past life before you.

Clear and vivid you remember. You are safe, secure, these are memories, clear and vivid memories of your past life. The metronome carries you through these memories. With each tick, that sound carries you safely through the memories. Vivid and clear memories. It all now fades to black.

You are going to continue your journey beyond the thresholds that you once expected. You are in a deep trance, deep sleep. You can go within your mind and remember. You are going further now, a far distance in your mind. You see a bit of light in the distance. The light becomes larger, larger, larger. You now see and remember vividly the past as now. Clear and vivid memories of the past. You feel safe and warm. The metronome carries you deeply into your memories. You are an observer. You can move freely about in your memories. Free and uninhibited in your memories that you see now within your mind's eye. You remember.

You now are going to go even further into your memories. In the distance, you see another spot of light. It approaches you. It becomes larger and larger until you become consumed by it. You see vivid and clear memories in your mind's eye. You remember everything you experienced. You will go into a deeper hypnotic state each and every time you have a session.

WARNING

The subject of the following chapter is not intended for all audiences. The language and content used in the following chapter may be offensive to some readers. Please be aware that this is not Eric's intent. Eric feels very strongly about including this information in its raw form with *minimal grammatical editing.* This is the same information that was presented in the video classes with Eric's students, in the order it was given. Eric feels strongly about being honest and upfront.

Again, the opinions and information presented in this chapter are NOT intended as offensive or sexist. If you begin to feel offended by the information presented herein we encourage you to skip this chapter and move on to the next. At a later time, if you wish to return to this chapter, please do so when you feel ready.

Higher Balance Institute accepts no liability for any mental, emotional, or psychological damage that may be caused by the act of reading the contents of this chapter.

Chapter 7

SEX

Sex is a very primal instinct. It is almost as strong as your need to eat, breathe and drink water. It is designed to secure the safety of the human race; so humanity has a very primal sexual drive. When you are looking at attaining that state to become spiritual, you must have a sense of balance between your masculine and feminine energies, organically, so you can move your mind to those places.

By questioning yourself, you can identify whether you are interested in females or males, and whether you are attracted to the opposite sex or the same sex. If someone suggested the opposite sexual partner of whom you are attracted to, you may have a big knee jerk reaction. When you are balanced, your level of reaction is a great way to get an idea of where you're at. It is a great way to find out how balanced you are. If you're a guy and something happened with another guy, or if you are a girl and something happened with another girl, how would you feel? Your knee jerk reaction to the idea is a great barometer that will give you a sense of where you are at. I am not telling anyone that they need to go and have sex with the same sex if they are straight. And I'm not telling someone who is gay that they need to go out and have sex with someone of the opposite sex either.

If you are one hundred percent gay, then you should have some polarity towards females, too. If you a very masculine female who is wearing macho clothing, you should have some degree of a feeling towards men. *So this is what I am trying to say.* A great way to do a sound check, is to say, "Well, how do I feel about that?" If it is completely repulsive, you are probably not as balanced as you think you are because it is all part of the organic machinery in your brain.

So, it is hard to figure out and you may wonder, "How do I tell? How do I truthfully know where I am at?" It is a great way to get a sound check. I don't want people to run out with somebody and do it. This is not what this is about. *It is about asking yourself in your head, "Where is your comfort zone? Where is your understanding? Where is your comprehension?"* And that is going to define your ability to move into a consciousness that has a masculine/feminine polarity. The God field, if you want to call it that, is neither masculine nor feminine, but it is a blend of perfection. God created life within Itself. So if you are going to approach that frequency, this is a great way to get a sense of your mind balance, your energy. Is it going to blend and move in, or will parts of your energy be so heavy that it bounces out of it?

Now that may be offensive to some people. Some people might say, "So God isn't interested if I am a masculine straight guy? Or a feminine straight woman?" And I would say to you, "When you are dead, it won't matter. You will have both polarities." If you believe in reincarnation, you already should be okay with that kind of thinking, but if you only identify with the organic body, "This is who I am," then you are really putting aside the idea of what your afterlife is like.

You are trying to have both polarities *before you leave your body,* so you can access stuff from the place you're in now. So, that is what I am trying to say. Jumping in bed with a guy or a woman, if it is the opposite of your sexual preference, is too much of a shock. If you do that, you're overwhelming the system. You don't want to create chaos. If something happens, you can decide what you want to do, but I wouldn't recommend that you actively seek it out.

The way that you view the world is through the lens of your consciousness. It is how you think of yourself, or how you see yourself. Also, the Universe sees you through that lens.

If you look at all the spiritual teachers, past and present, you could say some were probably gay. Historically, we will never know. Some were clearly straight, but when you really look at them they definitely had a perfect down-the-middle-of-the-road balance. I wouldn't necessarily say that Siddhartha, or Buddha was gay. He had a harem of women before he became spiritual. He also had a nurturing, loving, and compassionate aspect in his consciousness that is definitely more feminine. If you looked at his brain, it would have been masculine. Therefore, we will never know for sure. I am not going to put myself out there saying what I think it is because that is not what's important. I think that Buddha could've compassionately held a man with absolute love and conviction in his heart as well as a woman. It would not be a challenge to Buddha's masculine identity, because he could then let his emotion, his heart, and his true vibration flow.

I don't want my students trying to sack people. It's not necessary to do that. *I just want you to find the harmony in you.* If you do it in your head, you may find it helps you cross over because anything you are exposed to enough, you adapt to in your thinking.

So, at the end of the day, I realize it is a very strong knee jerk reaction. Because I am a teacher, not only do I have to address issues that are safe to talk about, I also have to talk about the stuff that nobody wants to talk about. Because I claim to be who I AM, then I have to talk about a very touchy subject that is going to make people feel potentially uncomfortable. If I ignore it, it isn't helping you to spiritually understand polarity. It is like never giving kids Sex Education in high school, or college for that matter. It is just irresponsible on my part. If you are going to ask me about my spiritual perception of all this, well here it is.

I am not saying the Hindus, Buddhists, or Hare Krishna's agree with this, but because you are asking my opinion, these are my thoughts. The big problem with religion is most people aren't knowledgeable enough to understand how deeply layered and manipulated religion really is. Right away we think about Christianity, but it's actually true for almost all organized religions.

At some point, the religious leaders probably asked, "Without getting dirty and without having to do any work, how do I make more money? How do I get people to give me money?" Then they had the realization, "I will be their spiritual leader, and like a school teacher, my job will be to do spiritual stuff in exchange for money. Now, how do I broaden my teachings for my followers? In thirty or forty years, my parishioners are going to be much older and I'll still be alive. What will be the revenue for each person?" There is nothing fruitfully gained by letting two men or two women get together. So it is wiser for me to say that only a man and a woman must get together. Then I will tell them to bring their children to me to baptize them and bring them into the fold. That is business marketing. It is revenue down the road. It is an investment.

When women were growing older, the men tended to be promiscuous, so the women didn't have a sense of security anymore. So the guys said, "Look, we will back up the women, who will nag the men to keep them from breaking away from us because we know that the women are more loyal." They are especially loyal if they know they have a strong voice saying, "Don't cheat on your wife. Don't wander. You signed a contract. You take care of her when she gets older because you don't age as hard. Your body is more muscle. She is going to lose her looks. You can't discard her. So we are going to hold you to your contract." That will make the women want to become part of that group because it is good for them. So the women wanted their husbands to be in that group so they would be obligated to provide for them. They fed off each other. Eventually, it became a control cycle of consciousness, of thinking, because it started to go outside of the group. It didn't just end there. So this is when society started to change.

The Greek and Roman cultures are very open-minded. Look at how the technological advances of those cultures compare to others. If you look at the sexual tendencies of that time, you will see flourishments and non-flourishments in big ways. That is religion manipulating and controlling the psyche of humanity.

So at the end of the day, I don't want my guys or my girls actively going to a gay bar. I don't want an actively gay man seeking out a straight woman to entice him to desire a female. It is not necessarily about the physical act. The physical leads to the mental. The spectrum is made of many lines. You don't have to be in the middle of the spectrum. You just have to be within the border limits, and that is usually enough.

We're going to be talking about sex, and sex is a very taboo word. I think that most people say, "What's the big deal? It's just sex." Most people who feel or think that way, even though they're being sincere are way off. People are still killed to this day because of the idea of sex, their personal belief systems about it, or different boundaries from one culture to another. Even in our day-to-day culture, sex is definitely a touchy subject. It affects people's careers, people's lives, and it affects people's moral perspectives and moral views. It is probably the most controlled subject that I can think of.

They say that there are three things you should not talk about when you're out to dinner: Sex, politics, and religion. You cannot talk about those things because someone sitting next to you may have a very strong difference of opinion. More than likely, they will feel enlivened enough to speak up and spar with you even though they may not know you. So, those are the three taboo subjects that you don't talk about.

I am absolutely certain that there are going to be people who hear or read this that will have very strong mixed emotions. They're going to be very uncomfortable. There are going to be areas that they absolutely disagree with. I think the question that comes to mind is, "Why is sex such a taboo subject for us, culturally? Why is it such a touchy subject?" The bottom line, in my opinion, is because it's the strongest, primal urge in human beings. Without it, there are no human beings! The survival of our species is dependent on the whole concept of sex. We need sex as much as we need to eat: as much as we need to breathe. Sex is one of the top instincts within us for survival. Therefore, it is very rooted into the psyche of human beings. It is also one of the things that most human beings use to try to control other human beings.

I cannot stress enough that sex is a very controlling subject. I believe that human beings have been trying to control one another since the beginning of its understanding. *In a sense, if you control sex, you control life.* That's a very profound concept if you really think about it.

I've been wrestling for a very, very long time about whether or not I should even talk about this subject, if I should go into it, what my thoughts are on it, and what are the spiritual implications in regards to it. The implications are profound. Hence, again, I will say procreation is the strongest primal urge in human beings.

I've spoken about this before. I was watching a National Geographic documentary many years ago and they were showing a lion that was dying of old age. You could see its ribs and its breathing was labored. The lion walked maybe about two feet before it collapsed. The narrator said that the lion wasn't expected to make it through the night. Somewhere in this process, a female lioness walked by. Of course, she was in heat and ready for mating. Lo and behold, this dying lion that was literally in its last few minutes of life struggled to get back on its feet and started walking, as if it was possessed, to catch up to the female. So the power to get this dying male lion, obviously in pain with labored breathing, to muster the will and the strength to actually think that it could mate is a profound instinct. That is a profound drive in a living creature. Human beings aren't much different.

I think that men are obsessed with women to control their orgasm. I think that a woman is obsessed to get emotions from a man through sex. Those are the two key areas and they have very complex thinking behind them. We're going to go into that.

What I am trying to decide is which direction I want to go first. This is a very lengthy topic. You have the physical aspect and you have the spiritual aspect. Not only that, you have the political and sociological aspect, and they're all so heavily intertwined that it's going to make for a very difficult subject to navigate or work through. There are also different sexual preferences, whether people are bisexual, gay or straight. You have all of these preferences, as well as a lot of different takes and perspectives on this subject. Are there any questions that anybody would like to start off with?

How did there come to be male and female in each species?

All human beings evolved from the ocean. I believe that we were sea creatures. We're not talking about the beginning of life here. We're talking about the beginning of human beings, our species. So, remove the equation of primates and such, we are talking about before all of that. I believe that we were a hermaphrodite type of sea creature. We were both male and female organically, meaning that we didn't necessarily have to mate with another species. We were a split species. We could produce children internally within us. I don't know how many people are familiar with earthworms or what a hermaphrodite is. There are very few creatures today that are hermaphrodites. In 2007, a female Komodo dragon shocked the staff at Chester Zoo in northern England when it became pregnant without ever having a male partner or being exposed to the opposite sex. It was able to procreate on its own.

When life crawled out of the ocean and became land bound, the male and female jointly created offspring. The male had to hunt for food and the female gather the food, but when they left the nesting area to find food, other predatory animals killed their young. This created an evolutionary urge for change deep within the psyches of both sexes.

You could say that evolution is a large part of 'the consciousness of God.' By the same token, our biology goes through a lot of emotional stress or duress with change but can adapt to meet those situations, like: "I have to get food for survival, or I have to stay and protect the young." That is what eventually separated life into two different sexes.

Male and female bodies of most species are similar in many ways. This is one of the sensitive subjects that we're going to talk about. In rare cases, men have lactated and given milk from their body. And if you look at the clitoris, some people will tell you that it's an under-developed penis. This is how our bodies are mirrored. Evolution propagated most of the species on the planet and all living organisms in the oceans. If you look closely, you will still find some hermaphrodite creatures that have both male and female properties. Does that answer your question?

Yes.

One of the reasons that I'm doing this class on sex is because nobody else will tell you the facts from a spiritual perspective. Everything that I'm going to talk about is pretty much already out there. It's not like I'm the first person to say it. The difference is that most of it is buried to protect the spiritual teachings. If society finds that there are these peculiarities in their perspectives on sex having to do with spirituality, the funding will stop. It is a fear process, a control process. Therefore, you're not going to find this information very easily. If I don't teach this, I honestly and sincerely believe that I'm cheating people from awakening spiritually. The sexual drive is such a critical part of our humanness, and to not discuss it or avoid it would be to say that I am not the person or the teacher that I claim to be. This subject has to be addressed eventually. It has to be discussed and dissected. It has to be shown for what it is so that the people who are trying to reach enlightenment can understand and certainly have a good grasp of this knowledge. I would be doing a great disservice as a teacher to not go into it at some point.

Why don't we just ease into this subject by covering some of the questions that will wind into different areas? Does anyone have any personal questions that they want to start with?

Does it enhance manifestation or the connection with The Force if, during orgasm, you have an intention in your mind of awakening, or manifesting, or that type of thing? Is it more powerful during that moment of pleasure or bliss?

Absolutely. For starters, you have to look at what sex is and then get the elemental breakdown and the basics of it. Sex, to me, is not about the sexual organs. It is really in your mind, but I don't think a lot of people contemplate that. They just think, "Yes, you're right." But really, it is literally in your mind. So is walking, talking, and reaching for something. All of these decisions are determined right in your consciousness.

Sex is very interesting. It is such a powerful, dominating instinct. That is what makes it so critical to being a bridge to your spirituality and also a conflict to your spirituality. I often say that what makes you a Red Cell is engaging in heterosexual sex, not that there's anything wrong with heterosexual sex. And here I have to constantly be politically correct because people are ten steps ahead of me wondering, "What is he suggesting?"

What is the purpose of mating? We're mating because we're trying to create offspring. There were no condoms and no contraceptives with primal man. Mating serves only one function, and that is to create life. As a male, your sperm has your energy in it. It is literally the part of you that can take your soul outside of your main soul frequency. When your sperm leaves your body, it carries a piece of you. It's almost as if it's taking a piece of your existence with it. A woman is designed to take this frequency. The sperm holds data in it. It holds DNA. It holds information of your past ancestors that make up your genetic code. *It literally has a piece of your soul*, and you're giving this up.

When a woman makes love to a man, she wants that energy, whether or not she will tell you that. It's not thought of in those terms. I don't think that a woman is literally saying, "I want your energy." But I've really analyzed it, and I've spoken at great length to female students, as much as I have with male students, and I'm certainly privy to intimate secrets that are revealed in trust to me.

So I know that they want that energy. They want to consume it. They don't think of it as being destructive. They don't think of it as wanting to take your energy, or your life force, but there's a part of them that has an understanding that they need to create something within their womb, in their body.

There's a certain call that draws energy deep within a woman. And so when a man makes love to her, he wants to dominate the female by putting his sperm within her. In a very primal sense, he wants to put his seed in her. He wants to dominate her. Dominate is a very powerful word, but let's call it what it is. In our deeper psyche, a man wants to seed a woman by putting his sperm in her so that she is carrying his child.

Look closely at gorillas; they are also primates. What do they do to another male gorilla's child? They know which ones are theirs and which ones aren't. It's an instinct. What do they do? They kill the other male's offspring. Men instinctually want to seed women. It's domination and it's a control thing. A woman mates to create life. She is not thinking about dominating, but she is thinking, in some way, that she might want to have a child. There's an exchange on a spiritual level. You have to remove this. But you have to think of the mind power and the programming that's going into this. When a man is making love to woman, he's got this urge inside of him to dominate, control, and push his energy within her. And she has this energy to create something with it. Whether or not modern man is thinking that they want to create something with it is not the point. Right now at this stage of our conversation, we're just looking at primal layers.

Let's put aside contraceptives, the importance of making love, or the passion of love for a minute to have to look at the dynamics in our genetic code and what's going on organically because we're programming energy intensely. It's probably one of the only areas that we're programming intensely, unaware that we're doing it. If my students could take objects and imbue them with programming the way that people do sexually without thinking about it, you would have some very powerful programming if you think about it. Think about the level of non-thought you have going on in your mind. You have intent, and you're running with that intent, and you're invoking that intent. You're pushing that energy with that intent but you don't necessarily have a lot of thought going on. It's almost as if your mind goes into a different level of stasis.

You're functioning but there's a level of ecstatic gratification also. It is a fine veil between higher consciousness and organic consciousness. It has to ride 'the veil' to gather the Prana and pull it in to create life. The same goes for women to create life. They ride a veil; this is where spirituality starts to get into the equation. Can we poke our head and exist in this way? *Is it a back door to higher consciousness?* It literally is, but it takes skill in order to tap that because our programming is to create life and that's what we need to fool spiritually to get out of that loop. You must appease both of them at the same time.

So, a woman is drawing in energy. In spiritual terms, a woman is often thought of as being a negative/positive polarity. And a male is thought of as a positive/negative polarity. Now when I say negative, I do not mean this in a derogatory sense whatsoever. Remove that from your thinking. It's just polarities of energy, how we're moving, so people can understand; one is pulling and one is pushing.

So, a woman can absorb energy from a man. Hence, often a lot of men will feel depleted when they're done with love making and they almost have to push away from the female. A lot of men will understand what I am saying. What happens to the female? The female is almost rejuvenated in many, but not all cases. You must keep in mind that nothing being said here is going to be 100% accurate for every single person. There are so many different intricacies of perspective. I am trying to cover the majority, or the most basic of constructs and then get into the details of things that could delve a long time into the future. Any person should be able to work their way through all these areas with some rational knowledge of what they're getting now.

A woman can actually be energized and empowered from love making, as if she just absorbed an enormous amount of energy while the male feels depleted, and rightfully so. It's not to say that a woman may not feel depleted. If a woman feels depleted, the man is over-dominating her and she is rejecting that dominance. And the reason she feels tired is because her energy is fighting that wall, organically. She is just going for a ride to appease the man.

Here we are back in to the physical, the energy, and the dualities, again. This topic can get into some gray areas; so a lot of times women will make love with their partners when they don't really want to but feel obligated. This is where that exhaustion is in reverse. Yet, if it's someone they passionately want to be with, they can literally absorb that energy and they'll feel rejuvenated because they wanted that energy; so it's not as much a duty anymore. This is where their energy polarities can switch.

It makes a lot of sense if the male readers will listen to what I'm saying. The same thing can happen with men, but not as often because men will just think it's not a necessity, and a woman's not allowed to push for it, but this gets back into social structure again.

There was a very strong female on the Navigator site who was talking about wanting to feel comfortable making love to people whenever she wants. There is one thing that I think women are often frustrated about. I've been doing a good job trying to get away from my potty mouth and now I must go right back to it to make an impact on what I am saying. There is no other way around it. I need to use the word 'fuck.' When a man is allowed to make a conquest, they're honored in the male world as being a conqueror and held in great esteem. Men will say, "Oh my God, you got to fuck twenty girls! You're awesome! If it's 100 or 1,000, you're a God." But if women do this, they are considered whores and unwanted. They're vile in a sense and it's derogatory. Right away, everybody can instinctually feel it in their 'feels-like.' Yes, it's programming. This woman wondered, "Why does it have to be that way?" I'll tell you why it's that way, but I don't agree with it. And then I'm going to empower the women. When I told most of the guys on the staff that I was going to tell you this, they couldn't believe it. I said, "No! I promised I was going to empower the females as much as the males from here on out." I've said this before and I intend to keep my word.

Here is the reason. It starts off very basic. One, a male penis is exterior. It's a function. It's on the outside of the body, if you will. A woman has her sexual organs within the body. The body is a temple in perspective or psychologically. If something gets inside of your body, it's like a virus, an illness, or a sickness. Right away, all of us instinctually know that we don't want to get an illness inside of the body. So, we see a woman as being vulnerable. When a woman takes sperm within her, she's taking it inside of her body. If she has a man going inside of her, it's as if this energy from a male is inside of her. Keep in mind something else: go back to the male gorilla killing the baby gorilla that was conceived from the female. It doesn't kill the female. It kills the offspring from the other male.

Men, inherently, *because of needing to insure our species, or our genetics, have this thing about wanting to exclusively dominate the female who is the productive source that will create the genetic pool.* As humankind became more intellectually complicated and more learned from the primitive state to the intellectual state, the *"thinking"* started to get dressed up in a suit and tie. But if you took it all off, it's still the same gorilla; they just dress it up to look at a certain perspective of how they want to do it. It's still dominating and controlling the female. It's just that our social structure got so big and complicated that men lost the origin of why we're so obsessed with sex and why we make women feel so violated. We were going to kill your offspring, but in modern times we can't do that, so we might as well kill your belief in yourself instead because you're the controlling factor. We think, "We can't kill your offspring but we'll kill you psychologically. We'll control you so that you don't wander around. We can control you."

So, I would imagine that the female gorillas are less likely to mess around because if they do, they know that there's a dominate gorilla close by. They know that they're going to lose the offspring. They have to carry this child with them for a certain amount of time. There has to be a certain amount of love but they know their offspring is going to get killed, so it's a way of controlling the females from mating with other males because they know there's the always the dominant silverback. With the human race, it's similar but different. This is why women have been considered dirty, vile, and all of those things.

Sperm is taken within the body. A man feels he can go and shoot it around because he's taking something from inside of him and he's putting his isism, his sperm, his force of energy inside of a female. When a man looks at another man, it is a lot like the hate that the gorilla has for the gorilla child that isn't its offspring. Every man looks at another male's sperm as competitive. So if a woman is the source of his fixation, then he wants to psychologically control her because he can't kill her offspring. He can't beat her since we live in a modern society. There are certain governorships that have to be controlled when a male is frustrated. So, I think that these concepts became interwoven into society.

You have to look at the effect of religion and how it has always been obsessed with controlling women. If you control the vagina, you control man. If you control man, you have the power to create empires. Just look at Christianity. The most powerful asset in Christianity was the power to consummate marriage; if you were a Christian, you were brought in. Of course, in those times, men were very fearful. You would burn in hell if you did something wrong. People had a limited education, but you weren't allowed to fuck as a man unless you came to the church. The church consummated your marriage. So if they consummated your marriage, they controlled whether you were going to get laid or not.

You could always get a little hussy, since prostitution is the oldest business in history, but if there was a nice woman that you really desired, you would have to become a Christian and submit to religious laws in order to have her. You would agree to anything if that's the vagina you wanted. That's how it was simplistically put. Man had a fever to get laid. So the church, understanding this, said that you have to consecrate your marriage. If the church consecrated your marriage, you could have her and she'll be exclusively yours.

Here we go back to the gorilla thing about exclusivity. So it becomes very complex. And this is how they built their numbers because when the child was born, it didn't have a choice about its belief system until it was 18 years old. At birth, they were baptized. This bolstered the numbers. Every religion does this; every culture does this whether it is Jewish, Catholic, Protestant, Islamic, or whatever. This is how you control the numbers. It's all controlled through sex. If you control the sex, you control the people. You control the men; you control the warriors, you control the armies, and the psyche of the people. I hate to say it, but everything in life is manipulated by sex.

Most successful people's careers are often motivated by sex. Young boys start off by having to wear their clothing or their hair combed a certain way. They read books on how to meet and talk to girls. It's an obsession. Even architecture has this mindset interwoven in it. Some people would say that is hard to imagine. No. In the end, we are all organic creatures of the Earth, of Gaia. We serve a primal purpose. If you look at evolution, it's about keeping the genetics flowing by keeping the organic body going. As intelligent as we've become as a species, it only makes sense that the most important source of our survival is integrated into our society. If you look at the Oval Office at the White House in Washington D.C., you will see what looks like a vagina or womb. The shape of a vagina or a penis is everywhere. Even the Washington Monument represents the penis. This makes it all too simplistic but realistically, the United States has the biggest penis in the world! And that's really what it is.

When you study ancient history, and you research the Christians and the battle that took place between the Freemasons, you see all of the sexual stuff and innuendos that's purposely put there. If you look at the Vatican, they have rows and rows of bushes. There is a bush in the middle with two rounded ones near them. These are penises. They know. They're doing this on purpose. The common person will not recognize this as we've become so accustomed to it that we don't think about it anymore. It's just the way it is. How many shapes are there? You have round and you have oblong. It's a matter of perspective.

So, a woman is designed to create a child within her body. Modern science comes along now and says, "Here's a contraceptive; it lowers the risk of pregnancy." At one time, having sex was a very high risk because it meant there was a good chance that they could get pregnant. So, in a sense women weren't really allowed pleasure. With men, it was all about conquest, seeding, and irresponsibility. In the battles, what inspired the Romans was the ability to rape and pillage. It was to rape the females. This is what gave the men the willpower to march forward and to get money, but it was really the raping of the women, this obsession again. That's what drove them forward. The military leaders all knew this. That is why they let them do it. If they didn't, there would be no conquest. Believe me; they would have no armies.

So, a woman wasn't allowed pleasure. Now all of a sudden, she is allowed pleasure because she has been given contraceptives. There are contraceptives for men and women. The risk factor has diminished, so now there's an explosion of being able to have pleasure. There is an explosion now to have freedom. She can explore the sexual areas and go from having one partner her entire life to having multiple partners, but to keep it down so that nobody knows her business. Where a man can boast about it, a woman certainly cannot, at least until recent times. Now we have TV shows like, "Sex in the City," and women's liberation, and woman's rights. Thank God!

So the bottom line is, "Why is sexual freedom wrong for a woman versus a man?" The bottom line comes back to control. It is man's dominance over women. Remove the contraceptive and you can see what the risk is really about. People just haven't caught up to the fact that the risk factor is removed now. And it's the first time that the playing field is equal for men and women. The psyche of people must now catch up in society, but it is going to take many generations from where we are now to accept that you have that kind of power.

You have to take it for yourselves. You have to feel unashamed. My advice is for the women to go out and do it. Just don't tell people your business. That's the bottom line, but you must share that information with other women because you need to empower one another. You need to laugh about the sexual flaws of the men and gain power from that, from cackling, as I call it. Men make comments about women, how their conquest was over her and her breasts. You have to create your own inner society amongst females that belittles the men. I hate to put it that way, but that's what's going to make you feel stronger and more empowered to be more selective.

Now, it is true to say that women are not always a one person kind of mindset. We know sociologically and scientifically that women cheat. We know that they look to cheat. We know that they will choose a mate because of the nurturing sense in them. He must be more of a provider: work, money, able to create a home, a shelter for the children. But we also know that when they get the mating urge, they will put on their war paint as I call it. This makeup enhances their attractiveness. When they go out to the bars, all of the studies show that they are looking for a robust, strong, strapping man. If they become pregnant their husband will raise the child. They'll go home and say that it belonged to their mate. It was shocking when all of this came out in research. Now, of course, this is not true in every single case. The women are thinking, "Oh my God, I never thought about it that way." Of course, now we have DNA testing and everything else, so the accusations fly and there are repercussions for everything. Society and science is changing rapidly.

So, we do know that women have desire. We know that they want to go out and have conquests. It's just that the price they have to pay is much greater for a woman than it is for a man. A man is able to go out and fuck in almost every culture, and cheat. But in most of the other cultures, women would suffer consequences for that, as in the Middle East. In China, you could get beaten to death for infidelity. It goes on and on. It's still only in a very few select parts of the world that you have this progression. Even sociologically, women would be outcast still.

How can a woman get more energy from a man when they have sex?

Just take it. Want it. Do you think its vampirism? Is that why you're afraid to take it? This is what I said to my students when they were saying that was vampirism. I'll say to you, "Most men, and I'd like to say all but I'm trying to be kind now, but I'll say most men want to control you. They will take it from you if you will give it, so why should you give them back any less? That's the truth. Make love to a man and if you're a student of mine, drain the life from them." I want warriors. I don't want weak women. I've thought about this for a long time. Should I reveal this or not? How does this affect my male students when they make love to females? By revealing this, the field is now even.

So you need to say, "Okay. You're going to push? That's fine." Instead of being gentle and not taking their energy, or feeling guilty about taking the energy, take it! Leave them spent. Make yourself youthful and beautiful. *It will affect you genetically*. It will affect your cellular body. It will slow the aging process. I guarantee it. Do not be afraid. Drain them. If you're with another White Cell and you have a fair playing field, or if it's someone you care passionately about, you can control this. But if you're going to go out and play around, then take their energy. They will recuperate.

To make them ill would take a little bit more effort, but White Cells will get more powerful. If they could dominate you, if they could impregnate you they would even though they don't want you to get pregnant in this day in age. They want to fuck you but they don't want the responsibility. Still in their mind, they're just fucking and it is dominance. It's back to the gorilla. That is really what it is. And if a man tells you anything else, such as, "I love you, or I just want to plant flowers with you," then it's bullshit and there's probably no interest in you anyway because they need that robustness.

A woman wants to get that energy still but they don't want to believe that they're doing it purposefully. Drain them! When they're done, when their seeds are thrown, nine times out of ten, they will say, "See you later! I'm done with you now." Why should you not do the same thing? You should say, "I feel glorious today! See you later. I'm heading out now." They'll do it to you! I think some women do it a little bit, but they don't really take full advantage of it because there's a Governor in the back of their mind that's saying they're only allowed a certain limit. You don't even think about it anymore. It's internalized. Take the energy! Take it all. Let them have their lesson.

Eventually, they're going to know to back off. But you're going to escalate your power in life dramatically. It will come out in business. It will come out in how you handle matters. It will come out emotionally. I will tell you this, "Sperm has something in it that prevents depression in women. I think that, yes, absolutely. I can't give you the scientific proof but I do believe there are some studies on this already. It will never make it into public knowledge though because *they* don't want women to know about it. But there is something that happens to the dopamine in the body.

Now with condoms, you don't necessarily want to take a high risk. Of course, you have to worry about venereal diseases, but if you know the situation and you can control it, then work with it. But take the energy. Take it from men. Don't be shy. That is the bottom line.

In a relationship between a man and a woman who are both White Cells, we're going to talk differently about how to work with this energy because, naturally, you don't want there to be conflict. If they can switch their energy in their head correctly, a man can draw as much energy from a female because the switch changes the polarity. Without training from someone like me, or understanding these things, most men would never know anyway, so it doesn't matter. And if they did, you would sense it. You just have to be aware of what's going on and then you end it. Or you say, "Okay. Bring it on. I'll fight over it." I would hope my women would say that. I would say, "Take them down. You know that they're going to take you down, so have no mercy. We're not talking about harming somebody here. They're just going to need a week or so to recuperate. But they would have left you anyway. They wouldn't have cared about your condition." You should never forget that. Does that help to better understand this?

Yes.

So the real question is, "How do you take their energy? When's the real moment that you pull their energy?" *The moment is in the window and the window is in the orgasm.* The orgasm is more than just the ejaculation of fluid or the release of the sexual energy within the woman's body. It is a moment in the mind that is so occupied when the body is in so much release, but there's an opening in the mind. You have to consciously will, desire, and have intent. At that moment, be aware of your intent and literally, like inhaling your breath, feel it move up into the lower chakra, and then the chest area. Move it up and claim it as your own. Have intent and think, "I'm going to take it; I'm going to take it." You'll feel it down in the lower chakra. You're going to pull it in, just like you do with lower chakra energy. You're pulling it in and you'll say, "It's mine. It's over." Then get off. You're done. Literally take it in. It will go into the lower chakra and it will move up into your chest center, and then up into the mind chakra area. If they have a lot of energy for you to take, it'll even hit your crown area. And if you really know how to work it, you can even manipulate it into your own orgasms. A woman can go into seven orgasms, where a male can go into four. You can literally hit levels and they won't even know what the hell's going on with you and you won't even care what they're thinking anyway. And you can ride it.

Just like the In-Between.

Yes. I can always tell the powerful women from meeker women. I can tell that with your energy, you'll take the energy. I believe some women reserve it and don't know what to do with the energy. You need to take it more. But I can always tell by personality. The men will look for the women that have dominate energy, that are able to take the energy because they know that there's something strong about them and they want to dominate it. Nobody wants to dominate the weak one. They want to dominate the stronger one because that's merit for you. And you can switch that very easily.

I have a question about a marriage between a White and a Red Cell. How does that work?

I think that a Red Cell male will try to dominate, no matter what, period. He will take on the organic role in the male/female dominated relationship. If it's a White Cell that is male, as he evolves he will balance the masculine and the feminine within himself and this gives them equality in their relationship and allows for a lot more growth. I find that in almost every single case of a White Cell female with a Red Cell male, the male will constantly try to take control. This is because the White Cell female is still bringing in that masculine energy over time and she is getting stronger. He feels intimidated by that, so he has to constantly reinforce control and keep attacking whatever he feels is empowering her. It is his security. And this goes back to his primal nature, and so it is a very difficult situation.

Therefore, I would say absorb the energy or live a life of depression because you're constantly dominated, unless you can train him. And when I say to take the energy, I really mean to take the *power*. If you take the power, then you control the relationship, and it does happen. I've often seen in many cases, where the White Cell female accepts the role of power and takes over the dominant role in their relationship, and then the male is more docile. It doesn't mean she abuses him. It just means she has empowered the direction of her life. I'm not concerned at all with Red Cells. My concern is with my White Cells and empowering them in life. Anything that I have to say is going to be giving them the advantage because I think Red Cells have the majority of control in the world as it is.

So, I would say dominate and take the energy. It's up to you. You may have a suppressive husband and you feel that he's constantly riding you, or belittling you. This is usually a male thing since a male always goes after the psyche of a female by telling her that she is stupid, weak, and useless and can't get anything done when she has to. This is belittling and this is willfully done. It's not honest. It's not the truth. It is done to break the will of the female because, at some point, the female must have shown that she had some strength and she is being punished now. That punishment can last for years, even from an incident that happened many years ago because a man can't get it out of his head.

So, I would say, take him in bed. Seduce him. Take that energy. Keep taking it and you're going to switch those polarities. All of a sudden, he'll become very docile. Happiness comes first. What do I always say in my teachings? It's good as long as you're not controlling someone else. That is a sin to me. You're not controlling the male. You're liberating yourself. It's just how you choose to use that power. Then afterwards, you have to do the right thing to them.

If he doesn't treat you with a certain amount of respect, get out of that relationship. You'll suffer for one year because of the transition but you will adapt and your life will be better for it. Do not be afraid. I don't care if you have ten kids. It's better than twenty years of misery. I bet that since you met me, your relationship has changed. That's from the teachings and it has probably affected him by now, and that's a good thing. It's a wonderful thing. But what I'm saying is that many students are dominated by the males and it drives me nuts, and I cannot stand a White Cell that is docile. I just want to put a fire up their ass and feed them lead pellets. Get in there now. That's just how I am. I want them to be happy. What matters to me is that White Cells are happy whether they are male or female. I honestly do not discern a difference between a human being as male or female. What I see is a White Cell, and I see both polarities as a soul.

We esteem to be like our creator and our creator is neither a male nor a female. Of course, man has created God as a male in the history books, in the Bible, and in religion which is ridiculous. If God created the Universe and this was the birth of its existence, then who did God mate with to create the Universe? There had to have been a yin/yang. There had to have been a positive/negative. God is a hermaphrodite. There was nobody before, during, or after. It's just simply God. God created life within God. This is the feminine aspect by creating within himself. The act of creation, or the will to begin it, was the male aspect. The act of creation of birthing was the female aspect. So if we are souls, we go from life, to life, to life. We talk about reincarnation yet we shun people for their sexual identities. Yet, we'll say we believe in reincarnation. Well, doesn't that mean that you were a female in a previous life? Doesn't that mean that you were in a male body before? Should you suppress the female if you were a female in a past life? How did it make you feel? This is ignorance. The bottom line is that you're neither male nor female in the spiritual aspect.

If I am to teach my students, I can't look at them as being a male or female. I have to look at them as a balanced being and say, "You have to bring your polarity up from this side, or you need to bring this up so that you can hit perfect pitch." A tuning fork, that's the pitch you want. And when you find that, you will find happiness in your life. You will find peace. You will stop looking for a counterpart in your life. You will stop looking at your mate, trying to make them into something that they're not. You'll be able to accept them more because you found inner-peace. Inner-peace isn't found out there. Inner-peace is found within you. All White Cells know that but we never have put it into practical terms before. It's about finding the yin/yang in you and finding that balance.

Look at any spiritual teacher, whether it's Krishna, Milarepa, or Buddha. When you look at them, can you honestly say that they were masculine? They were feminine in their aspect but they had masculine qualities. They had perfect pitch. Even myself, I'm not masculine and I'm not feminine. I'm somewhere down that middle road and there's a reason for that. And that is what makes perfection.

What makes enlightenment is finding inner balance. It goes back to the same thing. I think that men got away with it because they put it under philosophical thinking and teaching. So they historically got away with it and that's what allowed them to find enlightenment. But a woman who acted too masculine would get beaten to death. If she empowered herself too much, or dressed masculine, she would be beaten to death. So I don't think in terms of, "Well, that's not the way it is." My mind branches thousands of years. To me, that's yesterday, in certain ways. Just sixty years ago, there were only certain things that you could do before main-stream society. You could push the feminine all you wanted but if it was masculine in any way, people would say, "Oh my God." And there was a price to pay in our society.

There are so many dynamics to sex; therefore, teaching a group of men and women is very, very difficult to do. There are just so many challenges sociologically. There are so many things that need to be mentioned for women. As females, you are forced to become dependent on males in many ways. It has only been recently that women have become more independent. But that dependence on men is still sociologically interwoven in society, so you have to compromise constantly. Unfortunately, there is a spiritual compromise as well.

Men don't think about the spiritual aspect. This is why a woman shouldn't care about taking their energy. Men are not concerned with whether or not a woman is going to find enlight-enment. Men are only concerned with whether or not they can find enlightenment themselves. It's just like medicine. A large percentage of medical research funding goes towards men's health and medicine. Very little funding is given for female med-ical research.

It's no different than the job market in the United States. According to a 2013 Institute for Women's Policy Research (IWPR) paper, women are paid somewhere from twenty-one to twenty-three percent less money for the exact same job as a man.

In the end, it is all about sex, self-importance, and dominance. Since women aren't the dominant sex, they haven't been able to counteract it because they were not designed that way. I would say to all women, "Go out there take the energy from men. Take the power and you will find the control." Absolutely.

On an energy level, how does sex affect men? Do men give energy away?

Men don't give energy away, they use it to control. Men give energy with conditions. I don't think there's one orgasm that's given just for the sake of giving. Men always have an intent behind the orgasm. It's usually for conquest and power. It can be used to feed and nourish, but it's almost always directed. There's always a program behind it. That's why a female is always giving something, but it has a directive. Women are not allowed to make the choices they want so they feel threatened.

Women hold onto men through sex. That's their way to men. They're not stupid. The bottom line is that women take men's energy through sex. In many schools of spiritual teaching, the sperm is the life force of the man. It's very connected to Prana. When a man's sperm leaves his body, it takes a piece of his soul with it. When a woman does the same thing, it creates a child. In essence, it's just Micro-Macro in a different perspective.

There was a study done on sperm at a college. They put the sperm on a machine that acted like a Geiger counter. Not far from this machine was an open door. When people walked by, the sperm actually jumped. It could sense human beings, male or female. When a person entered the room, the sperm jumped even more. But if the sperm donor walked by, the sperm would just go off the charts. Distance wasn't a factor. Can you imagine the amount of distance that would be in ratio to the size of the sperm? If we had the same ability, it would be like being able to sense something across an entire city, or maybe a state. The sperm senses the donor, and it senses other people. It can feel and detect energy fields. The sperm reacts to energy fields. It gets excited when it senses another energy field.

A woman's sexual organ is negative polarity, whereas a man's is positive. It's just polarities. A woman is designed to absorb a man's energy because her body is designed to perform one task. It's not a good thing or a bad thing. A woman's body is made to create life. That is what it's designed to do. So when a man puts forth his sperm, his life force, his soul energy, women consume it. They're consuming a part of his frequency and he is giving it because he's thinking, "Oh, it's the dominating thing."

Spiritually, a man gives a piece of his soul away and a woman takes it and absorbs it. This is why many spiritual teachings encourage the man to hold his sperm in and not release it. Then the man can retain control and recycle the energy. I disagree with that. I think it's wrong for a man to recycle the sperm within his body. If he's going to ejaculate, he should keep it near his body and just rest for a few minutes before discarding it. The energy will cycle back to him.

If you don't do this, you're allowing yourself to age faster. At thirty years old, the process has already started. At forty, it's increasing even more. As far as evolution goes, the meaning of life is to procreate. Your body wants to know that your cells are reproducing. Every living organism in your body has a program. If your cells aren't reproducing anymore you're saying, "I'm not functioning anymore." You're really telling your body that you've stopped serving the biological process of life as a living creature. So, the body tells itself to start aging and declining. Your body starts to collapse because sex is the primal force for the survival of the species. By holding the sperm in, you're telling yourself that you're no longer serving the biological order of life.

Whether you're a man or a woman, you definitely want to at least masturbate to tell your body, organically, that it still has a reproductive process. There is a necessity for this. There is a reason why your body produces these cells. Why do men have wet dreams? It's because there's a certain point when the male has to release his sperm. His body is just trying to get him there.

When a man willfully uses his conscious mind, his will controls it. So, I think it's wrong to recycle the Prana.

Men have to be very careful about the distance they are from a woman when they ejaculate because females are going to absorb that energy. A woman's natural process is to seek out that energy. The biological need to reproduce keeps most human beings as Red Cells. It's a safety switch that nature has built into itself to ensure that there are always enough Red Cells on the planet for the security and future of the planet as a living organism. When a man's energy drops, the woman's energy elevates. This whole absorbing of energy process is designed to create life.

Science has given men and women more freedom now with the availability of contraceptives. Hence, they are mating more than ever before. So there is more cycling of women taking in this energy, creating a stagnancy in the big scheme of things for the progression of the Gaia consciousness. You have to choose wisely how you're going to have sex.

Is there any way that you can conserve your sexual energy?

Yes, absolutely. There is always abstinence, but nobody wants to hear that. I could never tell anybody not to be with a woman or not to be with a man. For a woman, there is an advantage in a way. So, I can't preach the same way to a woman as I can to a men. Men think, "Well, that sucks! Why can't it be just the opposite?" Well, I didn't make it that way. Nature made it that way. Do you see what I'm saying? Science has made it more convenient for women because they get the energy and with the use of contra-ceptives, there are fewer repercussions like pregnancy, morning sickness, and depletion of their body of nutrients. Before, it was altogether a different playing field.

So, if you're going to make love to a woman, don't make love to her every day. If you do, you're having sex like a rabbit. You think like a rabbit; therefore, you are mating like a rabbit. If you're going to make love to a woman by all means make passionate love to her. Do it maybe once every two weeks, or once a month, but make it passionate and fulfilling. Then, your orgasm will be better and your sensory will be higher because you haven't had sex all the time.

In our day and age, making love has become just a casual process of mindless sex. It's lost all of the excitement. The big orgasms always come when you meet somebody new. It's fun for the first week or two. Well, it can be fun like that all the time if you're not acting like rabbits. Don't treat it like blowing your nose with tissue. The idea of making love is lost. It's become more of a quick release valve of, "Let's fuck and get it over with," or, "We're tense today so let's fuck," or, "I feel a little horny so let's fuck." At one time, it wasn't like that. Women would know when they wanted to make love. They let the men know and they would then sense it or smell it with the endorphins in the air. And children were made out of passion.

Dull sex creates dull people. One has to be mindful of the level of passion when having sex with a woman. I want you to think about sex differently. A lot of spiritual teachings tell the man to hold the energy within because of the depletion of their energy. Somehow, these teachings got misconstrued over time. When a man is with a woman, it is very difficult to remain spiritual. And the same goes for a woman, but more so because women are forced to survive sociologically. Women force it more. That's the reason why there are fewer enlightened women.

When you couple, nature says that you have to produce offspring. If you produce the offspring, where's the time to intellectually grow within an average lifetime? This cuts down on the amount of time you have to awaken, practice and hone your skills. It minimalizes your ability to discover, recognize, and take it to deeper levels. All of this takes time and dedication. This is the reason spiritual masters always end up running off, leaving the women stuck with the kids. Therefore, the women can't run off and find their spirituality. So when you're with a woman, you get the sense of having children because the children must be nurtured, sheltered and fed.

When do you have the time to pursue your spirituality? It starts to become a greater and greater time constraint. Each child takes a certain amount of energy from your life force. In part, they are tuned in to your frequency. The woman gives the majority of the energy to conceive the children, but they take a certain amount of energy from the man's life force as well. You want the most for your child so your mindfulness is always on your child. Your mindfulness is a kind of energy that also goes to them. Can you deny that? This is the safety feature of the planet for Gaia to insure that the species continues. If you have wax wings and you fly too close to the sun, your wings will melt. So you have to realize that you have wax wings. If you choose to ignore that, then you suffer the consequences.

The battle for your spirituality becomes much more challenging. It becomes more difficult to be creative and find the time to grow spiritually. It's very rare to see co-habitable relationships between a male and a female with children where one can pursue their spiritual growth. It usually ends with the female feeling that the male is going to abandon them. So she starts to constrain more and becomes more fearful to draw the male in. He becomes more resentful because he feels this going on. It's not that she is trying to control. She's fearful of losing him because she has to provide for the children. What will the children do? Women really have a tougher situation because they are the ones who bond the most with their children. Society places most of the responsibility for the care of the children on the women.

You could say practice abstinence, but I don't know. I'll be very honest. A lot of people want to know whether I'm gay, straight, or bisexual. What am I? I'm the same thing that most spiritual masters are. I started off extremely straight, heterosexual, but probably was a bit more open to bisexuality than a typical male because of the way my advanced spirituality sees the body. Most men don't register it the same way. You develop a different sensory. This sensory is more developed in spiritual masters, so it's hard to discern just the body. I could have been married already. It was a very close call and I seriously considered it. I could also have been a father once. However, I recognized the power that women had over me, the lust, the sexual drive, the captivation that they hold. Both physically and biologically, the curvature of a woman's body and their breasts has a certain power over me. But, I was able to recognize this. At some point, I knew that I could gravitate towards males because they would never have power over me that a woman had because I was not so naturally inclined.

It's a place that I can be passionate and not have a sense that they could take my heart. There was a chance I would fall madly in love with a woman and I would then have children. Spiritually I would be in conflict and it would be a big thing for me. I'm also very loyal, so if I ever did have children, I would never abandon them. I would never give up my children for my spirituality. Hence, I found the wisdom in time to make a very extreme decision.

Being an enlightened person and having that level of knowledge was very helpful because it gave me a greater advantage. I knew that if I cultivated the opposite direction towards males, I would have a better chance of surviving spiritually than if I kept playing around with females. That's why a lot of spiritual teachers isolate themselves from women. It wasn't a matter of being gay. It was a matter of spiritual survival when you're young. Only with age do you get enough power and self-control. Now that I am over forty, I feel more confident that I'm not going to allow certain things to happen. It was a matter of recognizing what I wanted.

This is where I don't want to scare the women because some women might be afraid their husband is going to hear this and don't want him to leave them. Or they are in a relationship where they love the person and don't want to leave them. My job is to be absolutely honest and try to give both perspectives. I took the extreme path to my enlightenment because I knew I was biologically attracted to females more than I was attracted to males. As an awakened master I knew that if I gravitated towards males, I would be able to balance both polarities within me. That is the choice that I made. That is where I found inner balance within myself, giving me a masculine/feminine polarity. That's the base of my consciousness, allowing me to approach God frequency and integrate masculine/feminine polarities. I am able to be in unison where there's not a vibrational difference. That is what it's all about.

It was definitely a strategy. Even today, I certainly am attracted to women but I can sense when I need to take three steps backwards because I can feel that power. I simply recognize it for what it is. You can have your cake and eat it, too! You do not have to lead the life that I am leading. *You just have to understand polarity.* If you want to pursue your spirituality, then you have to find another White Cell.

That's why it's wonderful that the Higher Balance Institute is growing and getting so many new people involved because I'm finding more and more powerful females who are in it for the truth of learning, rather than having their boyfriends drag them into it. They're more dedicated. You can now find females in our inner circles that understand these things. They have a practical understanding of energy and frequency and their goals are the same as the men's goals. They want to attain enlightenment also. So, now there is an equal playing field. I don't allow any of the males in my circle to dominate the females. I have issues with that. I prefer to have equality in the relationships. I find that those relationships last longer than relationships where one has a dominate role versus the other. As Higher Balance continues to grow, I'm hoping that there will be some very stable relationships coming out of it down the road as students intermingle in our circle and find one another. It's very hard to find another White Cell.

Is abstinence really a benefit?

I disagree with abstinence without ejaculation. I'm fine with abstinence with ejaculation. In that aspect, it's the same for a woman as it is for a man. One should masturbate in order to keep the body healthy so it can send the right signals through the body. When the body doesn't find some kind of stimulation in that area, it's going to become tense. It knows what it needs to do and you're preventing it by not masturbating. It's going to show up in your psyche, psychology, and personality. It's going to come off in intention. It's a bit different for women, but not that much different. It's just more taboo so you can't address it. Women have the same drives and needs as men do. They've just psychologically suppressed them more.

Would it be beneficial for a man to ingest his own ejaculate?

I hear this all the time and my answer is no. It's simply your own frequency, your own energy. It's a fair question and this does come up in advanced spiritual circles. There are no boundaries in this discussion and I want everyone to have an open mind. This has been brought up before; I've heard about it in different teachings. As far as I'm concerned, the energy is released and it's a matching frequency.

It's socially acceptable if a woman does that but it's not acceptable if a man does. I'm not here to talk about sociological structure. I'm here to give the facts and information for both women and men. If a woman ingests a man's ejaculate, most men want them to swallow it as a sign of their love for them. This is dominance again.

Sperm is a man's frequency. Sperm carries data. Now, granted that data is more designed to go into the womb and the ovaries to combine its DNA within the egg, but there is also frequency energy in it. There is data of that person's frequency and as I said before, "It's the only way for you to move your soul outside of yourself temporarily." Do you follow me? How did the sperm know when other people were going by? What was the intelligence of that? That was its frequency sensing. It's just not as advanced, per se. It's fading but it is still a part of you.

So, if sperm is consciously taken from a male, no matter who is consuming it, they are literally taking a part of the male's energy.

One of my biggest pet peeves is that students think since I am bisexual, they should run out and be with a gay male. If you go with a gay male, I'm done teaching you because the vast majority of them already have over feminine energy which is the same thing as being with a female. The only difference is they don't have the sex organs for intercourse but their polarity is the same. A gay male desperately wants the sperm of another male because he wants to do the same thing that a female does. Since they don't have the ability to absorb the energy through the womb, they take it in orally, so they're consuming the energy. They're taking life force the same way and *it empowers them.*

Energy follows a pattern because the organic body acts like a railroad track. It says this is the pattern. It's easy for a woman to absorb energy whether they're a Red Cell or not because she is designed to create life. If the consciousness starts to take over, it controls the energy. So, if the male wants to act like the female counterpart, the consciousness finds a way to make the energy work similar to a female's. They're still commanding that energy to work in a certain way even though it wasn't necessarily designed organically to work that way.

So, I get very concerned when male students talk about being with gay males because I think that the gay males have double the aggression to take that energy than a female does. It could also be because the heterosexual part of me is more prone to lean towards women, so maybe I feel more relaxed with that. I'm just trying to be absolutely honest here. Gay males have a very strong desire to conquer other males and absorb their energy. The same goes for lesbians who are overly masculine. They are lethal for a female to allow into their energy. They have the dominator and the absorber built into them. So, not only do they want to control you but they want to drain you. So, it's a double jolt. Maybe that's why I feel so strongly against those two complete polarities.

If you're a male heterosexual, you can bend your sexuality but you'll never completely go the other way because your organic body knows what it really wants. It's a matter of working with that energy to prevent you from becoming overly feminine as a male. You change the polarity so the organs are the same but the energy is more balanced.

I see the middle as being heterosexual. If you're on either side of the middle, you're bisexual but you're heterosexually rooted. The extremes on either side of the middle are where there is a complete shifting towards the opposite role of your gender. This is definitely where you *don't* want to go. These are definitely the people that you don't want to end up in the sack with because they will ravish you. When I look into the psyche of these people, I find there's just such a clingy, controlling dominance there. You can see the dysfunction in the energy. *It's too dominant.* If you're a lesbian but still bridging towards that heterosexual balance of energy, that's perfectly okay. The same goes for males who have that counterpart of a balanced energy where they still under-stand their role, as long as the females are not trying to be males and the males are not trying to be females. Just enjoy the beauty of being with another person.

There are lesbians who embrace their lesbianism but they don't like makeup or over femininity. They're not overt yet they're very feminine. They also have that balance. *That is excellent pitch.* The same goes for a gay man. A gay man can still embrace his desire to be with another man but also have very masculine energy. They haven't lost or given up their masculinity. *That's a good pitch.* Spiritually, they're keeping both their energies wishy-washy, but there's still that root core of their main organic balance. It's very hard to explain. And it's very difficult because this is a very taboo subject. I'm finding that even I have reserva-tions saying certain things.

Can a man lose energy if fantasizing or masturbating to a woman? Can a woman gain energy from a man who is masturbating this way?

Well, yes and no. This is the way it is. A female can gain energy from any male she has had intercourse with even if he is three thousand miles away. If the female fantasizes about that male and she's been with him intimately, she knows that man's frequency and pattern so she can gain energy from him any time because of that programming. There's a certain smell that every human being has. There's a certain *feels-like* that every human being has. *I call that feels-like their code.* It's like having a little bar code on you.

Everybody has their own frequency. When a female is intimate with a male, there is that one moment when she gives in and takes your energy and you dominate her. Well, you're the fool who put the code in there. So now when she masturbates, all she has to do is envision you, giving her absolute mind control. These are the best trained people sexually. Since they can invoke your frequency, they can invoke you. They're invoking your energy. When they invoke your energy, they can open up a portal and that presence moves through time and space. Again, this is the power of sex. They're tapping into the grid, but they can never consume as much of your energy as if you were in close proximity. They could be a thousand miles away and they can invoke your spirit and take your sexual energy. It locks onto you and it will hold you.

Most people think of sex as dirty or vile. I don't. To me, sex is beautiful but it's really about energy. I'm not thinking about the organic, sweaty part with all the bodily fluids involved. That's not the part of sex that I am talking about. But yes, if a woman's been with you she can take your energy. The same goes for a gay man. Men can't do it as easily because they're dominant whereas females can. They can tune into your energy. They project you. They recreate you in their mind. They recreate your vibration and that tags you and draws you in. They have a desire for you to want them. They will call you. They're like sirens when they go into that state of mind. It's a power and they can then bring your energy in. Hence, you have to use High Guard (from my book *Igniting the Sixth Sense*). Use psychic defenses like your pyramid. There's a reason for all of this. You will recognize this *feels-like* when suddenly there is a huge energy drain on you, as if something is pulling on you. We can't say in the mainstream, "Some woman's masturbating over you and she's drawing and calling your energy." It's a taboo. You just can't really say that. So I say, *"Build a pyramid. Cut those energy ties."*

When you're with a woman, you give her your energy and she marks it. The same thing goes for a completely gay man. They have the same ability once they lock into your energy. So you should always be conscientious of that. Any White Cell who understands what I'm saying can do that now. It's just easier if there's lust involved. The organic body is willing to work with you one hundred percent if lust is involved. The organic body is the Babbler and when the Babbler says, "Alright, I'm working with you," you can achieve non-thought and push the parameters.

Does a man project energy out when he lusts for a woman?

If you're masturbating to women you're projecting your frequency out. Instead, masturbate to a woman that you don't know personally. *Never masturbate to a woman who you really have feelings for.* This is about control. Men tend to break that barrier, but women do it, too. Control is the same thing as desire. It's just different slightly but it's still the same thing. They want you to want them. That's control.

If a man invokes a female who he's been with, he is sending out his energy to dominate her. So, he's really sending his energy out but he's also depleting it. If you can astral project, this is energy that is consciously moving outside of your body. It's your frequency, so whatever it experiences, it reciprocates back to you. When you're masturbating, you're projecting the energy versus pulling it towards you. I don't see a woman projecting it out and I don't see a man calling it in. *It's what the design of the body is copacetically working with.* Did you catch that? I thought that was an interesting thing to point out.

A man projects this energy through masturbation. He will get the same kind of clarity. He's still dominating but he's surrendering that energy to the woman. Nine times out of ten, the woman doesn't want the energy. It's usually the man trying to dominate her again, so the energy is wasted.

Whenever you do this, you're willfully giving your energy away. The funny thing is that a man, in the heat of the moment, doesn't really care because it's what he wants! Therefore, it takes great discipline. When one can fantasize about a fictional woman who doesn't have a locked frequency, it's much better than to have somebody you're fixated on to send that energy to. I think it's a good piece of new information that I hadn't discussed before. So it's good that I'm talking about it now.

I encourage White Cell females to take the energy from a male. If you don't want to do that, then create a fantasy male the same way a male creates a fantasy female. Your energy doesn't lock-in then. But now you're also programming your sexual identity.

So let's talk about sexual identity. We know through science that a man will predominantly use the left hemisphere of the brain. We know that a woman will use the right hemisphere. If a man predominately uses one hundred percent of the left hemisphere, a woman will use around seventy-five percent of the right and twenty-five percent of the left. So women are actually using a little bit of both. That's what makes women more balanced than men.

Bisexual men and women, who are really balanced, use both hemispheres of the brain equally. This is what allows them to become poets, artists and writers. When you look at all the great minds in history, an astonishing amount were bisexual and gay like Michelangelo, Joan of Arc, and Alexander the Great. Again, the women in this group have been historically suppressed, but they do exist. Considering that only ten percent of society is gay or bisexual, that is a huge proportion of the greatest minds in history. So, that tells you there's a big difference between gay or bisexuals and heterosexuals. The difference is that they embrace their passion. They embrace a fearless sense of sexuality where many of them have been intimate with both men and women. I suspect this is the main reason why they use both hemispheres of their brain.

Over a long period of time, I know that both my male and female students have played around with the whole idea of same sex relationships. When they play around with that concept for about two months in their mind, they get over their anxiety and you can see a difference in their personality. They start to grasp literature and music like they never had before. They see art and poetry differently. It's as if their whole world goes from black and white to color. There's something richer about life. I believe it is because the hemispheres of their brain are now equalized. It's like going from one engine to two, or from one computer CPU to two. Which is obviously better?

If you're just using a portion of your brain to conceive reality, how much more could you understand if you used all of what is already there? So, finding inner balance and a comfort zone within your own consciousness allows both of these hemispheres to turn on. Sociologically you're taught to fit into society and suppress any interest in the same sex. This in turn creates character roles for your identity, psyche, or intellect. This leads into your spiritual vibration and it moves you to a polarity that becomes very Red Cell to serve the organism as a planet versus something that's trying to balance itself and emerge with the Universe frequency, which is a masculine-feminine polarity. Does that make sense?

What about the whole idea of people being born gay?

Well, I think there's no doubt that people are born gay. Honestly, I think that society needs gay people. I think gay people are the peace makers. Women, have you ever imagined how much different your life would be if you were born male? Do you feel that you would have been respected differently? That you would have had more say? That you would have had more opportunities in life? That you would have more control in life? So what if you had a penis but you still had your same personality? Then you'd be gay. What would that mean that you could do? You'd be allowed to affect the rest of the dumb males saying, "War, war, war!" And you'd be like, "Listen, I'm one of the guys but I think we're rushing things a little bit. Let's be sensible here." Do you think that you could have had an effect on the world? That's the point!

I think that gay people, as well as masculine females, hold a critical role. One of my students was talking about how the gay American Indians are very prissy about certain things. Well, take the faggot or the feminine, which are both powerful negative words, out of the equation and what do you have from primitive humanity? "Let's not drink the green water. It looks a little murky. Let's go after this clear water. It looks like it would taste better." Or, "Let's not camp out over there where there's what looks like red bacteria growing all over. Let's go over to the green pasture that looks flat and clean and airy from the pine trees." I think that these people had an effect. I think that American Indians would consider gay people as being very special and mystical. So, I think they would really listen to what they had to say. Hence, the brilliance of certain individuals.

Historically, this was very closely scrutinized, and the survival of the human race had a big part of it. Look at society. Look at art. Let's look at Michelangelo. If you discard him, then you get rid of the Sistine Chapel and all of his creations and sculptures, where does that put society in modern day? Let's get rid of the drive and vision of Alexander the Great. Let's get rid of all that he contributed to society. If you take these people who were obviously gay and you murder them, where are we as a civilization? I've got news for you. We would still be clacking rocks and beating each other over the head. We'd be dragging the women by their hair and having our way with them.

There were also huge contributions from heterosexuals. When you look at the brilliant minds, a lot of them like Einstein were not gay. But there is without a doubt a massive contribution from this ten percent of society who really stand out if you look at their sexual orientation. If you look at the percentage of society that is gay versus how many people stand out, it's disproportionally big. You can't dismiss the effect they've had on society.

Other than brain hemisphere balance, is there another biological component?

Well, if they had been too feminine, I don't think they would have contributed any more than anybody else. If you look at Alexander the Great, he had both masculine and feminine properties. He walked that middle line. His sexual preference doesn't matter. His persona understood what masculine was and he could walk an even line. Michelangelo, same thing. If you look at all the great Greek philosophers, every one of them had both feminine and masculine properties. So, you have to define that line that I'm talking about. It's the secondary line from the core. I think that you could be gay but if you're not overly feminine, you're still masculine. It's just your sexual desire is towards males. You don't have the need to put make-up on and feel over feminine.

Gay men who become overly feminine are in a much more challenging situation because they're trying to be like heterosexuals in their relationships, but their organs are male, so it is extremely difficult for them to fit into society. When a man is gay but looks masculine, or a female is lesbian but looks feminine, because of their outward appearance, they can move easier in society and they're more accepted. They can influence society and work with it better than the ones who are on the extreme end of their sexuality.

People on the extreme end of their sexuality are in such a battle to be accepted by society that it consumes them their whole life. If a male feels like he should have been a female, he doesn't need to put on feminine clothing, a wig, or make-up just because of the thrill of it. In his mind, he already is female. Neither does a female have to shave her head, tape her breasts down, or put on trousers and walk like a man. In her mind, she already is male. It's just that their organs don't match what their brain perceives. On a spiritual or creative level, both are suppressed because they are shunned by people so aggressively since it's such a vexation to society to conceive this total transformation.

So, if a man is dressed in female clothing, most people don't want to sit down and even have a cup of coffee with this person.

But if you never do that, how will you know whether or not they are a genius? Whereas, if it was a male or a female who loved women, you can't really tell what they want. You don't judge them then. They can get underneath the radar. So, you have a cup of coffee with them because sex isn't the topic. What the heck are you going to talk about? The universe, mathematics, and architecture! Then you will be listening to what they're saying and they will be like, "Wow!" Society is progressive and digressive in life.

Concerning the ones that have more of a balanced hemisphere, how much does the amygdala play a role in that?

We're doing exactly what I don't like to do. We're getting over technical about something that we can keep very simple. There's no loss of knowledge here. We can call it this or we can call it that, but I prefer to keep it simple. The bottom line is that it's hemispheres of the brain. So, we want to keep balanced hemispheres rather than having one side more dominant than the other. Somebody can be born with a very feminine consciousness. Does that mean they are balanced and will get more advantages than most people do? No. They've gone too far over. They were born that way. My mother was definitely born super feminine and my father was definitely born super masculine.

My parents couldn't even imagine the idea of bisexuality or anything close to that. They can cope with it but it comes down to the brain hemispheres. You have to understand that my parents could accept that. They're progressive so they will accept it, however, they could never bridge over to even think about being bisexual. Never. That isn't necessarily genetic; it is sociological programming. In the 1960's, television portrayed gay or lesbian characters in the worst possible way - as the feminine weak ones. They never showed them as masculine. Yet, some of the most famous actors and actresses were gay or lesbian.

It's only in recent generations that new attitudes about this have started to emerge. People are a lot more accepting of it.

There are now terms like *metrosexuals*. People are starting to become indifferent about who sleeps with whom. What difference does it make who they sleep with? Who cares what kind of bodily fluids are flying around? It's sex. It is what it is.

Sexuality is starting to become irrelevant and people are starting to see the bigger picture. It's about who the person is but it required an evolutionary process to get to that point. The ironic thing is that earlier in history people had already progressed enough to understand this. Then religion came along and constrained sexuality again. People are now figuring this all out again and sexuality is becoming less and less relevant.

I'm always asked, "When are the aliens going come to the earth? When are the spaceships going to come? When are other aliens going to come to earth and say hello?" It will be as soon as we can stop judging each other for our sexual identities and different personalities. How can you expect aliens to come down here? God knows if they have a third sex or a fourth or a fifth sex. Who knows if they birth their offspring or have sexual organs? We kill each other already over trivial shit. How can we be expected to be broad minded enough to accept other civilizations that look completely different than us and may have completely different customs than us when we can't get all along?

What happens energetically during group sex?
How is White Cell group sex different from Red Cell group sex?

Okay great! So I opened myself up to this one, didn't I? This is the first time I think I'm blushing. I said, "I can answer all and know all." By answering this, it does not mean I've actually done any group sex. I just happen to know everything from my collective memory of thousands of lives.

Group sex is very interesting. I often think of sex as an exchange of data, of information. I think data can flow. Information flows between a man and a woman during an exchange of sex. I believe that information can be exchanged between two males during sex, and I believe that information can be exchanged between two women when they're having sex. I see it as everybody being a harmonic of frequency that holds their data. What do I always say? Consciousness is your knowledge. When you leave your organic body, there's only one thing you're going to take with you. It's not your car. It's not your dog. It's not your boyfriend or girlfriend. It's not your mother, or your couch; it's not your house. It's your memories, your consciousness. Who you've become is your frequency. It's your vibration.

Consciousness is multi-layered in itself, like the organs of your body. Different weights and values are added to your identity. This is what makes the mass or the flesh of your energy, per se. When two people have intercourse, it is meant originally to create life organically. When you take the life process out of it, and it's just for pure pleasure, for pure sex to dominate, receive, pull in and pull out, there is an exchange of frequency. When you move into a spiritual level, you become masculine and feminine. So, therefore, you're receiving and you're giving, if you really think about it.

When people are with each other and it gets to a point, it doesn't necessarily have to be an orgasm. Let's simplify it and then we can put it into a big salad bowl in a minute. When two people are together, usually there's going to be one dominate person, and that's going to be the stronger of the two. One will usually take the role of the receiver; call it the feminine, if you will. A male can take the feminine role and a female can take the masculine role. We're talking about energy now. If it's spiritual, usually the person who has the lesser energy memory, the lesser energy frequency, gains data from the one with the most energy frequency.

I guess I'll explain it this way. I don't know if you have read *Interview with the Vampire*, but there's a very interesting line there. I don't want to say it's in a negative or positive way. But when a younger person is bitten by an older vampire and draws their blood, they become vampires if the vampire chooses to make them one. He drains the blood. He takes the energy and he gives forth his energy to them, or his blood. Depending on how powerful the vampire is, the power is going to be imbued into the new vampire. So it doesn't mean the young one has to live a hundred years before they obtain a certain amount of power or a certain amount of abilities. The effect is a slingshot up because of the older vampire giving the date of his blood to them. They automatically rise almost to the same level.

So, in essence, there's a little truth in these vampire stories. Anne Rice, of course, did her research. These stories are based on an element of fact. I don't think there's a fairy tale out there that doesn't have some truth to it. I think when they were talking about vampires, they were talking about old souls, and an exchange of energy, including sexual energy. This is what makes it so erotic, the biting and the blood, and how it became vampirism in these stories. But there is an exchange between people and spiritually one can gain power from the other. This is what it's all about. If it's not dominated by just physical sex, there's dominance in an exchange for energy because we're still in a human body. But there's this higher vibrational consciousness going on.

Am I going to get myself in trouble for this! If I was with somebody of lesser energy, and they were with me and they go into this intimate level and there's a lot of emotion and sexual energy, the consciousness is down. The Babbler is saying, "Okay," because it doesn't distinguish between male and female if you're okay with it. It's a merging.

What happens when two people make love? There's a merging. Everybody understands that; it's universal. It's not about penetration. Women understand that it's not just about penetration. With women there's this certain passionate moment that's very much like having two tuning forks, and if you bend one and if the other one is close, it becomes the same pitch. There's a harmony where the frequencies of two become one. Men don't understand that so easily but women understand this. It's one of the advantages they have biologically – the ability to understand this. A woman can find the deep healing she needs mostly only from another woman. A man wants to dominate that healing, whereas a woman doesn't know how to approach it. Only a woman can nurture another woman's spiritual health back. There are certain things that can only come from a man to a man if they have a polarity shift in them and know both sides, then they can do that for one another. So it can be very passionate.

There is an exchange of consciousness at a certain moment, whether it's just before or during the orgasm. But there's a moment that one can go into when two people become one. When you separate, you take a piece of that. It's not a bad piece; it's not like you're taking their energy away. It's an exchange of energy where you learn a different pitch than you knew before. It's as if you learn something from that person. Whenever you make love to somebody, you have their frequency. There's a piece of them that you carry inside that makes that memory inside of your mind. There's something living in them. Anybody you've ever been with, you can say there's something that you carry from that, if you really, really analyze it. It's within you. It's the same thing.

So when you have group sex, it depends on the passion. It depends on the circumstance. Group sex has the potential to be automated and machine-like, which is purely sex at its rawest level. More likely, you would get more energy out of something that's going to be one on one, maybe two with a third making three. If it goes beyond that, there's so many things popping and happening sexually that it keeps you very organic with the whole sex thing rather than letting it become a deeply sexual experience. It can be deeply spiritual but it depends on the mix of people involved and the level of evolution of their mind. If you have a bunch of Red Cells in there, it really becomes less about energy and more about dominance and sex. Whereas, if you get some people that understand energy, they can get into the whole sexual part but there's also something inside of them that feels the exchange, an energy that's happening on another level that makes it very intimate, very sexually intense. Does that help?

Yes.

There's truth and then there's complete truth. It's like *Eyes Wide Shut,* the movie with Nicole Kidman and Tom Cruise. Cruise's character comes across this very elaborate sexual group where participants are masked and identities are hidden. If no one knew who you were, could you really set yourself free? Our society is very constrained in its attitude towards sex. There's a reason for this. If we don't have a certain control over sex, then it's a problem, too.

Society tells us that you can't be with a woman and her sister at the same time because it makes enemies of the sisters. This is envy. They wanted you to be with one person and they wanted to control this for social growth. It was a way to keep men from killing each other. It also kept the women from killing each other because of envy. This was a way to control the sociological order. The ironic thing is that in most systems where they have multiple wives or multiple lovers, they get along amazingly well. In fact, in some ways, these systems are more efficient than your single relationships. So, to me, it always comes down to religion messing everything up. See guys, we used to be able to have ten wives until religion got into it! In either case, there are certain truths.

Are there advantages to having one partner as opposed to having multiple partners?

Well, this is where I can get into to trouble giving one opinion or the other. Everybody wants a sense of security. This is where it all comes from. You want one partner because you're afraid if the second person comes in that they're going to abandon you, or you're getting older and becoming undesirable, or you're not as ideal. So you feel that if you have an equal partner and they're growing old with you, there's a sense of security that is non-competitive. But now, you have to look at it on another token. What if you took a younger partner and you were getting older?

The younger partner could take care of the two of you guys. Or your sense of libido might be a little more driven because you're attracted to a little bit more youthful body. But then, it makes the other one feel like they're in an inferior position or undesirable. Well then, they should get a younger guy. When you look at the economics, having three wives at home to raise all the children gives you six pairs of hands versus two extra pairs of hands. I think there are advantages to everything.

It all comes down to a good working system. Couples that are in pairs of twos can be very isolated sociologically so they become very depressed. They isolate one another. If you have a third or a fourth, it becomes a better social circle. When you have families living all in one house, you have that social aspect so you won't be alone. I think single couple relationships are also under great pressure, especially in this day and age where they deteriorate just as if there was competitiveness. In my opinion, it comes down to the dynamics of the group and how well it is organized to keep things functional.

How about when two people go to swinger clubs?

We have to talk! I guess we needed somebody to be brought in to spice things up! Well, you know what it is? I'll point it out. I think you're a masculine warrior in a woman's body. And you have a very masculine energy within you but it's very powerfully feminine at the same time. You're like an Amazon warrior or Amazon woman. I think you're hunting and I don't find anything wrong with what you're doing. It is no different than what a man would do. If I were going to teach you and work with you, I would teach you as I would a male rather than as I would teach a female. So when you talk about swinger clubs, and this is extra taboo because you're a female, I think this is what excites you because you like breaking rules that you are told not to do.

The reason I asked is because I have a partner that is like that and I go because I am very curious.

And that curiosity usually leads to what?

Knowledge.

Knowledge, which means experience.

I didn't say I don't do it. I do it because I'm very curious. I'm just thanking him for taking me.

That curiosity is good but you're also breaking the taboos as a woman.

I am.

Well, that's a male role though. Now I'm not saying that quite literally. We can argue this all day long but that's a masculine property to go along with. I think a lot of men can get their woman to do those things also.

It's not like he made me do it. I said, "Yes."

I would say this. Do it because you want to do it. If you're saying you're okay with it and you want to investigate it, that's good. But eventually it's probably going to lead to the demise of the relationship with your partner. It's a numbers game. It's going to open up a door where you're going to invite a third person in who is going to be attracted to one of you. But right now, it's equal.

You both are serving the same interest and it's working out for you. But there's a chance there's going to be a third person and you're going to be told, "Well, you need to accept her because I'm in love with her now, too, and I'm in love with you." Now you might get upset and you might not like that, or you might decide to leave the relationship. All I'm saying is, "Nothing is for nothing." Somebody might say, "Well, there you go. That's what a lifestyle like that brings." And I would say, "I know plenty of heterosexuals where a guy is having a relationship on the side regardless and the woman doesn't know about it. In this case, at least she knows about it. There are also cases where the female is having relationships and the guy has no idea about it. At least, there's honesty." So I don't like it when people try to get mightier than thou and say, "Well this is the way it is. They lead a bad life." At least, they're honest. That's the bottom line. We're talking now about sex in the sense of exploring it rather than the sense of sex in energy and frequency. So, I think, it's almost getting a little off topic.

I want to check out the energy there. What's going on?

In that situation, you're dealing with a lot of Red Cells, so it just breaks down to raw sex. If you like it, go for it. Explore it and enjoy it while you can but be careful. Be sensible. Be reasonable. And once you have your fill, then you can decide what you want to do with your life. I don't think it is right for everybody. Everybody has a different approach to it.

I don't even think it's so right. It was good the two times I've been there but it's not like I want to go there every week.

Right. I think it is okay to explore but with caution and reservation. I would probably not approve of my students doing that because I don't want their energy so concentrated in the sexual arena. I don't want them to become so grounded out that it's all about sex, sex, sex! I want them to explore the intimacy between relationships, the energy exchange and the dynamics of that, rather than the rawness of just having sex.

Were there schools in the past that used group sexual activity to enhance consciousness?

Well, let's break it down. I don't think an exchange of information can happen if it's not two White Cells. I probably haven't said that. If it's between a White Cell and a Red Cell, it's unlikely the exchange can happen because the Red Cell doesn't have the capability to absorb the data. So it's nullified. If it's between two Red Cells, it isn't going to happen. It's sex so it's either about creating a child or it's just fucking. If it's between two White Cells, it's about sex and intimacy just like it would be for anybody else, but there is an exchange spiritually because they're both in this understanding. White Cells have a sense of feeling energy and a sense of recognizing it.

Red Cells don't recognize it. It's not a function that exists for them. At some point, White Cells can consciously choose to become aware of it but that is an act of will. That's where our training comes in. All of a sudden, we can consciously breathe it, feel it and move into those higher levels of the sexual experience because we can consciously ride with it. I call it surfing it. You're working with it. Whereas, people who just have sex or it's just about sex, they don't stop for a moment to really feel the energy. Sometimes, in the very beginning, I'd have to say maybe some Red Cells do. It can get pretty intense. But I don't think they really recognize it as energy so it dissipates.

Could you use the group sex activity as a form of teaching?

Yes, you can but it's extremely difficult. I hate to say this because it probably puts me in a questionable position, but I think a lot of gurus exploit their students. Without a doubt, they're indulging themselves sexually. But I also think it's a puritan concept largely from western cultures that makes it so taboo that the teacher shouldn't be having sex with the students. This again gets into Christianity, because if you look at what you were bringing up earlier, a lot of this was a non-issue. It became a Puritan thing like, "Oh! Taboo!" I think it's mainly jealousy between students and non-students who are getting it and who aren't getting it. There's a feeling of who is getting ahead and who's not.

There's always motivation when it comes to sex. There's always a plot. There's always a scheme. Can there be group sex where there's an enormous amount of energy involved? Absolutely yes, but the likelihood of that happening is extremely unlikely. Once you start to get beyond three, which is the maximum number, in my opinion, I think it becomes over complicated. Even three people are a lot for some people to take into consideration, let alone the configurations working here for sex.

When it gets into group sex, it's too easy once it goes beyond three, which is the threshold to control the experience, and it becomes too much of a meat market, even for White Cells. We are still organic. We still function with lust. We still get turned on erotically by the erotic environment. So when it becomes so many varieties and so many people coming at it from different moments, it's not unison. It's too many rhythms going on and it's chaotic, and it just becomes about sex, sex, sex! So I think it's certainly possible but I would probably say it would not be something I would encourage anybody to pursue. It would be a waste. Maybe that helps, in some way, to answer your earlier question.

So that's pretty much what happened to Tantric Yoga, meaning the spiritual practice of sexual yoga, in the modern age?

Tantric yoga is basically a form of mysticism that was developed purely based on the concept of sex and sexual energy. In my very strong opinion, it was truly developed to exploit sex by people who wanted to be spiritual but could not control their heterosexual drive for sex. They wanted both so they created tantric sex to exploit females and say, "I'm still a spiritual teacher."

One of my students asked me whether we could envelop heterosexual sex as a form of spiritualism. He said that, "This is good and it's going to take us spiritually." In fact, that's not the case at all, but they cannot let go of such a powerful heterosexual drive when they realize that it's going to ferment them in the Doe. Again there's this delicateness between having a lover and having it be spiritual and equalized. In this case, it is a heterosexual male who wants to be spiritual, but he wants to completely dominate the female. That is no longer being spiritual. That is no longer being a White Cell. And they're trying to present it any way they can because in their mind they just can't jive it any other way. So there's a big problem; there's a big conflict there.

How do you move beyond that? How do you train yourself? How do you approach that?

I knew I was going to get hit with this one. The second that I say what I'm going to say, it's going to put me into a noose of trouble and I know this. But my job is to be as absolutely honest as I can be or I'm cheating people. You have to train your mind. Your sexual identity is rooted very deeply in your mind. And if I'm going to say, "You should explore sexually in your mind with the same sex," now I'm going to be accused of being a gay spiritual teacher trying to get all my students to become gay and fuck them all up. It's not the case at all.

The bottom line is this, "If you are a very heterosexual male, don't go out and do it. But *fantasize* and try to introduce a male into your sexuality as if you could be intimate with them, whether you're controlling the other male or whatever. I would really suggest basically having a female in your fantasy with a second male. You don't have to do anything with them but it's the first way to introduce that concept, that energy because the brain is so highly geared for sexual orientation. Again, it is absolutely the most dominating, driving force for procreation in your body, in your mind. Therefore, it ferments how you think and how you perceive. It's what dominates your hemispheres.

As I said in the very beginning, you are half woman and half man organically. Even men have lactated. You're not going to lactate nor is a woman going to start producing sperm. It is more in the mind. Sex is up there in your mind; it's not down in the groin. So if you want to convert your energy to be more balanced, you have to decide, "Am I more masculine? Am I more feminine?" If you're a feminine guy, then you're going to have to try to become more masculine. You just have to find out your polarity - what you desire. Having said that, the best and fastest way would be to literally fantasize about the same sex *in your mind*. It's like a train stopping and just building up. It's going to be hard for you to tackle intellectually and say, "I can't believe what you're asking me to do." Well, as I've always said from the very beginning, if it's what you expected, then it's probably not worth shit to understand. Or if it doesn't challenge your thinking, or it doesn't hit you in a certain way like, "Ah!" If it's what you expected, then everybody would be enlightened. It is in the curves and the turns. It's in between finding the hidden truths that are going to get you to breakthrough.

If it was a woman and she's very feminine, I would say fantasize about another woman. Bring another woman into your fantasy. Be salaciously lustful or take it gently and see how it stimulates your consciousness. It will affect you in your everyday life. You will feel a different kind of empowerment because you're almost taking on the masculine role. Or, pretend in your mind that you're a male with a female and that you're pleasuring them. In your fantasy, if it's a woman and you're a woman and you're pretending you are the male, you're going to discover stuff about yourself because you're going to mirror your desires. The only difference is that you're going to see what those inner desires are because you're not physically doing it. You're going to fool yourself to release inner desires, but it's the brain. It's the little electrons turning on engines in your brain that you've never turned on before. It's like pulling the cloaks off the dusty machinery and firing it up. And then you think, "I've never perceived it this way."

You have the mechanism for everything. As an entity, as a soul, are you a man or are you a woman? Well, if you're a White Cell and you're trying to reach enlightenment in this body, the most powerful, gravitating, Doe-ifying thing, the best way would be to throw it off guard. Would it not? The one thing that holds you in your identity is your sexual role as a human being. And the fastest way to convert you into a spiritual frequency is to challenge the very thing that says this is your identity and role in this life, in this moment, and say, "No, It's not! And I'll jack it all up if I have to." That's what you're doing. You're challenging it. And by challenging it, you're turning on the other hemisphere of the brain, which means your consciousness. That would be your feminine aspect. It can now utilize that part of the organic brain where before it was in a stasis because you had to choose an identity role of frequency. This is why all spiritual teachers seem very feminine and masculine all at the same time. They get it.

So by fantasizing, pardon the pun, it's a way to stimulate your brain to go, "What the hell?" And be like, "I've never thought about it." It's going to fight your inner being. It's going to be like, "I can't accept this! I don't want this! Blah!" And either you're going to get past it or you're not. Now does it mean I would stop teaching you because you can't handle this concept? Of course, I would still teach you. But if you want to *accelerate*, if you want to push for breakthroughs, and you're willing to shock yourself intensely to do this, that would be the way to begin. Shock your inner brain by introducing other sensory in the brain that is actually capable of experiencing it, and you're forcing it to create a hologram of an experience which makes it almost surrealistically real. And then, all of a sudden, it has to turn those hemispheres of the brain on. In my opinion, you are now using both hemispheres just like all these other geniuses throughout history have been doing.

So the idea is to shock the brain to get it to work with the complete soul, dimensionally, that you are because you're not a man; you're not a woman. You're both, but you're neither – just like God. And when you hit that frequency, how can you approach God's frequency? When you hear the Aums and you hear the ringing that comes in, that is perfect pitch. *It's what you're trying to learn without learning that you're really learning what I'm trying to say*. Did anybody catch what I just said? It's teaching you about harmony. If you're out of harmony, you're not in sync. If you're in harmony, you're harmonized. You're one. Do you understand?

Your frequency is not male or female. God is not a male or female; it is both frequencies. You can't approach that harmonic in your one half, fifty percent frequency. You have to be both frequencies. So if you want to do it now, you're going to have to somehow break the system into working. You have to get your brain to somehow fool and just cope and then break through the programming, society wise, that you've accepted. You have to get past the fears and the control of, "If you do this you'll be outcast, you'll be unwanted! You're bad, you're evil! Let's stone him or stone her!" That's what's holding you in place spiritually.

If you can mess with your harmonics organically, it spiritually allows you to come more into pitch. When you get pitch, you then have harmony. You have the Aum with the second ringing in there that's actually one. And then you can enter into the frequency of God because now you don't have to be dead without an organic body in order to do it. You can harmonize with this ultra-powerful frequency and bring it into this body and channel it out being able to do the miracles that the masters were able to do. They harnessed the frequency from God. But they have to be in harmonics organically to do it. You're in harmonics when you're not organic. When you're energy, you match the frequency.

When you get old, you take on the opposite role of your gender. Women cut their hair shorter; they start to put trousers on. They start taking the masculine roles after they've gone through menopause. Men do the same thing only it's not as evident, but they will take on feminine roles and start doing stuff like gardening or feminine roles that are more personified. Or they get more emotional, more talkative, and more contemplative; whereas a woman's had enough of that their whole life and they start to get sterner in their energy. That's preparing you for the death cycle already. You're trying to beat the punch.

Women would never admit it but they are attracted to other attractive and youthful women. Older men are attracted to younger men because they esteem and see the physical beauty of their youth and lustily desire to have it. But that's actually the harmonics in them preparing for the death cycle. It's not about being nasty. It just gets that way because you're still in the body. This is what no one will talk about. This is the big secret. I'll be crucified for saying all this. "Motive! He must have a motive behind it!" It is the truth. *It is the truth*!

So if you want to get yourself to accelerate spiritually, you need to understand that there are tricks that have been around for thousands of years. This is nothing new. This has been done for thousands of years with gurus and teachers. They know what the deal is. They teach it to very select groups of people. If you go into the colleges and dig into their research, you'll find slivers of it, but you have to know what you're looking for. And then, all of a sudden, it's going to become very obvious.

So just to summarize, masturbate to mystery partners of your less inclined preference whether you're gay or straight. If you're heterosexual, fantasize more about same sex partners to balance that.

Your brain is organic; you can teach yourself anything. If you introduce something slowly enough into your psyche, you can overcome certain things. So that's what you want to do. If you have issues with that, then bring in a female to your imagination with a male. Find ways of introducing it slowly, depending on your comfort level. It will have an effect on you. I guarantee it. It will have an effect on you. You will find that, as a male, you're much more comfortable. You're much more at peace. That's the feminine quality that the masculine needs in order to reach enlightenment.

The women let their emotions go out of control. They need the masculine aspect to control it, to dominate it. Then they find inner peace. They balance the part that's out of balance. And that's what we're doing when we're looking for partners in life.

We're just trying to do it physically. In truth, it doesn't really work that way. We're really trying to do a reflection of what our soul is trying to fix. It's just stuck in a body that's chemically telling it that it has to be one way or the other. If you don't want to take energy or give your energy away, think about an imaginary opposite sex also. Keep that in mind; we covered that when I was talking about that brain thing. You have options!

What if you're a guy and you're masturbating to a picture of somebody you've never met before, or something like that?

That's fine. A picture isn't going to do it even if it's on TV. You must have been physically near them before. You can take energy from someone you've been in close proximity to. For instance, you can get somebody's frequency from a hug, if you really pull it in. You can draw it in even from this distance. I always have to be very mindful of my energy with all the people that I meet because they're very fixated on me and I'm a great energy source for everybody. It's the truth.

The bottom line is that if it's somebody from a magazine, you don't have that frequency lock because a magazine isn't going to give it to you. Although, as you get more, I hate to use the word powerful, there will come a point where you have to be careful. I can certainly look at pictures and scan their eyes and lock into their frequency.

What about if you're masturbating to try and draw someone's energy? Is there someone that would be more ideal that you'd want to look for to do that with?

This getting into psychic warfare, or vampirism now because now we're talking about taking energy and choosing who that person's going to be. If somebody doesn't willfully open themselves up to an energy exchange and you're just taking it and not giving back to them, then it's dominance and a control factor. So, just keep this in mind about energy: be careful what you ask for. If you choose somebody that has a really crappy personality, you can take that quality into your own body because you're not trying to filter it out. So you should try to be more cautious about doing something like that.

About the psychic warfare, if you're a woman and you're masturbating and you're saying, "Take the energy. Get the energy!" Is there ever a point where it becomes psychic vampirism? Should they worry about that or not?

Well, a woman generally takes energy. It's not very often that they'll give it. But when they do give it, it is quite profound. But it usually comes in the terms of the nurturer. They will give their energy to a male, a child, or even to a woman in a programmed sense of nurturing. It's less negative than a man's intentions. Usually, it's more life giving and empowering. It's done in such a way that it becomes very organic rather than spiritual, but some women can become advanced enough that they can make it spiritual. That takes training.

If a woman takes the energy from a guy, it absolutely would be psychic vampirism. Remember what I said about a little truth in every myth, and the stories of the succubus? They were the daughters of Lucifer, and they would come in the night. They would sexually ride the men and basically seduce them. I think that women were lusting for certain men and were so psychically engulfed by it. You have to remember, women were cooped up then. So it was a very powerful passionate thing rather than, "Oh, I think I'm going to get horny and masturbate to somebody." I think they literally connected. The men were also very sensitive to sex because they were so restrained. They were told spiritually that they weren't able to masturbate. They weren't able to have sex. When it happened, it was very intense for them. And they psychically linked up, immensely. So yes, it could be a certain level of a psychic attack. Absolutely.

What about people who masturbate to bigger things like solar systems or galaxies or even atoms or molecules?

I think that is excellent. Most people don't have the ability to fantasize that much. They're so stuck in the organic level of the idea of sex being a penis or a vagina. It's very hard for them to go beyond all that. But if they were capable of doing that they could take in enormous amounts of energy. It takes a more advanced Navigator to hold that level of sustaining one's direction with it.

Can a male and female having tantric sex navigate to other dimensions?

Yeah, right. When you get two people who have progressed and are very spiritually trained, if they can sustain the sexual intensity and prolong it, then they can enter those levels. It doesn't just have to be man and woman. In other words, there are different moments in sex. There's the initiation of sex. There's the intimacy. There's the heating up of it. Most people are in the body at that point and they remain in the body of pleasure. They don't realize that there's a different level of pleasure also going on that's interwoven with it. They're only seeing the body. If they could go to the outer-woven, they could let their mind ride while their body was busy. So if you can learn to do that, you can then move your consciousness up here, let the body automate and you're on a different level. This is when you're moving into these higher frequencies, if you will. Now you have to be able to move. And it takes a second person because one is the boat; one is the wind. Together, you move. So, in essence, you can use your mind then to fold time and fold space, if you can sustain that.

Most people don't understand that they think it has to take place over a great length of time. The actuality is if you go to that place it'll be very, very, very intense but, it would be a very long time condensed into a very short moment. When you're done you're like, "Holy shit!" and you're just reeling. Not that I want to claim my intensity or not, but there's many people who've been intimate with me and it's been so intense on that level that they literally think they're going to get up and walk away and they collapse to the ground. The whole room is just vibrating, or they'll see everything vibrating molecularly. There's data there. Their brain can't process it. You need your higher consciousness and you need to come down and go into a meditative state so that it can unfold. The second you have thought, it's too clunky and it binds it. The body can't cope with it very well but it will cope and it will empower you. The more you can train and calm yourself to absorb it after the fact, you can actually re-experience where you just went. Time changes.

What about having sex with entities?

Well, the problem with having sex with entities is that a lot of entities are the problem, not you. There is a certain need or envy of the organic body. You're grounded, so it's like electricity in a plug. They're not grounded because they don't have an organic body at the same time. So when the intimacy of the energy fields combine, there's not a sexual organic sense for them. So to match your frequency from where you're starting and from where they're at, it makes it extremely difficult and unlikely, unless you were just energy. When it's just energy, there's not a sense of sex as we understand it.

Sex, for the most part, is very organic because we're in organic bodies. It's biochemically initiated. As entities, we have a constant orgasm of pleasure. It's very different. You exist at that level. When you meet another being, you combine and there's an immense amount of pleasure, but you don't have an organ or a place in your body where it's coming from. It's an ecstatic vibration. To explain it in human terms is almost impossible because we relate it, all the time, to our body and how we feel. So it's possible but it's very, very, very difficult. It's not too much different than to say that one can make their energy move to another person. It's happening much like a succubus, but the difference is that you still have a platform in this dimension, which is your organic body. So the entity is going through certain motions but you're operating on this other level.

If a woman is masturbating and there is no man or woman around, and you 'call' somebody ...

You invoke.

You invoke and you feel it.

You're just putting it out there as if saying, "I'm open, come get me. I don't care who it is but I need somebody to ride the stallion, somebody good. But if you're not qualified, you're out! I don't want to waste my time!" Well, you're opening up your energy then so you want to be very careful. When you have an open invitation, you don't want somebody to come along that you don't want. There are plenty of people on the Darkside that would seize that opportunity in a second.

You can feel it in a second.

Yeah, but it may be too late! You definitely want to watch what kind of energy is approaching you. You don't want to just say, "Bring it on!" because you want to play. Sometimes, you might play with something a bit too intense. Let's imagine. What if I was a bad guy? And I see a little snack. "Oh, you want me to come and play? I'll come and play, but I'm taking everything." Do you understand?

I would never do such a thing but there are very intense beings out there. If you're putting that message out there, they are going to want to come and take this energy from you. How will that affect you physically? It could affect your health. It could affect you with aging. It can affect you with your psychology where, all of a sudden, you become depressed and you don't know why. They take something from you. That's why you have to be very careful and very selective. When you ride, you better be the winner. So always size it up. There's no shame in saying, "No, I changed my mind." That's the point. You have to know to say, "No, I changed my mind!" Okay? That's my advice.

Can two astral probes have a sexual encounter?

Yeah. It's just sex differently. It's much cleaner. It's very different but, you can project it back. If you have sex in a dream, it has very much the same properties. You're still dealing with an inner dimension or you could be dealing in a reality but you just haven't accepted that reality. And your body simply reacts to it as if it was, touch sensory, the real deal. That's all that's happening. So, it's still good in the end. Maybe some of the properties of how much energy is exchanged would be lesser because there's less proximity of closeness. That's the only difference. Whenever you're in close physical proximity, again, it's like my dominating energy versus somebody else. Mine is very dominating because of the intensity of it. But hopefully you would want that energy because it's like the vampire issue, "Bring it on!" But it's literally like a tuning fork. One has no vibe; if you bang the other one, it's going to take on that vibe. If this one has a higher bang and this one has a lower bang, which one is it going to mimic? Is it going to go down or is it going to go up to the higher one? It's going to take the dominant. Do you see? It's no different.

Speaking of proximity, what about a man and a woman sleeping in the same room? What happens to the energy when you do this?

For a dozen reasons, I think that a man and woman should either have a king size bed and have the extra, or they should have separate beds in the same room. The very best would be to have separate rooms. I think it makes for a much longer sexual life, a much more appreciated life. You will find that the relationship lasts a lot longer. When you're lying in bed constantly with the opposite polarity of what you are, you will find that there's a mingling of the two and you become very similar as one another. You can get bored of one another, but the energy can also draw and fight. In your sleep, you can have battles with your energy. It can overload into the day and there's anxiety towards one or the other. It all has to do with the psychic energy.

I think the whole idea of a man and woman sleeping in the same bed is horrible. It's horrible spiritually. It's horrible physically. It's good for a while when you're passionate. But there's a point where you know that it's time to have a little bit of space. Having space makes you appreciate one another when you see each other. When you're around each other 24/7, you tend to become immune sociologically to each other, like you don't really appreciate each other as much. When you have space, you keep your identity. So when you see each other, you tend to really enjoy each other's company more. This all comes down to energy in the end.

Very heterosexual people, that are very Red Cell, insist on sleeping together. I honestly think that's mainly for insecurity reasons. They need a sense of feeling secure. That's why they tend to need a partner consistently in the same bed with them. It's a nurturing thing. It's a lot of things. I could go on and on. It's always better spiritually and psychically to not sleep in the same bed, especially if you're at a point where you're really working on your energy. You don't want to sleep in the same bed because you're expanding so rapidly and your consciousness is so open.

Now you have somebody with a lower tonal lying right next to you and their energy is going to have an effect on you, if you consistently let it keep rubbing on you. Sorry for the pun.

How often should couples spend some nights together? What's an average number you would put out there?

What are you saying? Like how many times should you have sex in a week? If it's hot and passionate, go for it! Get it on for a week or two and just guard your energy. But at some point, you have to say, "Alright, we need to lean it up a little bit." Be hot and passionate when it's hot and passionate. But when it starts to be just about sex like, "Oh, I've got a boner. Let's fuck!" or, "I feel like doing it," then it isn't about sex any more. It's just a function. When you're not holding each other and there's no kissing or feeling deep in your chest that you need to be holding her, it's just someone that you're fucking. Well, go jerk off or go masturbate because you're starting to act like an organism.

When you get to that point as a White Cell, you just have to know, "Now I'm just functioning. It's not about passion anymore." Some people will say, "My passion can last a long time." Then let it ride. It'll pass. Then you have to look at the relationship from a different perspective. And spiritually you have to say, "Now's the time for me to get back to business." When you feel hot and heavy, you might want to jerk off for a while; get it out of your system. Work it out.

Then, all of a sudden, you'll continuously see your partner in that light of beauty. Then you can go with them and maybe do it once a week, instead of once every other week or once a month. When it wears off a little bit, wait a month and then do it. Ironically, women sometimes need it more than men. Sometimes men need it more than women. You have to know the other's needs. But whenever you're giving into those needs, you also have to understand you're making sacrifices on your energy, too. So you have to weigh it all out. Abstinence does not mean no sex indefinitely. It just means you value the sexual relationship rather than just making it an organic function. Your relationship will be doomed if that's all it becomes. It'll come out in how you treat each other and how the relationship functions because the other person then becomes just an object. You might say, "Well, how can I always keep the passion going?" When you shut yourself down for a few weeks, they get real hot looking very fast again. And then you are like, "Oh yeah, I'm taking you out for dinner now! We're going to have a good time!" That's what it is.

You said guard your energy during sex. Is there any way for a man to stop the energy from leaving or the energy from being lost?

If you can find a woman that can do what I'm going to say, then you can have all the sex you want. If you can find a man that can do this, you can have all the sex that you want, too. As the moment is getting more intense, there is an energy exchange. The energy exchange usually becomes more intense within about fifteen seconds before the orgasm and during the orgasm. Then usually after, it's a quick drop of about five seconds to maybe ten or fifteen in some people. Totally, there's about a minute and a half cycle where the energy is at a critical point that's happening before, during and after the orgasm.

For a woman, if they can knowingly think of their energy in the groin area and just push it down, that's all it would take. Almost take it but think about that area. It's as if they are tightening a muscle, or as if they are just saying, "No." But the guys try to push through that wall and they're saying, "Well, why not let it in?" I'm not saying push the penis out. Energy-wise you just want to hold back a little bit. You almost want to push consciously as if your energy is saying, "No." And that's usually enough to prevent a great loss of energy in the male.

That's like taking a spoonful of food when you're really hungry and chewing it and then deciding to spit it out. Your body wants the swallowing mechanism. Doesn't it feel a bit awkward to spit it out? But you could. You need to have an intentional purpose to do that. It's only easy to spit out food when it tastes bad. Then it's not a problem, just like the man's energy. It's easier to not take a man's energy that you don't want to be with. That's whose energy you should take in the first place. There's never a win-win situation in this dimension.

It's just like a guys' energy. It's easier to not take the guy's energy that you don't want to be with, but that is the guy you should take the energy from to begin with. Do you get what I'm saying? There's never a win-win situation in this dimension. I swear! For a man, it's the same thing. If you don't want to give your energy, at the moment of orgasm, you almost have to intentionally withdraw. Well, it goes against *everything*, organically, you're designed to do. It's the same thing for a male. When you have that moment of orgasm, you almost have to breathe in and focus as if it's your chakra pulling in as you're ejaculating out to get it up in there. It's extremely difficult. You can have all the sex you want if you can find a partner who's doing the same thing. Between the two of you, there will be no energy loss whatsoever.

So you mentioned it's like a lose/lose situation, like there's no easy route.

Sex is designed for procreation to create a life form. When lesbians or gay males have sex, the energy they exchange can't create new life. It's like trying to get a river to flow backwards. It can be done, but it takes greater discipline because there are negative and positive polarities.

When two females have sex, the energy is not neutralized because the mechanism isn't there. The energy knows it can't do that, so it creates a nurturing cycle. With two women, there is a need to be loved.

Anyway, with women it's very different than guys. A woman, in my mind, has a need to be loved. It's extremely rare to find a man who can really love a woman. Usually, the men who can do that usually have a very balanced quality about them. Most masculine men that women are attracted to don't have that balanced polarity, so they're constantly trying to pull emotion from them. In many cases, when a woman makes love to a man, she wants to have an emotional experience. A man wants the woman to have an emotional experience, too, but it's based upon where he's commanding her to go. It's like a symphony and he's going to control it. A woman isn't trying to control it. She is trying to get the man to release it. It's very hard to explain. I don't know if you understand where I'm going with that or not.

When a woman gets together with another woman, it's not that they can't be sexual. It's not like that for them. They can fall in love just from touching one another, not even stroking the vagina. Men have a very difficult time understanding this. There is an exchange of beauty. It's like when they reach out and they move; it's something that only a woman can really feel.

They try to get the same experience from a man but it's very hard to get it. But if they allow another woman to give them that nurturing, it can really heal their soul. A woman's soul is very beat up in life because of man's energy. Yet, women endure it. They're always the sufferers, enduring pain. When they give birth, it's painful. They're so used to pain that they find coping mechanisms. There is a certain energy that can come from them being with another woman. They become very spiritual and very balanced because they're not constantly having that other dominating energy on them. Do you see what I am saying? But organically, if they're straight, they're going to be just like the rest of us. We're all prone to do organically what we're designed to do.

If you can break out of that, there's a lot of very intense passion that can come from two women. They can literally have an orgasm without even touching those body parts. They can really let their minds go there, but it has to be a very intimate moment for them. And if men could learn that, well then they would have very satisfied women. They could do anything they want afterwards. But they don't get it. It's all about rush through sex, hit it and, "Yeah, didn't I make you feel wonderful!" "Yeah, sure you did." So it's about perception.

With two males, it's different and there's a different kind of energy that comes from it. Usually the males will eventually relax with it instead of dominating. They don't feel the sense of energy or the need to dominate. Usually one of them takes on the dominating role. For the first time, they accept the role of the feminine which is the same thing that's happening between two women. One is going to bring the other one there. They just know how to go there, the same way two men would go. You have to reverse it. If you let the male take you there, it's not a docile role. It's not like, "Bend over; let them hit your ass," or something. That's not what it's about. And for the record, there is no chakra on your ass. Okay? You're after energy; this is not what you're interested in. If you want to go there, go there but we need to cover everything here. It's a little bit simpler than that. For two males, it's about the other one almost relaxing, allowing them to find more feminine quality inside of them. They find that they could still be dominating with the women, but they like this other place, too. Of course, it's turning on the other hemisphere of the brain intensely. For the females, it's turning on the other hemisphere of the brain intensely.

Two heterosexuals can't do that because all the equipment is designed for a specific function. Now, you could say, "Well, how do we know that this is acceptable?" Some people say, "Well, nature says, 'It's the birds and the bees.'" Bullshit! Look at the research that's been suppressed. Almost eighty-five percent of animals sexually prefer the same sex. This is just coming out now. Dolphins are bisexual. They have to come together seasonally for the mating period and do it. When they break up it's not like, "I want to hang with my woman." It's not like, "I want to hang with my man." They want to hang with the sociological one that they prefer. And they're having sex or copulating. And this goes for the females and the males, not just one or the other. And all this research now is coming out.

So what does that say? It says predominantly that the heterosexual dominant alpha males control the media. They control the science communities. They control religion and they're really controlling what's acceptable and what's not. And that's what's training the vast community, rather than giving people the truth and the facts. So if you want the truth, I'm going to give it to you. Whether you want to hear it or not; whether you want to discern and argue it forever and ever, that's up to you. I'm telling you these are the things I believe. You don't have to believe me. You can go do whatever you want to do. All I know is, "I'm enlightened. You're not."

The bottom line is do as you will, whatever your comfort level is. Certainly never, ever do anything that you don't feel comfortable with. And don't let somebody take advantage of you or exploit you. There are plenty of people who definitely just want to play with your package, or whatever, and they will in a heartbeat. They'll tell you anything under the sun in order to do it, so use rational common sense. Feel your heart and go with things slowly. But there are certain advantages.

I'm probably going to get in trouble for this, too. Look at the situation of the disciples. If you think nothing was going on, I keep saying to you guys, "Think again." They knew. It's the same reason why I have preferences that I choose if I'm going to have a relationship; I've already explained this. I have sexual interest, just like anybody else does. And if any guru, any spiritual teacher, any priest tells you they don't, they're full of it. At least, I'm honest.

I make a conscious choice because of my understanding of polarities. Believe me, I can go towards women like a raving maniac. It's about me needing to be in a certain place. And it's not to say that I don't dabble occasionally, and I shouldn't even put that out there. There's a reason behind the madness, and there is logic behind it. Everybody has to find their comfort level and their level of understanding. My libido certainly is not what it used to be. I'm at the point now in life where I'm just not even interested in it physically. I don't know; maybe I've just done it all ten thousand times so I don't care any more. But it is what it is. Those are the things that you have to understand. That's your triangle; there's your magic number, again three, and it is what it is.

Are there advantages or disadvantages in staying alone and not having a relationship?

I honestly think that people should have a partner. Life is tough. We live in an organic world and there are certain demands. If you have a good community and you're really at peace with the idea, I think it's okay. It's better to find a partner who is going to work with you, and putting your energy into finding the right person and making it work. Trying to be on your own can be just as challenging. Now, I'm not against it and I'm not for it. All I'm saying is that if you choose not to have a partner, I'd say it's a nine out of ten chance you're going to fail. It's that high, spiritually, because you're going to be fighting so much with looking or denying or suppressing your sexual need for a partner. Do you see what I'm saying? Again, sex is one of the most powerful drives.

I think it's better to find another White Cell and have a reasonable understanding of your expectations of life. You need to ask questions like, "Do you want kids or not? If you have a kid, how many kids are you going to want? How do you want to raise them? How do you want to work it? Will you respect my need for spiritualness? Will you give me a sabbatical once a month for a few days? Will you give me my time? I'll give you your time. I'll watch the kid." Most guys won't keep their word about watching the kid. So ladies, you need to have a good contract. Find somebody you can work with because the biggest factor is sex. If you can find a partner, sex gets old.

Having a relationship isn't about sex. It's about having a partner and someone that you can count on. If you get sick and you're in bed and you're ill, you need to know that person is going to bring the bedpan to your bed. They're going to wipe your ass; they are going to wipe your face. They're going to bring you your medicine. They are going to nurture you back to health. That's a partner. That somebody's going to be there when you're down and low and be able to bring you back up. You want a partner. I don't want my students to be single in life; it's tough. The sex will get old. It's only if you're bouncing around a lot that you're constantly getting yourself back in the same pickle. Find some-body that you can work with and have a relationship with. Then the sex gets old and you're not wasting your energy anymore because she's like, "I'm not interested. Just leave me alone." And you're like, "Oh, I'll go jerk it off."

Well, now we have something here. You can have your own space, your own bedrooms or a king-size bed. Or you can have a certain understanding. I think you could say, "No, this is my partner in life. We have a contract to take care of one another, to look out for one another and to achieve a common goal in life. And this is our particular spiritual path and it is strengthening us because we both believe in it. We both agree on it, and it upholds our beliefs. I'm supportive of it." It should be good.

There's going to be ups and downs in a relationship; it is what it is. So, you can have your cake and eat it, too. I think it really comes down to the same thing for anything spiritual. It takes effort. If you have effort, you can achieve anything spiritually. And some people would say, "Well, historically, guru masters went off and separated and left their wives and their family." Well, you know something? We live in a modern age and things are very different now. You can take your guru along with you on your mp3 player. There you go.

So I think it's about making a relationship work instead of trying to find excuses to dissolve the relationship because it's not fitting your spiritual needs. You need to have a partner that is saying, "I'm compassionate and understanding of it but you can't be over-demanding of those needs and change them on me every month because now it's just about you gratifying yourself and making it work for you instead of contributing to the rela-tionship." You have to make it work. Women are at a disadvantage. They end up having kids and it changes their energy field; they're about producing life. It's very hard to focus on your spirituality when you have to focus on taking care of a child, creating a place for the child that's safe, and making sure they are nurtured.

Then the guy's like, "Well, that's all good but I don't want it." Now I can see a conflict. So, it means that the other person has to be conscientious of that and say, "I'm a spiritual person and part of being spiritual is being compassionate and being there through this." There has to be compassion from the person that's carrying the child that has to say back, "I understand that you need some time for your spirituality and I don't want to dominate it but as long as I feel secure that you're helping me and you're there for me, I won't have a problem with your needs."

It's all about being reasonable. That's what it comes down to. I think you can get everything you want. It's funny; we focus on females wanting it because they're the most vulnerable, but males want it too. As long as your partner can feel a sense of security and you can reinforce that security, that you're not going to abandon them over your path, I don't think you'll have much of a problem. They'll be like, "Have your own room. I expect you to be home on Friday nights for dinner, and I expect a good sex session at least by ten o'clock at night before I get tired." There's a reasonable level to everything. It's just about working that out. I think one wants a partner. The secret is finding the right partner. I want all of my students to find a partner but I want that partner to be the right person, someone who is not going to suppress them or make them feel bad. When you find the right one, don't be so quick to throw it away. If it's semi-working, make it work more so.

Are there some areas like advanced Black Box techniques in your knowledge, in your teaching, that require longer than a three-day sabbatical?

Well, guys have been doing this to women for millennia. They go off to war in the Military Services for months at a time. Women don't like it but it depends. Men can be selfish and be like, "I'm leaving for whatever," when they really just want to get away. It depends on each person. The funny thing is that a guy can go on a sabbatical but often a woman feels guilty if she wants to go on sabbatical. That's what is unfair. If the man leaves on sabbatical for a week, then the woman should have a week to go on sabbatical while the man is stuck with the kids. I think that is fair. Do unto others as you would want done unto yourself. You just have to make it fair. You both had a kid; you're 50/50.

So, it's just convenience. If you don't want to have kids and you're in a relationship where you both don't want that, fine. If you go on sabbatical because you want to focus on your spirituality, fine. If that person's spiritual, then you need to do the same. If they're not spiritual, and they are in a relationship where they're allowing you to have this and they're not making you feel guilty over it, then you have to still give back their week and let them go to the Bahamas with their girlfriend. And you have to trust them that they're not out slutting around, because that'd be the first thing you'd say to control them. It's trust. They don't know if you're slutting around.

I'm being honest here. They could be sleeping with a guru. The bottom line is trust. It's understanding that if you know the deal, they know the deal, too. You both agree and understand that; then you have to keep your word and you'll have it all.

There's a couple that I know who are both White Cells but they're a bit on the New Age side. I knew them out in California when I lived in Tujunga. His name was John. I don't remember her name but it was a very interesting name. They both had to be in their seventies. And they both had spunk. They invited me to their house once. They had the ultimate house in a residential area in California. They had a strip piece of land with a big fence around it and it was in a foresty area. There was a little creek that went through the whole property. They had a lot of big crystals all over the place because he had a big crystal business.

As you walked into the property, to the right there was a workshop. There were all sorts of wood carvings and crystals, and then you went further down and the house was down there. It wasn't a big house. It was a regular size house. Down a little bit further on the left was another little house, a small one, the same size as the first one, and it had all sorts of painting and artistry stuff. One was her space; one was his space, and they lived together in the middle and they had a perfect relationship spiritually. I found their energy very, very balanced. So, it showed me that it is absolutely capable of being done. They both had a very good understanding of each other's energy. They both understood each other's space. And I found them about equal in a lot of the things. Certain ones took on the roles and they were in unison and I thought it was a very good working system.

In the end, ten-to-one, you're going to end up alone. One of you is going to die before the other person does. I often think about the saying that women have to put up with men's shit their whole lives; so when the man dies ten years before the woman does, in general, the woman gets her last ten years to whoop it up.

When you focus on your female energy, it gives you a certain feeling. Male energy also gives you a certain feeling. When you have the desire to combine both, it gives you a very gratifying feeling in your sexual chakra.

Well, it's a very gratifying feeling in your sexual chakra. You need to let it move all the way up, and that will come with time. You'll find that you feel very balanced. Don't I look balanced to you?

You do.

Okay, thank you. Well, this is what it's about, unless you catch me on an off day. The problem is that you get the foo-foo moments where the girly part comes out and you're like, "God damn, my hair just won't work right," and then the guy part comes out and says, "Shut the hell up; let's go! Who cares?" So you get very confused, but you're really at peace with yourself most of the time.

Could you talk about the sexual practices of enlightened masters? Krishna, Buddha, Christ, and the disciples?

Well, I'm just going to say it. In my opinion, they were either bisexual or they were gay. Krishna was notorious with women, but he really had great control over his energy. I'll probably get shot for this by the Krishnas. There was also a passionate love affair, in my opinion, between Arjuna and Krishna. It's evident. The scholars will admit this. The scholars will admit that Christ was gay. They'll tell you he was gay, "We know he's gay. We're Christians. We love Christ. We're anti-gay. He was gay but he never puffed." Bullshit. If you read the letters of John, those were love letters. Re-read them again. They're love letters. What do you think they did for months up in the cave? There's other stuff that you don't see that other students of mine have been more privy to. There's certain stuff that we're taking out that's just recently resurfacing again but they talk and hint about certain things. Clearly once you know this and you look at it, you think, "No shit!"

Buddha is the one that's really the hardest to get a fix on, but it's there. I know what the Buddhists do. I know what goes on behind the backdoors, per se. It's there too. They're very balanced; there's an indifference between one and the other but they obviously want one, but it's probably the same perspective that I take. If you're going to have to act on this, instead of doing something stupid, find somebody that you can work with and feel comfortable with and at least you can release that organic level of anxiety. Some people might want to say, "Well, we don't want you guys. It's dirty to think that way." No, it's the puritans that are pushing that as being dirty or clean or bad or dominant. This is all perspective, and that is really what it comes down to. Does that help answer anything? I am trying to be very dodgy with it, and I think I've said more than I wanted to. Clearly they were all bisexual. *Clearly.* I would have hit myself in the head with a frying pan and not seen it.

What's the Mary Magdalene relationship with Christ?

This is again the heterosexuals working it so it works for them; that's how I feel. It's so much bullshit. This all came out from the book. And if you look at half the stuff that's pointed out in the book, it's rubbish. The History Channel analyzed it all. It's all rubbish. You want to accept it because it's romantically accept-able to believe, "Oh, he's a heterosexual and Mary Magdeline got together, and they were banging it up. It makes perfect sense. And they had a kid. Oh, it makes me feel good as a heterosexual guy. It makes me feel good as a heterosexual woman." Bullshit.

This is what has been done to most stories in history. It's so manipulated. The truth is so extrapolated, and manipulated to fit the agenda of what needs to be fed to the masses of people to make them the 'flock.' There is an old saying, "Keep the sheep stupid. And then fleece the sheep. Keep them close. If they wander too much, you lose them." What is wandering? It means educating. "If they get educated, you lose them. Keep them stupid; keep them fearful. If they wander too much, they're going to lose themselves; the Devil's going to get them." And they want to keep them stupid so they can fleece the sheep. It's the money. It's the business. Every religion has this, all of it. It's just the way it is.

If one truly wants to find the truth of spirituality, then I'm laying it out. You don't have to believe me. Do your research, but do it with the sense of having a different filter and see if it fits better. When you read something, they're not going to tell you outright because it's all been edited out. But re-read it with the thought, "Well, what if he was? Let me pretend this is what he was like and he couldn't say it." And you read it and you're like, "Oh, this makes sense now. Where this didn't make sense or this seemed a little funny when he said it, now it makes sense." That's what I'm saying. That's all you need to do and the truth will come out. The Mary Magdalene thing? Ask your Navigator if that makes sense. It doesn't make any sense.

I'm just getting it on the recording. That's all.

Yeah, alright. Boy, we better head down to Mexico; that's all I have to say. Oh my God; I can't even believe I just I said that. I am relieved to say it. Trust me; I am relieved to say it. But I'm a bit nervous to say it because I know what I'm saying. I know the effect it could have.

I can obviously speak more freely when I'm not being recorded than when I am. That is a great advantage. It is a simple truth. Everybody here knows it. Now granted, if you have a one-on-one with me, I'll shut off the recorder if you ask me the right question and I'm going to tell you the right answer. Then I'm going to turn the recorder back on. It's the truth. It's a matter of me trusting you so I can freely speak my mind and that you've evolved and educated yourself and you're familiar enough with the material that you're ready to handle what I'm going to say.

Now, after tonight, I don't think there's really much that they've been privy to, minus the fact that I can say Jesus was this way or that way and he did it with this one and that one and this is why. Look at the literature and so on. Or, let's look at the Jews or let's look at the Muslims. I can be more specific, but I don't want to insult anybody. If somebody turned around and said they'd been with my momma, it might be true but I'm still going to be insulted.

So, I don't want to be disrespectful, but on the same token, I have an obligation to the people who are coming to me saying, "Eric, I know there's something here. I don't know what it is and I need to have it unraveled and you're my guru. You're my teacher. Will you tell me?" I can't say, "No, I don't want to get involved." If I'm true to you, I really say it the way it is, and what I think is on my mind. I have always told you this, "Believe what you want. This is what I think. If you want to adapt to it, that's fine. If you want to analyze it, analyze it. If you don't want it, you don't want it. All I can say is you want to know how I got to where I am? If you believe I am where I am, this is what I think. This is how I got to know what I know and this is what it's done for me and I can share it." That's my intention. So there it is.

What are the building blocks of becoming more aroused to galaxies or atoms or the Universe or The Force? How can that propel you to higher spaces?

Well, I like to say focusing on your guru would be better. I know that sounds horrible but I'll try to explain this better. It goes back to the same thing about wrapping your mind around a concept. I said earlier that there is a way to make love to the Universe. First of all, the real question is why would you want to hump the Universe? Most of you guys already have the answer, because it's not about humping. It's about giving something from yourself that you feel is the ultimate and the most beautiful and the most pleasing. Do you see what I'm saying? Absolute ecstatic passion is what you are trying to express. And you're like, "My orgasm is the most private thing in my life. It is the most personal thing to me. It is the one thing that I exclusively share with only a select few people in the most intimate times." And to me, it is one of my most prized and valuable things that I would not want to give up. It is the pivotal moment of giving life or the creation of life on a micro level. If God created the Universe, what would you say the moment of this creation of the Universe would be called for God? It would be an orgasm. We all know that.

So on the micro level, we want to give an orgasm back but some people think, "Oh, it's the whole mating thing," or "It's dominating," or "It's a sex thing." No, to a White Cell, it's an expression of giving selflessly. You have to take the whole organ thing out of it. You want to give it but it's very hard to take it out of that visual concept. So you have to see if you can move beyond that and make it into an energy giving thing and hope that the Universe is going to get back.

When we meditate, at the end of our meditation, what do we do? We surrender to the Universe and we ask the Universe to put us back together. A male gives out energy during an orgasm. A female can give energy out also. When you give out energy during an orgasm, it is to say, "I'm giving you all this energy because it's the easiest way to get through all the loops." We already talked

— 254 —

about tying up the Babbler because it's part of the mission now. You've got it signed on board. The one time it is going to work with you is for an orgasm. And you're in that zone. You give, and then you just basically say, "I give unconditionally. You don't have to give anything back." And you expect the Universe to bring it back into you.

Now the trick is that if you were to do something like that, you don't think about the galaxy as a galaxy like you do visually. You don't think about planets or solar systems or any of that; although that could be considered foreplay. One would think about just the absolute love that you feel in your spirit towards the Universe and you'd want to give it back. I think ultimately that's what you would end up at anyway. Do you see what I am saying?

As I have said before, God is not so clingy with emotions as humans are. God doesn't have those emotions that we have for trivial stuff like sex. It's not about squirting your sperm and having an orgasm with God actually fucking you! It's not about that. And that's the thing, God moves and feels frequency. That is God's communication. And the greatest way for you to express to God, at least at the level that you're at, is to express it in an orgasm. It's something that you can give that's very personal; it's very deep.

But it takes great skills to really make love to The Force. It's not an easy thing. It's easier to envision somebody else because it's commonplace and something that you do in your head all the time. The problem is that most of the time as human beings, when we do something, we expect something in return. When men have an orgasm they want to please and they expect their partner to have an orgasm. In fact, most of the time, men are more interested in their partner having an orgasm than themselves. So, when you're making this concept of giving yourself to the Universe sexually, or this orgasm, you have to be very careful that somewhere, ever so lightly weavered in there, you're **not** saying, "I expect you to have one back now," or, "Give it to me." You have to be a little bit careful because then you're setting conditions. So you need to be very careful about that but it's not really a major issue.

What about other enlightened masters of the past? Would one invoke them?

The problem is now we get into the debate of sacrilege. These are very difficult things to talk about because it sounds so diabolically nasty. I expect Hustler magazine to do an article on this next: "Sex cult!" Again, it goes back to the same thing, "Why is it about sex? What is the connection to sex and why connect it to other spiritual masters?" I think that there is a need for Navigators, or people who are spiritual, to express their love and they know they can't do it with money. It's a matter of saying, "I want to give the most passionate thing from me, and that is my orgasm because it's not just a sexual release for me. It's a moment of spiritual release for me. It's a moment of passion; it's a moment of love. It's the most sacred and most profoundly personal thing for me. If you rejected it, I'd be crushed." And that's really what you're saying emotionally and spiritually.

Hence, the need to want to give something like that to a spiritual being. It invokes the idea that you're making it all about a Red Cell sexual mating thing. And it's very important that I bring this up because I think that one has to understand that's not what it's about. You have to be careful because if you're going to see Jesus sexually, or you're orally fixating on him in your fantasy, it's too Red Cell. Do you see what I am saying? This is where you have to really be careful. If that's all it's about, then it's just about sex again. It has to be about the passion, love, energy and the intimacy. At the moment of it, then you switch bases and you can surrender it out to that person, more so than the copulation concept with that person.

I don't want to have people on my energy like I'm riding them or they're orally doing me and stuff like that. To me, that is grounding. They don't know better but I know their intentions are good so I'm not offended. What I think would be beautiful is that they reach this pinnacle of their sexual energy and they say at that moment, "I'm giving it out. I'm going to send it to you." That's a very profound and very special thing to do. But it gets very tacky as human beings when we think about it.

Find the inner pleasure within yourself and then, at the moment of surrendering, you can choose where you want to send it or how you want to send it. If you want to be intimate with a spiritual master, by all means. I just don't know. To me, it's all trivial in the end. It's all trife. To me, at that one minute thirty second marker, what are you going to do with that moment? Where are you directing it? What are you going to turn it into or invoke it into? A blessing? It surely should not become your main and only process of giving or expressing energy. You should move beyond that.

Could you use it as a way to get used to it? And then do something like that in your meditation?

Well, you wouldn't do it in your meditation. I'd hate to see that you are sitting there masturbating while you're meditating. You should be meditating and it should be a different level of giving. There can be a different passion of sexual energy, but it's not actually sexual energy although it would be read as sexual energy from a human perspective. Do you see what I am saying? You have to take out the equation of all the humping, and sex. It gets into very intricate levels.

Is manifestation during orgasm more powerful?

Well, again, if you can remove the Babbler and get it to work with you, is that an advantage intensely or not? When you get the Babbler occupied, which means it's so focused on the sex, if you can switch it at the last moment, it can be powerful. Of course, it can. I don't want a bunch of people who are so fixated on the easy. Now everybody's fixated on manifesting only when they're having orgasms because it's easier and more convenient. You should recognize the power of an orgasm, but the bottom line is that you probably shouldn't exploit it consistently to meet those goals. It's okay to utilize it on rare occasions. And plug in any of your teachings to work with it. But don't fixate on being the only way you do it.

I don't use my orgasms for anything spiritual at all. I can do those things now by will. Don't handicap yourself because of a quick fix that you get fixated on because you end up using it all the time then. So yes, the answer is you can manifest. You can do many things using sexual energy and intensify it at the right window of time. You have to work with it, but in the back of your mind you have that other consciousness that has a will of where you want to take it or what you want to do with it.

I guess is what I'm saying is that you can manifest that you want to buy a house or sell a house or whatever, and you want to use an orgasm to do it. Well, the second you start thinking about a house you might lose your orgasm. Then you have to start all over again so it could take a whole night. So you really have to know how to operate those two levels and to make it into feels-like and intertwine it to the pleasure, and then make it happen. It's perfect for manifestation, because if you can interweave the feels-like with the orgasm, what are you doing when you're masturbating? You're creating. What do you want to do with manifestation? You want to manifest. Manifestation falls very much in line; it's a synchronicity with creation. You're creating life through your orgasm; it's just that you're not copulating with somebody, so you have all the mechanisms in your brain in the right place as if you were trying to manifest. You're just using your sexual energy now, to occupy the body, which is all the things that ruin your recipe normally. You just found a way to work with both of them.

When you manifest, it's very hard not to let your mind babble. You can also have desires without physically hearing them. That gets your mind off of concentrating on your manifestation. It's all in the details. It's in the precision. From the start, the better precision that you work with concentrated through your whole manifestation, the better.

Whenever you have an outer thought or an emotion or a feeling, it waters down the quality of your work. That all comes from the occupation of the organic brain. It's from the Babbler. Hence, you're sitting there and you're masturbating and you're getting this orgasm, and then you go into this manifestation process but you're holding your orgasm – *I can't believe I'm doing this recording and putting this into a book!* – You're holding this orgasm; you're manifesting, and you get them to come out of the racetrack together; they fuse together and it becomes one creation that you're giving that would normally create life; you're seeing the creation of this house manifesting as life.

Do you get what I am saying? So you're directing your spiritual ability to affect reality with the organic part that's the most spiritual, the approach to create life, which is the most powerful thing to do. And you've found a way to fuse them together. The alchemy of it. But it takes skill. *That's a profound secret, ladies and gentlemen.*

On a greater level, can you diminish your energy fields by making it a habit of doing spiritual practices?

Absolutely. If you do it all the time, I don't think it's a bad thing. You just have to do it correctly. But if you have a paved street, what will happen with nature underneath it eventually? It's going to come through the pavement. If you keep manipulating sex consecutively for your goals spiritually, it's going to find a way to water you down and the Babbler now is going to find a way to come back into its power because it's going to sense you're constantly exploiting it. Hence, the reason why you want to have respect for it and not do it consistently. I don't think it's good to do it constantly like that. You have to let your mind flow and be passionate. It's okay to be a male-male or a female-female, in that sense. But to start using upper abilities, and mixing it with your orgasms consistently, I don't think that is a good way to go. In certain moments, you can do those things. You just don't want it to become repetitive. You don't want it to become a habit. You want to learn the natural way of doing it beyond that.

Can you deplenish other areas of your energy field?

I would say eventually yes. But we're getting into a whole other category now. I pretty much feel resolved that I've answered your question in that way. So I'll say, "Next question," and move along real quick.

Looking at it on a planetary scale, is the Earth a hermaphrodite?

It's very hard to explain that. I would say the Earth is definitely a hermaphrodite but ironically, it's a different species altogether and it is still necessary for it to procreate. I was saying before that I look at the human race like sperm and I see it like pollen. And when we develop technology and we go to another world, what do we do to the other world? We pollinate it. We terraform it. The technology and the DNA that we send to it, that we're carrying, intermingles with the DNA from that planet and it creates its own life. It becomes the third. Well, who's to say that an alien planet can't send a pod of their sperm to our planet and it indoctrinates into our society? So, it's very alien for me to try to explain how it would function if it was in a sexual way. But I think what I gave was brilliant. It's just alien. And this is why I don't think aliens will ever come down here until we stop stoning each other. We have to broaden our perspective of how we see things.

You were saying you look at it as a sperm, as an alien coming down here. So, is that sperm from another planet?

Well, I think that as a hermaphrodite, you could say that the planet can send aliens out and go to another planet. Then that planet becomes the egg. If it projects out, then our planet becomes the egg, rather than the sperm. It's a hermaphrodite. It's balanced.

Do you think that has happened already with the planet?

Yeah, I think there's constantly an exchange. The Universe is very promiscuous. They're always fucking one another whenever they can. No really, think about it. So, there you have it. There's always meteorites shooting different pollens inside the meteorites. That's what brings bacteria and stuff, if you will. It goes to other planets; other planets explode. It could be a big orgasm, and then it dies. It sends its stuff for millions of years in hibernation into the Universe, comes down in meteorites to planets that are fertile but nothing seeding it yet, and boom, there it is. It comes down and busts open and takes hold on the planet, and now it's got that genetic code on that planet and it starts to grow. So it's promiscuous.

What about an alien species that's compatible with this human host?

Are we talking about sex now or are we starting to ride off into another field? I don't want to get into alien sex anymore than what we have already.

So, at this point, I think we have covered everything there is to cover on this subject. I think that I have answered all of your questions and it should give you much to ponder!

Chapter 8

What Are You Waiting For

I can feed you the knowledge and you can expand your mind in order to understand a lot more, but it also takes a course of action. There has to be a course for meditating and utilizing the tools that are given to you in order to reach a higher state of awareness. If you're not going to do that, what is the point of all this?

There's no point.

You must want to help yourself so you've got to try to help yourself by taking action. If you want to achieve higher states of consciousness, you have to apply what you've learned. Bad habits are hard to break, aren't they? You must discipline yourself by taking action.

Whenever life stresses me out, I forget to focus on my spirituality. When I forget to focus, it's hard to get it back. The desire is ultimately there, but the desire fluctuates. It's not a matter of when I wake up every morning, I automatically meditate. It's not very systematic.

Everybody knows about the Doe. You know how hard it is to stay focused. You know that life throws stuff at you. Everybody knows all of that. The question is, "Where do you get off and when do you really start focusing?" When do you honestly and wholeheartedly make a commitment in your life to the idea that this is something you want to achieve? How do you evaluate that level of commitment?

One of my aggravations is the expenditure of time and energy for zero results. How much of me do I want to give away consistently? That's my concern. I don't expect you to be perfect. The question is, "How much am I willing to put out for you to accept that?" That's all. So you must ask yourself, "What do I want, spiritually? What is my ultimate goal?"

To find the truth.

Anybody else?

Enlightenment.

Okay.

**To be one with God and The Force
and perform my duty as it is anticipated.**

Next student?

It used to be to find the truth, but I've been struggling with that lately. I don't know what I want because I'm looking for a role. I'm looking for a purpose, and I don't think there is one there.

So, maybe you should give this up altogether?

I know that I don't want to do that.
I know that I want Spirituality.

Settle down. Have some kids. Get married. It's much easier, you know.

I know it's easier. I'm looking for a reason and it's more than just the truth. I don't know what it is. But I don't think there is a part for me, so I know that's not what I want.

Well, there is always a higher role and a higher purpose. Either you're going to meet that standard or you won't in your lifetime. Everything that you *need* to know, you already know. It's a matter of exercising what you do know. *I think you should focus on carrying your own load while the teacher's walking, that way you can walk beside him. A good student is going to carry their own weight. They're not going to weigh the teacher down.* Ask yourself, "Are you here for the ride or are you really here to learn? Are you really here to improve yourself and your skills, knowledge, and abilities? Are you willing to put forth the energy to do that?"

Let me ask you another question. "Is Prana constant? Do we need to go in psychic mode here?"

No.

Why? Give me some arguments on that. Quickly.

It fluctuates.

How does it fluctuate?

It might fluctuate, but it's always there.
Take the seasons of the year as an example.

Do you have constant access to Prana? Is Prana constantly being worked on you?

Prana is only there if we realize it's there.

Only if you think about it?

But it's there if we want it.

It's there if you want it. But if you pour a glass of water, does it have Prana in it? No. If you think about the Prana going into the water, is the Prana in the water?

Yes.

Because of quantum physics and its mechanics, scientists know that certain things are mentally receptive. In the classic physics Double Slit Experiment, the result changes depending on whether you watch it or not. The very act of measuring, or observing, which slit an electron goes through changes the result. *The electron acts differently as if it's aware it is being watched!* It's something that's inexplicable. It's just one of the mysteries. There are a million things like this that can be described without me getting into it. So, if Prana is not present unless you think about it, this somehow makes Prana connected to your awareness. The recognition of it changes your dimension.

You must think about the Prana. The moment you start thinking about the Prana, what happens? All of a sudden, you start to become more spiritual and more aware. Isn't that positively amazing? It's absolutely subtle, yet absolutely effective. Tell me what do you do to trigger that recognition of Prana?

**Whenever I'm at work, every time I drink something,
I think of Prana.**

Well you can't just think about Prana as a drink. You've got to think about the Prana in the air. You've got to think about the energy everywhere. What is the difference between a believer and a non-believer? Why is it that a believer sees spiritual things and a non-believer doesn't see anything at all?

The believer is in tune. Their tonal is higher.

Give me some examples.

If someone doesn't believe in ghosts, then obviously they're not going to be able to see anything spiritual because they have a mental block. But if someone believes that they can actually see ghosts, they're more open to the possibility of seeing a ghost. They can sense that something is there and they may actually see its presence. Believing in something that is a higher tonal would raise their tonal the same as talking and thinking about Prana will make us receptive to it.

It's a self-feeding process. It is the act of believing at first. But it's the believing that propels you forward when you focus on the spiritual. You have to think about it to make yourself go to a spiritual level. You have to think about spiritualism. You have to be inspired by the things that you have around you. It's not that believing is the power. Think about it. It's not that some higher dimension doesn't radiate some power that keeps me there. But it radiates something within me dimensionally that inspires and propels me to a spiritual level that allows me to see everything in my world as spiritual. In order to stay in a spiritual realm, you must inspire yourself to be spiritually there. Then you remove the layers that you went through to achieve that state of mind and you're there. You're there to experience.

You have to find your inspiration somehow. You have to find your motivation. You can't be so hard on yourself and expect everything to be there written in stone.

Since you introduced me to this and you pushed it, I still look to you for motivation and inspiration.

Well, you have to be your own motivator and create your own inspiration. You can utilize me, but you have to create your own inspiration. If I died tomorrow, what would happen then? It's about taking baby steps. I can hold your hand, teach you how to walk now, but sooner or later you've got to do it on your own. I'll spoon feed you until you learn how to eat on your own. Once you learn how to eat on your own, I'll boost you up into the chair to sit at the table. After you can climb into the chair at the table, I'll make sure I still bring the food over to the table. After you learn how to get your own food, I'll be sure to cook it for you. After you learn to cook your own food, I'll be sure to provide the food for you. After you learn to provide for yourself, I'll still be there to nourish your spirit. But you have got to progress.

I've been struggling because I want to reach this certain state of enlightenment and I've been trying to push myself to get there, but I'm getting nowhere. The only way to get there is by not following any structure, so I've been trying to free myself, give myself to The Force and letting It take me there. It's not about pushing myself and getting to enlightenment by myself.

One of the things I want to explain about that concept is that a lot of people don't understand how I teach. The state of mind that has taken some people ten years to achieve, you can achieve in a short period of time because of my demands on you and because of the way that I teach. It gets you there faster. But each person is different.

Let me explain something to you about learning. Maybe this will help answer your other questions. We know that The Dark Side is *structuralization*. Absolute structuralization. With absolute structuralization, there is a beginning and an end. We have *fluidity*, which is the opposite of structuralization. Fluidity has no beginning or end; it just is. It's almost chaotic. People say that chaos is evil because it can't be predicted or controlled. Not so, even chaos has its law. It is ruled by law and that's what we learned from Chaos Theory. Let's push this all aside. That is for those of you who want to get into the scientific, hypothetical argument of this.

I generally start students off with a level of absolute structure because I have to break them out of their mythology of reality as they see it. I have to direct them in such a way that they are forced to come to an awakening.

Here is a perfect example of this. A young student came to me with Christianity concepts: fears, phobias, and mental confusion. I had to construct and direct her in a way that would bring her to a metaphorical open ocean; it broke down all of her walls. She saw the expansiveness of truth. Then I told her, "Okay, now you can do what you want to do." That's the idea, more or less.

There has to be a balance of structure and fluidity. You can look at it any way you want: yin/yang, male/female, whatever works for you. But there has to be a balance, a happy medium. We're in a physical world so we have to deal with the temperament of structure on all levels. Even our bodies are structured in comparison to being pure energy. Those of you who have been around me for a while know from experience about this dimensional level that seems to be pure energy consciousness, that you're complete, but you move as energy. There's fluidity.

Another student started off with absolute structure from me trying to structuralize all my concepts, so he had a strong foundational understanding. Now, he's gotten to such a point where he thinks of 'structure' as he tries to temper his willfulness to control what his destination will be. He now has to use *fluidity*.

The first student, that I previously mentioned, needs more structure. She has too much fluidity because she has a much higher level of feminine energy. Everybody's a little bit different, so you have to find the right way to reach each individual.

In either case, our whole conversation was that the structured student was really frustrated. And I said, "Well, you have to surrender." He felt that surrender was a sense of being weak. I responded with an answer that I've given a hundred times, even though I dislike repeating things. But for some students, this is the first time they hear it.

I explained to him that there is absolute power with fluidity, if you can just learn to work with it. There's the concept in the movie *Star Wars* about, "Trust The Force, Luke." What does trusting The Force really feel like? How do you even know what it is? And what does it mean?

Well, it means to have structure but to surrender to the fluidity and trust it. You must have discipline to surrender fear and the Babbler. Everything needs to simply be. You have to shut it out through your will. Once you use that control, then you surrender to the fluidity, letting it move you, feeling what it wants, trusting how it's going to move you. It takes time, skill, practice, trust, and in the end that's what you are trying to learn. You're trying to learn to have a balance between your masculine and feminine polarities. You're learning to use your feminine fluidity with your masculine structural direction. You must have both. That is the secret. Too much of one and too little of the other is not the perfect combination.

I always go back to this concept because it is the perfect state of mind. It is the perfect place to be. It is the reason why we do the things we do. You want the mind to become flexible so you have to open the barriers in the brain. Utilize every single advantage and every single tool that you can enter that perfect state of mind.

When Jesus calmed the storm, he didn't do it with passion, which would collapse under fluidity. He had to control his biological and biochemical thought processes while controlling the mind babble. This helped him to work with fluidity to become one with it. The hardest thing to do is to project it. If you try to do that, it's control.

You must have a level of control, but you also need to have fluidity. It's difficult to do, but it is absolutely the highest state of consciousness you can achieve. That's how to do the amazing things you all want to do. That is how I do "miracles." It is how I have the power that I have. Even I have to bring it all together and pool it so that it's just right. But it's easy to do if you can walk that balanced path. No matter how you look at it, scientifically, mathematically, philosophically, it will always come back to balance. And you have to feel it. You have to be it. You have to biochemically work with it because you're in a body. You must utilize every single advantage you can to attain it. The structured student has too much control. He's being too masculine. He's too manly. For him, it's all about control, structure. You have to figure out where you are on the masculine/feminine spectrum and make adjustments accordingly.

Many years ago, scientists did a study to determine the difference between how boys and girls play. What were the results? They determined that girls play with dolls, making homes, and have nesting instincts. They have higher emotions, a higher sense of feelings, and a higher sense of compassion. The boys like construction. They like to build stuff. They dug and made roads. They used Tonka trucks, tractors, and other types of vehicles to build and move around things. Basically, they were constructing. What does that tell you about their consciousness?

One is constructing the Universe. The other is into fluidity of feelings, emotions, and energies, but both operate with the lack of the quality of the other. This is why we constantly seek out partners. We think it's going to balance us. In the end, we don't realize we are looking for an internal thing rather than an external thing. We physically act on it in an attempt to try and complete ourselves. We think if we find a partner, we'll be complete. No, it's internal.

I can look at you and in two seconds know where you began and where you are now. That's what I'm trying to work with, but

I don't have the time to work with everyone individually. You have to do it yourself. I know it's hard. I know you fall off track. I fall off track as well, but I don't sit around and complain about it. I take action. I tend to have more willpower than most people to get back on track. Or at least I'm more familiar with the signs so I can adjust faster. *Think of yourself as two lines. Both of the lines are waving. Inner perfection is achieved when they crisscross. At that point you become the duality of both. That's a moment of perfection. That's when you can do miracles. That's when you can do everything.*

Now, really reflect on this because this is brilliant. When the lines come close, that's where you are when you're in a spiritual state of mind; you can feel it. Then life sways you back apart. *You need to take those two lines and roll them together. That's how I reach my state of mind. That's how I reach that level to operate in and hold it together. That's the point from which I operate.*

You can call one line male and one female, whatever dualities you want. It still comes out to positive and negative. It still comes down to duality of dimension and space or matter. You think you are just matter, but you are both an energy being as well as a physical being. You are matter, yet you are composed of billions of living creatures that collect that sensory perception that individually are not you. However, as a collective, they become you. There is an infinite amount of dualities to compare it to. Ultimately, you have to bridge it all together. Then when you're in that place, that's where you operate from. It's passion, but it's also control; too much of one or the other spins you and snaps you right back out again.

Every time I teach you, it's always the same class. It's always the same thing. It's just from a different perspective to try to get you to understand. When you understand, it's about getting you to do it. Do you want to heal? You have to do it when you're in that state of mind. Do you want to open up a dimensional vortex? You have to do it when you're *there*. Do you want to talk to spirits and see entities? You have to do it from *there*. Think of it as using dowsing rods. You hold the dowsing rods. You walk until they cross. The difference is that you have to get the dowsing in your mind to work.

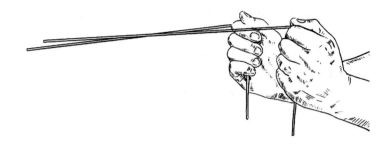

In *Escaflowne*, a Japanese anime, she used her dowsing device to discern which way to go by the direction it was pointing. Eventually, she learned to do it in her. That is truth. It's the same thing. You have to find that place where it meets. Then you can operate from there, but you have to do it so skillfully. Your actions, your conscious thoughts must be skillfully controlled because, if you step out of the boundaries, you snap out of it. That's the problem. You don't know how to get there. You don't know how to stay there. I've taught you well enough so you have an idea, but the idea is to continue working until you can get to that place. When you meditate, it helps you to get familiar with that feeling.

If you want to do anything spiritual, you have to operate from that level. There is a level of control and conversely a level of fluidity. Imagine a young student who is too structured and tries to control everything in his (or her) life. If he gets upset with the circumstances in his life and tries to take control, to take the bull by the horns, he is heading towards his own destruction. This is what the Darkside wants him to do.

Finding that place is like finding a house you've never been to before. If I say that I want you to go to Bobby and Martha's house, you may not have a clue what I'm talking about. But if you have been there once, do you think you can get there again without instructions? Yes, because you have a sense of direction now. We are trying to get you to this certain place, which is a level of enlightenment.

Until you can dedicate yourself enough to achieve that goal, you will never know what it is until you have achieved it. You will never know what Bobby and Martha's house looks like. You will never know who they are except their two names with two basic descriptions of them and what you perceive them to be. You can only imagine it. They probably don't look anything like what you imagine, but you won't know until you finally put forth the effort to get there. If you say every day is a rainy Sunday and it's too cold and you don't feel like driving out there, you'll never get there and you'll never know for sure. But the answer to everything that you're looking for will likely be there. It'll be the doorway to it all.

Hundreds of millions have looked for it before you. Every culture, every race of people, all had seers. All have wise men and women who had followings. All have dedicated people, but only a few have really found it. Those who found it are the ones who were the best students. Those are the ones who were the most dedicated, and certainly those who listened, word for word, verbatim, to their teacher. Otherwise, it's pointless. You might learn a lot, but then you walk away from the table feeling pretty smart. If that's all that you want, fine. We'll catch you in the next life. You'll be a little bit ahead of your previous life, but that's it.

Why do you always talk like, "That's what 'we're' trying to get you to do. That's what 'we're' trying to teach you?"

I sometimes use 'we' because my mind is connected to the Akashic Records or beyond when I teach. That is a vast, multi-collective consciousness, and when I get into that level the data's coming in so fast, I already want to say something else. So I'm almost pulling my words back. This is why I slur my speech sometimes. The 'we' probably has to do with the fact that I believe I'm not just speaking for myself. I'm speaking for a galactic level of beings who really want to influence the direction of your path so that you're beneficial to the world.

But, you know this whole thing about finding your purpose? Your first purpose is to learn. You aren't any good to anybody until you've put in five to ten years, period. Five to ten years of learning at a minimum. Then, it's decided whether or not you can teach. If you can't teach, then you're really not any good to anyone. You should never have been taught because, if you can't reach out to others to teach them, to awaken them with the knowledge that you have gained, you're not advancing the purpose. The second thing is to become a teacher. Develop yourself. Become a teacher. Do not choose a role because you are fluidic. Choosing a role is the desire of the Darkside for you. Choosing a role just to have a purpose is foolish. *Develop yourself to become fluidic.*

Do you understand what I'm saying about that place, that state of mind? That's really what this is all about. I have to keep going back to it. When I say we are walking out in the canyon and we're walking on the stone, you go into a certain state of mind. It's about getting there. You're getting close. You can feel it. And when the lines get close, they can arc towards each other and it's such a peaceful feeling.

Now, you're getting to the fluidic part, but you don't have the sense of control to make something happen. The second that you try to control it, all of a sudden you're back to not feeling that feeling. It snaps you right back out again. It's all about learning that. That's what the meditation is all about: wax on, wax off. Wax on, wax off. Wax on, wax off. You'll get it, but not if you don't practice it. Remember, I said, *"Thought without thought. Action without thought."* Not reaction. When you think without using words, you'll think faster. You have to utilize every single thing.

When do you decide how much you want enlightenment? How much do you really, really want to get there? Do you think that Jesus wanted it, whom we know learned it in only a few years? For how long was he gone? For how long was he missing in those lost years? Vanished!

Fifteen years.

I think eighteen years, actually. Anyway, he vanished for a period of time. What was he doing? He was learning. He dedicated himself exclusively to learning. Do you think when his teacher said, "This is your new direction; this is what you're going to do every day," that he just said, "Okay, fine," and then didn't do it? What did Siddhartha do? Who is Siddhartha?

Buddha.

Did it just hit him on the head one day and suddenly he was Enlightened?

No, he worked his butt off.

What did he do? Did he just go out for a year and learn everything he knew? How long did it take him?

About twenty years. He didn't become enlightened until he was much older.

Do you think he worked for it? Do you think he suffered for it? Do you think he dedicated himself to it?

Yes.

You just want the instant oatmeal. Just add hot water, right? Is anything ever as good as homemade?

No.

Do you think the food that you get at a fast food place is going to be the same as what I cook in my kitchen? Did Krishna just become enlightened? Do you get the analogy? Everybody worked at it. Either you work at it or you don't. You can take the red pill or you can take the blue pill; that's really what it comes down to. Now, you say, "Well, I have a job, and I have to work, and I have to do this or that." Okay. What makes you more special than Jesus or Buddha? Do you think in those eighteen years that Jesus was educated that he didn't work? Do you think that the teacher just gave him knowledge and room and board for free?

He probably worked a lot harder than we do.

What do you think he did? He just had it made and that's it? He didn't have to do anything? He just sat around and they just fed him and taught him everything? Did his teachers just say, "Good boy. We're proud of you. Keep it up. Great work." You think that he didn't have many ups and downs in his progress? They worked him like a dog. It was only near the end that he became the teacher he was and went out and found students. I repeat. Went out and ...

Found students.

They didn't just come running to him, did they? He strolled around the countryside, probably fifty miles at a time. Who knows how long it took between finding those students, weeks, or months? But he actively sought students every day until he got a few gems out of the rough. It's a lot of work. Even Buddha, at different times, starved or lived off the land, but at other times he performed many other services of labor.

If you want the easy route, then this path is not the answer because to get you to where you need to be, you're going to have to pick up your own feet and help yourself get there. You need to sit down and meditate. You need to dedicate a portion of your life to your path. Period. God and spirituality, or money. What are you really about?

Most people are more about money and selfishness because money satisfies needs. It's about fulfilling themselves. They don't necessarily feel that their spirituality can fulfill them. We all know you have to work to make a living and that you have basic needs. But can you honestly say that out of all the available time in your day, you can never find time to meditate for your spirituality? Most people are willing to take on a second job to earn extra cash so that there is money to go out and eat, find entertainment, or buy stuff at the store. How much do you work to earn money for your simple needs and how much of it is earned for selfishness, things that you want and desire? What does that say about you? The Force is well aware of it. Can you not put aside fifteen minutes a day for It?

Do you think it would change things if you were offered one dollar for every minute that you meditate? Do you think that you would sit down and say, "Okay, I need thirty bucks; I can put in thirty minutes right now. Then I'll just go out to the movies and have a good time afterwards." Think about how that feels. Well, how do you think God feels? How do you think you are going to become a master? What do you think your chances are with this kind of mentality? In the end, you're still owned by the machine and the machine is owned by the Darkside.

Value is still estimated by your gains, which brings you right back to this world. That means you're caught in another illusion and you don't even know it. Do you see the interweaving nature of the illusion? Do you see how deep it goes and how much we're a product of these things? Convince yourself of one thing that I can tell you is the truth. For every minute you meditate, I guarantee you will make a dollar for every one of those minutes. It may come in a different way. You'll get better jobs. You'll feel better at work. You'll excel more, which means you'll make more money. You will have more opportunities presented to you, no matter what they are. I'm telling you, doors open when you meditate.

Who knows how much you've really committed to this, but I can tell you right now, when I go for an interview I do some serious meditating before I go. And I always land the job I want.

I've never gone for two interviews in my life. Doors open to you when you meditate. If it's money you need, justify it in that way. Equate it to refining opportunities to make more money. When I meditate the night before, I tend to close more deals the next day because people can feel my tonal right through the phone.

Tell yourself you want to make thirty bucks. Then convince yourself that if you sit down, you're going to make thirty bucks from meditating. It's just like a check. You might not get it for two weeks. Maybe that's the line of reasoning you need to enact in order to get where you need to go spiritually. If that's what motivates you, fool yourself. Fool the brain.

I want you to think about finding your spirituality versus making a buck. Can everybody feel that inside themselves, how they feel when they think about making a buck a minute for every minute you meditate? Doesn't that somehow inspire you to meditate, like you could just sit down and earn a whole paycheck in one day? Think about it. If you got paid a buck a minute to meditate, how much meditation do you think you could do in a day? How much do you feel that you'd want to do? I'm just curious.

I could do five hours.

You think you could do that every day? You would get up. Take your shower. Sit down. Put your music together. Write a little time log of how many hours you're putting in. How much do you think the structured student could do?

I don't know, four or five hours.

Four or five hours. Do you think you could do it often? Would you love your job then? How about someone who is searching for what she wants?

It's difficult to think about it in that way.

There's a point to all of this. How many hours do you think you'd put in?

Okay, if this was seriously my job and someone was going to pay me to meditate all day, I would easily put in fifteen hour days.

How long do you think it would take for you to reach where you wanted to be spiritually?

Like a month.

You would be floating around. You would come to work and you'd be glowing people, illuminated, not even moving, just going "Auuuum." You would get together for a minute and, instead of having meetings, you'd be communicating telepathically. Do you think, for a million dollars, we would up the frequency on the planet another octave?

We could do it. It would just take one of us being rich.

But if you were rich, you still wouldn't do it. You'd need to be motivated. And the only way to be motivated is by want, desire and fulfillment. If you were a millionaire, you wouldn't have the incentive.

**I just need a rich guy to say,
"Here. A dollar a minute, buddy. Plan it out."**

A dollar a minute. I can see it already. You would start off putting in thirty minutes and you'd be tired. You'd be winded saying,

"Okay, I just need a glass of water. Let's crank up the music. Let's go. I need that new car, man. Let's go. Car payment."

After the first week, it would just be pssshhhh, going over a cliff.

Think about it. You want to go to the movies later on, "I'll put thirty minutes in and I'll have thirty bucks."

Do you understand the point that I'm trying to make here? You want spirituality but technically you're bought and owned already. To be Jedi knights, you cannot be tempted by anything. Your soul is owned and inspired only by one true thing. When you're inspired by something else, it means you can be bought, and so can all of your knowledge and all of your training. The way I have lived my life serving only The Force *proves* that I can't be bought.

When I started getting paid for my grades, I got straight A's.

On an average, how many hours do you work for thirty bucks?

Around three hours.

Three hours for thirty dollars at ten dollars an hour to be out in the cold and the rain, walking up to strangers and catching their cold. I can pay you that. I can pay you ten dollars an hour to meditate. Do you think you could do it for ten dollars an hour? Sit down for three hours to meditate?

Of course.

Maybe that's what we should do. Should we just open up big schools and pay people to meditate?

I think people would meditate for free if they were taken care of, if they could do their chores together in a community. It's all about community.

I don't believe it. I hope you think about what I said about the money. I hope you set your values to what you esteem them to be, what you really are, and it puts that in perspective. Try to see yourselves for what you really are. It's all about greed.

I wish I got a dollar a minute just for meditating. It would be a lot of money. Just last year, I was conversing with a student about having no money and I said to The Force, "Look, give me a break here. I'm willing to work for it, but give me something where I can at least make money based on my skills. Cut me some slack here. Do I really have to be poverty stricken on this planet?"

I had to give that whole argument to the Universe about three thousand years ago. You know it wants me to live in caves and suffer. Times have changed. Let's have a little leniency here. Jesus had beautiful white robes, which would be pretty wealthy by today's standards. White robes at a time when they didn't even have a washer and dryer and he was living in the desert. Tell me how those robes stayed white. That was a miracle in itself, a luxury. Think about it. How luxurious was that? There's humor in all of this!

Chapter 9

MAYAN STORM

(Note: This class took place in March 2008 in Mexico
and was revealed to Eric's students before 2012.
He knew what was in the forecast long before 2012.)

I've been trying to think of a way to express how I feel right now and what I want to say to you. There's a song that expresses that emotion. It's called *Yellow* by Coldplay, one of my favorite bands. In this song, the artist tells you to look at the stars and how they shine for you and everything that you do. I'd like you to listen to this song in a different way. Think about this song as if it was singing to The Force or to God. If you are singing this song to God, how does it change the words? For me, when the band says yellow, it's talking about The Force. It's talking about the Universe. It's the relationship of a person approaching the Universe or a person approaching a teacher. It's someone who's showing them the Universe. When you listen to the song with that mindset, it's amazing. It brings me to tears because it's powerful and you catch the feeling of that. So the next time you listen to that song, reflect on it from that perspective.

Like Hawaii, Mexico is a line chakra point on the planet. You cannot necessarily say that a chakra point on the planet is going to specifically be a hard line. Ley lines are like pathways or meridian lines in the body. At different points on the planet, they adjust and move over the centuries. When they crisscross, I believe it intensifies a culture to be very creative or artistic. The first one that usually comes to mind is Egypt. At one point, I believe that the Mayan culture was heavily influenced by the ley lines that cross in Mexico, cultivating the intellect of the people and inspiring them. A lot of the Mayan temples are really pyramids. Most people don't know that there are actually pyramids all over the world. There seems to be this geometric pattern that's inspired by the Universe. People sense it and want to somehow articulate creatively and bring it out of their subconscious. So it comes out in different designs from different cultures but it's basically the same pattern.

A lot of Mayan culture was expressed in the Yucatan Peninsula of Mexico. If you go far back in history, you will find that this is literally the hub of its culture. So there is something very important there. There's a frequency that emanates for you. When you are in a place like this, your consciousness harmonically begins to resonate and you will feel this effect.

When you go to a place and you meditate there, you take on the frequency of that place. It is imbued into you. When you travel to these other parts of the world, it is also a very good thing spiritually because there is something that happens within your frequency that inspires you to reach higher levels of awakening and higher levels of consciousness. There are very specific places that imbue data into you. Whether they realize it or not, most of the people who went to a Higher Balance retreat in Hawaii would probably agree that something from Hawaii is not *just* Hawaiian. It's a certain experience that came from this. It's inside of them now. It is a tonal and it's very real, although it's not easily definable. Mexico is a different frequency but it's very powerful and very unique. Anyone who visits there is going to be imbued by that tonal before they leave there.

If I had to narrow down what Mexico represented, it's really just the longitude and latitude. There was a very dark period in Mayan culture but also a very beautiful period. So for me, there is the intermingling of a battle between the Darkside and The Force. There is also a hallucinogen that comes from South America called ayahuasca. It's not a good idea to go out and try it unless you have done your research beforehand to ensure that you will be going to a safe area and that you have good information about the validity of the shaman, as well as a clear understanding of the process you will be using to eliminate any risk.

I don't advocate it or any drugs. As you know, I'm very anti-drugs. Having said that, ayahuasca is a very interesting hallucinogen. It's used in a very unique shamanic process but it's very difficult to get. Synthetic versions of ayahuasca are now being produced. They are completely different and don't produce the same affect. The bottom line is that ayahuasca comes from the jungle. It holds in it the DNA of Gaia married with the celestial universal consciousness. It's what I would call the Gaia mind of our solar system or universe. So when you ingest ayahuasca, it's like data going into a computer and making your energy and your consciousness go holographic. Ironically, those who take it usually experience things having to do with snakes. It unveils a very earthy, jungle energy.

The jungle in Mexico, unlike in any other part of the world, was infused with what I would call the Gaia consciousness. Something occurred in Mexico between the Universe and the Earth. There's a very unique frequency there that the people took in them, and these two frequencies merged creating a third. Then the Darkside came, wanting to integrate into it. This is where the dark features in the Mayan culture come from. When you see snakes and reptiles, that's the Gaia consciousness influencing the people. The pyramids are the influence of the Universe. So there are three very specific energies there.

At this Higher Balance Retreat in Mexico, because of the merging of these three frequencies (Gaia, The Force, and the Darkside), I feel that it's time to discuss a topic that I have avoided talking about for twenty years - the nature of the Darkside. When you invoke the Darkside, you invoke that energy. My job as a teacher is give you the best data, the best information, the best knowledge, and the best skills so that you can understand your opponent. The more that you understand your opponent, the greater position of strength you have. I don't talk about the Darkside to empower the Darkside or to enliven it. I talk about it so that you can say, "I know your next move!" That is a great power and it's something that the Darkside does not want you to know about. To know it is almost sickening, but it's something that you have to understand if you are going to confront it at some time or some place. You have to understand what you're dealing with.

I'm also going to discuss The Force. I believe the greatest way to tap into energies is to learn the science and logic of them so they become something concrete that you can sink your teeth into. Without realizing it, science is already acknowledging the Darkside and The Force in the universe. What is that source of energy? I'm going to make it very tangible and understandable. By understanding and seeing the logic behind that, something clicks inside of you.

With astral projection, you can only go so far before your body snaps you back in because there's an instinct that says, "No, this can't be happening." Your brain is your worst enemy because it adheres to the way society has programmed you in a certain way. So I have to unravel your logic. Everybody that's attracted to me is a thinker. You analyze things to death. You like me because I can give you the logic and say, "Chew on it and try to disprove it."

When you have this revelation, it makes things more tangible and real compared to your previous perceptions of reality. When that happens, you're going to be able to consciously tap into a source of energy with fewer restrictions.

American cars have a governor built in to the system that restrains the level of speed you can drive that car. If your car can do 180 miles per hour but it has a governor chip inside of it, you can put the gas pedal to the floor but it isn't going to go past 120 miles per hour, no matter how hard you try. You have the same thing in your brain. So if you're going to heal, or move your mind, your Governor will restrict you. By explaining this to you, I'm helping you to remove this chip so that you can release whatever's in you. So you need a lot of logic to disassemble that computer chip. That's what it's all about. I'm giving you that logic so you can understand that, "This is real. This is fact. It makes sense and now I understand it. Now I can conceive it; now I can approach it." If you can conceive it, you can control it. You can grasp it and utilize it.

The people who are attracted to what I teach are White Cells. We have a warrior-like vibration about us but we are also very loving, compassionate, and kind. We're not about free love, hugs and kisses.

There are movies that I love, like *Dune, Donny Darko*, and *Renegade*. There are certain things that I see in a movie that I believe is the Gaia consciousness trying to communicate to the planet as a global organism. Creatively, it comes out in music, movies, art and poetry. Now obviously, one the greatest sources right now are movies because they are so accessible and they're getting better at communicating this internal knowledge. I think many of the people that are creating these movies are probably using both hemispheres of their brain. They are the meditators, spiritualists, philosophers, and highly creative people. These are the people who are *producing and writing* these movies and a lot of people don't give them enough acknowledgment.

Usually, the people who get acknowledged are the actors, directors and producers who put the money into it. But the real people who put the nuts and bolts together are actually the creative writers. Then it gets hacked a little bit by what they can or can't afford and what they are able to do technically. So there are things in movies that are great examples to show people a concept that they can understand. I'll give you an example.

In *Dune*, there is a point where they have what is called the navigator, and it has the ability to fold space. So it can jump from here to there without moving linearly though the space between point A and point B. It's like folding a piece of paper so that one side overlaps the other so they just jump from one point to the other. It works in science fiction. There's a point where they go dimensionally and for me, it was an 'Aha' moment!

Donnie Darko has this great concept where this consciousness that comes out of his chest center, which I refer to as *feels-like*. It's where your true intelligence exists. It's like a conscious brain for your dimensional body. Women understand it much better than men. When the writer wrote about it, he probably meant it to be one thing and the director probably told him, "Listen, people are too stupid to understand that. Let's just simplify it." By referring you to movies, you can get those 'Aha' moments. It's just another tool for you to understand those concepts.

As for the movie *Renegade*, it took ten years to make it. The creator of the movie was into shamanism and he took hallucinogens. So he put the emphasis on the visual effects of the hallucinations in this movie. It's a Western and the special effects are jaw dropping and very accurate. I was just blown away. As for the hallucinogen, I don't want you to do it, but this movie gives me a way to explain it so you can walk away with fantastic data at zero risk. In the movie, there's The Force, the Darkside and Gaia. So it's a highly accurate depiction of ayahuasca. You need to learn to integrate in with society and still be spiritual. You can go on a retreat, do your spiritual thing, and leave. It's good but there is a softening process that actually can come from that. You don't need to build an altar and a sanctuary to be spiritual. I want you to take your spirituality with you, rather than having it behind two doors that you have to open and a room to sit in. Your greatest power lies within you. If something negative happens, then you can simply step forward because you have that great spirituality inside of you. That is something profound! You don't need to go to your sanctuary, meditate on this and heal yourself because *you are that place* and you need to integrate yourself with society.

We are really the guests here because we're dimensional. We're really universal. We're not of this place one hundred percent. So we resist it and we fight it.

White Cells are here to bring in a vibration of consciousness, of frequency, into this world. The more spiritual you become, the more you want to withdraw from this place. If you withdraw from this world because it is too difficult for you, you're no longer serving that purpose. You're not here to save yourselves. You're not here for you. You were asked to be here by the One, so you need to integrate with society. You need to be patient, like a parent is with their children. By integrating with the world and moving among the people, you will become a better person.

You've got to make a living. You've got to function in the world, so deal with it. The more that you're angry with Red Cells, the more you're separating yourself from them. You need to look at them like children, or someone that doesn't understand the world as much as you. They're just simply not capable so you need to accept that.

You're learning to contain, release, and cohabitate peacefully with them. You're here to take your neighbor's consciousness and just raise it up a notch. He'll get it just from your vibration. You don't even need to help him. He'll be inspired to do it on his own because he'll be thinking in his head, "There's something about this person that's very special and I don't know what it is but I think I'm inspired." They won't stay inspired. They just know there's something there and it's seeding them like pollen.

Build your life around your spirituality. When you walk and look at nature that is meditation. That is a communion! You can sit down on the beach and not go into your meditation, but you'll be in a meditation just from looking at the ocean. When you choose something to inspire you spiritually, you are feeding your soul. It's not what you're looking at it; rather it is what makes you feel a certain way that all of a sudden attracts Prana to you. That's how you feed your frequency. That's how you survive and feed your soul. Meditation is a tool. When you need it, go to your toolbox and pull it out.

In your spiritual toolbox you have many tools. You need to make a point to use those tools. Don't get down on yourself if you slack off. You have to find beauty in the world. I don't want meditation to extract you from the world. Meditate as often as you feel like it. When you feel that you're getting off course, go meditate. If you feel like you're really in alignment and you're expanding your consciousness, that's great. If you're really thinking and applying yourself in mastering those things, that's good. That's progression. That's all that I can really ask.

If you are meditating daily and you're not having the break-throughs you want, there is probably a reason. It may just be that your Governor is washing away the memories of those experiences and breakthroughs. Maybe you just have the "Evil Richard" syndrome, from the book *Bending God*. Evil Richard is the nick-name I gave a student of mine. He saw things that no other living person has probably seen. One day, Richard and I went to the park and some crazy things happened that day. There was a storm and the clouds rolled backwards across the sky. The wind blew crazily and then just stopped. Then it started up again. Tree limbs broke and it felt like God had just belched on the park. Richard went home to watch the news because he couldn't believe what he had just seen. He was in total denial. He thought that this couldn't have happened. It didn't happen! It couldn't happen! If you say it enough, you'll believe it. That's why I don't 'perform' anymore.

So you're probably having experiences but you haven't had the kind of experience that will give you closure to reach the next level. You're still *filtering*, which is a very normal, intelligent process. Everybody has a different level of doing that. So I think that you are having experiences but you just expect them to be bigger, more spectacular and more amazing than what you're getting. There is no simple answer until you finally have that experience. You just need to continue doing what you're doing and you'll get there. Until that happens, you're a psychic vampire because there is a hole in you that's just not going to be satisfied. So no matter what is thrown at you, you're just going to find a way to dismiss it. You could have some pretty profound experiences, but a part of your brain is going to find a way to dismiss it. You probably had experiences but you do not fully recall them. It's like having an amazing dream. You don't want to forget it and by the time you try to write it down, you have lost about fifty or sixty percent of what you thought was so amazing from your dream. You're left with a sense that something astonishing happened, but the memory of it has already evaporated.

Anyway, you're going to need an impact that just pummels you into submission. That is going to be a life changing moment for you. Whether that happens soon or not depends on you. Your heart has led you to the right people, so be patient. Do not set a standard on the Universe of what you expect it to be. Want for nothing and gain everything. I want you to think about that and meditate on it. *Want for nothing and gain everything.* That is your mantra. That is what you really need to think about. When you can surrender that, you're going to hit the level that you really want to hit.

In The Handbook of the Navigator, it says that the seeker is guided by an inner Navigator that is a part of the Higher Self. If a Red Cell is taught spiritual knowledge, he creates a new energy body, a soul. At what point in that process is the Navigator created?

The Navigator is a big part of the fabric and consciousness of God. As soon as you say, "I consciously think of myself; therefore I am," there's a moment of self-reflection. At that moment of self-reflection, the mirroring is not you. It's God. It's the Universe. It's The Force. By doing that, the Navigator is created, but the new White Cell is probably not going to be aware enough to recognize it right away. It just depends on whether or not that seeding takes root. If the roots managed to take hold, then that person will keep asking that same question. And that question is going to come from the Navigator. If it doesn't root, they are going to forget to ask that question and they are just going to keep functioning through life.

One day, I was walking in a cemetery while I was In-Between. As I shifted, it appeared that the shadows on the ground were actually moving to meet me. You called it an invitation. Could you elaborate on that?

If you're going to a graveyard, it's probably because you sense the presence of spiritual beings. A graveyard is a collective of spiritual beings, a collection of frequency. You're drawn to something that's on the other side. Not only that, but we're Navigators. We're White Cells. We're compelled to help, protect, give and heal. We can't help it. It's in our nature.

When you go to a graveyard, you're almost saying, "I want to communicate. I want to experience. I want to exchange." You're not walking through there just to look at the grass or the trees. It's a place of solitude. For White Cells, a graveyard is what a park is to Red Cells. It's a place to unwind. I've always found graveyards more relaxing than actual parks. For White Cells, there's a yearning to go there. There's a connection to life after death. We're drawn to something that seems very dark but we really don't see it that way. We almost yearn for it.

When you're In-Between, people don't necessarily see you. Entities don't necessarily see you like you see people. They see your frequency like a shimmer of energy. That is why they're drawn to you. You already know this. In fact, you're probably quite willing to experience this. You're may be a little intimidated, but probably more curious than afraid. So that's an invitation. It's a frequency. It's a feeling. It's like a catchy musical tune to them. When they hear it, they're drawn to you. If you presented a sense of fear, you probably would have come out of the In-Between state. If you presented a sense of not wanting them, they would have moved away. They don't understand words, but if you have an emotion behind it they would hear the emotion but they wouldn't hear any sound. They would feel the emotion but they wouldn't hear any sound. So why are you there? It's because you find solace in a graveyard, almost like a healing. If you went there, you invited something unearthly. Maybe you were really there for something spiritual. That's an invitation.

At one point you mentioned a place where Buddhist monks go in their deep meditations. Sometimes, there are confrontations. How do you know you're there?

Recently, I was talking to someone who said they were able to see things from other people but they couldn't really hear things audibly. So I explained that if they wanted to add the skill of hearing things audibly, I suggested that they start wearing ear plugs. By doing that, you're telling your body to not externally hear. Before you get to that stage, it's not that you really hear it. All of a sudden, you just know it. It's normal to question yourself, "Did I just imagine this?"

Here's another example. When is the last time you actually had a conversation in a dream? You obviously communicate and do things with other people in your dream state, but there are almost never any words. Most of the time, there are no words but nobody ever realizes that. It never seems to dawn on anyone to think about that. It's like you're telepathically talking in your dream and you just don't think about it. You're having a conversation, yet you know things and you believe the next scenario.

When you go into hyper-dimension, at first you're going to think it's your imagination, but it's not. You're going to wrestle with that, but eventually, you're going to know it is real. That comes with skill. That comes from quieting the Babbler. It comes from all your other skills. You're going to know that you're somewhere else. You're in two places but you're firmly in this one so it dominates ninety nine percent to one percent. You know that there's something else going on. The key is to begin to acknowledge that one percent, even though you can't see anything. You don't want to imagine something that's not real, but you've got to take a leap.

There comes a point where you need to have a belief to quite literally empower the quantum physical realm to take effect. There's a line from a Spanish movie called *The Orphanage* that says this perfectly, *"Seeing is believing but believing is seeing."*

So, believing is seeing. You're anchored in this dimension because what you see is what you believe. You yearn to get out of this dimension, but your organic mind is dominant. It's saying, "No, these are the rules. This is the way is going to be. This is what you're allowed." But your other consciousness in your chest is saying, "No, there's more! There's more! There's more!"

So there's this constant conflict between the two until you start to exercise your chest consciousness. As it gets stronger, you have better and better experiences. So you need to pull the one percent and make it into two percent; then make it into five percent; then make it ten percent. To do this, you begin by indulging yourself in what may seem like a dream or a wishful fantasy. You should have enough skill now to not let your imagination run rampant. This will allow your sensory to interpret what you see.

You have to remember that you're still using your organic brain. Most people will envision monks shooting electricity at each other. Well, a floating monk means you're seeing a physical body. How did you know it was a monk?

When I say that monks go there and they have battles, you immediately visualize or tag this in your head. This tagging has now limited your ability to get into this real space. So it's very complex. You almost have to play with going there. Don't let your mind tag things so easily. You've got to discipline yourself and envision it more as energy. Let it decide what it's going to look like. You've got to be in the second person looking at what your brain is doing or what you're projecting. It's a lot of work. It's not easy. It's like driving a car when you were a kid. The car is all over the place because the kid doesn't know how to steer or how to brake. At some point, you can drive a car, chew gum, put your lipstick on, tilt the mirror down, change channels on the radio, and look at what's going on outside. You can do twenty million things and not give it a second thought. You grow into these things.

At first, it seems overwhelming to really visualize all this but you eventually get there. Then you ask bigger questions. You take this one percent, two percent, three percent and it starts to manifest. All of a sudden, you're going to see these frequencies. You don't want to say what frequency you are in because if you do, you just organically solidified it. This is what restricts you to certain bands, dictating where you're allowed to enter and where you're not. When I cruise, there's no conscious thinking but there's brilliance of intelligence going on. It's just that I've learned to rub my head and tap my chest at the same time. A lot of people would say that it's hard to coordinate those two movements. It's the same kind of concept.

You cannot conceive, "Why am I here? What am I seeing?" It's so natural for us to do that and it immediately holds us in place. We know it so we get very frustrated. In this particular place where these battles take place, there might be a time when you want to heal. You're not going to go to that other place. You're going to go to a place where there are people suffering and you're going there to heal. That becomes the reality of your perception.

If you go to a horror movie, and then you go camping, what happens when you hear something in the woods? You think something from the horror movie is coming to get you. If you watch a UFO movie, and you go to the woods, what happens when you hear something? You immediately envision that it's a UFO or that there are aliens are in the woods. *Your perception is what you're going to project.* Seven times out of ten, whatever you expect to happen is exactly what turns out to be the situation. The moral of the story is, 'Don't watch horror movies before you go camping!' So, are you creating your reality?

You feel like you need to fight something. There's a reason for it. It's like the Universe is saying, "You're needed." The problem is you're like a baby eagle. You haven't learned to fly out of the nest yet. You see your parents doing something and you want to join in but you lack the ability to get there. So, it's frustrating. That feeling is coming from communication. You feel it all the time. Sometimes you feel it more than other times and you dismiss it. Or you don't know what to do with it and you feel there's nothing you can do. Regardless, there is a communication and you're receiving it. What are you going to do with it? And what are you capable of doing?

Now, this is how you learn to enter into that particular bandwidth. You feel an urge that you're needed to fight, or something's being attacked and you need to help defend it. When you're feeling that, you go to that place. How would you know that's the bandwidth? That's because your instinct will take you immediately there. There's no distance. It's a frequency that's constantly here. You just simply switch to that channel. The TV doesn't move. It's the same thing. In that place, you'd just adjust your level of fighting to whatever you believe you're doing even though you can't visualize or see it. Feel The Force. Trust yourself. You're doing more than you can imagine. You'll know when to step out because you'll feel it. You'll also know when to push forward. It's almost like you're playing with your imagination. You have to use your toolbox. You have to be sensible.

If you go deep into your mind, deep into your consciousness, you're going to know immediately that you're not on the map in this dimension right now. When you allow yourself to go there, you'll see the red come in. You'll see then what looks like light reflections from a gold glass. It looks wavy, like a distorted colored light hitting the wall. You would look like this distorted, bent, sharp, light energy. You'll see them hit other lights, like they're fighting and almost fusing. Or you'll see light move. You can see its frequency fighting to dominate, eradicate, or remove the other one. That's what it looks like there. You'll see all these like squiggly lights but they're not orbs. They're moving into this place. There's not a high. There's not a low. There's not a sense of up or down. It's just like this space. When you're in that energy form, it makes perfect sense. If you feel it, you'll know what I mean. It's very comfortable there. You communicate like a radio, by tuning into it and sending the same way. It's hard because you're doing it from an organic three dimensional space and you're trying to interpret what you need to do there. You really should be focusing more on being here than babbling out there, but it's irresistible to you because it's your nature.

How does 'believing is seeing' tie into the In-Between state of consciousness? How is it linked to the realizations that might come from that?

In my mind, the In-Between state is like tree branches. You have to consciously take the In-Between into a certain direction. When you consciously choose, it will explode into a whole other level of abilities and experiences.

White Cells are very intelligent, analytical, and skeptical of information. It's the truth. We need to have a logical, reasonable approach to things. We have breakthroughs when we realize in our mind that it's not fairy tale stuff but something is as real as the carpet or the fan on the ceiling. We know that there's some other form of confirmation. Unfortunately, science is just like another religion. They change it as they go. We've been internally trained that science is fact. We're trained to believe that science can heal us better than a witch doctor who blows smoke on us. When I see science having major breakthroughs and when they are really on top of something, I like to utilize that.

So every time you show that something's possible, it's like fire. Imagine lightning striking a tree, creating fire and smoke. What if this was the first time you ever saw fire? You find wood around you so you use that as firewood, but one day the rain comes along and puts the fire out. After sitting around for three months without fire, shivering from the cold, some guy comes along, sits down, and starts rubbing two pieces of wood together. You're wondering, "What's this guy doing? It's cold out." And he's rubbing these two pieces of wood together until it smokes, eventually creating fire! And it seems unbelievable to you!

The possibilities in your mind just begin to explode! Then you no longer see fire the same way. You internalize it differently, allowing you to see all these other possibilities. Eventually, you don't even think about those possibilities. It just becomes the norm.

I want you to think about something. Do you believe in vampires? Do you think aliens have visited this planet? There are probably more people who believe in aliens than those who believe in vampires. So, let's put another little twist on this. How many kinds of aliens do you think there are out there? Do you think there's more than a hundred species in the universe? Probably some of those different aliens have visited the Earth, right? Do you think that any of them have ever been abandoned or lost here? Do you think any of their ships broke down, marooning them here? Do you think any of them might resemble a vampire in any way?

Maybe we should open our minds to the possibility that there are just so many amazing things out there. No one wants to appear dopey, ignorant, or foolish. We all want to appear open-minded. Therefore, you should always have three reasonable explanations when you see something that seems a little out of the ordinary. I think most of us are pretty stringent on how we approach and look at things. I think we're pretty level-headed. It comes down to how it's communicated.

When you really don't think about it, you narrow your ability to see things. So, perception is very important. You have to remain mindful of how you perceive things, and how you make a judgment call in your mind. If you don't believe in vampires, but you believe in aliens, you may need to rethink that. Or if you believe there could be vampire-aliens but there can't be vampires, you may need to have another look at that. You have to be broad-minded, but also sensible. You have to take into consideration how you look at all these things. When you narrow down certain ways that you think, you limit yourself spiritually. That puts a cap on what you're going to be able to see or experience.

In South America, when the first European ships came in, the natives could not see the ships that were anchored offshore. The ships were invisible to the natives because they were very simple people. They were unable to imagine the possibility of ships manifesting on the horizon. However, the shaman was able to see them because of his elevated frequency. By imagining what he was looking for, the shaman stared out to sea and eventually he was able to see the ships. The shaman could do this because he was open to the possibilities of strange things from other worlds. He then was able to point them out to others until everyone could see the ships. They would start to see different pieces of it like the mast and the sails. This tells you the power of the mind and how it edits things. It tells you the power of what you can perceive, what you can't perceive, and what the brain is capable of allowing.

We think that we're so advanced, sophisticated and open-minded that this would never happen to us. I guarantee you that it happens. I proved that in the *Handbook of the Navigator*, with the count of how many letter F's you see. You probably counted only five but there were actually eight F's in that sentence. Most people don't see the F's in the word "of," so they only see five letter F's. Your brain lies to you. You always have to be mindful of what you perceive as your level of reality. Nobody wants to be way out in left field either.

In the 2002 BBC Science documentary, *Parallel Universes,* they scientifically speculate that there are other realities and dimensions. The graphics that they use to explain this are wonderfully done. More so, the documentary talks about the Big Bang *before* the Big Bang. In relation to all these parallel universes, our whole universe is merely the size of the point of a needle. In theoretical physics, a brane (short for *membrane*) is an object which can have any number of allowed dimensions. When the surfaces of these dimensional objects (or branes) touch, they smash into each other creating other dimensions. You can't see them moving, but in the other dimension you can see a Big Bang, so it's like parallels of God. The parallel universes move like waves. Like any wave, these parallel universes rippled. It was these ripples that went on to form the clumps of matter after the Big Bang. This is where God entered this dimension. The documentary really defines this well.

When you are able to observe a concept, it gives you a fundamental ability to see what's going on here. That helps you in your meditations. It helps you in your ability to affect and manipulate reality because you realize that these other realities are just as real as ours. We have to constantly confirm that. Whether you think about it or not, just being exposed to this allows your meditations to take off better, giving you better experiences. It's removing the limitations that your Governor imposes on you.

I believe there are other dimensions functioning with laws of physics that are different from the ones here. When we hear about stories from ancient or medieval times about fairies and fairy rings, I do believe there's a level of truth to that. When folk tales get woven into that, the stories become a little bit more whimsical.

There are stories of fairy people in almost every continent on Earth. When you find different cultures that have never really been exposed to each other yet they have similar stories that are very much the same, it makes you wonder if there is a level of truth to this. At some point, the fairy people just vanish. When this happens, I think whatever allows them to come in and out of this dimension switches. The gateway or rift that allows them to enter or leave this dimension disappears. It's like the ley lines moving and touching on different continents. Then these continents cultivate intellectually and build. That's a gateway of a different sort. It affects your consciousness, rather than allowing these beings to come in and out of this dimension.

I believe that science is finally realizing that these parallel universes are feasible, but they don't understand how they react with this dimension yet. I think they're even afraid to talk about that possibility because it opens up a bigger door that could create a level of hysteria for people who live in a religious bubble. You really have to be broad-minded to understand this.

When I am looking at a topic like Mayan history, I do the best that I can as an intelligent person. I am not an expert on the Mayan culture. I try to extrapolate truths with the help of my higher consciousness, using what I would call the Gaia consciousness, the consciousness of the solar system, the galactic consciousness and so on. I sift through them to pick out the truths. According to true Mayan culture, the years that led up to 2012 were a time period of great change. If you really research it, you probably would shake your head in wonder at the people who focused on making this the end times. Everybody just loves doom, gloom, and death. It doesn't make any sense to me. Regardless, the subject is extremely fascinating. I'm going to try to simplify it for those of us who aren't as sophisticated in the scientific realms.

The planets, including Earth, move around the Sun in our solar system. As we're moving around the solar system, so is the whole solar system moving around the Milky Way Galaxy in an oblong pattern. It's like the gears in a watch. The Milky Way is like an oblong beam stretching across the sky. It's very hard for a lot of us to relate to because the lighting in the cities keeps us from seeing the Milky Way. Even in the rural towns, there's so much lighting that you're likely to only see a few stars. Many years ago, I remember driving out into the boonies of Massachusetts into a big field at the back of a friend's house. It was really dark. When I looked up, the Milky Way was so thick with stars that it looked like a crustation moving across the sky. There were stars every-where. I was just amazed! It was just like some other unearthly place. You can go to other parts of the world and the stars are very bright and so big you just want to pluck them.

There is something that looks like a black ribbon in the Milky Way. It's black as if there are no stars in it. That is what the Mayan people were referring to as the point that our solar system was going to cross under. They referred to it as a dark time - a very bad time. Isn't it amazing that they knew that this was there? How did they know about this black ribbon? They stared at the skies night after night. When you stare at the skies all the time, you really become familiar with what's out there. They saw this ominous dark ribbon up there and they thought it was significant. They took notice of it in their mathematical charts. As the skies were changing, they could calculate about when the Earth was going pass under it. That became known as the End Times, but it really was a time of change.

What is that black ribbon? It's called the Dark Rift and con-sists of overlapping, non-luminous, molecular dust clouds that are located between the Solar System and the Sagittarius Arm of the Milky Way Galaxy at a distance of about 300 light years. This is somewhat speculation, but I believe the molecular clouds of dust are also responsible for creating the Dark Rift. What makes this metaphysical? You're probably thinking, "Isn't It the Darkside?" Don't worry; we'll get there. I like to use actual facts because there's no point in having fantasy if, in the end, you realize that there is no Santa Claus. Let's get to the point of it.

Everyone reading this is coming from various levels of knowledge, so this is the simplest way that I can break this down to give you a very basic level of understanding.

The planet is a living organism. We are affected by the electromagnetic radiation that not only comes from the sun, but also from every star in the universe. All of this radiation hits the Earth, and some level of that will get through after it's affected by our magnetic field, which serves to shield the planet from this massive radiation. However, there are different formats of energy permeating the magnetic field that we're not even able to measure yet. Before we had a way to be able to measure ozone, we were not aware of how much there was of it. Until then, we were oblivious to it.

So all of the stars in the universe are like the neurosystem to God's body. In your body, you have pivotal points. It's an exchange of information. You could call them meridian lines, or ley lines, or information lines, but they are nerve cells that send information. They are like an amplification point. There are large ones and small ones. There are 100 billion nerves just in the brain, so there are trillions of them throughout the body.

An article in the *National Geographic Magazine* written by Michael D. Lemonick states that our universe likely contains more than 100 billion galaxies, and each of those galaxies may have more than 100 billion stars. There are more stars than there are nerves in your whole body.

In my opinion, the stars act as a form of communication for the whole neurosystem of life in the universe. They send electromagnetic radiation impulses or frequencies and life on every planet reacts to it. The solar radiations of the sun are what determine the color of trees. On Earth, we have many green trees. On some worlds, because of their star size or its density or its radiation, all their trees could be predominantly purple or red. If you went to that kind of world, it would just look completely unusual and alien to you because of the pigmentation.

What happens to life if you give it the right lighting and temperature? It explodes. It follows a genetic pattern. It knows what to do. Where did that pattern come from? In the end, it really came from the electromagnetic radiation of the sun. Every bit of light hitting us is like a number. It's like code. It's like the Matrix numbers hitting us - just different.

Radiation and other factors including the atmosphere and gravitational pull of the planet determine the color and design of plants and animals. I don't believe in astrology. I don't believe that the planets have an effect on the Earth because of the gravitational pull. There's more impact on us when somebody passes gas on the other side of a room than the impact that other planets have on us right now. But what does affect us is the stars, including the Sun. They have an effect on our moods as a collective, as a species, and as organisms.

Our Sun is the most dominant, so it's the one that's the most relevant and influential for us. That's not to say that the other stars in the universe are not having an effect on us because they are. The electromagnetic radiation affects the culture of the people. It affects how we think. It affects whether we're aggressive or passive as a species. It affects whether we're dreamers and builders or lazy and lethargic. It all has to do with the scheme of things that influence how our minds are developed.

Some people compare two cultures and conclude that one culture didn't do anything with their land and live in mud huts while another race is superior to them. You have to take into consideration where they live. If it is one hundred degrees out and there are no trees growing to build into houses, you work with what you have. If you live in a desert, you're lucky to have mud. It has to rain to get mud so you carve out what you can. Ultimately, that's going to slow down the whole civilization process. So, you have to look at the environment and the land that you have to cultivate. Everywhere in the world is different. There are different opportunities for civilizations to move ahead or fall behind due to weather, land, environment, and whatever is available from lumber to minerals. Do you have steel and iron to beat up the other cultures that have wood sticks? If they had the ore in the ground, you probably wouldn't be here now unless they were much nicer people than we are today. Anyway, there are many factors that affect life. As much as the factors of life on the planet have an effect on us, so do the stars of the universe have an effect on our consciousness and why we collectively are the way that we are.

Now, remember the planets are all moving and rotating and we're going to get ready to go under this Dark Rift. Envision that we are plants. Now envision that this is a very sunny day but the difference is we love sunshine because we're plants. All of a sudden, we have this gigantic umbrella that we're getting ready to pass under and all the sunshine that's fed us to make us grow suddenly tapers. All of a sudden, we're not going to have any more sunshine hit us. It's going to be blocked out. So, we're still going to receive a substantial amount, but what difference does two percent or ten percent less make? It's a huge difference! It makes a huge difference.

If you took about ten percent of the light out of the jungle, the whole jungle would change. The temperature would drop and it would go from ninety or one hundred degrees down to sixty degrees. Maybe the jungle plants wouldn't be able to grow and other plants would replace them so everything would change. *Life would change.*

How did the Mayan's arrive at the date December 21st, 2012? When I researched the ancient Mayan's and delved into their history, I discovered that it's actually about a thirty year period where we cross under this dark area of space. The planet Earth and all the other planets of our solar system are spinning around our Sun. Meanwhile, our whole solar system is spinning around within the Milky Way galaxy, gradually moving underneath this dark rift. Also, during this thirty year period, there's a bandwidth of intensity. It's like the effect that sunlight has on the shade. There's darker shade and brighter shade. As we moved further under this dark area of space, it became denser, making the effect stronger. As the planet moved into this period, it affected all life, especially human. That is why people were easily agitated. They could feel it. For those people who are sensitive to this kind of phenomena, they could feel that something was happening to the collective consciousness. And the effect of moving through the dark rift will continue for several more years.

When I was a telemarketer selling newspapers, I noticed something which was very interesting. I really believe that the Universe put me through this torrential life system like everyone else so I could learn some valuable things. In every job I had that I hated, I always gleaned something interesting from it. I am who I am. The computer system placed the phone calls for us, concentrating all the calls on a particular region of a city or town. *The Oregonian* newspaper covered a huge area. When we called certain areas, the people would be less than receptive to us, often hanging up and telling us to never call back. When that happened, we complained to the managers to switch the area because every salesperson would get the same effect. Then, all of a sudden, the machine clicked audibly and we'd call a new area. And we'd be able to sell without any problems. In fact, everyone wanted to buy in those areas. It was perplexing to watch it. I kept seeing this pattern. How is it possible that it could change so dramatically from a positive area to a negative area? What difference does ten miles or twenty miles make? There are different energy movements that are flowing across the planet affecting our consciousness collectively. I truly believe that. The electromagnetic radiation is one of the things contributing to this. What energies actually move through the planet? And what effect do they have on consciousness?

So, as the planet moves into this zone, there is less influence and direction for the Red Cells. If you're a Red Cell and you're told what to do your whole life, you learn to automate. On the other hand, White Cells don't want to automate. They want to have an aware consciousness. So, in the 2012 scenario, White Cells could function much better than Red Cells. What decisions did they make that were radically different?

The longest cycle in the Maya calendar is 26,000 years, which is the approximate length of a so-called 'Platonic year' or 'Equinoctial cycle'. The Tibetans, ancient Egyptians, Cherokee, and Hopi Indians also refer to such a cycle of 26,000 years in their mystical belief systems. It has been 26,000 years since the Earth moved through this band of space, so it's difficult to see what took place back then.

Terence McKenna and John Major Jenkins got together, did their research, and wrote a book called *Maya Cosmogenesis 2012: The True Meaning of the Maya Calendar End-Date.* Terence McKenna was a brilliant guy who used a lot of psychedelics. In the mid 70's, McKenna's experiences with psychedelic mushrooms led him to study the King Wen sequence of the *I Ching*. The Yin and Yang are two complementary principals of Chinese philosophy. Yin is negative, dark, and feminine while Yang is positive, bright, and masculine. The negative and positive aspects refer to polarities not value judgements. Both are always present in everything yet the amount of influence of each varies over time. The individual lines of the *I Ching* are made up of both Yin (broken lines) and Yang (solid lines). When examining the King Wen sequence of the 64 hexagrams, McKenna noticed a pattern. He analyzed the "degree of difference" between each successive hexagram and found a statistical anomaly. He believed that the Ken Wen sequence was an intentional construct. He worked out a mathematical wave form based on the 384 lines of change that make up the 64 hexagrams. McKenna was then able to graph the data. This became the *Novelty Time Wave.*

Peter Meyer and Terrance McKenna worked out a mathematical formula which enabled them to graph and explore the dynamics of it on a computer. The graph was fractal, meaning that it exhibited a pattern where a given small section of the wave was found to be identical in form to a larger section of the wave.

McKenna identified notable events in history like population growth, peak oil, pollution and the dropping of the atomic bomb on Hiroshima that helped him locate the time wave's end date. This worked out to the graph reaching zero in mid-November 2012. When he later discovered that the end of the 13th baktun in the Mayan Calendar had been correlated by Western Maya scholars as December 21, 2012, he adopted their end date instead.

As these earlier cycles ended, the people returned to normal and there were no wars. It was a stunning difference. In essence, when the Red Cells do not have the full influence from the universe, they turn into savages. They are more likely to be more aggressive than passive. During earlier cycles, the people were all warring and chopping off each other's heads. Now we've got nuclear bombs and all sorts of high tech weaponry we didn't have during the last cycle. Things have changed. This was the concern heading back into this cycle. It was not specifically about 2012 or a certain moment when something happens. It was about this time period where human civilization could have gone haywire and turned on itself. There could have been more devastation in this cycle than there has ever been in known human history.

Without the embodiment of the Universe affecting the consciousness of the people, it allows for Red Cells to feel like they have no control because nothing is directing them. White Cells don't want that. They don't need that direction so they fight it. White Cells already exist without it and have learned to be at peace because they've inner-harmonized with the presence of the Universe. Meanwhile, Red Cells haven't learned to inner-harmonize. They've externalized, becoming part of the organism of the planet.

What is the role of White Cells? What is the role of the spiritual? I believe that White Cells need to embrace the Buddhist monks and other spiritual groups. There's this huge brilliance and intellect coming from them, although not as much as White Cells. They're broadcasting, in their heart, the right vibration. I've talked about harmonics before and how our vibration collectively affects the people around us. Right now, Red Cells control this world. When they try to define us, we may have to disassemble our spiritual vibration and become like a Red Cell. Like any other species, Red Cells look at other people and if they smell, see, or hear something outside their accepted norm of how things should be, they intellectualize it moralistically and sociologically and judge it accordingly. It is the same for any species – including whales, dolphins, monkeys, and gorillas.

When I worked for *The Oregonian* and I got on the tram, even if it was packed, no one would sit near me. I used to think, "Do I stink?" It was rare if anyone sat next to me. Then I realized that I really didn't want people around me and the people who sat close to me were either children or they had some Buddhist or other spiritual symbol on them. There is a vibration from a White Cell that pushes Red Cells away from you. You may not know what it is – it's your tonal. That's your energy or vibration emiting out.

You've got to learn to like people. You have the harmonic of God within you and you emanate it out, getting brighter when you meditate. You get stronger with this vibration when you feel and embrace your spirituality. You can intensify the sound, that sound that's not an *audible sound* but it's something there. People can feel that. You have to really embrace humankind or you're defeating your purpose. That means that you're not doing what the One asked you to do.

Some of you are probably wondering, "What happened to the light saber stuff? What happened to thrashing the Darkside? Eric, are you saying that our job is just to be harmonic? Are we only here to surrender our vibe? If that's what you want, we're happy to do it."

Everything is multi-layered. It's like turning coal into a diamond. As a White Cell, there's not one purpose that you serve. Your service encompasses that whole spectrum, that whole diamond. It's just a facet of an important thing that you serve. It's not just about you passing on harmonic balance. As the Earth continues to pass through the Dark Rift in the coming years, you can affect the planet globally.

Let me put it a different way. There are other people helping us with the Earth's harmonic energy. It's not just us. There is a difference between Navigators, Buddhist monks, spiritualists, and the people who have love in their heart. They're all good. They all get it. For the most part, they could talk with us about harmonics, energy and love. We have to look at them as allies. When we were at war with the Germans and the Japanese, we may not have understood the Chinese people. At that time, their culture had not even opened their doors to outsiders, but we knew that we needed to accept friends who had a common cause. We accepted them as our allies so that they could help us fight the greater cause.

We need to look at the Hindus, Buddhists, and Christians as allies and understand that they contribute some facet of the vibration that is needed. Even though, in some ways, they're closer to a Red Cell vibration, there are some that are harmonically above the people they associate with. Therefore they could affect those people. We are amongst them, so it's about function and purpose. I see all these different groups as being collectively different, like organs of the body. There's the liver, the kidney, the heart, and so on. Navigators are like the brains. We have in us a need to feel it, a need to direct, a need to explore, and a need for knowledge. And we want to move things, so there's a sense of us directing. We're frustrated with society because there's quibbling among other countries. If we shared technology instead of hording it, we could get off the rock!

Navigators need to direct the consciousness of the planet to continue a progressive growth while the Earth moves through this point of turmoil. I don't see it as being bad, but I don't see it as good either. Either we do what we need to do or we let the dice roll where it's going to roll. Personally, I would rather have some say in how those dice are going to roll.

Shiva is the god of destruction. We need destruction to create new life. When everything is passive or good, there is no need for change. There is no strife in us to have to reinvent the wheel when we are too relaxed or too comfortable. We need a little chaos in order for us to adapt, to make better rules or improve things. We need to get prodded in the butt to fix things. There has to be prodding to make things better. This is why I always say 'Shiva' when I refer to 'destruction' or 'change.' There has to be upheaval.

When I look at all the upheaval in my life, I realize that I wouldn't be the person who I am if my life was any different. I didn't like going through all that upheaval. And I wouldn't want to go through it again because I've done it already. I don't want to give it up because the disruptions in my life made me learn. They made me suffer and they humbled me. I'm grateful for that humbling. I'm grateful to realize what can happen if I don't pay attention or if I'm not graceful or considerate of other things. Even now, my life isn't one hundred percent in my control. I realize that I am a guest here, so I have to be polite and considerate of other life. That's the only time that I truly have power over my life - by making those decisions about how I'm going to communicate and work with others, because it's going to affect me.

A Navigator's job is to use our minds to move in a sense. As the planet approached the 2012 date, there was an alleviation process. There's a bonus in that for us. As Navigators, we are always trying to be mindful. The Red Cells need that direction. We get less direction which is great for us because we're always trying to fight it to keep from being automated. It increases our possibilities spiritually.

The Babbler controls Red Cells and is fed by the cosmic rays as much as anybody else. White Cells have recognized the Babbler, whereas Red Cells don't know about the Babbler. They think they are just talking to themselves. One could say there's chaos, but the Universe is saying, "No, I've sent something that will take this moment of chaos and elevate humanity because there's nothing interfering with that possibility." White Cells can substitute the voice that they need to hear.

Could you imagine in that moment we chose to shine our brightest? If they were looking to feel something but there was no sense of direction for them, they would be willing to take direction from anything. We could help them. That is part of our job, our purpose. That is why we're here. There's such a huge population, more than ever in history. God wants to proliferate life. God wants to pollinate life through our solar system, into our galaxy, and on into the universe. And we have to ensure the future.

If we have wars, there are no starships so there is no future. Would you like to go on a UFO? I would guess that most White Cells would want to explore space. If not, do you want better technology? Do you want the body of a 20-year old? When all the nations start getting along, it will change things. There will be better health and a better quality of life. That's what I want. But you're not going to get that if you are in conflict with the other cultures of the planet. Everyone is so worried about what the Russians are doing. And the Chinese are worried about what the Americans are doing. Every culture has something to offer. With all the knowledge I have, even I am influenced by culture and TV. At times, it makes us afraid of other cultures, so much that we don't want to travel.

What if we all got along? What if we could take someone's skin technology and put it together with some other group's technology that can accelerate it and make it compatible so that the body will accept it? What if we could just all share that technology instead of guarding, controlling, and being fearful of it? It really all comes down to education. I'm a huge believer of putting our money into better education. If people could just get along, they'd get over their fears. Then we would be able to cultivate life on this planet to an almost unbelievable level. *Education is truly the answer.* Religion is not the answer. Big government is not the answer. Education is the answer.

As a Navigator, you have an ability to affect other people through your energy and through your frequency. If you think about your energy moving outward when you meditate, you can affect people all around you. You can affect Red Cells so they are able to feel something from you and so they become calmer and more loving. I think you probably know that already. But what if it was ten times stronger, more intense, or easier to affect?

I always see everything as water. When I'm in a pool, I move the water. When you were a kid, did you ever walk around in a circle in an above ground pool? If you did, you started the water to spiral in a certain direction. If you turn in the opposite direction it pushes you. If you were to stand still and make your body tilt a little bit, you could siphon it off in a certain direction.

As Navigators, I see us being able to navigate, direct, show the way, and maneuver around obstacles. We have the ability to harness the beautiful Buddhist and Hindu energy. To us, it's like sunlight emiting outward only without a sense of direction. It is just there, but it's not shining on the people it needs to shine on.

So the Buddhists are saying, "Hey, Red Cells, come smell our glowing flower," and the Red Cells say, "I don't want to smell that damn flower. I don't even know what it is." Then one or two people smell it and say, "Oh, that's it." Then they join in. It's not that I want to control them. I just want to open their eyes. I want them to see. I want them to understand. It doesn't have to be what *I see*. It doesn't have to be completely what *I believe*. I think that if you just gave it a chance, you'd go, "Aha!" That's all, just give me an "Aha." That's all I want.

Our consciousness can mingle with all of these other good harmonics that are not being efficiently applied. My gripe is the efficiency of that energy. The Buddhists put out an enormous amount of energy but it isn't being efficiently directed to affect the consciousness of the people. It's not that it's not having a good effect. But if they could learn to direct it better, thay could harness more.

As Navigators, I want us to acknowledge all of those beautiful frequencies that are out there. If it's not jus like our harmonic, it's still good. Otherwise, that's just like saying that orchids are the only good flowers. Or daffodils are the only good flowers, or jasmines are the only beautiful smelling flowers. I don't see it that way. I'm stunned that they even grow. I'm stunned that they have the colors they have. I'm stunned about how the bees pollinate them. And their smell! What a great gift! They're showing me all these beautiful colors and how the silkiness of the textures feels on my skin. It's so much to give. I am not selective. I look at all the beauty in the world. I just want to spread the seeds.

I want to harness that energy instead of it being just passive in the jungle. We need to bring it into the cities to convert the streets from concrete into plants and life that flourishes. Life doesn't have to be just plants. Life is about energy which affects consciousness which affects the organic life to come in. Then it becomes symbiotic. You have to affect the consciousness of the people.

When you're meditating or when you're in the zone, you can choose to enter this hyper frequency because your intent understands that frequency. I've exposed you to the concept. I've given you visualizations but I've also sent you the data so it's in you now. You can take that data and enter that bandwidth.

When you think about these other beautiful bandwidths that are not being efficiently applied, with your intent you can harness them, mix them in a big colorful bowl of consciousness, thought and energy. Then you can go to your chest, feel it, and just send it out. Then breathe it in and breathe it out.

You don't have to see to believe. *Believing is seeing, seeing is believing.* You have to believe. And you have to know that not everybody's going to feel it. Out of a certain amount of Red Cells, there's only going to be one or two. Then all of a sudden, you're just going to see a look in their face. It won't even be a smile, but it's a smile. Have you ever seen somebody smile but not smile? I see it all the time.

I'm going to show you a technique that's going to just drop you to your knees when you unleash it. Inside of you is a multi-dimensional gateway. It is a wormhole of sorts. And it is living. It is right in your chest about three inches deep. A part of it acts as your Navigator. It acts as your consciousness. Your soul is intertwined around it, almost like a guard. That gateway is like a very thin membrane. Have you ever seen a membrane? If you crack an egg and look inside, there a little skin inside of it that has the airway pocket in it. It's very thin, very fragile, but it's membrane. The other side of that membrane goes through all the dimensions, all the layers, until it gets to the final one dimension. *The One.* And it's radiating everywhere. It's just like the sound of "Aummm."

At the right time, you will open that through your consciousness harmonic, like a key. It's a certain thought process. If you just have that thought, if you can hold your Babbler and your other consciousness at bay and hold it still, it will then know that you're like a temple. All of your skills will release the greatest power that this Earth, this place has ever seen. It will simply open because you're able to open it with your Navigator.

It is the box that cannot be opened by anything. But it can be opened by one thing. Just like a flower, you can't force it to open. You can't do anything with it, but when the Sun hits it and the right moment hits it, what does it do? It blossoms. You're going into this place as a Master, because you are a Master. You wouldn't be here on this earth right now during these times if you had not been a Master in at least 3,000 lives already. You made a sacrifice to be here. You brought it in under the radar and it's under the hood. And when you go into the right place, people feel spiritual. That's just like the petals of the flower opening at the right time. At the core of that red flower in the very center is that brilliant orange-yellow, gold star. You will open at the right time at the right place. You will open if you choose to. When you open, it will just come out.

The Darkside senses weakness so it will move in and you will be in its shadow. And when it is at the darkest moment, the darkest time, you will release throughout the Earth, throughout every continent. It will be the One, "Aummmm." And the Darkside will go away ... leaving *The Master*.

The song *One* by U2 is about love. I often use songs to convey thoughts that are difficult to put into words. For me, this song says that you need to get over your hang-ups, whatever they are. At times, you think I'm great, you love me and want me to be your teacher. In the next minute, when you are unhappy or something goes wrong with your life, you blame me. Or you blame The Force. One day, you're meditating and doing all the things you think you should be doing and everything's wonderful in your life. Then your wife sends you child support papers from the lawyer. All of a sudden, you're angry at both God and me wondering why this is happening to you. Well, you shouldn't be angry at me because you didn't pay child support for seven months. That has nothing to do with God. It has to do with the decisions you made.

Everyone goes through dark times in their spiritual evolution. There are points when you can become frustrated, feel lost, cheated, or let down. These are human emotions. We are still biochemical in this dimension. There are still other people who wear you down, no matter how high you get. There's a part of you that's mad because you really liked where you were and you can't understand why all this crap just happened to bring you down.

So, you find reasons to be angry with me or the material I teach. When time passes, you rebound and wonder if you can return as a student of mine. And I'll tell you right now, there's not really anything that you can do to stop me from loving you. There's nothing you can do that can discourage me from not wanting to help you. And I mean that sincerely.

For those of you who have read Eric Robison's book *Bending God,* there is the whole thing about Evil Richard. He really put me through the mill on many different levels. And that book never really captured what I went through with him. None of my students could put me through what he put me through! I'm very honest and I'm very open. Most spiritual teachers are very much like me. When another well-known spiritual teacher started off as a teacher, as a guru, everybody had access to him. He would sit at the table with him. They could hug him and have just a moment to talk with him, but as time progressed, the staff kept people at a distance. And he became more reclusive and less accessible. At some point, you just couldn't even approach him any more. If you wanted to just say hi, hug him or even wave to him, you literally had to go through a process to get to that person. At some point, I think that may happen with me, but it is not my preference. When something happens, I personally get involved and I will do that for as long as I can.

These people are so guarded that you never see them get upset, fart, or even cough. You'll never see them ecstatic or sad. All you'll see is a very sterile product. These people are not always saintly. I don't buy that. That's just not real. If you only get to see their beauty, how are you supposed to attain that when it's not real? Jesus Christ got angry with some of his students. Krishna did the same thing. You just see slivers of the facts because it is impossible to capture the whole truth when the records are written. You are getting an already refined amount of information, but you think this is the way you should be. Well, me too. I wish I was always in this happy, blissful mood and I wish that my students around me wouldn't crash my car or run over my dog and stuff like that.

This is the real world ... and I love this world! I'm a teacher who said you shouldn't go into a cave and exclude yourself from the world. You can go into the cave once in a while but you have to go into the world, too. Have one foot in each world. You cannot just be a monk and live a spiritual life in a monastery, isolating yourself from reality. You want to find God, but didn't God create all of this so that you can find yourself? Isn't that really what it's all about? You can't live life and feel these emotions as energy. As energy, there are no major highs or lows. Those are biochemical releases in your body. We don't want our I's, but you can't just get rid of them. Just be aware of them even if you let them run rampant. You can recognize them. Most Red Cells can't recognize that's the point of it. They function but they never see themselves in the second person acting in a certain way. If they do, it's for a few seconds but is very limited. It is not about how much control you have over your I's. Just acknowledge that they are there and that you have some say at some point over them.

I certainly do not believe that all of those other enlightened people were always totally refined perfected beings. Maybe that's the let down. Maybe you're disappointed with that. You know something, I think that they laughed; they cried; they got angry, and they felt emotions. The difference is that I'm not afraid for you to see my emotions and I know I will be judged for that. Just make sure that you judge me overall and not for five minutes here or there.

I've mentioned Gurdjieff and the Fourth Way in previous books. Gurdjieff believed in what was called 'shock.' He would be at the dinner table with all the students and some intellectual or respectful guests who weren't really part of these teachings. At times, a student would do something that would upset him and he would slam his hands down on the table and berate them.

Everyone would be surprised at Gurdjieff's reaction. His answer was, "Well, that's shock. I need to shock you because if I don't, you're always going to be in this stasis where you get used to being yelled at and afterwards you adapt to my pattern." It's just like music. You get used to the music, so you adapt and then you become numb to it. Therefore it has no more effect.

So when someone is shocked by such a manner, it is almost like they're thinking, "Oh my God! He is angry at me," and you really reflect about what you did. In a way, it's a horrible thing, but it can be a good thing. By the fifth or tenth time you're thinking, "Oh, he is upset with me. He'll get over it in five minutes. It doesn't matter." It is important to say things in a certain way because we can get callous otherwise. Some people are more sensitive than others, and some people function at higher levels whereas others function at lower levels. I think women are much more reactive. I don't have to scream and get to that point with most of the women that I know because they get it. They're just smarter in some ways. There is a different processing mechanism with different people. Some guys actually get it the very first time, whereas some women can be off, too.

I have thousands of people who want my attention. Every year, there's another five or ten thousand. Fifteen years ago, I only had between 20 to 100 people, so there weren't so many consciousnesses focused on me looking for hope, help, energy and love. Every year it gets more and more intense, not that it's a problem. It's just that everybody wants a piece of me. I want to give to everybody. That's my nature. I would give so much that my heart will stop. And I wouldn't even think about it. And so I have to stop and check because I know that I can't make everybody happy.

I remember being devastated when somebody called up Higher Balance to complain, or sent a disparaging letter, or sent our stuff back because they thought I couldn't speak properly. Other people didn't like my grammar. I told my friends that I didn't want to teach because I knew people would say these things but they made me do it anyway. They said, "Who cares?"

But I would be devastated and really depressed because I wasn't able to reach this person to help them. That's what I'm thinking all the time - I failed them. How can I help this person if they don't like the way I express myself? How am I ever going to help them?

Can I change the way that I talk? I have to get them to listen. If they can listen, then I can reach them. I can show them how to build the foundation of Consciousness and find what they are really looking and yearning for – God! That's all I want to do. I realized that I can please most of the people most of the time, but I cannot please all of the people all of the time. Not everybody's going to understand you. Sometimes, they're just going to walk in and catch you at a really bad time. That's the first time they ever see you, and that was your moment. That's going to be recorded in their mind for the rest of their life and they're going to leave. For others, it doesn't matter how much you show them, teach them or do for them. If you cut your chest open and gave them your beating heart, they would just go, "Eh, that's not enough. I don't think that you really care that much." I'm telling you the truth but I'm taking it to an extreme.

I passionately want you to know that someday you must teach others. I'm trying to hand down the lessons from the scars that I bear to my children whom I love. I want no harm to come to you. I want to protect you, I want to shelter to you. I want to nurture you and that's truly how I feel. I have both polarities - the masculine and the feminine. When I say to you that I feel that motherly protective instinct, I really feel that. But I know that you are going to be disappointed because you are going to try to please other people and they're going to hurt you. It's not necessarily you, although you're going to believe it's you the way that I believed it was me.

I practically killed myself trying to please *Richard*. Then he would break down and cry, "I love you, and you are my teacher. You are my master and made me see the light again. I don't know why you try so hard and I'm not worthy." That was all great and wonderful. I didn't let him know that it felt like a sledge hammer had just hit my heart. I would never show him that heart. It took so much of my spirit to resurrect his spirit that I didn't stop to think about my own spirit. And he did this for over a decade! Three months later, the same thing would happen again. He was constantly challenging me because he wanted to see if he could master me. It took me a really long time to realize that. *Richard* had psychological problems. Human beings are biochemical so sometimes the brain can be deformed. Or it doesn't have all the right motor gears. As White Cells, we give so much we don't think about ourselves and that can be detrimental to our health.

For all intents and purposes, *Richard* was broken. And I kept trying to fix him. By the laws of physics, *Richard* shouldn't be able to be fixed. Yet, I did the miraculous. Every time, I fixed *Richard*. He had a history of destroying people including his family and his psychiatrist. He was just a destructive Goliath.

I've realized that I made *Richard* happy in one way because he's been through all the psychic schools. I didn't speak with him for five years. After five years, I started to warm up to him again. We remain friends. About eleven years ago, he made the mistake of not accepting me as his teacher anymore after I kept pushing him to say it. Now I say to him, "You relieved me of my responsibility so I have to go because I have things to do." Anyway, that's really the truth to the matter.

In my heart, letting *Richard* go was the hardest thing to do because I felt that I was failing him. Shortly afterward, the Higher Balance Institute was born! Look at how many people I have been able to reach since I gave up the one student that was draining me. When you teach, choose wisely. Know when to hold them and know when to fold them. There's nothing wrong with that. It's not giving up. You have to realize that there's only so much you can do to teach someone so you've got to choose wisely. Just don't toss them to the curve. If you are having issues, you've got to work through them like a good teacher. At some point, you have to ask yourself whether you as the teacher are the problem. Or does the student have psychological problems or other issues? Could you be teaching five people for the one that you are working with now? That is maybe the hardest decision you are ever going to make in your life as a teacher. But you are going to have to make it and live with that.

I give you permission to let them go. Proceed and find the ones you can work with because by the time you have hundreds of people that you were able to reach, you will have helped make The Force stronger on this planet.

We are going to go really deep into The Force and the Darkside from a scientific perspective. Once you understand that, you will be able to draw ten times more energy, even if you don't like or care about science. Believe me - it has an effect on your psyche.

I usually teach right from my consciousness and just lay it out. I feel the room and try and find the right frequency to communicate. The problem is that I am not a scientist. Science to me is a language. So, I'm going to read some scientific facts and then translate what that actually means to me so that you can interpret it for what it is. Keep in mind that there is a percentage of error in translation. Whenever I say something, generally it's like gospel and it will hold up, but now I'm taking something that's not specifically my arena and I'm using it to help show you something. There can be a measure of miscommunication if I get a photon confused with a micron or something else.

In the *Handbook of the Navigator,* I communicate what I understand within my mind, my hyper dimensional consciousness. It is a knowing. It is a memory. It is a language that is unlike anything that is vocalized inaudibly. Like when your tongue rolls and you have different languages. Can you imagine the complexities of trying to speak a different language? Often when I teach, my mind is trying to grapple a very sophisticated piece of knowledge for you. I'm translating that into English using the vocabulary I have to the best of my ability. When I think the vocabulary just isn't quite going to cut it, I generally start to describe or try to use different things that are familiar to you and say, "It's like this, it's like that." Then everybody 'gets it.'

When you can internalize that, it becomes you. It becomes your frequency. Your frequency is the totality of your experiences, your knowledge, and your intelligence. It is the fabric within your soul. It's like the essence of your frequency. When you move through the Universe and another entity moves towards you, you are on a different frequency. It's like when you look at somebody who is very old. You think they must really know a few things. We all learn, but not all old people actually know an awful lot. Some do. Some don't. Teenagers think they know everything and they usually don't know an awful lot.

Anyway, it's similar to when your frequency becomes aware of another frequency in the Universe. There is a sizing up that happens in a tenth of a millisecond. It's an acknowledgement that this energy has a certain texture to it. You recognize it as being old or powerful because powerful really means more knowledgeable and more experienced. They can manipulate the frequencies and energies because they have a better attunement. There's a communion because they get it. Not only am I trying to translate something from my mind, but now I'm taking something scientific from the exterior and distilling it down into something you can comprehend.

Recently, scientists had a huge breakthrough on something that I talked about twenty years ago! No one is listening to me because I don't have the scientific credentials. To be accepted scientifically, you have to be able to reproduce things in the lab. Even though most of it cannot be reproduced in a lab, it's accepted as gospel "truth" because it's mathematics. Well, what is mathematics? It's a language. That's all it is. In this dimension, science is probably what I would buy into the most as far as a form of data based information. It's the best quality.

Storytelling is good, but I know that it has lost a lot of its content because it's translated through a human consciousness. Science is like a collective of thought that is meticulously compiled but where they are constantly going back and forth over the details of it. With science, about every ten years there is literally an explosion where their whole understanding of things changes by about 30%. That's huge when you think about it. I never say it's gospel truth. You can't just assume that what they say is the way it is. If you read the lines carefully, they'll admit that. They'll lay it out like, "Here's the numbers. This is what the data says. This is the best explanation we have to work with." Nine times out of ten, it turns out to be accurate.

So having said that, science has a huge effect on the human consciousness through what I would call your Governor - that microchip in the back of your head. You have an understanding of how electricity works because of science. You have an understanding of where your heart, kidney, liver and other organs are in your body because of science. It is ingrained in your consciousness. In a way, science is almost worshiped, like how God is worshiped in church. In a way, I see science as being a religion that literally competes with religions. I think that's a very good thing because competition is good. A lot of people don't understand that, but I do. Within reason, a friendly, respectful, helpful, loving, nurturing, and encouraging competition is very good. There is a certain trait in a human being that likes that and it makes you want to be better. As a spiritual teacher and guru and as a person, I like to use science to help confirm what I'm teaching or what I'm sharing because unknowingly in your consciousness there is a reverence and respect for science and it's directly connected to your Governor.

The reason why you are attracted to me as a spiritual person is because I embrace science and appreciate common sense and logic. I know that science will dictate what you can do and what you can't do. The more that I can utilize what scientists disclose, the more you will be able to see the logic in it. When you see that it makes sense, you can see how it works and you realize it must be so. And when you say something must be so, all of a sudden you can do it.

When I wrote *The Handbook of the Navigator,* I talked about the creation of the Universe and vacuum energy, which is friction energy. It is a frequency that I can see in my mind. I try to find ways to describe that energy. The very beginning is the substance from which God ethereally was more or less created from. It was like the water with the microbes bouncing into each other that finally created complex life from that. I've talked about The Force, Prana, and energy. I know that if I can come at it from different angles, you can see different aspects of the same thing. If I want to talk from a spiritual angle, I'll explain Prana and God's consciousness. That's good but there is some part of us that wants to know more about the scientific part.

I believe that vacuum energy is the energy in the Universe which we call Prana, or what energy is in the Universe. Scientists are re-approaching and trying to understand it so they can tap that energy because it's still very mysterious to them. I purposely took all of this information from published sources so that it is recorded and videotaped. It's pretty simplified, as much as something complicated can be. *Wikipedia* describes vacuum energy as, "An underlying background energy that exists in space thoughout the entire universe."

Even when there are no stars, no planets, or anything else, there's still vacuum energy. So before there was a universe there was vacuum energy. Think about that. Wikipedia continues:

> "The effects of vacuum energy can be experimentally observed in various phenomena such as spontaneous emission, the Casimir effect and the Lamb shift, and are thought to influence the behavior of the Universe on cosmological scales."

They don't have the proof of this yet. In standard terms, they're saying they know there's this vacuum energy and that it existed before anything of matter existed, like stars, planets, or anything physical. They don't have a way of demonstrating yet but they're pretty sure that its presence had a major effect on the universe with the cosmological scales. They are really trying to say that it's part of creation. I call it The Force. Wikipedia continues with the Origin of Vacuum Energy:

> "Quantum field theory states that all fundamental fields, such as the electromagnetic field, must be quantized at each and every point in space. A field of physics may be envisioned as if space were filled with interconnected vibrating balls and springs, and the strength of the field were like the displacement of a ball from its rest position."

When they are talking about fundamental fields, they are talking about gravitation, magnetism, and the all the other areas of physics that have an effect on our reality. In one of my classes, I talked about when I really zoom in that everything comes down to these orbs and that there's a frequency in that. I suspect they're talking about exactly what I'm seeing. Or they are starting to get there in science and in technology. The reason this is very important is that we are on the fringe of tapping time and space. In this lifetime, we are on the fringe of time travel and quantum jumps. This will give a new definition to the term 'navigator.'

In the movie *Dune*, they use spice, which is a drug that expands their consciousness. Once their consciousness is expanded, they don't necessarily need to keep doing it. They just kept doing it to maintain that expanded consciousness. Each member of the highest evolved species that used spice developed an array of skills or abilities. The most advanced ones became navigators. Other civilizations loaded their spaceships into these huge tubes. Then a navigator went into the cockpit of the tube and used her mind to fold space. In other words, she took whatever was in that tube, including all the space crafts, and she traversed space to the other side of the galaxy. Navigators fold the space between those points in a matter of seconds. You wouldn't even feel it. The door shut when everybody was in. When the door opened, you'd look out and be in another galaxy.

The people from other worlds who didn't have access to the navigator ships had to fly through space from one point to another. That takes a long time! The Universe is over 27 billion light years across so if you were going to travel across it, even at the speed of light, it would take you over 27 billion years! But if a navigator uses his mind, he is able to fold space and take with him the cargo that is within the ship. When his mind moves, you reappear in a different place.

At some earlier time, navigators probably journeyed to or saw that destination. In the early phases of history, navigators had to see a destination in order to know how to get there again. They kept travelling through space by traditional means, but they were able to go further because they had a better way of utilizing their consciousness. When they went back again, they could do it in one leap instead of having to do it in small distances. So over hundreds or thousands of years, their species collectively mapped the galaxies.

A navigator goes deep into his mind just like he is meditating. When I talk about the different frequencies I go into, these different places, these different dimensions, they do the same thing. Their technology doesn't have the capability of doing what the multi-dimensional consciousness can do. The multi-dimensional consciousness is too advanced. But the technology can work with and enhance the multidimensional consciousness in other quantum physics ways. It's like taking two particles that are moving and stopping one. The other one will stop without having any reason to stop. We know this from scientific research. In a similar way, the navigator envisions or sees very clearly this place that he wants to be and he builds the vision in his mind so clearly. Then he convinces himself without a doubt, almost to the level of delusion, that it is reality so it becomes reality. When he comes out of this meditation, he assumes he's there along with all the beings that travelled with him; and so they are. They were in a tube that was sealed completely shut, so their consciousness had no thoughts of seeing what's outside because it would've weighed the navigator down. The same thing happens when you meditate with me. You drag me down with you.

There will be huge breakthroughs in science in the next ten to thirty years. I'm already aware of a number of them that are not noted anywhere. You're not going to see them on TV. In my opinion, they are going to need to start dabbling with time and space. They are literally going to need 'White Cells,' who have disciplined their mind like a martial artist so that they have this flexibility in their consciousness to affect what I call 'quantum physical ripples,' by moving through time, space or a dimension, and acquiring data from these places.

Navigators will do more than just helping the harmonics of the planet. Don't ever think that you have just one role. Also, there will be a difference in harmonics between males and females in how they choose to apply their abilities as Navigators. It's not that the male can't do what the female does; and it's not what the male or the female can do. It can also go vice versa. There's not a limitation. It's just a natural interest that will lead you in a certain direction. You just have to define that. You will find that the majority of White Cells, because of biological reasons, will naturally want to be that way by choice.

In the future, schools that are based upon my teachings become 'houses.' There will be schools which are going to be very much like in the movie *Dune*. The people in one house might follow the philosophy of a teacher that mastered healing. That house will take the teachings and serve as healers. If you want to go to a house of healing under HBI's teachings, this is where the master healers reside. You can go to them for help and they can teach you. If you want to be a long distance seer, you will go to the Navigator house. Could you find a healer in a house that's predominantly long distance seers? Absolutely, if someone wants to master a certain area, they can go to the house that specializes in that even if they belong to a different house. They will interchange and share.

This is where I see the future of HBI going. It will become a necessity and literally a part of the dynamics of the planet. I believe that science is going to discover that Navigators have the ability to work with science to manipulate particles and have an influence on energies. This is already true. We know this from the *Princeton Engineering Anomalies Research (PEAR) studies* where a mechanical device dropped balls down a peg-covered board and people concentrated to make the balls move more towards one side more than the other. If somebody concentrates on affecting the balls path, it is significant if it goes past 50%. Literally, you wouldn't think 51% is a big difference but when it's consistently 51, 52, or 53% when you're affecting it and 50, 50, 50% when you are not, that is significant.

Well, scientists are going to find that for people who are drawn to stuff like this that there's almost a distilling level of the other ones who are interested in it. There is something inside of them driving them further. It's like the drive that the main characters had in *Close Encounters of the Third Kind*. Since the teachings are so advanced, the scientists are more than likely going to recruit the people who have studied my teachings for ten years rather than training their own people for ten years. I can't say specifically how it's going to happen because you're talking about a matter of time.

When we have a guild, our protocols will state that we will help science as long as science is in line with God, The Force. If there is a fine line, as a guild, we will refuse to assist them and might even turn on them if we think they are going down a road that we disagree with. If they want to work with us and want our technology, then they are going to have to work with us on our terms. I would hope that we stand by that and not sell out. And remember that there will always be sell outs, so don't be bitter about it. It wouldn't be any fun if it weren't that way. Wikipedia continues:

> *"The theory requires "vibrations" in, or more accurately changes in the strength of, such a field to propagate as per the appropriate wave equation for the particular field in question. The second quantization of quantum field theory requires that each such ball-spring combination be quantized, that is, that the strength of the field be quantized at each point in space. Canonically, if the field at each point in space is a simple harmonic oscillator, its quantization places a quantum harmonic oscillator at each point. Excitations of the field correspond to the elementary particles of particle physics. Thus, according to the theory, even the vacuum has a vastly complex structure and all calculations of quantum field theory must be made in relation to this model of the vacuum."*

In other words, no matter where we go with any of this, it all comes back to the vacuum, to The Force, to the primal energy. The Wikipedia article on Vacuum Energy continues:

"The theory considers vacuum to implicitly have the same properties as a particle, such as spin or polarization in the case of light, energy, and so on."

Scientifically, they are saying what we've been saying the whole time. We refer to The Force as *The Light*, as *The Energy*. They are just making it more scientific sounding. I've always said that science and spirituality are going to come head to head. This is happening already. Wikipedia continues on vacuum energy:

"According to the theory, most of these properties cancel out on average leaving the vacuum empty in the literal sense of the word. One important exception, however, is the vacuum energy or the vacuum expectation value of the energy. The quantization of a simple harmonic oscillator requires the lowest possible energy, or zero-point energy of such an oscillator to be:

$$E = \frac{1}{2}hv$$

Summing over all possible oscillators at all points in space gives an infinite quantity. To remove this infinity, one may argue that only differences in energy are physically measurable, much as the concept of potential energy has been treated in classical mechanics for centuries. This argument is the underpinning of the theory of renormalization. In all practical calculations, this is how the infinity is handled.

Vacuum energy can also be thought of in terms of virtual particles (also known as vacuum fluctuations) which are created and destroyed out of the vacuum. These particles are always created out of the vacuum in particle-antiparticle pairs, which in most cases shortly annihilate each other and disappear. However, these particles and antiparticles may interact with others before disappearing, a process which can be mapped using Feynman diagrams. Note that this method of computing vacuum energy is mathematically equivalent to having a quantum harmonic oscillator at each point and, therefore, suffers the same renormalization problems."

Scientifically, what is The Force? What is this energy that is everywhere that you can see, that you can feel, that you can tap and utilize? I would say that it probably falls under this vacuum field of energy. God is probably something finer still and yet beyond this. In this dimension, it is abundant. They are trying to tap this as 'free energy.' There are a lot of videos on YouTube of wheel spinning magnetics that are supposed to create energy without having gas or any fuel in the traditional sense. They'll say that it uses this vacuum energy. They are trying to use The Force to power cars in the future. And why not? That's what it really comes down to. It's fascinating to see that they are starting to catch on.

The Large Hadron Collider (LHC) is the world's largest and most powerful particle collider, built by the European Organization for Nuclear Research (CERN) from 1998 to 2008. The LHC was built in collaboration with over 10,000 scientists and engineers from over 100 countries, as well as hundreds of universities and laboratories. It lies in a tunnel 27 kilometres (17 mi) in circumference, as deep as 175 metres (574 ft) beneath the Franco-Swiss border near Geneva, Switzerland.

The LHC is going to delve much deeper into these energies in more practical forms. There have been other Hadron colliders built at CERN and Fermilab, but they were not big enough. The LHC's aim is to allow physicists to test the predictions of different theories of particle physics and high-energy physics, and particularly prove or disprove the existence of the Higgs particle and of the large family of new particles predicted by supersymmetrical theories. The Higgs particle was confirmed by data from the LHC in 2013. The LHC is expected to address some of the unsolved questions of physics, advancing human understanding of physical laws. It contains seven detectors, each designed for certain kinds of research.

In essence, by smashing these particles and proving the existence of the Higg's particle, *the God particle*, they can potentially tap the source that created the universe - the Big Bang - God.

While they were building the LHC, there was speculation from some factions that it would open up a black hole. They really believed that was feasible so it could affect all of us in a horrible, horrible way. Other people speculated that it wasn't going to do anything. Anyway, I suspect that when they actually are able to achieve this they will have the data and information they will need to get the technology and mathematics they will need to affect time and space. There is very critical information that will come out of it. I do not believe it will be the end of the world because how else would there be future people if we blew up the world?

Let's move onto the Darkside. *In science, the Darkside is known as dark energy, dark matter.* Now the ironic thing is that the spiritualist is going to say that dark matter is the Darkside because it uses the word 'dark,' so it must be what's evil in the universe. There are several things I want to say about that. The Gaia mind speaks to us through movies, concepts and ideas. And these ideas become our perception of reality. If you were in a different culture, your perception might be different because it was isolated from this culture. You have to keep in mind that the world is now really falling under one culture. Today, the dominate culture is probably the United States or the English language, which came from England. Inevitably, our TV programs are now being seen all over the world and people are learning English just from watching those TV programs. They are also watching how we act and how we move.

One of the things I've noticed when I travelled across America was the loss of accents, especially from the South. Years ago, younger people had more of a drawl and had heavier accents. In the younger generation, you almost can't find that anymore. Even the Australians don't have much of an accent, unless you really pay attention. The accent is still there but it's fading out. To me, this indicates that slowly the collective consciousness is becoming one collective perception. We're losing our diversity, and we're becoming more single minded and more like-minded. I don't think that is a bad thing, but I don't think it's a good thing. In a sense, I think it's probably more of a good thing. I just don't know what the loss means.

I would love to see a one world government because I want us to move into space. I want medicine to be available in Africa just as it is in the United States and Europe. That is not going to happen until we treat all these other countries like our neighbours. Then what affects them is what affects us. We have to get along and we have to share. I think culture is beautiful and amazing, but if we all hang onto our separate identities, I see it as a self-defeating thing in its own way. It keeps us separate and in fear over who has what, who has an advantage over the other, and who's going to get this and who's going to get that.

It's very complicated, but this has been happening ever since we first started trading by ship thousands of years ago. Over the past two decades, there has been a dramatic increase because of the speed that data moves via the Internet. When an event happens somewhere in the world, that information is instantly available everywhere else. As the data transfer becomes faster and faster, the whole consciousness of the planet reacts to events simultaneously. This has a huge effect on the consciousness of the planet. The Internet and television are flooding us with data. The human brain is the same way. The human brain started to speed up information so it became more cognitive, more memory oriented, and more complex. It shared data to one part of the brain faster than the other. In a way, that's what separated us from other species.

What does all this have to do with the Darkside? There have recently been movies talking about anti-matter and the Darkside. Star Trek has really jacked up the whole concept of anti-matter. Forget about anti-matter. The proper scientific term is actually dark matter and dark energy. One would think they would come up with some technical name for it like 'Quasar triple space.' In my opinion, the scientists didn't decide to call it dark matter and dark energy because it was a black void space. They choose dark matter because, intuitively, they felt something was very wrong about what they were seeing. The collective consciousness deemed it dark matter and dark energy.

Dark matter is different than dark energy. They're two different things, yet they're synonymous in a way. When I say dark matter, I'm talking about matter - something solid. When I talk about dark energy, I'm talking more like the vacuum, the frequency, the energy. You must have that separation in your head when you are trying to wrap your spiritual hyper dimensional consciousness around this, because you have to work with your organic brain. This is why we are doing this now. Hyper dimensionally and spiritually, you understand the Darkside. You know the vibe, but you still have to process organically as long as you are in this physical dimension. In the past, I've taught you that this is a dark energy but I've never gone into it too deeply because you are still young in the sense of awakening yourself. Also, you'll drift towards what you become interested in. Your consciouness is determined by what you think so you gravitate towards what you think, because it's all intuitively connected. By approaching it this way now, you are going to deal with the organic state which has that microchip and remove that microchip and its limitations by talking about this material. That will give you a better ability to confront and deal with this energy. Here's what Wikipedia has to say about Dark Matter:

> *"In astrophysics and cosmology, dark matter is a hypothetical form of matter of unknown composition that does not emit or reflect enough electromagnetic radiation to be observed directly, but whose presence can be inferred from gravitational effects and visible matter."*

They know dark matter is out there because when they look at the universe with their telescopes, they see the stars. And when they look at the stars, some of them have a blurred effect to them like something is not perfectly symmetrical. When they look at the blurred effect, they can see there's a whole section of them that appears to be stretching. When light comes towards dark matter from behind, in our angle of vision, it hits the dark matter making the light bend. By seeing where these bends in the light are located, scientists can actually determine the size of the dark matter that's out there. They can detect dark matter by using the light. Wikipedia continues:

> "According to present observations of structures larger than galaxies as well as Big Bang cosmology, dark matter accounts for the vast majority of mass in the observable Universe."

There's dark matter in the universe that we can observe. That's the trick here. It's what we on this little tiny planet can see. From what we can evaluate, there's more dark matter than there is actually life, or matter as we'd see it in a positive way. In a way, that is a scary thought though – you have to admit. The Dark Matter article on Wikipedia continues:

> "The observed phenomenon is consistent with dark matter observations as the rotational speeds of galaxies and orbital velocities of galaxies in clusters, gravitational lensing of background objects by galaxy clusters such as the Bullet cluster, and the temperature distribution of hot gas in galaxies and clusters of galaxies. Dark matter also plays a central role in structure formation and galaxy evolution, and has measurable effects on the anisotropy of the cosmic microwave background. All these lines of evidence suggest that galaxies, clusters of galaxies, and the universe as a whole contain far more matter than that which interacts with electromagnetic radiation: the remainder is called the "dark matter component."

There seems to be a relationship between the existence and expansion of the universe and dark matter's role in the creation and evolution of the universe. The dogma from some religions and belief systems say that the Darkside is necessary in order to have the good. I don't buy into that idea, but I would say that you need destruction to create life, like Shiva. With dark matter, there is a push-pull effect with the energies. When you push something and it moves forward, it's not the object that is moving forward in the pushing. The vacuum that follows behind it is the mysterious effect, or what we want to pay attention to.

In this dimension, I believe that God is matter. Part of God solidified and became the planets and the stars. God's essence is The Force that surrounds and binds. It became matter which is still another form of energy to experience a law of physics. God is curious, inquisitive, and wants to experience. There's this whole universe here for God to experience. We are a fragment of that experience for God. We're still collecting little rain drops of air and somehow give our data and our experience to God because we're interconnected and we're evolving independently at the same time. So – Alisone. Wikipedia continues:

> "The composition of dark matter is unknown but may include ordinary and heavy neutrinos, recently postulated elementary particles such as WIMPS, and axions, astronomical bodies such as dwarf stars and planets (collectively called MACHOs), primordial black holes and clouds of nonluminous gas."

Primordial means from the very beginning.

> "Also matter which might exist in another Universe but might affect ours via gravity would be consistent with some theories of brane cosmology. Current evidence favors models in which the primary component of dark matter is new elementary particles, collectively called non-baryonic dark matter."

I don't necessarily think they're right because it starts off by saying that "dark matter is a hypothetical form of matter of unknown composition." Everything they say is speculative. As they begin to study it even more, I believe their thinking is going to change a lot. Wikipedia continues:

"The dark matter component has vastly more mass than the visible component of the Universe. At present the density of ordinary baryons and radiation in the universe is estimated to be equivalent to about one hydrogen atom per cubic meter of space. Only about 4% of the total energy density in the universe (as inferred from gravitational effects) can be seen directly." Remember, they said that only 4% can be seen directly. *"About 22% is thought to be composed of dark matter. The remaining 74% is thought to consist of dark energy."*

So, in our Universe dark matter and dark energy are the dominant components. I believe that dark energy and dark matter are the scientific equivalent of what we would call the Darkside or the Dark Force. Looking at those percentages, then scientifically the Darkside is more powerful than The Force in this dimension. Doesn't that suck?! Fear not, there is hope yet. Some people ask me whether the Darkside is stronger than The Force. My reply is, "No, but you know you have to understand everything that I understand to really come to that conclusion."

"The remaining 74% is thought to consist of dark energy, an even stranger component, distributed diffusely in space."

It's diffusely spread, not concentrated in any specific spot, just like rice being thrown into the air.

"Some hard- to-detect baryonic matter makes a contribution to dark matter, but constitutes only a small portion. Determining the nature of this missing mass is one of the most important problems in modern cosmology and particle physics. It has been noted that the names 'dark matter' and 'dark energy' serve mainly as expressions of human ignorance, much as the marking of early map with terror incognita."

The consciousness named it 'dark' because intuitively there's a truth behind it. So we are already arguing with science.

"Observational Evidence - The first to provide evidence and infer the existence of a phenomenon that has come to be called dark matter was Swiss astrophysicist Fritz Zwicky of the California Institute of Technology (Caltech) in 1933... When Zwicky compared this mass estimate to one based on the number of galaxies and total brightness of the cluster, he found that there was about 400 times more mass than expected."

So this is how he figured out how to see dark matter.

"The gravity of the visible galaxies in the cluster would be far too small for such fast orbits, so something extra was required. This is known as the 'missing mass problem.' Based on these conclusions, Zwicky inferred that there must be some non-visible form of matter which would provide enough of the mass and gravity to hold the cluster together."

As for dark energy:

"Cosmologists estimate that the acceleration began roughly five billion years ago."

They're really saying that the Big Bang was God entering this universe. We know the universe is expanding because we can measure it. We know there was probably an epicenter, and the universe is moving outwards from the epicenter. Also, there's evidence that the epicenter is fading away. I believe the universe is expanding and that it started off with the Big Bang. That's when God punched into the universe.

In the diagram above, the circle on the top is the Big Bang. In that explosion, the Universe comes in and it starts to expand, which is shown in the downwards arc. It keeps expanding, expanding, and expanding, moving out from the epicenter. Eventually, it's evolving and changing. Slowly, it's deteriorating but growing and becoming new things as it's going through the Shiva process. Civilizations live and die in the universe and technology evolves. Somewhere in the picture is the human race, along with the millions of other races. *Eventually, God solidifies its energy into a slower vibration which becomes matter.* All the stars and the planets are all matter. Within the circle, there are galaxies and within those are solar systems composed of planets. Let's have each dot within the circle represent a galaxy. Keep in mind that it's not drawn to scale. To give you an idea of the scale, if you look at a beach, as far as you can see on a clear day, one grain of sand would represent a galaxy. Inside each grain are billions of solar systems just like ours. That really doesn't even do it justice.

Time is an effect. In my opinion, the easiest way to evaluate time is deterioration and restructuring. A mountain grows and deteriorates, crumbling back down; deterioration is an easy way to generalize time. Everything is changing and metamorphosing. It's experiencing and data is being collected. Souls probably have not even fully gestated until the universe is at least 25% into its beginning phase. There may be living creatures but the mechanism to create frequency and hold it together to exist after the organic body dies has not necessarily happened yet. After that, intelligent life comes about when a being asks, "Is this all that I am?" When they take in Prana, they start to build a dimensional body that can exist outside of the fundamental dimension that we see here, allowing them to be birthed into the next life. This is reincarnation, which allows the planetary consciousness and God's consciousness to grow on another level. It means that God is learning because God is adapting.

In the above diagram, grey represents the physical matter. Trace amounts of energy are mixing on a higher frequency with the physical matter, compounding and becoming stronger. In my opinion, it is getting so strong that life is now gaining intelligence to recreate itself as life again. This is the birth of the soul.

In this dimension, for every action there is an equal and opposite reaction. In this case, the reaction to God's presence would be the Darkside. I've noted it in the diagram above with red. Yhe Darkside has also been in this dimension since the Big Bang. The Darkside also represents dark matter, so the truth of the science is correct.

The Universe is learning as it expands in this dimension. This is important! God is expanding into the nothingness, but for God it's not about expanding because that's a problem. God doesn't necessarily want us to expand. God wants us to stay in this amount of space for as long as possible because God is gaining information here that God can't get in any other dimension. It's not to say that God is not in any other dimension. Like us, God seeks out knowledge. As God experiences this dimension, God is rushing and struggling to stay here for as long as possible to acquire the information It wants. On some micro-level, we're in this game play. Science says this universe is about 15 billion years old, but I think it's closer to 20 billion years old. Anyway, I'm just trying to give you a mental concept.

The universe is expanding but it's becoming more fragmented. Eventually It dissipates into nothing. It just disappears, becoming complete energy again. All matter breaks down into energy, to molecules, to photons. Eventually it will dissipate into this vacuum form of energy. Imagine your brain expanding, and expanding, and expanding. What eventually happens? The information traveling for those short distances on your neural pathways is not able to transverse fast enough. It takes more time to get there, making it more difficult for the energy to communicate. As the universe expands, it also deteriorates. The planets and solar systems are falling apart. Eventually somewhere in the far distant future, the universe is going to fade away. It might as well be infinity compared to how we perceive time on this micro level. As a group, we have a bigger vision so we can conceive this.

In my opinion, God came in as energy. God will leave as energy into the next dimension. It doesn't mean that God is gone. It means that God's hand dipped into the cookie jar that is this dimension, grabbed the cookie, and got out fast. God is standing wholly in these other dimensions where God is predominant and exists and will be there an infinite amount of time before this. This is nothing in comparison. It's not to say God is gone. God wants to be in this dimension for a certain amount of time.

Dark matter and dark energy are a major factor in this dimension comprising 96%. The remaining 4% is matter. While pushing the universe apart, dark matter seems to be the major contributor in the expansion of the universe. There is this constant struggle between The Force and the Darkside in our universe. God is trying to accelerate and collect as much experience in this dimension from all these worlds, galaxies, and universes, and time is infinite. We can't really look at time in that sense because we're trying to understand the big picture. Why is this happening? What is going on? What is the reason behind it? What's the motive? If we can understand the motive – that knowledge gives you power. That's what I'm trying to give you - power. You understand something that no other person on this planet fully understands! The people reading this book are some of the few people on the planet who can perceptually understand this. Dark matter is pushing the world apart. When scientists look at the universe, they're seeing these huge sections of dark matter. In this dark matter, they are going to find dead worlds, dead galaxies, dead stars, and other forms of life that have died. That is the handy work of the Darkside. That's the aftermath.

Dark energy also permeates the space you're in now. We also know that The Force is in this same space. This is a constant. Dark energy has been very successful destroying matter. That is the role of the Darkside. In my opinion, that is the source of the Darkside's energy.

So The Force is struggling to exist in this dimension so It can experience, gain what It can, and protect the life that It's symbiotically a part of. It looks at you the same way that you look at your body. Do you love your body? You don't think of your body as being separate from you but it really is, isn't it? Are you going to stick your hand into a fire? No, you're going to try and protect it. Just as there are billions of living cells in your body, the body of God is comprised of billions of tiny living things. To God, we're all a part of it. It's fighting to exist here in this dimension, but eventually it's going to lose the battle in this dimension. It's not a bad thing because God got the cookie from the cookie jar which is what God was really after.

I just feel like I need to say this so that you understand. God has all these upper levels dimensionally. If I drew thousands of lines, each line would represent an entire universe or dimension. That's how I see it. Inside of one of those lines could be our entire expanding universe.

This whole thing is happening over an area that's a tiny little speck in one of these lines. God wants to experience what's here. As God pushes down from the upper levels, the intensity gets much darker because that's the vibration of what we would deem the Darkside. And the Darkside is oozing into this dimension while God is pushing down through all the higher levels. The further God gets, the higher the level of resistance. We're collecting data on the Darkside which it doesn't want us to get. With knowledge comes power. God takes this information and absorbs it into the God 'collective', reformatting it so that God can push down and take another one of these dimensions.

In the end, it's like a big chess game between God and the Darkside. Having the scientific background about the Darkside gives you a better way of looking at it. By giving you this knowledge, you will be able to feel it. There's a knowing.

Earlier, you said that you will be drawing energy down from the highest dimension. Is that another factor in this equation?

No, it's not. I'll show you how it's all connected. Everything I've told you is absolutely pertinent information that you need to know. As the world approached 2012, the Darkside encroached upon our world. It was an opportunity for the Darkside because the Red Cells were going to lose their programming that comes from the stars. The stars use solar radiation to send data. In a sense, I believe that the stars are also multi-dimensional. They're operating from these other frequencies, emitting outward into space in this dimension. It's almost like finger tips coming in, sending data or information to living planets. As life advances and becomes more complex, the possibility increases that these beings will create souls which they can then use to articulate this information back into the higher frequencies.

Most organic intelligence is contributed back to the living planet. Some of the organic intelligence that goes back to the planet can be uploaded to a higher frequency for God. On a micro defensive level, a white cell that is part of your immune system has to be a hybrid cell that's able to move the data up into the higher dimensions and then return back down, interfusing with the organic life again. When the planet started to go through this dark, shadowy space that has nothing to do with the Darkside, it was an opportunity for this energy to move and try to accumulate or have an effect on the consciousness of the organism. It could influence, infiltrate, and move on different levels. Some human beings became Sith warriors, instead of Jedi. Many of them live in the corporate world manipulating things. There are different levels of operations going on.

You might say that we're the winning team but you have to remember, if we slip an inch, the Darkside will move a mile. If we turn our backs, it will move a mile. And if it has an opportunity, it will annihilate and destroy us. And eventually one of the two are going to win. In the diagram, light stretches across the higher dimensions whereas the dark is condensed in the lower dimensions. As far as size goes, this dimension is a lot darker. So that is a concern.

Anyway, we can move our data but God wants us here to create a higher vibration. God is willing to move into us to preserve the life on this particular planet. It's not to say that we're the only precious one in the Universe. It just means that none of the other worlds are running under the umbrella at this moment. That's what makes it imperative now - to infuse White Cells into the planet's culture and people. Genetics plays a role in this, too. If there's not enough illumination here as it reaches that pivotal moment, we must create the illumination so that when the Darkside touches down, we can turn into such a hot flame that we burn it.

So, let's just take a few seconds to do that. Close your eyes. Relax and go into the zone. This is important now. I am going to show you a technique that I call *chuning*. Then I will show you how to activate it. I have been waiting for this moment for 10,000 years.

I recommend that you watch the movie *Dark City (1998)*. It starts off in a setting that feels like the 1950's. It has the feeling of an old movie even though it isn't one. Everything seems like it's always dark because it's always night time. There's never any daylight. In *Dark City*, everybody goes about their life routinely every day. The main character (John Murdock) starts to question his reality. He begins to have issues with various things. To make a long story short, the whole city was removed from the Earth in one big chunk of land. Or it was created to look like a city from Earth. And it's traveling through space. The inhabitants of the city were abducted and transplanted there but they didn't know they were abducted so they're living their lives as if nothing has happened. It turns out that bald-headed aliens control the city and they look like Shadow People.

I think that's what first caught my attention about the movie – the similarity between the bald-headed aliens and Shadow People. They both wear a hat and a long trench coat. The screenwriters of this movie must have tapped into the collective consciousness of the planet to come up with this material. As I continued to watch the movie, it became more and more interesting. It turns out that the aliens are looking for the human soul because that is an element that they don't have. The writers did a really great job making the movie very realistic. I think any spiritual person can relate to this story.

The humans don't even know that the aliens exist. In the movie, the aliens have a very strong telepathic ability that they call *chuning.* The aliens gather together, willing the whole city to fall asleep. Everybody just stops whatever they're doing and drop their heads – as if someone flicked a switch turning them off. All the humans just become unconscious. Then thousands of the aliens went out in groups, injecting things into the people's brains. They switch people's personalities by injecting something in their brains. One minute you are somebody's wife; and the next minute you're a divorced woman. The whole environment, including the walls and even the building structures, shifts and changes. Apartments become big and fancy because this chuning allows the aliens to control the whole layout with their minds. They constantly immerse the people into micro condensed life-time after lifetime, trying to see what happens to their energy and to their soul.

It's fascinating to watch how the lead character, John Murdoch, awakens and realizes he has abilities, just like the aliens. He ends up getting into a battle with the most powerful alien there. I recommend that you watch this movie because it's really cool.

Earlier in this chapter, I explained that our consciousness shifts as we move around our solar system and galaxy. When our solar system moves under this black ribbon area of the Milky Way, it blocks the stars that normally bombard our planet with frequency. That affects our reality as human beings, which impacts society around the world. There's less influence from the stars during this thirty year period. The difference in solar, or *electromagnetic radiation* affects our human consciousness. Do you understand that the stars have solar radiation and the solar radiation impacts the earth to a certain degree? It gets distorted through the magnetic field. These stars are the same influence as Red Cells, and they influence you somewhat. It's like your Babbler, or your desire, or your inspiration and it culls you along, along with other vibrations and frequencies. When we move under this ribbon, this black ribbon, it's like an umbrella and it's going to prevent these affects or filter them. It's not going to prevent it 100%. It's going to filter a certain *quality* or *quantity* of this radiation that we're used to getting for thousands of years.

The Universe communicates with the living organisms of its body throughout the galaxies via electromagnetic radiation. The stars really represent the consciousness of the Universe. When the electromagnetic radiation is reduced, human beings have a moment of free thought, giving the Darkside an opportunity to jump in. As White Cells, we tune into a frequency that cannot be manipulated by the Darkside. We always have a higher level of clarity.

Red Cells are really affected by the different levels of electromagnetic radiation so that affects how they function and react to it. It's not as much of a crisis for White Cells as it is for the vast majority of the human race, but it does become a crisis for us because the actions of Red Cells inevitably affect everyone. If they are in a war and they use nuclear bombs, the war will be devastating. Hostilities will grow. Then it affects all of us. We need to take an active interest in what happens.

In the years that were leading up to 2012, a lot of people felt this 'shadow phase,' even though it was not literally a shadow. Every year during that time period, it slowly increased. It was not a dramatic change. Yet, it was there growing in intensity. The year 2012 was the time when we entered the deepest part of the filtering. It's like a color chart going from soft grey to thicker grey to darker grey to charcoal grey. During 2012, it looked like solid black. Now we're moving out of that solid black into the charcoal grey.

That black ribbon of space is not the Darkside. It also doesn't affect how many stars you're going to see in the sky. You'll see the same stars you've always seen. The amount of energy that reaches Earth from the stars is reduced, but it's still enough to have a dramatic effect on us.

It's not about moving under that shadow. The shadow does not represent evil or the Darkside. But there is a dark energy. Wherever you are, it is ever present just as The Force is ever present. Scientists know there's dark matter or energy all around us. Dark matter throughout the universe devours huge globules of galaxies and just has its way with it. Now, it exists there as matter. *But it's energy. It's frequency.*

It's illuminated wherever you are, but it's kept in a semi-neutral level. This is why there are skirmishes between dark entities and light beings of The Force. We're constantly battling to exist here. When our solar system moves under this dark ribbon, the Darkside can have a greater effect on the human species during this period.

You have wants and desires. You have I's, but you're not actively telling your organs to function because they know what to do. Electromagnetic radiation impulses from the brain go to all your organs, telling them how to work. You're just not consciously aware of it. But if you get really depressed or go through some kind of psychological shock, you can really affect those signals. That impacts your immune system, making you vulnerable to illness. Laughter and joy boosts your immune system. You can indirectly affect them, too.

It's not really a disadvantage for The Force or the Darkside. The stars are that indirect communication with the Universe to keep it moving and functioning. In the same way, your brain is constantly working with your body and all the organs. Its inner-verse is constantly functioning for the whole, for the one. You are the one for your trillions of living organisms, as we're the one for the body of God. It's just Micro-Macro.

You might believe this is not a good opportunity for The Force because it's losing some influence on the Earth. That is not true because of the Shiva concept. There has to be some upheaval. Will you progress if you always have bliss? Could you progress if everything in your life was perfect and every want and desire you had was there? If you had all the money in the world, everything that you wanted, just absolute perfection, could you evolve? If nothing disturbed your world, why would you bother to get off your butt to make something better? Human beings naturally are lethargic. There is a small percentage of people that will actively go out and do something in the world. The vast majority of people are lethargic if there's a comfort level. They will take advantage of this and just sit around doing nothing. Could you imagine just absolute bliss?

The Universe doesn't want that. It wants you to actively deal with issues and overcome circumstances. By forcing you to think, adapt to a new situation and make it good, it progresses your consciousness. You're not going to make a situation worse. You're always looking to improve it, make it better or correct it. That's a positive thing. In a sense, it's negative. For example, if your house is destroyed, you get mad because you think it is a perfectly fine house. But now you're going to build a better one with better materials – like a shingled roof instead of hay, and brick walls instead of clay. Now you can put in windows and solar panels. Sometimes, there's very little desire for change unless it's forced on us.

In a way, this is cyclical for the planet. It's like when the tide comes in, a new cycle starts and life flourishes. So, as we headed into this questionable period, both sides saw it as an opportunity. The Darkside saw it as an opportunity to manipulate people to become frustrated, angry, and destructive. The Darkside wants people to become destructive enough to collapse the growth of consciousness on this organism called Earth. If it's really lucky, it might just wipe out life completely. This is something it's never been able to do yet because there have never been nuclear bombs or biological or chemical weapons that have the capablity of destruction on that level. Until now, the destruction has always been restricted to an area, like a country or maybe even a continent. There was enough firepower to kill your neighbor, but other continents and civilizations thrived because there was no conflict there. They argued among themselves and had their own issues.

The Force saw this as an opportunity because there's not as much influence so It could intervene and raise the tonal, the spiritual vibration of the people. By the time it pulls back out to where the energy is starting to come again, so that the planet would again be running like in the movie *Dark City*, everybody could be awake. That could make things better for the next 26,000 year cycle, allowing the human race to advance and move out into the stars and the universes.

If the Darkside has its way, we're going to beat ourselves down and we're going to have conflict and wars. We're going to stay separated or worse. I don't like to talk negatively because it helps manifest that scenario. You can see where the possibilities could go. Both the Darkside and The Force want to program. The Darkside sees it as a circumstance in the universe that is going to happen inevitably. So out of these two energies, one will be the dominant one, creating a domino cycle into the next 26,000 years. One is a prolific life, making it greater and better. The other is a destructive path that is going to self-implode, which is exactly what the Darkside wants. According to science, dark matter makes up around 73 percent of the universe. That means it's won a lot of battles through this process, enabling it to create a foothold.

God wants to gather experience and knowledge, protecting and preserving its existence and the life that's here. In some ways, God is wounded in this particular dimension. God is bringing different kinds of energy in to battle and push the Darkside back. Just as the Darkside is figuring out stuff, so is The Force figuring out stuff.

A White Cell has many purposes. When the time comes, you are all going to feel it and you'll know that you have to chune. Hopefully, the whole globe will have at least one White Cell in every 10,000 people who knows how to chune. Then we can be like a microbe all over the planet by our existence in different places. It is a frequency that we pull from deep inside of us. Then we release it out for a moment. We don't have to do it constantly. All it takes is 15 to 30 seconds; and it will permeate. It's like when you ring a tinshaw, and it gets louder and then you're done. It rings for a while, but that could last three years on the planet. It's a different time scale. If you were looking at a small bowl, or a tinshaw, and it was as big as the planet and it rang, that vibration's going to permeate and travel through time and space for an infinite amount of time. We're creating this vibration for the planet that is like an embryo. It's like a special membrane that's surrounding the Earth piercing and burning the Darkside energy when it moves in. It's almost like the sea urchins in the ocean that are covered with little tentacles. If anything touches the sea urchins, they're poisoned. We're willing to let life in as long as it's positive.

The Darkside just can't permeate enough. The Force is going to keep it at a minimal. At some point, we may be able to push the Darkside out totally, burning it out of the energy field around our planet. We're not the only ones who know this. I believe the Buddhist monks, Christians, Hindus and Muslims have known this for thousands of years. It's a place in their mind. Each of them uses their own cultural method.

The New Age people say that you've got to be able to love to raise the consciousness. Unfortunately, none of them specifically knows how to do it. Have you noticed that? We've got to make everybody happy. We've got to send free love. We've got to all feel good. That's great, but in my School of Hard Knocks reality there's a method and an approach. You've got to whack it! We're a different breed. *There is a warrior in us.* We tell ourselves that we are supposed to be nice. We're nice. We are good. We are beautiful. We shine. But there's a part of us that's almost like the little kid that get's bullied at school. You're a really nice kid and you've always been good but the bully's always pushing you and pushing you. One day you punch them in the nose. That's what we feel. There's this mighty powerful thing that's inside of us and we feel it. How do I let it out? I want to let it out! We know that we have to let it out.

I think that other spiritual people feel the same thing. You get the evangelical people speaking in tongues. It's because they're buzzing so fast. They're trying to tune in, but they have no skill. It's quality versus quantity. There's a truth to when they talk in tongues. They're locking in hyper-dimensionally to data but they haven't really trained their brains to filter it correctly. They get some experiential level. In a sense, it's a piece of God and it's beautiful for them. Can you imagine any piece of God not being beautiful? That's amazing to them. When they're speaking in tongues, they're doing their thing and they're feeling it. When I watch someone speaking in tongues, I see this energy just being wasted. Direct it! Direct it!! Direct it!!!

When I see the Hindus chanting, I see that as wasteful. You need to direct it. Focus it! Channel it! Send it a certain way. You need to be the rudder. You need to capture the wind to move the ship. That is the problem. I see all of these spiritual teachings and they're just feeling it. I'm glad that they are feeling it and rolling with it. But what good are they doing? When an evangelical person is feeling the spirit and says, "I heal you in the name of Jesus," What is that? *It's belief.* It's an absolute belief. They have convinced themselves that Jesus is going to heal them.

The Buddhist monks and the followers of Hare Krishna chant. When they're healed, it's because they're feeling it. Everybody who has that absolute belief in their heart, they're healed. It's cellular. In the spirit of their energy, they actually open something up. In my opinion, that is what healed them. After a few days, many of these 'healed' people revert back to whatever illness they had. By that time, they've given their car, house and everything else to whoever 'cured' them.

There is a genuine feeling that is undeniable. That feeling comes from God. It's love. It's passion. Sometimes, I think it's manipulated for corruption and money but there is a lot of legitimacy out there, too. There are spiritual people who truly believe and they're sending that energy and love to one another. They're feeling it and they're trying to understand what to do with it. They feel the passion and they want to share it with other people.

We need to understand that passion inside of them because we have it, too. We can feel the spirit, too. Trust me. We do it secretly. We're just cool and calm about it. I feel it. It's genuine. It's real. All of them have a different way of expressing it. They feel it. It's a real feeling. It's a real vibration. It's a real energy. I love them all. I just don't necessarily agree with their approach - how they direct and use that energy.

I think sometimes there's too much politics involved with it, but when you get to the genuine part of it, the spirit inside of them is very real. They just don't understand what that is and what they need to do with it. Their information is limited, misdirected, or misguided. If they don't have an answer, they just say, "It's the Holy Spirit! Feel it!" To me, it's The Force. You can give it any name you want. I don't think it has a name. It is God. It is The Force. You can feel it. You can love it. You can cherish it, but it isn't just for you to revel in it. There's a reason why it's there and it has more than one purpose. That purpose is *chuning*. You can use it to heal and help others. You can use it to broadcast a frequency to others to help raise their energy up. Then they can experience that frequency, making their consciousness expand.

I see religions on different levels. For me, the Buddhists and the Hindus are on a higher level than the European belief systems. I think a lot of the European influenced religions are more vocal asking God to give them something with a little internal reflection. For me, some Hindu and Buddhist sects seem more sincere and genuine. They have more of a commitment to their spirituality. I think that has to do with the economy, environment, and social structure.

When I was in Cambodia, I saw a lot of Buddhist monks and I watched what they had to do. A lot of them became Buddhist monks when they were young. There's nothing else to do. All of them get fed and feel stimulated. They do chants and various other things. They are very organized and that gives them a sense of purpose. I think that they excel because they have less exterior distractions. It's not by choice. It's because of their environment.

The same thing goes for Hindus in poorer countries. In my opinion, the reason why those in these poor countries are the most spiritual and have the greatest energy is because all they really have to focus on is spirituality. Therefore they excel at it. Westerners have many things besides religion for stimulation and entertainment. The economy and social structures are totally different. They have more things distracting them and pulling them away.

I think that the majority of priests aren't as spiritual as their counterparts in these poorer countries. Also, there's a different vibration from many of the priests in western countries. When you think of them, you don't get the same vibration, reverence, or respect that you get when you invoke a guru or a Buddhist monk. You immediately feel a greater level of respect internally for a guru or a Buddhist monk. There's brilliant spiritual priests also, but all of them have what I call technology. Technology is the spiritual format of your religion. It's how you breathe, how you don't breathe, how you pray, how you don't pray. What is your technique? What is your method? They all have schools of technique. That's what I see as technology.

How do you harness The Force? How do you choose your relationship with God? All religions have an affinity towards God. None of the people are better or worse. You're lucky to find what you find. If that's the best you can find, you have to work with it because you believe that's as good as it gets. Fortunately, there's a small percentage, like you, that have a very strong Navigator that weaves through a lot of the bullshit. You know something is not right so you keep searching until you find the right thing. That's how you found your way to me. Our technology is an extremely high caliber. I believe it's a 10.

Sometimes when you meditate, you feel God move on you and you weep. *You weep.* When you're alone, your relationship with God can just be profound. When I'm alone, at times I get on my hands and knees. I lie on the floor and I say to God, "I am the floor mat for you, God. I'm not worthy." That's how I feel about God. If God just told me, "Well, I'm not happy with you today," that's it! I'm dead! Gone!

Don't you feel the exact same way? These are the things we never talk about. We want to talk about it, but society has trained us to be a little embarrassed about this. It feels a little awkward. Do you know what it really is? We have been introduced to so many religions that we know are bunk. Somehow, we have been trained that feeling God and feeling our spirituality has become a commercialized thing. We feel that by expressing it, we will be portrayed as religious. Or that we will be misinterpreted. We've learned to hold it, hide it, and be careful how we let people know about it.

Since we're highly spiritual, we're madly in love with God. We don't even like using the word 'God.' Even *I* don't like it. When I use the word 'God,' I feel like a preacher. It's so indoctrinated in us that we're not allowed to talk about it. We have to break that conditioning so that we can feel God, express God, and be with God without feeling like we're being put in a box.

If we call it The 'Force,' we can work with that. But if we say 'God,' you would think we are going to talk about Jesus or Buddha or Moses. And that would have been the end of it. It's different if we use words like The Force, Energy or the Universe. Those are better words. We've been conditioned to have a certain feeling about how we are allowed to talk about God. And our relationship has been kept a secret. Haven't you kept your real feelings for God a secret? Even I do it. I know you do. We talk about God and we say that we love God. We're not afraid to say that because we are spiritual people. But we're spiritual instead of Godly. It's almost as if they've got a trade mark on those words so we can't use them. When did that happen? If you use those words, you feel like you could be a Christian. But you don't want to sound like a Christian, so you can't use those words. You have to find something better because you know there's a better way to find that spirituality, that closeness to God.

So we have been conditioned to hide our frequency and our compassion for God. We secretly meditate. Secretly, we weep and share our heart with God. We do all these things in private and we shouldn't. To be honest with you, I like privacy. I like my relationship with God behind curtains. I can tell you how I really feel! I'm ecstatic about God. I think about God all the time. I can't stop. I have a closet filled with all these little petals that fell off a tree at Chase Park. I once had a surreal experience where the petals looked to be falling off the tree. That was my moment. It was when God said, "Hi," to me. "Don't tell anybody." That's really what we're doing.

I think that by me coming forward and addressing it, we all acknowledge it. We can acknowledge that we have a very deep loving reverence for God. I can't even think of a word in English to express what my heart feels. It's as if my heart is broken but it's not broken. I feel so much love and it's so powerful that it cripples me. I can't even function with my body if I think about how much I love God. I want to ask God, "What can I do for you? What do you need? How can I serve you better?"

I know that's what you say to me all the time, "How can I get more spiritual? How can I do better?" You're really saying to me, "How do I serve God better?" It's the truth. You are just afraid of saying it in so many words. I think that you get so upset and disappointed with yourself that you're suffering. You wonder, "How can I do more?" There's a certain feeling that comes from that. You sometimes almost think, "I deserve to feel bad because I am not doing enough." That's not good.

You have to admire how far you've come. I've said this many times. It seems like it's always the same thing. I want you to think about where you were before you found me. I want you to think about how many things you went through. How many experiences did you have before you found me? Since you've found me, now ask yourself. "What did it do for you? What kind of experiences did you have?"

Those experiences confirmed and strengthened your confidence in me. Somehow, you knew that there are more than the floors and walls of the room you're in - what you see with your eyes and hear with your ears. If you've ever seen an aura, you earned that! You applied yourself. That is amazing. It's confirmation that there's more than what you see here. And it tells you, "What more could there be? I was right the whole time. I was right the whole time!" And you get a shiver and you feel so liberated. It makes you stronger with The Force. It makes you stronger with God. It binds you to God. It makes God move through you better.

You come to me and say, "Eric, you're my teacher, my master, my guru. I want to know how I can have a breakthrough. I want to know how I can get closer to God." I asked, "Have you had any experiences?" He replied, "Well, yeah. I went over across this universe and then I went through this dimensional gateway." And on and on he continued. He had an amazing amount of experiences! I said, "You've had so many experiences. How can you be sitting here telling me you want more?" I understand you want more. And you're absolutely right. I already know that more just means that you're trying to get closer to God because you want to be absolutely sure when God says, "This is what I want you to do. I want God to talk right into my ear because I want to be absolutely certain the instant I hear it that I've heard it right."

When you are hounding me, I'm not mad at you. How could you ask for more when you already have so much? Think about how much you had before you found me. You had morsels, crumbs.

The Hand of Hands:

Is a hand posture that has a unique vibration. Thumb out, first two fingers extended together, and the remaining two curled back. The two fingers out ignites multi-frequency consciousness. It's why you can be here physically and multidimensionally at the same time. It's what holds your consciousness there. Your hand should have some tension, allowing your energy to pop.

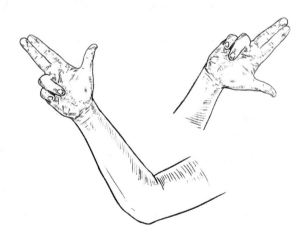

Chuning

Is when you can build up an extreme amount of emotion and passion for God and then release it. You can use Chuning on your own to clear your town or your house of bad energy. Or you can join with other Navigators to push together and project that frequency. It can be very intense because you're opening a gateway for God to come through. Then you're projecting that out. When you Chune, you pull a frequency from deep inside of you and release it out. That vibration permeates and travels through time and space for an infinite amount of time. When you see negative chaos and beyond-coincidental destruction going on in the world, you'll just know when to use this technique.

Before You Begin

I want you to sit. Clear your mind. Put your two feet on the ground. Put your hands in your lap. Feel your chest area. Become conscious of it. And this is what I want. It's the only thing I think I've ever asked of anybody. This is the first time I'm going to ask anything of you. *I'm asking you to be proud of what you've achieved.* Be proud of how far you've come. Be proud of how well you have served God. You're not lost. You've managed to survive and learn. You've managed to find something. I'm ordering you to take a moment and say to yourself, "Good job! Maybe when you can finally say, "Good job," to yourself, God will also let you know, "Yes, I'm very proud of you," because I know God is very proud of you. I know God is. It's a fact. You are in such denial and you feel so unworthy. Do you realize that when you feel unworthy, you take a piece out of my heart? It kills me. It kills me when you feel that you're not worthy enough yet. When you say that you'll try a little harder so that you can be that much more worthy, you have no idea! Nobody's so perfect! It's okay to want to be better. It's okay to be great, but every so often I just want you to stop and sit. Don't revel on the view, the trees, the flowers or anything.

I want you to sit there and just feel what it is to be you, the fact that you're reading this book now, and that you can understand everything that you see. You actually understand there's this living Force moving through all things, and that there's an inner harmony dancing around all those things. That is profound! Do you know how many people walk through life, and everything is just Styrofoam? They don't ever think about it.

Every time you think about it, you heal God. You nourish God. You make God feel appreciated and loved. *As much as you want to be loved by God, God needs to be loved, too.* God created the universe so God wouldn't be alone. The closest relationship that God has is to the people who can communicate and be close to God like a confidant. They're with God every step of the way. That's you! That's the constant feeling in your chest. It's that constant, little heaviness that you feel. *You're holding God and that's what holds God in this world.* Other people have it but they don't have it as much. You are like God's rock.

You've probably had friends, lovers, or children in your life. But you're lucky if you have a companion, mother, or father. And they're your rock. They're your ear, your shoulder to cry and weep on. Well, that is what you are to God. Believe it or not, when God is hurt, God turns to you and weeps on your shoulder. And you give God this love that makes God stronger. God is all knowing, all powerful, all this and that. God created the universe so you wouldn't be alone. God, the Universe, wants to feel these things. You are a micro version of God. It mourns when the Darkside takes life that it birthed. It mourns like a mother over its child. It mourns over you. It protects you with *ferocity*! It gives its own life at times, fighting here to keep us here so that we can grow.

Every single time that you don't stop to say, "Good job," and pat yourself on the shoulder, you deny that to yourself. Every time that you feel you don't deserve that, you cheat God. That's how I feel. I want you to pat yourself on the shoulder. I want you to know that I, Eric Joseph Pepin, the ancient being that I am, have a great relationship most of the time with God. I know as a fact that God has whispered in my ear, "I feel so loved. Would you let them know that? I know that right now they can't fully hear me, but if you tell them, they'll know."

So I'm telling you. God loves you. There's no running from God. There's no hiding from God. There's nothing that you're going to do that's going to disappoint God. There's nothing you can do. I challenge you! If you kill me right now, the Universe will still love you. That's how beautiful you are and how much love you have in your heart. God absolutely trusts you. You have to stop feeling that you're not quite good enough, or that somehow you're disappointing God. In the end, you're the one who has to work it out. If you run over your neighbor, God might say, "Okay, you are probably going to jail. It's going to suck but that'll give you more down time to talk to me. Don't worry because your neighbor's energy has moved on. It's so much better where he is now."

If you do it with wicked intention, you'd feel like shit. Shit happens. Mistakes happen. Sometimes you just get angry and you do something stupid. The Universe, God, loves you. You're beautiful. You're perfect. You are worthy of being my student. You're worthy to walk with me. You're worthy to talk with me. I honestly don't think you are lower than me. I honestly don't see that. I know I'm the one teaching. I'm the one talking. I don't see higher or lower. I've obtained consciousness. Yes, I have some advantages.

You have been in other worlds and universes fighting, clawing and battling side by side with me, for the same cause, for the same rights and privileges, for The Force, for the Universe to be where it is. You are my comrade. You are an ancient being who is standing with me. You have stood with me in other places. You know I'm telling the truth. It may not be a solid memory but it's a solid instinct in you. There's a solid instinct that knows, that there's something that had happened in time past. There's something inside of you that says something happened and I was a part of it. I was part of it probably more than once. It is that warrior. It's that fight that we have. We won some and we lost some. And the Universe asked you, "Will you come to this place? Will you come to Earth?" It wasn't in those words but these are our words in this dimension now. It asked you and you responded absolutely.

Low and behold, you are now stuck here. Stand proud. Let your wings roar and shine because when we have to deal with the shit, I don't want self-pity. I want brilliant light walking over the hill. I want the Darkside to shit its pants - not from the sight of us, but from the illumination of our approach, let alone what it's going to have to deal with when it sees what it is.

Chuning Technique

It's a good idea to sit when you're Chuning – either in a chair or on the floor. If you hit a really intense level, you literally could pass out. Be aware of that possibility. It doesn't matter which hand you use. You will likely feel more confident with your dominant hand, whether that's your left or right.

For the sake of simplicity, let's say your right hand is the dominate one. You'll use that one to do the Hand of Hands. Take your left hand and put it palm up in your lap as if you're going to meditate. Your eyes should be open to allow a connection of consciousness there. If you need to shut your eyes to concentrate, that's okay. Put your right hand on top of your left hand in your lap, holding the Hand of Hands position, with your palm up. Now pull both hands up so that your left hand is just above your belly button. As you pull the energy up from your chi to your heart center, breathe in. This increases the energy in your multidimensional consciousness.

When both hands are up to your belly button, take your right hand and turn it over so that the palm is down. Point your thumb toward your body and pull it up like when you're doing energy movements. When your right thumb gets up to about your neck, turn your hand so that the Hand of Hands is pointing upward and out in front of your face. Then project out to the universe, breathing out as you release. Let it come naturally.

In your soul, in your energy, your consciousness is in tune like a Kung Fu master. There's no thought. There's only pure God love emotion. That genuine feeling is undeniable. It's God. It's love. It's passion. We need to have an understanding of that passion because we have it, too. To us, it's The Force. You can feel it. You can love it. You're invoking this intensity from within you and broadcasting it out into the atmosphere at the Darkside. Chuning broadcasts a frequency to others, helping raise their energy up. Then they can gain experience and their consciousness gets bigger. And it is done! Bring your hand down and relax.

Chapter 10

DIRECT MANIFESTATION

M anifestation is to will, or to will upon reality as we exist in it and to effectively create your will. To manifest is to create. What we're going to be talking about is manifesting or creating what you want. Now, I'm not just talking about manifesting happiness. I'm actually talking about manifesting money, a house, or a relationship with a specific person that would be more ideal for you. The idea is to show you how to manifest. Manifestation is the active will to create something in our reality, to make something happen.

Most spiritual communities talk about manifesting things, like money. They tell you to visualize money coming into your life or to want it to come through. For me, that's very vague; it's a very broad statement and I find that there is not a lot of success with that concept. I think the effectiveness and its true potential is really watered down. Direct Manifestation is about applying a method that is very strategic, very matter of fact, very pointed in its creation to give you a much higher achievement of your expectations.

I'm going to teach you how to manifest a specific thing and get almost, if not exactly, that. It's very complex, but I will teach how it's done and how it works. I've always said that the more you understand something, the more powerful you become in the way that you affect reality around you, and the more your spiritual and metaphysical experiences will evolve.

Is there a difference between intent, manifestation, remote influencing, and programming the matrix?

Programming the matrix is similar to *direct manifestation*. This will give you a much broader and more useful tool that will help to enhance that area. *Intent* is to have an expectation of what's going to happen, which is a much milder form of what you are going to learn. It's effective, but it's not nearly as effective as what I'm going to teach you. Intent is often used in meditation. It sets a premise and usually the Universe will gently respond.

In this particular case, you may have a very specific need or a very specific desire, and instead of having the intention for positive things to happen and to come any way they can on a very broad level, you're being more specific by working with the Universe to give you exactly what you need. It is more of a specific need that's being taken care of. It's not to say that you can't get that from *intent* but that is generally used in a format where, let's say psychically you're trying to find information out about someone. Your intent is to find out about their love life, or to find out about their health, or to find out about their finances so you gather information. It's not really requesting a specific thing to happen or a result to affect your physical life. It's more like a request or an inquiry.

Remote influencing is influencing maybe a specific person that you are aware of, or a specific thing you're aware of. It's very similar to direct manifestation, but again, it's not. For the most part, everything I've said before is interconnected. They're like little rings or loops. They're separate by themselves, yet they're somehow touching or weaving through another loop.

So you could say that it's a fine 'braidedness' of links that create one big piece of sheet metal or something to that effect, but when you look at it closely you can see the individuality. And in this particular case, there are similarities. How this all works is that all of this is somehow connected. But you can get very specific about a need or a desire or an outcome. Direct manifestation is more about you specifically creating the oncoming future to have an effect on you.

If you want to look at the future as a wave coming towards us, as if it was somehow being prewritten by a greater program, such as the matrix or call it whatever you want, all the variables are affecting us. What you're doing is effectively creating something in the future to come towards you until it becomes a reality and integrates into this whole concept of what we call the *now* or *reality*, which it would not have necessarily been part of.

What would you say is the main difference between manifesting and just praying to a particular God or a particular faith?

I would say that prayer is a lower level of manifestation. I'm not saying that in any derogatory way to insult people's religious beliefs. It is a form of putting that desire out and I think, in many cases, it does work. You can look at prayer in many different religious groups where it has helped people. They prayed for people to get better. They prayed for certain circumstances to happen. On the same token, a lot of horrible things happen in life where people have prayed and it's done nothing. You could say then, "It's God's will it happened."

We look at prayer and say it works or it doesn't work, and we try to take a closer look at it. If you look at what prayer is in the sense of what I'm trying to share with you right now, there is a sense of desire. There is a sense of hope. There is a sense of requesting or asking. And I would probably say that the best prayers are done with the greatest amount of intention and expectation, but even more so, with emotional communication to what they deem as the Universe or God. And I think that you will find that these people will have the most success with manifestation.

When you observe healers and you look at different variations of healing, you will find that some of the greatest healers are the most emotional people. I find that if you look at other religions in the world that have amazing things happen, they use a very high level of emotional broadcasting. I'm not saying that this is the rule of thumb for everything. There's always room for diversity, but what I am talking about is *manifestation* and specifically *direct manifestation*. I believe the people who prayed were manifesting and that can have many highs and lows.

If you use this technique, you are being a lot more specific. You understand now the secret element is *emotion and broadcasting* and *presenting that emotion to the Universe with a level of intent, expectation, wishing, and understanding what all of that is* by using the sixth sense.

I think people unconsciously manifest all the time. Let me give you a concept to really think about. It may not sit well with some people. Reality is based upon a collective consciousness of us all similarly believing and thinking in the same thing. It's to say that as a collective, we are the grid. We are noids, the data center points where information comes in and goes out. That our will as a whole, all intelligent life on earth, collectively creates reality or holds reality in the format that we see. We hold this frequency, this matter, this structure together in the form of walls, cloth, or fabric. Our perception of how we convey this belief is what creates it.

Now, if we want to go into religious teachers, you could say that their will, in some ways, influences the people around them. The people around them believe so much in what they think those teachers can do that when they are ready to do something, they practically make a presentation or an announcement or a suggestion of what they're going to do. And the other people are so confident, so sure that it is going to happen that it really isn't the spiritual teacher who makes the miracle happen. It is the collective belief the teacher initiated that acted as a wave. It's similar to a pebble thrown into the water creating outward rings. Their belief shifted so greatly it manifested or created this new reality, hence water to wine, or baskets that were empty and then filled with bread.

It's not to say that the religious individuals needed others to believe in them in order to create these things. You could say that one individual's will could be so powerful that they can change the matrix or reality as we understand it. It becomes so much stronger than a thousand people's will or belief. Unconsciously, I think that people will react sometimes to statements such as, "Oh, I was just thinking about that," or "I was just thinking about you," or "I was just thinking about something like that happening," or "I just knew something like that was going to happen."

You could say that perhaps they manifested it to happen subconsciously. Or that maybe, subconsciously, you're being affected through another person's consciousness. It's a little intimidating to think about those things, but in the end, there's really nothing to worry about. The idea is that you should practice the tools that were given to you in *High Guard*, the techniques for energy defense, as well as various other tools Higher Balance Institute offers. That is what will make you rise above it all. This factors into why White Cells evolve to a higher level than Red Cells and how they separate themselves from the general matrix. I said *general matrix*. Other people tend to stay in this remote controlled or remote operated level to a higher effected level.

Obviously, we live in a world where we need a certain level of monetary gain to exist to pursue our interests. This is a very difficult topic to cover because there are so many passionate perceptions of what is acceptable for a spiritual circle, or any circle, to discuss and whether you should be profiting or not profiting. For many years, I've had reservations about putting all this material out there, as many of you know. I've always felt that I was selling myself out, expecially my beliefs or what I personally believed in until someone from another spiritual circle (who had seen some of my material) said that it just had to get out there. How else am I to do it but through monetary gain, using that monetary gain to create a greater abundance of information and then re-circulate it? That individual explained to me that there's nothing wrong with money; it's what you do with it. I agreed with that concept. It paved the way for me to feel more comfortable with monetary gain.

Having said that, we live in a world where we must have money to survive. And I stress this to everybody. Before I teach you how to tap into creating money or manifesting it, you must have self-control. You must have a sense of self-discipline and a knowing of what is right and what is grossly out of control. Even when you directly manifest something, there are always repercussions. You can affect something so much that it takes from somewhere else, or affects something somewhere else; therefore, you could create what I call an influx – a suction or a vacuum that eventually pulls you into some greater circumstances that you may not like.

In other words, reality has a set level that is balanced and necessary to create that balance. It has an agenda, which is to grow at a steady rate to expand its consciousness. When people become too gifted or too advanced but have not advanced themselves inwardly, spiritually, balancing their inner-harmony, then greed, money, power, and manipulation take over. It creates negative beings or negative people; they don't care about what your needs are. They just think about themselves, and when they're selfishly manifesting that way, they may be taking from others.

The reality is that you're affecting the flow, the balance of this universal energy and if you affect it too much, it's going to turn on you. It's going to say, "Hey, there's really a problem here and it's starting to become too big of a problem." It will need to resolve the problem and it's going to backlash on you. It's going to try to correct the problem, but not in a subtle, slow building way. It's going to dramatically react to you if you don't treat it with the respect that you need to treat it with, hence, the concept of respect The Force or respect the Universe.

Don't will your demands so greatly upon the Universe. You must have a level of respect. It will allow you to have some advantages, but you have to project a sincere heart and sincerely do what you'll say you're going to do for it to manifest because if you don't really feel that way, if you have doubt in your heart, it already knows that and you're not going to be able to manifest it.

So it polices itself, in a way, but you can also become so wealthy that it corrupts you. That's where the problem arises when you start manifesting all the time to create more and more and more. That's when you will have repercussions.

So it's important to have very pure intent when you go into this?

Yes, because pure intent is really a key element that you work up to while directly manifesting what you want. It's as if it's a standard check. You're basically attempting to rewrite reality on a small scale compared to the big picture. You're trying to fly under the radar because if you were to fly in the radar too much, it's going to bump you back out and you're going to be right back to square one. That's what happens to most people when they try to manifest. What I'm actually going to do is teach you how to get under that radar, learn not to ask for so much, yet ask for an awful lot and get it.

What everybody wants to hear is how to manifest money but the reality is, as a spiritual person, everybody expects me to say, "Well, you've got to be poor because it is the way of a spiritual life, and so on." I just don't necessarily accept that. I think that financial excessiveness is a horrid thing, but then everybody has a different perception of what excessiveness is.

The bottom line is it's what you do with the money that really matters. Make as much as you want, but what you choose to do with it is going to be the key element. You can manifest financial stability, finances, work, and employment. You can manifest a specific kind of person to come into your life, anything. The sky's the limit. But what you have to remember is, as much as I say the sky is the limit, pushing too much, too fast, too great is going to cancel out your manifestation through the Universe. You can't set too high of an unrealistic demand. You've got to really think about what you're asking for and where are you're going to open up the potential of possibilities.

Let's say you want to meet someone new in your life. You would sit down, clear your mind, and go into a meditative state. Get yourself as clear as you can so that your intent is clear and high quality as possible. Express your sincerity and with intent you need to say, "I want to manifest this particular person in my life." That's what your intent should be without actually saying it in words. The Universe doesn't need you to say, "I want to create this perfect person in my life because I'm tired of being lonely." What you really are saying with emotion is, "This is the frequency of what I'm asking for."

You reflect on that desire or need to find someone and then you need to throw in expectation. Expectation is a desire or, not really a desire, but an expectation that this is going to manifest for you. Now, after you throw your dash of expectation in there, you need to start designing what it is or who it is you're trying to find in your life. And you need to visualize someone perhaps with blonde hair, or a brunette, that has a certain body build. You have to 'see' a certain nationality, eye color, and skin texture. Be specific yet somewhat vague. If you say, "They must be this person specifically," forget it. What you're really doing by being vague but specific is you're saying to the Universe, "These are the variables and possibilities I'm giving you to work with." And if that person is within a reasonable distance of, say 20 or 30 miles, the Universe is going to say, "This person will find you desirable."

The Universe is going to take that person and generate a desire for them, let's say to go to the organic vegetable store that you usually go to. It now has to put in the equations of right timing and right place in order to fit you in there. If you suddenly decide this week that you're not going to go out shopping because you just don't feel like it, you lessen your opportunity for the Universe to put this person that you're trying to manifest in your life. You have to work with the Universe to a certain degree and not expect this person to just find you and knock on the door. But there is a measure of prewritten information in the Universe that has to be followed. If you try to get something completely impossible to happen, it's not going happen. You have to say to yourself, "Now, I have to make myself more available." Then somebody might say to you, "Well, the only reason you found this person is because you started going out more." And I would say, "Well, what did you ask for?"

Weigh it all out. I guarantee, there will be a huge correlation. Now, that person may be a brunette instead of a blonde, but the body build will be correct, the personality will be what you asked for, and you're going to put this into your manifestation when you directly will it. You're going to go over what kind of personality you want this person to have. You want to go over how they're going to feel about you. You're going to go over creating all of this, and you'll find that it's really about setting up the dynamics for the Universe to find this person.

When you're doing this and you're manifesting, it's almost as if you have to *wish with expectation*. To wish is like asking for it but you aslo need to have a certain level of expectation. You believe by wishing for it that you understand it may not be *exactly* what you're expecting, but it's going to be the best probability within reason for what this person will be like that is coming into your life. And you have to understand that. So, when people say, "Well, you're just putting yourself out there," I would say "Fine, but how long have you put yourself out there over the years and still haven't found the right person? Then all of a sudden you run into the right person?" Don't doubt what you've just created for yourself.

If you want to find a person that you can love and settle down with that will be ideal for you, the first thing you want to do is sit down, relax, clear your mind, and then put the intent out there. You want to put the expectation out there. You want to put the wish out there – all in a frequency, an emotion. And you can talk in your head, but you have to talk from a good place in your heart like you're having a one on one with the Universe. And you have to say, "Okay, I need to find somebody and I know that you understand," and the Universe is going to understand that. And you're going to say, "Well, I really need this person to feel a certain way. I really need them to love me, desire me, or physically desire me, or cherish me. I don't want it to be all about sex. I want this person to like me for my intellect, or vice versa. I want them to like me for who I am."

Now, let me give you a piece of advice here. Not all guys or gals are the same but the first thing that most guys are probably going to think is, "I want this totally smoking hot blonde that's a model, and on and on, and she's got to be totally into me," but you're physically not the most attractive person to look at. I'll tell you right now, if you truly manifest that out, you still will get it. You may not believe in a million years, but they're going to be attracted to you. You are also going to find, perhaps, that this person may become so obsessed over you.

I'll tell you this right now and I will swear on it – the ideal, most perfect person that you want in your life, no matter who you are, is definitely out there. There's not just one person either, there's several of them if you manifest and create the opportunities that will help the Universe to help you.

It means putting yourself out there so it can work them towards you through a city, through hundreds if not thousands of people, opportunities, everything. It has to work with all of those variables. You have to contribute to make that somehow happen. You can't make it so impossible that it just can't crunch the numbers. That person is out there. I promise you.

Now having said that, you wanted this person to be totally infatuated with you but I'm telling you, you will eventually get tired of this person. You will want to get away from this individual and you will want nothing more than to escape from the situation. At first it's going to be great, but afterwards, in the end, it's going to be horrid. Now, you're going to try to break that relationship, and you may. What's going to happen now? You're going to go back now and try to manifest another situation. This is when you're using and abusing manifestation. That's what you have to recognize. That's what using and abusing is, and the Universe now sees you knocking on the door too much too often.

If you realize you made an error; you made a mistake and you acted rashly upon lust rather than passion from your heart, give it time. Wait a year or two. That may sound like a long time, but that's BS. You made the error. You reacted on lust rather than what you passionately want to find as a good balance in your life. You need to give the Universe some space, otherwise you're going to get that backlash I'm talking about. Maybe every person you meet's going to be a nightmare. Maybe you're going to start meeting people left and right and you find that it's just not going to work; your life is in chaos. Who's to say? But what I'm saying is that the Universe will try to resolve that problem, somehow, someway, and usually not in a manner you would like. It's just really fast with us. It's a whole different concept of time and how we deal with it.

You want to really take into consideration what you're manifesting. You want to take into consideration, not only what this person is going to look like, but also what this person's going to be like and how they're going to react to you. Are they going to be understanding? Are they going to be compassionate? Are they going to be nurturing? Are they going to be good to you?

Now let's look at some other variables. There is no such thing as a perfect person. There is no such thing as creating exactly the most perfect person you want. You have to understand that we are all growing. We are all constantly changing. We are all affected by not only emotional things, but biological and biochemical things, too. Okay? Life happens to people and they all have ups and downs. Tragedies happen. Joyous things happen. You must not expect that everything is going to be exactly and perfectly what you want it to be. When you can set that parameter, or that realistic standard, you will then truly find the next best thing – I would still call it perfection. And remember, you yourself have to grow.

If someone manifests love or friendship, is that love real or are they controlling it? If they manifest a bunch of friends, will those friends truly like them?

If they are manifesting to make friends, those are going to be real friends because the Universe is going to attract what it takes to create what you feel is friendship. Your genuine desire is to genuinely be liked, so the Universe is going to seek out those qualities. Each quality I see is a frequency number. I'm not saying I see everything in numbers, but what I'm trying to give you is a way of understanding this. The Universe looks to match the best variables of those qualities, and if a person doesn't have all of those or most of those, it moves on. The world is filled with millions of people. In this sense, if these people live within a reasonable distance, sometimes even a greater distance, it doesn't matter. If your manifestation is good, it will find a way, within a given amount of time, to connect those things to make it happen. But these people will genuinely like you for who you are.

If you're a funny person, you will manifest funny people. If you've got a dry sense of humor but no one understands you, you're going to find the people that really get that dry humor. If you are a person who likes obscure things, you're going to ironically bump into somebody who has the same tastes and interests as you do. It is that perfect.

So, just to confirm that train of thought, let's say you manifest a job. You don't have to keep manifesting to maintain that job. You have the job that was suited for you.

It was suited for you. The key people and circumstances will somehow be attracted to you. The Universe is going to fit your calibration and match it with the other calibrations instead of you randomly bouncing around in life. You need friction in your life to learn. At times people look at strife as always being a bad thing. And I'm not talking evil now; I am just talking about growth. If you never had any challenges to face, you would not grow. It is only when you are challenged that you actually are forced to think about a situation, overcome it, work it out, or resolve it. That's how you grow as individuals. You learn from it. You reflect on that experience and that's how you learn to resolve those situations in the future, or make it so you don't have to deal with them anymore. You have to wait for the next equation to come so that you can grow. Then you have to learn to deal with the situation.

What you are saying to the Universe is this, "I am directly manifesting because I just want a little break. I will deal with whatever else is thrown at me." And rest assured it will be. You're going to have all sorts of problems in your life. It's part of growth. Believe me, if you can look at it this way, your life will get much easier than if you look at it out of context. You've got to look at everything as being a challenge in life.

I often remember a suggestion I once read to find something good about everything in life. Find something good about everything that's bad and learn from it. Acknowledge what you learned from it. Well, what that says is that these things help you grow. As horrible as you say something is remember you are a spiritual being seeking to understand life; whether it is death, or life, or joy, or sadness. Whether it's sexual, or monetary. These are all part of an existence you require, that you would not necessarily be able to experience as an energy being.

You have to really look at everything and say, "God, this really sucks but I'll get past it." Look at older people and their accumulated wisdom. With wisdom, the reason it is always old chiefs or wise people is because they've had to complete more equations than you. They can say, "Look, if you don't want to go through this to make it a little easier on yourself, let me give you some answers to these equations I, myself, have worked out." Then it's a choice of whether or not you want to accept it. That's what wisdom is.

When we manifest, what we are trying to do is cheat, maybe just a little bit, or bend the rules a little bit and say, "I'm okay. I know I'm going to have to deal with these equations and situations so that I can grow and enhance my frequency in order to keep moving forward." On the same token, "This is something I would like to divert to make my life a little different, or a little bit better without having to go through the logistics of things." And that's really what you're proposing. And if your proposal is good enough to the Universe, the Universe is very cool and very loving and it is very understanding and when you propose it correctly, *that's the big secret, correctly*, it's going to give you what you're asking for. It's going to say, "Okay, fine. I'm willing to work this out to see where it takes us."

If you don't manifest correctly or your demands are outrageous, you're not going to get anything. You're still going to run into that same problem if you try to control other people with good or bad intentions. So you have to think about how you are manifesting. If you are trying to manifest money and you're trying to say, "I want my boss to give me more money." That could be a problem if you really think about it. Are you trying to influence your boss to make him do something he wouldn't otherwise do? Or are you really presenting your case and saying, "I need to increase my income." And letting the Universe see if that can fit naturally into the equation and create an opportunity that just happens to start working for you. Or maybe some other opportunity would land on your doorstep.

You've got to watch out for that gray area because that gray area is what's preventing a lot of opportunities for people to actually have good manifestations. You have to put out the right terminology. When I say inner, I mean emotional. Expressing emotion is how you want to create this and then speak it in words, but try to feel it. Don't say, "I need this. I need that. This should be this way," or "that's how I imagine it."

No. Feel, internally, what you're saying with intent but feel the emotion of it, feel how things are. That's how the Universe talks. That's the Universal language. I've often said that if an alien landed on the Earth and talked to you, you probably wouldn't understand a word. But if you saw it crying, or expressing joy, or reacting to something beautiful, you would get it. If you could just feel things as if you were a radio receiver except you receive emotion, you'd be able to internalize those emotions and they would become things that you understand, or that you've experienced in your own life. You'd have data to compare it to. But if you don't have any data for it, I'm betting your Universal communicator, meaning your older soul, will have some way of quickly finding that answer. And then you're going to have these revelations in your mind, and this is what people call tapping into a higher consciousness. Think about what you're manifesting and think about how you're manifesting it.

Does this mean that you only do one manifestation? No, you've got to keep working the equation into the Universe. You've got to bounce it out there every so often. I think the biggest flaw in every single spiritual or metaphysical practice, or any growth is that people do not have consistency. If you are consistent, the possibilities would be just absolutely amazing. The only way to do that is to set a schedule that you abide by to work on your manifestation and do not deviate from it.

You can't make it more specific. You can make it a little bit broader because maybe that's the reason why it's not manifesting. Maybe your manifestation wish list is too complex and there's just no way that the Universe can realistically bend the laws of the bigger programs to get this person to move. The only feasible person might be 10,000 miles away. It's just not going to work. You have to consider lowering your demands and that will increase the possibilities. That's usually the case. And ten to one, it's usually the thing that you least expected.

Can you clarify that? Because right now you're talking about being vague to increase the chances of the probability. Yet in the beginning, you were talking about being very specific.

You can be specific about whether you want a man or a woman. You can be specific about wanting a lot of money versus a little money. You can be specific about wanting a mansion, or a small, two-bedroom house, or a one-bedroom house, or an apartment, or any home for that matter. Different things mean different things to different people. But in some ways, you've got to be specific as to what it is that you want. The vagueness comes in with – let's use a house as an example.

You know that you can only afford X amount, or maybe something slightly over your monetary range right now. Well, you're not going to go for the million dollar house because now you're asking the Universe to have to crunch too many equations and to bend too many rules. You're not going to get it. But, if you realistically knew that you could pull it off, yet there are some challenges that would be better to manifest, well, here's the specific way to do it: I want to manifest a two-bedroom house with two- baths. I wouldn't even have to put an amount of money on it, because by just creating that intent, the Universe already knows. You already know. It's probably going to be, depending on where you live, about $120,000 to $200,000.

You already have that woven into the intent. You want to be vague so you shouldn't say it has to be a *blue* house. You don't want to say it has to be two floors. You want to be vague whenever you can get away with it because that expands the possibilities.

You said that there's a ten to one chance that you'd get the exact person that you want, or the exact apartment you want, or the exact house, or whatever it is. How do you put yourself into that one out of ten chance to get it?

You've just got to work on being specific. It's about how creative can you be with your verbiage with the Universe. How creative can you be? If you lived on an island with only houses availble but you want to have a condo and you don't want to leave the island, well, I would say you've got a problem on your hands. But who's to say that, all of a sudden, somebody buys you a lotto ticket and mails it to you as a gift – you win and you collect your millions and build the condo?

The possibilities are endless, but what you have to think about is how realistic would that be for you to get that lotto ticket? It'd be more realistic to say that you're going to have to move to a largely populated area with more possibilities for things to happen. And then manifest that because the Universe has more material to work out all those equations. It's got more possibilities to work with to give you those chances of running into that right moment, that right place, that right opportunity. You may see it coming. You may not see it coming at all. You may forget it was a month ago that you worked on it for a few days. And you might have just completely forgotten about it and all of a sudden you're with this person. You build a relationship or whatever. Then, all of a sudden, it hits you and you really recall all these things that you wanted, and you realize this person's already right in front of you.

Well, what about something like money? You want to make more money but it's really impossible with your current job.

If your goal is to make more money, you want to open it up to the Universe to make a feasible opportunity present itself to you. Your expectation will already be in there because you have an inner sense of standards. You're not going to do something you don't want to do, like something illegal or something unethical. It already knows that. That's already interwoven with that emotional information. The data's already there. What you're saying to the Universe is, "I want to manifest more money."

You visualize money. You feel the sensation of that liberation. You create that liberation for yourself with the expectation of something reasonable, so you want to say, "I just want an opportunity to make more money," and you see that money. You can visualize it. But remember the key emotion. What would it feel like to have that security or that money? And that's what you have to broadcast because then the Universe says, "Oh, I know what you want. Let me create that vibration for you all the time."

The only way you can have that specific vibration is if those things happen. Having a lot of money has a very specific feeling. Having your hair caressed has a very certain feeling when you think about it. Everything has a frequency. A frequency is numbers. It's a code. To the Universe, it's information. The Universe doesn't necessarily understand pictures. The Universe doesn't necessarily understand the word 'money'. But if you think of money, then you create the feeling of it and you share this as a form of communicating because it's an art, then it gets it. It says, "Oh, I will create this feeling for you. I will create that frequency in your life." And then that frequency turns out and it equates to cash. You get it now?

You have to put it out there as a feeling that you're looking for and you have to project it out there to the Universe. And then what will happen is you'll either get a raise, or who knows, maybe somebody will rear-end you without harming you and all of a sudden you get a big fat check in the mail. I mean, it's hard to say how it will happen. The Universe doesn't look at semantics. It's not going to harm you. It wants the progression of life. But it doesn't really see opportunity, like a car being rear-ended, as the other guy's bad luck. The bottom line is that it all works out in the end. More than likely, because your expectation is not going to be anything like that, it will come in ways that seem more feasible to you. Perhaps somebody in your family is going to say, "Okay look, I came into a lot of money. You're my son. Here, I'm going to give you a lot of money to help you get your house, or start your business." These unusual things will begin to happen.

What could also happen is you may get awarded a grant, or a new opportunity, or somebody offers to pay for more education for you. You may not see it then, but that initially opens a doorway for an opportunity to become an entrepreneur with a peer or someone at school and you could start a huge profitable business. The idea is not to set a very specific date, but you can have some expectation of what you think would be realistic. If you want it to be tomorrow, you're limiting your possibilities. If you say a month, I would say depending on what you're asking, it's certainly feasible. That's a frequency.

You're saying these are all things I'm willing to work with and you're putting it out as emotion. It will be more likely that those opportunities will arise. Somebody might say, "Well, in three months anything could happen." Well, I would say, "Have you been asking for money? Did you desire money anytime during the past five years?" The answer's going to be, "Yeah." Well, here it is. You applied this manifestation; you gave it three months and what happened? Well, you tell me if it was random luck or not. Now do it with something else and see what happens. But don't abuse it.

I'm very grateful for spirituality as a whole, whether it is Christianity or Hinduism or Buddhism, because I think there's a great amount of dedication in groups to put out a very positive level of energy for the planet. What I get disappointed in is when certain groups become more controlling in that broadcast in their perception of, "If you are not one of us, you're against us." That's when it loses the quality to really register with the Universe. But as a whole, it is one of the most contributing factors to the planet as a living organism. The bottom line is that everybody has a will for life. Everybody is projecting goodness or something that's expanding life, and life is good and we want that. We want that energy. We want that concept broadcasted out and that is the dominating energy from all of these groups and organizations.

I think that there is a positive aspect in each one of those groups that counters the negative, providing we're not looking at this on a global level of intention. Let's say we're looking at it in a group level of maybe four people to twenty people, or even larger. The secret to it is that everybody should have identical, or close to identical, intentions. You may feel that everyone in the group has the same desired outcome or goal as you do, but you would be surprised what each person emanates, and that's when it gets very confusing. That's why sometimes the best work can be done individually.

You have to make sure that everyone's on the same page. Hence, the reason why a lot of religious groups that have been around a long time use chanting. Chanting gives a certain rhythm, a certain pattern, and if emotion can be installed into that, you'll be projecting a harmonious vibration. Keep in mind that singing in groups, if it's done with the intention of manifesting, is also done for that reason. When you get together with a group of people, try to have someone sketch out with pen and paper what the sequence of conveying a certain emotion will be. So, by communicating and talking on that level, everybody will be on the same page. And then you go step by step explaining how you want to do it.

It can be very complicated if you really want to do a good manifestation as a group. Sometimes it is better just to keep it simple. Let's just focus on the sense of having shelter or a teaching place. But then again, you have to talk and get that narrowed down or refined to that concept. Do you see? Instead of saying, "Let's focus on a school," say, "Let's just focus on the *feeling* of having a place to teach from." And that might be broader and better to create and manifest for the Universe to work with than specifically imagining a brick building, or a wood building, or a stone building, or whatever. Yes, it can have benefits, but it can also have drawbacks. Part of the creation of the Doe is conflict. It's what creates the Doe. It's what prevents a lot of stuff from actually manifesting. It's because everybody has a certain expectation. By cancelling out one another it also contributes to maintain things the way they are.

Do the benefits outweigh the potential drawbacks if you do it well?

If you do it well, obviously you're going to have a very strong broadcast. But, didn't I tell you before? I think one person can broadcast just as well as twenty people can. It really depends on their level of spiritual progression.

How does the sixth sense fit in?

The sixth sense is a form of navigating in all of this. The sixth sense allows you to communicate with the Universe and broadcast your intent. You have learned to understand intent and expectation in a different way. The sixth sense is experiencing and projecting them because you are now communicating with something that is no longer physical. It is vibration and energy and a different kind of consciousness that we somehow are able to interpret as a very real thing. Had we not had that sense, then we would say it simply does not exist. But our sixth sense says we can *feel* this force. We can feel the Universe and its subtle and gentle nature. We acknowledge its existence and can share in that existence and we believe that there's a format through the sixth sense to communicate.

Is this communication between you and the Universe or is it more like a thought projection as in thought influence?

It's a little bit of everything. It's psychological. It is also spiritual. It is also frequency. It is also a thought projection. It's all of those things. But what we are actually doing is being very specific rather than a little vague. We're being very specific in what we're trying to manifest rather than just experiencing things, or observing things, or sharing things, or working on a problem to resolve.

If it takes so much work to get the Universe to acknowledge you spiritually, why would the Universe care about your biological needs?

The Universe sees all life as part of itself. Are you aware that you have organisms that are creating more organisms in you? That is part of existence. We are all a part of that chain. It's not that you're trying to get the Universe to say, "Oh, I'm going to do this for you." You're really doing it for yourself by intervening with the Universe. When I say, "*Will* it on the Universe," I don't think the Universe is solely thinking, "Oh, look who's asking for something from me.

As I said before, you're really flying under the radar. I think the Universe will trust certain individuals to make requests if their frequency or their intentions are good. If your frequency is the right calibration, it's going to let you get away with a lot more than it would with other people.

In a sense, it's really about us being a bit selfish. But on the same token, we have to govern our own selfishness and if we don't, well, then there's going to be a reaction. You could say that you could put healthy creams on your skin, but if you use a bad quality of cream, what's going to happen? You clog your pores and then your body pops it out or pushes it out through acne. If it's a good quality cream, you get healthy, rejuvenated skin. That's a choice, making you the applicator now.

You are a shared experience with the Universe. Never forget that. You are sharing in experiences, so what you experience, the Universe experiences. What the Universe experiences, you experience. Instead of the Universe saying, "Okay, this is the layout that I'm going to give to you," you're saying to the Universe, "Well, I'm sharing in this experience so let me contribute a few thoughts of my own or what I would like to see written into this game plan." I mean, this may be a novel idea to some people, but there's nothing wrong with that. You've just got to stay away from certain elements. Don't suppress other people. Don't harm other people. You know the basic laws of right and wrong. Put that into your equation. If you're going to, let's say, desire a specific person and you're going to directly manifest that person using this technique, ten to one you're going to fail.

You're going to fail because you're increasing the odds of failure. It's like the lotto, you've got to stack as much as you can in your favor for the probabilities to happen. I'm not saying it's impossible, but this now gets into forcing someone else to do something they may not really have an interest in doing. You now have to work ten times harder to reprogram reality to fit them into your equation.

The bottom line is that maybe the Universe would never have selected that specific person. It's finding a person that will be attracted to you: whether that person has blue eyes or brown eyes, is heavy or skinny, whether they are a foreign person or a non-foreign person, whether they are tanned, or white, or black, or yellow skinned. The bottom line is you've got to trust the Universe to figure that all in. And it's going to selectively find that person and then you've got to put yourself out there to help the probability of that person bouncing into you.

When you try to force a specific person to have those qualities, the probabilities of that person being attracted to your hair color, your eye color, your weight, your personality, your interests, and your personal traits may not be even remotely close. Now you're really *forcing* that person against their will or using a form of psychic attack to get them to do what you want. You've got to work with the Universe for it to selectively work with what you really are looking for. But on the same token, you can't be trying to control other people or manipulate other people in that sense.

There are good people and bad people. This is about having a respect for life, a respect for one another, and a respect in the unity of progression of life. This should be done in a way that is not harmful or suppressive or negative to other people. Now, absolutely, people can manifest and hurt other people. This is where you get into your darker side or the individuals that use this for darker purposes. Why did we have to come out with a product called *High Guard*? It's because people are manifesting or willing their intent on other people. Whether it's in a negative or a positive way, this person doesn't understand what's going on and it feels negative to them. They're freaked out because they don't know what's going on. It doesn't take a rocket scientist to start figuring out ways to use this information in a negative way against other people.

If this really works and people can really manifest anything that they want, why would you teach that?

Because I believe that the people who have found this program have found it because I have manifested with great will that I only find the people in this world who will do great, great good. A decision had to be made whether or not to help them become enlightened or to let the other factors bypass them in their struggle to awaken. They needed certain advantages. I have to trust that this material will find the right people, and I believe it has. I believe that the people I'm working with are reaching out to other people. They will become more knowledgeable, more awakened. The gifts that they herald inside of themselves from the Universe are so needed. They are just going to expand and will reach out to other people to do whatever they need to do individually. I believe that's the case. I believe that the people this is wrong for, well they won't have the consistency to do what they really need to do or to pull it off. But, that's my will.

Is it possible to manifest something you can't conceive?

Yes, this is the beautiful thing about using this technique. When you are asking, you can be vague. The vagueness is to say that you're opening yourself up to an experience that would somehow open you up to greater places. You're not saying, "I want to see an entity. I want to see a UFO. I want to see people floating in the room." What you're saying is, "I desire a greater experience. I desire something beyond what I can perceive at this moment."

I stress to you about emotion. Find the emotion that best describes your expectation. When you think about it, it's a very unique feeling. It's unique; it's an open-feeling. It's a very beautiful feeling because you want something beautiful to happen. It's almost as if you want to say, "I want to embrace God, but I don't want to say that God must be this way or that way." Or "I want to experience something that is special, like a secret that God decided to whisper in my ear and my ear alone."

That's what it is you're trying to create. Think about that before you sit down to create your manifestation. Think about the best way to describe what it is you want and feel it. Try to remember that feeling; when you're ready, release that feeling out. You can definitely ask the Universe to share something that goes beyond what you can perceive as a human being at this moment. Now something beyond what you can perceive is to say that you wouldn't be able to understand it, but on the same token, when you're saying, "Give me something that is beyond my perceptions," you don't have to worry about those kinds of details.

Here we get into details again. The Universe already understands that it has to be something that you can conceive, otherwise there's no point in showing it to you because it wouldn't register. It has to show you something that you could eventually absorb and get it. What you're really asking for is, "Teach me something new. Teach me something that I have never experienced before. I don't care if other people know it, but for me, teach me revelations that I have not yet been exposed to."

That's all you're really saying when you really think about it. This is why I say to give it some thought and with us looking at this now, I would say that's what you're asking the Universe. "Show me something I've never seen before. Show me something new." New to whom? New to you or new to me? "Show me something that no one's ever experienced before." What are you doing? You're narrowing down those opportunities now. The point is you have to give that some consideration and then you have to propose that emotionally, a little vague yet specific again.

So, how can a person manifest an object right in front of them?

Well now, you're going into a whole other level. Now you're saying, "I don't want to manifest something that is within the realms of feasible probabilities." Now you're saying you want to take it to the extreme level. You want to manifest an object in front of you. You want to manifest something paranormal to happen. Now you're dealing with dimension, time, space, and all those things. That is writing the program intensely above the standardized program. You're no longer slipping under the radar. You're very clearly saying, "I'm going to take notice now and I'm going to rewrite reality."

That is going to take a great amount of skill, spiritually, mentally, call it whatever you want, to make it happen. And this is where you're going to have to override the collective consciousness. You're going to have to step above that and that's what an enlightened person is able to do. For that moment, if they so desire, they are able to do it. And different people can do different kinds of manifestations in that way. This is what all of the great spiritual masters have achieved.

Say you have the ability to fly well above the radar and manifest things that are outside of the range. What are the repercussions of doing that continuously?

Well, the Universe is going to deal with you however the Universe decides to deal with you. It's going to be very vague and specific. There are spiritual beings that are here to counteract negative people or beings. Hence, conflict and what we would deem as negative beings imposing negative things and positive beings becoming very powerful to effect positive things.

There is always a measure and counter-measure going on in the Universe as it is expanding. There are always problems arising and forces that would like to dismantle or destruct this process of growth. Therefore, the Universe reacts in ways of creating beings or in itself intervenes on its own part in some other way. By making you much more gifted, you really *are* now acting as part of that reaction from the Universe because you are that part of the Universe. This now gets into the whole concept of good and evil, or battles between spiritual beings, which is the reason I hesitated on whether or not I should present this material.

Having expectation can be a tricky dance. Could over focusing between manifestations be the reason it's not happening?

Absolutely. That's a negative expectation – be careful of it. It's the same thing when you meditate. If you have expectations when you meditate, your meditations will not be as profound as when you choose not to have expectations because you're telling the Universe the rules and guidelines of what *you* think is going to happen. Well the Universe might have something much bigger, grander, and more intense in store for you, but you're saying you're not open to that now. You're saying that it has to fit in these things. The Universe feels emotion, and expectation is very much a projected emotion. Hence, there is an expectation of something. What is that? You don't realize you're doing it, but you've already created that something in a very *vague* but specific language. It's kind of a parallel to what we're talking about.

The bottom line is that you don't want to get frustrated. You put it out to the Universe. You put it out in a very good platform. You can have some expectation. Just don't let yourself get frustrated with it. Just because you're not sitting down and having a session specifically to do it, it doesn't matter. The Universe only acknowledges what you're putting out all the time. You've just put out a bigger beacon for that at a certain moment, and then you're going back to the normal projections of everyday life. But if your mind's on it all the time, you could be projecting that back out. I say do it; do your session; forget about it. Move on with your day. Wait a few days; do it again; move on with your day. And then that's what you're going to do for about three weeks and then stop. See where it goes. Let the Universe do its thing.

Basically, from what I'm gathering, just by knowing that manifestation is a possibility makes all the difference.

Yes, it's a positive outlook; it's hope. The Universe will always give you hope, always. That is one of the greatest things of creation. Creation was based on this sense of hope. Something came from nothing. If you ask me, that's hope. That was an intent. That was a desire because it is the grandest miracle of all. The word *hope* may not necessarily mean much to you, but don't use your organic brain to think about it. Stop for a moment and *feel* hope. Feel it as an emotion. It is a very unique and a very beautiful emotion and that is a key in itself. It gives people hope.

So how can you use Direct Manifestation to accelerate your spiritual growth and development?

You want to open yourself up to have the Universe teach you things that you haven't been exposed to. You also want to open yourself up to asking the Universe to correct the things that may be the flaws or errors that have prevented you from having that huge awakening. You want to put it out to the Universe that you want to become ready or more prepared to have a greater awakening. You want to tell the Universe to manifest, to create the balance you need in your physical life and your spiritual life so that you can mentally be able to transcend all this.

I think that by helping people to create a better balance in their life, this will enable them to find the time to also work on their spirituality without being so distracted. This is not just about money. It's also about finding a balance in your life with other people. It's about creating balance in general. I believe very strongly that one has to commune with physical life as much as their spirituality. To be so focused on spirituality disconnects you and prevents you from leading a quality life. By not leading a quality life physically, you can't really transcend very easily spiritually. There must be a harmony.

Understanding that, I have to help people find a balance in their physical life in order for it to reflect into their spiritual life. I'm just trying to be a good teacher by conveying this understanding to you instead of telling you to put money out of your thoughts and God will come down on your doorstep and say, "Okay, here are the answers to everything you want." It's just not realistic for me to suggest that to people. I don't believe that. I do believe that God helps those who help themselves, and the Universe will also help you if you ask. There's unification there and it's about finding that happy medium.

I trust and only ask that you turn inward and ask yourself to be sincere in whatever it is that you're going to request and the questions are deep within you. The answers are also deep within you. What you're really asking the Universe to do is to help reveal those answers for you, or to help manifest that outward and I think that's the ultimate request.

You spoke about not working against the program or not working against the matrix.

Let me elaborate on that. You're always going to work against the matrix. Remember there's a difference between the Earth matrix and the Universe. Matrix is a word now that's caught on and everybody has a very visual concept of what that is because of the movie. What I would call *the Gaia Mind*, or the *Akashic Records* is all really the matrix still. But there is a greater matrix and then there's an even greater matrix beyond that. There's this big influence until you get to the maximum, which is really going to be the consciousness of God, the greatest collective.

What we are primarily dealing with is this matrix - the Earth, but somewhere inter-fibered in all this is a greater matrix and then another one upon that. I would say that the simplest way to understand this is to look at the planet as being one organism with all the micro life on it, the Earth is part of another microorganism within the solar system. Then the solar system is a microorganism of the galaxy and the galaxy is a microorganism of the Universe. And there are billions of galaxies which you can break down to the smaller particles, or smaller elements.

Now this can be overwhelming when you think about it, but what we're really trying to do with this is to primarily understand what is affecting us at this moment. That is the biggest element of how we're going to direct our lives, and that would be the Gaia Mind matrix. It's not to say that these other levels aren't here and present, because they are, but what we need to deal with right now is working through this matrix to get to these higher areas or higher frequencies.

When I say, "Don't change it too much," what I'm really saying is to fly under the radar as much as you can without making too many waves. Waves bring too much attention to you, which means it's going to prevent you from succeeding and if you make too many waves, you're going to get pushed into the Doe. The Doe is going to affect you. The planet can't have everyone instantaneously become spiritual. It defeats the purpose for the planet because the people who are spiritual are really working for the Universe. The Universe still needs people to work for the planet because there's a big agenda down the road for that. It's just in millions of years.

When you mess with the matrix too much because you're really trying to push yourself spiritually, or you're doing it through spiritual methods, you're manipulating reality. Well what is it going to do? It's probably going to react to you in a Doe vibrational wave by creating more bills for you, or some physical trivialities that are going to consume you and pull you out of that higher vibration, the place that it senses you're operating from.

Now that you've drawn its attention towards you, it's going to try to find ways or invent ways to bring you back down into the Doe to readjust to the pattern - to this matrix. Once it feels that you've come down from that vibration again, it's going to leave you there. But it's going to work very hard to get you to come back down into it. That's why we meditate all the time. We're trying to move up and then life brings us back down because the Doe is constantly affecting us. The Doe is the mechanism - the safety latch for the planet to finish its agenda. The Universe understands that there are going to be people who break out of that for the good of the planet, but that doesn't necessarily mean the planet always recognizes it in those terms.

Could you manifest personality traits within yourself?

Absolutely, and that is a very, very good way to raise your own frequency. I don't want to use the word "powerful," but basically what you could do is create better traits that are more loving, more nurturing, and more positive. We all innately know what a good thing is and what a bad thing is. By doing those things you start to create that vibration.

But be very careful that you don't ignore internalized issues. Don't pretend. Don't be fake. Don't convince yourself that you don't have issues. If you don't really feel it, then it's probably not real. But you can have those things and still be very happy and very positive. They're real. What I would suggest is to manifest a need to resolve those things so that you can grow and so that maybe you will find a way to work out those problems. Whether it's through a therapist, a friend, a family member, or through an experience the Universe will show you and you will say, "Wow, I never thought of it that way. That makes me feel so different about those negative things that I've been holding inside of me."

Just ask the Universe to help you work it out and make yourself available for those things to happen so that they can be worked out. The more positive you become, it is an inviting vibration that allows you more free reign to work within the Gaia matrix and into those higher vibrations. It's to say that the more loving, the more positive, the better your energy becomes, it is ideally what the Universe wants to see. Therefore, it gives you greater opportunities to do things, to intervene, and to work with it. It's a level of trust. When you don't have the right vibration and you can't fix it, it knows that you're going to have destructive intentions and, therefore, limits you more. Unless you try to find ways around it, but that gets into a negative perspective.

I think people constantly manifest themselves into ruts. If you really think about it, how many times have you said, "Boy, when my luck gets so bad, it's like one thing after the other?" What are you doing? You're creating the vibe, the feeling, the vibration. You're projecting it and you're requesting it because you have expectation and intent now. It happens all the time. I see it all the time and this is why I say to meditate and clear your energy. Work with the energy around you; do this; do that; practice your *High Guard*. All of these things aren't just to prevent other people's energy; it's also to help you psychologically remove a lot of negativity. When we say, "Get rid of the Babbler," we're saying clear all those programmable vibes because that's where the negative thoughts start.

When you meditate, you're clearing the slate and it's allowing the Universe to approach you better because you've got a cleaner vibration without all those intentions and demands. The Universe wants to work with you. I told you, you're co-creating in the Universe. You're a contributor and it's sharing with you. So, unconsciously you're constantly putting in and putting out.

Red Cells are a necessity for the planet but the Universe acknowledges that there are spiritual beings that are progressing, advancing, and trying to guide the rest of life or mankind. They've chosen to do this and it is a contribution of awareness. I think most people can see those things happening. If you've ever watched someone who has a lucky streak, it's almost as if anything they touch turns to gold. They seem to have every opportunity in life.

Now I'm not saying it's everybody's fault and that you manifest negative circumstances, but I do believe that your state of mind greatly contributes to this. You could ask, "What can I do about it?" Meditate. Meditation is the answer. Clear the slate and then reprogram by using other products that we put out there, other material. All of these things are designed to circumvent this programming. It's made to give you the tools to shape, empower, and steer you in the right direction.

I don't think it's anybody's fault that they specifically turn out a certain way. I think it starts from very early on. Your parents were a big influence in your life. Your social life and the circumstances that happened in your life, whether fair or unfair had a big effect on you. They all created certain vibrations in your perception. What did I say? Life can mold you. Life presents challenges. It's up to you to overcome them. It's how you want to perceive the things that happen in life. If you want to hang on to the negative things that have happened and constantly reflect on them, what are you doing? You're recreating that vibration over and over again, impacting it, reinforcing it, and putting that out to the Universe; that's how it's going to respond to you.

What you need to do is acknowledge that. Dump all that crappy programming. Dump all that negative information and find outlets to create positive vibrations. Those positive vibrations will begin to manifest and opportunities will begin to arise from that.

How do you start that cycle? And when you do run into a major problem, how do you prevent it from happening? It's all in how you perceive. In my youth I was always told to learn from every negative situation. Always find humor in things, even the bad things. That's because it's going to control your frequency. And you will hear this from very successful people all the time. Now I'm not saying that every successful person falls under this because there are some pretty ruthless people that have success. I'm saying, as a rule of thumb, you can find happiness, success, freedom, and almost everything that you really need to progress in this life and this day and age. How you choose to see it is up to you.

I'm not saying that bad things don't happen to people. Bad things do happen to people but at some point you have to empower yourself and choose to overcome those bad things. At first, it may seem overwhelming, but I promise you that all you have to do is put out your intent to find the solution and it will present itself very quickly. Manifest it. Manifest a solution. Ask the Universe, "This is what I'm looking for," and put that vibration out there.

If a person gets cancer or gets into a car accident and they've been involved with this type of development, this type of work, there's a tendency for them to feel guilty for something that they aren't even aware they've done. They feel like it's their responsibility it happened.

As I said before, bad things happen but what they need to do is take the bad and try to turn it into good. That's the first thing. The statistics for their success will elevate if they perceive themselves getting healthier and they develop a more positive outlook. The odds go up and they will either heal, or overcome the illness, or it will go into remission. Their state of mind has a big effect on them. The people who don't have the will to create that state of mind tend to have a more difficult time trying to heal themselves or turn it into a positive situation.

They can use manifestation to will upon themselves to have a positive outlook, to have good health, to have those things and to tell the Universe this is what they need. But it's very difficult to manifest healing physically when someone is feeling ill. That's why I say to use the next best thing. *Wish for it.* Desire for it and then share that with the Universe and ten to one, it will work with them. It will help them.

Do you have to put the guilt aside to heal?

We are our own worst enemy and there's a reason why that statement exists. Guilt is part of experiencing. It's also a part of self-reflection. I think that growth comes from challenges, and guilt is another form of challenge. Either you can let the guilt consume you or you can look at the guilt long enough until something inside of you says, "I've accepted this guilt." What do you do with it?

Okay, so you've accepted responsibility. Well, I've often said if you say you're sorry for something that you've done to a person you have wronged, then there's not really much else you can say. If you don't say you're sorry, they're going to keep attacking you because they don't feel as if there's a resolution yet. Well, you're resolving this by taking it out on yourself. By accepting guilt, the first thing you need to do is to say, "Okay, I must have done this to myself." Stop hating yourself now. You've accepted it and it's time to move on. It doesn't mean it's the truth. It doesn't mean that it really was your fault at all, and ten to one it wasn't. But you don't necessarily fight the psychology at first. Be vague but specific with yourself.

Now, start to look for some answers. When you start to realize that you have to work on making yourself get better, you can stop pounding yourself into the ground with guilt. I think that there's a process you have to go through and each person is a little bit different. You can't take that away from them at first. I know that sounds crazy and they're not going to want to hear it. There's a reason why they're doing this to themselves. Now, be supportive and still tell them, "Hey look, it's not your fault. "And try to explain it to them, but there's an inner level of communicating with yourself.

What they need to realize is that they need to help themselves and stop worrying about how they did this to themselves or that it's their fault. This will eventually come in time, but for some people it never does. Don't focus so much on trying to get them to believe it's not their fault. You're going to have to get them to start thinking that they need to help themselves. If they can just look at it in terms of helping themselves, they can then realize that they probably had nothing to do with the problem to begin with. It's a perception. It's a point of view. I would say that they want to punish themselves.

Some people are martyrs. By punishing themselves, they feel vindication in that. Don't focus on that at first with them because they're just going to get angry and it will empower their guilt. You need to tell them, "What's done is done. What we have to work on now is how to turn this into a positive situation or how get you to start thinking more positively." When they can acknowledge that they need to start thinking that way, then ten to one they're going to begin to look at their negative perception of themselves and realize that there's nothing they could have done to prevent whats happened.

I'm not saying to let the person suffer. What I'm saying is that sometimes suffering is something that each individual needs to go through, whether right or wrong. You can't just say to someone, "Well, it's not your fault." It sounds shallow. There are things involved that only they understand. If you really want to reach them, get their mind off their guilt by trying to get them to see that they need to work on the positive. Say, "Okay, well that's all water under the bridge. It doesn't help us at all. Right now, are we both on the same page? You need to get well. That's what we need to focus on. Getting well means you need to stop dwelling on this."

You approach it like that and then you move on. Don't keep talking about it. You start a regimen of meditation, positive music, plants, life, fresh air, and positive information coming in on the radio or television. You help create a positive atmosphere for them and then you start with manifestation classes to create positive manifestations. You can't just say, "Well, you've got to start doing positive stuff," without first explaining the importance of self-reflection. Again, if you feel like crap, you can't create positivity. You've got to create a positive environment for the person to even psychologically get a footing to start manifesting it internally.

Moving on to your own personal stuff, what you're trying to do is stack up as many things in your favor as you can. If you stack a lot in your favor, odds are that you'll probably come out ahead. You can't stack everything in your favor. It's very unlikely because life is life and there are other people that have other intentions and their intentions are going to affect you. That's a part of the whole Doe system.

You want to try to help yourself to project things in a more positive way. That, in return, affects other people. Other peoples' effect on you then is more positive. That escalates that positive energy. That positive energy then can also help you manifest the ability to mentally focus and stay attuned to what you want in order to continue to manifest in that area and expand that positivity.

If you're miserable and you're upset and you're trying to get yourself in a mental zone to create positive energy, you'll find that it's very, very difficult to do, unfortunately. Therefore, stacking as much in your favor as possible is what you're going to do to create that momentum and unfortunately if you think that, "Oh boy, I've got all this to my disadvantage." Finding something positive in a negative situation is realizing that there's a lot of other people in the same boat as you and you can laugh about it. That's your first step in enhancing the positive and that's where you start. You have to level the playing field and not have a lot of self-pity. First you have to be able to acknowledge that rather than being in it.

What is your intention? I think the intention is going to be a vibration. You can't hide it from the Universe and that's what it's going to pick up on most. When we're talking about Jesus turning water into wine and manifesting loaves of bread, what were his intentions in doing that? I think they were very clear, very positive intentions. He had the ability to do something specifically on a much higher level and still fly under the radar because he could balance himself through his highly developed skills. Psychic things aren't completely against the matrix because I do believe that psychic ability is still organic the same way I say animals can do certain things that are psychic. Certain things are perfectly okay in the realm of psychic abilities.

When you start pushing those levels to try to manifest objects, or change the real matrix (the bigger reality of how we perceive things) then it really comes down to how you're going to get around the consciousness of the planet, the matrix, and how it's going to affect you. If you have a very steady mind then you're basically learning to override the matrix at that point; it's just to what level. You now have become a co-writer in the Gaia mind.

Now to do something like that is going to take a great amount of will, manifestation, and creation, and it's going far beyond standardized manifestation. You're specifically rewriting things, you're plugged in, and it's a level of enlightenment. It's not to say that a person could be negative and still do the same thing, but it's very rare for it to happen.

Over the years, I've taught a few people and some of them had experiences during the class while I was teaching them. I was explaining certain techniques that you taught me throughout the years. I know that, in some cases, I was affecting the experience, but at the same time, it's like I knew that somehow I was supposed to. It's like what you were saying about flying above radar. I felt like I knew that I had to think a certain way, or I had to feel a certain way, and I knew it was okay to feel that way.

When you go into that spiritual state of mind, you've moved into a different frequency and you're no longer one with the Gaia mind. You're now connecting to what may be the solar collective of a different kind of matrix. You could say the galaxy, which isn't necessarily exactly how it works, but the point is you're moving to higher frequencies. Now these frequencies are working with you because your intention is to help raise the frequency of others which, in turn, are going to help this planet combat negative situations.

Now it's saying, "This is what we need you to do: We're going to assist you, or the Universe is going to assist you in this lower frequency so that you can reach these other people to give them the information they need so it can raise their frequency." It is helping you write the code for this planet, but keep in mind that even it is saying, "We're going to work with certain variables. We don't want you out manifesting tea cups. We want you raising tonals in certain individuals," because that's what the Universe's larger plan is to help this planet, to help elevate civilization. What you do today is going to have an affect 20 or 30 years from now."

That playing field can get very extensive which gets into a whole different thing about miracles and what level people are capable of doing them. And just for the record, the Darkside, which is alive and very real is always going to extend the same invitation to the people who want to put a wrench in the mechanisms of the planet, which is trying to achieve what we see in our society in life. It's going to mirror something very negative opposed to making positive contributions.

Is it naive to think that there will be times when you should just trust the Universe, or surrender to the Universe? Would you be creating or manifesting the intention that everything is going to be okay?

Well no. When I surrender to the Universe, and I certainly do, I'm really saying I love the Universe so much and I'm deeply compassionate to the Universe. I'm like, "Look, you can roll me up into a ball of mud if you want. I'm anything you need me to be. All I want to do is serve you with all of my heart," and I'm simply opening up that in the sense that I don't want to have any intention, or any expectations for myself. My only intention is to communicate to whatever is my highest level of perception of what is good and beautiful and life giving to the existence that I am in right now.

Let's say you have a situation going on that you don't like but, for whatever reason, the Universe needs you to be there because there's something that you're going to get from that. How do you know when to surrender and when to manifest a better situation?

The Universe doesn't want anything terrible to happen to you but sometimes, this may sound odd, the Universe doesn't necessarily recognize that it's a negative situation. When something becomes a bit overwhelming, well then I think you're saying, "Okay, I think I need to intervene here a little bit." If it was a life and death situation, or an aggressive situation, or suppressing your life, or in conflict with what you think is suppressing your life, then it's time to turn to the Universe and say, "Okay, we need to start working on this; this is an overwhelming problem. This is not about moles digging up my vegetables. This is about me losing my home, or someone trying to take it away from me," whether it be legally or aggressively, or who knows what.

I think it's perfectly okay to want some stability in your life. And even when you're confronted with situations that seem overwhelming, I wouldn't necessarily say to surrender. I would say, "Look, I need help to resolve this." All you're doing is saying, "I want to learn from this experience. What I'm asking for is for you to give me the tools to properly disarm this situation faster than whatever I would have to go through to learn the same lesson."

A few of our clients have asked, "Who am I to manifest?"

They are God's reflection. They are made out of the same molecules that created the Universe and they have every right to ask, every right. That's it! It's as simple as that. You have a right to live. You have a right to ask. The Universe has a right to say no but you have the right to ask. You are a living creature and you are part of the Universe. You're part of God; therefore, you have every right.

What makes them so sure that they shouldn't be asking? Maybe, what gives them the right to *not* ask?

There is a certain – I hate using the word ritual – etiquette that I think all of us universally understand. You need to be alone because you are now ready to open yourself up to the Universe, God, The Force, and you're asking or requesting a *one-on-one*. You need to have some space and if you can't have that space, it's okay because the Universe won't mind one way or the other. But what I'm saying is, from our perspective there are certain things that you need in order to get into the zone. Therefore, you want a quiet place where you won't be disturbed. You don't want any phones ringing. You don't want any cell phones on. You don't want any TV's on in the background, and you don't want anything even next door going on that you can hear. You want to enable yourself to get into a certain state and you don't want anything to disrupt the work that you're about to do.

I can explain how I would go about it and then you can decide how you want to do it. I choose a private time when I'm by myself. I prefer to either sit or kneel on the floor. I think you can lie in bed and do it. I think you can sit in a chair and do it, and I probably have in the past depending on the circumstances in my life, or what trials and tribulations I was trying to cope with at the time. For the most part, I just sit on the floor. I probably take a little time to clear my mind, to relax myself, to feel at peace with myself or create a sense of at peace and if I don't feel that, then I know it's not the right time. You may want to meditate, or listen to some nice music, or prepare yourself for that moment. I personally am not one to light candles or burn incense. I don't even like the idea of turning down the lights. I think these are not really necessary things, but to other people they may contribute to their environment and their ritual. It's really a matter of preference. What I do then is I close my eyes and I begin to approach whatever it is I want to achieve.

Now, we'll talk about money. I hate talking about money all the time, but I know that is a key element that most people are going want to know about and they're going to say, "God, I wish he had talked about money." You know the old saying is that "money isn't everything" but it certainly is an awful lot. I hate saying that, but if it was a money concern, *I simply put out the feeling to the Universe of wanting to express it. I'm going to put out the feeling of what the Universe feels like to me. When I think about the Universe and I feel its absoluteness, there's a moment of expansion. I don't have to worry about how big it is or how small it is; I'm not doing that. What I'm doing is just opening up myself to the Universe, all matter, all life, all energy, all existence, and how that feels. And then I'm going to put out hope to the Universe that my greatest desires are received. And then I'm going to express or say, "Forgive me. Forgive me for intruding. Forgive me for even thinking about asking, but this is something that I need to do, and I'm almost ashamed to even ask."*

That's really how I feel. Sometimes I feel that I need to communicate that, but it's the guilt thing that we were talking about earlier, yet not exactly in the same context. I really don't feel that the Universe should be bothered with such petty things. On the same token, I may feel so helpless with a situation so out of my realm in how to deal with it that I turn to the only thing that I know I can turn to whenever, wherever, and however there is a need to. I present those emotions first and I know what the Universe is going to say to me. It's going to say to me, "Eric, I love you. You can come to me with anything you want. I'm always here for you."

It's unconditional love and there's a part of me that feels guilty knowing that I would even intrude knowing that the Universe would never turn me away. That's crazy in itself. Having gone through the ritual of knowing what's going to happen, what I do next is evoke a sense of monetary gain. When I see visually, I will see money. I will see whatever I associate with money: whether it's a home, or a business, or work. These images help evoke a certain feeling, so when I see the house, I throw in a sense of security that makes me feel like I have a place to reside and operate from. When I see the money, I see it presenting the ease and the ability to reach out to other people, to find them, to give them this information, and I express that this is the best way for me to do this.

The first ten minutes is really me feeling like I have to explain myself to the Universe to justify why I'm presenting it this way. And what's happening now is it's checking my intent: is this is what I really feel. Is my intent really to make money on the side, or am I sincere about why I'm approaching in this way. Or do I feel like I could do it other ways? And then it would know if I'm not being sincere. I guess what I'm doing is I'm trying to approach it for a loan, like I would my parents, but it's very different. There is this part of reasoning that I'm going to project out.

I approach it very delicately; I don't just sit there and say, okay this is what I want. It depends on what I'm doing. If I'm doing something on a higher level that's with a negative entity, I'm not asking for permission. I know I already have ultimate permission to crush the situation immediately and I'm going to react that way. Where I think that I have to ask permission is when I'm looking out for my own gains and whether I have the right to ask for that.

There is this level of internal ethics that I'm always working with. I really just put it out there as more of a wish and say, "Look, I need to manifest this," so I put out the feeling of money and I visualize money and project it as the answer to my problem. This is what I need right now and I don't really specify a certain amount. I trust that the Universe is going to know what that amount is so I don't specify dollars. I don't say a million dollars, although I already know what it's going to cost to do what I want to do with it, so that intent or knowing is already there. Those are all details that aren't necessary.

There is a certain feeling, a certain level of security, and I can do things with this and all the things that the Universe needs me to do, I can do. And, so I project that and I say, "This is what I need – I need this – I need this to happen." I see this integrating into my life. I see this as something that the Universe is going to give to me. And I present it in such a way that I'm asking, but it's more like a wish. I think sometimes when people pray, they say, "I need money – I need ten thousand dollars – *I need.*" I think that's just too direct. I'd rather say, "I'm wishing for a large amount of money. I'm not really demanding; I'm not really saying this is going to happen. I'm really saying that I'm open to whatever you have in mind, but I'm saying this is what I need."

To me, it's just a little different and so I visualize money or I visualize whatever it is that I need and associate it with the correct feelings or emotions. I think the biggest error that people make is visualizing without any emotion. It becomes routine. And I'll tell you, it's difficult for some people to remember that they have to be emotional about it all. That's the element that they forget and that's the missing link to make it actually happen. You have to sit there, and everything you see or you do, you have to feel what it is to have that money or what it emotionally represents to you. It's like extending your hands and saying, "Feel this emotion." Do you get it? And they're like, "Oh" and the Universe is like, "Oh I understand that now. I can make you feel that way. Here."

It creates an emotion and emotion turns into physical matter because that's the Universe's intent – to try to create that – that's the secret. Of course, when I am done I bow very humbly, doing my thing, or I say "thank you." Whether or not I get it doesn't matter. What matters is that I present this to the Universe and approach the Universe, or God. I am very grateful for all that; I make sure I don't have a list of things to ask for.

To make a request is different than approaching God because you're dying, and "Gee, it's so wonderful to meet you" – It's just, different circumstances. You're going to a different frequency. You're going there in a very humble way and you're making requests, not specifically, that you're seeing someone. You're presenting it to this vibration. You've opened this doorway because you've asked for the representation of what you believe God is, for a vibration, or at least that part of God that these things are presented to.

When I see this money, there is also the intent of reaffirming, "Ok, that's it. Now that I've presented it, I just know it will manifest," It usually always did in my youth, about three or four times. But for me to talk about money, you've got to understand that for the most part I've lived relatively humbly. Everybody has a different perspective of what being financially humble is, so it's very hard for me to equate how I would have done it if I had more money. To me it's like, okay, I've got to pay my rent. I've got to pay it and, of course, it would always work out.

Again, it's a very complex matter and I think that the simpler you approach it and the more sincere your intentions are the higher probability of success. That's really what it comes down to, and when you talk about meeting someone, you've really got to tell the Universe what you want. You assume that the Universe knows what you want. Well, I've got news for you – I don't necessarily follow that path all the time. In this particular case, I want to be sure I'm going to get what is going to be compatible. I'm trying to put what I need out there, but I also trust the fact that by being a bit vague the Universe will know what I want and that I'm looking for the best solution. Hopefully, that will override whatever I think is good for me. It might set up a whole different senario for me because I still left out that greater possibility and trusted the Universe knows what is best.

How would you go about manifesting a relationship or a partner?

If I was going to manifest somebody, I would probably go through the same thing in a humble way saying, "I don't want to be alone," and put that vibration out there and that is why I'm presenting this. I think that if you very humbly and passionately present this to the Universe, it will respond. It's like being a parent. There's a part of you that cannot deny your child or someone that you love, so when I go to the Universe there's this guilty part of me that knows it doesn't want to say "no" to me. I know it loves me unconditionally, so there's this guilt of asking something selfishly. What do you decide as being selfish or unselfish? That's always a problem for me.

Reflecting on that, I think it's fair to say that you feel that you need someone in your life and I think it's fair to ask for that. You might put out there, "This is my situation: this is what I am projecting, what I'm asking for. What I really would like is someone who I'm attracted to." Attraction is different for every single person. You could be a very physically attractive person, but what you desire or want may not be what someone else thinks is physical beauty. That's the first thing to remember. You present, "I want to meet someone who is a brunette, or has blonde hair, and I would like them to be tall, and have a certain build." And you might describe what your typical model is, for that matter, but you better realistically say to yourself, "What really is feasible to manifest in Timbuktu in the middle of nowhere?"

You have to be realistic and say, "I just want to meet somebody that I'm attracted to." Then I would start thinking about what personality this person should have. What personality would best get along with me? I want them to be this way, or that way, or whatever. You can think of your desires but then you eventually keep working in that emotional area.

Wanting all those things, especially the physical part is very easy to do emotionally when it comes to desire: I want them to desire me; I want them to be hot for me; I want to have great sex. Usually for a guy that's at the top of the list, but not necessarily for everybody. Some of us have matured past that. Most women, I think, are looking for things like emotional support, maybe financial security, stuff like that and, of course, loyalty.

Everybody's a little bit different. But the bottom line is to think about the list before you start to request it. Write it down. Think about emotion, physical appearance, money, spirituality, all of these things because, I'll tell you, usually manifesting somebody in your life is the easiest thing to do compared with everything else. And for some reason, it worked very well for the people that I've taught to do this. They manifest people or they make that connection with someone right away. If you're not careful, you could really get stuck in a situation before you realize, "Wow, I really overdid it." Keep in mind that you have to have balance.

Really, really think about balance and that having too much of a good thing can be – too much of a good thing!

How have you personally used manifestation in the past?

In my younger days, as I approached or developed the higher states of consciousness, I was already unknowingly working on manifestation. One of the biggest things I did was to open myself up to God. I asked, "How can I open up more to the Universe? How can I make it so that I am more capable of allowing the Universe to work through me to shape, to mold me so I can become a better person?" And those are the things that I worked on when manifesting. It was more about – I hate to say being humble because sometimes I don't feel like I'm a very humble person at all – but essentially I asked to become more humble. I asked to become more open. I asked, "Show me" and I learned a lot. I learned that being humble doesn't necessarily mean be a pushover. Humble doesn't necessarily mean weak.

That is what I learned from those things and the Universe taught me those things. It showed me things very quickly when I opened myself up. It was very eager to work with me as I think it would with anybody presenting the right questions. I think that's where you have to start off, by asking to become more humble, but don't become naïve.

Also in my youth, I think I had a very big desire to have a greater relationship with God, and the Universe, and understanding what that really was, not wanting to accept concepts that were force-fed to me. I just basically asked for the truth. I would certainly ask to develop spiritually or psychically too. I'm sure I did in my youth and, of course, I did. I asked to manifest greater abilities, not to the extent of what I could do with them but just that I wanted them to expand. I wanted them to make me more gifted or, in a sense, to open myself to the concept of psychic abilities so that the possibilities would be boundless.

What I really was saying was, "Please help my sixth sense improve so that I can perform better." It's like saying, help me become a better painter, or help me become a better musician through my ears, or my hands. I already felt early on that the sixth sense was simply another sense and I just asked to enhance that sense so that I could better find you. I think that a lot of people will present this and when they think about the Universe and approaching it in humbleness, it's very hard not to get caught up emotionally; you know it's going to happen. For me, if I talk about it even right now I'm choking up a little bit just trying to keep it together. So, you just open yourself up to it. If you want to experience God then you have to open yourself up to God.

Meditation helps you to manifest better because it helps you steady your mind so that you can remember to broadcast more emotion. It makes you more conscientious on that higher level of consciousness, that higher level of thinking that I speak about often. And that's what you want to do. You want to try to be conscientious of what you're doing. There's nothing wrong with that. There's nothing wrong with being conscious of directing what it is you're trying to communicate. Remember that above all, even though you're making requests, or asking, or wishing; you're talking to the Universe. You must intelligently communicate. You are simply setting emotions, but you have to formulate what you want to say.

It's okay to have a list of what you want to ask for, or what you're trying to say. You must, at some point, ask for it but you're going to ask for it emotionally. And you're going to request that you want this to happen. I think that there's a fine line between *willing* it to happen and *wishing* for it to happen. I believe the results are much greater when you wish, and I think I said that earlier but I want to reintegrate that.

The results are going to be based upon the quality of the vibration that you're at so I would say there is no need for working on chakras, or doing any form of meditation while you're doing this. The reason that you want to do all these things is because you're making yourself a better person so that when you do try to manifest, you're access level is going to be greater. That's why you're doing it. You're trying to make yourself as pliable as possible so the Universe can work through you to do whatever It needs you to do. That's why you're doing all these other things. You're designing yourself to be the best performer that you can be for the Universe.

Manifestation - Walkthrough

Before You Begin

Make sure that you *feel* that you're ready to begin; make sure that your *intentions* are something that you *feel* you need to do. You're overwhelmed by it so it's important to you. Don't feel guilty about it but also don't make huge demands. Let the Universe decide how it wants to help you. Don't specifically tell it how it has to help you.

Go through a ritual of finding your location. Go through the steps that we talked about. The most important thing to remember is: emotion, emotion, emotion. Project your emotion – try to be aware of your emotion.

Do not suppress other people. Do not try to control other people. Do not try to make them fall in love with you. Ask the Universe if this person has the possibility of love for you in them, if that's what you're after, and that it manifests the best way that it can. That's the gentlest way you can do it. But don't ask the Universe to make this person fall in love with you because a lot of times the heart is blinding and you always have to be in check with that. You don't want to control other people, so always try to be aware of what you're asking.

Visualize, visualize, visualize. Visualization is very important combined with emotional projection. You're talking to the Universe. You're going to talk to the Universe through emotion. For us to correctly find what we want, we need to visualize.

Manifestation - Technique

a. Find a place where you can be alone and free of distraction.

b. Sit for a while in silence and take a few deep breaths in order to clear your mind. You may also want to do manifestation exercises after you have meditated.

c. Create the feeling of inner peace within yourself.

d. Humble yourself before the Universe as you ask for your desire to be received and acknowledged by it.

e. Remember, it is a matter of feeling respect towards the Universe and that you are indeed asking for a favor or gift to be presented to you.

f. Understand that the Universe loves you unconditionally. If you come to it with true intent, it wants nothing more than to give what you need.

g. Now visualize what you would like to be given to you.

h. Produce certain details that will give your manifestation an outline for the Universe to work with. (You do not want to get overly detailed or too vague with your visualization because it will be less likely to manifest).

i. Now create the feeling of how the manifestation would make you feel. Concentrate on that feeling and share it with the Universe by projecting it out.

j. Present your desire to the Universe with a similar feeling you would have as if you were making a wish.

k. It is important that you concentrate on one thing at a time and stop for a while if your desire becomes too jumbled. Clarity of thought and consistent visual flow is the key.

You don't always have to be specifically broadcasting your emotion. You don't have to say, "Brown eyes." How do brown eyes feel? What you do is just go through a checklist and say this is what I'm looking for. I want them to have brown eyes, brown hair, be a certain height, a particular weight, and have a love for music, art, and travel. Then when you've said all those things, you imagine what that person feels like to you and that's what you broadcast because all of those variables are crunched into that one broadcast. I think these are the most important things, and remember to do it maybe twice a week for three weeks. Don't set a date or an expectation, just wait and see what happens. I often say, the moment you really forget about it, that is when it's going to manifest. It's almost true every time.

Put it out of your head when you're done and just give it time to see where it's going to go. If nothing pans out after three weeks, go back and reevaluate it and ask yourself if you think that you pushed it too far? If you're asking for a six foot Asian woman, elaborate and exotic – you've got to be realistic – you better go to Japan. You know? I mean give the Universe the opportunity to create that manifestation for you by putting yourself in the right circumstances. If you're going to ask to meet somebody, but you stay indoors your whole life, well fine. You can ask for it; there's a chance it may be able to manifest for you, but you're going to have a better chance if you at least try to go out to the grocery store once a week.

You're giving it more variables to work with. You're stacking the odds in your favor for It to work with you to give you what you want. If you're going to make it impossible, it's going to be impossible. But then again, if your manifestation is strong enough and you really are doing your meditations, and you're doing everything else, well then I'd have to concede that I would not be shocked at all if there was a knock on the door. I've seen it happen.

**You've spoken throughout the class, for example:
"The Universe will say this or the Universe will say that."
Can you speak a little bit about how it actually works since
there's not a person checking out your intention,
or is It a separate being?**

How does your body know what to do? How does it know how to process all the chemicals? How do all the organs know what to do? You are the main consciousness of it but you're not aware of any of it. Then how is it able to react to all the needs of these things? The Universe reacts in the same way; it's almost inconceivable to us. The Universe is a different kind of intelligence. All the other lower cycles of that life, whether it's the galaxy, the solar system, the Earth, so on and so forth. Even with us, there are microorganisms living within us; there's a whole other universes within us.

The Universe reacts to those needs by creating and manifesting, whether it is molecules, protons, or photons, to create this reality of what I call fluidic consciousness; which is God's dream in a way. That would be the best answer that I can give you that I think we can sum up in a short amount of time. You present it to the Universe, the Universe uses its wholeness, all of its knowledge, to respond or echo back to you what it is that you're asking. And it's the echo that you hear back that becomes the manifestation.

Why not manifest everything?

Why is there a purpose to randomness to creation? Because God created the Universe to experience. God wants to learn things. Well, if you start manifesting everything, you're not really creating anything new; you're just creating what you already know. There's no excitement in that for the Universe.

Chapter 11

Discussions with Eric: Manifestation

L et me take some time to address some questions asked by Navigators regarding manifestation.

I have tried many different courses on manifestation. The results have been doubtful. Mostly when all the veneer is stripped off, all manifestation methods focus on removing the blockages that are stopping you from manifesting, entering a state of deep relaxation, and visualizing and feeling what we want to manifest. My question is, "Does your manifestation course basically work along these lines or are there other things taught?"

I will agree with you that all three of those things are certainly key factors. They cannot be removed; they are key factors in creating results.

Well, I can tell you there are a lot more things taught than that. These are what I consider very basic steps: removing the blockages, entering the state of deep relaxation, visualizing and feeling what we want to manifest. First of all, there is no simple way to manifest. If someone's going to tell you to just remove your blockages, enter a deep state of relaxation, visualize (and feel), these are all foundational steps. This is why it's as extensive as it is. There is a method to the madness. There is a unique process. One could say it's like baking a cake. If you don't add all of your ingredients correctly, your cake is not going to rise.

So, the million dollar question is, "What is the specific process?" And the answer is in the *Direct Manifestation* chapter. Removing your blockages, or talking about subjects that are on your mind as you learned to do in *The Foundation System*. If you are not familiar with this system, you can find it in my book, *Meditation Within Eternity*. The second thing you mentioned is deep relaxation. You're going to learn that with the Foundation system as well.

Visualizing and feeling what you want to manifest is the third key step. You've got to pick a subject. What do you want to manifest? Do you want love? Do you want money or success, or spiritual connectedness? This is where all of those other programs drop off. What I'm going to do is to teach you a method to design or implement *your desire*. I'm going to show you *how to construct it* and *how to broadcast it to the Universe.* You can't just ask for it because the Universe simply doesn't understand English. Yes, you have to learn to emotionalize, but you also have to learn to broadcast. That broadcast has to be done in a very specific method. If it is tainted or if it "has a virus" within the emotional process, you're going to cancel out your effect.

It's one thing to talk about blockages that are preventing you from manifesting; it's another to understand actually how to remove them. I think a lot of programs say that if you have a blockage, you need to get rid of it. Well, this is why you need to read the chapter on *The Power of Surrender* in my book, *Silent Awakening*, because it specifically addresses the process of removing those blockages whereas other people just say you should just release them.

That doesn't mean anything to me, "Release them." What is the science behind releasing? What is the method, the technique, the methodology? This question is loaded on many levels. The bottom line is that in order to go beyond the other programs you have to realize that you are the actual designer of your manifestation. And I would say that is where it's at, the architectural design. You have to have a design built within your dimensional consciousness, within yourself.

What you're going to do then is launch it, release it, and broadcast it. If it is of the correct pitch, the correct frequency in design, it will be received. Then the master architect, meaning God or the Universe echoes it back to you. That echo starts to design and implement into your life, meaning that you suddenly reach the right people that you're looking for, or the right person you're looking for, or the right opportunity starts to manifest itself. This is all very compressed energy movements and flows, so it's very, very important to have the right design. Again, we're going to take all three of those steps and we're going to go far, far beyond all those to specifically teach you what you need to do.

What is the maximum number of steps necessary for manifestation to work?

I've never counted them to be honest with you. In a lot of ways, I think differently than most people. When I start to see questions like this, I realize just how people think and it is one of my pet peeves. Most people have a way of organizing things, structuralizing things, tagging things mentally and verbally with names, numbers, or structures. I'm naturally inclined not to do that.

When that's done you lose the context of the Universe. The Universe wants flow and when you start tagging things, or overly tagging things, you prevent that flow and you prevent things from happening. So, when you ask, "how many steps," my answer is going to be, "As many as it takes." It's a process that you're experiencing inside of you. You're going to obviously go through the first three steps that we talked about, but there's significantly more. There's a part of you, once you've had the training that has an inner knowing. It is a different kind of intelligence that does not come from your organic brain. It's a knowing.

This knowing is the same thing that tells a baby to suckle milk from a breast; it's instinctive. It's all of a sudden; it's something inside of you once you've been immersed in this knowledge. You have an intent and that intent is to achieve a particular goal or a manifestation. It's as if it takes over and you start to think on a different level, from your heart area or solar plexus area. And it starts to unfold itself and there is a process of steps. But it's very dimensional. The only way that I can explain it, given the limited usage of words, is that there is something being built, or designed, like a package and you're actually designing your request on a dimensional level. You're releasing it to the Universe or God, who's going to understand it, be able to interpret it, and reflect it back to be brought into the reality of this holographic dimension, this holographic reality that we live in. I hope that helps a little bit.

I've got several things I would like to manifest. One of them is abundance of money. Another one is health, and another one is organization.

Let's stop right there. We're going to talk about each one of those things. The first one is abundance of money. The second was what?

The second one is health issues.

Health, and the third?

And the third one is that I've just been feeling really fearful. I have to do this and I have to do that, and I have to do the other thing to be better, better, better.

So these things come to me. I wind up with all this stuff and some of it's finished and some of it isn't. Our business is travel, so we are selling honeymoons and romantic travel, and so it's been a matter of attracting brides to us.

And the market has changed from doing wedding shows to doing mailing lists to doing email lists. Now it's just really scattered. And then we have farmland that could give us money, or we could just sell it. And then there are other sources of income as well.

Let's deal with abundance first. Everything you have listed here is going to be exactly what everybody else is interested in manifesting. Everybody else who is sitting here is thinking, "Those are the questions I have, too: abundance, health, and being fearful of certain circumstances." The first thing that I'm getting from you, which is *rule-of-thumb*, is a lot of static. Static means you're all over the place for your manifestation. Can you imagine talking to the Universe and throwing out all of the questions you just did to me?

Well, that's why I want to be able to focus. How do I get this to the Universe in a more focused approach?

Sit down; Use *The Foundation System* – Clear your mind. The most important thing is to have a clear mind. You have to get rid of all the static, all your questions. However, this is the million dollar answer to your question. *What do you consider to be an abundance of money?* Is it a million dollars? Is it a hundred thousand dollars? Is it just a regular paycheck coming in? What does that mean to you?

No, more than that.
Our family goal has been like four million.

So four million dollars. Now, I want you to sit down and clear yourself for a minute; just take a nice deep breath. Now think about or internalize what four million dollars feels like. It feels different than a million dollars and it feels different than five dollars. What does four million dollars feel like to you? Now, you need to dissect that feeling or decode it even more than that.

Right now, you're feeling the first layer which is the relief of what it can offer you. But that's not what four million dollars *feels like*. That's what it *offers you*. There's a science behind this. *What does four million dollars feel like?* Everything has a specific vibration, a specific feeling. You have to determine what four million dollars specifically would feel like to you. Imagine a pile of money. Feel it. Lift it; four million dollars; would it hurt your back to lift four million dollars? Maybe if it was in twenty dollar bills.

So, the point is, what does four million dollars feel like? And when I say "feel," I'm not talking about the touch of the paper. I'm not talking about how much weight there is. I'm talking about a certain knowing, a certain knowing that is internalized inside of you. It means that four million dollars represents a certain frequency, a certain code, a certain feeling.

My fingers and toes and nose are vibrating.

But you're still not decoding it yet. You have to distill it down even more. It's not easy. If it was easy, everybody would be able to do it. This is why you use the programs and you have to really think about what it is saying. It's the words in between that stand out that are helping you to decode what the problem is, to get to what the actual vibration is. If I was to will in four million dollars, I would have to internalize all these different kinds of ingredients into my pot, if you will, or my pan. The first one is that I'd have to realistically realize that I'm not just going to have four million dollars handed to me in one lump sum necessarily.

I need to say to the Universe, "I'm okay with getting it in several payments. I can't have it trickling in because I need all of it within a year." You have to think about these things and you have to create a feeling, or a sense of security, which could be a feeling of, "It's alright if I get this amount over the next year, or over the next two years. I understand that we have to work within realistic levels."

The second thing is that you're fine with that, that you don't feel any guilt, shame or anything. You have to be like, "I'm okay with this. It is going to work for me." Then you have to "show" mentally, what four million dollars is so that the Universe goes, "Oh, I see what you want." Four million dollars to the Universe is just dirt.

It doesn't have a conception of money because It doesn't have a use for it; it doesn't have an understanding of it. You have to convey what you need in a feeling that it needs to provide for you. And this is why I keep saying, if you can figure out what four million dollars feels like and say to the Universe, "This is what I need to feel in my life." And ask it to give that feeling to you, it's not going to manifest this four million dollars in your physical life.

In other words, I'm not going to quantify where it's coming from?

Exactly.

And I'm not going to necessarily say I'm going to have a house or a car.

Exactly.

It should be more a lifestyle and a feeling.

Yes, the Universe needs it to be simplified. It needs it to be broken down into concepts it can understand. The Universe doesn't necessarily relate to a house. It relates to a sense of shelter, comfort. If you were to say, "I don't have a home and this is what I need," what would it feel like to have that home, what does it provide for you inside of yourself? It provides shelter; it provides warmth, goodness, family. You want to say to the Universe, "These are the feelings that I want." If you decode what a home is, you're going to decode it down to a feeling of safety, love, and protection. And you need to say, "This is what I need." And that's what you have to broadcast out to the Universe through your chest area, through your heart chakra.

But if I'm asking for an amount of money like that,
it's going to be not only for a home.
It's going to be the health; it's going to be the lifestyle.

I would say that the more that you pile into your manifestation request, the more complicated it's going to be to create it. You want to go after these things separately. Maybe you focus on one for the first month. Then you focus on the second one the next month. The third one, you focus on the third month. And you just watch them come in. If you say, "Well if I have four million dollars, then it's probably going to help me with my health because I can afford better doctors and everything." Why focus on the health then? Just focus on what you think the main solution would be. You want to keep it simple, because the simpler it is, the less room for the Universe to make a mistake.

And that's what you want to make sure that you do; you want to keep it simple. I would stick with the four million dollars. I would come up with what four million dollars feels like. Picture the house you should have; picture the release you should have; picture all those things. Find all of those feelings or write them down on a piece of paper. Then find one word that condenses all of those, or four of those, then another four, so you have two groups condensed down to two words. Take those two words and try to find one word for the two. And then feel that inside of you and broadcast and say, "This is what I need to feel." And say, "That's what I need; please provide this specific frequency, this feeling, to me," and what it's going to do is it's going to provide exactly what you need.

I'll tell you a little story here. I had a lot of problems with deciding whether or not I should open up Higher Balance and whether I should do it for money and all of this other stuff. And I never really knew how I wanted to go about it. Other things I had tried, generally in business, had failed. And I'm a smart guy. I understand business. I know all of these things. Finally I decided I want to do this for the Universe. I want to do this for other people. And I need to feel good about it. I came to terms with that and I've talked about that in other programs – I put it out. Once I came to terms with that, I sat down and manifested what I needed to make this happen. Now, before this all happened, I didn't have a pot to piss in, to put it plainly. I think that I was down to forty dollars, eating Top Ramen noodle soups, working on getting Higher Balance off the ground from a small apartment room. In that amount of time, Higher Balance has become a multi-million dollar company. That's not sheer luck.

That's intentional.

That's right. That's manifestation. Every time when things got a little slow, I would sit down. I would decode and come up with the feeling of having a lot of people suddenly become attracted to what I'm offering and tune into it. I would ask the Universe to wake the whole planet up and to bring them to Higher Balance. Or take notice of our advertising, as limited as it was. And lo and behold, all the phones would ring off the hook for the next month or two. So, these things took place because of manifestation and the secret really is broadcasting, but also decoding and knowing what that feeling is because you can't say to God or the Universe, "I need four million dollars." It means nothing; always remember that. "I need a new house," means nothing. You need to say, *"This is the feeling of what I need; this is the vibration; this is the frequency. Provide this for me and I will have what I need to serve you greater."*

Is it important to have proper intention or can a person manifest whatever they want? Other studies that I've done, like Kabbalah and stuff like that, they always tell you that you're not going to get anything from the Universe unless you first, do this, and that. And if you're not a good person, you're not going to get it because of karma.

Well, I'll go over it and from another perspective, everybody has different takes on this so it's important to hear it in different perspectives. Sometimes that's what helps people. For me, in order to have the achievements I've had, I had to come to terms with being able to accept the fact that it was okay to take money for what I'm teaching, bottom line. And I realized that it was going to take money to find people, such as you and the people who will read this. And it's just the way it worked out. I came to terms with it. What it comes down to is that every person knows the difference between right and wrong deep within themselves. I don't care who you are or what your background is. No matter what you say, you know right from wrong. It's designed within us.

Instead of worrying about karma, I would say to the Universe, "If I could get to this point, then I'll do my best to do the right thing." I'll give you a simple example. I think that crime is driven by lack of income in many cases. I think that people fester into crime levels because they just simply don't have an income. They see those people who do and it affects them, so they make poor decisions. I think that if people had a certain level of income, it would remove the drive to create certain crimes.

This is why you need *The Power of Surrender*. It teaches you how to remove the blocks inside of you that are preventing you from doing that manifestation.

It's within you. You're the one who's preventing yourself from manifesting. And, of course, you're beating yourself over the head saying, "But I really want to make this happen. Why would I do that to myself?" It's like chewing your nails and then somebody says, "Are you aware you're chewing your nails?" And you're like, "No, I don't chew my nails." The mind is very peculiar. When you meditate, you can calm your mind and then you can use *The Power of Surrender* to release those issues. Then you can use the manifestation material to start to create and design what it is that you want.

As far as what you want, I don't think there's any problem unless you're looking to harm someone or kill someone or something like that. I'm sure there would be a big problem with that. If you're trying to find a companion in life, or you're trying to find success in life, or you're trying to find the right job, or you're trying to get your business to take off the ground, those are all good things. You need to internalize that and accept that, and then work on designing that manifestation.

And anybody who just thinks they're going to sit down, listen to the material, and create a manifestation in the first thirty minutes is crazy. If you're going to have success with it, by all means, you've got to sit down and really take that material in. And dissect it for five, six, seven days and work on how you want to design that manifestation. Once it's done, it's done. But no, I don't think there's a limit to what you can manifest. I've heard it all and I've seen it all.

I've been asking the Universe to let me win the Powerball.

The more specific you make it, the more you limit the possibilities of what the Universe can give you. It is difficult for the Universe to create that because there are probably six million people all trying to manifest a Powerball win just like you are. You have a conflict of interest there; so there's a problem.

I want to find a job, but I don't really want to do what I did before. I want to maybe become a massage therapist and give back to people as opposed to a company bottom line. I feel like my heart is in the right place.

If you put out to the Universe what it feels like for you to be a massage therapist and what it would feel like to make that your source of successful income and lifestyle, then you need to use the program to design that decoding down to its very basic core. Then you need to broadcast that through the techniques that have been taught. And you're going to have it. It's going to happen.

If you think you're going to get the manifestation material or any of the other materials, and you're just going to do it and sit around on your couch or your chair, and somebody's going to come knocking on your door or a letter's going to come in the mail, it's very unlikely. It's not what the Universe can do for you, but what you can do for the Universe. Meet it halfway. Put out through the manifestation what you want. Go out and then achieve your goal. If you already have the schooling behind you for doing massage, then you need to start putting out there to build a clientele, or to find the employment you selectively want.

Now you may say, "Well, I went out and I made it happen for myself." Well, that may be true. But I would say after twenty years of teaching, there are people who go out and they never get one response from doing it. They work on the manifestation; they broadcast it; they go out and within three or four days they have the job of their dreams. Was it manifestation or was it luck?

It proves itself over and over and over and over and over. Manifestation works, but you've got to help the Universe help you.

Well, I think the tools that you're putting out are going to help. What does it feel like to have the money to do the things I want to do? Not that I want money in my life or I want financial freedom in my life, but what does it feel like? That's what you told the last student; it makes a lot of sense to me here.

I share more secrets than any other teacher or self-help coach out there; believe me. Just decode what I'm saying to you. Listen to what I'm saying and apply it. It works; I swear to God, it works. And you can do it and anybody else can do it. Apply it. It works.

The other schools that I have been involved with have disciplines about manifestation and abundance. If you want to manifest abundance, you need to somehow come to terms with not being in lack, knowing that you're not in lack and having that knowingness.

When you say, "In lack," what do you mean by that?

Thinking that you don't have it instead of knowing that you already have. It's like living every day like you were already abundantly wealthy. I was just wondering if you had specific guidelines or disciplines, or a structure. Those are the only words that I can think of.

I'm not sure if I understand this lack, or if you have a lack, and whether or not you're deserving. One thing I've learned is that different people have a different income level and that's how you see the world. Some people may say, "I feel guilty asking for money when there are poor people living in certain countries, third world countries, who have nothing." My answer to that is the same thing that got me over my level of manifesting Higher Balance and actually making it the huge success that it is. It was coming to terms with a Buddhist philosophy that there's nothing wrong with making money. There's nothing wrong with it. The real question is, *"What are you going to do with it?"* That's what's going to decide whether you're honorable or not.

That's going to decide whether you are worthy or not for the Universe to help you. What I would say is to ask yourself that question. And it's perfectly okay to request abundance from.the Universe. There's nothing wrong with it, okay? But the real deciding factor of that will be what you decide to do with it once you have it.

Right. Well, the reason why that just popped into my mind as I was listening to you was I heard you speaking about blockages. And the first thing that popped up in my mind was that somebody might have a feeling that they weren't worthy of abundance.

That's right, and most people do but they won't say it. They'll say, "Oh no, I'm worthy," but secretly they feel that they're not. Those things that are in the deepest part of your psyche really prevent you from achieving your goals. By getting those out of your system and finding acceptable psycho-therapy, you'll be finding answers to dilemmas inside of you that are unresolved. This is why we put together the surrender program because that really teaches you to very powerfully and very quickly dissolve all of these issues. But you can remember something and all of you know this; everybody reading this is a White Cell, in my book. You're deserving, no matter what errors you made, no matter what your situation is, no matter what you're income level is.

I believe and I know that you are. And it's the reason why I've decided to come clean and teach all this knowledge; it's really been kept under wraps for the most part. I believe you are all going to do the greatest good. I know that you have all the greatest intentions inside of you. I believe in all of you. And I know that by me helping you, you're going to help the world.

Don't worry about whether or not you're deserving. You wouldn't be asking if you didn't need it. Bottom line – you wouldn't ask if you didn't need it. You'd be asking for something else. You can only do so much, so fast. Everybody knows right from wrong; just resolve it. The money makes the world go round in this particular day and age.

What will you do with it? Go ahead and ask for it; you've got my permission, but the real question that I hold you to is, "What will your honor, what will your integrity be once you've achieved it? Once you've settled your finances and paid off all your bills, and you've gotten your house finances under control, your home, your car, and your family, what then will you do with it?" And I expect for all of you to hold the same to me. I hope I will be tested and proven as being honorable in the end. We'll see.

I know a lot about gurus and manifesting material objects and that kind of thing. How does one do that and how does that apply to actually manifesting something like dreams and desires?

Well, I'm going to be very honest here. I'm going to probably get into a lot of trouble. I'm the rebel in the spiritual teacher arena. One, I've talked about this before in a live lecture. I talk about these people who claim that they manifest material objects. I don't want to talk smack on any other spiritual teachers out there. But my job is to be absolutely forthcoming with the people who come to me to learn information. And my job is to make sure that you don't waste your lives, your years, your weeks, your days, and your minutes believing something that just isn't completely true. Most of these spiritual teachers, without naming who, what, where, he, she, whatever, I don't believe are really manifesting. In fact, I'll go as far as to say that I think some of them are using sleight of hand.

I do magic myself.

So, when in doubt, be in doubt. A lot of people have heard about different things I've done. There's are some recorded interviews from students who've actually witnessed me doing some phenomenal things, but my philosophy is to show other people how to do it themselves because there's no denying it then. If you experience or you achieve something on your own, then you can't deny that it actually happened. You can say you brainwashed yourself or it was self-hypnosis, but the evidence is so strong that you can't deny it.

Most of the claims of people creating jewelry, or any other kinds of objects is pure rubbish. Getting caught up in that is just going to waste years of your life; you could be developing yourself into a higher being. Now, I'm not saying it's not possible. What I'm saying is there's a lot of fraud out there and you have to be very, very careful about what's real and what's not. So, about your question about dreams and its relationship to manifesting, can you be more specific?

What's the scientific method? How do you simplify it now that we know your thoughts on the physical manifestation of objects? How do you simplify your request? I'm still unclear how you simplify that to put that out to the Universe in the Universe's language, if you will.

Okay, you mean decoding?

Yeah.

You have to listen specifically to what I'm saying. You obviously come from what I call a *mind center*. Your mind thinks a lot like mine; we're very rational. The problem is that human beings generally think in terms of words. And those words are secondary with emotions behind them, in my perspective. What you need to do is realize that everything has a specific emotion, a very specific feeling. If you were to look at a coffee cup without touching it, you have a feeling for that coffee cup. You could say it's cool; it's soft; it has a smooth contour. You could imagine what your lip feels pressed against it and then hot liquid coming from that.

If you were to just say to yourself, "What does a coffee cup feel like?" Everybody has a universal feeling for it. And the problem is there's not a specific word in our language for these things. But if I had to define it, it's like this firm smooth structural feel. And that's what a coffee cup feels like. If you took that and you said to the Universe, "this is what I need," not in words, it already knows; it's an intent. You're not sitting there in your room in a half lotus or in a chair and having a clear mind for nothing. Your intention is already part of that secret process.

Your intention is already saying to the Universe, without actually uttering a single word, "I have a request." And that request is this feeling of an object. And you're going to project the feeling of a coffee cup. But what you're projecting is the design or the decoding, the final distilling of an object, what it is in our dimension. And you're saying, "This is what I need." And lo and behold, you're going to have a ton of coffee cups start showing up in your life.

That is the secret. That is what writes into the matrix. That's what writes into our holographic Universe. So, it's not easy to start doing more and more complex things. When you start thinking about a house or a lover or those things, these are much more specific. But if you were to manifest a lover, you could define a personality. But you would have to have an idea of what that personality feels like; maybe you knew a friend or a family member who has that certain personality. You build the ideal person.

And do you focus more on the physical feelings that you get from that person or the mental?

It's more like you focus on all of those things and when you put them all together, you ask yourself what does that person, as a collective, feel like? Again, if you go to a symphony and you listen to a piece of music, you can identify the different instruments. But in the end, there's one total experience that you actually get from that piece of music.

Once you distill it down, you could say, "It made me feel as if I was flying over a valley in Italy. How do you define what that is? How do you know that's what it is? It's an *internal knowing*. And that is what we don't have words for. This is why it's so hard to describe what it is to decode something because we just don't have the words in English, or any other language, that has really gone into this in-depth. The closest thing is to say "emotions" or "feelings" and I would say that they're pretty close to what it is. But it is an overall feeling. If you listen to a piece of music, there are words in it; there are instrumental sounds in it. But in the end, it gives you a certain feeling.

Well, in a sense, everything else has that feeling, not just music because it's audio, but also visual and touch too. It's just a matter of how you want to input that data. Your brain can distill it down to one particular vibration that's made of all these things, and that's what the Universe understands. If it was easy, everybody could do it. If it was easy you could sit down for five minutes and say, "This is what I want." Then everybody would achieve it. The more you distill it, the more you can find the exact frequency you want and put that out there. The simpler and cleaner you can make it, the faster the response is going to be from the Universe.

In general, what is manifestation? What do you consider manifestation to be from a religious standpoint? Could manifestation be a result of prayer or things like that? Are you talking about something that's similar to that?

Well, yes and no. Let's talk about meditation. When I talk about meditation, I say that when people pray, they talk at God. And I'll emphasize that, *they talk at God*: I need a new pair of shoes; Mary needs a new roof on her house. Or, they outline their other problems. When you meditate, you *listen* to God. You clear your mind. You don't have any babble; you don't have any wants; you don't have any desires. You just are open to whatever God wants to talk to you about at that moment. That's meditation.

Now, where does manifestation come in? Manifestation is another way to talk to God. I believe that a percentage of prayer gets to God but I don't think that God specifically is a man sitting on a throne up in Heaven. I don't know what Heaven is; I see God as being a part of a living Universe. And we are part of that as micro-beings within God.

Now, having said that, we have to assume that there are thousands of different languages on our planet alone and in the Universe, there's hundreds of millions. When somebody says that God can understand them all, I agree with that. The question is, "Does he understand it through words? Does he understand every single language and speak it fluently? Or is there some underlying language that communicates something we don't clearly understand." We say it in words, but is God receiving or understanding this on some other level? It's that other level that is key to manifestation. It's about learning and decoding what verbal communication is.

When most people generally pray to God, there's about a 50/50 chance of them being answered or not. Then people say when something good happens, "It's an act of God." But then when the church gets blown over in a hurricane, they don't really say anything. Well, was that an act of God too? We tend to selectively choose what we think God is doing for us and we try to always focus on the wonderful things that happen. When something bad happens, we just assume the devil had something to do with it. I just don't believe it's that cut and dry. I think the Universe wants desperately to communicate with us.

Most people are so inebriated in what I call the 'Doe' that they no longer have a strong relationship with God in its truest level. I believe that God wants to help us and is willing to help us in our lives because we'll help God in exchange. It's just an even exchange in the end. Manifesting is a way to communicate to God, or to the Universe, The Force, or whatever you want to call it, with much more clarity. Meditation is to hear God and manifestation is to communicate to God.

How do you communicate that manifestation and once it's happened, how do you address that?

If it's happened, then you can thank God in the same way – through a manifestation. Who says that you always have to ask for something from God when you manifest? Why not broadcast your appreciation? Sometimes I get on my hands and knees, just like somebody deeply in prayer, and I pour my heart out to God in how greatly humbled, appreciative and unworthy I feel.

To me, it's my way of really saying to God that I absolutely love him for everything that God is and I live to serve. I don't know how else to put it. But there's no better thing than to give a gift to someone. It's one thing to give it and to not need appreciation, but boy, I'll tell you, it's wonderful to be thanked also. And so, I believe in thanking the Universe consistently. I'm not talking about a cheesy quick thank you like, "Oh God, thank you!" For me, I can thank God for over two hours. It depends on what's going on in my life. But, it's a matter of personal feeling. It's a matter of personal perspective.

So you can thank God or the Universe even if nothing has come to pass?

I trust that the Universe has better knowing than I have and if it's denying me, then who am I to continue requesting that? My job then would be to be a little bit cleverer in my request. I hate putting it this way but find a different angle on asking for what I want. Maybe there's a reason that I'm not getting it if I'm trying to manifest four million dollars. Maybe it's because it could be the end of me. Who knows? Maybe it because I would buy a helicopter and then crash it into a building? Everything I've ever manifested has come to be, so it's hard for me to think of manifesting and it not happening. If it hasn't manifested for you yet, then you're doing something wrong. It's that simple.

Once you've manifested something, do you need to continue to focus on it or as you say, keep the vibration on it to be able to maintain it?

Well, yes and no. I often say that if you're really good at manifesting, you would have put that into your request already. When you originally manifested, you should have had in there, that it was self-maintaining.

I made that same mistake on many occasions. With me, particularly, let's say with the business, if I feel there's a slow spell. Or the advertising just isn't getting to the people that we want to find. I have to sit there and manifest it reaching people and, of course, the phones start ringing like crazy. The bottom line is that I probably didn't do a good enough job when I made the master design to manifest people for HBI.

This is why I say take five days to seven days to think about what you want to manifest. Make notes. Read the material repeatedly. You want to become a specialist in it. Start off with a few small projects because sometimes when you manifest something, it's very hard to re-manifest something similar. It's as if you now have to manifest special components to it and that's where the maintenance comes in.

Make notes, be very specific about it. If it's a person, you better make sure that you've thought about any faults that you didn't want him or her to have!

If you see any faults, should you put it down on paper?

Why not? What you're trying to do on paper is develop your structure, your content, and when you've done that you want to create the code. You want to distill that vision, so you want to use your imagination to create that perfect person. But in your imagination you have to create a real feel for them as if they were real. And you have to implement all of the feelings that are on your list so that you can combine that into that person.

Now, you might wonder, "How do you get all of that out of one person in one moment?" I would say rubbish, it happens all the time. You might meet somebody and they're laughing, they're talking, they're being philosophical, they're doing all these wonderful things. Then all of a sudden you're like, "That's the perfect person for me." And they have a feeling for you and that's it, that's your code.

Yeah, I've met somebody like that and we're on and off.
I don't even know what's going on at the moment.
Yet that's the quality I look for and the feel that I get.

I would say that right now that you inwardly probably want that person to work out for you. That's where you're starting to get into some trouble because there's some inner conflicts inside of you.

And that's going to be a challenge. What I suggest is to say to the Universe, "This is exactly the person I want." But I want you to remember the double-edge sword I'm talking about. If there are some issues now between the two of you, it doesn't mean that those issues will be gone. You might create a better connection but there will always be those issues.

Maybe this person's not the perfect person for you, but you're trying to convince yourself otherwise. That's something you might want to think about. What I suggest is that you trust the Universe, which is hard because you know what you want. You're like a spoiled child, I do it too. We all think we know what's best. And you need to say this is what I'm looking for. Then you need to put the faults into your recipe that you're having with this person. Then say, "These are the things I don't want, this is the remainder, this is how the vibration should feel, this is my code now and this is what I'm broadcasting."

And I'll tell you, I've gotten so good with this, and in some cases in trouble in my younger days. I mean I could literally pick the hair color of the person, the eye color, their physical fitness. I mean, literally to a T. It's all in how creative you want to be.

You talk so very briefly in Direct Manifestation about how meditation really helps with manifestation. Would you elaborate on that some more? Talk a bit more about how you can enhance your manifestation through the meditation processes.

Absolutely, it's a good question. First of all, one of the things that you're learning in meditation is to have better control of your brain, your mind, your Babbler. When you create a recipe, it's one thing to develop your information for you to distill it down to a code but most human beings, without any formal training from the HBI material, have a lot of static. They have random thoughts, random emotions. They don't really have a way of controlling it or a method to control it even a little.

When they attempt to manifest or they buy the material they're like, "Okay, I'm just going to do this now." They're success level isn't as good as it could be. When they're getting ready to broadcast, their signal is weaker or dampened because they've got a second, third, and fourth layer of consciousness. And what I mean by that is, sometimes you can have problems in life and while you're doing your manifestation you feel this anxiety in the back of your mind. There's a reason why you feel tense, your body's tense, but you're not really mentally acknowledging it or aware of it.

You haven't found a way to recognize it because you're not in-tune with yourself. Through meditation you really tune in to yourself. You learn to release a lot of stuff and your tuning ability is much greater. What I am saying is that your second and third layer become your primary. Then you're going to manifest.

Your second layer might get wound up because you've got financial issues going on. Your third layer is wound up because your mother just called and needs a place to live, or she's having some trouble so you have that on your mind. But, without meditation, you haven't learned to put those issues aside and not have them affect what you're going to do.

This is where meditation comes in. It gives you a method or a process to remove yourself from these things so that you can focus on other issues that are going to bring greater ability for you to solve those other problems. When people try to do manifestation, they tend to let these second and third vibrations into their code without even knowing they're doing it. And when that happens they're breaking down their initial broadcast to the Universe.

When the Universe gets it, It is like, "Oh, four million dollars from your husband who's very angry at you for buying all those shoes. I see that your mother wants to move in, and ..." It's confused. You end up doing exactly what I said you don't want to do. You want a clean signal. You're trying to distill it down to a specific vibration of what it should be and without you knowing it, you have hitchhikers on your broadcast that you're not even aware of. And that's what's jumbling it up and the Universe is saying, "I don't know how to deliver this to you."

Meditation is a skill, wax-on, wax-off that allows you to move into these other areas. This is why I say you should read

The Power of Surrender. Another suggestion is to read *Thought Reflection* from my book *Igniting the Sixth Sense.* These two chapters will make you an expert. It's all about creating the proper stage for that broadcast.

What I'm saying is that if you have a big challenge ahead of you, particularly like the person who called up about wanting four million dollars, that's what I would do. I would sit down and say, "This is a serious thing. I'm not going to do this for an hour and assume that the Universe is going to give me what I want. I'm desperate, I'm serious. How serious am I? I'm so serious that I'm going to read the other material over a weekend which could be ten hours. And I'm going to be bleeding from my ears, but it's going to get me so in the mood and so focused that I can't go wrong and it's going to bring it home."

My question is about surrender because it's come to me that I need to surrender. But I don't know what it means. I feel like I've been given a strong message which is, "you need to surrender."

Well, let me talk to you about some of the parameters of surrendering and see if that helps you. Surrender, to me, can be done on several levels. It sometimes means that you have to surrender the ego. The Universe wants something from you and you feel very strongly about serving the Universe. But your ego is saying, "Well I'm going to serve it the way that I want." And the Universe is saying, "No, you're not." You need to surrender that ego. You need to say, "Let me put aside my wants and desires so that you can purely, truly communicate with me what it is that you want."

Surrender is also letting go of certain negative individuals in your life. Letting go of feelings of regret, like maybe you have to send your mother to a nursing home and you feel guilty about it. In some ways, it's preventing you from moving forward. You need to surrender that guilt and let it go. The surrendering method can be used for a vast variety of things that are deep within your psyche.

Remember one thing: Everybody reading this is looking to develop their mind, their higher consciousness. We are spiritual; we don't just reflect on the physical but also what affects us mentally, even subtly, is going to have a profound effect on our enlightenment cycle, our awakening. The idea is for us to look at what's mentally ticking around in our mind and remove certain weights and certain caps that are on us that we may or may not even be aware of. It's important to have the tools to do that. If we do that, then what's remaining, what's allowed to come forward, is profound.

**Well, I think I need to answer my own question.
I need to figure out what it is I need to surrender.**

Exactly. Well, I'll give you a little help. Why don't you try to think about surrendering whatever it is that you need to know? Let me explain. We're going to get a little deep here, so bear with me or maybe think about it. Sometimes the problem is wondering what it is we need to surrender. The overall thought is that, "Well, I don't know what I need to surrender."

Then surrender the search. Stop looking. It's when you can stop looking or assuming that there's something that you need to surrender, that you have a huge breakthrough.

**I'm wondering why I even got the message to surrender
because surrender wasn't even on my mind
until you brought it up today.**

Then there's obviously something there. This is what I'm talking about when I say second, third, and fourth levels within your mind. I would suggest you read the *Reverse Engineering the Self* chapter from *Waking the Immortal Within*.

Anyway, it's really in-depth stuff. I don't recommend it to people who don't want to mess with themselves a little bit. But I have a hunch it's exactly what you're looking for. After you finish that material, come back and ask yourself the same question about surrendering and I think you'll find what it is you're looking for.

I don't want to break out of myself only to find more of myself. I want to break out of myself to find my creator, to find my destiny and my call and I don't have a picture, I don't have a construct of that specifically. So, when can you trust that you're really outside of yourself and in the divine? When can you trust that it's not just you constructing a bunch of stuff that is not meant for you?

I'm going to go right back to *Reverse Engineering the Self.* Believe me, if you're interested in what I'm talking about you're definitely an intellectual person. *Reverse Engineering the Self* is powerful stuff for someone who's very cerebral. You're literally going to dissect your brain and start removing all these things that you think are you. They're just as real as the table or a glass or anything in front of you and you're going to realize that. And it has a tremendous emotional impact in the end.

Is it possible that you may be doing the direct manifestation correctly but that there might be other things involved like if you have other people that you work with that are very negative energy, very selfish, greedy, unethical ... Those types of people and you're trapped there and can't get out. Does that affect the ability of the Universe to help you with your direct manifestation?

Absolutely. Sometimes people are imposing or manifesting without even being aware that they're doing it. And this is creating another form of what I call "static". This is why we put out a program called *High Guard.* And *High Guard* is actually a method and technique that is used to move all these energy fields away from you to actually destroy linkages to your energy fields and how to set up barriers. Literally, you can feel like what feels like an emotional ton lifted off of you. Absolutely, there are other people that can affect you.

A lot of people aren't thinking about this but there are people who are manifesting their will on you. It doesn't necessarily mean that they're directly doing it the way you are because they're not that skilled. They're not going to be able to manifest better jobs or better money, but I've often said that negative manifesting is a lot easier than positive manifesting. If somebody's constantly willing negative emotional energy at you, it will have an effect. And this is why I strongly urge that people use the *High Guard* material because it works. You already know what the problem is; you just have to choose to react to it. My answer is that you should look into the *High Guard* material.

But in order for you to do powerful manifesting, you should already have the *Foundation Set* and be implementing the meditation. That, in itself, is a very powerful deflector of negative energy to begin with. If you really feel that you're dealing with an extraordinary amount of negative energy, then I would say read *High Guard* in the book *Igniting the Sixth Sense.*

When people ask questions and they're coming up with a reason, nine times out of ten they're actually correct. And if you're feeling that it's the environment you're in and the people you work with, I would say that you're probably right, and you're probably sensitive enough and aware enough to recognize what the problem is.

If I see, feel, hear no difference during meditation and I'm not getting any feedback from it, how can I improve the process? In other words, sometimes my Babbler is a little quiet. Sometimes I go ten minutes and I know I have to change position. Sometimes I'm guessing. What can I do without feedback from the process?

My feeling is that you have expectation. Do you know what I mean when I say that?

I'm aware that I've always had expectation.

But, what I'm saying is that your expectation, I feel, is affecting you when you actually sit down and do your meditation. You're obviously meditating for certain results and you're asking yourself, "Well, when am I going to feel these results?" But what I'm saying is that when you actually sit down to do the meditation, don't analyze. Don't have anticipation, try not to have hope of what to experience.

What happens is that sometimes we start to manipulate, from the deeper parts of our consciousness, what we want to have happen or anticipate a certain experience. And what I'm getting from you is that you want a specific result. Sometimes, without knowing what that is, you're creating it. You're saying, "Oh, I want to see lights, I want to float, I want to have this experience or that." Maybe not in so many words, but there's a kind of inner mind thing that you're projecting out. And God's saying, "Well, I'm not going to give you any of that. You just going to have to take what I'm going to give you." When you have a certain expectation that you're not aware you're projecting, it's preventing you from having the breakthrough that you're looking for.

I was just wondering where and how did you develop or find all this information and these techniques? I've studied this kind of stuff with a lot of different people and I find your information and techniques fascinating.

Well, I'll be perfectly honest with you, I have probably never really studied anything that's out there. I'd like to say that I know what I know, if you know what I mean. You know, like the song. I'm enlightened. That's what it is. It took me a long time to accept that. I feel that I don't deserve to say that, but I guess it is what it is. My state of consciousness is extremely high in a spiritual aspect. If you ask me to fix a car I may have a problem with that. The knowing I have is from being a very old soul and learning how to direct that knowledge into this physical dimension. And it seems as if everything I come across in this dimension from Reiki to Gurdjieff's material, I breezed over. Over the years I've had many students who were experts in these disciplines. And this is why I know what these things are or know of them.

You know, I try not to indulge myself in reading other material so much and I know that may sound horrible, but I feel that it would corrupt my consciousness and that I would start to think the same way. I like the fact that I come from a different perspective, and I think a lot of the people who are attracted to me share that same perspective. But I have to say that I'm enlightened. I mean it's been this way since I was a child. I've been talking about quantum physics since I was twelve years old, I think. You know, I've been talking physic work since I can remember.

I've had spiritual experiences since childhood. My family lived on a small, little Island in New England. It had six houses on it and the island was built up about maybe eight or ten feet high with a wall going around it. There was a lake and I disappeared. I was probably about three years old, or five years old, I'm not sure.

They search all over for me and I was standing on the edge of the wall with water running off of me. And they asked what happened to me and I said, "I was in the water". And they asked, "How did you get out of the water?" It was impossible to crawl out of the water and up the wall. And I said, "Well, the light came down and took me out."

And I could give you hundreds of stories like that since my childhood. It's fair to say that I've had a unique advantage that most people may not have had. But I'm the unique advantage that you have now and I'm doing my very best to give that knowledge to you.

Chapter 12

THE IN-BETWEEN

The In-Between is an absolutely unique state of mind. It's a fluidic state of consciousness. It's almost impossible to really describe what it is to be in the In-Between state. It is truly something that you need to experience for yourself to really understand it. Those who have experienced it will say it's almost like taking a hallucinogen. In other ways, it's not hallucinogenic because it becomes very physical. It's more than just visual. I often tell people to try to imagine when Moses did his miracles, or Christ, or Buddha, or Krishna, or Milarepa, or whoever. The real question isn't about whether or not these people did miracles. Everybody thinks about the physical act of the miracles. They don't stop to think about what was really going through their mind.

If you're a musician, artist, or poet there is a certain state of mind you go into where you focus on what you're trying to achieve. You go into a set function in your brain. When spiritual masters created or manifested, they were in that state of mind. So, what is that state of mind? What does it feel like? What was it like for them? If you can get into that mindset, can you do the same things? The answer is yes, you can do those same things! The state of mind they were in was *the In-Between*.

All the things that you can learn from me can be greatly amplified if you can learn to do them in what I call the In-Between state of consciousness. The problem is that you use so much forward thinking and so much verbiage. You're trying to create this other state of awareness that goes beyond your normal state. You're trying to quiet your mind using non-thought. As I've said before, there's a different intelligence and awareness. It's a knowing. When you go into an In-Between state, you'll find that you're naturally flowing in that state of mind.

Most people who go In-Between simply experience what it has to offer in the environment they're in. They walk around in awe of what they see, smell, hear or feel. They aren't focused on actually doing something that has a direct effect through the will of their consciousness, whether it's something paranormal, telepathic, healing, or something like that. It takes a certain amount of skill to get to that point. It's as if you're doing two things at one time, like rubbing your stomach while tapping your head. It certainly can be done the same way a musician learns to play a guitar, or an artist learns to paint. With practice comes perfection.

The secret is first being able to experience this mythic state of consciousness called the In-Between. I believe I'm going to have a lot of success in helping you achieve that.

Much of what I teach, how I teach, and how I know what I know depends on me reflecting and studying my own actions and my own consciousness. I discovered these different personalities called the I's (you can read about them in my book *Waking The Immortal Within*). Once I achieved a very refined level and got to my *Middle Pillar* (see Glossary), I was able to observe other higher functions of what I was doing. When I was doing something miraculous or something on a higher level, I actually was able to analyze what I was doing to achieve that.

During years of going In-Between, I still didn't realize that's what I was doing. I had no idea that this was a "thing." You don't really reflect on, "How am I doing something?" You just reflect on what you are experiencing. Of course, over time I was able to look at myself and analyze what I was experiencing in that state of consciousness. That was the first realization of this higher state of consciousness. Over time, I began to refine it and sort it into our current human language so that I could communicate it in a format that you could better understand from your state of consciousness.

Is the In-Between different from just shifting really hard?

Well, it's a little bit of both. You can shift your consciousness and that's an In-Between state. The question is, "How much can you do when you shift and how long can it last?" Most people will shift and remain in the environment they're in. They won't really act out and do too many things beyond experiencing or being aware that they're in some other state of consciousness. When you're In-Between, you're learning, first of all, to recognize it rather than just being in it and not understanding what it is. Once you can understand it and recognize it, you can then utilize it and do more things with it. Once you are able to do more things with it, you can apply greater techniques or methods to begin greater experimentation or attain profound levels of knowledge.

I call it the In-Between because you're still in a physical body. You're always going to use a level of your biological brain because you're connected and rooted here. This is the main dimension that you currently exist in.

When you go In-Between, you're literally in between two different frequencies. Instead of projecting yourself fully into what I would call this hyper state of pure consciousness, which I think is a multilayered energy environment, you're actually stepping into the In-Between. It's a level between that dimension and this one. It's the crossover that allows you to see what things really are or a very unique version of how you perceive or experience reality. Therefore, it's an in between state.

If you completely cross over, you would definitely have some problems because the physical body just isn't going to let you do that. You might leave your body to project or move into other dimensions with your mind, but this is such a physically oriented level that you really are tapping into your other five senses which are somehow being amplified along with your sixth sense. Your experiences are absolutely unique versus a standard psychic state of consciousness. Again I repeat, it's very difficult to explain this and it's something that you almost have to experience to really understand the complexities of it. It is a state of hyperconsciousness, a level of higher awareness more so than your everyday state of consciousness.

All the psychic things that I teach are largely done from a standard conscious level utilizing your sixth sense, which I believe is within the brain. You're trying to develop the sixth sense to eventually allow yourself to move into higher levels of awareness. The In-Between is literally achieving this higher state of consciousness, this multidimensional consciousness. It's a different level of awareness; it's the In-Between. Again, it's something that's very difficult to explain and something that you need to experience yourself. You're more in the hyper-dimensional consciousness that I talk about tapping rather than utilizing your normal everyday level of consciousness.

Do you become more aware of your causal energy?

Absolutely, but there are certainly levels to that. When you first go into an In-Between state, there are a lot of things you're experiencing that can be very overwhelming. Imagine a fireworks display on the Fourth of July. How aware are you of the people around you? Or what they are eating? There are so many different stimuli and experiences that you're really not able to focus on more direct things at first. Once you've done it enough or you continue to do it, you tend to be able to expand and master it. That is what allows you to delve deeper into other areas.

You have mentioned in other classes that there are seven bodies total, but I think we really only covered the first three. Does the In-Between state actually build all seven of those bodies?

It's certainly going to help build those bodies but you have to remember that your organic body is currently your main body; it's the most developed. By going into an In-Between state, you are utilizing the functions of this other body. As you learn, develop, and explore self-awareness, that's naturally going to contribute to those other dimensional bodies.

The problem is that the extent of information or data that you can conceive or understand is going to be limited because you're largely based in this dimension, in this physical body. There are things that will just not compute in your mind or in your brain. You have to try to absorb it slowly or it'll be too overwhelming. Your brain will just start going into heavy edit mode.

Once you learn to exercise these other dimensional states of consciousness, or your multidimensional consciousness, you will be able to exercise other consciousnesses, other brains, and they will be able to hold that data. When you go In-Between, you'll be able to use the full spectrum of this information. There's going to be a point when you have to stop because you're just going to feel like you need to come down from this. Often people who use hallucinogens will, at some point, peak in whatever they're doing and things become so intense that they need to come down. What does that mean? It means they have to come back to this reality, bringing themselves back to their comfort zone.

As you progress, that comfort zone will change and you will feel more comfortable in higher states of consciousness. If you climb a mountain every day, it eventually becomes easier. When the things that are difficult to do become simple, you've adjusted. You can say, "Where does my mind reside?" It would certainly be somewhere beyond most people. That's because you've exercised all the time in these higher places, making you more buff now than others.

Because one is in a dual reality moving into the energy dimension, is there a chance that one might go temporarily insane or simply not be able to handle it?

Yes, everybody's different. This is why I struggled with the question of whether or not I should release this material. I gave it a lot of thought, and my final feeling was that you obviously are going to come down. You may end up being so mentally overwhelmed that you just fall asleep. Your body is going to instill a certain level that it can tolerate. If you can't come down on your own, you're just going to end up shutting down and going to sleep. You're body's going to shut you down eventually.

Mental fatigue is just like physical fatigue. Enough is enough. You're not going to do any damage. It's as if you've been really stimulated or really overwhelmed and you might want to come down. Your first instinct is going to be to lie down, just as if you drank too much. If you had too much alcohol, and you lie down, your bed is probably spinning and you're going to vomit. The body's going to make you come back down to a level where it feels more comfortable.

In an extreme situation, you're going to go to sleep. When you wake up, you'll be perfectly fine and you're going to have a lot to think about. You certainly need to approach this with caution. I hope that everybody who reads this understands that you need to put your foot in the water a little bit before you jump in. But if you decide to jump in, I don't feel that anything horrible or terrible will happen.

There are natural safety precautions. It's like when you're holding your breath. Inevitably you're going to naturally force yourself to breathe. It's going to have the same effect. This is the Universe. This is part of life. It wants you to grow. It wants you to find It. It wants you to experience. The last thing the Universe wants for you is death. It's what every living thing is instinctually aware of, whether it's a plant, animal, or human being. It's self-preservation. I do not feel that this is a threat in any way, unless you already have a psychotic problem. If you do, you seriously need to rethink about doing this.

We offer an 800 number. We're here five days a week. Talk to us and we'll walk you through it. There may be a few people that this is too intense for. If it's too intense, you need to put it away. You need to decide what is too much and what's not. A vast majority of people have been looking for this teaching their entire life but nobody would give it to them. It's the one thing they needed to plug into something profound. It's part of the journey of awakening.

No one teaches anybody about the In-Between. After seeing no real material for decades on how to achieve this in a format that most people can access, I've decided it's time to teach my students. With technological exposure as it is today, and with all that we are exposed to in theaters, movies, video games, and television the concepts are pretty much the same. Like anything else, it takes training to attain a level of mastery.

If you were to go into the Air Force because you want to be a pilot, you don't just get put into a jet plane. They start training you and one of the ways they do this is with a flight simulator that gives you situation awareness and knowledge of what to expect. There isn't anything exactly like this for In-Between training, but watching the Matrix movies and other Sci-Fi movies, especially ones dealing with dimensional and energy concepts, is really a form of training. Even some children's animations are good training tools. All of these forms of teaching are coming from the Gaia mind, and it's really looking for White Cells.

As a modern spiritualist, I feel that you need a more informed perspective so you should embrace technology to a certain degree. The people who are going to experience this already have a much higher awareness of these things, so they know what to expect. I don't think there's going to be any new revelations that are going to shock them. The only difference is that they will be the ones who experience the *real thing* but they won't be too overwhelmed because of what they've already learned through this technology.

When the movie *The Exorcist* first came out around forty years ago, people hadn't ever seen anything as crazy as that before, so there were people in the audience who were throwing up. Others with weak hearts were having heart attacks.

Most people have now been desensitized to this material. We see ten year olds eating popcorn and trying to sneak into the theater to watch horror movies now. Of course, they go to bed scared. The point is we are much more experienced through what life has shown us. This is why we're constantly looking for a new level of stimuli. That could be a problem someday. For the vast majority of people, the things we are exposed to on a daily basis now would shock somebody about fifty to eighty years ago. It would have blown their minds.

This is the reason that the In-Between was considered a secret teaching available to only a select few accelerated level students in the ancient teachings. The bottom line is that students were carefully prepared for the In-Between. The common people would never have been able to handle this.

When we were talking about other dimensions and you look at these mandala paintings with their brilliant colors, you realize that these are people who are going to these places and coming back trying to put it in a format for the vast majority of people to understand on a much simpler level. We're looking at it and saying, "Oh, those are pretty colors. Oh, they're very brilliant. Oh, look at these geometric designs they're making." We don't realize that they're trying to take something that's very complex, intense, amazing, and beautiful, and put it in a simplified context. Again, it's something you must experience.

There's always the possibility that it's going to be overwhelming for some people. If it's overwhelming for you, call us. We are definitely setting an incredible benchmark for a teacher-student relationship on a global level. We're reaching out to people in ways that you had to teach face-to-face in ancient times. Of course, this limited opportunities for a great many. We are simply not watering down anything. We're really putting out the real deal.

What kind of preparation would you suggest for a person who wants to go In-Between?

I would certainly suggest that they have a lot of experience with other Higher Balance material that has been put out there. Again, it's somewhat like a flight simulator, but different. If you want to learn to fly, you need to have a very good concept of what to expect. Work with your energy a little bit. Be a little bit conscious of how your mind works, how your energy works in your body, and certain elements that are really going to train you and fit very, very well with going In-Between.

Already, I'm beginning to shift into the In-Between. While I'm on it, I'll explain a little bit of what it's like to go In-Between. First, I am having more difficulty communicating, more stuttering, and more slippage in my communication because I'm really moving out. I'm fighting to stay in this rudimentary state of consciousness so that I can communicate with you. The other part of me is very excited and wants to move into the higher dimensions because it just feels more natural, now that I'm conscious of it. It's what makes me feel more whole. The stuttering basically comes from being in a higher speed of consciousness and trying to funnel ten pipelines of information into one to get it to this level.

One of the things that I experience, which is very typical of shifting into a higher state of consciousness, is a very bland taste in my mouth. For some reason, it often starts off with a metallic taste in my mouth. It's almost like a strychnine taste. A lot of times when people use LSD, because of the chemicals they use in it, they say there's a strychnine taste. It always comes to mind, but I know there's certainly a big difference between the two. Right away your mouth gets pasty and feels a little bit unusual. You also can feel it in your jaws. For me, there's sometimes a tightening or a weird feeling because I'm becoming more conscious of my physical body.

It's like a high pressure hose that's flapping through the air. If you don't gain control of it, then you're not going to like what you're experiencing very much. It's nothing harmful, but you're going to be thinking, "Wow, these are weird experiences." You become conscious of your jaw bone, and you can really feel it. It's like you can feel the whole bone. You can feel your tongue. You can feel the glands in your mouth, and you can just feel those strange sensations that you're not normally conscious of. Then the training kicks in, and it straightens you back out again. It's really very mind oriented. Again, it's one thing to explain it. It's a lot different when you're doing it without having to talk because you really don't want to talk. You'll understand that when you get there.

Sometimes you will feel a lot hotter. That could be Kundalini flashes moving through your body; you'll feel heat moving up from your lower body through your chi area and up to your chest. Not everybody experiences exactly the same things; it can change for different people. Hearing becomes very unique. It is definitely a way to begin shifting. I discovered in my youth that hearing is an excellent way to begin moving into this state of consciousness.

One of the things that you also have to be conscious of when you start to shift into the In-Between is the room or space that you're in, particularly if you're indoors. Most of the time, the outdoors is not as bad as indoors because there's a lot of plant life. But indoors can affect you and make you nauseous, so you should be really careful about how much food you're going to eat before you start doing this.

For some reason, everything starts to take on a very plasticky feel. Everything seems to be fake; it's not necessarily real. It's like you can feel things with some other sense that's telling you all this stuff is synthetic. Your brain says it's plastic. This is because when you think about the most synthetic thing in your environment, it's generally plastic. That's how the brain works.

When you start to use the sixth sense, this higher sense starts to work with your sight because your sight acknowledges something and the sixth sense ties in with it. Or it's like looking for a source of music. Using your sight, you can hone in on the radio about ten feet away and, all of a sudden, you can clarify what you're listening to. It's like you've focused on it, so your hearing now joins in. You become visually conscious of the carpet and the furniture and everything. All of a sudden, there's this other space inside of you that most people aren't aware of. You have to become aware that you're feeling with another sense that you're not used to.

Your brain is trying to loop it into your normal senses and say, "Well, you're feeling it from here, or you're feeling it from there." When you start to feel the environment and how plasticky it is, it's not touch; it's not smell; it's not really sight; it's not hearing, but somehow you have this feeling of knowing what all these objects are and that they're synthetic. That knowing is part of the sixth sense. You are interpreting information from your sixth sense. Your brain is telling you to begin somewhere else. It's telling you not to think about where that source is. You're just accepting that you know it. The real question is, "How do you know it?" What's telling you that it's synthetic? And again, it's something you need to experience, but once you do it you'll know exactly what I'm talking about.

You're going to feel that everything is synthetic. You may start to feel a level of panic that is going to say, "I don't want to be here; this is not real." You're going to want to escape to 'reality.' The only way that I can explain it is to imagine going to one of those burger restaurants with a play area full of plastic balls. Then imagine that feeling applied to everything else.

I hate to use that kind of restaurant as an example, but sometimes when I go into one of them with the hard colored chairs and tables, the hard floor, the bright colors, and this very sterile overhead lighting; there's a part of me that says, "This is just so synthetic; there's no life here," and wants to escape from that. Well, it's ten times stronger than that. When you're at one of these restaurants, you can just go out the door and see some trees, smell the air, and feel life again. In a way, there's a part of you that needs to escape and you need to be able to control it.

You don't need to panic. You need to know that you're not going to feel that way when you're done. Everything will eventually normalize. I can say that with certainty after numerous times of going In-Between. But there's going to be that little part of you that says, "What if? What if it doesn't go back to normal?" That's going to create panic in you because you're, all of a sudden, completely out of your environment or your environment sensory has completely changed. The sixth sense is what's created the feeling. You've got this whole new sense of information coming in and you're not sure how you know what you know. It's telling you, "Nothing is real."

Well, imagine if you were blindfolded and you were feeling everything with your hands and everything was fuzzy. It just would not make sense. It would make you feel a little overwhelmed, mentally panicky if you will. When you start to go In-Between, these are very normal feelings and they will pass.

Be calm, steady yourself, use your training from other things that I teach, and allow yourself to just flow with it and move beyond that. If you do feel overwhelmed, the best thing is to go outdoors and look at the trees and nature. I'll be very honest with you. If you start heading into higher levels of the In-Between, everything can start feeling very plasticky and you're not going to have a very pleasant experience. You may want to stop for a while. Just walk around. Turn on the TV and watch anything that will bring your attention back into this dimension. Then you'll slowly come back down. You just have to stick yourself in front of a TV or talk to somebody. As soon as you're forced to have to communicate or relate, that will bring you back out of it. And you'll be completely out of it before you know it.

Here's a few other things. Just so you don't panic, you can hit certain levels where it's so intense that you can forget how to physically walk. The muscles in your body are just not going to cooperate with you. Don't panic because it will pass. My body feels strange right now, but I have so much experience with it that I'm okay because I can control it. There are certain things you're going to feel, such as your muscles feeling weaker than normal. They may even feel gelatinous. You will feel a variety of different sensations, but these are things that you learn by placing yourself into that experience. You will adapt. If somebody throws you in the water, you either sink or swim. Nine times out of ten, you'll start to swim. With all of my experience, I'm positive that you're going to adapt.

Your natural drive to experience will override and take the data that you're ingesting and digest it. That's where you're going to go through the panicking because it's trying to figure out what to do with it all. Then you'll adapt. It will absorb the situation and say, "Okay, get it under control." You will master it very quickly compared to normal things. And then you'll be able to move on to something else. But each time you go into it, you might have to go through those phases until you get it down. At that point, they just go even faster.

Should one have a certain amount of Prana absorption to spark the shift to the In-Between? When we are In-Between, can we absorb Prana at a higher level?

You will definitely absorb Prana at a much higher level when you're In-Between. When you begin to go In-Between, you're taking on Prana but it's a unique kind of Prana that's designed to move you In-Between more than it is designed to actually enable you to do paranormal things or to affect things in this dimension. You're really just moving your consciousness. Then that affects your sensory in your body. Whereas, if you are going to do more psychic things, or if you're inclined toward psychic abilities, which is more rooted in this dimension that takes a different format of Prana energy. I talk about which chakra you choose to bring in your energy in *Meditation Within Eternity*. The chakra you use determines the kind of Prana you're taking in.

Why is there such a repulsion of the grosser form of Prana in physical objects when you are in that state of consciousness? Why not see the beauty in it?

You can see the beauty in it, without a doubt. The problem is that it takes time to see the beauty and you've got to digest it first so your brain can interpret or understand what it is getting. It's an overwhelming amount of information. If you were to smell hundreds of very potent roses all at the same time, it will be intoxicating for you. It will become overwhelming and nauseating for you until you learn to break it down or refine it to a level that's acceptable. Going In-Between is the same thing; you're just flushed with this whole new sensory so that your body is nauseated by it.

You'll literally feel a little bit of nausea in your stomach, but you will adapt. And when you adapt and you get it under control, then you can take it to this other level to experience it differently.

There is an intense, immense beauty when you go In-Between, a beauty that will change you for the rest of your life. Enlightened people don't just become enlightened for no reason. There's a development to enlightenment. When they start to enter this doorway and go In-Between, it really begins to unfold them and make them so unique and special because they can see so many things in life.

In your daily life, how much time do you spend in the In-Between?

I try not to go In-Between but it's so easy for me to do that because I begin to shift within the first five seconds of even talking about it. When I have to do classes, I start to go In-Between. That is where the stuttering comes from. People who know me know I don't generally stutter unless I'm really in teaching or communication mode. I try to stay away from it because I have the opposite problem. You are trying to reach these higher levels but I'm trying to remain here so I can help you to find this place.

When I go there, there's a part of me that doesn't want to leave. Yet I know that if I'm to help others, I need to separate from that. In a way, it's very sad and emotional because it's like going blind or losing one of the senses that really taps you into the beauty of life. I have to ignore that in order to remain here because they just don't mix that well. It's much a higher place. You're really attaining something that you will retain after you leave your physical body, providing you develop your dimensional bodies. You'll understand it better because the mechanisms now are not limited by the main body that you have for this dimension.

When you leave this body, and you're in a dimensional body that's of a higher frequency, you're going to have the same problem trying to experience this dimension. It's just a different spectrum. Of course, there's a part of you that will have more knowledge of this dimension so you're going to want to return to it at some point. Then you're going to have difficulties because the machinery just isn't designed to absorb it. Enjoy life now; that's why you're here. It's beautiful. But for those of us who want to know more about what's out there, well now you know. You have to understand, that's why you are doing this.

When you come back from the In-Between, how is your thinking process changed?

When you come back from a trip to some foreign place, you see the world very differently. You might go to a poverty stricken part of the world and come back and look at what you have. At one time, you might have thought that you had so little. Then, all of a sudden, you're disgusted with how much you really have and how indulgent you are in certain things that the other people in the world don't have. It enriches you; it really expands your perspective of life; it really gives you a greater depth of understanding life in this world. You are enriched because you see life differently. You see human beings differently, and you see the characteristics of how they communicate differently. You can look at art, or listen to music. Anything you do from the In-Between state of mind takes on a whole new level.

Imagine what it would be like to lose one of your senses. Imagine if you never had it your whole life. Somebody could explain color to you but could you really, truly grasp it 100% without sight? It's the same thing. You're going without certain senses for your whole life. When you go In-Between, this whole other symphony of incredible things suddenly turns on for you so you can't help but be enriched and deeply moved when you come out of it.

When you leave this world, there's one thing you are leaving with – your data which is your experiences and your knowledge. You don't take anything else with you - not your car, house, money, nor the people you love. You're really leaving here with what you've experienced and what you've gained. As a consciousness, as a frequency, it's going to make who and what you are. By going In-Between while you're in this physical dimension, you're really adding a whole new level to what surrounds you in this world. It really highlights everything and puts it into a greater spectrum of understanding.

Is the In-Between something that can be accidentally attained through the use of hallucinogens?

Well, in one aspect hallucinogens would be great. The problem with hallucinogens is that you don't have the self-control you really need to have. Hallucinogens are so overwhelming that they rip open the corridors in your mind and you start flooding with information. When you're done, you don't remember half of what you experienced. And the things you do experience are really trivial compared to the big picture. You know that you had some profound experiences but you really don't know exactly what they were. They don't make so much sense here and now. In the In-Between, you have a lot more control. You remember everything. You have clarity of mind and you're working with the brain to move into these higher states of consciousness instead of forcing it. With hallucinogens, the brain is stumbling to give you this information and you're doing damage to it.

In the In-Between, you are literally working in such a form of poetry within your mind that it's as if the brain is able to sing and the song is the mind. The mind becomes this profound flow of information that's really supposed to be shared with you. With hallucinogens, at least the ones I have experimented with, I was either bored with them or greatly disappointed at how they damaged my mind and how long it took me to repair that damage, both spiritually and psychically.

What about people who don't use hallucinogens?
Is there a way they can accidentally slip into an In-Between state,
like people who have Kundalini awakenings?
Is it possible just to fall into it by accident?

Well, nobody needs any hallucinogens to experience the In-Between. Most of the people who have the shocks are people who have been messing around with energy work. You don't hear very often about people who are not involved with any form of spirituality suddenly having these energy experiences. On rare occasions you do, but they're probably old souls who were never fully awakened in this life but have hit this level in a previous lifetime. Like a lot of things, they didn't know what it was and they didn't go anywhere. They didn't know how to ride the wave. They were in a swell, as if they were swimming in the ocean and went back down instead of riding the wave or doing something with it.

You have to recognize it. That's the number one thing. What is the In-Between? You're going to say, "Hey, I'm starting to feel these things that Eric was talking about. Let me just try not to fear it or try not to bring myself out of it. Let's try to see where it's going to take me and amplify the experience." That's what's going to proliferate it. I think people have experienced it before. They just haven't known how to work with it, or known what it was.

How do you ride the wave of the In-Between and amplify that?

By acknowledging it. When you are aware of it, just try to feel whatever it is you are feeling. Try to acknowledge whatever it is you are experiencing. Most of all, don't try to think. Don't use your forward thinking. Don't use your brain, "What am I thinking?" You don't realize it but you suddenly start experiencing on a higher level. A thought becomes a faded thing and you're not really thinking. You just don't realize that. You're really thinking super-fast so you're going to have a different kind of awareness. It's only when you realize something weird is going on that it grounds you and brings you back down. If you know what's going on, and you're okay with that, then you can just move around your environment without thinking and you can start to experiment with it.

How do you communicate in the In-Between?

Well, you try not to but it's hard. If somebody is In-Between with you, there is a synchronization between you. I often relate it to schools of fish in the ocean. Or, I've heard Rupert Sheldrake talk about starlings that synchronize all their maneuvers. It's as if there is this field of consciousness that they are tapped into. It's very much the same thing. When you shift with other people, they're with you, and when you begin to feel something or you think something, they feel or think it, too. If you allow it, that precedes words. You're just aware of each other. It's a level of very advanced telepathy. Instead of words or just emotions (which is what we use for telepathy) being projected, you can literally decipher so rapidly that you're really on the same page.

There is this synchronicity of consciousness among the people who are experiencing the In-Between. There's not a need to use words; there's just a knowing that you don't really want to talk. The only reason you would talk is if you're with people who are just learning. You might want to use words to help guide them but once they've done it a few times, there's this perfect synchro-nization of consciousness.

When new people go In-Between, does it have an effect on the collective consciousness?

I would say that everybody has an effect on the collective con-sciousness, whether you're new or old or whatever. It's nothing that's going to damage it or anything.

Does it have a positive effect?

I've never seen anything negative come from it. The only thing that would be negative is if they were a Red Cell and it was just too mind blowing for them to conceive that these things are pos-sible. Anybody who's reading this, or anybody who is remotely seeking this, is probably a White Cell. For them it's feasible. But for somebody who doesn't buy into the In-Between to suddenly slip into this state, acknowledge it, and be aware of it, I think they would be in shock. I do think there's a shock level there. And I think they would ground themselves out quickly because the other mechanisms of being a White Cell aren't there so it would just evaporate away from them as if it never happened.

You said before that there are battles on energy levels going on as you attain these states of consciousness. Are you naturally fighting those battles from within yourself in order to achieve this?

Well, there are instincts you've been programmed with, as we've brought up in the books I've written and the material that I teach. Of course, there are the natural inclinations that you've learned so you've got to bypass those and try to see them, just like the F thing from the *Handbook of the Navigator*. There's a certain pro-gramming in your brain that's designed to edit the information you receive and this is how you perceive reality. If you've gotten this far with my material, then it shouldn't be that much of a prob-lem for you. There's going to be some upheaval and resistance like the nausea and the plasticity that you experience.

These are all phases that you have to go through in order to move beyond all that. This is the resistance that's designed into your body to keep you in this place. That's why you experience those things. It's because the body's going, "Yeah, something weird is happening." Once your body has done it enough, then you can move past it rather quickly. The only reason why I'm re-experiencing it is because I'm choosing to, so that I can give you a map to what you're going to experience before you get to these higher places. Otherwise, I wouldn't reflect on it so much and it would have been a quick little bleep.

Without a Middle Pillar, how would a Red Cell shift into the In-Between?

Well, they have organic properties. Like everybody else, they have psychic ability because it's within the human brain. The psychic ability that's there is really designed to be the building blocks for the final level to bridge you over to the building of these other dimensional bodies. It is nature giving you the poten-tial to reach these levels, whether you use them or not. Getting there is another thing. White Cells instinctively reach for these other senses even though society says they don't exist. So, that's a challenge. Once someone accepts that they exist, they can start to work with them. That's what begins to bridge you or give you the tools to start reaching into hyperdimensional consciousness, or using this other state of mind.

You teach us not to have intent when we meditate.
Should we have an intent while going In-Between?
How would you prepare someone to go into the In-Between?

When we say in meditation, "*Do not have intent,*" we are trying to teach you to open yourself to the Universe. The Universe already wants to tell you what to do; it tells every plant how to grow. Every flower knows when to bloom because it listens.

Human beings are the only things that really don't listen. That's because our minds are so complex and so evolved that it really distorts that ability. You're trying to learn to be quiet. When you go into the In-Between, you're trying to discover a different type of consciousness that is going to step forward and communicate with the Universe through that quietness.

When you go In-Between you're using your Navigator more and a different intelligence to guide you. It takes practice because it's not something that comes easily. There's not necessarily a word for it. Again, it's something that has to be experienced and reflected upon to really understand, but it's an inner knowing using a different intelligence.

Can human emotion, like love or sadness,
spark this state of consciousness?

This may be disheartening to some people, but I find that when I'm emotional it grounds me down. When I go In-Between, I'm really relieved of any emotions. I'm not sad; I'm not happy although I have that possibility because when I see something I feel this immense joy. I think the difference is that when I think of joy in human terms, I think of it being connected to someone I love, sex, food, or monetary gain. It usually has some kind of physical relationship. When I feel happiness in the In-Between, it's very different; it's so much cleaner. It has a different feel of happiness. It's very difficult to explain but it's definitely positive. When I feel emotions in this physical level, they are tied to these things. Emotion is so powerful to the mind because that's really how communication happens. It's more on an emotional level rather than verbal communication and I find that it grounds me out. The best thing is to be placid in your emotions when you're going In-Between. If you start to have emotions, they are very grounding because they're so connected to something physical.

What things should one exercise, look for, or observe in that state of consciousness?

Everybody is uniquely different. I think that you have to go through a definite process. If you gained the ability to hear for the first time, I don't think that I can say to you, "Well, pay attention to the bumble bees," because you wouldn't necessarily know what the bumble bees are. I think you're going to spend some time just being in awe of anything you can hear. I think that when people go In-Between, they can't do this or that right off the bat. They're so in awe of what they're experiencing that they're not really able to define any specific thing.

I think that you need to spend your time absorbing your experiences. Once you've saturated yourself enough with that, you'll move on to something else. Another way to explain this is by comparing the In-Between with art. You can look at an art piece and think, "Oh, wow, that's really nice. It almost looks like a photograph." Or, "It looks surreal," and, "It's very pretty," and, "It's cool." If you've educated yourself in art, or worked in that field, you're going to see things you never noticed before when you keep looking at the same art piece whether it's the strokes of the brush or different hues of color. You're suddenly going to see something that moves you emotionally. And you may not have realized it had that power until you had the knowledge and the intelligence built up from your experiences, decoding the different layers of information that the artist encoded into it when she imbued this emotion onto canvas. In essence, she recorded something in the art piece.

It depends on what intelligence created it. And that goes for music, art, poetry, or whatever. One person can hear poetry and be moved to tears while another person may not know why. There's a decoding level based upon how much you can understand something. I think everything is written by an intelligence. In my opinion, the whole world was created by an intelligence: the Universe. Part of moving your consciousness forward as a dimensional being is to decode all the things you may not have had access to before. This is why we live life after life and we continue forward - to experience. We're really here in this world to decode things that we didn't have the mechanisms to decode while in a purely energy body.

When you took me In-Between, there were objects that I saw, like a fish in an aquarium that I felt like had been specifically placed there for me to experience. There was a whole other beauty behind that fish. One time I saw this chemical spill on the ground where I worked. Instead of seeing it as something I had to clean up, I saw the beauty of the spill. It was almost as if the Universe wanted me to experience that spill from a whole different perspective.

Well for starters, at that point I had brought you to a very deep level of In-Between, so you were pushed to a higher level of decoding. The level of coding you can decipher depends on what level of In-Between you're in. I was much younger then, and I probably would have done things differently now, being a little older, wiser, and more experienced. But you were able to decode what I would consider high compilations. You were able to see the beauty as a molecular design. This is what you were experiencing. You were more aware of the hues of color that reflected the light. You were more aware of the roles and the structure of the fluidity. You were more aware of all it was doing with everything around it; it was more like watching a dance. And this is something people will experience as they achieve greater levels of going In-Between.

I felt like the spill had a purpose.

Well, everything has a purpose. Everything has a design. Everything in the Universe is developed by an intelligence. Everything is numerical, just like the scientists say. You don't have to think in numbers. If you don't understand numbers, it's perfectly okay so remove that thinking. There are other ways to experience the same harmony.

When you shift to a significant degree, why do you feel that things happening all around you are for you to experience?

Everything in life is for you to experience. God created the Universe for you and all you have to do is choose to look at the beauty of what was given to you. Most people simply function like they're robots. They're just functioning like organisms. Everything here is for you. The Universe was created to be experienced; therefore, it is a given thing, not an expected thing. There's an intelligence; there's a creation; there's a want. The Universe wants you to look at what It has done. When a child hands you something they've made, what do they want from you? They want acknowledgment. Not just to hear you say, "Oh you did a good job." They want to say, "Look at the coding I put into this. Look at the beauty of what I've created." And it's up to you to decide if you're going to reflect on that beauty or not. I think a mother can. Other people may have a little bit more difficulty, but a mother sees the beauty in it. They have the decoding designed in them already.

So the Universe has created all of this and its saying, "Well, I know you're busy and I know you're doing whatever you're doing," and you're thinking,"Oh, I've got to pay bills," or, "I've got to meet with my girlfriend," or "I need to buy a car." And the Universe is saying, "Here, look at all this stuff!" It's like a kid wanting to show you something. God doesn't have to be this profound, deep thing. It also has a child's heart and this passionate love to share with you. What happens when something is shared with you?

What do you get out of it? You've gained something out of it. It's making you more complete by evolving you. You're evolving to reach higher states of consciousness. Everything that you are is based on the harmony of the vibrations that create your experiences. Your experiences are living. They create your perception, your understanding; they add to your ability to decode to understand greater things.

Was there something that you did in your experiences growing up in your youth when you started to slip into these states? Were there things that you paid attention to that propelled you in these directions?

When I was a kid, I walked out in this field and I lay down on a big stone at the edge of a pond. I looked into the water at the tadpoles and then I looked up at the sky. That was an In-Between experience. I learned early on in my youth that sound was the doorway for me to go In-Between. That's one of the keys I want to share with everybody. One of the techniques is sound. When I heard the hum of the insects, I cleared my mind, and I allowed myself to flow into this other state of consciousness.

I'm going to say something even though it's not the most elegant thing to say but it's the closest thing that some people can relate to. When you're going to the bathroom and you're having a bowel movement, there's a point where there's a certain stimulation when you're releasing your bowels. There's a nerve there. And it's very relaxing. There's a point when your mind shuts off; keep in mind that one of the seven main chakras is on the tail bone.

You go into a quiet state of consciousness. If you let yourself go, there's almost a point when you're just enjoying the release from your body and your mind is feeling really pleasant. When you experience this quietness, there's the potential that something more could come from it. You don't know what it is and it just ends there. Well, somehow, I think that those nerves in the spine create some kind of frequency that is very similar to the threshold that springs you into going In-Between.

I know it's a difficult thing to talk about but you will never get this stuff if it's pre-scripted. This is the real deal. Now you know. My job is to use any tool I possibly can to communicate what I'm trying to say to you so that you understand. I won't bar myself even from that.

When I sat out on the stairsteps where I used to live, it was a summer day and the heat from the sun hit me in a certain way. The quiet also hit me in a certain way. The quiet can take you to the In-Between if you let it. At that point when it was so quiet, for some reason I wasn't rattling in my brain. I wasn't thinking about what I wanted to do next. The quiet became the reflection of what was on my mind.

When I noticed how quiet it was, the quiet mirrored back into my mind, propelling me to go deeper and experience the hum of the insects out in the field. Then that hum became mesmerizing, almost hypnotic, which again is like when you hear Aums or ting-shaws. It's these sounds that we hear in different spiritual and religious processes that quiet the mind. They create or mimic something that's trying to get the mind to be quiet.

We meditate with music with no words in it. We're doing the same thing but this is a very refined, pure form of that. Yhe insects, the warmth, and everything else relaxed my body, while my mind focused on the quiet. I wasn't counting cars because I'd be like, "One, two, Chevy, Dodge." I wasn't looking longingly at any kids playing and wishing I could be out there doing that, too. There was nothing to really think about. *I chose to reflect on the nothing*; but the nothing turned out to be something incredible. It turned out to be the Universe really just saying, "Hey you, come here. I've got something to show you." And show me it did!

When I allowed myself to go into this quiet state, it compelled me to walk out into this field. I don't know why I chose to go out to the field. I recall that it felt inviting. It felt to me that it would love and caress me. There was something very loving and fulfilling that I desired from that field. It seemed to be all lit up. Visually, it was beauty from the shimmer or the glow that might have been coming off of it with the blue sky above and the trees in the distance. There was something that was calling me, inviting me to come. It turns out it wasn't necessarily the field; it wasn't the sky; it wasn't the humming. It was the Universe saying it wanted to teach me something. I didn't understand it fully then but I trusted whatever was calling on me, not that I even knew it was a calling. It felt right so I went with it.

I went into this field and because I was in this state of mind, I could acknowledge the insects. Again, there was this plasticity thing with the structure and texture of the insects. If objects in your home look like plastic because your sensory is so intense, imagine what living organisms are to you. I remember seeing the blades of grass with the design of their molecular structure. The more you focus on something, the more you begin to see even more complex things. Sometimes you don't want to look at something too long because it's just too overwhelming for the mind to perceive.

I think at that stage of the game, I wasn't really looking at the molecular structure but I certainly was aware of higher levels. Children take greater notice of these things. As a kid, I remember lying down in the field and looking at a blade of grass. You see the blade of grass as a pasture of grass. Then you notice the coolness of it when you lie down on it. Then you notice the patches of it being more defined, then you zoom in on the blade and you start to see little lines. Then you start to see the fibers of the grass and the hairs coming off of it. You become more aware of the smell. It's like this hyper awareness. Well, this is what leads you into the In-Between. Fortunately, I was able to take it to the next level. I think the Universe is always calling on the children first because they're more open-minded. But they are still biased because they're preoccupied with our world as much as we are.

This is what showed me the In-Between, although I didn't know what it was. I was feeling and experiencing at this profound higher level. By the time I felt compelled to lie down on the stone in this state of mind, the stone didn't look like a stone to me. I was aware of every divot of every structure, little grains of sand and little hollowed spots of it. I was aware of all of it from dried insect wings to you name it. It's just how much you can communicate and how much you can define.

When I talk about the story, I don't talk about in so much detail but there was so much more to it. There's so much lost when you communicate in words. I was aware of everything and it called to me. The warmth in the stone called to me, and it said to me, "Lie down on me and I'll warm your body." It said, "Hold me." And I didn't see it as this hard stone that was uninviting to lie on. My body called out to press against it as if it was something more. And it was. Of course, this led to me looking into the water in the same state of mind, In-Between, seeing the living organisms. Then I rolled over and looked at the sky, standing up, looking all around me. When you're In-Between, let me tell you, it's profound. I looked at the sky and I could see the stars for a few moments. You can only do that in the daytime while you're In-Between; it changes reality.

By having these experiences, one out of many already at a very young age, this eventually led to some point in my life that I started to say, "What the hell is it that I'm experiencing to learn, acknowledge and understand these things? How do I know?" Then I realized I was going into this different state of consciousness; it wasn't normal. This was not an everyday occurrence; other people weren't telling me, "Oh well, I was aware of this and this and this." I realized there's something very different between what I was experiencing and what everybody else was experiencing.

Then you can refine and narrow down what it is and you can isolate it. When I isolated it, that's when I began to discover all these things, and discovered how I was going into these altered states of consciousness. Then I was able to do it at will instead of it happening randomly to me. When I could do it by will, that's when I decided to try to show other people how to do it.

I learned that not only could I show other people how to do it but I could literally make myself go In-Between and shift other people and get them to go In-Between as well just by the vibration I was feeling. You literally can move it into other people. I experimented more with this, gaining more experiences and sharing more information about it.

You mentioned that the silence and the state that you were going into somehow catered to what was on your mind at that point.

Well, my mind wasn't on anything; that's the point. When it called me into silence, it gained my attention. Then it held it and I became the observer without really talking in my head. It's like looking at a beautiful piece of art or listening to a beautiful piece of music. There's a moment when it captures you. In this particular case, it called me into it further and the depth of where it took me was profound.

It's the rabbit hole. How far does the rabbit hole go? How far are you willing to go? I went down the rabbit hole pretty far. On the other side, there is a whole new level of this dimension. The main factor is how far you choose to go into it.

How did you obtain your knowledge? Did you have a teacher? And can this state be used as a means to learn about things specifically?

Well, let's put it this way: I obviously believe in other lives and I do believe that when you come into this life that most of your knowledge is recessed because you couldn't emotionally function if you remembered everything, or even just a little. It's too overwhelming until you at least develop the ability to cope. I'll repeat that: develop the ability to cope. There's a part of me that was strong enough from past lives to push me to start to learn to experience these things. It pushed me in the right direction. This was my Navigator. Having these experiences taught me the skills to cope by then allowing me to release greater pieces of knowledge that were recessed in my deeper consciousness dimensionally. That's how I began to awaken so rapidly to this higher state of consciousness. That's exactly how I would explain it.

In the Handbook of the Navigator, you talk about sleepers and how they have to incarnate asleep so that the Darkside does not notice them coming in. When you come back from such a high state as the In-Between, how does the Darkside react?

The Darkside doesn't want anything to do with you when you go In-Between. When you're In-Between, you're closer to the higher frequency of God than you probably have ever been in your life. You are really harmonizing with a higher frequency. It's the first time you've learned to become a conduit of some type to God. If anything, the Darkside is a little intimidated as to what to make of you. Is it going to poke you with a finger in this state of mind? I don't think so. If it pokes you, it may awaken ancient knowledge of who or what you are that you could tap into. It's like poking and awakening God!

I've never had a bad experience at all. If anything I felt profoundly powerful, but not in an egotistic way. There's really no sense of fear when you're in this state of mind. There's common sense so you're not going to jump in water or do something to hurt yourself. You're fully conscious but there is such beauty around you that the last thing you're really reflecting on is the Darkside.

If the Darkside was to make itself present, I really think that you have so much profound awareness that you literally can brush it aside. If I have to deal with something negative, I just go In-Between with the intent, "Let's dance." It then becomes a play toy for me. The Darkside preys upon weak minds. If you are tapping into hyper-dimensional consciousness, you are just too profound at that point. It's trying to prevent you from going there. When you're there, there's nothing the Darkside can do to prevent it. The best thing it can do is stay out of your way. If you turn your mind on the Darkside, it's not about absorbing into the Darkside. It's about you really simplifying the Darkside. That's the last thing the Darkside wants because you're taking its power from it.

After Buddha reached a state of Enlightenment, he puts his hands down as his final testament to the level he reached of being In-Between. The Darkside tried to do all these crazy things, and Buddha just brushed it aside inferring it's not a problem anymore. When you reach this level, you'll understand that. As I said before, you don't really have emotion the way that you normally have emotion. You don't really have the fear that you have on a human level, so you don't internalize it the same way. For human beings, fear is really a survival mechanism. When you reach this higher state of consciousness, you don't necessarily have that kind of fear any more. It's very different.

When you're in this world and you're using purely psychic abilities while you're dealing with entities, ghosts, spirits, or other people, I feel like they're wearing clothes. It's not literally the clothes we're wearing but there's these other kinds of characteristics to them that are made for this dimension, whether they are bad or good. When you're In-Between, you really see everything being naked and transparent. You really see what they are. There's nothing that they necessarily can hide from you. Therefore, you can feel their intentions. You can feel whether they're positive or negative but in this place there's an understanding of not intruding on one another. It's a very complex form of communication that happens.

Most people going In-Between will not have much of that communication until they start to hit much higher levels. I guess that's what I'm trying to explain. I don't want people to think they're going to communicate with entities and the like; it's very different. In a way, communication itself is a very human concept. I don't know how else to explain it. When you're dimensional and you're hooked up with the higher collective, you're aware of information so you don't really communicate. You are just aware of what everything else is doing. It's part of you. It's a knowing. You don't even need to ask. You just know what they're up to and they know what you're up to. There's just a much higher level of what's going on.

Are you able to manifest or summon beings personally?

I don't feel that there's a limit to anything. Therefore, the answer is yes; I can do both of those things and probably have in the past depending on the situation. It's a profound state of consciousness. When I think of this, I often think of the movie *Dune*, particularly the Navigators. They were the most evolved of all the users of the *spice* and it expanded their minds. In Dune, navigators fold space. That was so important for the rest of the Galaxy because other civilizations were dependent on them to go great distances. Most people imagine distance as being from point A to point B. They wonder how much time it will take to get from point A to point B.

When everybody was in a tube that had no windows to look outside, the navigators were able then to use their mind and think about where they wanted to be. Wherever they believed they were is where they went. In my opinion, their belief moved them. It did not move them in distance but made them appear across the universe. They faded from the place they were in because the navigator was so sure they weren't there anymore. Then the navigator made itself believe that it was floating above a planet halfway across the Galaxy. Thus, they re-materialized there. The people in the spacecraft couldn't see anything because they were inside of the tube. There was no way for them to see outside of it. In a sense, that is what prevents their collective consciousness from affecting the ability of the Navigator to move his mind. Of course, I'm reading more into the movie, but that is my interpretation of what happened. If they were able to see their planet, that would have prevented them from moving through time and space. Since the people couldn't see what was going on, they didn't think about it. Therefore, they re-materialized across the galaxy. When they opened the doors of the tube, they expected to be somewhere different. They knew this is what happened; they just didn't know how it worked.

In my opinion, anything's possible. When these highly trained great minds went into this state of In-Between, they were able to perform what we call miracles. I don't really think they're miracles. I think they are acts of willing consciousness because of the circumstances. When Jesus turned water to wine, people expected the act to happen. That is what made it work in the favor of changing reality. The ancient tales contain stories about how some wizards brought down the fog so they could go into battle and not be seen. There were also legends about how the wizard then moved the army across to the other side of the continent. When they came out of the fog, they were hundreds of miles across the land.

Of course, they didn't know how to explain it. This is a really profound level of the In-Between. These are levels you want to work towards. In a world that has inter-webbed its beliefs through the Gaia mind, it really takes profound White Cells to do truly amazing things to separate themselves from that grid for even short amounts of time; that's what you're doing. I think you're falling off the standard grid when you go In-Between and you're moving into some higher level grid.

How do you experience time in the In-Between?

Well, I would say that you don't. If you do, it takes on this very strange perception, becoming very different. Again, it's one of those things you have to experience to understand. You can watch the hand of a clock and a part of you knows that it represents time. There's another part of you that looks at the clock, sees the hand moving, and all you see is the movement and grace of it. You forget what it represents and in itself, it becomes the dance that we talked about. In other words, when you reflect on the concept of time, everything stands still but you realize that everything is moving and wavering like a big wind. Everything is shimmering and constantly changing. Does that represent time? What is it changing to?

It becomes irrelevant. It's more or less the consciousness of God. That's what everything manifests towards. Time is perceived as a very physical thing. The more physical you are, the more you are in this dimension. Hence, the more relevant time becomes. The more that you move away from this dimension, the less relevant it becomes.

If you can learn to go In-Between all the time, is there even a need for meditation anymore?

Yes, absolutely because you still have to exist in this physical dimension. You still have to develop things from this physical dimension that you're going to utilize in a different way. The In-Between is a higher state of consciousness. They go hand in hand. You cannot escape being in this physical dimension; it's a necessity. When you go In-Between, you are probably only going to stay there between fifteen minutes to two hours. You constantly will be anchored back here though, largely because of the Doe.

When you meditate do you go In-Between at all?

When you are meditating, you can go In-Between. However, you're not as aware of the shift because you are in a state of mind that's directed for a very specific purpose. When you meditate, or when you do other spiritual practices, it allows you to catapult further In-Between. Rather than having the hose flapping all over the place, it allows you to go to deeper levels because you're more aware of it and you're able to direct it. If you don't understand the I's from previous material and you don't understand energy, the hose is going to be flapping out of control. If you have knowledge of these other classes and you apply the material in them, you immediately get control of the hose and you are able to do really cool things. It's just a matter of how fast you can adapt. That adaptation is going to be based upon your experiences, knowledge, and the data that you have to decode from what you're experiencing. Decoding is your tool; it's going to allow you to be able to experience or manipulate certain things.

Is the In-Between where awakenings that eventually lead to enlightenment take place?

Yes, it is the path to enlightenment without a doubt.

Is age a factor in your ability to shift In-Between?

I would say age definitely has its pluses and minuses. With age, I think that you become more conditioned by this reality and you start to reflect on your body and how long you are going to live, so this is a grounding thing. Those of you in your thirties, forties and fifties are perhaps more concerned about attaining homes and cars rather than when you are free flowing in your early teens and twenties. There's different conditioning and other things going on in your brain. Those are the things that anchor us. On the same token, I think that there are things about age that are definitely a positive: wisdom, experience, and patience. You really learn to harness and control a lot of emotions, thoughts or feelings that would rage out of control. As some people grow older they become disenchanted with life. All the amusements of it become blander; this can also happen as you become more intelligent. If you can utilize this in the right way, it can also allow you to detach so you can move into higher states of consciousness more easily. There are pluses and minuses to it, absolutely.

Is there a difference between men and women going In-Between?

No, I think women can achieve it as easily as men. I think it can be a dual situation depending on the person. Women have both an advantage and a disadvantage because they're more emotional. If they can cultivate their emotion, they can use it to guide them and move them through the In-Between. On the same token, it can also anchor them in much the same way that certain emotions can hold them here.

Most men, but not all, have less of an emotional level. Therefore, they have the advantage of being able to detach in that way. The problem with men is that they have more problems moving because it's more unnatural for them. They can't project their emotion or figure out how to use it to propel them. Again, I'm trying to explain distance with movement. To me, experiencing something is a type of movement because if I look at something, I see structure. For instance, when I look at a blade of grass, and I see the details of it, I move into it. I begin to see the layers of it whereas you just see the blade of grass. That whole scenario to me is movement. The details and the complexity of it become energy; to me that's movement. I don't want to confuse it with distance but I'm trying to use the best words I can to explain this.

Women sometimes move better that men do, but they can be anchored. Each gender has a different advantage and disadvantage. It is better to find a balance in your core because emotion is a factor, as is will. Those are things that men pride themselves in versus what women pride themselves in. You're trying to go down the middle path constantly to cultivate both.

As I said, a soul isn't male or female. It's both and it has both polarities. We are limited because we think of ourselves as just being a male with certain male aspects or a female just having female aspects. When we can get past that kind of thinking and allow ourselves to feel or to remove ourselves slightly from it and trust, that is when we discover new things about ourselves.

**Would it be counterproductive to use an emotional state
in order to bring in and amplify that energy?**

Forget it! You won't be able to do it and if you do, it may pop you
right out real fast. The In-Between is like fifth gear and everything
else is second and third; there's literally that big of a difference.
You are trying to interpret what makes logic in this way of thinking; but in an In-Between state you'll understand immediately
what I'm saying. You're going to be like, "That doesn't quite jive."

**You said that slipping into an In-Between state
just happens when you rest in that place.
Can an emotional surge take you there?**

I'm not going to rule it out but the In-Between is so unemotional
that emotion is basically the opposite of what really slips you into
it. I really stand by the fact that emotion will anchor you out of it
instead of propelling you where you need to go. You'll understand
when you experience it.

**Once a person has experiences in the In-Between, does the
emotion that you feel during the heart chakra focus change?**

You have an inner knowing of different forms of joy. There is a
joy of seeing a friend you haven't seen for a long time. There's
the joy of watching a puppy playing and jumping around; there's
a joy of winning the lotto. There are different kinds of joy versus
heart chakra or such with different kinds of emotions. They're
just undiscovered to you yet.

Could you go into the phenomenon of animal behavior and how animals respond to you differently when you're in this state?

I suspect that when you're in a normal state of mind, animals are just on a grid with you so they know to stay away. It's interesting to watch animals that are not predatory in nature. For example, a bird will sit on a buffalo's butt and walk around with it and other animals will walk around those animals. When a human being comes by, they instantly know there's a problem. I think most animals are In-Between. There's not so much frontal lobe thinking and they are more in contact with this other frequency. As I said before, you know the intentions of other creatures when you are In-Between. If you think about this, they know if something's going to eat them or not, in most cases.

When you are In-Between, you can project your intentions without realizing you are doing it and this is why animals seem to be less frightened. If you think about it, then that's a problem because they're going to detect that you're aware that it's not afraid of you. That will instantly repel it from you. Use what you learn in meditation: don't have intention in that particular case.

In one case when I brought a student In-Between, we were walking past a stream and a beaver was literally two feet from us and wild peacocks were just walking right up to us. Then they walked along with us. When we weren't In-Between, they would not come near us. There were some aggressive dogs that were being really friendly. I've had birds come up to me and practically sit. It makes you think about the story of Saint Francis and other people who communed with animals. It's just a choice that person made for their In-Between. Then they probably refined that choice to become their specialty. That's what they became very good at and very comfortable with and learned to project this in the right way.

Other people may develop it and master it to become really incredible healers. Or they might master it to be great yogis who we hear these amazing stories about. They really get very specific in a certain area. I've always focused on teaching and sending people in the right direction. Maybe it's not as amazing as everybody else, but without it where would you be now?

How do you relate to yourself and your identities when you are In-Between?

The identities really are not very important because you're separated, in a lot of ways, from the majority of your I's. When you are really in this higher state of consciousness, you are removed from a lot of it. You're very comfortable; it's a very peaceful state of mind that you're functioning in. Anybody who saw you would say you look saintly, or you appeared very placid to them. There's nothing threatening; there's not really a sign of what you would normally see in a person. You might even appear beautiful in a way, like spiritual people often do when they are in spiritual states of consciousness. When you think about them, that's usually their vibration. They're not really in this zone so much.

I am actually more comfortable In-Between than normal everyday consciousness, like I had been there before. It's very comfortable and familiar, like I've been waiting to get back there my whole life.

If you are an old soul, you obviously have existed in this state of consciousness as your natural state. When you return back to it and you haven't remembered it for a long time, the shoe fits. You don't want to take it off when it is a comfortable fit. Your body is still anchored into this dimension, so this is where the conflict comes between the two. The body will always win out because you are really anchored to it. Again, whatever you focus on becomes like the blade of grass; you just keep seeing more layers of it. How many layers you see is really based upon how far you let yourself go. I don't think focusing on people is necessarily a good thing to do because you see different aspects of life. You can see them just as pods, or robots, walking around. A lot of times that's what it's like for me. It is nauseating because it makes me feel very detached as I don't want to be part of what I think is synchronized.

On other aspects, you can look at somebody and you see what they are. Then you move through them on an energy level. You can see their intentions and if you go to deeper levels, you can also see the passion in them. I'll tell you, even in the darkest of people you can find love or light in them if you are in an In-Between state. Also, when you are in an In-Between state you can see somebody who's really beautiful and discover their negative aspects. Nothing is hidden from you depending on how far you let yourself move through things.

I think the most important thing is that *you allow yourself to be fluidic.* Be open to whatever you experience. Don't be judgmental because judgment is based upon our culture's perspective of ideals. And when you add that to your experience, you really cannot move well in the In-Between. It limits how far you can move. And remember how I explained move. When you can comprehend that different cultures have different beliefs and ethics, you cannot be judgmental because being judgmental is emotional and it's an anchor. You're going to experience what you're going to experience. Analyze it when you're done, when you've come down or come out of it. Then you can try to make of it what you will. When you become judgmental, it will usually bring you out of it. It also greatly limits what the Universe is trying to show you.

If you're going to tell the Universe what it can show you, there's no point in learning because you're only going to learn what you've already figured out. What you're really after is what you don't know and what you can't yet conceive. That's really going to be what you want to learn. If you are judgmental, you are really filtering what the Universe wants to show you. Again, remove any judgment or any kind of thinking in that way. You just want to remain in non-thought and learn to navigate differently.

It seems to me like going into the In-Between state takes a little stamina, like it would wear out your sensory very quickly if you weren't used to it. Is that true?

Yes, I sometimes tire very easily doing it. At other times, I can keep going. It depends on what else I have done that day. That's why it's no problem to get back to this dimension. You definitely don't have to worry about going out there and not coming back. You're 99.99% guaranteed to come back – most likely after the first fifteen minutes to thirty minutes. You're definitely guaranteed to come back down after an hour. It can be exhausting until you build the stamina to stay in that zone for long periods of time.

Do you think the reason why some people might be so attracted to drugs is because it might unintentionally remind them of going In-Between?

Most people who have addictive personalities or use drugs for some outside stimuli are usually White Cells to begin with. Unfortunately, they haven't found the right course through their Navigator and have been detoured. The Darkside will destroy as many White Cells as it can. When I look at drugs and what they have done in our culture and in our world, I see oceans of beings just pushed to the wayside, so it's very sad. They've gone towards the addictive drugs which rip the brain apart, giving them the experiences or tapping into the feelings or sensory that they want. In the meantime, it destroys the actual mechanism that allows them to reach enlightenment. If you destroy the car, how can you drive the distance to get to where you need to go?

When you're using drugs, you've gotten to the point where you've got the hose but you don't have any way of controlling it so it's flapping all over the place. Some people may develop certain levels of control, but the reality is they're only fooling themselves.

What about shamans or Native Americans that use some kind of ceremonial drugs to reach these states of consciousness?

I have an absolute respect for them because our Western culture doesn't realize there's a difference between recreational use and spiritual use. Often Westerners will say, "I am doing it for spiritual purposes." No, they're doing it for pure entertainment. Shamans utilize it with the strictest concept of creating a pathway of direction. They've also spent a lot of time on breathing techniques, developing their psychic mind and determining the correct dosage. They know what amount is going to have a positive effect and how much or how little is going to have a negative effect.

You'll find that a lot of shamans who have used various forms of hallucinogens will also eventually move past it so it's not required anymore. Just because shamans are able to go past that doesn't mean that anybody can jump on the band wagon and get the same effect from using hallucinogens. Most shamans dedicate their life to spiritual development. That's all they do 24/7. They're not out doing what typical people are doing on a daily basis. Eventually, they realize that it's a limited tool so they need to move beyond all that.

The In-Between can be brought on at certain points. Usually it's brought on when you're deeply reflecting. When you're listening to or reading this material, it is like sitting out in the rain. You're going to get wet so it's going to transform you. This is data. This is you developing the ability to decode. Therefore, the more you listen, the more you are going to shift or the more it is going to build you so that you'll be able to go into these different states of consciousness. If you ponder my teachings, there's going to be a time when it's going to shift you. These are glimpses or step-ins to you moving temporarily into these higher states of consciousness.

You just have no way of fully recognizing what they are, so you think something really cool or amazing just happened. The

In-Between is a direct line to activating that. It was a big decision for me to go ahead and do this. Instead of just popping in and out of the In-Between, I'm actually going to show you how to directly go into it.

Has anyone you taught to go In-Between forgotten how to do it?

Knowledge from the Universe is an interesting thing. If you are not ready to hold it, much like water in a glass, eventually it will evaporate. You must exercise this knowledge. This is why you should meditate and practice energy movements. If you don't feed your body, what happens? You starve so you diminish and you could die. Well, your dimensional body is not much different. If you exercise it and you work with it, you'll make it strong. But just like a weight lifter, if you stop lifting weights during your prime, what will happen? You won't stay at that level and what you have achieved diminishes. You have to feed your spiritual energy body. You do that by exercising what you know.

It's a living thing. This knowledge isn't necessarily designed to exist in this frequency, this dimension. If you are not actively pursuing it, working with it or filling your life with it, it will evaporate. You will forget how you did something. In fact, you will forget that you even did it. During a conversation somewhere down the road, you will vaguely remember some piece of it and then have to really pull it out of your mind, "Hey, yeah, that did happen to me." Some of the most profound things I've seen people experience become an evaporated moment to them shortly after. They did not have the developmental level yet to hold it here in this dimension.

Is it a different experience if you take somebody else In-Between or they take themselves?

I think they're both good. If I take them In-Between, obviously, I'm leading the movement which means that I can probably make better choices for them to walk away with more useful information. If they go in on their own, it's going to be beneficial no matter what in the beginning. After they've gone several times, it's more or less a question of, "What else can I do?" They're going to be thinking, "What can I do with this?" Obviously someone who has done it a lot more can say, "Well hey, let me show you what I discovered here," or "Try this or try that." So, it has its advantages.

Why don't you perform miracles and take everybody In-Between to prove who and what you are?

I think everything in life should be earned. There was a time when I did what I would call profound miracles. All the amazing things that I did really didn't do anything for them. They certainly were dedicated in their love and passion for who and what I am but it didn't help them on any level spiritually. It didn't transform them to work on their spirituality to become enlightened. In a sense, all it did was make them lazy and fat. They just wanted to be fed all their experiences by me. Every time they wanted to experience something profound, they were dependent on me to bring them In-Between. They were dependent on me to show them how to do something or give them the energy to do it. Everything in life takes energy.

As I grew older, I realized that the reason why I did things was because I thought that would be the best way to convince them that this is the way to go and they would be motivated to achieve it on their own. The other reason was my ego. I received a lot of praise and awe when I showed people what I could do. That was for ego. I grew out of that eventually as I became older and wiser. I moved past that when I realized that I didn't need the praise anymore. I felt very comfortable with who I was and what I could do.

It really came down to how I could be the most beneficial to the people that I am teaching. The best way is to show them how to do something on their own. Show them how to achieve it on their own and not with me actively making them do it. I'm not always going to be here. Which is better? Moving them all to the In-Between so I can awe them? Or giving them the knowledge to do it themselves? Then they can go In-Between and make of it what they will.

Hearing is a one of your five senses. What is it about hearing and not touch?

Well, it's like going number two to the bathroom. The body is hard wired so it's like an acupuncture point. If you hit a certain nerve in the body, it may crisscross and have a different effect somewhere else. I think that hearing has somehow crisscrossed the wiring in the brain, looping into the ability to go In-Between. There's a connection with sight, smell, and all the other senses but in this particular case the easiest is hearing. The one that seems to be a sure-fire way of achieving the In-Between is through hearing.

Will you be giving examples for people who are hard of hearing, who have very limited hearing ability, or people who have tinnitus or something like that?

There's a way that you can enter the In-Between through touch. If you simply touch your hand back and forth and with some other techniques I'll give, you should be able to achieve it also. And there may be some advantages to that. The idea is for me to just give you the basics and a sure-fire method of achieving it. Then I'll say to you, "There it is. What do you want to do with it now?"

Other than just achieving it, is it necessary to eventually direct it in some way?

Well, you definitely should move into whatever area you want. Eventually you move into so many things that the only one way to take it is to places you haven't conceived yet.

Are there any physiological changes to the body when a person goes In-Between?

I would say, absolutely, without a doubt there are physiological changes but I would be interested to see some testing done on it. The human brain has some chemicals, like DMT, that are also found in hallucinogenic drugs so they must be there for a reason. I believe that God is the most brilliant intelligence in the universe. It *is* the Universe. Those chemicals must serve some purpose for us to release them naturally to achieve these things. If LSD is in the brain, which it may be in trace amounts, I wouldn't doubt that there's a perfect release amount that harmonizes with some other chemicals we haven't yet discovered that allow you to biochemically attain the electrical conscious levels which become a different intelligence all itself within the human mind.

When you go In-Between, you allow yourself to create the best chemical level that lets you retain information and not lose it. I think that will make more sense to people who use hallucinogens. If somebody uses hallucinogens with this, it's going to amplify it significantly; but is it positive or negative? I would say there's really not a need for it. Train yourself how to go In-Between and you'll be perfectly happy. It'd be a great way to remove yourself from certain drugs. I can tell you that much right now. A lot of my students have been addicted to serious drugs. They all kicked the can, which is unheard of. They did it through training because they were looking for a different kind of stimuli.

Does a healthy mental state help to get you to that state? For instance, if you're lacking something, is it harder to get there?

You don't want to be on an empty or full stomach. You don't want to be thirsty. Take care of the other intelligences in your body that are going to make demands on you. They make very powerful demands because they're tied into your survival. You shouldn't be tired. You don't want to be hungry, or so full that you become tired because of a big meal you've eaten. These are natural factors you've got to take into consideration and be a little bit conscientious of.

One of your students who went In-Between said that he started really grounding as soon as he ate food.

That's right. I can't eat food when I'm In-Between. Just the thought of it makes me cringe right now. The thought of biting into an apple while In-Between may as well be a basketball. That's what it would feel like to me. If you had the ability to imagine biting into a basketball and gumming it, tasting the rubber and the powder, that's what an apple is like. My brain says, "No, there is juice there," but all I can feel is this crunchiness of the flesh, and the skin of the apple. Your whole mind works differently.

In summary, what would you do to your spirituality by learning to go In-Between?

Spiritually, you are an embodiment. What is your soul? What is it? You soul is energy. That energy is data; it's you; it's your consciousness. Your consciousness is made up of your experiences, emotions, thoughts, the things that you reflected on in life, the things that happened to you, and how you reacted to them. Even smell is an emotion. Every single thing has a feel to you that creates a certain emotion. Everything is coded with some emotion, if you think about it. You know what a carpet is going to feel like. That's an emotion.

When you go In-Between, it really makes you see a higher level of the fabric of this dimension. Therefore, it adds a vast amount of new data to your experiential level. It enriches you as a soul, as a being. Your perception greatly changes after this experience because your whole spectrum evolves. You see life in a much broader picture rather than just trees and plants. You look at water as being living organisms. You can look at your table as being a molecular structure that actually coincides with a living organism. It makes the same molecular structure that gives inanimate objects life. You can't help but have this deeper, greater passion for all things which enriches you. Of course, it makes you see things in a perspective that's probably truer to what the Universe wants you to understand.

For people who follow other teachings, would this be like a turbo button for them to do healing?

This is a massive turbo button for any path, no matter what they do. Their whole level of ability should leap forward, depending on how well they train themselves. But it is certainly a leap.

Would a select group of supplements or nutrients greatly help your ability to go In-Between?

Of course it would. First of all, let's start with the basics. If you have to study to do exams and you eat Twinkies and drink soda all week long and nothing else, do you think it's going to have an effect on your ability to stay focused and retain information? You are a biological machine. The food you take into your body is the actual fuel that generates the organic building blocks of what you are.

If you're an athlete and you live on the same diet, it's going to be the same thing because your brain is biological and your body is biological. Your body is searching for the right elements to use. When you use something, your energy is converted from one thing into something else. You need that resource to propel yourself to do whatever you are going to do.

In this particular case, I believe all psychic abilities basically rely on the pineal gland of the brain. I think it integrates with the other parts of the brain, but that is the core. There are certain minerals that definitely contribute to your ability to achieve In-Between states and all paranormal abilities for that matter. I'm aware of some people who have certain quantities of specific minerals that are higher than the norm. Those people would be defined as being more gifted or more talented. That can diminish if they lose that mineral in their brain. It doesn't mean that the average person doesn't have the skill. It comes down to whether or not they have the right material in their brain to fuel those engines - the glands or chemicals - to create the right electrical currents.

Several years ago, we began to develop a product that I'd been working on for about a decade. We understood what elements were needed to make this product, and after production we tested it out with different individuals. The results were profound! So, we now have a product line called *The Magnetic Pill* that we're offering to our clients because I want everybody to experience this. It's that amazing and that profound.

In-Between – Technique

Before You Begin

Before you start, I think it is very important to clear your mind of all expectations. Do not have an expectation of whatever level you think you're going to reach or what you're going to experience. When you have expectations, your organic thoughts will control and limit exactly what you're going to be able to experience. You can't suggest to yourself, "I should be able to do this," or "I should be able to do that," because you're simply going to go to a level that you may not have ever experienced before.

When you start to assess or have ideas of what it is that you're going to achieve, that's a big no-no. *Don't have any expectations.* That's really the best way to start. I can tell you that regardless of how much you start off experiencing, the more that you experience or the more you can move towards that experience, the more intensive the sessions are going to become. Each session should be more impressive than the last. It's just simply that you're starting to learn more. And during that process you're going to be able to expand upon your experiences.

Reflect on what was extraordinary in your own experience versus other people's stories that you may have heard. Simply stay focused on your own experiences and they will become very profound in time. Again, do not have any particular expectations other than the basics of what I've explained to you. I can't emphasize that enough.

I'm going to basically do a walkthrough. If you follow this formula, you should achieve the altered state of consciousness that's going to start sending you into the In-Between. The formula must follow the sequence that I explain.

In-Between – Walkthrough

The first thing I want you to do right now is just relax your body. Clear your mind. Use the meditations that you've learned to just clear your mind. Let the muscles in your face relax. Let everything sink down. Keep your eyes open. That's a big one.

Do not close your eyes at this point. You want to use your normal senses to amplify this state of mind. You're going to work with your senses in such a way that it's going to help trigger this state of consciousness, this unusual sense of awareness that you're going to move into.

So just relax, clear your mind, and again become a little bit aware of your physical body: how you're sitting in the chair, the weight of your body, the clothing, the weight of your arms, perhaps resting. Take a nice slow deep breath in through your nose. And as you're breathing, I want you to become aware of your breathing. At this particular point, visually make a note of everything around you and how everything is silent.

Very slowly choose a few items to look at in the room. If you can see auras, try to see the aura but don't think about it. Become conscious of the floor – whether it is carpet, wood, or plastic. Become conscious of whatever environment you're in. If you're outdoors, it's the same process. At the same time, remain aware of your breathing. One of the first things you'll notice is that your breathing will seem a little unusual. It's almost as if you're a little nervous. Then be aware of any frequencies you may see, or illuminations, and things like that.

Now, I want you to concentrate on your hearing. If there's anything that's in the distance, become aware of it. Then use your eyes to look around slowly. Pay attention to all the sounds. If you're outdoors, start paying attention to any barking dogs in the distance. Listen for any surreal sounds - things take on a surreal-ness.

Currently, there is another frequency coming in. You can hear it as a high pitch. I want you to focus now on your breath in your upper chest area. It's very important to become conscious of your breathing. Your breathing should feel as if you almost have to think about it to make yourself breathe. It's weird but it almost becomes like fog in the air, but you don't necessarily see it. It's as if your breathing almost doesn't want to take in the air. That's part of the shifting process. As it begins, you'll usually feel that a little bit. You may not necessarily want to stay completely still. You'll want to be a little bit free, but you should also be conscious in this state of mind and ride the feeling that you feel.

So, let's go back. I want you to clear your mind. Relax yourself. Feel the muscles in your face relaxing. Feel your body relaxing ... the weight of your body ... clearing your mind. Choose the floor or some other space to just look at. Let go. Become aware of the light in the room. See if you can make it illuminate in your own eyes. See the light intensifying.

As you are intensifying the light, trying to see frequency in the air, become aware of your breathing. Let your breathing intensify you as if it's helping to make the light illuminate. Hear the high pitch in your ears ... the frequency. At the same time, feel your breathing. Try to fill the illumination that you're trying to create. Look around the room and choose an object. Attempt to feel it without physically touching it. Feel it in a different way. Become aware of it. In a sense, breathe it in. When you see it, breathe it in as if you were acknowledging what it feels like for a structure, for an object.

Stand up. Getting ready to walk, I want you first to relax your body. Clear your mind. Don't think about anything. Rather, listen to things. I want you to just walk all the way down the hallway in the house or the building you are in. Then come all the way back. Or, walk down the hallway. Go upstairs to the furthest point that you can go. Open up a door, but listen to how that door sounds. Then come back and just quietly sit down. Then start taking notice of objects.

Try to think about the things that I just said. Pay attention to your breathing. Pay attention to the sensation of the environment, the temperature of the air, and your body movement. If you're outside, pay attention to how the wind is moving against you as your body's walking. Pay attention to the sounds of your feet. Choose an object. Look at the object, and try to breathe it in. Become aware of it.

If you have a painting in your house, look at it. See what it makes you feel. Pay attention to your breathing; become aware of your body. I want you to go to the sink. Turn the water to a comfortable temperature. I want you to feel and observe it as it's running over one of your hands. Become aware of your hand and just stare. Absorb the water moving on your hand. Listen to the sounds. Look at the structure. Notice the feel.

When you come back, I want you to just stare at a chair in the room. Have you ever just zoned out, just spaced out on something? I want you to space out. Zone out on the chair. I want you to just stare at the chair. Zone out on it. Let your mind just space out on it. Remember what I said about sitting on the toilet. As you sit there, you don't have anything on your mind and you get this certain stimulation that just zones you out while you are looking at the floor or whatever. That's what you want to do right now. You don't want to have any thought going through your head.

I want you to be aware of your breathing. Staring at the chair, I want you just to breathe. Just be aware of your breathing - in and out. Hear the distant sounds that move through you. Be aware of that. Focus on the chair and be aware of your breathing. Become conscious of how you feel right now. That's the key: recognizing what the In-Between feels like. Now slowly choose another object near it to look at. Become aware how things look very sterile. Very inanimate, unalive in a way. Remember how I said things look like plastic when you are In-Between?

Become slightly aware of the unusual taste in your mouth, the feeling in the back of your throat where your tongue is, your jaw. Become aware of shadows now. As you are still, become aware of a very faint shimmer that's on certain things. A transparent faint energy. Remember your breathing. If you stay focused on the breathing, but you observe with your eyes, it'll hold you in the In-Between. Focus on your breathing. Pay attention to it. Let it hold you there and just move around with your eyes in non-thought. Stay in non-thought. Get up and be aware of every sound you make. If your location has stairs, walk all the way up to the top of the stairs slowly and come back down now. Pay attention to the sounds you are making, the movements of your body, and enjoy it. Let it flow as if it's natural. Find an object to stare at. Let your mind go into non-thought.

Now, just look around the room with non-thought. It's almost as if you're feeling with your chest. Become aware of energy, illumination. Focus on it. Look at the carpeting and see if you can visualize almost a three-dimensional effect to it, like a fuzziness coming off of it. Focus on the static energy that's all around us. Focus on the fuzziness in the air.

Now you're going to take another walk. This time I want you to touch objects. Experience them but don't say what they are. Listen to a door being opened and the feeling of how it opens and turns. Then feel the door open, the air pressure changes, the texture of the metal, the coolness, the sounds! The sounds! The sounds that they make, the sounds of your body moving, how the air moves on your body. You can feel it on every hair on your skin, on your face, on your cheeks, as it's gently moving. As if you're cutting through the thickness of the oxygen around you. It's thicker then you've ever known it before. Become more aware of it. The heaviness of it.

The sounds! The sounds! The sounds! Touch things. Become conscious of them without thinking about them. Experience the sounds. Experience how the air feels moving against you like a soft wind. Not too much, just a little here and a little there. Give it extra sense - pay extra extreme attention to what you're feeling. Feel the sound that makes the clanking, the mechanicalness in objects.

Now go into the bathroom and turn the light on. Shut the door. Sit down. Close the toilet, and just sit on it. Listen to the quiet and just stare at the floor. Be aware of the light in the bathroom. When you turn on the light, leave it on. Now go back and sit down. I want you to look over into a corner of the room. Keep your eyes fixated. Of course, you can blink but I want you to find any shadows or differences on the wall that you can find. There are things there that technically just aren't there but they are.

One of the things that happens when you go In-Between or you are attempting to go In-Between is that you begin to see shadowy things that are on the wall. Or something that actually has no logical reason to be there. Some do but some do not – it's like little tiny details or illuminations. Or leveling of three dimensionality starts to appear.

Now become conscious of how you're feeling. Something is beginning to change. Breathe in and feel your interior energy rising. Breathe in, lifting it, back down again. Up. Down. Pay attention to your environment. Pay attention to the room. It's begun to change in its frequency. It's not an awareness that you can necessarily tell with your standard senses, but it's something that you internally know or can feel. Sound is adjusting. Frequencies are adjusting. Breathe in and feel yourself and the energy move in you. Do you feel a difference in your state of consciousness right now? It is a wave. You have to let it flow. Do not have thought. Let yourself experience it. Be aware of feeling, touch, and sound. Sound ... sound ... sound is changing.

Focus again on the furniture and think to yourself how unusual it is for those chairs to be there with nobody sitting in them. In the In-Between state, it seems almost odd for a chair to just be there with no one in it. It's as if they need to be reorganized or moved. It's something you feel.

Chapter 13

IN-BETWEEN EXPERIENCES

Note: This was a class where Eric took a few of his students
In-Between; in some cases, for the very first time. They each had
different experiences that might be beneficial for you to learn about
before you take that first step of going In-Between. Remember, every-
one experiences the In-Between differently, but here are just a few
things you might experience yourself.

Everyone is returning to class now after taking some time to experience the In-Between outside in nature. It will take them some time to transition back down.

Baard is having a harder time shifting because his mind chatters a lot. He tends to talk a lot, so he's having a harder time getting there. Anna is doing fairly well but Shana is shifting pretty hard. I think that we've managed to tap the elements that are necessary to go In-Between, so we'll see what happens. When they return, we'll get them to come back into the zone so we can talk with them.

Is your stomach nauseous?

Whenever you shift, it's nauseous.

My stomach is aching.

That's because you're feeling frequency. Anybody who is a little bit sensitive is going to feel that vibe if you tune into it right now. When someone shifts, they shift a lot of energy. Anybody who's sensitive can feel that because the energy fields are manipulated slightly. You can actually feel it yourself and carry it with you if you want. It's definitely a very telepathic vibe. A lot of people can zone in on it pretty quickly.

The first thing that's very important is to be aware of sound. Sound is definitely an indicator of shifting. The environment somehow carries sound differently. For some reason, being aware of that helps you go In-Between. The second thing to pay attention to is your breathing in the upper respiratory area. That will definitely also move you In-Between. Being conscious of your breathing and paying attention to it removes you from thought.

It's important to become aware of air pressure, temperatures in the room, and temperatures when touching and feeling things. It's also very important to acknowledge shadowy backgrounds from lighting. When you begin to shift, you'll start to see shadows that either have some three-dimensionality or don't seem like they naturally belong there.

Go sit down in the bathroom with the light on and look at the floor. Just let yourself space out. Acknowledge that you can begin to see energy or what looks like illumination. Then look at the walls and begin to see the fluctuation of them almost breathing in and out. The more that you acknowledge, or the more that you allow yourself to experience, the more labored your breathing becomes. Don't panic. It's normal. Nothing horrible is going to happen.

Then maybe move around slowly being conscious of the environment, taking in what you're doing. That's definitely the first level to it. Then you can begin to make greater discoveries as you begin to explore this three dimensionality with the walls, shadows and energy moving on things. You may also have some difficulty if it's cold out because that starts to ground you.

Alright, you're going to try to come back into the zone. It's going to take a little bit of time. You'll still feel a bit weird and you'll adjust slowly. You'll eventually come back down to normal. Rest assured, it's already begun. I'd like you to talk about your thoughts and your experiences now. You can take a minute.

Anna, would you like to talk about your experience?

At first, going outside was hard to adjust to because it was so cold. After thinking about my breathing and listening to my footsteps, I started to feel that detachment from what I was doing. At one point, it was difficult to take steps.

If you were having trouble walking, you were shifting harder then.

Yes, I was. My legs started shaking.

Now you understand why it's hard to function with the body. It takes a lot of endurance to get everything under control.

The air seemed very thick. It was hard to see at one point. Things went out of focus and it was just really strange because I knew my eyes were wide open and it wasn't that dark outside.

So you knew you should be able to see.

Yes.

But something was happening visually. Maybe it was biological or maybe it was something else. That's good.

At one point, I reached down and I touched the grass. I could hear and feel something, but I didn't know what it was. The minute that I tried to focus on that, I lost it.

That's correct. This is why you shouldn't really try to focus. Just experience. Would you say that it was a positive experience?

It was positive, but at one point I touched the branch of the tree. Then I felt the ground and I felt a little bit sad that it didn't feel the way I was used to.

So you let your human emotions influence you. That can also mess you up a little bit because it's just a different perspective. All of you seem to be stuttering a little bit. Now you know why I stutter sometimes. Baard, you seem to have a lot harder time going into the zone. What are your thoughts?

When I came out, I realized that your voice had changed. Something happened when I realized that your voice had actually changed because I didn't know what to answer. Then I started to feel the tingling in my jaw. Then I felt the tingling all over.

That's good. Did you also feel the tingling and the energy moving all over your body? Would you say it's something that you experience in your normal everyday life?

No, not to this extreme.

Are any of you on any kind of drug? Do you use drugs of any type?

No.

Do you use any antihistamines, alcohol or anything like that?

No.

Have you ever experienced anything like this before?

No, not to this extreme.

Would you say that I have definitely tried to explain to you some good examples of what you'd experience in the In-Between state of consciousness?

Yes.

Okay. Good! Do you think that you could follow this same method to achieve the In-Between state again?

I think so.

Would you want to experience this again in different ways?

Yes, definitely, for a longer period of time.

Okay, that's very good. Can you see that you're now starting to come down? It just happens if you let yourself go there. There's a part of it that will never leave you. That's a very good thing. Just feel how quiet and at peace you are right now. There's a relaxed zoning out that comes in afterwards that is very healing and very peaceful. That must be how plants and trees feel because they're very peaceful and so are you.

I feel very relaxed.

Yes, that is good. I'm having trouble vocalizing my thoughts. I'm forcing it so that I can teach this. Is there anything else you want to add? Can you verbalize any more of your experience at all?

When I was outside, I focused on my hearing. I could hear the sirens but they weren't that loud. I knew they were there.

Right, but they intensified, or you became more conscious of them. It's hard to pick the right words. This is why there's always a problem. You can't explain it, and you have to experience it. Sounds are very important, aren't they? There's something about sounds that shift you. There's also something about sight and feeling. When you go there, you amplify all of your senses. Or your sixth sense seems to amplify the other five senses somehow. They complement each other into this other level of awareness.

It was intense. When I ran my hands across the rocks outside at the same time, I could feel it. I could hear my hand running across it.

It's a whole different emotion, isn't it?

Exactly.

So, they're all new and different emotions that you haven't necessarily experienced before.

**I think that I was trying to see the aura of the tree.
When I came over here, I tried to figure out if it was plastic
or what it was made of. It seems like it was plastic.
When I touched it, it felt like plastic.**

That's correct.

It was very weird.

How much of the plasticity did you guys notice? Do you now real-ize how things start to take on a very hard plastic look or feel? Did different textures seem odd?

**The texture and the plasticity wasn't something I was
focusing on, but nothing felt real anymore. It just felt fake.**

Correct.

The texture of it was just different.

Good. Once you've gone In-Between, you'll slip in and out for a while. You noticed it tonight. You're going to have different things happen. This is an amazing thing to experience. One of the things you notice right away is that it's going to change who you are and how you perceive things. In a psychic way, you're going to become more sensitive. You might be in the dark and start to see more energy than you ever have before. Or you're going to start feeling things that you weren't even aware of before because it really teaches you to tap into that sixth sense. In essence, it's going to really amplify your abilities. If it is all too much for you, just ignore it and it'll fade away. The more you are conscientious of it, the more it's going to continue to expand out.

Can you imagine what it would be like to touch somebody physically while you're In-Between? Or to turn to that feeling of all the other life? At first, you're going to acknowledge it. Then you're going to be really turned off by the human body. You're going to feel that it's just too weird. If you allow yourself to move in further, you'll feel other people's souls and their energy. That's going to be a wonderful interesting thing for you to experience. You might want to sit by a brook and experience the water running because water is liquid and you can see through it. Eventually, it becomes almost like gelatin. It seems like a gelatin structure moving over stones but it seems solid. It's different than what you would think it would be.

When you had us go into the bathroom and run our hands under water, the water had a different feeling.

Exactly, and that's what I wanted to show you with the water. It's as if you are using a different part of your brain or data is assembled differently on a higher level. If you continue to work with it, your comfort level is going to increase. As you absorb information through experiences, you won't think twice about it. It's as if you already acknowledged it so you start to get into more complex things. Don't be surprised if you see a being walking across a room or outdoors. At first, it might scare you but you've got to remember that we're not the only beings that populate the world. There are things out there now that are going to give you a whole new level to experience, making it that much more interesting. There are numerous things for you to experience yet so don't be afraid of exploring them.

On a scale of one to ten, how was your success rate of experiencing the In-Between? Ten being "definite" and one being "absolutely not."

Well, I've never experienced anything like it so I don't know how to compare it, but I would definitely say it's a ten.

Good.

I've never experienced anything like it, so I'd rate it a ten.

Okay, so none of you have experienced anything like this? Baard, how about you?

When we touched the water, it didn't feel like room temperature water. It felt cold and hot like it sort of separated from the water.

That's very interesting. Do you understand how fascinating it becomes when you're in this state of mind? It's like a whole new exploration of things. Can you imagine now how you're going to see your ordinary world? Do you think it'll ever quite be the same as what you understand now?

No.

There's this whole other part of it that you were unaware of and haven't even experienced yet. It adds a new understanding now. Do you understand now why a spiritual person would say that everybody seems to be asleep? Now that you've started to experience this higher level, can you understand how spiritual people function in this other world? Maybe this gives you a different understanding of that now. Do you understand now why there's no real simple way to explain it until you've experienced it? Do you feel that you're really doing it justice at all trying to say what you experienced? Or would you say that you have to experience it to really get it?

You have to experience it.
Yes, you really have to try it for yourself.

Okay, great. I don't think there's a precise method other than what I did. People can also read this chapter and learn about it that way. We are for real. This is a real thing and we're not rehearsing this. It's not something I think that you can necessarily say, "Do this, do this, do this." I laid it out the best that I could to take you there and it may not sound all that impressive. But believe me; the end result is rather profound. Don't be discouraged if you can't hit it the first time. It takes practice.

Look what happened to Baard. At one point when everybody was definitely going into that zone, Baard said, "No, I'm not feeling it." He walked out the door and suddenly he shifted hard. Don't let it catch you by surprise. Just keep working with it and trust that flow. It's there, and it's going to happen. Just work with it.

In the time that I've gone scanning before, it sounds similar but not to this extent. Have you noticed how everything relates to one another? For instance, have you noticed how the frequencies of each thing synchronize together like a dance and the energy becomes one? It's hard to explain.

Hurray! I'm not the only one! Now you can appreciate how well I do under these circumstances.

I fully understand. The first time Eric took me In-Between, I said, "Oh my God, Eric, we've got to tell people about this!" Eric said, "Oh sure, grab a pen and write it down." I said, "Alright." I grabbed a pen and a pad. I sat down In-Between and wondered what I should write. I was all ready to do it. Then I told Eric that I didn't know what to write! Eric replied to me, "Now you understand my problem!" I felt this coming. It became surrealistic.

It is very surreal.

I didn't understand it. I didn't know what to expect.

Well, there's two things. Some people will think that it's like self-hypnosis, or perhaps hypnosis on my part. If you understand anything about hypnosis and you experience this, believe me they're like night and day. Again, it's something you need to experience. Hypnosis certainly is a way for you to free your mind. That's the purpose of it - to get past your inhibitions. Of course, this is what I keep saying. Remove your normal state of mind to let this other part out. It's a very big part.

When I came in and saw you, I thought that you actually changed but at that moment I didn't realize it.

The process that I decided to do for Baard was the biggest trick. I use the word "trick" because it was a difficult process. In a sense, it's crafty. It's like learning a move on a snowboard and trying to get it down perfect to get the right effect. The second you realize that something's very different is the moment that you actually are able to leap into a deeper state of consciousness. There's a part of you that's dopey because you're thinking with your organic brain. Don't think with your organic brain! Just pay attention to what's going on.

There's something different going on and I'll point that out to you. Did you notice it? Everyone is so automated that we're like machines in this dimension. When you start to pay more attention, you realize there's something definitely happening. When you do that, it's like catching the wave. That's when you begin to harness that momentum. That's what I had to do. I sent two students off because I knew they had caught the wave. I even acknowledged to them that they caught the wave.

I was trying to get all of you to pay more attention to it because the second that you realize that there's something different happening, that's what allows you to get past the Governor. That's what opens the floodgate even more. This is what creates the movement in order for you to reach this higher state of consciousness. The more you do this, the greater the movements are going to be because you're mapping out something. When you start off, you've got a map to assist you, which means that you can be that much quicker about it and then continue on beyond that. Were you going to say something, Shana?

I've seen energy to a certain point before.

Sure you have! Just for the record, Dan has been a student of mine for many years and the two of you are basically in a marriage. You've been exposed to certain things but this is the first time you've had a direct teaching from me. I want the readers to be aware of that.

That's right. I've seen energy before, but I've always been afraid of the unknown. As soon as I relaxed and I wasn't afraid, I just went with the flow.

That's correct. You harnessed the wave and opened up those sails, letting it move you.

I walked upstairs into a totally dark room and I could see the energy more than anything. I wasn't scared anymore, even when I went outside.

That's right. You didn't find it intimidating. You trusted The Force. You trusted the Universe. It's a very positive place. You just have to let yourself go there.

I understand what you said about the movement. When I came out, I realized there was something different. As I realized it, that's when it happened. It came in my jaws.

Right, you had the tingling in your jaw. That's exactly what it is; it's the moment of realization. When you start to realize, that's what allows you to keep going with it. You just have to let yourself flow with it and acknowledge it! Don't analyze in your head. Just let it happen. When you realize something's happening, that helps you to amplify the direction you're heading in. You want to catch and harness that wave. That's what you want to do.

When we first came back up into the room, I could feel a thickness in the air. Was that from you or them?

It's from all of us. I really pushed in the end to intensify and help to gravitate them there. I'm still shaking it off because that energy is still in here. I think most of you can still feel the remnants of it. In either case, it's definitely a thing that most people can feel. I think the people that aren't sensitive might come in and not feel it right away, but I'm almost sure that the vast majority of people, regardless of their level of development, are going to feel something unusual. It's just natural. In fact, if my pets were here, I'm sure that they would probably be reacting to what's going on in here also.

My body is really bothering me because my limbs are numb.

Well, that is because you are familiar with that sensation. When you are around people who are actively using hallucinogenic drugs, or something to that effect, if you have ever taken drugs in the past, you can feel the drug's influence on others even if you are not taking anything yourself. You start to get that sensation yourself. It doesn't surprise me that those are frequencies that you learn and become familiar with. Again, this is an effect that can catapult you. When you get around people who have shifted before, you actually can create a vortex of shifting.

Christ said, "When two or more gather in my name, I am there." It really puts a very interesting spin on those words when you associate someone's frequency and vibration with how they might have moved you or affected you. If you can get other people to talk about that person, even when that person's not there, you can get into the zone. You start to shift and that creates that person's frequency, energy or vibration. I think there's a hidden knowledge in there that most people don't understand. We always get fragments of what really happened in those stories. Perhaps, we have to try to figure them out so we know what they really mean.

My body feels very, very heavy right now.

That's because you're solidifying now. You're starting to feel what your normal body feels like. You're just more aware of it.

I never felt like this before. I have this tingly feeling all over. It almost feels cold. Then again, I feel really excited.

You're adjusting. Again, several things come to mind. There's a point where your body gets clammy and moist. Different people feel it in slightly different ways, but it's very normal. Your body reacts by going through some chemical change that creates euphoria. Some people might say, "The chemicals in your brain are changing and that's what's creating reality." I could tell them, "Well, you could say that it's a hallucination," or I could say, "Aren't the same chemicals in a different frequency in my brain creating my normal everyday reality?" Which is the difference? Which is the right one? Which is the wrong one? That's something to keep in mind, but you'll keep adjusting to the one that you're used to.

Here's one of the things I want you to reflect on differently. I want you to respond with your first instincts of what you're aware of now because you're a little sharper than normal. After you've done this a few times, do you think that you could learn to apply the things that you've learned, like healing or telepathy? Do you now see the possibilities of functioning in that state of mind? If you could see energy in general, do you think you could become more sensitive to these things in people's bodies and environments? You'd be able to literally say, "Yeah, I can distinguish that now whereas before I really had no way of knowing whether that existed or not." Does that make sense now?

Yes, it makes a lot of sense.

Yes, it appears logical. Do you remember what I said in the last chapter? When Jesus, Buddha, Krishna or Milarepa performed miracles, they were in a state of mind like this. It might have been even more intensive. That's when they were able to change reality, even outside of them. You can eventually get to that point and be able to do really interesting things. It's a whole different kind of logic.

**I noticed something pretty intense.
Shana doesn't feel like Shana at all.**

Right, right.

I don't feel like myself either.

Well, you're not really yourself. You're still reverting back down to normal. We can all feel that. Soon we'll break this conversation because the conversation keeps you there. Remember what I said: *Thought is a living thing.* Since we're talking about being In-Between, that's really what's holding you there. Once this conversation dissipates and we move on, you'll come back down and you'll reflect on it. You're going to lose a certain amount of it. It's almost as if the organic brain needs to digest some of it. There's a vast quantity of information here that will never be spoken in words. It's something that you can only internalize and it's just not something you can verbalize well.

Again, it's something you need to experience more so than what you can explain. You're changed forever now. You'll never be the same person. You're now going to have a greater view of the world that you exist in. There's something even more profound than what you originally thought. Among the three of you, two people are about average with their spirituality, which is ideal for this. The third person is someone who has actually been heavily immersed and could be considered more advanced. Yet, all three of you look to be pretty blown away with this experience.

When I saw the weather today, I really felt that it had attributes that related to our group consciousness from yesterday.

Well, I don't like to get into major things. As a group, I think we're well aware of some pretty profound things that we're privy to. I don't want to admit what you're saying, but I'm not denying it. It is what it is.

It really just felt like what's happening was a mood.

Well, this is a very powerful state of consciousness. It has a rippling effect on the Gaia mind in a positive way. In a sense, I think that you can affect reality. Now, I'll give you a bigger picture. I would like to see many awakened masters on the Earth at the same time.

Imagine if this knowledge gets out and awakens many other White Cells who are now asleep. If I can affect a group of people and they evolve, they're going to affect other frequencies around them. If we could get this to move all around the planet over the next five years or six years, what effect is that going to have on global consciousness? I would think it's going to have a profound effect. I would even be willing to say that because of the frequency that's emanating from here right now, the people who are living in the houses within a few miles around me are feeling what would be deemed a very spiritual or surreal vibration. They just don't know why they feel that way.

So, at any moment, were you preoccupied or scared as you were experiencing this?

I was at first.

We're afraid of anything we don't know or don't understand. It's normal.

I'd gotten to the point before where I could see the energy of things swelling, but I was afraid of what would happen next. As soon as I thought about that, it snapped me back to reality. This time I just relaxed and let go.

That's exactly what I've explained. And voilà, you rode the wave and you got something out of it.

That's actually what's happening. It's just like a wave going over the whole room. I could see that as well.

You could see the energy waves? I wasn't sure that you had gotten that far. That's good. A lot of words that I say are analogies, but in some ways I'm really pulling out stuff that describes exactly what I'm seeing or experiencing. That's why I say it's a wave. So, Anna, did you go through any moments of fear? Sometimes I know you get nervous with certain things very easily.

Well, I didn't have fear but I did have this feeling of a rush of excitement. When I was sitting over there, I saw the aura of the microphone really intensify.

That's good.

As soon as I saw that, I got really excited! Then it faded away. That's when I remembered how you said that we should focus on our breathing. That brought me back and it slowly came back but not exactly the same as before.

Right, but that's very interesting because we're getting more bits and pieces here. You will never hear *everything*. This is why it's good that we're talking about it. Go ahead.

When you told us to look at you, I could see your energy change.

So you could see change. When you hear people say they see this big aura around me or other people, do you understand now?

Yeah, your aura was growing bigger and I could see colors, too.

When you start off seeing auras, don't look for color. The color will come to you as you get more skilled. I think it's interesting that somebody who doesn't really work with it at all is seeing not only a full blown intense aura, which I'm sure was several feet in some cases, but brilliant color as well. Do you understand how this can literally catapult you ahead in your psychic development? How do you guys feel now? Are you a little tired or perhaps fatigued in a way?

Yeah.

Some of you are tired but one of you isn't. Well, good for you. You must have good stamina.

I'm trying to raise my arms, and it feels very difficult.

I think Anna's experience with the microphone is a great explanation of how thought yanks you out of this. The organic thought pulls you out of the higher vibrational consciousness because that sees things on a different level. It computes on a different level. When you acknowledged it, and you saw it going up, you got excited. When you got excited, you lowered your energy because that came from an emotion from the organic level that you're used to. That's why it faded again. When you calmed yourself, it started to come back up, but there's a limit to what you let yourself go to when you do these things. As you practice, you can let go even more.

**I am looking at how plastic things look. When I look
at two other objects, they shine out in the background.
Then something starts to happen and I think,
"Oh, no wonder! It's because it is plastic."
Then that grounds me again.**

Thought is what controls a lot of this. So, the less thought that you have, the better. Just experience. You're already thinking. There's something processing thought but it doesn't have to be words. It's very fast, very accurate, and very clear.

Yes, definitely.

The things that you're pointing out are very good. It is through this self-awareness and self-study that you advance. When you acknowledge it, something starts to happen that's really amazing and profound. You're seeing this glow, this three dimensional thing. It's definitely not something ordinary. It is mystical. These things that you are experiencing are what mystics call the *mystical state of mind*. This is a very bona fide experience, just as much as theirs is. They have been out there doing these things 25, 30, or 40 years. Here you are – family members, taking care of your kids or doing your own thing. Yet, you are here experiencing similar things.

The second that you thought with your organic brain, it diminished again. Again, it really emphasizes the need to learn to steady your mind and your thinking. Focus on your breathing. Move around in that state of consciousness and just try to experience. This is where your meditations pay off. All the techniques that you've learned through all the other material really helps you to move through all this, understand it, and really be aware of what's going on. When you are aware of something changing, that moves you into it. When you think with your organic mind, it can move you out of it.

I usually have a big problem with the Babbler in my meditations so I'm always babbling. This time I managed to hold my mind steady a lot more because of the way you directed me. When I went outside, I was amazed that there was not much babbling going on.

One of the amazing things is that you can really shut it off like that. If you can catch the wave, it shuts right down and you just go with the flow. Don't think about thinking. Don't analyze. Just let yourself flow. The more you can let yourself flow, the more intense things are going to get. You're going to have a very powerful, mystical experience. It just gets more amazing.

I did not go out with them. I let them go out on their own because I wanted their experience to be self-directed. I wanted to take myself out of the picture so that I couldn't influence the direction of the experience. That's why I didn't go out with them.

I could feel the wind and I didn't even know if it was windy out. I could feel the air moving.

I'll let you in on a little secret. You can entertain yourself with the wind in that state of mind and other people can feel it if you *will* it. When you are more practiced with the In-Between and have a certain level expectation, it will respond to you.

I put my arms out when I was walking and I could feel the air on my hands, fingertips and palms. I felt it was windy, too. Wasn't it windy?

I don't know. I don't think it's windy out.

I didn't feel wind. I did feel cold though.

So you didn't feel wind. They felt it was windy, while you felt it was very windy.

Yes.

You were working with the wind, even though you probably didn't realize it. If you can understand how things really happen in this state of consciousness, you can perform 'miracles'. I don't want to create a whole planet where everybody is fighting over what to manifest. That's not my goal. If that becomes a problem, it will self-regulate. When you're doing healing, telepathy, or things like that there's no limitation in this state of mind. You really can do some pretty profound things.

Some people might come back to me and wonder how I could actually just release this information in a book or on audio CD so just anybody could listen or read it. I want to make it very clear on the record that I don't think anybody is going to read this material if it's not something that they're earnestly seeking already. There's a reason why they want to listen. There's a reason why they're intrigued by it. Their inner Navigator is seeking this knowledge. If I don't release it, the world is going to consistently have the same problem trying to find this knowledge. There are going to be people consistently tainting it and watering it down. I'm trying to keep it as pure as I can without any particular belief system saying it belongs to them. It doesn't belong to anybody. It belongs to everybody.

I feel that this knowledge can be freely given at this time. On its own accord, it will find the right people. That's the point of it. This is a modern age. The world is vastly more populated than any other time in history. Technology and the way of life are very different. This is the way that it must be done. I'm confident that it's going to find the right people. Through these experiences, there are going to be a lot of people who are going to find enlightenment. There are going to be a lot of people who are going to find a much higher state of consciousness. It is a form of learning.

Not all learning is from a book, listening to audio CDs, or watching DVDs. Not all learning is through watching somebody else doing it. This is a form of teaching. I'm showing you how to go to school. That's really how I feel. When you go In-Between, I feel like you're going to school for a higher education. Hence, Higher Balance. This is what's going to start changing you. All of you already look different to me. There's already this wealth of knowledge that's moving around you. You don't even realize how many volumes of knowledge you've just learned. Where could you have learned this? How many books would you have to read to get everything that you just experienced in thirty minutes? I don't think you would have gotten that same effect by just reading about it without experiencing it, too.

I know I wouldn't have.

This is something that you'll never forget for the rest of your life. When you look at things in life, you're going to appreciate them on a much greater level. And it's something that you may not have necessarily done. You might appreciate life, but now you can really say that you have this deeper understanding. That's why I've done this. This is why I've broken the constraints of keeping it all a secret. And I'm going to continue doing this as long as I can. It's time that this knowledge is freed. It's time it's given out freely. It belongs to everybody.

Thank you.

You're welcome.

I really feel confident that I'm able to do it on my own now.

I do not doubt it for one minute. Once you know the process, it can be done again. The thing that I want to emphasize the most is that it really helps to have the other material I have previously released. Either read the other books I have written or listen to the modules. If you haven't listened to all the material, even if you don't think it's relevant to your particular interest, I strongly urge that you listen to it, or read the books because it's going to profoundly advance you when you go into this state of consciousness. It's literally going to open up avenues that would have taken you much longer to have achieved otherwise. You can only appreciate that once you experience it. Then you'll understand what I mean by that. So, definitely, use everything that we're putting out there. It's going to catapult you forward significantly no matter what the topic.

At this point in the book, some of the more 'seasoned' students that have gone In-Between in the past will share their experiences with YOU, the reader!

Eric R.'s Experience:

I've only been In-Between once and it was after I'd known Eric for four years. I had a lot of crazy experiences before that, but this one was completely different. After that, everything else made so much sense.

I think we had just launched the Higher Balance Institute to the public so this was probably early June 2003. At the time, Eric and I were still living in a small apartment. It was around 9:30 or 10:00 pm and we'd just come back from having coffee. I remember feeling really tired and all I wanted to do was go to bed.

After parking, we started to walk up to the apartment. It felt like it was still early spring, but you could smell it moving towards summer. There were clouds in the sky like a storm was coming. Everything had that *halfway there but not quite* feeling. It was like summer but still spring. It almost felt like it could storm, but it wasn't quite there. There was a feeling of electricity in the air. Everything was just *halfway*.

It was a very strange feeling and Eric pointed this out. He looked up at the sky and he said, "Wow! There's some kind of space there. Do you feel that? Do you notice that strange feeling in the air?" I felt it and said, "Yeah." Eric said, "It almost never gets like this. We should take a walk."

I remember complaining, "Oh, I am so tired." Eric insisted, "No, we should take a walk. You don't understand. Sometimes Gaia's consciousness moves around because weather patterns are like thoughts moving around Gaia. Sometimes, you'll hit a certain spot where everything gets quiet and you've got to take advantage of it. This is the spot. You've got to look around. Look at the clouds. Feel the air. Everything is quieter than it normally is."

He was right. Everything was really quiet. It looked ready to storm there but it wasn't. It was like this weird, quiet moment, like the calm before the storm. I said, "Fine, we'll take a walk." I thought he just wanted exercise, or that he wasn't ready to go to bed.

So, we walked around the apartment complex and we didn't really say anything. He just walked with me following him. I remember we walked around half the complex before he pointed out some lights and said, "Look at the lights. All the outdoor lights remind me of lanterns." They weren't bright. They were dim, almost foggy. They were a shade of orange or a dim yellow. They weren't bright lights. Occasionally a breeze would come through and Eric would just say little things like, "Listen to the breeze." As the breeze blew through the pine trees, he'd say, "Listen to the pine trees."

In this apartment complex, there were little streams that went through it and there were bridges that went across the streams. As we walked across a bridge, Eric said, "Don't just walk around. Pay attention to the sounds of things. When the wind blows the trees, pay attention to that." Someone's wind chimes were blowing so he said, "Pay attention to the wind chimes. It can be very surreal. The surrealism can put you in this state if you pay attention to it." So, I listened to the wind chimes and I listened to the wind. As we went across these bridges, I listened to the babbling brook.

Eric talked about the surrealism like you just have to experience things. Everything in that moment seemed very surreal. You could hear the babbling brook as you walked across the bridge but you didn't really think about it. You just experienced it in that half-light. The lights from the apartment gave everything a really strange glow. Nothing was bright. You couldn't see everything clearly. Yet everything seemed very quiet. The whole place was just dead asleep. We never saw any people or any cars. It was like the whole place had shut down. It was like going to an amusement park after hours when there was nobody there.

Then, we started walking back towards the apartment. I was paying attention to how surreal things felt, but nothing really hit me. I didn't know what was going on. I was just following Eric while he's saying, "Pay attention to your body. Listen to the stream. Listen to the wind chimes. Listen to the things going through the trees." Then Eric started talking about this state that he used to go into when he walked around. He said, "It was the *In-Between*." I'd heard him mention it a few times. Other people who learned from Eric had talked about it, too. Yet, I really had no concept of what it was except from some of the descriptions other people had given me. It seemed like it was this real crazy psychedelic inter-dimensional place. Then Eric reflected, "Sometimes I can put myself in that place and I can carry people there. I haven't really done that in a while."

As we walked back towards the apartment, there's this big, tall lamp post and underneath is a bush of wild flowers. This was my first indication that something had happened because when we looked at the wild flowers, Eric said, "Doesn't this remind you of little universes?" I looked at these flowers and they had really long, tall, thin stalks. At the very end of the stalks, there were all these bursts of yellow wild flowers. They were just these little round things, but all really yellow. As I looked at them, I remember Eric said, "Universe." I remembered going into them and seeing them. All of a sudden, size didn't matter. There was no perspective of, "I'm big and they're small and the universe behind me is even bigger and the molecules inside them are even smaller." It was like they were these enormous things and I was this other thing experiencing the space inside them.

And it didn't matter. It was this spatial loop. All I could feel were these flowers, and I just stood there in awe, "Holy cow, they are this universe. They're not these small flowers. They're just as big." I remember feeling this circular loop of me moving inside them and somehow coming out the other end of the universe. And the universe was moving inside me going into the flowers. Size didn't matter. That's the best way I can explain it. It was a really bizarre experience to know that they are really this little universe. Then I realized, "Wow! That was a really strange experience." Then I looked at Eric and suddenly I was in this state where I was spinning through all these things that I just started understanding. That's when I realized something had happened. Suddenly, I started to feel really good.

So, we walked up the stairs to the apartment and there was one light on the bookshelves in the living room. I remember suddenly looking around and everything started to make perfect sense. Everything was just perfect and I understood everything. I didn't even question anything because I knew the answers. I could look at objects and just know things about them. There was a light that came in through the window, hitting a spot on the wall. Eric said, "Look at that spot." When I looked at the spot, I realized the spot wasn't there because the light was shooting in through the window. The spot was there because it was there and everything was going backwards. The spot was there, creating the light beam going out. The light beam had to adjust to the fact that the spot was there. It made perfect sense in that state.

There was a spot on the wall. When you're not in that In-Between state you think, "Okay, the spot's there because the light beam is coming in through the window, hitting the spot on the wall. That's why there's this light spot on the wall." In the In-Between state you think, "Oh no, it's backwards. The spot needed to be there. So, there had to be a light there because there had to be a beam there. In order for that spot to be there, that's how it had to happen. The spot was the first thing and everything else went backwards from that spot. When Eric said, "You should go up and feel that spot," I went up and I felt the spot on the wall. It felt warm even though the light beam was 500 feet away coming through the window from across the apartment complex. I felt the wall beside this spot of light and it felt cold. When I felt right on the spot of the light, it was completely warm. That's where the spot was located. I literally felt heat from that spot which seems unbelievable.

So, I just sat there trying to absorb being in this space. Then Eric said, "Okay, I'm going to bed." I just said, "Good night." I just stood there for five minutes because I didn't want to go to bed.

All I had to do was just look at something and I could start feeling things from it. Normally, in psychometry, you have to touch everything to open those lines of communication. This was perfect psychometry. I didn't have to touch anything. There were some beads hanging on the wall. When I looked at the beads, I could feel all the past owners and see images of them in my mind. I experienced each of them getting the beads, owning them and the significance of the beads for them, just from looking at the beads on the wall. I could just flip through everything like that, perfectly.

Everything was alive with its own memory. It was like going up to a person and asking, "What was your life like?" Then they explained to you all the things that happened in their life. It was like this with all these objects. You could ask, "Where do you come from?" and "What is your memory?" and "What has your journey been like so far?" Then they told me. It was just a perfect communication where I didn't even have to touch them. I just looked at them and suddenly this conduit opened up where I could experience everything that those things had experienced. It was just perfect in my mind. I didn't even have to think about it. I wasn't even trying to do that. That wasn't even my intention.

I just looked at it and suddenly I saw them and everything was just perfect and alive.

I remember standing there, looking at all these objects and just trying to absorb all of this while thinking how perfect it was. I didn't want to go to sleep because if I did I was going to lose all this. I was so tired but I wanted to stay up as long as I could. There was only one light on behind me on the bookshelf and Eric's cat had come up from behind me but I didn't know that. I saw this shadow on the floor with the two pointy ears. I looked at the shadow and it felt as alive to me as the cat. I didn't even connect that the two were related. It wasn't that the cat was behind me and the light was hitting it, creating the shadow. The shadow and the cat were in a symbiotic relationship. They were both living things, just as separate but just as connected. I looked at the shadow and it was his cat but this completely different thing, but I knew they were shared somehow. I just sat there and experienced its shadow, almost as if it was just a different form of his cat, just as alive but different. It was quite profound.

Then finally, I started to think in normal terms, "Oh wait, this isn't a thing by itself; this is supposed to be connected to something." I had to think about that in logical terms. Then I had to put it back in a space that I'd understand if I wasn't in the In-Between. I thought, "Oh, there's supposed to be a cat here. This isn't a life form by itself. There's supposed to be something else." That's when I turned around and I saw his cat. Then I realized, "That's how it's supposed to work. The cat makes the shadow. The shadow doesn't just walk around by itself." That is how I experienced it when I first saw it. It didn't even occur to me that there was supposed to be a cat connected to it. I just experienced that perfect living shadow.

So I remember looking at the cat and experiencing him in a completely different way. I was just going around in a state of total wonder. Everything was alive. Nothing was inanimate. These objects weren't just made of molecules and atoms. You could feel this different life behind them. They were there, but everything was connected and you could feel the connection of everything perfectly. It was just this completely extraordinary state where everything made sense. Before you could even form a question, you knew the answers. They were just there in your mind and it was perfectly natural. It was like being alive for the first time and completely different than any state you could ever shift into, including during meditation. The Babbler wasn't there but you and everything else was there. There was just this flow of communication where everything made sense. It was just perfect. Everything had its memory and you were just connected to that. Nothing felt disjointed. Everything felt in perfect harmony and in perfect rhythm. It was separate but it wasn't. You could feel the unity in everything so perfectly.

I had such a hard time trying to comprehend how Eric was going to explain the In-Between before people experienced it. The things that he talks about in the course make sense because I can take the experience of In-Between and then *Reverse Engineer* it. If I never experienced that, I would relate it to all the wrong things. After my awakening, I was in these really different states. Since I didn't have any way to define it, I didn't know what it was. You can be in some profoundly aware states where you really feel like you're buzzing and cruising on a dimensional level. You can see the strobe flashing and you can see and experience the white fog of different dimensions moving into this one clearly and physically.

You can even feel the hum of your internal and your outer bodies. You can feel that black space of infinity moving into your consciousness and see things and feel it behind everything. You can feel the connection of everything and you can hear things and feel the surrealism of it. You can hit those Gaia grids where you see energy and download information about people or really profound things. You can feel really aware, look at someone and just open up that conduit of data flowing from them. Or, you can sit there and be in a state of ecstatic bliss, laughing to yourself because everything makes such perfect sense.

It's different because when you're hitting those peak aware states, it almost feels like you are moving towards the frequency of The Force, by trying to use your sixth sense. You're hitting a really peak state but it's still somehow you moving towards that state. As amazing as those states are, even though you're using a fluidic state of consciousness, they still feel mechanical and structured to me when you put them along beside the In-Between. If it feels more human to you than the In-Between, you are still trying to use too much of your sixth sense while approaching those states.

When I think about my experience with the In-Between, everything moves backwards. Eric said several times, "You've got to start thinking in reverse. When you start thinking backwards, that's when you'll start to understand things." When I think about my perception of things in the In-Between, everything was backwards. I saw the spot and I knew the spot was the first thing. It's not that there was a light that was turned on by electricity that was shining and moving through the window that created the spot. It was that everything was going backwards from the spot. With the cat, there was a shadow. It wasn't that the cat created the shadow. They were both there in this weird, symbiotic, shared relationship and that's what made sense. It wasn't that the light created the shadow. The shadow was there and it needed to be there.

It is only when you go out of that state that you have to logically think of things like, "Oh, there's this light that hits the cat that makes the shadow." It doesn't work that way. It's only when you leave that state that you believe that there has to be some kind of reflection. The In-Between is a true fluidic state because it's not you mechanically using your biological sixth sense to move towards the state of The Force. You've somehow flipped the conduit. Eric says that you are a conduit because that's exactly the difference. *You flipped the source.* You're not moving towards The Force, trying to experience those peak states of awareness, like you do during meditation. It's flipped, and The Force is moving through you and you're experiencing everything from the perspective of The Force. When you have a human perspective, you are moving towards the source of all creation. When you're in the In-Between, you're the source of all creation moving towards the human perspective. That's why everything is backwards.

Dan T.'s Experience:

When I was In-Between, I noticed all matter had patterns and textures to it, even glass. Glass is made by melting minerals at very high temperatures. It becomes a clear hard substance that we make glasses and windows from. Everything has a pattern to it, down to its molecular structure. While I was In-Between, I could see the flow of all of those patterns. When I say the flow of things, I literally mean the flow of time. I was so deep in the In-Between that I saw all positions, or all points that every piece of matter would go through in its lifespan, somewhat like the flow of energy. At this point, I realized how it was possible in this heightened state of awareness to actually see into the past and into the future because I could watch the flow of things. I could see the absoluteness of the origin of everything. I could look at a crack in the paint on the wall and I could actually trace with a pencil where that crack would go all the way down the wall. If you'd watch it over time, that paint would crack exactly where you marked it.

It's not like I was seeing the future, the past, or the present in individual moments. I saw them all coexisting, almost as if I was aware of all of the states that the crack in the wall would be at all times. In other words, I was aware of the totality of the crack in the wall, but it wasn't just that. This happened, no matter what I looked at. I could actually see all the characteristics of any object that I looked at, the matter that it was made of, how it formed, where it was going to break and how it would break down.

Another excellent example is the time that Eric and I were traveling on the interstate and we stopped at a hotel room. That night we had some spiritual conversations and Eric ended up shifting me In-Between. This is probably one of the deepest times that I had ever been shifted. I was in awe because I was watching this napkin on the table molecularly break down. I could actually see the molecular fragments of the napkin breaking down. I don't know if I was observing where this napkin was going in the future or if I was actually watching it on a molecular level break down in the present. All I know was that I observed this napkin break down. I have no way to reference how long it takes for a napkin to break down so I don't know if I was actually watching time. I don't know how long I was watching the napkin break down. All I know is that I could see it break down all the way to the point where it basically became dust. I also saw it all the way to where it is currently, which is a full-fledged crumpled up napkin sitting on the table. The reason why the napkin stands out in my head so much is because it's such a light, cloth-like material. The lamp above the napkin just made it illuminate. Since it was such a light cloth, it was easy to see it breaking down as opposed to looking at wood from the furniture that it was sitting on.

At one point in time, I realized that I was in this higher level state of consciousness. I was a part of a frequency, like a flow of energy if you will, but simultaneously I coexisted with my body. I was in a higher state of consciousness because I wasn't using words. In fact, I was incapable of using words in that higher state of consciousness. If I kept trying, I probably would have come down. When you are that high in the In-Between, there's no part of you that wants to be grounded. Eric had to force me to come out of the In-Between by making me play a video game that I didn't want to play.

When I was in this higher state of consciousness, I wasn't as concerned with my bodily needs in my life as Dan. I was more aware of the global life consciousness that was around me because I was more a part of it. As a matter of fact, I had to actually look at an object to relate to something in my life. I was so deep into a universal state of consciousness of the synchronicity that was in my life that I almost lost my identity. I was a part of the higher circle of life, if you will, which is so incredibly moving. Obviously, by listening to what I experienced in my life, you can imagine why I would be. I knew that Eric could just take me In-Between at will, so I no longer wanted to work for it. I knew it could just be handed to me. It took me a long time to realize that I have to do my own work. The beauty of it is that the In-Between has many levels and anyone can obtain them. It's an open book.

Matt S.'s Experience:

I'm going to talk about the time that Eric took me In-Between in 2002 when I first moved to Oregon. It was a night where we had gone to see a somewhat thought provoking movie called, *Minority Report*. After the movie, we had a conversation that was pretty deep. As we were driving home, I asked Eric questions about the differences between Red Cells and White Cells. Eric's answers started to shift me because I was deeply internalizing it as I listened to it. He obviously felt the shift that I was going into because he told me, "Oh, you're starting to feel it now. Look around you at things. Look at the people next to us on the road." Then, he started to mention how synchronized everything was and how you could see that there was some kind of order at work. Eric paused the conversation to give me a chance to look around and feel the heaviness of my body. I had a really heavy sense in my chest.

I remember looking out the window at all the trees and the different things we were passing by, especially the people on the highway. Staring forward, I could almost feel what they were thinking from their facial expressions. It felt like I was in a vein like a neural pathway in the city. I was in this hub of a macro, like the neural pathways in the body with its little nerves doing their business for the whole. I have thought about that many times, but this time I looked over and I started to feel it. There's no way in the world that I could logically break down the information that I was picking up on. It was nameless information, nameless data, like the same nameless information you feel when you have love for someone. If you look at one of the people driving on the freeway when you're in this state of mind, you start to shift into seeing more of the macro element of what's going on. There's no terms for the data that you feel. Over the span of our lives, there's data being transferred, and I was able to pick up on that information. It wasn't specific thoughts.

During those states of shifting since then, I've discovered that I can go into the specific thoughts. At that time, I saw more of the big picture. That happened pretty much throughout the whole drive home. I felt like a microorganism in a vein, carrying information or carrying out a duty that I couldn't describe. It was just very interesting. There was an immense level of information. It was just a really complex feeling. My senses were definitely enhanced and heightened. Everything shimmered. I could hear beyond the walls of the car. It was almost as if I could project my hearing out to listen to things that were going on outside the car around a building. I looked towards two people who were standing next to a building that was really far away. I could almost hear, or feel, what they were saying. It wasn't a conversation. It was an energy relay, but it was information, nonetheless. It was very deep and it had a big impact on my perception at that time.

When we got to our destination, Eric got out and he smirked at me. Then he started to direct my attention towards various things that we were walking past. He told me to look at the configurations of the berry bushes that were off to our right and the way that each one grew in a unique pattern from a seed; that cellular unfolding that ended up being this bush, looking a certain way in its current state. In that state of mind, as Eric directed my attention towards it, I could feel the entire lifespan of that plant and how it burst from the ground through the earth and grew into this totally unique shape.

Eric directed my attention to sound and how it almost had a three dimensional quality about it. You could hear what a cube was, if a cube had a sound. That's the only way that I can explain my perception of sounds in the In-Between. There was one very particular point that made a big impact in my memory. As we were walking upstairs, Eric put his key into the lock in the keyhole. The key went in and he said, "Do you hear the music?" The metal against each of the teeth inside the lock, rubbing up against each tooth of the key, slowed down to where it actually produced a musical element. He looked at me and he said, "Even that produces a melody in the universe."

I was floored at that point. I don't know what it was about the key but every time I hear a key going into a lock now, it can shift me. That was like taking a gift back from that state. When we got into the living room, I sat down and went into a meditative state that was totally effortless and felt so natural.

It was different than simply being aware. The amount of information that I brought in was just staggering. It didn't matter whether I directed my attention towards something like the freeway with all the cars, the people on the freeway, or things that Eric pointed out like the key and the various sounds. The difference was that when I normally come out of a meditation, we don't have measurements for that level of termless data. When you slip In-Between, the amount of data is inconceivably more than your normal sleep, the mechanical patterned state during the day, or even while you're watching a movie. It's just immense data. That's the difference.

If you go into the In-Between state, it's going to enhance anything that you do. The In-Between is a place in your consciousness. Most people don't know how to open the door to that place. It's a vibratory location where the data comes in so unbelievably fast that you just slip into it. It's the movement that Eric talks about where the ability to be fluidic opens up the pipelines for data to just stream in. The deeper you go In-Between, the deeper the information goes to the point where talking about it is fruitless. It's fancy to say that but to wholeheartedly believe it and really experience it takes a certain state of awareness. That's incredible data. It's not just the realization that something happened for you. He's not talking like that. He's in a totally expanded state.

Anna's Experience:

This is so hard to put into words. I can describe what I felt, what my body felt like, and what thoughts went through my head even though I was trying not to think at the time. I had to think in order to experience what I was experiencing. I was going through some form of thought. There were some points when Eric was guiding us through the process where he had us walk up the stairs. When I came back down and into the room, I immediately experienced a haze, almost like a fog, in the room. As I walked into the living room, I also felt a drastic change in the temperature. My body just turned cold.

When Eric was walking us through the process, I found it difficult at times because I was looking for changes. At first, he explained what it felt like to him when he was shifting. He mentioned the tightness of his jaw and the metallic taste in the back of his mouth. Since I was trying to look for things like that, I wasn't really paying attention to what was happening until he told us to focus and pay attention to our breathing. Then I saw shadows or shapes coming off the wall. The feeling of the temperature in the room changed, too. After that, my mind was actually quieter than when I'm regularly meditating. It was just immensely quiet.

Also, Eric asked us to go outside. At one point while we were walking, I was struggling. My body just felt very weird. The only other time that I can say I've felt like that is during an astral projection when I was trying to move around. There's a feeling like you have like weights on your legs. It's also similar to the feeling when you're trying to fly in a dream and you're trying to get that momentum to take off.

Afterward, I analyzed myself and the one thing that I learned was to forget everything and ride the wave. Don't expect anything. Pay attention to what's happening, but be careful while paying attention to it. At one point, I experienced the aura in the area where Eric was sitting. I remember seeing the aura around the microphone illuminate. It was just so vibrant that I got excited because I saw it. As soon as I said, "Wow," it just completely turned off. Then, I had to go back to the breathing and try to bring myself back to that place where I was so that I could start seeing the aura again but it wasn't as vibrant as it was before.

The experience itself was so wonderful and amazing. It completely changed how I look at life. There're so many layers and the whole meaning of life is to experience.

Baard W.'s Experience:

Since I have been studying with Eric, I've heard about many students who have been In-Between, but not all of the students have been there. Everyone talks about how it's supposed to be awesome, so I really wanted to experience it. I think I had so many expectations for the In-Between. I was imagining that it was going to be a drug-like feeling that was just going to hit you like, "Bam!" And there you were in the In-Between!

When I was In-Between, I had most of the experiences that Eric or some of the other students mentioned, so I'm not going to say much about those experiences. I had a lot of problems moving myself into the In-Between because I had so many expectations. So, when Eric said, "Now I'll shift you into the In-Between," I thought, "Oh my God, this is like a movie. Why does it have to be surrealistic? This is so artificial. Why does it have to be like that? Why can't we make it more natural?" So, when I came out, it hit me, "That is how it is to be in the In-Between. Everything becomes surrealistic." As soon as I internalized that, I moved into it, and I think that I got the same experiences as the others.

After being In-Between, one thing that really struck me is that I felt God. I felt how beautiful God was. I could never imagine anything as beautiful as that. I felt as if God came down and touched me! It was so beautiful. I never wanted to use the word God before. I always used The Force or something higher but never God. I never felt comfortable with that word. God is just so big, so huge and so intense! I could never imagine something would be that beautiful. When I came back in to Eric and the other people waiting in the class, and he wanted me to talk about my experiences, my tears just came out. I started to laugh and cry both at the same time. I didn't know how to handle it. It was so strong. It was so beautiful and it just came out. I don't know if the people there noticed it but I was really touched by God.

After the class was finished, I felt this God force coming from Eric, so I felt attracted to Eric somehow. I had to go over to him and he's like, "Baard, what are you looking at? It seems like you're gobbling me up. Are you going to eat me?" And I caught myself looking at him in that way, but I didn't want to leave Eric. I just wanted to stay around him the whole night. He basically told me to leave because he needed to rest. And this feeling of the In-the-Between stuck with me for two days. Suddenly, when I sat in front of my computer, the whole room started to wave and shadows became alive.

After that experience, everything about me changed – my whole spirituality, my meditations, how I look at life and how I perceive God. Everything has changed; everything. I'm not the same person anymore. I feel it. When I feel myself, I feel different. It was just the most amazing experience I ever, ever, ever had. There's no way I can put it down in words. It just feels so beautiful and if you think about something that's the most beautiful thing you ever experienced, times that by one thousand, it's just vibratory beauty. That's all I want to say.

Chapter 14

THE HUNT

New Orleans, January 2010

When you are In-Between, you can feel everything. It's not something you can touch with your hands, but you do feel it. It's a different kind of knowing. You can feel all the dips and curves of the curtains. Everything has a spongy texture that you can feel.

There is a big chandelier in my room. I remember looking up at the chandelier and thinking that it felt like one of the sponges from the ocean. If you could fill it with water and squeeze it while the water comes out, you could see the pressure of each little squirt and the texture of it squeezing. That's how the whole chandelier felt to me. Interestingly enough, if my eyes were shut and I felt that chandelier somewhere else, I would say, "Oh, that is a chandelier."

When you are In-Between, your brain takes on sensations very differently. That affects how your brain interprets what you see. Rather than looking at it and saying, "I acknowledge that is a chandelier," or "I know that's what it is," use your feels-like, or assimilation, or tagging. *Everything comes from an In-Between state of mind*. To me, an In-Between state of consciousness is a higher state of consciousness than the state that we normally communicate in. Everything you have learned is a technology that has come from that place. Everything you have learned can be integrated into this dimension as a tool. When I am In-Between, I never analyze it. I never think, "What is the In-Between like?" Interestingly enough, I realized that it is all of the things you have learned, happening at the same time to you.

You are constantly scanning people. You are constantly assimilating things. You are constantly doing a feels-like. You are constantly feeling everything in your chest consciousness. It is like a symphony of all of the skills you have ever learned. Instead of seeing them from your dimension as an individual tool that you apply, you have to function with all of those skills, bringing your awareness to your reality. That was very hard to communicate right now, but I think I did a good job.

I know that I have to come out of the In-Between to link up with you a little bit lower. There is another part of me that doesn't want to because I like being in that state of mind. There is a struggle inside of me that goes, "No, I don't want to." The other part says, "It feels so good here." It's like waking up in the morning and knowing you have to get up, but your bed feels so inviting, soft, and comfortable so you just want to stay where you are.

I have several concerns about having everybody go In-Between. Some people who go In-Between have a lot of trouble getting back out. All of this talk about being here and being there will make a lot more sense to you once you start shifting because it is a very distinct place. I want to ease your fear because then you will transition much better. It is very easy to come out from the In-Between if you just go to your room and relax. It's almost like you're going to take a nap. Lie down on your bed and close your eyes. You will probably go to sleep fairly easily. When you come to, you will be out of the In-Between and back to normal. That is in an extreme case.

You may be walking along and all of a sudden objects will start to transition to that place where things feel very differently and you will see yourself going there. If you panic and say to yourself, "Oh my God, I am back in again," because you will feel yourself slip into it.

The best thing to do if you have trouble staying out of the In-Between is listen to some pop music like Madonna or Lady

Gaga. It is the most grounding thing you can do. I normally never listen to that kind of music because of the simplicity of it. Ironically, I just felt myself go down a notch just thinking about it. It's like feeling yourself coming out of a bubble. It's like having air pressure in an airplane and having your ears pop as you come down. You can feel your mind shifting and everything takes on a normal structure where you can't feel the walls so much. You may feel anxiety because you don't want to stay in that place. It is so different and so overwhelming for your sensory. It's such a different state of mind that you will want to come out especially if you feel stuck. You will feel, "Oh my God, now I can't get out of it. I can't deal with it anymore."

Another way to get out of the In-Between is to drink some orange juice. For some reason, orange juice helps snap you out once your body starts to metabolize it. Don't think that you will come out instantly after you drink it. It will take a few minutes. The problem is actually drinking the orange juice. You won't want to drink things. Things will take on a slightly unusual taste for you because everything switches in your sensory. If you drink orange juice or citrus, it tends to help bring you out of the In-Between. I think it has something to do with the Vitamin C. Another thing you can do is touch objects.

Right away, I could feel another slight shift because even thinking about the In-Between will shift you right into it once you know how to go there. Another way to get out of it is by just touching objects. When you think about your chi chakra below your belly button, it helps bring you out of it slowly. It is interesting because when I think about that, I feel the fluctuations. It feels literally like you are getting heavier and denser. When you are in that In-Between state, you don't think about your body but when you're popping out of the In-Between, you begin to feel the heaviness of your body. When you touch and feel things, it snaps you out of the In-Between.

If you know somebody who is In-Between and they want to come out of it, talk to them. Better yet, take them outside in the cold air. That will help shift them, too. I have been doing this for over twenty years and it is only recently that I started to teach more people. In the beginning, I really didn't know how to take people In-Between gently.

Dan and Frank can attest that I powered myself up in the In-Between and I took this spiraling energy and just pushed it into them. They felt themselves ramping up slowly but it was so intense for them. Over that twenty year period, I've learned to slowly gravitate people into it and be gentler in shifting their consciousness. I am sure that everybody is thinking they want to feel that extreme level.

When you have groups of people In-Between, you should try to keep an eye out for people who you think are just too deep or are in that zone too long. If you think they need to come out of it, just talk to them about their hair style, or ask them about their job. Or you can go for a walk in the park and get some fresh air. Remember, it's all in the details. Your mind will be fixated on very unusual things.

Often, when I look at the ground and see the cracks in the pavement, I shift In-Between because the pavement starts to take on a three dimensional lift to it almost. It reminds me of a mother of pearl being rubbed when it has that rainbow glow hazing over it. It is like the pavement, although not literally. It's very hard to explain because then everybody thinks that is what they should see. *Words cannot define the actual experience.* So, whatever I am telling you, only take it as a rule of thumb. Don't assume that what you see is not the correct thing. It probably is. There's a notching up effect. It is movement into that state of consciousness, so what you see is going to ramp up in levels. I may be ramping up faster so I may see something in a different way than you. When you're entering the In-Between, you're probably just doing it a little more slowly because you are adjusting to it. You just get absorbed into detail, the dips and curves, the feel of the fabric, and the textures. *You feel everything.* I'd like to ask for some people who feel comfortable explaining their personal experiences with the In-Between so we can get it from a different perspective.

In Hawaii in 2009, one of the coaches shifted us and told us to hold it during lunch. I started to feel the effects of the In-Between in line, but I didn't know what it was. I just thought I was shifting really hard. I was just really quiet, holding non-thought. Once I got onto it, I could keep my head clear, hold it and almost ride it. Once I got up to the food, I said, "I will take that, that, and that." I had this big plate of food and I walked back to sit down. I was listening and everyone just sounded like one tone. My food was just like textures in my mouth. I was chewing and swallowing and it wasn't fun to eat but I just knew that I had to, to fill my body with sustenance. I stayed in it for a while and just dumped the rest of my food in the garbage and decided to go on a little walk. Then I bumped into a guy named Bob. When I started talking to him, he slipped me out of it a little bit.

You won't like Red Cells. They will be very annoying to you. They will be like, "Hey, how you doing?" And you'll be like, "Leave me alone!"

We talked for awhile and he was explaining something to me and I was still shifted, but I wasn't as deep as when I was at lunch and then I was slowly getting out of it towards the end of the day and it was like having a different sort of hangover. Of course, I tried hallucinogens in the past so it wasn't that big of a deal.

When you heard talk of the In-Between, did you ever think, "I don't know if I could do that," or "I don't think that is ever going to be able to happen to me."

I figured I could do it because when I got the In-Between class last year, I tried it out but the cat screwed me up and I never got there.

That's funny. It's very interesting because I have my pets for that reason. Sometimes, when I am by myself all the time I will go into the In-Between too much. When you have a pet, they tend to ground you out and keep you in that zone. If you have a pet or other things that are going to distract you, it's very hard to stay In-Between. You almost want to extract yourself from them. When they are around, it's almost impossible to go into that state. When I go In-Between, my dog freaks out. He'll come over and start bumping into me and rubbing on me and I'll say, "Alright, go away." Pets know that something is going on so they want to bring you back to where they're at so they can relate to you. Pets can sense that state of mind. It is very interesting. Anybody else want to talk about their In-Between experience?

Steve?

One of the most memorable times for me was when we were at the Mexico retreat. A lot of people shifted In-Between during a class so I ended up spending the whole day in the In-Between state. Later that night, I finally got out of the In-Between. I didn't want to walk past people in the In-Between because they were like a black hole that grabbed you and pulled you In-Between. It was only the second day of the retreat and I thought, "If I go In-Between, I will be so burned out that I won't make it through the week." I got to the point where I couldn't even look at people who were In-Between.

When someone who was In-Between walked up to me, I had to pick my feet up off the floor. Just being on the same floor that they were on pulled me back into that state. After 12 hours of being there, I was so completely burned out, I just had nothing left. It was like, "Oh, don't make me go back there."

Yes! Exactly. It's almost like you are afraid to go there. If you spot anybody who is In-Between, you just want to run away. There is something that puts you into that state of consciousness. It is very powerful, but it is exhausting, so after a while you just want to get grounded. It can be very consuming. After you learn to tap into it, there'll be a part of you that is almost a little afraid of it. There will be another part of you that will want it. So it is very interesting.

Are you consuming Prana in the In-Between state? Is that what exhausts you?

Your physical body cannot cope with the amount of data that you're absorbing. It's using facilities that just weren't necessarily designed to do that. Your brain has to interpret everything for you while you're in this state of mind. The data is so overwhelming, so unique, and so potent that it is a major process for your brain to have to chew on it. I honestly think that you are using more of your dimensional consciousness, your true consciousness, than you are using your organic brain.

One of the interesting things about being In-Between is that you have almost zero thought. There is no talking. You know how hard it is to meditate without thought and here you are for an hour, two hours, or even three hours doing these huge leaps with nothing in your head. Yet you are fully aware, thinking, and functional. It is from a whole different level, but I can feel it like a pressure in my temples and my skull. It's like there is this different arch inside of it that somehow forces it to communicate still, but you literally achieve non-thought. You literally function on a higher state of consciousness, in my opinion.

All of your sensory and all of those psychic abilities kick in and you almost have the desire to do one of those things in order to function with it. It takes time for you to learn to balance all of those things just like walking, talking, or anything else. It can be overwhelming at first. As you play around with it, you get to stay in that state of mind longer and do more interesting things because it is not as exhausting. The first few times can be very exhausting. I am going back and forth right now to explain where

I am so you can recognize it. You can sense the shifts when I go higher or lower. There should be a sense that there is something a little odd or unusual going on.

It's very important that you get as much data as possible before I start pushing those of you who haven't been in the In-Between. In fact, my consciousness is already playing with you a little bit. I am trying to get you tempered somewhat before we push for the deeper levels. My goal is not only to be In-Between here, but to take you In-Between and have you go out and engage with entities. Do you understand how unique that is? You will use all the skills you've learned, and you'll find that they operate at a much more intensive level when you are in an In-Between state. It should be very interesting.

If you even think about an In-Between experience, it's difficult. You're going to understand after a while. When you think about it, your mind just goes there. The hard part is getting there the first time. If you have found it once, it is easy to find it twice, but the first time is the hardest.

We're talking about it now so that you know what might happen when you go In-Between. It's very important that I take the time to give you information because if you can't walk, all of a sudden, you're going to get freaked out. She had that experience where she couldn't walk but she is walking and talking now. When you're in that state, it can be overwhelming. Once you know what can happen, you can get past the fear because you know it's going to pass. You instantly get your motor gears back faster. Or you may need a little while because your mind is so absorbed with other stuff. It's important to have these conversations. It's important to have people who have been In-Between who can say, "I've been In-Between. I had this experience. I've come back. I'm normal again. Don't worry. Don't panic. If you go there, don't have a meltdown. You'll be fine later on." You can snap out of it. If it is too intense for you, you can snap out of it. It's like being drunk when you want to be sober. You know you have to take a while to come out of it and just deal with it. If you're really concerned whether you are prepared for this or not and you don't want to do this, then you should not participate.

When you go In-Between, I want you to also be careful with getting up and moving right away. Play around with it. Take your time. You're going to still be cognitive. It's just like another bubble of consciousness. You're still going to be yourself, but you're going to be able to sense things on a much higher level. There is no way to fully explain it until you've done it. You should be careful because when your goal is to not only go In-Between but to go into and explore a paranormal environment in that state, you're are going to be in positions that are unique versus being at home. You have to know what your limitations are. You need to know your boundaries.

If you're new to the In-Between, maybe you should explore with someone who has been In-Between before. For me, it's not that big of a deal. I've been doing it since I was a child. I have to put myself in another person's shoes who has never been In-Between before. That's why I have to exercise some caution. That's the reason why we have all this so that you understand what you're getting involved in, what could take place, what you should be concerned about and what you should not concerned about.

The reason why we chose New Orleans for this event is because when you're In-Between, everything takes on a very unique position. New Orleans is probably one of the most unique places in the United States, whether it's the colors they chose or the structures. More importantly, it's one of the last places where the consciousness of the people is a little bit different because of the languages, dialect, and the culture that's still blended here.

I have found out from travelling across the United States that it's all been homogenized. New Orleans is one of the last pockets that I'm aware of that still has that unique diversity. One of the things about going In-Between is that you definitely want to be in a place that is uniquely different. It adds to the amount of experiences that you can have, versus a place where not many things are going to stand out for you.

The people who live in New Orleans have a slight disadvantage because they've done a lot more tagging since it is their environment. Their mind has associated things that are this way, and things that are that way. This has solidified as a reality for them. For the people where this is new, everything has a different smell, sound or dialect. It leaves room for the mind to try to define those things. If you can do that in an In-Between state of mind, your experiences are probably going to be a little bit richer in a way because you haven't a set structure for your mind to relate to it. If there is something unique there beyond what you would normally see, it may likely tend to come out more. That's one of the reasons.

This is something that I think you will find exciting, assuming that everybody accepts that I'm an enlightened being. The opportunity to meet somebody like me is a billion to one. I have come forward to let people know what I am and the things that I can do, but even more so I am breaking all the rules by showing others how they can get to this place. *I am not the only unique person that's like this. All of you have the same ability that I have.* That is true.

There are others. Some people call them vampires. Some people call them immortals. Some people call them ancients. There also may be aliens that appear to look like humans that are visiting us. It's a stretch to talk this up because nobody wants to talk about something way out in left field. I'd like to think that I have given you a solid footing to look at this more sensibly and logically. These beings are not unicorns and fairies. There are unique people that coexist with us, mostly to study society. Nine times out of ten, they could be aliens. It is like having a foreigner who looks like an American until they speak. These people again seem to be attracted to places where they are not necessarily going to stand out so much. It's the same thing that I pointed out about Playa del Carmen in Mexico. If you're going to go somewhere, you are going to stand out if you're a bit different. People are going to pick up on that, so you want to go to a place where there is such a uniqueness that the people have become accustomed to that. Even though something or someone stands out now, you're used to it.

Whereas, if you are some place where everybody has a similar vibe and everything is very homogenized, and someone very different comes into town, they definitely stand out. Then you observe them much more than the norm. When these beings try to move into societies, they choose locations that have very unique diversity so that they don't stand out in the collective of that environment. One of those places is New Orleans.

Tim, tell them about the couple in Portland you came across.

I was living in downtown Portland right next door to a convenience store. One night around 11:30 I was walking to the convenience store and I saw an SUV with a really big antenna on it. It was like those CB antennas, going about ten feet high, so it looked weird. In the vehicle, I saw this couple who immediately stood out. Some people are going to stand out obviously, psychologically. This African-American couple had to be in their late 70s or 80s. They were all decked out in a Mardi Gras look with shiny glass beads. They looked like they had done a lot of traveling. What was up with the CB radio? No one has that setup if they're not on the road all the time talking to truckers while they are doing their thing. They had these big glasses on that looked like they might have been sunglasses, Mardi Gras beads, and neon colored jump suits. Just none of it fit at all.

When you come to a place like New Orleans and you see some of the cultural diversity where some of the things don't blend in quite the same, you have to ask yourself, "Is there a tag that you can associate with that? What are these people about?" Whether they were extremely unique or not, it is very hard to say. They did not fit the profile. They did not fit the consciousness whatsoever of the area.

If they were in New Orleans, I don't think people would have given them a second look because they wouldn't have stood out at all. If they're outside of a region like that, they are going to stand out. Who's to say they weren't space aliens who were dressing so that they would blend in? In their minds, they look like one of us but in reality we're thinking, "Oh my God! They have to be from New Orleans." In either case, any intelligent being knows that they don't want to stand out. They should go to a place where they can assimilate society before they start moving outwards - a place where there is less likelihood of standing out. They're going to look for a place of uniqueness such as New Orleans. There is a higher likelihood of running into unique persons in New Orleans than there is elsewhere.

Now, the second reason I'm bringing this up is because when you are In-Between, your awareness for detail is absolutely shocking. I think sometimes about a movie where there is a vampire and he is tied up. And the comic relief guy is trying to come up with ways to stall this vampire if it gets loose. He takes all these marbles and he throws them on the floor and he says something like, "Well, vampires have a compulsive need to count. They have to count everything." He thinks that if he throws all these marbles that the vampire is going to have to go 1, 2, 3, 4, 5, 6, 7, 8. Therefore the guy has time to leave because the vampire can't come after him to eat him because the vampire has to count to find out the number of marbles because it's a compulsion. In the end of the movie, the guy goes, "Wait, you can't get me. You have to count the marbles." The vampire goes, "3492," and the vampire goes after him. Putting all humor aside, when you are in a higher state of consciousness, your mind is aware of so many things. You may not know the specific number but if you move your mind that way, I believe you would be able to get that flow and the brain would just pull that number out.

When you are in an In-Between state, unique beings that are trying to move among us are going to stand out. There's going to be something you instantly pick up on them. You're going to know they look human, but there is something not right about them. You are going to know there's something unearthly about them or there's a different kind of vibration. You have to be prepared for that. My suggestion is that if you do have something like that happen, you can't just go up to somebody and say, "You're an alien! I know it!" You know you can't. You've got to keep control of your senses. If you're wrong, they're going to put you in a loony bin. Ten to one, that person is incognito and they are not going to say, "You've got me!"

The Hunt is not just about finding entities. That is really the least of it. The Hunt is about finding unique beings and unique things. My concern has always been that if I take students with me, how much self-discipline will they have? Are they going to act like buffoons if they see something absolutely unique? Or are they going to be Rico Suave? I just don't think they're going to keep it under control. Every time I bring my students out somewhere and they watch what I look at, especially if they know that I'm in that space, they will see me look. I have learned now to divert my eyes because I know that if I give something two seconds too much attention, they are on it. I'm trying to be really cool. So I am watching, doing my thing. I'm scanning and there's my students just standing there staring at something. That's frustrating because you've got to be cool. You can't let people know the gig is up because they are just going to take off and you are not going to be able to approach them.

In the end, I think you are hoping that everybody who wants to approach you is willing to engage you. If you are going to be the freak that's staring them down, do you honestly think that they want to have a conversation with you? They are going to play dumb and pretend you don't know what you're talking about. They are just going to go off because they are afraid you are going to expose them to everybody else. Being cool takes practice. Of course, if you've experienced a lot of stuff then you're not so excited when you see unusual things.

I remember when Jamison and I were out in Las Vegas eating at this one casino. I said to him, "Gee, there's an alien here." I just bumped into him and we looked at each other and he said, "Hey! I'm cool. You're cool." Jamison asked, "Where is this alien?" I said, "I don't know where he's gone. He must have taken off." I thought to myself, "This guy must have jammed the mental frequency because I just wasn't interested anymore." I was thinking, "Hey, this can't happen to me," but that it did, so there you go. I got sloppy and careless. If I take an interest, I'll track it but I wasn't that interested. I thought to myself, "Gee, there are an awful lot of aliens in Vegas." Do they like to gamble? I do believe that there is an interesting amount of extraterrestrial beings that tend to migrate there and I don't think it has anything to do with *Area 51*, the military, or anything like that. I don't know. Sometimes I think it's a specific species and I think that the climate is ideal for them, like wherever they come from might be dry and arid. Ironically, I think they like a lot of smoke for some reason.

Is the casino a good place or are there other places in Las Vegas?

I don't know. All I know is that I've run into them on a few occasions. I run into them more in Vegas than anywhere else. Take it for what it is.

Do we stand out to them? Do they notice us?

Nine times out of ten, they will notice right away because you aren't that slick yet. If you can control your body and your emotions, ten to one you can fly under the radar, but you are so excited that you think you have spotted something. It's like shouting at them. *They can feel you.* Think of it differently. When I was In-Between, you were starting to shift a little bit. You can tell I've come down quite a bit now. Just the fact that I thought of the In-Between, I have to hold it down now! You can feel it from me. How did you know? Obviously, I was probably acting different but you had to feel that. It is such a strong vibration. They will feel it that intensely as soon as you spot them. You've got to really keep a lot of control over that feeling or that vibration. You have got to be like a cat. When my cat did something, then I knew he'd want attention from me.

There is a way of diverting all that. You've got to play with that and you need to control how you react. One of the things is this. This week while you are in New Orleans, *you* are the most extraordinary and unique people in this whole city spiritually speaking. That's not to say that there are not some unusual beings here.

As a whole, you are going to be what other people are coming here for, like ghosts and spirits. Don't tell me if you guys are In-Between walking around town that there aren't going to be people thinking or saying, "What the heck is it with these people? My God, Henry, there is a strange vibe. I can feel it from them in my crystal." They are going to feel that from you because you are going to be so in tune. It is going to be hard for you to fly under the radar. Now, other people who aren't sensitive are probably not going to pay any attention to you. You cannot be concerned about other people picking up on you. You can't give it a second thought because if you do, you are in this really intense place so it's like somebody pushing you over. Or a spinning top standing still. It looks like it's still but it is spiraling, and if something touches you, you just can't care. What are they going to do?

The other interesting thing is that there is so much drug use and drinking in this particular area that a lot of the people will think, "It is just a local." In that sense, it's good that you can intermingle and maybe not really stand out too much. I think some of the visitors who are here to do the ghost hunts may have that ability or sensory. They are going to pick up on you, so you need to just be chill. If you get approached, it might be interesting to put the shoe on the other foot now and say, "Excuse me. I don't know how to say this but I do psychic work and I just felt there was something very unusual about you but I didn't know how to approach you. I don't know how you feel about that, but are you into spiritual things?"

Do you see how you would react to it? Do you really want to talk to them? Remember how I was In-Between. Are you going to want to talk? You're probably going to say, "Now's not a good time for me."

Think about it. You may be approached because you are so heavily shifted from looking at textures or feeling things. There are other unique things happening. If you spot somebody, how do you approach them? How do you engage that conversation with them? The best thing for you to do is just to be chill. There is some level of eye contact that happens. If they want to engage with you, they will give you a nod, or they will go, "Hey." That is their way of saying, "I'm approachable." If they don't, you just have to accept the fact that you don't get to say, "Hey, show me your teeth. Come on, I know you've got something in there."

You are going to be the unique one now. When there's thirty of us walking around a one square mile area, there's going to be a weird vibe. If I come in and you feel a weird vibe, can you imagine all of us affecting whatever environment we are in? It's going to have a strange vibe, a different sensation. I think that unusual things will likely occur to the people. It will be like there's some strange energy going on. As far as anyone is concerned, you are going to be the aliens who are visiting. As far as they're concerned, you are going to be the strange vibration that entered this environment. You need to be prepared for how you might want to deal with that. You should be aware that it's possible so don't let it affect you too much one way or the other.

The next thing about being In-Between that I want to bring up is that reality changes dramatically when you are in that state of mind. Reality is going to change for you. The supernatural world is hidden. You don't see ghosts and spirits every day. You don't see shadow things moving around every day. When people see these things for five seconds, I think it's because they shift to the In-Between, get a view and then come back. They just don't know that happened to them. When you are In-Between, you are so hypersensitive.

It's very hard for me to explain but reality changes. It's as if physics changes. You may walk up to a wall right now that seems like a wall. If you look very close, you might see a dark shade here, a lighter shade there, and then even lighter. A normal person wouldn't be able to notice the three different shades. When you're in the In-Between state of consciousness, something as simple as three lines can somehow shift your consciousness in a way that the lines become three dimensional. It's as if reality has changed that much, and literally it does. If there's a light shining there, you could see the bends and it could become very hot to touch even though right now it's cold.

Now, one might ask, "How do you know that you're not inducing your brain to a level of hypnosis and it's altering your consciousness? How do you know that you're not getting the brain to over-create psychoactive drugs within the brain?" I would say that all of the above is true. All of the above is happening. Then what is your reality based upon? It is based upon a set determined amount of those same chemicals that the brain produces, and it gives you this perception because that is the said frequency that is determined for you. If you could see reality but your consciousness is altered, which one becomes the norm? *Which one becomes the true reality?* That is something that you need to think about.

When you're In-Between, there are dynamics that are very interesting. For instance, when I was with Kerri and Eric, we went to a coffee shop after we attended a lecture in LA. I was very much in the In-Between. I had a glass of iced tea so, right in front of everybody, I tore the packet of sugar and poured it into my glass of iced tea and stirred it. When I went to pick up the glass, there was a neat pile of sugar underneath the bottom of the glass. This happened from an In-Between state of consciousness. I changed reality. *When you're in an In-Between state of mind, you can change reality.* The only thing that prevents you from changing reality is the set laws of how you accept reality, what is possible and what's not. The point is that neither Kerri nor Eric were In-Between and I changed reality.

Kerri and Eric weren't In-Between; they were in this dimension in that state of consciousness and they witnessed what took place. It was a real occurrence that happened in the In-Between state of mind. For me, it was completely feasible and logical. There wasn't a doubt in my mind that it could occur. In my mind, I poured the sugar and saw it go down and I just envisioned it going all the way down, but because I did that it literally went *all* the way down. I wasn't thinking about it dissolving. I just finished the thought of pouring it and letting it continue down to the bottom. I knew it was going to sink and I knew I had to stir it up. Because my mind shifted reality, it literally went right through the glass. It continued the thought rather than stopping in this reality at the bottom of the glass. In a shifted state of consciousness or the In-Between state, that made perfect logic for it to continue passing through like it did. I was like, "Oh shoot! I should have stopped it at the bottom of the glass instead of letting it go all the way through." That will make more sense to you when you are In-Between.

Is your brain altered? Perhaps, then how come it isn't an illusion? *Clearly it is not fully an illusion, because it can manifest into this dimension.* Every single thing that I have ever done where I have affected reality has been from an extreme shifted state of consciousness. It's even more interesting to see how easy it is to ground yourself out by interaction. If you think of anything you have done psychically or spiritually, once you experience the In-Between I bet you will recognize that you were in some state of being In-Between when it happened. Then you came out of it.

When scientists conduct studies on people who normally can do psychic stuff, all of a sudden they can't perform because they have trouble going into that In-Between state of mind. They are observing too much, so they are grounded. I think therein it lies an answer to observation. In the Double Slit Experiment, as long as you're looking at a particle or recording it, it can't split into two. As soon as you block it from your view, it will do it. As long as you are observing it, it stops happening. I believe this is what holds true. This is the bleed over from reality. This is how the program functions.

So when you are In-Between, you have a much higher level of observing that which is hidden. If there is a portal in a room, you have a greater possibility of seeing that portal. You are more aware of it. All of a sudden, you may look and you may say there is a very shaded square there. It's transparent; it almost looks like there's nothing there but you see a square. It looks like the tone right here, or the tone over there, which most of you may not even see. When I'm slightly shifted, I can see a band of shading going up. To me, it is very distinct. It is just floating in the air. If you go to touch it, you'll feel a spongy tingling moving through your arm.

To an ordinary person, that could be an illusion or it could be very real just like the iced tea. I believe that would be the portal that allows shadow beings to move from one place to the other. There is always a place for these consciousnesses to come and go. You are able to move into those states more easily. You may be walking and look at the ground and you see shadow overlaying shadow. You'll see it lift and you will think, "That is not normal! What just happened? What was that?" You are likely to see entities more so than in a normal state of mind.

When you do In-Between stuff, one of the things that is very interesting is light. I have been watching the lighting here. I don't know if it is me. This is where you can mess with somebody that's In-Between. It's like you're on drugs. You can affect light. Maybe it's because dilated pupils take in more light. You can make rooms much brighter and then bring the light down. If you focus on it, you can do it. Then other people will have that experience. They don't know you're doing it but if you ask them, "Did you notice anything?" They will say, "Yeah, the light just started illuminating in here."

Would you recommend wearing glasses or not wearing them?

I used to wear glasses. I don't recall it having an effect on me one way or the other so I would say probably not. I think that when you start to go In-Between that you can just take them off and hold them in your hand and put them back on. Once you're there, it shouldn't have an effect one way or the other. Being In-Between is very potent. Once you get there, you could pop out and then you are mad because you want to pop back in, but you should be able to do it fairly easily.

If the temperature is very cold outside, is it going to pull us out once we get into that In-Between state?

Well, I was experimenting outside on myself so I could decide how it's going to affect you. I found that it didn't hinder me too much. At first, I thought that it would, but it's sometimes very hard for me to decide how it's going to affect you because I am so adept at it. I am probably more disciplined, but I thought it might shift me out because it is like somebody jarring you around. It's cold so it's definitely very grounding, but I just looked at the pavement and it did its three-dimensional effect on me and that put me where I needed to be. I did find it hampered it but as soon as I went in, it just hit me full flush again. It's just waiting to come on strongly again. As you are playing around, even at this point, you should be fine with it.

Do the insights that you glean while you are in the In-Between conflict with insights that you glean while you are in a sober state?

That's a good question and it is a yes and no answer. When you're In-Between, things take on a new meaning. Your whole thinking process is alien, but it makes perfect logic. When you're In-Between, the strangest things will start to happen. Very surreal things start to happen. Reality starts to change. I would not be surprised how the unusualness will continue to happen, but I've listened to whole pieces of music In-Between when there's been nothing there. That's why you can almost get schizophrenic. You've got to calm down and just relax. It may or may not be. Don't search for meaning in everything. Just go for the ride and admire it like flowers on the side of the road. It's interesting and beautiful. Just wait until you're done to analyze it. If you analyze it too much, you'll miss the experience. It snaps you out. Just flow with what it's trying to allow you to experience.

In the In-Between, your thoughts are completely alien to your normal way of thinking. When I teach, I've gotten very adept at being In-Between to certain levels. It is extremely difficult when you specifically go In-Between to talk about the In-Between and then try to explain it. For instance, I often stutter when I teach because I'm translating. I'm trying to find words to explain and teach what I understand. I think my teachings are rather profound. I think I'm very good at taking something that other people just can't teach and translate it so that you can understand. That is literally the key. If you understand another language, you'll find that there are certain words or expressions in one language that do not translate well into the other language. You wonder how you can explain it. There's not a *word* for that in this language or there's not a *word* for it in that language. So, it's the same thing. I am trying to take this very high state of consciousness and explain to you in terminology that you understand.

At times, the information also moves; it swims and things take on texture. Sound is alive. The knowledge is alive. In this state of mind, it doesn't make much sense, but in the In-Between state of mind, it makes perfect logic. It is like taking an alien language and trying to explain it in words that you can relate to. It's not just trying to take Italian or French to make it into English. It is literally taking another dimensional language, outside of human guttural and human definition for structure and mass, and trying to bridge the two to communicate them. The stuttering happens when I'm struggling to find a way to explain it. If you'll notice, much of my teaching is in metaphors. I'll use explanations like how a tree will feel waxy and cool, but it's a living thing and you will understand. I'm constantly searching for ways to explain something to you. Also, I'm constantly broadcasting telepathically as long as you are with me. I'm always trying to give imagery to your minds while also deciding what I can use for words. I think that is what helps also.

How relevant are your experiences to the state of consciousness you are in? You can take a great deal of it with you depending on how much you can translate it to apply to here. When you go into deeper spiritual states of consciousness and you go into these other planes of existence, you have to work with the human body. So, as much as the mind can understand from that place, it helps you to get back there faster.

It's not as alien anymore. It starts to understand it, and the more that can happen, the more your mind operates on those two levels simultaneously and it becomes like a third. It's a hard question to answer. It is all relevant. Let me explain it differently. You can use the White Fire class to heal, but if you can go into an In-Between state of consciousness and you can learn to operate from that state of mind, the profound level of what you can affect is a lot more intense if you are going to heal somebody. The difference is that when you start thinking about it, you look at stuff differently.

In one of the science shows that I like to watch, I saw people whose brains were hooked up in a slightly different way. They say that they see colors for certain words. Other people can hear words and taste the flavor in their mouth. Those words will always taste a specific way. Or certain words will have that specific color in their head if they hear it. They don't necessarily see the color in their mind. They acknowledge it as the color. It is like an internal knowing. You may be throwing your brain off gear but there's definitely something extremely unique to it. When you heal, there are certain things that I can teach you to have a good effect.

When you're In-Between, an illness can feel like a piece of rubber. A tumor tastes and looks like liver to me. It's like a little, black rubbery thing that I can feel inside a person. Again, it's like how the sugar went through the glass. You perceive differently so you can operate differently. Since I can understand that, I may not be able to use that in a practical way in the conscious state. If I want to go in that In-Between state of mind, I know exactly what I need to do or where to go because I have been there to operate from In-Between to get around that.

I would say to somebody, "Take the liver flavor and switch it with the feel of lavender flowers." Now that always seems odd but that's a healthier healing frequency and I believe the body understands that. It's a weird way of communicating. I've always said that if you want to make something happen there, do something over here and it'll connect. It's this weird system but it makes perfect sense when you are in that other state of consciousness.

I think people don't fully realize that I need to go In-Between to do this. It's like juggling and trying to wash your foot. It seems weird and I would say just going to the one and the other one will happen from intent. When you ask if certain things can be used in a practical way, I'd say yes and no. I feel everything that I see because of being In-Between.

At certain points, I'm more like you and other times I feel like I'm more in this other state of consciousness. When I am in an ordinary state of mind, my unique intelligence still has an understanding that everything has a taste and a flavor, not just by the color that you see. This room feels different to me than it would to some other people. Some people wonder how I have such a good idea of feng shui. Or why I am the 'Renaissance man'. Choosing things is like tasting a salad. In an In-Between state, this room is like a salad. It's got olive colors which made my mind think of olive, but there is a different mechanism for how your brain puts it all together. It just makes sense. You know what you want in a salad. I don't think you're going to put pickles in your salad even though it's a vegetable. You might want to put cucumbers and normal stuff in there, but you might put lima beans in. I'll put some garbanzo beans in there or something. You feel it when it is happening. When you're not In-Between, you do have a relationship with reality that is more real, in my opinion, than when you are a Red Cell and you are just functioning here. Everything has its practical place. I think that you have a utilization of that knowledge without realizing you are doing it. I hope so.

When you start moving In-Between more often, it seems like there's a gradient where you move towards being in lower levels of the In-Between more often. Once you know something, you can't unknow it.

When you know something you can't unknow it; that's right. Think about that. Once you know something, you can't unknow it. I say that often. Now you should know where that comes from. Let me explain something a little bit differently. Every time you go In-Between, you can go to 100. You can even go to 1000 In-Between. You can go so deep In-Between that you can see the molecular structure of a wall vividly. You can actually see stuff live and die in front of your eyes, depending on how deep you go. Now I don't want to talk about that level of deep because that's not appropriate for where you need to explore at this point, but you can go that intensely deep.

When you go In-Between, what you experience you can't necessarily unknow. It's just that on a normal level your brain can't translate it into a useful format. It changes your intellect and your vision by a percent each time more intensely. You definitely are not the same person you used to be. You are more articulate, more visual, and more sensual in your mind. Something has changed. Something has enriched you each time you journey there and you come back.

In the Brazilian jungle, certain people use the hallucinogen, Ayahuasca. In fact, the tribal people will give a little bit of Ayahuasca to newborn babies so that it shifts their consciousness. They say that it enriches their mind. In a sense, you could say that makes them a little bit unique because that exposure changes the perspective of how they see things. When you go In-Between, it changes the perspective of how you see things in the same way, if not more so. I do believe that everything happens in a flow. You can be much more spiritually in tune. Then you could hit a lower tone which is more like a Red Cell. Then you can go up. The difference is, "What Is your peak?"

I think this whole piece is natural. I think that it is normal to move through these peaks and lows in your consciousness throughout your life. Sometimes you feel spiritually high. Sometimes you feel down. Sometimes you're not connecting with your meditations. Other times, you really like where you are at for a week or a month. These peaks are decided by how much exploration you have pushed yourself to, and then it becomes this higher point. The more exploration that you can push or that your consciousness can endure, that is how far or how deep you can go until you reach this enlightenment level. You become a duality that coexists in all of them; but that is the state that either you're there or you're not there.

Is the In-Between a way to enlightenment?

Yes, I do think it's the way to enlightenment. There is such a variety. I remember one time that I was discussing the In-Between, and shifting consciousness and I drew this big branch of trees with the different directions you could go with your consciousness. I can remember filling this whole wall up with this branch of where your mind can go In-Between. You don't just go In-Between. You can go In-Between, and meditate, and go into hyper dimension. You can meditate and use it to heal. You can go In-Between and use it to go into a state of scanning. You can go In-Between and it leads to all these diversifications of what you can utilize it for. Nonetheless, it is a state of higher consciousness. When you go In-Between, you are in an enlightened state. It's just how well you can operate from that place.

A person who goes In-Between has got to be a White Cell because I just don't think you can get it otherwise. Now if you have trouble with it, don't think that you're not a White Cell because sometimes it can be difficult to put your finger on it.

When you're there, you move in a different place for whatever you are doing. When I came in, I was In-Between but it felt so foreign. That's what gives you this euphoria because it's not made to be here. You're made to do something else with it. It's more of what you're like and how you think when you're not in your body. It's closer to that.

If I go In-Between and I think of my heart chakra, I go to such a blissful place that it is almost painful to come back here. It's such a beautiful state of mind. There are just no words that can describe it. It's just like being held in the womb of God, if that makes sense. You can move to a different place just by your intent.

Being In-Between is a way of going into enlightenment or moving into a state of enlightenment. When I say that you dip back and forth, this is the most grounded out you could be on a day-to-day basis. You can go into these peaks where you feel spiritual. Once you get up to a certain point, it drops but you are always in a state of consciousness. That's where I am. Even though I'm down here, I'm still in this higher state at the same time. It's just how intense I want to bring it forward, or how withdrawn I have to be to deal with everyday life. For me, I'm constantly at this point. You are working to get to this point where you just stay there. To me, it's definitely a process, or a movement into enlightenment.

At that point, are miracles driven by your intention?

Yes, exactly. You see things and you feel things extremely differently. There was a group of my students who observed me walk through a physical wall. I went into an altered state of consciousness, basically In-Between, and I just simply perceived the wall as being like fog. I wanted to move through the fog like swimming into water. I certainly could understand that it was a different structure but I perceived it in my heart center miracle-wise, if that is what you would call it, like moving or diving into water. I was standing and walking in, rather than diving in. That is how I allowed my physical body to work with the experience. It simply changed the dimensions of reality. So, absolutely, miracles are driven by your intent.

If you can learn to operate when you're In-Between, that is where the miracles take place. That is where the yogis of the ages went. If you go In-Between, don't think about doing a miracle. You can't think about doing it because if you do, it won't happen. You have to think with this other state of consciousness in order to do it. I think you are starting to understand that. This is why you've got to play around with it constantly. The more that you do it, the more durable you become.

When we were younger, I used to drive to places with Dan and he got so in tune with me that he could see me shift and he'd say, "You are moving In-Between now." He could feel it. If you go back to anything that you or other people see me do spiritually, you'll know when I'm in that place. You can feel it. You have to be in that place to do those things. If Moses parted the Red Sea, he was in one hell of an In-Between state of consciousness. Rest assured. I don't know if other gurus call it In-Between, but even their smaller miracles are done from that state of consciousness. That is how they do what they do. Most people see them as just a human being. They can't feel that shift that another White Cell can feel. Others can feel it but they just don't understand what it is. They know that this is some very intense spiritual vibe from this person. That is the In-Between energy. That is the shift of consciousness that they are in. That is the place where you operate from to do miracles. When I play with the weather, or when I do other profound things, it's from that In-Between place. If I scan a house, I don't even acknowledge that I'm In-Between. It's just a thing that I go to. I know that I'm there but I don't think about it, no more than you think to check in with yourself sitting in a chair. It's just a reaction and then you go there. With all due respect, I think that most spiritual people go there but they don't know how to explain the In-Between. They just say, "Well, I'm in this place," and they reached this state of mind. No, you literally move into the In-Between; that's what it is.

If you want a conscious communion with God, would that be like going into the In-Between and into your heart chakra?

Well, the heart chakra is that perfect pitch. We assimilate it with love. There's the intent that is made from this dimension, that heart love, so it helps to create. Some people will tap a singing bowl once and get it to kick in that way. It's a little harder if you do it from a dry rub, but you can get there also. Since you think of the heart chakra as this loving place, it's that ting. It helps build momentum for you when you know what direction you are trying to pulsate into. It just keeps amplifying. It's not that you have to think about it; it's just helpful to get there from this place.

The heart chakra also creates a blissful feeling when you meditate. Ironically, it is the same place. Maybe that's where the concept came from because it really does that. You enter from this place. In fact, that is a great interpretation. Whenever you are In-Between, whatever you want to do, and which chakra you work from is like 'gonging' so that you can head in that direction. That becomes the tree limbs you want to achieve.

When you're In-Between a long time, your body starts to feel very strange to you and you can get cold sweats, too. They come and go. If I do something psychic, I'll get cold sweats but I don't acknowledge myself as being In-Between because I'm not thinking about where I am operating from. I'm just doing. That's where I am doing it from. It's funny how all those things kick in.

Would you take someone who is sick In-Between to work on them?

Well, it's extremely difficult when the body is ill or sick to even go there. It depends on the sickness. If they have cancer, or tumors, it's an excellent place to operate from. On the same token, you have to be very careful. You have to ask yourself, "If they're going In-Between, do they have the discipline to navigate correctly?" If they are going to dwell upon the negative, they can make the negative more compounded.

When I put out the In-Between CD, I heard that people were playing around with it. One person said, "I can't get out of the In-Between. I just wanted to stop and I can't get it to stop." They let their mind go to this place and then that is what perpetuates it. It's like a speaker echo that goes boom, but now it goes bob

bob bob bob. It's out-of-control. I think someone who has the other HBI programs, as well as discipline, that this would be a marvelous place to work from. However, it is not easy. If it was easy, everybody would do it every single day. It is hard! To go In-Between, you are so overwhelmed with this other state of consciousness, that it is very hard to even think about your organic body. *It certainly can be done, and it certainly would be good for the right person, but it is not necessarily right for the wrong person.* It depends on who they are. If you are the right person, you can certainly operate from that place. Make sure that you have a good flight plan put together, because that is going to help stabilize your stay and keep you from wobbling out of control when you're going In-Between.

What about self-healing from that place rather than having somebody else heal you from that place?

Well, I would say that it can happen, but differently. When I used the In-Between to heal certain things for myself once, something very interesting happened. I guess that's why I call healing the *White Fire.* I can get so burning hot; I just get drenched. It's like I'm burning the center point of whatever illness I'm trying to work on right out of me. There is an accelerated cellular process happening and I wouldn't call it friction. Something is happening on a molecular level that creates the sensation of heat. I'm not sure if it's even real heat in the sense that if somebody touched you they could feel it. I would definitely focus on going In-Between; utilize that heat as much as you can tolerate it while centralizing it on the problem. I believe that it's changing the cellular structure. That's what creates this immense heat. Focus on the specific region of the problem with the intent of cellular restructuralization.

Would you incorporate a program of vigorous growth?

That's a different approach. When you're in an In-Between state, you've got to be careful. This is why there is so much need for conversation on this subject. You have to understand that things are a lot more intense. Once you set your mind to it, there is clarity in what you want to do. There is no babbling. There is no Governor. You are somehow able to bypass the biggest portion of it, so the plant life and everything would be great; but in truth, it would now become obsolete if you're in an In-Between state. If you're not in an In-Between state, focusing on using that burning or that intensity would not have that effect. If you want to have the best effect, think about what plant life and growth means health-wise. That's what is going to have that effect.

When you're In-Between, you literally can use the plant growth but you're going to start feeling hot. The plant is not just slowly growing. It is the rapid cellular reaction. Remember when I said I am very consistent even though I may sound inconsistent?

What did I say about time? Time is sometimes micro-compounded. What is one second here is like an hour of condensed packed information there. Electricity moves so fast it seems slower. *Sometimes to go fast you've got to move slower.* This is where these times come from. When I start talking In-Between, my perspective starts to change a bit because I'm in this high-speed power lane. I'm in a very powerful place. It's very hard to describe, but it is very empowering.

If your mind goes to pure velocity power, you'll feel it. You'll feel like you could just crush something with your mind. This is just one of those other branch-like places that you go to and it intertwines. That process will speed up, and it becomes this heating process. I believe I'm consistent. I just believe that they are two different intense zones. You have to play around with it so that you know these different regions. They will come very quickly if you play around with them. Most people don't have the stomach to do it all time.

Can you affect your DNA to re-pattern and program yourself?

Every time science throws some new breakthrough out to the normal community, it's the same thing. Science has said that vitamin C cures the common cold. We inject it and all this other stuff. People assume that if they eat twenty pounds of it, it's going to be more effective. Whether or not it works depends on how it's processed. It's different than how you would eat it. If you take more of something, that doesn't necessarily mean it's the right way to utilize it, or that it does what it was proven to do .

When science says that they figured something out, first they talk cellular and show us little pictures of cells. We can understand that. When you're talking DNA, you're getting down to these tiny, microscopic things. Now there's DNA within the DNA strand's coding. We understand it, but I think there is a dilution of understanding. When you communicate to heal your body, it's like talking to a child. You have to determine the age of the child and what you think they can understand. Your body understands a different language than what your intellectual mind understands.

When you think of DNA, you're thinking about healing a problem, whether it is the kidney, the liver or some other part of the body. You might say, "I'm working on my DNA. I see these little tiny things and I'm going to change them." Your body understands that you're really working something on a cellular level. It's maximum capacity when it gets down to micro and macro levels. You want to change something on an itty-bitty level. On its own, your body knows to change the DNA by default. When you start getting into the nitty-gritty language of telling it what to do, you lack the skill to describe the details of what it understands to do.

I think you need to apply the KISS principle, "Keep it simple stupid." In other words, *work with the desired intent that you want*. Don't get too specific because you don't understand the detail of what that DNA changing really requires. I believe that to heal certain ailments, there is an ecosystem of support. If you convert a tumor into something, you can work on the cells. If you work on the DNA to slow your aging, there are many factors that you are overlooking.

For instance, let's talk aging. There is more than one factor involved with aging, and it isn't necessarily DNA. DNA is one factor. DNA says, "This is the default process of events that are calculated to happen to you. You're either going to lose the elasticity in your skin faster, or your bones are going to deteriorate faster." It has these set rules, but it also governs how much the glands produce for that process to happen. It also governs other factors. Move that all aside, and science is still trying to figure out a lot of this.

Now I am not a scientist but as time progresses, the DNA chain links end up knowing when to let go of certain things. That is not necessarily your DNA that's telling these cells to do this. The cells have their own DNA longevity that works within your ecosystem. They work collectively on the whole. If you are centralizing your thoughts just on your DNA and you're saying, "This is what I'm telling you," you're not stopping all the other potential factors that contribute as a whole to govern the other aspects of your body.

Can you change a thought? Like the thoughts of a person who is depressed a lot? Or someone who's been trying to quit smoking and can't? Or a personality trait?

To me, all of those things start within the mind. The mind is the true Governor to all cellular life. I think there's a blueprint that runs things. We could say that it's the DNA. The DNA might be part of it, but it is also sociological and biochemical programming. It is also diet and other things. For depression, you can work with the mind.

Listen! The body has all of the programming in it. All you have to do is to create the *feels-like* and introduce that to it. It's like a book. It reads it, follows the directions, and mimics that if it overwhelms it. It's that simple. You don't have to overcomplicate it. If I talk to the DNA, it's going to be more effective. It's more important that you tell the body that *this is what you need*, and *this is the result that you want*. Be persistent in your broadcast. If that person says, "I just don't think that's going to work," they are resisting your efforts and filtering you out. That doesn't mean that you can't overpower them. It just means you have to broadcast a higher frequency, which is more work for you. Whoever is the loudest speaker is the one that is going to be heard to overwrite the program. Unfortunately, the person who you're trying to permeate is usually the loudest because it's for them. You're trying to affect their broadcasting.

If you're trying to do it yourself, there are many factors you have to consider. There is their belief system. In the end, you believe through observation. You're going to age. You are going to die. No matter how much you try to change that, your deeper subconscious isn't going to override that. You would really have to deeply brainwash your consciousness. You want to slow the process down and bring it to a grinding halt.

There are different methods that I have taught that you can start to do that. It almost takes a year of this practice to start to unwind and slow that process down. You can try to convince yourself all day long, but every day you walk by somebody who is a senior citizen, something in your deeper subconscious is saying, "Hey, this is your destiny!" You have got to find ways of meeting yourself halfway and find the terms to accept a few things. You want to stretch out the benefits of what you have rather than focusing too much on changing it because I think you're up against the wall then.

What would you tell people who have been working on going into the In-Between but get frustrated and can't seem to get there? You said that this unfolds when you're ready for it. Is going into the In-Between totally in your control?

I think that you need to have some basic skills to understand going In-Between. What you think about that decides that. I'm really not In-Between, hardly at all. We've talked about the In-Between and you are now internalizing it. I externalized it. I think that if you understand the basic fundamentals of what I teach, and you have a good understanding of those things, it's going to be easier for you to go In-Between because you are more self-aware. You can feel what is happening to you. That in itself creates the effect of shifting your consciousness. The people who are very scientific could externalize the process that is very hard for them to internalize, and that will help to make it happen within them. They can create and feel the sensation to amplify within them. They don't have that ability. They haven't learned to switch it inwards yet. Somewhere in their studies they must have that "Aha" moment. We teach moving the energy up and down with the hand but most people can't feel it right away. Then they think they're just imagining it. When they actually feel it, they have an "Aha!" moment.

When you think about simple things like the body, the bones and the tendons in it, you are turning inwards because you are reflecting inwards. These are the exercises you need to play around with in order for you to understand that something is happening inside of you. Then just let it happen. The second you start to think like that, you're constantly brought back to what is outside of you.

Think about your five senses. Are any of these senses designed to be interiorly active? Is your sense of smell made to smell what is going on inside of you? Is your mouth designed to taste what is going on inside of your lungs? Are your ears designed to listen to your ecosystem? Everything is designed to be exterior, so it is very difficult for a person to figure out the concept of how to turn a cup inside out. That's what happens when you go In-Between. You are externalizing but there is a part of you that goes inside and it shifts your consciousness to explore this other hyperdimensional conscious sensory. It is about being able to turn your reflection inward, or to feel what's going on inside of you from a different sense.

Whenever you do anything psychically or spiritually, can you honestly say that the majority of it is from one of the main five senses? Not necessarily. It's something you feel that amplifies and directs you to something. You can hear something but there's also this other sensory that says tthere is something there. You know you are using your other senses to react to it because that's intuitive. Usually it is this other sense that is more hypersensitive to that frequency, and the other ones are just getting whatever is spilling over from it.

To me, it depends on what classes that person has in order to understand how to psychically move inwards and externalize it by popping from the inside out. It's like turning your guts inside out. Then those things become the new feelers. It's a spiritual energy.

If you're more intellectual, is it more challenging going into the In-Between?

That's true, but then I would say that the vast majority of people who are attracted to me are intellectuals. Probably 90% of the people that are attracted to me are mind oriented. You can always tell the person who might not go the distance with us. They're all about feeling the love and feeling the heart chakra. They're not like Higher Balance people. We are very analytical. Give us something to sink our teeth into. Give us some logic. We want our logic to be sensible.

You have to go through the process of learning certain things before you can be ready to go there. The other thing is this that if you are shifted, you can shift everybody else. If they just give you a few minutes to move into your space, it will begin to happen. They just have to be able to let it happen or let it flow and then their consciousness will go there. I wish everybody could go In-Between. If that's the case, everybody would. It is a skill. It is another skill to be able to actively function in that state of mind. It's another skill to be able to use your expertise and your consciousness in a practical way and integrate it.

**Whenever I start thinking about the In-Between,
I consistently compare it to psychedelic mushrooms.
Is that recollection stopping me from going In-Between?**

What are you doing? You are analyzing your experience. You need to just learn to get past that. You'll be fine. Usually, it's like psychotherapy. It is a place of the mind. You just need to have that "Aha!" connection so that you can be alright with it. Then it'll happen.

To help you get that aha moment, just tell yourself you are doing hallucinogens. That's what I'm doing. For every hallucinogen that is out there, your brain is a biochemical pharmaceutical shop. It has the capacity to create most of those effects within its own mind. If you look at Ayahuasca, its main component is DMT which occurs naturally in the human brain. Scientists now believe that maybe DMT gives us our sense of reality, so it's already well within our consciousness.

You could say that maybe it is a key to reality. When we're shifting In-Between, maybe we are triggering some gland in our brain to overflow this DMT production that allows us to be in this state of mind. When we are ready to come out of it, it is just like a faucet that turns itself off. When we burn it out of our system, we come down. Instead of analyzing, "Well, this feels like this and it feels like that," you need to say, "Well, let me just continue feeling these things." You can even lie to yourself, "If I need to tell myself I'm on a drug at the moment," roll with it. Then, at least you can have the experience. When you are done, you know you didn't do any drugs.

Not everybody here is eating or drinking the same stuff, so it didn't come from me! Also, a lot of Higher Balance people have gone In-Between in their own homes. You know logically what you need. Once you are logically convinced that you are definitely experiencing some crazy shit, you realize it's definitely coming from this conscious shift in your mind. You will be able to produce it and you will be able to go back there to achieve higher states of that experience. You just have to find a way to be alright with it so that your analytical mind will give you a break and let you experience the effects of it.

**I'm also expecting it to slap me in the face though.
I'm expecting it to be as intense as you're talking about but
it seems like it doesn't ever get to that point of intensity.**

This is the earthly dilemma. This is nature trying to put a cap on you. Since you have this anxiety of expecting it to have a certain effect, you have an expectation for it. That's what prevents it from happening. Remember when I talked about the particle splitting? It only splits when you're not looking at it. You are analyzing it too much.

It's the same thing with your meditations. You're expecting to have your next breakthrough and it's not coming. That's because you want it to happen so you're anticipating or expecting it to happen, so you are setting the values of what it should be like. The second that you set the values of what you think it's like, it cannot meet those standards because it's not like that at all. Inadvertently, you're controlling the situation.

How do you undo that? That is the principle of self-exploration. That is what you're trying to untangle in yourself in order to achieve higher consciousness. That is the principle by which you meditate and why you go inside your mind. That is why you do self-analyzing. That's why you practice these things. The more that you practice them, the more you are going to get closer to achieving that goal. It's also the reason why you're reading this book. It's so that you can learn that much more from me, so that you can get to the level that you want to be at. The ironic thing is that you won't even remember this moment, even once you have achieved the In-Between. You won't remember how hard it was for you to achieve it. You won't even give it a second thought. You'll be just like, "I'll go In-Between now." Everybody has felt the way that you have. Isn't that the point where you really feel frustrated and you just don't know if you can get there? You're analyzing why it's not happening for you, and you're getting frustrated. Then it happens. When was the last time you reflected on that? You weren't thinking about the frustration it took to have an experience.

Everybody feels inferior. They may not have done it. In fact, if you ask them if they have experienced it, some people will say that they have. By their whisper, you know that they haven't but they don't want anybody else to know. There's nothing to be ashamed of! You've just got to keep working at it. It **will** happen!

If it doesn't happen, you can't sit there and go, "It hasn't happened." It's like trying to get a good night's rest. You need a good night's rest, and you're so worried about getting a good night rest and you're not getting it, what happens? You end up staying up the whole night fretting over whether you're going to fall asleep, "Oh my God! I'm not going to be able to fall asleep and it's going to be a terrible day tomorrow." Since you're doing that, you are preventing yourself from going to sleep to have the good night's rest that you need. That's exactly what is happening. You're fretting over whether or not you're going to achieve this incredible experience.

Anyway, for me that's amazing. That is why it is avoiding you. You almost need to have an "I don't give a shit" attitude. You experience whatever it is you experience. You can't help but want more. Of course, everybody wants to have those deeper experiences. Everybody wants to walk through walls. This is why I refrain from demonstrating a lot of this stuff because I know that everything I do: monkey see, monkey do. I've seen it innumerable times with my students. If I say something, you will run out there and try to do it or you'll get really frustrated.

I have to be so careful with what I do because if I make an error somewhere, if you yourself can't achieve it, you get so fixated on it that you implode. I can name a bunch of people who that's happened to now. They get really mean and they start going after everybody else, but they don't want to admit they can't do it themselves. Their own inner frustration prevents them from being able to experience it.

When you try to go In-Between, you've just got to let go of how far you think you can get. Stop worrying about what it is and what it isn't. How long did it take? How many tries did it take you? How many days, weeks, months or years did it take you? How long did it take from when you discovered the knowledge about it, to the point of wanting to achieve it, to when you knew you actually hit it?

In Mexico at Mayan Storm, I did it on the second day. Then when I went home and tried to do it myself, it took longer.

It was harder because you were worried you couldn't do it on your own; it's that anxiety. Everybody feels it. Everybody is worried. Earlier, when I was shifted nobody was talking about it and everyone started to get this weird vibe. That's the beginning of going In-Between. When you're talking about it, it becomes elusive. And when you're not talking about it and somebody is there, all of a sudden you go. It is like this parallel universe stuff again. Do you want to add to it, Ginni?

I had the In-Between module for about two years before I went In-Between.

I remember you being very upset because you couldn't go In-Between. Do you remember that? That's the truth. It's not just you. People need to hear this because they need to see how hard it was. The benefit is you have me here to walk you through it. Even if it doesn't happen now, you're going to understand that it's like a recipe. There are many recipes to going In-Between. I am just going to try and work with one.

When it happened for me, it lasted pretty much all day, but I don't think I realized it was happening. It was in Hawaii and I couldn't talk. I couldn't eat. Everything was weird. People told me I was acting weird. I didn't know. I had interactions with people. Another Navigator and I were in our own little vortex, laughing and having this whole non-verbal communication. It wasn't until I looked back on the experience that I realized that's what it was. I didn't know at the time so you may not know either.

You know what it was? You flowed with it but you weren't analyzing the two differences. As soon as you look at your exterior, there is part of you that goes, "Wait a minute. Something really is different. It's like Eric was saying. It took him a few minutes to realize that he was somewhere else." It may not occur to you because you have nothing else to compare it to if you haven't dabbled around with drugs.

If you have dabbled around with drugs, it's not going to be just like that. It's going to be very different but it's the closest thing that I can compare it to. If you have never done drugs, it'll be like, "I guess this is what being on drugs is like," yet it's not like that either. It's a lot better than drugs. It really is!

When you are In-Between, do you learn easier?

When you are there, everything is very different. I think you learn much easier. I just don't think that anything interests you so much. When you are there, you are interested in this vortex-like space because it's so alien to you.

Is it easy for you to teach us when we are In-Between?

No, because you guys are all messed up.

Is there a way to use the In-Between to connect into the Gaia consciousness?

Yes, absolutely. This is what we are going to be doing. You can have these really cool experiences like walking into an environment that is supposed to be haunted while being In-Between. Or walking in the city and looking for dimensional vortexes. Or looking for certain people in crowds. It is like entering *The Game* times ten. It's just very unique to engage stuff from that place.

I want everybody to relax. We're just going to go into it a bit lightly. Some people will probably go into it more so, but we are going to introduce it slowly and later we will push for a deeper level.

In-Between – Walkthrough

I want you to just become aware of your body. Keep your eyes open, not closed. It's very important to have your eyes open but spacing out. I want you to listen to my voice and sense it. Hear it echoing off the walls or on your chest. How it feels on your body, or how it feels around you. I want you to look at the wall and see the objects in between you and the wall. See how the objects stand in their position. I want you to take your hand and put it out in front of you. You'll feel almost a slight tingle inside of you when your eye adjusts to looking at your hands and the environment that's out and around it. Then put your hand back down.

I want you to think about the fabric of the carpet, how it feels. I want you to feel your breath going in and out slowly. Feel the temperature of the room. I want you to look at the curtain and see the texture of it, how it goes in and out, how it is rounded and how it moves. Hear the sound. I want you to breathe inward in a sense while you are looking out but almost as if you're turning inside out.

I want you to stand up now and move over towards the wall. I want you to look at the texture of the wall, and just have a quietness in your head. Just breathe slowly.

Listen to the sound of the room and the sound of my voice, relaxing, relaxing, relaxing. Breathing in slowly, feel it moving into your body, hearing the pitches of sound. Pay attention to how your body feels. Slight pressure, being aware of the objects in the room, the syntheticity of things. Feeling your body, hearing the people outside, seeing the environment inside. I want you now to just be quiet. Notice that your thoughts should be quieting down in your mind. Don't get too talkative, or too chatty.

I want you to take your time and look at objects. Look at structure. Move silently. Feel the temperature of the room. Be aware of the environment and the temperature. Just because you snap out of it, or you think that you are not there, there's a resonance there because you are looking for it. You can go back into it much deeper when you're alone. Just go to your room and sit on the edge of the bed. And just look into your environment. Focus on the little crinkling of noise, the sound, the ruffling of stuff when you are walking, the sound of your feet moving.

Does anybody want to share *any* of their *experiences, thoughts or insights* after the I did the walkthrough last night? I heard that some of you managed to get over to one of the graveyards last night. Steve?

We drove in someone's car down one of the streets to where all the cemeteries are located. We went to the farthest cemetery all the way on the edge of a residential section. It was really interesting because the houses were backed up right against the cemetery. They even had doors in the back of their fences so they could just walk into the cemeteries. They had a family plot right on the edge of their property. We scanned the area as we walked through and it was pretty cool. It was hard to be very sensitive but the most interesting place was a mausoleum.

As we were walking through the tunnel covered in marble, and we were trying to find the frequencies that are in there, one of the coaches told me to look for the frequency of expiring. I started thinking about worms and I got this really strong feeling of the recycling of life and that cyclical nature and I thought, "Now I've got the frequency! It was very interesting."

Just for the record, I want to be cremated when I die. I want to make sure there's no way of reviving me. I'm done. I'm done! I'm out of here. Don't bring me back. Anybody else have any insights, anything that they want to share?

One of the experiences that I had was at Muriel's. It was quite funny. Baard was sitting on that circular thing and someone came over and gave him a taste of his drink and Baard pulled a face. And I got Baard's taste of the drink.

That's the telepathic link I'm talking about when you do a lot of In-Between stuff, even though you may not think you are In-Between anymore. There is a residual link when you go In-Between and funny things like that can happen. I wanted to talk about that so interesting that you brought that up.

I was out with Frank. There was a guy who was there who was dressed up as a pirate. He was using the pirate outfit as a way to put people off scanning him, but he was out scanning people. I thought that was interesting. He was really good at stealth, too. Frank was having a hard time locking onto him.

Excellent!!! I wanted to mention about the person that was dressed in the costume. I don't know anything about this particular person. For people who are in that unique category, it's not unusual for them to sometimes dress in a format that seems to be so extreme that you will dismiss it. Don't just assume that it's a costume. Sometimes they do that on purpose but it's also what they are comfortable with. It's so pungent that people will dismiss it. Rather than being subtle, they realize that people will dismiss it rather than jump on it. There were other people dressed up, too, but they could just be blending. Or maybe it's just the way it was. I don't know about that particular person, but it's a good thing to point out.

The other thing that happened, I phased out as I was looking at a door that had lattice work on it. Next to it was a brick wall and underneath that was mortar with whitewash on. It was like going into Paul Revere's time and wondering what was behind the door.

That's awesome! Very good! It's interesting that you brought it up about the door. It's very hard when you're in an In-Between state of consciousness to have that intent for what you want to do unless you put yourself into that situation to do those kinds of things. So, you always want to be aware of those things.

There are certain things that will help you to trigger it. I always say, "It's in the details." If you look at the micro stuff, for some reason it helps slip you into that state. When I'm in the bathroom sitting on the toilet, I usually look at the wall because there's nothing better to do. At some point, I realized I could shift In-Between by looking at the wall as long as it had the right kind of patterns on it. There's something about tile and the echo. There's a certain feel in those types of environments.

Yesterday I took everybody in to the men's room to look at the urinal. Other than me, who is going to tell you to look at a urinal? If you just stare at it, there's something surreal that strikes you as odd. These are cues that can help shift you. You're always looking for something to snap you into that state of mind. I think that a urinal is just some place you go, do your business and leave. To look at it, what else would you do with it? The brain goes, "Well, what do you want?" I think it throws it off or something. It's the shine on the tiles, the smooth surface and then the squared out lines to it.

There was a time when Dan was visiting me when I lived out in Hartford, Connecticut. At the time I lived there, the bathroom had a tiled floor. I've talked about this before. It was built probably in the 1950's. They were little hexagon tiles, all white with black rimmed little hexagon tiles. Then every so often there was a black one. It got to the point where I could do a *lift*. For me, a lift is when you see the tile all of a sudden lift to a three-dimensional platform. Maybe you have played around with something like this where you can see it go up.

When I was in an extremely In-Between state, I took a key and I put it down and I slid it until you couldn't see it anymore. If I slid it too far, it would resurface. It's like bending light, or like a straw where it bends in the light in the water. Dan and I experimented on a lot of things. I told Dan to look for the key but he couldn't find it. Then I pulled the key out and he said, "No way!" That was an extreme case. I'm bringing up these extreme cases, but there's part of me that doesn't want to do that, because it took years to get to that space. And that was the most unique thing that that I have ever done playing around with the In-Between. In the In-Between, I believe you're playing around with physics in your mind, but it was such a perfect place to dabble with something like that. I don't want you to think that it was a big key. It was a little key to a lock or something like that.

At this point, how do you feel about your ability to shift into that mild state of an In-Between place? I'm at about a one or two state of In-Between, but it's so hard to communicate at this level and be there, even for me. It'll pop you out, and when you want to go back in it's hard because your brain gets all confused.

It is one thing to me to bring you In-Between in person at an event, but there has to be a way for you to trigger it when you go home. How do you start to get yourself to go into that zone? I started to experiment last night to see how I could do that. I teach by self-analyzing, "How do I do it?" I just normally do it without giving it much thought. I've found what I think is a very good trigger. It's a little bit weird, but that's the point of it. I think we are going to do some experimenting with this. There's a part of me that wants to do more dialogue, but I am afraid if we do more dialogue first, we will end up bouncing back out of it.

I want you to set your chair so that you're facing another person. I want you to have another person in front of you to work with and I'm going to give you this technique. I think it should work very well. I think that's what we're going to do, without engaging in too much conversation. If you are doing it with more than two people, have a row with their backs to the wall, maybe about three feet apart for distance. If you are just doing it with two people, have one person with their back to the wall. If you are not touching, that would be really good, too.

The most interesting thing I have noticed about doing this in an In-Between state of mind is that it almost evaporates when you go back to a normal state of mind. You have a hard time relating to what you experienced when you were in that state of mind. It's like vinegar and oil wanting to separate. When you pull them apart, you can only glean certain aspects of it after the fact. It's a very weird thing with your mind. You don't know if you can go In-Between but then you start going, "Okay, I am there," but when you come back out again, you say, "I'm not sure about that place." As I have said before, there is this very strange disconnect. In my opinion, it is like you are using an altered state of consciousness. It is this secondary state of consciousness that you're using at probably one percent as you are moving out of the organic brain. This is going to be a little more time-consuming because you are really trying to develop and discipline yourself to go to these zones and do things.

One of the things that is probably going to happen is face morphing because we're entering a little bit of that as we look at one another. I don't want you to get all giddy and into the whole face morphing thing. That is in the *Cycles of the Soul* chapter earlier in this book. It's almost like you are on a road trip and you have to travel through the towns you've been through before to get further out to the towns you haven't yet explored. That's how I would look at it.

For the people reading this book now, I'm going to give you some other techniques that I have not yet shared.

First, I want you to take a white sheet and put it on a wall in your room. I want you to turn off the lights temporarily. If you are in a bright room, just work with what you've got. I want you to imagine that there's another person in front of you when you are doing this. For the most part, it is not really that necessary to have a second person so don't feel like you don't have that connection. If you do have a second person to work with, that's great.

In-Between – Technique #2

So, the first thing you want to do is clear your mind and just relax. Pay attention to the subtle sounds in your environment. If you hear a clickety sound, that's useful. Without moving your head much, let your mind look around the room. Just set your eyes forward or down. It's okay to blink. If you have ever zoned off or spaced off, you want to go to that place.

Now try to find the tones, if you can a little bit. It's not necessary that you find them. It's more about the feel of looking for the tones; that stretched out mind feel that comes from it, like something is stretching out looking for it from your head. There's a very calm feeling, almost like a heaviness that's starting now. It can be chest oriented. It's like a spatial space within you, but almost exterior to you. It's ever so mild. You just want to relax with it. Now looking across from you in the person's body, be aware of the head, and the space behind them and around them. Instead of using your eyes in the sense of looking out at something, I want you to breathe everything in through your eyes, pulling it inwards as you are looking outwards. Just work with your breath and be aware of how that affects you.

When you breathe in through your eyes, as if you are pulling in, it is a trigger to slowly move your consciousness into the In-Between. It actually takes a few minutes, but it brings you into that In-Between state. Hear the sounds and then pull in with your eyes visually at the same time, as if you are multitasking very calmly. It's an unusual concept to breathe in through your eyes. Try to work with it. I want you to very slowly breathe in through your eyes, just pulling inwards. Look around the room like you're trying to move into the In-Between state. See the surrealism of objects. It is an ever so slight difference that you feel, not that you just necessarily see.

As you look with your eyes, and you see an object, look at it and pull it with your eyes, with your breath. Almost feel it with your chest area. Now you can make it more intense. I'm not saying to breathe in hard, but pull harder in with your eyes. It's almost a correlation with your breath. As you pull in harder, it will start to move you even deeper into an In-Between state. You will feel almost a heaviness in the front of your skull area or in different parts of your body.

If you feel like you are starting to go In-Between, I want you to get up and move around. If you decide to walk outdoors, make sure the weather is appropriate - that it's dry enough and the temperature is not too cold or too warm. If you go outside, I want you to stay in this 'place.' If not, just walk around the house and feel the surrealism of the house, the stillness of the house.

*I want you to walk around using the breathing techniques. Be careful of cars and stuff. Maybe walk by the buildings. Try to look casual, as much as possible. Be aware of the ground and the walls. Look at the detail of it, the detail of the cracks in the ground, the glistening effect, and just breathe it in. I want you to go for about maybe five to ten minutes. Then come back and take your seat. If it's cold, make sure you take your jacket. Look at the walls. Feel the spatiality of the structure around you. When you walk down hallways, stop and breathe it in. Stop and slowly breathe it in, and try not to cluster with others too much. Go on your own and observe the detail of things and breathe it in with your eyes. **The deeper the breath pulling in, the more of that floaty relaxed feeling you will get from the shift.** Look at objects; move your eyes around. Pull them in. Breathe them in. Slowly, slowly; don't move too fast.*

As a concept, I want you to breathe your environment in through your eyes slowly. The deeper you breathe in, the more you take in from the environment. If you decide to stay inside, I want you to take about five minutes, get up and move around your house. Hopefully, there are not many people there. If there are, you can just say you are doing a mental exercise and that you're going to need a few minutes to practice it. Breathe in the environment through your eyes; look at things that grab you, or take your attention.

When you're done, return to your seat. Be aware of the light in the room. I want you to breathe it in with your eyes slowly as if you are trying to make the room look brighter. Focus on the luminosity of the room. Do it very slowly and calmly and you will be able to almost dilate the eyes. Don't stare at the light. Look out almost in the distance, or at the environmental light. Don't look at the source of the light. When people are walking in, listen to the sound that they're making, like the roughage of their pants moving against one another.

Pay attention to how calm you feel. It is a likeable feeling, and at the same time a plateaued feeling. Calmly, slowly, slowly. Focus on the luminosity of the room, almost as if you are trying to breathe the light in from the room. Don't look at the source of the light. Try to almost make the room brighter with your eyes. Use your breathing in cooperation with your sight.

Take your hands and move them out front almost, like you're reaching for a ball. Put your palms outward; there you go. I want you to stretch out with your hands and almost pull the entire room, when your hands go apart and away. Just look at me. Away, away, okay. Feel the room as if you're moving the light, almost breathing it in into your eyes. Move everything by pulling it into your eyes. It's almost like you are holding a basketball in your hands. Imagine a basketball, the luminosity, but the room is the ball. Feel the ball. Feel it connected outward. Feel it in your chest and stretch it. Move the whole room in with your eyes. Then feel what it feels like inside.

This is environmental control. When you go to haunted houses, you will see the real use of this technique. You have to let your mind become almost the energy in the room. If you move your hand, it's almost like you have giant hands stretching the room. You'll feel it in your chest. Breathe it in, and have tension in your hand almost like a firmness.

Okay, you can put your hands down. I want you to now find a blank wall where you are and just look at it. You want a wall with a large flat surface without objects on it. When you find it, I want you to just calmly feel the wall. Look at the detail, as best you can. You can see the structure of the wall. You can see the little divots in it. Become aware of the energy on the wall. It looks like sparkles. You know how to look for Prana. You know how to look for energy. You want to tune so much into the fuzzy faint energy that you almost want to see if you can lift it. See the room get brighter. Pull the wall in towards you, and it will almost stretch it. The more that you pull with your mind, it's almost like it separates reality. It's not like the wall is going to leap out towards you. Do not have a set decision of what it should do. Just experience it for what it is by doing what I am saying. It's almost like you are breathing and seeing. You're going to see a very faint dim sparkle like a little static electricity. You will see other grades of luminosity wavered in there.

Work with it and pull it with your eyes, breathing it in. Then observe what you are getting from that. Once you have done that, move your eyes to another source and do the same thing. Then go to another source, like when you move from blank objects. Move them to structural objects in the room like chairs, people, whatever. Just do that for a few minutes.

Just study, almost like you're observing the aura energy. Try to get your mind to almost come forward and just be aware. Don't have an expectation. Don't think it should be brighter and more intense. Just experience it for what it is. Then feel in your chest how it feels.

To summarize that last part quickly, find a wall to look at in your environment. Look at the luminosity coming off the wall, the static energy. Breathe it in with your eyes, as if you're lifting it, and making the luminosity in your room brighter by very calmly breathing it in. Then work on objects doing the same thing. Put your hands out very tense like you are holding a basketball. Then breathe in, as if you're stretching the room outside of you. It's actually affected by the interior of your hands. Do that for a few seconds. Then just relax.

Remember, the key is to breathe it in through your eyes, like you are pulling it into you from your eyes. Your breath will help you mentally understand how to imitate that process. In a sense, it's like using your imagination to do it.

I want you to look at the white sheet on the wall now. Do the same thing - pull it in and look over it for the static electricity or any illumination that you can see in the space between the wall and yourself. Just zone off into it. At the same time, be aware of the brightness in the room and breathe it in. Pull it in. Feel free to use your hands to move the energy. Use your hands as if you're moving into the sheet, pulling it forward. Feel it in your eyes. Feel it in your chest. Become aware of your hands without looking at them. It's like you can see them in a 3-D effect. When you breathe in, you can see it ahead of you. As you pull it in, see your hands and observe what's there. Use your breath to slowly breathe it in. It's very commanding, yet gentle at the same time. After you have done it once or twice with your hand, you can put your hands down.

This works best with two people. Clear your mind. Then find another person to look at. It's best to have somebody you can look across at. I want you to use the same process of looking in the eyes of that person and breathing them in through your eyes. It's going to look a little strange when you're looking at the other person doing it. Just feel them. Then be aware of the room and the space around them, the background around them. Be very aware of the subtle feeling inside of your presence. I want you to reach out and hold the other person's hands like you are making a chain, just in your little group. Pay attention to what you feel in that moment of touching and then breathe in the person across from you. Be aware of the luminosity in the room. Try to make it brighter in the room. It's almost like having to multitask.

It's normal to get nauseous when you do that. It happens to me sometimes, too. When you get your sensory back, the nausea will leave. It's like going upside down on a plane or on a rollercoaster. You are not using your five senses anymore. You're adding something to the mix, so your nervous system gets disoriented, making you nauseous. It comes and goes. After you've done this a few times, it will just stop happening. It is a good sign because it usually means you're doing something correct. Use your five senses to orientate yourself back. When your five senses normalize, you will feel normalized.

It's okay if you get a headache doing this. It means you're working that muscle in your brain. Use your five senses, talk and feel things. You don't necessarily want to stay in that state all the time, so using your five senses helps to orientate you. If you look people in the eye, you will see a lot of dilated pupils. I think this technique nails it.

I was talking to my group last night telling them to try and dilate the pupils of their eyes. I deliberately tried to dilate my eyes. It's a great way to do it.

Were you are able to get the light to luminosity to work a little bit? Did you find that technique worked well for you?

I did it on the curtains, and I swear to God that I saw the curtain move out. I did it even better with the light coming in.

It's hard because everybody is at a different degree. I am trying to work with that happy medium. People will have much better effects when they are at home because they'll probably go really deep.

Does anyone want to share some of your new insights or anything of interest that stood out for you? How about the people who had the most difficulty shifting yesterday? Do you want to share your thoughts?

I have been shifting all morning long. It's been a lot easier to get into the zone, without even really having to try. When I was waiting for my breakfast, I was watching the people in the street just walking around, and I could feel myself going there. I wanted to eat breakfast so I started to breathe a little.

So you want it to stop! I told you to be careful what you ask for. You are lucky it didn't come so strong that you couldn't walk, because that can happen, too.

I felt all spongy. When I breathed in, there was a real pressure in my forehead, and a curvy feeling in my chest. It's hard to describe it.

Let me try to explain the In-Between. It's really difficult to explain until you've experienced it. It can be really intense and it operates differently depending on how deep or what level you're on. I am sure everybody feels like they are still a little bit plugged in, so that adds another element to it.

**I saw depth in a rug last night at the restaurant
and not much else. I saw a brick wall moving.
It had more depth and some parts were bending out.**

So the brick wall was moving for you! That's excellent! All the bricks stood out and were moving! That's excellent. When you go home, you are going to dabble with this. Your experiences will go from one to one hundred once you are not influenced by everybody here. One of the most challenging things with the In-Between is that you link up mentally. When you are shifted and you look at another person, they will shift if they have been In-Between, too. That is a plus because then you can shift somebody. The downside is that it's very hard for you to go deeper than them because when you are all linked, they keep you anchored. It is just a very interesting dynamic. Some people will percolate up while others move down. When you go out on your own, you will go really deep because you won't feel anyone near you with your normal senses. When you feel someone's energy, you tend to match it. You are going to have your best experiences once you get away from everything, so you had better grab something to munch on.

You've got to use your five normal senses like touch, smell, taste, hearing and sight. When you use your five senses, you tend to come down. Then you can just pop out of it, or try to take a little nap, because it can get very intense. All it takes is a little sample. Believe me, it's like a weed fire because it just takes a little taste of this. When you start to dabble with it, it just catches on. There were some people having a difficult time with it. Now they have a difficult time shutting it off. That's how it happens. It just creeps up on you and when you least expect it, you go In-Between!

I find it interesting that you weren't looking for it in the morning, but you noticed that your mind went there and you followed it. You can't control it with expectation. If you have an intent, your mind starts to go there. You can recognize that and let it happen, so you can't control it directly. In this roundabout way, you can control it if you let it happen. You've just got to learn to work it in a very strange way.

Different people will hit different peaks. Sometimes you can feel very nauseated. You just need to orient yourself. Use your five senses, and eventually it will pass. There is a part of you that can't let go of it, and you can get frustrated because you may just want it to end. You can break it by taking a breather or going for a little walk, but if you go by yourself, that's when it comes on even stronger. You are damned if you do, and damned if you don't.

Feeling nauseous is normal for the In-Between. You are using this other sense that your body is not oriented to, so it can be overwhelming. There is just no way to control how you feel. It's like being on an airplane, a roller coaster, or a boat. If you're not used to it it's an abnormal experience. The body doesn't know how to cope with it and that's where the nausea comes from. Since you haven't learned to control it that well when you go In-Between, it creates a nauseous feeling with a funny taste on the back of your tongue. Sometimes you feel it in your throat or in your chest. It can move around and it affects people differently.

If I shift hard on and off, I get air pressure in my ears. It can affect people very differently. It is just going to happen temporarily until you start to play around with it more. Then you adapt. I've had some people tell me, "Before I knew it, I was fine. Now that I know it, it happens to me all the time and I can't do my job now." There may come a point where you have to search for it to happen again because you wandered away from it so long. It will stop eventually so you shouldn't panic. If your body is really affected by the process, you could take some Dramamine because it seems that the body can't go where the mind goes.

Yesterday afternoon after your talk, I went back to the hotel room and the carpet was moving. The floor seemed to be about leg level. That was a strange experience.

It always starts with the floor for me.

At Muriel's Restaurant, the gargoyles seemed to be alive. The eyes were looking at me and its mouth seemed to smile at me. I saw translucent glows and objects floating in the air. The In-Between has physical effects, but it seems like it's not accustomed to the physical effect to amplify the In-Between, like the dilation of the eyes.

Clearly, you're affecting the biochemicals in your brain. Some people might say that you are creating a forced illusion. Maybe you are making yourself go to a hypnotic state. The gargoyle isn't really alive. I agree with all of that. You are definitely tampering with chemicals in your brain to some degree. You are also tampering with your sensory. If you understand the dynamics of consciousness, your brain is always creating a certain chemical balance that allows you to interpret reality the way that you do. Some people might argue, "Who's to say this is the correct reality? It's just whatever your biochemicals are set for," and I would agree with that to some extent. I think that you have to cross through that biochemical change where certain things definitely mess with your biological level. However, within a short period of time your body compensates for it putting you in what I would call a higher intuitive level.

So you are not necessarily seeing gargoyles coming to life. You're seeing energy patterns and movements that are clearly there. It is not an illusion, but your mind has to go through something like Neo (from *The Matrix* movie) when the matrix fluxes. When it pops back, he gets it.

There is a point where reality warps. That's the river you have to cross to get to the other side. When you are on the other side, then you suddenly see things with a different clarity. There is a transition period that you have to work with your brain because the Governor dictates to you what reality is. The Governor dictates to you what you're able to experience and perceive. It's just like counting the f's in *The Handbook of the Navigator.* The Governor removes things from your sensory that are clearly there.

Once you go through the transition of letting your consciousness shift, working with the light and breathing it in with your eyes, there is a place where you almost feel more relaxed but you definitely know you are in a different place. It's like being in a tin can. It just feels different. It is from that place that you have a clearer sensory to higher dimensions and crossover dimensions. You may wonder why you don't see certain things when you are there.

Once you cross, there is a whole different range of experiences you can move into. You are still on the grassy shore. You haven't yet had the time to explore. You almost have to break apart so that you are alone. Then you are going to find these other avenues or places that you can move into where you can experience seeing shadow people, entities, or other beings. You can also discover other truths or telepathically linking. The human brain can only handle so much in the beginning, so you get exhausted and you need to stop for a while. I'm sure you would agree there's a point where you've had enough. It's like working your mind. The more you dabble with it, the more you can go there. There's a range of places that you can move your mind into once you can make that transition. Once you know something, you can't *unknow* it.

When I went outside and looked up at the sky, I could see little sparkling things. If you pull them in with your eyes, it's almost nourishing. Yesterday, one of the coaches was moving us Into the In-Between. When I looked up at the brick wall above someone's head, I think the ghosts came.

Really? You definitely tuned into that frequency then.

I tuned in for a second and then I was shocked. That was a little strange.

That's what you want, right? You're looking for something. Give me a little morsel. We like strange stuff.

The first thing that I noticed was that the brick wall started to move forward like the background of the picture. When you look at those pictures, all of a sudden the background moves forward and takes shape. It was like there were three different dimensions or shapes in the wall. Then I noticed the flame from the gas lamps started flickering. Then my heart started to keep pace with the flame and I could feel it inside.

Interesting, very good. So you linked with the flame.

I linked and I started having this metallic taste. I also started to sweat.

Did you sweat? Did you have the metallic taste? If it happens, it's just one dynamic if you go into a certain range in your mind.

I heard a hum of energy and vibration sounds. I thought it was coming from a tree and I could feel the life.

Yes, I remember a time when I was out in Hartford at a city park. It was spring and I let my mind go to these flowers. They were budding and I could actually hear the crackling of the flowers in their blooming process. I couldn't see them fully bloom but I could see the light green piercing out of the shell after a few minutes. Interestingly enough, you can link with it and they're receptive to you. Think about it this way. When you are in that zone, and you look at something, what happens? It reacts. If your mind captures a flame, then you think with it. This is why I want you to go out into nature. If you want to tune into something, it's like you become one with it. It becomes alive. There are many experiences.

Go out into the desert. Go out into nature. Watch what happens when you tune into animals. The animals will react to you. There's no limit to what you can learn to do in the In-Between. I don't know if you have even begun to really understand the magnitude of this. Once you really get it under control, you can walk that way every day in your spiritual mind, so it is very interesting stuff. You can't unknow what you know.

When I walked back in, the parking lot had a shimmer to it. The wall had the shimmer as well. One of the coaches told me that it is just as important to be conscious when you're coming out of the In-Between as it is going into the In-Between. Last night I was conscious of coming out of it so it was a lot easier.

That's excellent. That is the shimmer that I am talking about. Everybody seems to find that breathing in with the eyes is a tool to help move you In-Between a little faster. I thought that was brilliant. It's an amazing tool. If you teach students, you will know the right time to share something like that. I think you understand these things and that you are at a point where you really appreciate their value. This is secret doctrine stuff. In the olden days, people had to work for this stuff for about thirty years!

Then they learned to move their minds. There are structures that are made to shift your consciousness. When people walked through these buildings, their minds shifted. Can you imagine being in one of these places breathing in through your eyes? That would really amplify the effect that these places have on your consciousness. I'm not sure that you can begin to fathom the possibilities of what you're learning. This is incredible knowledge, but there is always a price to pay for everything in the universe. When you are playing around with the In-Between, the nauseated or uneasy feeling is your payment. It's like childbirth. When you give life, it's not exactly fun birthing it. There's a price to pay when you break the rules to learn the hidden secret of reality.

When you see the shimmering around things, remember that none of this is real. When the yogi said to his student, "This is an illusion," remember that it **is** an illusion. When you think about what I am showing you, you have to ask yourself, "Am I normally locked into a certain frequency? Am I now pushing on these door-ways of reality? Is this really the matrix that I am playing with now?"

When I say that you are in a conscious place, it's like being in a specific channel. You operate like a machine, always automating. This starts to add a new element to how you think about life, and how you really perceive things. It really changes the rules on your ideals so that you are no longer just White Cells. At this point, you are like the Magi. You reach a level of being mystics. There's going to be something that slowly changes about you because you have these insights. This sensory is going to change your thinking a little. You'll forget about it. But at some point, you will be sitting somewhere and something is going to shift you. You are going to go into something and it will reveal what is hidden. That is what is absolutely fascinating and unique. There are so many possibilities that can come from this.

When we first started facing each other, I shifted pretty hard. When we started walking down the hallway, I could feel myself automating again. It was like a roller coaster going up and down. The more I stayed still, the more I could let go.

Yes, when you moving, it's harder because you're using your sensory to navigate through your environment and you have to deal with people walking by. That's one of the purposes of making you walk outside. I threw you into the mix so that you are prepared for it. If you think about it, it creates anxiety because you know you're going to have to do this so you can't shift as well. You need to put yourself into situations, set up a flight plan, but try not to think about it. You've just got to do it. Then you'll get a little experience that you will use to adapt later, knowing that you can still exist there. When you stop, it'll come on stronger again.

This is a key statement: anytime you are actively consciously aware that you're using your five senses like when you are smell-ing or listening for something, in some cases, that can bring you out of it. Be calm. Move slowly. Float. Try not to actively be aware of using your five senses. Use this funkiness as a feeling. It's a new sense.

I'm always amazed by deaf children who then get a Cochlear implant put into their ears. When the doctor hooks the implant up to the brain and the child hears for the first time, they are disoriented as if they don't know how to process it. Sometimes they turn their head when they hear the sound. This is what is happening to you when you enter the In-Between. That's where the weirdness and the nauseousness comes from. I'm sure the person who has never heard before is going to get nauseated because they are trying to process it but their brain doesn't know what to do with it.

I imagine the same thing happens to somebody who is blind when they get a new technology that allows them to see. There has to be a period when the brain just doesn't know what to do with this thing. The brain has to build neural pathways, or awaken the neural pathways in the brain to process that data.

For somebody like me who has a lot of experience operating from this place, it's just another sense. For people who are new to this, I remember the nauseousness. It still happens a little if I don't go In-Between for a long time. When I go into the zone, I know how to cope with it so I can move it past me.

Something else that comes to mind is a weird heat sensation. It almost flushes throughout your body. It's very strange how it affects people in different ways. Years ago, when Dan was over at my apartment and I was teaching him about the states of consciousness, I had a hanging plant. It was one of the typical green leafy ones you see in offices. As I was explaining to Dan about moving energy, I moved my mind into that plant. I went In-Between and I linked up with the plant. This is a key point. I assimilated the plant, but I also created in me a navigation of it coming to life and growing. I wanted it to flourish, so I moved my life force into it. Literally, the plant grew in front of us. It had water dripping from its instant growth of three or four leaves. Dan said, "Holy shit!" It literally happened right in front of us.

The power of what you can do is only limited by your Governor. If you can escape from that, you can just go there. Where do you think I learned about all of this? I was In-Between experimenting, training myself, and awakening. When I came to in the normal state, I took the things that I learned in the In-Between and I pulled them through so they could be used here.

You can bring it to a whole new level. You don't have to go so deep. You only need to go two percent into the In-Between. Here's another big pearl. *Since you know the truth about reality, you can affect reality.* You can't affect reality if you don't understand that it is possible. When you see the wall move, you cannot deny that something happened. You cannot deny that you saw the floor rise. You cannot deny that you're seeing something. You may not have seen these things before in your life, but you always believed they were there. Now that you're dabbling with these strange things, it's almost like you don't know what to make of it.

People often ask me, "How do you change reality, Eric?" I change it because I know that I can. I affect reality, and I can affect the consciousness because I know that I can. I know because of the experiences I've had and the things that I've done when I was shifted. I brought them back and I know them to be truth because I've experienced them. I'm as certain of that as I am that water is going to fall to the ground if I pour it. The first time I did it, I learned that's what happens. Now when I learn other stuff, I have an expectation that I am going to bend the rules of reality because I know it can be done. That's what makes me unique.

I linked up with a tree outside. It was looking at me and we were trying to have a conversation about what and who it was, and what and who I was. When we were inside, looking past each other, I could feel the consciousness of the other person.

That's excellent.

**I found myself shifting. Last night I saw energy
for the first time. It is very, very subtle. I think, at times,
that I am on the brink of crossing over.**

Well, you are holding yourself back. This is what nobody wants to hear. You're the problem. Other people have told me that they think sometimes they are almost there. It is almost verbatim what others have said to me. Keep exercising with it. Tonight could be the night. Don't get upset that you feel like you are not quite getting there because you know what is happening. You are getting mad at yourself. You're wondering, "Why everybody else? Why not me? I work hard at this." That's like complaining to the Universe. What happens when you are a child and you have a temper tantrum? You have to just let it flow. When you enjoy the little things, they become big things.

The makings for it are beginning, just like with the others who have struggled and have now broken through. You know it is now coming on. I am willing to bet the ones who have broken through have better experiences now when they are out on their own, because they finally knew what to look for. You just have to be open to it.

Once you are on your own in the quiet of your house, just feel the room and go through the technique and breathe it in through your eyes. I am willing to bet it is going to happen for you. If you have any pets, lock them away somewhere. Not everybody's experience is going to be the same as somebody else's. Not everybody is going to be sure about what they experienced. Different people are coming from different places, so you just have to relax with it. You can't tell the Universe to give it to you. You can't tell the Universe that you deserve it because you worked hard for it. The Universe doesn't acknowledge that. The Universe says, "You will bud and flower when you are ready to bud and flower. That is it."

As soon as you come to terms with that, it moves forward. I think Navigators are very demanding. I know I am demanding. I am probably worse than you.

We were talking about how to get In-Between in different situations last night. I realize now that I had experienced it more than I thought.

Other people have said here that they've been In-Between. They just didn't know what it was. That's what is important. When you come to accept that, the next time it will happen more easily. The only difference is that in the back of your head this little person is just going to say, "OMG! It's finally happening." Then another voice is going to go, "Shut up. Shut up. Don't. You're going to scare it away. No!" Then you're going to breathe in and you're going to breathe out and go into the zone.

I wanted to bring up the gargoyle again. When we create symbols of life like gargoyles and angels, I often think that the artist has imbued a consciousness into it. When someone sees it come to life, I believe that to be true. In the movie *Interview With a Vampire,* there's a part where he gets bitten and becomes a vampire. I thought they did such a great job with that scene. That is almost what the In-Between is like. In the movie, Lestat says to Louis, "Now look with your vampire eyes." Louis looks and he sees the life from the plants. It's ever so subtle but he sees this statue of an angel turn and look at him. It's really true that these things can happen during the process of shifting.

After reading this chapter, go back and read the In-Between chapter again. Better yet, listen to the In-Between class. When you listen to it with the new insights from this chapter, it's going to really ramp up your experience because there's other good walkthroughs for the process in there. You're going to hear stuff in there that you've never heard before that is going to help trick you into getting into that state.

I had the same experience with the statue of the girl when I was coming back into the building. I've always noticed her when I exited and entered the building, but when I looked this time I noticed that she's so sad. It's like her eyes were following me. She came to life, ever so subtly. Then you said to look at the wall. Until now, I never understood the shadow. When I looked at the wall, I began to notice the texture. It came alive and its shadows were moving and it was amazing.

I often exist in that place. When I saw objects moving, I'd duck right in the middle of conversations. Reflecting on it now, I probably looked ridiculous. I'm so in tune now that I can block that out. I can actually switch the channel so I just stay in this place but I always feel it. If something moves around, then I can sense it.

One time I was in my bedroom, I could feel an entire legion of these things moving around. When I say that you can feel them, this is what I'm talking about. When you go In-Between often enough, it's like a new sensory that's always with you. You may not pay attention to it all the time but if something is strong enough, you'll feel a pull. It's almost like the pull of a kite when the wind is blowing it in a certain direction. You'll know something is going on more so than you normally do psychically. Jamison was there, too. I remember he came down the hall asking, "What's up?" I said, "Well, do you feel it?" He's like, "Yeah, Wow! It's not a problem but it could have been like psychic war time." It felt like what Germany was probably like during World War II when all the airplanes were flying by. It was just a very, strange, interesting thing.

When I went outside, sounds were a lot louder.
A jet in the sky made me duck.

For me, sound can get very intense. Sometimes I'll be in my room and there will be a little sound way off. It could be a mile away and it will get so loud that my mind will track it to the source as if it's in my ear. I hate it when that happens because it even occurs when I am sleeping. I'll often do it in a waking state. These are good things to practice.

The creaking of the door seems really shocking to me. I heard water and wondered where it was coming from. I saw this waterfall that I never noticed before. My ability to smell is insane. I smelt bacon and then the flavor and the smokiness they used for it. Also, I didn't put my glasses on when I went outside because I didn't need them anymore. Everything was crisp. It was shocking, yet amazing.

It's really amazing when you think about it. It truly is.

**I feel like I'm just getting pieces of it.
Breathing in through my eyes was very helpful.**

I think that is a technique that you can do anywhere. When I analyze what I am doing to get into these states, it's hard because I have to step outside of myself and watch me move through the process. Now you know what to look for.

When I went to the ladies room, I felt this sensation of depth behind me and when I looked at the soda machine, I realized it actually went in deeper into the wall. Then I realized that I felt it first before I noticed. Just now, I can see the carpet waving.

Yes, that is excellent.

**When I went outside, I saw Prana in the blue sky.
I'd never seen Prana in broad daylight before.
Then I saw a thickness floating between myself and the sky.
Then the sky turned from blue to gray.**

Excellent, some of these things I haven't done in twenty years. I remember that I'd go In-Between lying outside in a field and I'd move my mind. You are going to have a better appreciation for this now.

Remember when I wrote in the *Handbook of the Navigator* about when I was a child and I looked into the water and I saw the micro? Do you realize what I was doing now? I was shifting, but I didn't realize at that time that I was going In-Between. I was just going into that place. I remember that I stood up and the sky turned to stars during the sunlight. Do you realize now what was happening to me? Could you imagine 10 years, 20 years, or 30 years of going to this state of mind? What kind of person does it shape you to be? What things do you learn to understand? From all the little micro experiences, you have now spent a little bit of time In-Between. You've seen how challenging and taxing it can be but you can glean some amazing insights. After a while, you accumulate them. Then it forms this state of being.

**Last night, everything was really funny to me. Everyone
looked so serious so I thought I'd better keep it under
control and not laugh but everything seemed funny. This
morning after our meditation, we were talking about
something but I think I've been moving in and out all
morning so it's been challenging to talk today.**

Now you know what I feel like when you want me to teach a class and I can't talk. Do you realize how hard it is to keep it altogether in all the classes I've ever taught? Do you realize now why I sometimes stutter?

**It's been so difficult to talk around the restaurant.
Nothing looks good to eat.**

Why do you think I am so fussy over the food I eat? I've complained because it's not cooked enough. It takes on a whole different level.

Today, we were staring at the wall. There was shimmering and a light that moved in and out. As I was staring at someone, she just disappeared. It was so interesting.

Do you realize this is all dimensional stuff? You can say, "Well, it's an illusion." How does a person disappear but everything else is still there? Granted, the mind can play tricks. Is your mind playing tricks? Or is your mind bridging realities? This is what spiritual shamans are doing. You've probably heard stories about me doing dimensional things like walking through a wall. After hearing these stories, you can see how this can happen. The more that you really go into the zone, and the more classes you take, the more you can understand and learn to move entire objects. You can move walls. This is why I'm trying to teach you. If I give you too much and you can't do it, then you feel as if you've failed. If I give you little successes, it makes you much stronger. If I give you a big challenge and you can't do it, you just give up the whole kit and caboodle because everything else seems too irrelevant. You need to start small. You don't start off lifting two hundred pounds. You start off lifting ten. Then you lift twenty. Then you go for forty. You've got to start somewhere; then exercise it. You can do these crazy things. You can affect reality.

When Matt was meditating with me shortly after I moved through the wall, his mind was so there that when he went backwards, he fell through the wall. *You can change reality*. It's not just what's there. It's what you choose to broadcast forward from you. You just aren't quite ready yet, but you are beginning to understand. I don't believe there is one single school of metaphysical teaching that offers this level of cutting edge stuff. I don't know anyone who can even go there. No one is teaching this stuff because they don't know how to tap into it.

I hate to ring my own chimes, but it shows you what kind of teacher I really am when I've got such a diverse variety of students. These teachings have only been available to great yogis but now you can learn them, too. Do not dismiss the incredibleness of what you are on the verge of. You have no idea where this is heading. Trust me. There is a big plan for all of this and it's just going to ramp up, but first we must take little steps.

If you think about where you started off from when you first met me, and where you are now, there has been a profound change. Pat yourself on the back that you could even figure out how to do this. You're not supposed to know all of this. It's not supposed to happen. You've broken all the rules.

Tim said something about doing a feels-like that really helped me. When you're in that spot, you have to try to appear normal. Everything else may slow down, but one of the things you can do is the feels-like that you're being pushed off by a pool of water and you're moving through. For me, that really works. I feel like I just pushed off the wall and I'm moving.

That's brilliant. That's excellent, Tim. Excellent!

I think you really nailed it with the description about the eyes because when I was playing around with it, I noticed that my eyes got bigger and felt like they were opening. It went from there into the chest and it became a breathing rhythm. As I was looking at the room and the people, it was like a breathing wave. Then I realized that everything was breathing. Everything's pliable and fluid. You can go back and forth with it.

At Muriel's yesterday, the whole room was breathing. The carpet was breathing. The curtains were breathing. Then I started playing with it further. As I walked down the steps, I looked at the grains of the wood on the steps. As I looked at the grains of the wood and felt it, I realized that the grains were not wood on the steps. It was the grain of the light of the tree. Then I felt the tree and the rhythmic growth of the tree through the grain.

These are divine universal things. They are secrets: something that humans don't necessarily tap into or get to experience. Just the fact that you're witnessing or sharing these experiences and insights is profound. I wonder sometimes why everybody is not shouting, "Oh my God!" What do you do with it? There was a time not too long ago when you just wanted to experience anything. That is something for you to think about.

Maybe now you understand why I have an issue with mirrors. The one thing I don't like when I'm In-Between is mirrors because there's just something that reflects. It's not that I'm afraid of anything. I feel like I'm going to get caught up into something. There's something a little intimidating about mirrors, like it's a bigger task to have to tackle.

Right now, everything that you're experiencing depends on whatever your mind happens to trip over. Then, all of a sudden, you just get caught up in it. The difference between where you are at and where I'm at is that I can choose what I want to experience. If I want the soda machine to move, I literally can move it out of the way. Do you now understand what happened when I put the key in the floor and then moved it when I was In-Between? Do you wonder whether I can take something from this dimension and move it into another? Those were the experiences I had in my younger days. Can I hide myself while I am walking? There are other dimensions that are almost in between the molecules, like a prism.

It's like the House of Mirrors where the mirrors all turn. Then, all of a sudden, everything vanishes because it's like a different reflection. Even though the person is standing there, you can't really see her. All of a sudden, the mirror turns and then everything comes into view. It's like that. It's just such a strange world. If you can stomach playing around with the In-Between, using the tools that you've learned from all the classes, and bring them into that state of mind, you eventually can use them to play with and change reality. You can change and affect things. You can affect people. You can do miracles. You just have to eventually play around in there long enough that you learn how to operate things.

No longer are you subject to how things react to you. Instead, you're able to trigger that reaction. When you walk through the city, there's going to be pockets like the one where the gargoyle interacted with him or where the walls move. Those are the places where there are higher levels of paranormal energy that pool in certain spots. You can literally find doorways that you can interact with that you would not be able to normally see. If you're in a normal state of mind, they just would not be there. Right now, you are just dabbling on level one. Imagine being the wizard who walks up to the wall and knocks on it. Then the whole thing turns into a doorway. It's literally like you're playing on that level. You just have to let yourself get there.

When I was out in that parking lot, I connected with the tree as well. It basically turned into like this gummy substance and we were doing this dance together. It was a really cool feeling.

That is excellent!

Last night, in the restaurant, the people in the pictures on the walls were wiggling in the borders. From my peripheral, I could see everything wiggling. They were just not standing still. During the meditation this morning, an area just started vibrating and fluttering like leaves. Outside today, I was looking at the bulb inside a lantern that was reflecting something else. The whole lantern just started vibrating. As I inhaled with my eyes, I noticed the lights in the pond start pulling out. I felt like Alice in Wonderland for quite a while.

That's really what it's like. I never liked Alice in Wonderland because it's just too much. There are too many things messed up from the way that they should be.

Yesterday, when we started the tone meditation, I shifted immediately and the two people in front of me just phased out. Then the Babbler, that little voice in my head said, "Oh, it's happening!" I had to quieten it. Then the medallions on the carpet started spinning in a counter-clockwise motion for a second. I thought it was motion sickness brewing from my meditation. When everyone around me made it through that, it was great then.

Last night at Muriel's outside of the séance room, there was a shadow on the floor that didn't belong to anyone. At the same time, I heard a conversation that no one was having in an area over two other participants.

When we went outside, I wanted to stay in but it wasn't because I was cold. It was too bright and I couldn't look around, so instead I looked at the pavement. I'm pretty short, but suddenly I was a giant. I looked down and exclaimed, "Look at the lengths of my legs." There were cracks in the pavement the size of the Grand Canyon, only it didn't matter because I was a giant. It was a great experience.

That's excellent! Reality is what it is because of the frequency we're locked into. You are now learning the Magi secrets about how you change reality and do these really cool things. How do I play with the weather on such a grand level?

When you practice things over and over again, everything becomes wax on and wax off just like in *The Karate Kid*. All of the tools that you have practiced and had success with are easier to use in the In-Between state. It's harder to use these tools in the state that you were originally taught to use them. The problem with the In-Between is learning to control yourself. Can you imagine how hard it is to bring you In-Between and then teach you the stuff that you've learned already? It is easier to teach that stuff to you for maybe a year before you play around with the In-Between. During that year, you could slowly integrate those tools as you learn to control your mind better. You can just be there.

Then you can take these tools and assimilate a storm. You can manifest something. When you're In-Between, all of these things take on the power of ten. They can be magnified if you can just let your mind go there and operate from that place. It's really profound, but it takes great skill. It's like learning to juggle and balance pots and pans, but it can be done.

Time can also be shifted in the In-Between. You can speed time up In-Between or you can slow it down. Just the other day, I asked, "Well, what time is it?" Then we went into this state. Then all of a sudden, there was no time. It just zipped by, but I think we see this a lot. You're going to see it a lot more often when you go into the In-Between. Time is going to leap. Enormous amounts of time can pass in what feels like seconds. So, it's just something you want to be aware of.

There's so many things to cover. I want to give you so much information so when you go home and you start to have more experiences you can say, "Oh, Eric talked about this or he talked about that." Obviously, I can't possibly cover everything. There's just not enough time. *I'm always looking for anomalies, like the time a shadow was caused by nothing.* There often are shadows that are portals. When you look at all the shadows and you can match up all of them except one, you wonder where that shadow is from. Why is it out of place? There shouldn't be one there. The sun is hitting it, but it just shouldn't be there. Those are what I call portals. They're almost like a consciousness.

Another very interesting thing to look at when you're In-Between is a mirror. When it rains on the street, puddles can be intriguing, too. For some reason, the concrete takes on this vibe to it. Then your mind can literally go right into this whole other place. It's very surreal. Make sure you watch out for the puddles.

If you get really good, there's a lot of experiments that you probably could start doing. There's one that you could do with the water element and the mirror. Some of you know what I'm talking about. Doesn't that sound interesting? There are certain things you can do with your collective. You don't have to be intensely In-Between. All you need is to be one quarter of a percent In-Between. Do your techniques from that place, being aware that you're In-Between. Then watch how your techniques are enhanced when you're in that state.

When you go to these haunted places, you can tune in to entities popping through into this dimension to scope it out. Hopefully, you'll have something happen there but don't just look for the entities. Use the indoor places to play with your environment some more, too. If you find the entity, that's great, but experiment with other stuff because you don't know whether there will be entities in these houses or not.

Can you use a mirror if you don't have a person sitting across from you to do the same thing?

Well, I'm going to be honest with you. I'm not fond of working with mirrors as I've told you. I wouldn't advise working with mirrors in the In-Between state. There's always the Darkside. I've told you before that if you want to move this, you've got to move that. Since mirrors represent a reflection in reverse, they facilitate this weird way of communicating with entities that can be quite vocal.

At one time, I had a friend named Gary who I taught how to shift In-Between. I also taught him how to use his chest intelligence. We were staying at this hotel and that night he went into the bathroom and he used his eyes to go In-Between. Then Gary heard quite clearly, "Go to the wall," so he looked at the wall which contained large cinder blocks that were painted over. Gary's mind was so In-Between from shifting that the face morphed and it was that person talking to him. Not only did it morph, the face was talking to him audibly, "Go to the wall." Then all the bricks in the wall illuminated. They just lightened up. When Gary looked at it, he said that the cinder blocks started to move into the wall. He could hear the blocks grinding. Gary said that he knew in his chest intelligence that if he let the brick wall open up, it would create a gateway for this entity to come through. Gary knew that the entity was trying to fool him into letting it through. I try not to allow these things to happen because there's certain other things you need to learn from me first. I'm very careful when I give you information because there's always someone who wants to do it anyway because they think they're ready.

Gary felt that if the bricks fell through, the entity was going to be able to come through because the wall was probably still very much there for somebody in another spatial consciousness. That's where normal people are. Gary created a doorway in his mind because he believed a portal was there. That's all you need to bend reality. Since the entity was there communicating with him and it wanted to move into this dimension, he assisted it. In a sense, entities need assistance. His belief was, "This is an opening." Gary linked telepathically with this reflection thing in the mirror. He knew it would come through but it took all of his strength. The wall was in front of him but he felt like he was sucked to it at the same time. He's a grown man but he said he ran to his bed and pulled the covers up over him. Then he came into my room yelling, "Eric! Eric!" I asked him, "What?!" Then he said to me, "I did some bad shit."

It was quite interesting. I went into his room and I could see what had transpired. It's like an after effect. It's not quite as intense, but I could see the waviness in the wall and everything! I filled the sink up with water, and I took a cup of the water and threw it on the wall. Of course, water has a very interesting effect. It's very mirror-like, but it's different. There was this fire-like heat coming off the wall. I knew that if I threw the water on the wall, in Gary's mind it's like putting out a fire. *I used his thinking to bridge the link and drop the effect.* The water cooled the wall and the heat subsided, putting the fire-like heat out. I looked at him and you could see it was over in his mind. I told him to go back to bed and I went back to bed. Gary never played with it ever again. A lot of those kinds of things happened in my younger days. What can I say? I scared a lot of people.

He did it with all the lights low and everything, so that was foolish. You've got to remember that your mind invokes the things that you're drawn to. They're like channels. I'm not saying that you can't do that. Just realize that if you're really In-Between, and you're really pushing it, you haven't exercised your own mind 100% to really know where you want to go with things.

What's the first thing that you would do if something like that started happening? What are you going to do? Pyramid! Sword! Right here! Hack, Hack, hack! There's a big cord (or chord as in frequency) between you and that person. You want to start choping those cords with your machete. In a sense, you're breaking that connection. You're creating the thought of releasing it. That's what breaks the link. It just takes a tiny bit for it to break.

Can you use the technique where you pull in through the eyes with sounds while listening to the sound?

Yes, you can use it with anything. That technique is brilliant. When you think about it and you look out, you can almost feel that your mind is going this way if you try to feel the subtleness of it. Your mind is always going out to see what's there. It's never going in it. Whatever you look at, it's like you're reaching out to it. You're seeing it from a distance but it's like you're reaching to grab stuff. It's always in your five senses. Even your hearing is looking for something, "Where is it? It's over there." When you look for something, where is it? It's never about bringing it back to you which is basically what's happening.

When you reach for this to affect that, think about it. Instead of reaching out with your eyes, pull it in. Breathe it in. That's what rolls your mind to start flipping into that other state. It's like it says, "Okay, take reality and let's see what's really on the inside out." That is what turns it and it works very well.

When you do a feels-like, you can feel this and it's very natural. It's hard to feel anymore because you do it without thought. There's literally a flow outward. It's very different when you pull it in. It's like something in your inside starts to work with it, other than your other senses. It says that this is something different than your normal sensory is designed to do.

Technique

There's another technique that I thought I'd explain to you so you can play around with it later. I want you to close your eyes slightly, but at some point you have to do it with your eyes open so you can learn it. When you're pulling in, I want you to imagine that there's a mirror in the back of your eyes. I want you to look at the reflection in the mirror in the back of your eyes, instead of outward. Your consciousness is trying to look behind you, as if you have eyes in the back of your head. Now close your eyes. Imagine what's in the room behind you, including the people behind you. Use your imagination. Then put a mirror there to see yourself in your mind's eye in reverse. You can either put a mirror behind you, or you put a mirror like it's sliding into your skull. It's on the other side and you're looking in the mirror at yourself backwards. These things seem simple to me. Everybody should be able to do it without a problem, but you don't have to actually do it.

To elaborate on that technique, I want you to sit in a chair. Close your eyes and feel the sensation of looking backwards. In your mind, imagine rolling your eyes in their socket so instead of looking straight out in front of you, they are now facing backwards in your head, almost like a doll's eye's move. Just do a feels-like of what that sensation feels like. Try to use your mind's eye as if you can see what's behind you. If there are people behind you, imagine the people behind you. You don't need to have an exact match. Just use whatever your mind says. It's the sensation that it creates in the biochemical part of the brain. It makes it so that your brain operates differently. When I do it, I feel it right away in the chest and the throat. You have to play with it for a while, but you can do it with your eyes open at the same time. When your eyes are open, you have the sensation of doing it in reverse but it probably takes some practice.

It jacks the brain up once you figure out how to do it. When you get it under control, it will shift you, too. I decided that breathing in through the eyes was an easier technique and it was just as effective, but it may bring you into a different state of consciousness. I already feel how well it works on me because I can feel the metallic taste in my mouth.

Now you know why I chose the other technique because this one is a lot harder. It makes your brain wonder what the heck is going on. That's what tricks it so that when you look out, it's as if you're looking through those reverse eyes as if they were forward. Just don't think about it. Do you remember what I said about turning things inside out by breathing them in? It's like you turn your consciousness inside out so you get to see the illusion for what it is, or you start to see the threads of it moving.

What about viewing collective consciousnesses when you're in the In-Between? The other day you told me that something I described to you was the collective consciousness of the trees. Could you then see the A.I.? Or could you see the Ancients or I's of the planet while in the In-Between?

There is no limit to what you can do in the In-Between, but you have to be careful because you don't want to break yourself. When you have mental pressure in your head, that's what is happening. Whenever I start talking about stuff or invoking it, your mind moves on it. You mentally seek it out, whether you realize it or not. I'll delve into this a little bit.

When he was in Hawaii, he was probably going In-Between without necessarily realizing it at the time. Anyway, he saw some beautiful trees so he went there. As he approached them, he saw what looked like a ball of energy. He really felt it was the collective of the trees. Plant life of the same species, or even partially the same species has a tendency to become a collective. Plants don't think and communicate individually. They tend to create a collective of shared aspects of their consciousness to make one shared consciousness. In my opinion, that's what he was seeing. How does that work for other collectives?

The problem with the Gaia Mind is size. Size matters. It's so big! Since you are in the thick of the Gaia Mind, that makes it very difficult. If you could take yourself outside of the planet and look at it from that state of consciousness, you would probably see fiber-like balls. Consciousness is like strings moving within strings where everything is in a spherical shape. This should give you a better understanding of the nature of ley lines. They are really the byways of the consciousness moving.

There are always layers and multi-layers of collective consciousness. Everything is one collective. It's very difficult to understand, but there are layers to that frequency. There's a ball moving within a ball of fibers and they're all made up of fibers. They're all moving in different ways, yet it's one ball working collectively. If you were to find one layer, you could really understand that one layer instead of all of them moving.

There's the collective consciousness of all the plant life. Then there's the collective consciousness of animal species like monkeys or elephants. Then you have the collective consciousness of all the humans. Of course, then you have the whole sum total of how it becomes one consciousness for the planet. They all become one, but there are individual levels to it all.

You could say that going into the Akashic Records is like moving into one of the spiral fiber levels and that each corridor is one of the fibers that builds into that level. Each is a different direction of information or time. It's very difficult to explain.

If you're going to sync to influence ley lines, a crossover of ley lines, or an Ancient, how would you approach it? Would you be able to visually do that?

Have you ever seen what happens to a person when they're hit by lightning out in a field? I know your intentions are good, but you have to be careful how you try to communicate. You may not want to use the word *influence* because that means you want to tell it something or affect it to do what you want. As far as The Force goes, everything in consciousness and even other levels of that aspect are very sensitive to control issues. So, the word influence has a vibe to it. It has a subtle intention. When you're in hyper consciousness or when you're In-Between, you're so sensitive that's enough to alert it that your intentions may not be good.

You're wishing to communicate or experience it. You want it to move in you. You intuitively know that you would communicate. You don't have to say that, but it will have to be this kind of thing. You have to approach it very delicately until it decides it can trust you, once it knows what your intentions are. Everything on these levels is uniquely different. Remember, they're alien. It's like communicating to a species that does not have hands, arms, a mouth or a nose. It can be very scary for it to see you open your mouth. It may wonder, "What is it going to do with that? Is it going to bite me?" You're talking, but it can't hear you talk. These things don't think. Just because we're a part of it, that does not necessarily mean it relates well to us. The only thing it can relate to is what you send in a vibration. Until you learn to communicate, you have to be very careful of what you put out there. The one thing it's sensitive to is vibration, especially when you're rough, because it's a new thing for you.

I'll give you another insider tip. Every Navigator seems to love storm weather. There's something about the electricity and the energy in the air. Whether you realize it or not, that's what it is. When the clouds are moving, that's consciousness moving for the Gaia mind. When you see electrical storms in different regions, there's something going on in the Gaia Mind. If you're in outer space, you can see these storms. You can see the lightning in the clouds. That is almost exactly what the brain looks like when you're viewing it under an EEG. When I go into an In-Between state while these storms are happening, I can always feel the consciousness as if it's moving around me. It's like spirits, but it's not spirits. It's like thoughts, but it's so alien that you have to go slower. In a sense, you have to go faster so you go slower to communicate. You could almost say it becomes a *micro Ancient*.

If it chooses to communicate with you, that doesn't mean that it's going to look like a human or even a being. It's a presence and that is what you have to accept, but it will put enough of its intelligence together so that it can cohesively meet you on your terms. It's like having to communicate with a baby. If you want to communicate with a baby, you have to go down to a level that it's receptive to. You are way more advanced so you know that the baby may not necessarily relate to some words, depending on its age. You fixate your consciousness on whatever level you think they're going to understand.

It will communicate but it's very difficult because the technology is very different. It's much like learning to balance balls and everything else while trying to find that inner peace. If you ever want to try to experience it, the only thing that I would recommend is to *surrender to the process*. Become the reed in the wind and let it work with you so your mind will bend and move with it and you'll walk away with an incredible experience. However, it's very complex and it's probably a four hour conversation in itself.

It's interesting because we are starting to cover areas that the Higher Balance coaches haven't really started with me. They have to some degree but you can see them wanting to interact now more so than they have in previous years. That shows you how advanced you are getting.

I noticed something when I went outside. You mentioned that we're not entering this dimension with the same perspective as the collective. This ripples everything and bends the rules. When everybody was outside in the parking lot, we were all staggering and everybody was facing a car or a tree. We looked really bizarre.

There was a guy who came up through the little corridor from the front desk. As he entered the parking lot, he looked at Eric and the students who were laughing. He noticed something was different but he wasn't wondering what we were doing.

When he started to walk from there to this building, you could almost tell that to him it just seemed a lot farther than it should have been. Not only did it feel farther, but you could feel on a micro level he had to try harder to walk from A to B, which to me was representative of the fact that reality was changing.

Yes, reality was changing! Since you are the nodes, you've created a field of presence that emanates probably about twelve feet out through each of you. That's a great observation!

You mentioned you were trying a technique that reacts completely different. Obviously, everybody created this warbling of possibility. Instead of having to think about the weather and the wind, we tune into it like you taught in the Mexico retreat, Mayan Storm. It was already pre-packaged to bend with you because no assimilation was needed for it to happen. It reacted completely differently.

I think you're going to find a lot of interesting things now that you are dabbling around with the In-Between. When I was younger, I discovered that sometimes if I went out into wind storms, I could feel tubes and literally almost touch them. It's like the wind becomes structural tubes against these fibers. Then I learned that they're almost like consciousness but they're invisible to us. It's like radio and T.V. waves.

Going In-Between in New Orleans seems to have a different flavor than when we went In-Between at either the retreat in Mexico or the retreat in Hawaii. Does the location have a very profound effect on us or is that because we are in different states of consciousness?

We picked New Orleans because we would not have the success of this flavor if we hadn't. Remember what I said in the very beginning? It is the collective consciousness. The age of New Orleans and its uniqueness affect the collective consciousness. If you put yourself in an unusual environment, it's just like grabbing an object here to affect us over there. I knew that your success levels in figuring this out would be much better in a unique place than in a place where you already associate with everything.

If you've noticed, it's harder for the locals than it is for people from outside the area. The locals would have a more difficult time because they associate with this environment. Even the locals within this group have a harder time shifting because they have already been to the areas we went to, like the exotic room at

Muriel's. Their tagging and relationship to that place is different than ours. The same goes for the whole city. There's no written program with the collective there for those of you from outside the area because you're not part of the local collective.

For those of you who are not from New Orleans but have visited the French Quarter more than once, you have a lot of programming there and you know the vibe of the people, so the program is able to push those buttons. The two people who are from this area had some difficulties shifting. I suspected that this would occur.

So, it's definitely a case of the ties that bind you. Everything I teach is consistent. A particular region, a town, an area of a town, individual homes, individual bedrooms or even individual people will all have their own collective consciousness. It depends on what level you want to look at. It's like tuning into that frequency. There are some towns where you go and you just don't like the vibe there. Other places have a really good vibe. When you're doing what we're doing, you want something to be so different that it doesn't impose the program on you that you're supposed to react to. If you already have a program for your home environment, it's harder to change it. If you go to some place where you're not familiar with the program, you don't just flow with it. You're poking your finger at it, so you're able to play with it differently instead of it having a strong effect on you. When you go back home, now that you've been able to experience the In-Between, you can't unknow what you know. You can dabble with it, but you'll find that you have the best experiences in other places rather than your home environment because that's the strongest programming of what everything is supposed to be. It's as if reality is written in a specific frequency for you there.

I've been waiting 14 years to ask you something.

Oh, great. Remember, that a simple answer from me can change your consciousness. It might be the catalyst that creates a revelation for your mind that changes everything! A long time ago, I was trying to explain something to someone and the thought of it made them fall over backwards. It just struck a chord with their neural system, not that that's what's going to happen now. I know you would all love it though. That's how you all feel.

The night after you walked through the wall, you and I meditated in pitch blackness. When we opened up our eyes afterwards, reality wasn't there. We were somewhere else completely. So, when I came out of it, there was phenomena happening.

I couldn't recognize the room at all. We were both looking at it, recognizing it and I just relaxed backwards and fell through the wall. That's when it clicked. That's when I realized I was through it. Then I panicked. When I came back up, even though I recognized I was supposed to be in my room, I tried reaching for the lamp. My hand was going through the area where it should have been, so it made it that more intense.

When you meditate with your eyes closed, do you go In-Between because you're just not recognizing reality?

Since you're still mentally linked with me, the programming copied that experience, that feeling, that vibration. You knew that it was possible after witnessing me do it. *I can do miracles because I know that I can.* When that happened, you witnessed it. You saw me walk through a solid wall. You were there. You knew that this was impossible, but yet I walked through the wall. So, you accepted that as being possible.

When you meditated, you cleared your mind. You were still blown away by that experience. By clearing your mind and think-ing about that experience, that is a code. It is a written computer code. You were able to integrate that without realizing it. When you went back, you literally did the same thing I did. You just did it without knowing you did it. When you meditated, you achieved non-thought and you replaced that non-thought with a program that creates a dimension. You changed the illusion to remove what was here. Thus, that experience was allowed to happen. When you pulled up, you had the revelation of what had happened. Since you had that revelation, you knew what happened was amazing, but it shouldn't have happened. That is the echo. It's what solidified and made this rubber reality bloop. Then it solidified again. So, you had the code. You have the code now. You've always had the code. Nobody else here has the code, but because you were there you were able to get that code. You just have never really thought about reactivating it.

You mentioned that feeling like you're in another reality is a way to distort your view of this reality so you can do other stuff. Is there a way to amplify that while you're In-Between to achieve that awakening? Is there some way of using your senses to amplify more than just the idea of that?

You mean to just literally move into another reality?

Yeah, or just watch this reality turn into whatever reality.

Of course, it's completely possible. In the few times that I've stopped being here, the question is, "Where did I go?" First of all, there is a necessity for people to be here. It takes a great deal of skill to do such a thing. That doesn't mean that you can't do it. It would just be unwise. Do you remember how I talked about cases where people just vanished? I'm not saying they had the skill to do it themselves. Maybe they were just at the wrong place at the wrong time.

It is true that you can create those moments to make yourself step into something else. But, it's far easier to find portals to look for that experience than to actually make it happen. The program here is so strong because it has to be. It's hard, but you can bend slivers of it.

It's a question that I don't really want to answer at this moment because I know that people will jump on it mentally. If that's the case, it's another responsibility that I'm going to have to deal with for people. It's like handing over a loaded gun to a ten year old.

There is an appropriate time and place for all of these things. At the Higher Balance center in Santa Rosa, people can come out to visit me for a week and we can talk. Until you can find your way to the center, I think it's better to continue working where you are. If it's too big of a step, it's too big of a step – but that's where the magic begins!

When you look at the night sky, you'll see thousands of little sparkles. You'll also see things move through the sky. One of the things I want to talk about is aliens. I believe that they cloak their spacecraft when they're moving through so you can't necessarily see them. Sometimes their lower end technology makes it look like a cloud to us. If they decide to land their spaceship, it will look like a tractor in a field to us because they know how to send the program. They have the technology to send the feels-like of a tractor to tell our brain that's a tractor that is sitting out in the field. If you look from an In-Between state of being, especially at the sky, you will actually see what looks like a faint outline of the structure of the craft moving through the air. If you really focus on it, you can see even greater detail. It's not easy to see it, so you really have to push yourself. Also, you probably shouldn't be telling anybody about this.

Can Red Cells see the effects that we make to the matrix?

Yes and no. It depends. You are able to separate yourself from the program but they're stuck in a reality where it's still the same for them. There are ways of sealing what you do and that's how you change reality. The program is so strong that it bounces back. When you're In-Between and you're doing stuff like that, this is a good point to make. You're in that hyper consciousness where things are happening superfast but you don't realize it. That's why time can get jacked up at certain states when you leap there. The simple answer is 'yes.' You can change reality and Red Cells will see those things happen but it's challenging to do that. In some cases, you'll do it without realizing you've done it and there it is.

Sometimes when I meditate, the room loses its dimension. I can make it feel bigger or shrink smaller. Does this elastic place move through dimensions while it moves through objects as they lose their physicality?

Yes, but now you have to learn to move yourself and hold that. It's not an easy task. Hold your imaginary breath; move your hands and pretend you're swimming. There's more truth to that than you know.

I entered this state of consciousness where anything and everything was just free. Does that have any relationship to the In-Between?

Yes and no. It sounds to me more like you headed into your true Middle Pillar for a moment. That is what it's like when we leave our organic bodies. We don't have any more biochemical effects because of our emotions. It seems like she separated for a certain amount of time. That is like what I was talking about the other day where you don't have this feeling of connectedness like sorrow. In a sense, your whole life changed completely but you're still the same.

Chapter 15

BENDING REALITY

The following chapter is a collection of stories and experiences from various students who have trained with Eric Pepin. Permission was given to use names.

Jorge's Experience

I've been studying with Eric for many years now. Shortly after meeting Eric for the first time, I received news from my sister that her son, who was five years old at that time, was diagnosed with lupus. The doctors told her that he had six months to live. Of course, that was devastating for her and our family.

She went to several different hospitals to get second opinions, holding onto the hope that perhaps there was a mistake in his diagnosis. Despite going to three different major hospitals, the results were the same; he had lupus and he didn't have much time to live. There was no denying his condition. The blood and urine tests confirmed his diagnosis time and time again, and you could see he was pretty sick. He had spots on his skin and his urine was literally the color of Coca-Cola.

When I initially received this news I immediately thought of Eric, but I felt that I didn't have the right to ask for his help because I barely knew him. He had been teaching me for about two months by then. I knew what he was capable of and the knowledge that he had, but I felt guilty about asking for his help and putting him in that predicament. At the same time, I felt that I had to ask even if Eric's answer was "no." I felt that I owed my nephew at least that much. The next time I saw Eric, I told him what was going on and asked for his help. He immediately agreed to help me right away, which didn't surprise me because he's such a giving person. Eric and I lived in the same building at that time, so he asked me to go get my nephew and bring him up to his apartment, which I immediately did; not a second was wasted.

I ran down the stairs, knocked on my sister's door, and I brought my nephew up to his place where he proceeded to scan him. I imagine that he was pushing his own energy into my nephew's body. My nephew, this five-year-old boy, was just standing there with innocence in his eyes. He wasn't scared; he seemed comfortable and had the slightest smile on his face. That's all my nephew did; he just stood there with his hands over his head and that was it.

The very next day, my sister took my nephew to the hospital again as part of his weekly checkup. The doctors ran the same blood and urine tests that were run before but this time, they were surprised to find no trace of the disease whatsoever. Everybody was absolutely dumbfounded. After Eric saw my nephew and healed him, all of his disease was gone the next day.

Physically, he was able to function like a normal 5-year old boy again because there was no sign of the disease. Of course, the doctors did the tests again and still found nothing. They couldn't explain to themselves, or to my sister, what was going on. Eventually, all they said was that they didn't know what had happened; they had no idea. After all these tests that showed no sign of the disease, somehow the hospital mysteriously misplaced the initial test results that indicated he had lupus in the first place.

My nephew is about twelve years old now (even older as of the writing of this book) and he's completely healthy. He hasn't had any reoccurring problems with lupus again. I definitely believe that it was a miracle that I saw Eric perform. I'm still very grateful for what he did, and so is my family.

This experience taught me that anything is possible. Reflecting on it, I am able to appreciate the significance of what happened. A boy was given a death sentence by his doctors. He was diagnosed with a terminal disease and given only six months to live. All hope was gone. My family was devastated, and all of a sudden, everything is fixed. Eric showed me that miracles are possible. That experience showed me that, not only do miracles happen, but also *how* they happen, and *how* you can actually do them yourself. It just showed me that anything is possible; you just have to believe.

Eric R's Experience

Eric Pepin, my brother Matthew, and I made a trip up into the Santa Monica Mountains. At that time, Eric had a big four-by-four Baja California runner truck. We went all the way up to the top of the Santa Monica Mountains. There's not a lot of foliage or vegetation in those Mountains. This national forest is a joke, because there aren't really many trees, just scrubs, brush and stuff like that. But you've got a great view of the sky. While you're up there, you can see the lights of Los Angeles off in the distance. Up above, there wasn't a cloud in the sky. All you could see were stars everywhere. On the left was the constant glow of Los Angeles and on the right is desert; it's pretty much pitch black out there.

Anyway, we're up there hanging out in the back of the truck just talking and suddenly, it was as if for a split second the whole sky flashed white. It's like what it would look like if you've ever experienced an intense lighting storm – how it flashes for a second and everything gets real bright – except there was no storm. There was no lighting, there were no clouds. L.A. is notorious for having absolutely zero weather. Of course, I froze and started to look around. I was thinking, *what was that? Something just happened in my brain. Is something going on with my head?* However, I didn't say anything to Eric or Matthew. I just looked around.

Maybe thirty seconds later, the whole sky flashed white again. It was around midnight and there was light coming from L.A., but the white flash wasn't a search light because the entire sky lit up. I asked, "Man, did you guys see that?" And Matthew and Eric just started laughing. They start mocking me, "Ha, ha, ha real funny ha, ha." And I said, "No, seriously." They respond mockingly, "Yeah?" "What's going on?" It's important to note that Matthew's always been a little more open to unusual or paranormal things, so I think they liked to give me a hard time because I was Mr. "This Stuff Can't Happen. This is all crazy talk," whenever they discussed paranormal things.

So they were laughing at me and I said, "No, really, did you guys see that?" They said, "Yeah," and I asked, "What was that?" And Eric looked at Matthew and said, "Oh, it must be a search light from L.A." I said, "No way, L.A. is way over there and a search light's going to be one little beam; that was like the whole sky just lit up white." And Eric replied, "Well, must be a radio tower." I looked off in the distance, you could see these little blinking red lights. I said, "Come on, the radio tower's way over there, it's just one little monotonous blinking light, it hasn't changed in the last hour." Although I may have been a little slow on picking up on things, this was the whole sky that flashed white. And Eric asked sarcastically, "Well, I don't know. What could it be?" I let it go then.

Sure enough, thirty or forty seconds later at about the same rhythm, the whole sky completely flashed white and I blurted out, "Whatever you're going to say, just tell me what it's supposed to be because it's not a search light, and it's nothing coming from L.A. I'm looking at the lights over there and there are no clouds in the sky, so it's not lightning." I went through this whole big list of everything that I didn't want him to suggest. These guys had a good time making fun of me. Finally Eric said, "Well, it's the rhythm, the shift of the planet. Just like how the human body has a heartbeat and sends electrical impulses through the body, the planet has a similar thing."

This was when my brother and I both had time off from work and we'd been around Eric for a while, like four or five days straight. When you're around him for a while and you get saturated with his frequency, it gets a little intense. This experience was like the tail end of being around him for all those days. Eric said that what we saw was the shift of the planet and that it is possible to get to the point where you're able to tune into that and physically see it take place. It continued for the next thirty minutes. It was a steady beat, just like clockwork, every thirty or forty seconds, 'boom', the whole sky would flash white. That was a pretty crazy thing.

Jason's Experience

Eric and I decided to visit a local hotel that was known to be haunted. While we were there eating at the hotel restaurant, we talked one of the waitresses into showing us the haunted part of the hotel. We went up with her and scouted out the area. Almost immediately, we began to notice some very interesting things happening. The first thing that I noticed was the smell of old fashioned perfume. I asked the waitress if she was wearing any perfume and she said, "No." The scent was almost like an old rosy smell. It wasn't a modern perfume because no one in their right mind would wear such a flowery scent.

As we walked around, we picked up on these things and we could sense different energies. Eric was really tuned into everything that was happening. He could feel the entities leaving one room as soon as he came in. We'd open a door, the entities would scatter. He started to empathically pick up on a situation with this particular room. Apparently there was a murder he was picking up on. He could sense the people that lived there, how they were feeling, their sense of dread, and a feeling of suffocation.

We were picking up a lot and we were seeing a lot unfold. As we got to the last room, one of the windows in the room swung open by itself. This was very interesting and, of course we did a little scientific check because we wanted to make sure that it was authentic. We tried to push open the window, push it back, to see if it was maybe air pressure or something like that. The window was so rusty that it took a lot of force to move it. The entity that moved it used a lot of strength and energy to do that.

I have a hypothesis about the whole situation: Eric doesn't like to be in stuffy places. He likes fresh air, and I think the entity was obliging him by opening the window. I find that to be true because of the way spiritual beings acknowledge him. Just his presence up there was like shaking a beehive. They knew he was there and so they were scattering about, doing all these things, and we were picking up on all of it. I think if I'd gone by myself, I wouldn't have picked up anything. I wouldn't have stirred the nest. Hang around Eric long enough and you're going to see him stir a lot of nests.

Dan's Experience

An experience that comes to mind is one of the first things I actually saw Eric do. It was just absolutely astounding and it was only the second day that I knew him. He had a large leafed house plant. It was definitely sickly and looked like it needed some serious Miracle-Gro.

When I first saw it, I made a comment to Eric about how he needed to do something with this plant; it looked like it needed be thrown out or something. He made a comment to me about how it just needed some good love and care. Then he reached up and stuck his fingers in the dirt over the top of the pot and said, "Yeah, it'll be fine." My mother raised me where I have compassion for plants, so I really felt bad for this poor thing. However, I just left the situation at that and figured it was a goner.

Shortly afterwards, we left the house and went out to eat. When we returned approximately four or five hours later, Eric asked me, "Did you notice the plant?" I looked at him dumbfounded and said, "What do you mean – your plant? The one that's downstairs?" And he answered, "Yeah." I said, "No, what about it?" He said, "Go look at it. Tell me what you think."

I went downstairs and looked at the plant and was absolutely amazed. The plant had grown, and this is not an exaggeration by any means, a good two feet in that short amount of time that we were out. As a matter of fact, it grew so quickly that the leaves and the stem were white, almost transparent. I ran upstairs and asked, "Eric, how can that be, how can that be?" He said, "I told you I was going to take care of it," just nonchalantly.

Kerri's and Eric R's Experience

My name is Kerri. My experience happened in the year 2000. Eric Pepin, Eric R., and I had gone to see a lecture at the Philosophical Research Society on Egyptian metaphysics for a paper I was writing for school. During this lecture, the speaker talked about various things and then did a guided meditation of sorts. We stayed just to enjoy the day and have that experience.

When we left, we decided to go to a restaurant. It was a hipster diner type of place, but was really busy and chaotic. We sat down at the table. It was Eric R. and I on either end with Eric Pepin in the middle, and he had the Sunday Times. He set the paper down in front of him and we had all ordered our drinks. Eric always drinks iced tea. The tea came in a large glass that was packed full with ice, actually packed to the brim. They put all the ice in the glass before they put the tea in, so there's just a little bit of tea in this glass.

Eric's glass of iced tea was on the newspaper which was set in front of him, and he took some sweetener and poured it in the glass. The entire sweetener just sat on top of the ice. Eric took a spoon and started crushing the ice to try to stir it up. But the sweetener was just swirling around in the glass and wasn't dissolving like normal. Eric then said, "I hope it makes it to the bottom." Then he took the spoon out, put a straw in, and goes back to looking at his menu. He took a sip of his tea and had a very strange bewildered look on his face. He took another sip to make sure before lifting the glass off the newspaper. When he lifted it up, there was a perfectly dry pile of sweetener where the glass was. It wasn't wet with moisture from condensation from the glass. It wasn't diluted with tea. It was just a perfectly dry pile of sweetener on the newspaper.

Eric R.

We both saw him tear two packets of sugar at once. We both saw him initially put the glass down. We both saw the sweetener dump out on top of the iced tea, and we both saw him stab the spoon in the glass. Neither of us left to go to the bathroom, nobody moved. We saw him pick the glass up, and we both saw a pile right there in the middle of the wet ring and the sweetener dust around the outside of the glass where it fell off. I remember he just laughed about it, and made a comment like, "Whoa, gotta be careful."

It seems like a small thing, but when you think about what actually happened, it is staggering. Because he had a desire and he was in this certain state of mind, he wanted the sweetener towards the bottom of the glass. He projected or moved it there. It sounds insignificant, but there's this dry pile of sweetener *underneath* the glass. The sweetener was stirred into the glass of tea! Then it ended up on the bottom of the glass, perfectly dry, in this neat little pile when he lifted the glass.

Eric R's Experience

In the summer of 2000, I was meeting a group of people at Eric Pepin's house. It was me, my brother Matthew, Kerri, and Jeff. I don't think anyone of us feels any different, but it was probably the biggest experience, moment, or event in our lives. It was certainly the biggest experience or moment of my life up until that point. So, we were meeting at Eric's place and some of us happened to be late. This had been happening a lot more often than it should have, almost on a regular basis.

When we got there, Eric told us not to sit down; we were not staying. We thought he was upset because being late is a little disrespectful. He simply stated upon our arrival that we're all going for a ride. We went out to my truck and nobody really said anything.

After getting into the truck, Eric starts to tell me, turn by turn, where to go. The truck had an uncertain tension of nobody being quite sure how the day's going to go or what's going on because we were supposed to meet for a class or a lecture, and here we are in the truck.

Eric took us down a road where I've never been before. We went through a neighborhood and pulled up to a relatively small park. This park is basically one giant hill. There weren't really any trees, at least not where we were. It was pretty grassy and there was a paved path that went up to the top of the hill. The path curved up, spiraling around towards the top of this big hill.

So, Eric started walking up the hill without saying anything. He didn't say why we were there or what we were there to do. He just got out of the truck and said, "Get out." We all got out and he started walking up the hill. I think Matthew and Kerri were right behind him and I made sure nobody was lagging behind because I didn't want to irritate him any more than we already had. I made sure that Jeff was following too.

The way Eric was walking with his hands behind him and his head down like he was thinking about something was very different than his normal walk. He walked maybe halfway up the hill, and that's when I noticed another sidewalk curving around from the other side of the hill. The sidewalks merged into a single sidewalk and then continued up to the top of the hill.

Walking on the other sidewalk was a Sikh-looking person dressed in very traditional garb: he had the turban, cloth slippers, and a white robe. Los Angeles is a very culturally diverse place, but it's very rare to see someone walking around in such traditional looking garb. This man was maybe 70 or 80 and he had a big, thick white beard. He was wearing all white, had big flowing robes, a big turban. Basically, if you have ever read a book on old

Indian Yogis and flipped open a page to see of any of them from the earliest times, they would look like this guy.

The interesting thing was, when he merged into the sidewalk, he and Eric were basically side by side, and neither of them changed the way in which they were carrying themselves as they were walking. When we first got there, this man could not be seen from where we started. He walked around from the other side of the hill. But he and Eric were walking in the exact same manner. Both of their hands were held behind them, one hand holding the other. Both of their heads were face down, like in deep thought.

When they merged onto the sidewalk, it was almost like they were a mirror image of each other. They were both holding themselves exactly the same way and walking at almost the same pace. The Sikh had his head down and after he'd walked maybe three or four steps beside Eric, he lifted his head up, looked at Eric; Eric lifted his head up, looked at the Sikh who nodded his head in acknowledgement of Eric being there, and Eric nodded his head back.

Then they both turned their heads back down like they were walking before. That was it. Eric was walking faster than the Sikh at that point, so he sped up and walked ahead of him. The interesting thing was, as other people passed this older man, he never looked up and he never broke his train of thought. The only person he acknowledged as each of us passed by him was Eric.

We quickly got to the top of the hill where we found that there were more trees. The rest of the hill was very bare, yet very grassy. There was also a big playground with lots of playground equipment and sand.

Playing at this playground was an Indian family; two girls and a boy and the husband and wife and they were swinging. At that point I started to become aware of how surreal it all seemed. I think one of the little girls came up with a ball and looked at Eric. It was almost like these two separate worlds came crashing together; there was our group and there was the family enjoying the Sunday afternoon. But something didn't seem normal, that's probably the best way I could explain it. We got to the top of the hill and Eric made some comment about how we all needed to start being more aware. We had to pay attention.

So we all looked around and noticed that the park went up to the peak of the hill, which is a playground, and then it goes back down into a valley below. That's when we confirmed that this park was really just one giant hill. We looked over to the other side and started walking towards it. We followed the paved path for a little bit as it went down, and then we broke off the sidewalk and walked down the side of the hill into a grassy point where it was more of an open area, not in the trees.

We were sitting there for a little bit, in a semi-circle around Eric. He's talking about how much we've been meditating, and about consciousness and how we have to start exercising our consciousness and being more aware. All of a sudden, he started swishing his hand in front of his face. All around his head was a huge swarm of gnats. I didn't notice any gnats around me. He said something about how gnats were attracted to higher consciousness. When we started to shift, all these gnats suddenly swarmed him. After a minute or two he said, "We've got to move."

So we all stood up and started to walk back up the hill in the direction that we came down. About halfway up the hill, he asked us if we noticed the wind. We all look at each other and nobody dared to answer. Then he said, "Was it normal or paranormal?" Again he told us, "You're not paying enough attention. You're not being aware. You have to exercise your awareness. You have to move yourself to that place."

He then instructed us to sit down. We were all in a row. Eric was sitting on the far right; on his left were Jeff, Matthew, Kerri and I. Eric told us, "Pay attention to the wind. You're not paying attention." We all sat there trying to pay attention. He said, "Fine, close your eyes and try to be aware." Before I closed my eyes, I half-shut them and I looked over at Jeff. I noticed that Jeff's eyes weren't completely closed either, and that Jeff's head was slightly turned to the right, looking at Eric. I decided to see what Jeff was peeking at.

I noticed Eric's right hand was not resting in his lap in a comfortable position; it was slightly above his lap, and his other hand was straight out. His fingers were all together and he was moving his hand ever so slightly. At that moment his palm was facing down towards his lap. He took his hand and he swept it upwards a few inches.

Barely a second after he moved his hand up – almost as if it was following him, like he was raising the volume of a stereo – I felt the wind pick up. Then he turned his palm down, facing the ground again, and moved his hand back down a few inches. A second later, almost like it was following his hand, the breeze died down. Then it was totally calm, totally dead. There was nothing happening at all. There was complete stillness.

He stopped; I closed my eyes again and turned my head forward. Jeff did the same thing because we didn't want to be caught peeking. Eric then asked, "Did you notice the wind?" And everyone says, "Oh, yeah, that was pretty strong." We definitely noticed everyone was paying attention. The wind was definitely something we wanted to pay attention to that time.

Then he asked, "Normal or paranormal?" Jeff responded, "Paranormal" to which Eric asked, "Okay, how could you tell?" Jeff paused for a few seconds and I was thinking, "Ah, why did he say that? He should have let Kerri or Matthew answer because the reason he knows is he was looking at Eric." He knew, the same way I knew, which is why I wasn't going to say anything. Jeff responded, "Well, it's because I was watching you and I saw your hand move when the wind picked up. I saw your hand go down when the wind died down. It's almost like your hand moved before I even felt any wind and then the hand went down before it even started to fall away."

Eric said, "Okay, that's an honest answer." Then Eric asked how else we could tell, and that's when Kerri said, "Because it felt different, it had a different feeling." And he said, "Right."

I remember feeling something almost like sprinkles, like some kind of sparkle drops; that's the best way I can explain it. For some reason it felt like rain, but there were no clouds in the sky.

Eric then said he wanted to move farther down the hill. We all stood up and moved about ten feet farther down the hill towards the bottom.

That's when we started looking at the trees. Most of the trees at the bottom were tall white birch trees, but there was this one tree, in particular, directly in front of us. It was very round and looked like a dogwood, but was much bigger than a dogwood would ever be. The whole tree was basically filled with flowers. It was just exploding with flowers.

It was about four thirty or five o'clock, late in the summer. The sun was just starting to go down, so the light was hitting the hills and cutting through just perfectly. It was hitting this tree in a way that it was illuminating these whitish-yellowish flowers. The light basically made it look like the tree was on fire, like it was this melting pot of gold that was glowing with its own light. It was like a vibrant light bulb, very magical, especially when compared to the white birch trees which were very plain.

Then Eric asked, "What do you think about that tree down there? What does it make you think of?" Jeff says, "It reminds me of Valhalla," which is the Viking heaven. And Eric responded, "Okay, I can see how you think that. You know what it makes me think of?" We told him we didn't know and he said, "Let's get a closer look." We all stood up and moved about ten more feet down the hill and sat down again.

As we were looking at the tree again, the wind started blowing all the branches but there were no leaves blowing around anywhere. All we saw was this blazing tree because of the way the light was hitting it; the light was reddish-orange.

The whole tree was just on fire and all we saw was this crazy glow; it really did look magical. When Jeff said Valhalla, I thought to myself, "He's right," I could see that. It looked like a tree you would see in mythical tales of the afterlife because it had a very different quality; the way the sun was hitting the flowers and the way the flowers were capturing that light. They were exploding; they looked like little drops of gold.

At that point we were all captivated by the tree that he's

pointed out, and Eric said, "It reminds me of the Bodhi tree, the tree Buddha found enlightenment under." When you've been around Eric for any length of time and you've had experiences, you know when someone like Eric tells you, "this reminds me of the tree that this person found enlightenment under," it hits you pretty hard. You're like, "Holy cow, that's a pretty profound thing to say."

Eric then said, "Everyone, get up again; we're going to get a closer look." We all stood up again. We were all paying close attention to the tree and every single thing that was going on. Just think, if Eric told you this tree reminds him of the tree Buddha sat under when he became enlightened, you'd be looking at every aspect of this tree blowing around, and the wind coming and going just as we were.

Eric was walking in front of us and we were following after him. We got to about ten feet away from the tree, which was at the very bottom of the hill. Nobody said anything. Everyone was just trying to pay attention and hold on; trying to make sure they didn't miss anything.

At this point, an interesting thing happened. Jeff, Matthew, Kerri, and I were all walking basically in the same line we'd been sitting in. Eric was still walking in front of us and started to walk underneath the tree. For whatever reason, all four of us simultaneously stopped about ten feet away from the tree. Eric was still walking. We didn't know when he was going to stop walking, but we all stopped in that same line so we were all lined up and nobody was behind anyone.

Eric finally stopped underneath the tree, turned around, and looked at us. The sunlight was coming through the flowers of that tree and it was like Eric was bathed in this strange golden light. At that moment everything seemed to slow down, and it became this very surreal moment. It was almost as if time paused for a second. I can clearly recall almost every single movement or gesture that he made in that particular moment. As Eric turned his head to look at us, his eyes had this expression of mischievousness, like a little kid about to make you the subject of a really good prank.

In a sense, the look was playful, it was mischievous, and had this knowing, like he knew what was coming and everyone else was about to find out. In another sense, his expression was really caring; like a parent just before they're about to share some profound life wisdom with you. One second his look is mischievous and playful. Because of the way he held his face, mouth and eyes, the next second, his look conveyed a sense of peace, a sense of "here it comes, are you ready? I'm about to share something with you."

I was watching that and reading the feeling. The feeling I was getting from it was solely by his facial expression because he still hadn't said anything. In fact, nobody had said anything.

Eric raised his water bottle to his lips, but it seemed like slow motion. My mind was capturing so much that it was like a frame by frame playback. The second Eric closed his eyes, I caught this flash of light and my eyes darted just above him to try to find it. There was a bunch of flowers all spiraling down from the tree.

These flowers were just raining on him. It was like the sky started raining flowers; there were so many. Because of the way they spun, they flashed this golden light and it looked like it was raining gold; that's literally what it looked like. The flowers were just hitting his shoulders and head and were falling off him; it was this perfect moving moment. It was unbelievable.

Every single thing that I can remember looked like it happened in extremely slow motion. I remember seeing the light; I remember looking up to see what it was, and seeing all these flowers coming down from this tree. This could have lasted thirty minutes; it could have lasted two seconds. I don't really know because time wasn't working the same at that point. I don't remember feeling myself breathing or being aware of anything else. I was just capturing the moment that, for all intents and purposes, shouldn't be happening.

It was beyond surreal, it was beyond strange, it was *unreal* that all these things happened at once and the way they happened; how everything slowed down, these golden flowers, and the way the sun was hitting them. The sun was at the perfect angle to capture these petals as they were spiraling down, showering on him.

Eric then took the water bottle away from his lips and it stopped. All of a sudden the flowers just stopped falling. He put the water bottle down by his waist and he gave us this look of perfect contentment. If you've ever seen someone even close to feeling perfectly peaceful, just perfect, just completely at peace, contented, that was it. That's where he was, that was the look that, until that moment I'm not sure that I knew. However, the second I saw his face, I knew what it was like. He was feeling what I want to feel; he was in this place that I want to be in, and that expression on his face captured it perfectly.

Next, Eric turned and started walking towards the other side away from us, to the trees. I thought to myself, "What in the world just happened?" We all started to walk underneath the tree and look around like we were trying to wake up from this weird daydream we were just in, trying to figure out what happened. I remember looking over at Kerri and I noticed the wind was blowing. I remember looking up into the branches of the tree and seeing all these flowers still up there. The whole tree was full of them. The whole tree was still in bloom.

I saw all the branches blowing and the whole tree being stirred by the wind, but not a single flower was falling. Not a single one. I remember thinking at that moment, "How is this possible? Why are there no flowers falling?" I remember looking around on the ground and there weren't many flowers. There were a few, maybe a handful. But a moment before it was like the whole tree just dumped all its flowers. It was raining flowers. It was like they just came down like drops of rain; there were that many flowers coming down. It was as if the whole tree just shook loose. And now I was looking on the ground and there's barely any.

To this day I cannot explain what happened; I can't even come close to explaining how it was possible. Even knowing what I know and experiencing what I've experienced, I do not know why, with the wind blowing, there were no flowers coming down, and why, when I saw that many flowers coming down in that moment, there weren't many flowers on the ground. But I know what I saw and I know what I experienced. Everyone who was there that day will tell you the same thing. They know what they saw and they know what they experienced.

At that point, Eric was walking away and, in this weird stupor all we could do was follow, scratching our heads and wondering, "What does that mean? What does that mean about our reality? What does that mean about our spiritual path?" You can experience some things in meditation. You can experience some things outside of meditation, but nothing of this magnitude, nothing of the feeling of The Force, of the just complete mind-blowing nature of this.

We followed Eric through the birch trees and Eric turned to us and asked, "So, what just happened?" I remember Kerri saying something like, "Well, you controlled the wind or controlled the weather to make it happen." When we were underneath the tree and I saw the wind blow through the tree without knocking off a single flower, I knew it was more than that. I remember Eric saying something like, "I prefer to think of it more as a dance."

Something he told me later, which I always went back and reflected on, was that no miracle can be performed by yourself; it's unison, it's the harmony. When he said, "I prefer to think of it as a dance," and that's what he has always said, he meant *it is a joint communion or effort between you and the Universe.*

After all this happened, we walked towards the other side of the hill where we had started. We sat on the hill, back over on the grassy part of it. Again, we formed a semi-circle around Eric, facing him. He started talking to us about the future and about how, at some point, each of us will have to make a choice. He said it doesn't matter what choice we make. We can go as far as we want in the pursuit of our spirituality and that it was okay if we weren't willing to find enlightenment in this lifetime. He told us to devote what we want to our spirituality. Alternatively, if we want to have a family, we would feel held back. He basically told us to decide what we're going to do.

We had to make a decision. We had to make a choice because if we were going to be what he needed us to be in the future; we couldn't just keep waiting around. We couldn't be indecisive. "You have to decide what you're going to do and you have to go for it," he said. He went on to say that we had already done so much and that this path wasn't for everyone. We shouldn't feel bad if we wanted to just have a little bit of spirituality or just go a little bit of the distance. He said it takes a very distinctive determination to go all the way.

At that moment, these two gangster-thuggish looking guys came out of nowhere and they started walking up the hill. They began to harass us saying, "What are you guys doing? What are you talking about, some weird meditation stuff? Are you guys meditating?" They were being a little hostile, a little aggressive. They were definitely throwing some attitude our way trying to get us going. Eric said, "Yeah, we're talking about spiritual stuff. You guys should sit down and join us." That threw them off. They looked at him as if thinking to themselves, "We're making fun of you. Why did you just ask us to sit down and join you?" They talked some more crap and then just went off on their way. Soon after that, we got back in the car and we drove maybe ten minutes away to eat.

The second biggest lesson I learned that day happened next. As we're all sitting there at the diner maybe about fifteen or twenty minutes after our experiences in the park, we ordered our food. We were all sitting around the table and my mind was just spinning. It was like my whole world, everything, changed. I felt that before this event, my reality had changed enough. I had accepted a lot of things since I'd known Eric. I experienced a lot of things, and a lot of things that any normal person would consider crazy. But this just blew them all out the door.

I started thinking back over the day because I didn't want to forget a thing, I didn't want to miss anything. What happened? How did it happen? It was deep and it was out there, but I knew I caught it. I captured it and I didn't want to lose it, I didn't want to forget it. I remember looking up and someone said something like, "Oh, look at Eric, Mister Serious," or something like that.

When I did look up, Matthew and Kerri were laughing and carrying on about Kerri's dog Duncan. They were talking about how Matt had some kind of fight with the dog. Matthew lived in the basement and Duncan had burst in through his windows and Matthew had been wrestling with him. They were just laughing about that, how funny Duncan was, and how they had had a good wrestling match; stuff like that, saying how maybe Duncan should have been wearing a wrestling mask. They were laughing and having a good time. At that moment, I remember looking at them thinking, "They've fallen back asleep already." Just like that. Just twenty or thirty minutes; that's all it took. They were already asleep. The Doe had already come in and carried them on their way.

Eric has always said that he stopped bending and changing reality, and stopped performing miracles because it didn't make a difference. The things he did didn't change them. It didn't make them appreciate or understand anything. Just because he showed someone something didn't mean they could do it themselves or even want to know why or how it happened. It didn't help them spiritually. Basically, they just thought, "Oh, wow, neat." And then they wanted to go on to the next thing.

There's too much stimulation to compete with nowadays. If anything, it just made him a magician of sorts in their mind. He said that all they ever said was, "What are you going to show me next?" If he didn't show them anything, then they would just get bored and move on. When I saw the rest of the group, I understood, and I thought, "We just witnessed something so unbelievable that maybe nobody will believe our story. If they do, it is something that people can live lifetimes without ever experiencing."

What we witnessed is something that you only ever read about. Even then, it sounds like some kind of fantasy! Here we have a group that just experienced what should be fantasy, and thirty minutes later were talking about trivial things in life like nothing ever happened. To go back to normal that quickly is almost as equally profound as the miracle itself because it shows the reality of the Doe, how quickly it works and how hard it is to maintain awareness.

That was a moment that inspired me to make some really difficult and profound decisions in my life. I don't think I would have ever had the courage to make them because I could never have conceived what was beyond those choices had I not experienced that event in the diner. I think it's fair to say it changed my life forever.

Matt's Experience

I've been studying with Eric Pepin since February of 1995. The most profound experience I've ever had with Eric was an event that occurred about a year after I had originally met him. He was preparing us, the group that he was teaching at that point, for dimensional experiences. It was on a Sunday night and there were seven of us in his bedroom where the class was being held.

The bedroom was big enough for all seven of us to fit on the seating that he had prepared on one side of his room. Eric was standing and teaching us about tonal, dimensions, and how your body can shift up to higher states of vibration where you don't interact with matter. The teaching was fun, the intellectual material was fantastic, and then he decided to do a demonstration.

We'd always heard stories about the types of abilities he has displayed in the past; legends, you could say, from his older students. I had many experiences up until this point but they were all level one experiences like telepathy, or something along those lines; nothing like moving through a wall or something to that effect.

We were sitting on one side of the room and Eric was standing by the other wall, maybe six inches away from it. Hanging on that wall was a dark red Persian rug – not too dark. It had light patterns on it, but overall it was a darker rug in contrast to the off-white wall. It was a pretty big rug. It went from the ceiling all the way down to the floor, but the wall was visible on either side of the rug.

The room was well lit and measured approximately fifteen feet by fifteen feet, so everything was very visible to all of us. Eric began to enter into a certain state of mind while he stood in front of the rug. He started breathing in a very particular sequence. He moved his hands and arms in a very interesting fashion and suddenly everything became extremely thick. The atmosphere in the room became very thick. Not to breathe, but to feel. It felt solid and he asked us, "Do you guys feel that?" I told him that I did.

Eric continued breathing for two or three minutes and it gradually got thicker and thicker. It got to the point where the space between me and the objects around me seemed to move. It was as if I was looking through a room filled with gasoline fumes. The air was so thick and so interesting that whatever I looked at appeared to shimmer or move.

Eric explained this by telling us that he was essentially raising our tonal along with his. He was bringing the frequency of the entire room up a few octaves. This continued for another three or four minutes, and then he said, "Can you see me?" The air was really thick and everything was moving. Then he asked again, "Can you see me now?" The density was so thick I couldn't really see. His body was phasing in and out. I could see his color, I could see the shade of his clothes, and I could see the contrast of him before the rug, but it was all starting to blend together.

It was a very visual experience; I was not paying attention to smells or anything else. I was only paying attention to the thickness of the atmosphere, the breathing of the people that I was sitting next to, and the visual element of the room. That's what really stuck in my memory. The second time Eric asked if we could see him, the atmosphere was even denser. Everything was blending, fluctuating in and out. Then something really interesting happened. Eric said, "What about now?"

It looked as if he and the rug had blended together; I couldn't tell which was in front of the other and my mind was racing to figure it out. Then he said "Okay, can you see me now?" Just before he asked, Eric was in front of the rug, or should I say *in* the rug, or what looked like in the rug. It looked like he was further back at that point, inside the color of the rug pattern. Then he asked if we could see him and he moved behind the white wall. He disappeared. It looked like he took a side step behind what I could see as the white paint on the wall behind the rug.

At that point, my heart skipped a beat, and adrenaline totally set in. I heard everybody gasp; everybody was really struggling with this. I just about broke down. I didn't know what to do because that's not supposed to happen! I was definitely panicking, my heart started pounding as soon as he did that.

I closed my eyes for a second and when I opened them, everything in the room was still really thick and moving. Eric was there again. After a few seconds, everything started to solidify. The atmosphere started to return to normal and Eric was smirking. It was too intense for me to ground back down. I don't think I spoke for the rest of the night. I don't think anybody else spoke for the rest of the night either.

The saving grace of that night was when he came back, when everything came back to *'normal*,' even though there was a definite zing that remained in the air; that state of mind remained in the room. Everybody was at a higher state of consciousness.

Eric definitely knew what we were experiencing, the shock, everything, and he further explained what had happened and basically grounded us back into the room by teaching us how it happened. Eric gave a detailed explanation on why it happened, how it's possible, and why this is arcane or secret knowledge that the Governor of your brain isn't ready for. From that experience, I took away the reality of the Governor and learned there's also a very real ability to train yourself to remove or heighten the Governor so that you can experience more of reality.

It was single handedly the most profound class that I ever had. There have been many profound classes, but that class validated the other knowledge that he would reveal later on in my time with him. All my senses, sixth sense included, experienced that incredible moment. When I learned the rest of what he taught me throughout the years, I was able to listen from a completely different viewpoint.

Frank's Experience

I've been a student of Eric's since 1991. One day Eric and I went to a hilltop cemetery in Connecticut just to check it out. While we were up there, Eric was showing me how to change the speed and direction of the wind. After doing that for a little while, Eric had me lie down in the middle of a street. My brain, of course, told me I shouldn't really expect a car to come down the street because we were pretty much in the middle of nowhere - out in the sticks as they say.

I don't remember the events that led up to what was about to happen, all I know for sure is that one moment I was lying down in the street when I noticed a car was coming at me. It was maybe a quarter mile away coming towards me, and next thing I know I was blank. Suddenly, I felt the entirety of the planet. It's not so much that I felt this huge thing or huge rock, I felt *the planet*. I just felt it in its entirety.

The experience offered amazing insight into consciousness. It's not like I had lost myself in that moment. I experienced what it was to be the planet. It was completely alien to who and what I was as a human. Yet, I also experienced it from the perspective of being a part of it and existing within it. I understood the planet and understood its enormity in relation to me. But when I was experiencing it, in the moment, I did not feel enormous, if that makes sense. *The craziest part is, all this happened before the car reached the spot where I was lying.* Eric has a way of pointing out that time works in mysterious ways.

A few other students and I went camping with Eric at the Grand Canyon. We drove down a dirt road for quite some time and found a place to camp out in the middle of nowhere. We deliberately made a circular, spiritual space in order to solidify in our consciousness that this was a spiritual thing that we're doing.

At dusk, when the sun was just starting to set, we made a fire. It was still ninety percent daylight, it was still pretty light out, and although I don't remember what we all were discussing, I do remember Eric asking, "Did you notice what happened?" We all looked at him stupidly, not having a clue what he meant. He looked over and said "Well, is it very light out?" or something to that affect. We all looked and realized it was full on dark; it was nighttime. I was asking myself, "Where'd the sun go? It was here a second ago and now it's nighttime, what happened during the last two hours?"

I also noticed that Eric had moved his place within the circle too. He had actually gotten up, moved his chair, put it in another spot, sat down and none of us even noticed.

Thinking back on it now, it was as if our consciousnesses were placed on hold. I don't know exactly how it took place, if time was accelerated or skipped entirely, but essentially a couple of hours were allowed to pass with none of us being aware of it passing. Obviously, after this was brought to our attention, we realized this was very odd. That experience really makes me think about time and how irrelevant or how non-structured it really is in regards to the Universe. It's not a linear thing; it's a lot more pliable than that. It was a very profound experience.

Dan's Experience

I have been studying with Eric for about eighteen years. When I first met him, we were both very young. At that point in time, there was a lot of chaos in my life. I was not necessarily tied in with the best of people, and I had a lot of family issues.

The very first day I met Eric, he did a reading on me. He told me all about myself; incredible details about some of the more traumatic things that I had gone through in my life. I remember just sitting back some days while in the midst of that chaos and thinking, "Oh my God, why would anybody have to go through this?" Back then, I didn't realize that someday it would all be behind me. As a teenager, I think I wanted a level of recognition for what I had been through. It was incredible to have somebody unexpectedly come into my life who *knew* and understood what it was like to be me. I didn't have to explain it.

I've had incredible experiences on multiple occasions with Eric. We call it *the In-Between*. Well the In-Between is the point at which energy is solidifying into matter. The very first time that Eric took me to this place, this In-Between state, there was no coming back. I knew right then and there that anything else that I had seen was trivial in comparison. The fact that Eric knew details about my life can technically be argued and disproven by questioning whether he met people and got information from them before he met me. I know that is not the case, but let's face it, there's an argument that can be made. The In-Between, however, can't be put into words. It's a place of knowledge. It's a place that a teacher can bring their student to learn. The teacher can't give you the knowledge, but they can help bring you to the place so that you can find it yourself.

Once I found that place through Eric, I knew I understood that I had found the truth. I don't know if people reading this book are ready for what I'm about to say, but I'll say it anyway. Eric is an enlightened individual. He was enlightened when he came here. The Force - God - moved him to this place because it is only now in this day and age that we have the ability, the intelligence, and the technologies to understand this knowledge.

Think about if there was a major disaster a hundred and fifty years ago. It would have taken a month or two in order to get that information across the planet. It is only now in this day and age that the technology evolved enough to spread knowledge and data across the planet at lightning speed. If The Force is ever to communicate with the human race as a whole, if you really think about it scientifically, it has to wait until technology capable of communicating knowledge to the masses exists.

Seeing and knowing someone like Eric and knowing what he's capable of, what he's teaching, and what he's trying to do for the world, I understand that *now* is the time for this knowledge to get out because the global consciousness is ready for that movement. When someone like Eric comes into the world, his presence, his being is a vibration. It's a signature, just like you have a vibration to your being. It's your identity. It's your soul; it is who you are.

Eric's vibration is multi-dimensional; he's an old soul, so to speak. He's experienced so many things in his existence that his energy, his vibration, is very complex.

To bring me In-Between was simply a matter of him allowing part of his own vibration to overtake my own vibration. It's like sharing his identity. I had the opportunity to see through his eyes. For a six, seven, eight hour period I was super, super psychic. That is what happened. I got to see through his eyes how he experiences life here because he defines life differently than 'normal' people do. His concept of the way the world exists is not the same as normal people. Normal people are taught from the day they're born that there are a set of rules to this reality, such as gravity; there's no getting around gravity. I've seen Eric do things that defy gravity. I know personally, it can be done.

The In-Between is a shift of consciousness. I think that concept can be frightening because the average human associates it with drugs or alcohol. Neither of those is involved in the techniques that are used to achieve that state of mind. This place is something that can be achieved through diligent meditation. Having said that, I don't want to create any level of anticipation for beginning meditators because I think that's what I'm doing with this statement; and that's not what I'm trying to do. Trying to achieve it will prevent you from achieving it.

From this In-Between place, you can understand why it's possible to see the future and the past. *You understand that all time is happening in the same moment in the consciousness of God.* It's all one moment, it's all one thing. Time only exists here in this dimension because of matter. It is the breakdown and decay of matter that is the measurement of time.

The In-Between is a shift in consciousness. Perhaps the best way I can put it is to tell you some of the things that I could not do in the In-Between. For example, in the In-Between, I could not use words. I could not even think in words in that place. You can't form them because your consciousness is moving at such a rapid speed. In the time it would take for me to verbalize a sentence right now, while In-Between, I could convey the data of an entire encyclopedia set. I can only use analogies because there's really no way to put this place into text. It is the ultimate understanding.

The first time I experienced the In-Between with Eric, I felt it was the most amazing experience that anyone probably ever felt in all of time, in all of history. I was like, "Oh my God, this is just so incredible. I've got to share this with people." I remember turning to Eric and he verbally said to me, "Well, write it down."

At that point, I was scrambling. I remember I was trying to find a pen and when I finally got the pen in my hand, I looked at the paper and realized there was no way I could give this experience to anybody. I was experiencing the most incredible thing I've ever experienced in my life and there was no way I could share it. I couldn't even talk very well because I was in a higher state of consciousness. You can't form words very easily. You can do it but it's not easy because your consciousness and your body aren't in sync.

Trying to walk was very, very difficult because in that state your consciousness feels larger than your body, almost filling a room. When you're not In-Between, you're aware of only your body. Your consciousness fits inside of your body. When you're In-Between you're still aware of the body but you don't have the limitations of the body.

Everything I looked at was just so beautiful. I saw the Prana in everything; even a door or a wall. I could see how the energy, The Force, was making up the structure of everything.

One time while In-Between with Eric, I was staring at a crack in the wall paint in Eric's bedroom. The paint was chipped at a certain spot, but I was actually watching the paint before it was chipped. I actually watched the crack form and I watched where the crack was going to go.

For me, I thought it was very interesting that I was able to experience, on a very minor level, how it was possible to see into the past and into the future from this state of consciousness. I'd always wondered how Eric could tell me things that were going to happen long before they happened. From that state of mind, even though I was only seeing paint peeling on a wall, I could see where it was going to spread in the future. It was very enlightening because I was able to see how time spent in the In-Between didn't work the way we experience it in a normal everyday state of consciousness.

In another In-Between experience, Eric, Frank and I were in this park and Frank had asked Eric something along the lines of, "Did you drug us or something? Is this experience caused by a drug?" Even though Frank and I were both In-Between at the same moment and at the same physical location, we were both in different places. I had been In-Between many, many, many times before, so by this particular point I was already in a totally different place, even though I was still aware of the conversation that Frank and Eric were having.

I was meditating at the moment and I was In-Between when Frank said something about drugs to Eric. I remember Eric getting a bit upset and he asked, "Is that what you think, Frank?" Eric put his pointer finger forward and, at that moment, Frank and I both came out of the In-Between and back to a normal state of consciousness. Eric then asked, "Frank, are you in or out?" As Frank was figuring out what was going on, Eric brought his thumb back, and suddenly we were popped back In-Between. Eric was taking us in and out of the In-Between with just a twitch of his thumb.

When you're In-Between, you're in a higher level of consciousness. Your consciousness is moving very, very rapidly. You could be in front of a building and know everything about that building inside and out before you even walking in. You're just in tune with everything. If there was anybody that had any sort of negative intent towards you, you'd pick up on it in seconds.

Another time, Eric and I were in a park and I was In-Between. There was a guy coming towards us who had a horrible vibe. Instinctively we knew that we needed to maneuver ourselves in a different area of the park to stay away from this particular individual. I remember looking at the individual and I just felt like he was one from the Darkside or something. It's the only way I can explain it. I think even normal people that weren't In-Between would stop and look at this person and think, "Ehh, he looks like a shady character," but I really felt this person's being. I knew that this person was no good.

There are different levels to the In-Between. One time I asked Eric why being In- Between is like being drunk. He told me that when a person is In-Between, their consciousness is somewhere else, so their body and motor skills are sluggish; the body is like jelly.

In one instance, there were two ladies riding their bikes down a path, they were slowing down as they were approaching the parking lot. Eric was standing there and he looked up to them and asked a question about the map and I could feel what they were feeling about me. They were feeling like, "Oh this poor guy, he's all messed up." They thought I was mentally disabled or something.

Well, right about that point in time, Eric started shifting them In-Between with me. So, all four of us were In-Between. Of course, they were in a total stupor because they had no clue what was going on. They were just standing there in awe of this experience and sharing a knowing glance like, "Are you experiencing what I'm experiencing right now?" They came to realize it was like being in the presence of God.

I noticed that there was some physical movement. Eric had to position his body in them for some reason and he signaled to me, behind their backs, to walk to the other side of them. I didn't know what the purpose of that was but, for some reason, where I was standing had an effect on their consciousness.

As we were walking away, I could feel that they were shifting back to their normal state of consciousness. The second they were back to their normal state of consciousness, they knew that something had just happened but they didn't know what it was anymore. The experience had already been extracted from them. The second they were out they just got back on their bikes and started riding away. They lost it. It was already gone. I remember thinking, "Oh my God, they don't even realize what the hell just happened to them." That was one thing that stood out in my mind. I just couldn't believe it. How could they just lose that? Of course, I was still In-Between then.

Frank and I both had experienced the same place. You have to understand that when you touch a part of God of that magnitude, there's only one thing you can really take back from it. It's not really something to describe with words, but it's the value behind the words that lingers. If you find this place and touch it, and you're capable of experiencing it, then you understand something about the Universe. When I look at Frank, I know that he and I have both touched this place. We both have that beauty within us now; what we experienced, that value, is there. I know I could trust my life with Frank because I know that beautiful part of his soul that values my life is there.

Eric once described a meditation; he had gone so far out into the universe that he looked back and saw God and it filled his soul enough to last him a lifetime. Well, I think Frank and I experienced a place together to such a degree that it formed a bond between us that will last a lifetime, and beyond. Even though we weren't childhood brothers, our bond is even stronger than that.

Imagine being lost at sea for many, many days. You were scared, running low on food, and just didn't know what was to become of you. Then, all of a sudden, you stood up and saw a lighthouse. I think it is safe to say that this lighthouse would probably be the most incredible sight you have ever seen. The feeling that you would have from seeing that lighthouse brings you the knowing that you are going to be alright. Eric is that lighthouse in my life and I have the upmost respect for him as a spiritual teacher. I have to say that I get lost a lot spiritually. Even knowing all that I know, there are days that I get lost in my life. Eric is that one person that makes me sit back and go, "Oh yeah, yeah, yeah, I remember now, I remember now."

The In-Between in Frank's Experience

My perception of everything was different when I was In-Between; that is, everything visual was very different. I could see the life force, on everything, around everything, and in everything, as plain as day, without trying. It was just there. I couldn't deny it; I couldn't look away from it. I couldn't close my eyes. It was just there.

There are different levels and different perceptions of the In-Between. When you're In-Between, as well as with any altered state of consciousness with your eyes open, you externalize the experience. I'm referring to visually seeing things happen.

Imagine watching a flower materializing on a molecular level. Imagine looking at that flower as a whole thing, then seeing the petal, and then seeing the cells, and then seeing the molecules of the cells, and then just experiencing the coalescence of energy into matter and the whole dimensional aspect of the In-Between at that level.

When you close your eyes and you go into your inner-universe, your own consciousness, rather than projecting your consciousness outward through the In-Between into this dimension, you're experiencing the Universe from a reverse direction. Obviously, you'll have a much different perception, a much different experience, at that point.

When I did that while In-Between, I was experiencing things of a dimensional, universal level that I couldn't have experienced with opened eyes, externalizing things. It's simply a different application of a different state of consciousness. Obviously, they both have their place and it's important to have these different experiences and understand really how they are one and the same, just viewed from a different angle.

This is not to say that the In-Between is the be all and end all of Eric's teachings because there's a lot more to it. It's really about changing your perceptions, changing your understandings, and changing what's important to you. It puts your life into perspective.

When you ask yourself what you want out of life, the normal answer is, "I want a house, a car, a good job, and a family." The whole concept of impermanence becomes so solidified in your consciousness that you live impermanence, so to speak, without even thinking about it. You realize that the house, the car, the job, have no weight, no meaning. They certainly take a backseat more so than before you had that perspective shift.

Your life goals change from a more, to use Eric's words, Red Cell priority base to that of a White Cell. No longer is it about personal, materialistic gain; it's about knowledge, energy, experience, and consciousness. Your priorities shift from, "What can I buy?" to "What can I know? What can I learn? What can I do?" and "What can I be?"

Part of being In-Between with another person is the bond you create. Dan and I didn't really know each other that well when we first met Eric and started going In-Between. From my perspective, Dan was this older student that Eric really put a lot of time into and I was just starting out. Dan just had that label of knowledgeable, 'older student.'

Eric foresaw how that experience together would affect us on a bonding level, on a level of spiritual brotherhood, if you want to call it that. I experienced him as an energy being rather than a physical being. I still didn't really know Dan afterwards, but I was as comfortable with him as I would be with anybody else.

Even though I didn't really know him,
I knew him ...
"You are a shared experience with the Universe."

—ERIC PEPIN

THE 7,000 YEAR OLD MASTER

Thousands of years ago on a warm summer's morning a human being walked amongst other men the beaten path to the distant village where the day's work would begin.

The suns warmth penetrating the flesh and warming the blood within always calls for a moment of appreciation, inward.

"Every morning you have walked this path, I have been there to greet you, touching your cheek and warming your soul"

Unconsciously slowing their walk to momentarily savor the morning presence, a sound is caught in the webbing of the silent mind, a faint distant buzzing rapidly approach's from behind and peaks to a sudden eruption of rhythmic pattern and as quickly as it came it fades into the distance. In an instant one takes in the shape and form of a dragonfly passing by.

"Because you were with me in the moment you savored my touch upon your cheek a window of truth was opened and you reached out to the dragonfly drawing it to you, as it passed your mind was so fast the dragonfly had become so slow. Your eyes met as they crossed paths and in its reflection you seen reality truths"

The dragonfly echoes a feeling within that seems to remain longer then it should. Holding their mind to it as they observe themselves experiencing its fleeting impression.

A loud bellow vibrates through the air breaking the moment of reflection. To reveal it's self on the banks of the river as a water buffalo being bathed by its master.

The sun dancing on the surface of the broken water although familiar this time it's as if triangles were shaped as light pieces between the waves, seeming interlaced as a hidden design that draws the minds attention to investigate further. The water settles and its mystery with it.

They become aware of the sudden breath inward they take as their mind is released from the moment's captivation, for a moment acknowledging that perhaps they had not breathed during the entire observation?

Walking the long and distant path they observe their feet, bare and naked pressing into the soft dry powdery earth. Admiring the detail of the veins, muscles and bones orchestrating each changing step... rhythmically... Each step imprinting into the earth, pushing small mounds up and around each toe and each mound having crumbling grains separately rolling down from the top.

The eyes dilating and awareness expanding wider the patterns on the ground reveal the treaded path of man and beasts have taken for years. Mounds of dry soft earth dipping and lifting all around each foot. Slowly revealing the waves in the water and then the shimmering triangles in-between them?

Shaking their head, and breathing in suddenly to clear their mind they return to normal ...

Emotion becomes perplexed and the mind engages to wonder and the chest feels full ...

"Find me ..."

Along the river the forest has a twin reflecting back at it. There is a small old bridge that crossing a line between the banks and today it calls their name. Crossing the bridge looking forward they see the path fading into the forest and decide this day they will take the risk and the consequences of not arriving in the village center if only for a short while.

The presence of the trees towering from above makes them feel ever smaller in their presence, as if they were fading away into them. But the beams of sun light in between the leaves draws them upward.

There before a grand tree dancing with light beams the earth calls out invitingly. They sit into a meditation position. Closing their eyes, breathing deeply and releasing the weight of day with their breath. They surrender into the divine.

After sometime they slowly open their eyes upon seeing a wonder. Ever so still one settles upon their lips ever so gently breached a whisper is spoken from them... Reality is an illusion ...

"Only now are you ready to do the work you are needed for"

Eric J. Pepin

CONTINUE YOUR JOURNEY

Thank you for joining me on this journey. My hope is that you take what you have learned, apply it, and watch your life transform as your spirituality flourishes. The light of knowledge is vital on your journey, but you must apply it. That is why I am giving you additional tools, you cam download for free, to assist you in putting the methods you have discovered here into practice.

Before you do that, there is one thing I would ask of you: leave a short, honest review at Amazon.com or wherever you found this book. Higher Balance Institute is a dedicated, grass-roots organization. We rely on the power of people to help spread this knowledge. Assist others out there searching, like you, find this book.

ADD TO YOUR EXPERIENCE
READERS ONLY FREE MATERIAL

As a reader you receive special reader-only bonus material you can download for free. You will get new tools and knowledge to enhance all the practices found in the book.

Receive:

Guided Past Life Regression: Eric Pepin takes you deep into your soul to uncover forgotten lives. By bringing these memories into your conscious awareness, the wisdom of lifetimes allows you to accelerate your growth and raise your consciousness in this life.

Guided In-Between Session: Eric takes you on a sensory journey that allows you to slip into the In-Between, a state of mind that proves elusive for many. Whether you are new to the In-Between or are just seeking deeper levels, this audio will evoke new experiences for you.

Reflections of Then: A very rare and intimate class, Eric divulges incredible secrets, answering all of the unspoken questions of white cells. It is the calling of the Universe finally put into words.

Go to *www.prescientvisions.com/readers-only*

Appendix · Glossary of Terms

Akashic Records

The *Akashic Records* is a term for the dimensional data of the Gaia Mind (see *Gaia*). It is an energy vibration that contains a record of any and all planetary events, actions, thoughts, and feelings that have ever occurred or will ever occur in the future. These records can extend beyond the planet into all universal experience since the beginning of time, and are stored permanently in an energy substance named "Akasha."

Astral Planes

Astral planes are really dimensions. Culturally, there were times when people didn't know how to explain these other realities. Sometimes they were so surreal compared to how they perceived reality that they deemed it the 'astral plane' or the 'ethereal plane.' (See *Dimensions*).

Astral Projection

An "out-of-body experience" often occurring during sleep or a meditative state during which the ethereal or astral energy field of the body separates from the physical body and travels over great distances to other locations. It is a process that sends conscious energy out from the physical body to collect information to bring back for experience.

Awakening

The phrase used to describe the transformation or process of becoming conscious from a prior state of unconsciousness, or unawareness. A dynamic of discovery during spiritual development. To wake from sleep. (see: *Enlightenment*.)

Babbler, The

A term to define repetitious, involuntary thoughts pervading through the mind.

Uncontrolled babbling will naturally occur as a result of never learning how to manage the rational thinking process while growing into adulthood. It is also referred to as "Mind-Chatter."

Calibration

A word to explain the conscious or unconscious adjustments or optimizations that take place in one's energy, mind, or physicality. These different energy calibrations are often very subtle and not noticed; they occur all the time as a person adjusts to experiences in life. They are most often felt during meditation or clear states of consciousness.

Chakra

A name for the intersection areas of energy meridians (or electrical pathways) in the body. There are seven primary chakras along the spine. They extend from the tip of the tailbone to the crown of head. These seven are located (from the bottom up) in the rectal area, near the genitals, behind the navel or solar plexus, at the heart, at the neck, between the eyebrows, and on the crown of the head. Each chakra corresponds to certain states of consciousness, emotions, body organs, nerve networks, colors, and energies. There are over 2000 of these energy centers or intersections of this energy in the human body.

Chuning

Chuning is a technique you can use to clear your town or your house of bad energy where you pull a frequency from deep inside of you and release it out. When you chune, you're opening a gateway for God to come through. That vibration permeates and travels through time and space for an infinite amount of time.

Collective Consciousness

Humans serve as the planet's central nervous system; the collective consciousness is a term for the planet's mind state. It is the planetary energy field of humanity's entire evolutionary experiences and expressions. This mind-field or collective consciousness is enriched as humanity develops, whether the development is in language, art, music, technologies, cities, spiritual awakening, or any other area of endeavor. As this consciousness evolves, each succeeding generation of conscious individuals will inherit and be influenced by this collective consciousness and add their own experiences to it.

Darkside, The

A term commonly used in the movie trilogy *Star Wars* to describe a destructive energy in the universe that destroys any manifestation or potential of creation.

Dimension

One of the countless realms of reality or space. Alternate dimensions of reality can be experienced in degrees, from subtle to total immersion. There are countless dimensions of reality. These concepts are now being used in modern physics to develop theories of reality, such as String Theory. The term referenced by Eric is usually one of parallel dimensions where entities exist.

Direct Manifestation

Direct Manifestation is a simple but powerful technique used to create anything you want in your life: money, love, a new job, friendship, self-improvement, understanding, and more. Your imagination and the sincerity of your desire are the only things that limit you!

Doe (or Do)

'Doe' is the first and lowest tone of the diatonic scale. This term is used to define the primary vibratory state of the planet's consciousness. Spiritual states of existence are much higher in tonal. The "Doe" signifies a vibratory state that is limited to the immediate physical dimension which does not recognize higher energy frequencies. Within the 'Doe' state, immediate desires of the body outweigh the subtle urge for spiritual awakening. It is sometimes termed 'Doe.'

Empathy

The ability where one can tune into another person's feelings or emotions and then experience them as if they were one's own. This is experienced primarily through the heart chakra, although the understanding of the feeling would be enhanced by bringing the mind chakra into play. Empathy without understanding would be of limited value.

Energy

A term that refers to the simplest essence, condition, or state in all things. A dynamic and flexible word that can be used to express the relativity, vitality, and intensity of anything that exists.

Enlightenment

A higher state of consciousness in which a person transcends beyond his or her ego, and becomes aware of his or her divinity; a state where a person is one, or whose consciousness is existing near or at the frequency of the Multidimensional Universe or God.

Entity

A term that defines any living thing in existence. It is also used to describe a spirit normally assumed (often wrongly) to be that of a dead person. Sometimes in reference to a spirit or a being from another dimension.

Feels-Like

A "tag" or "feels-like" is what something feels like in your chest intelligence. Everything has a feels-like - a computer screen, a table, chair, pen, and paper. Without touching an object, you can imagine the texture, temperature, density, and clarity of it. You know how the object feels – its frequency.

Force, The

A term and concept for the positive life enriching conscious energy of the Universe. It is commonly used in the *Star Wars* movies to describe the life energy of the Universe which binds any manifestation of matter together.

Frequency

A term used for the property or condition of an occurrence taking place at frequent intervals. Any form of existence has a range of frequency in order for it to exist.

Frequency is a form of energy.

Gaia

(Greek - Goddess of the Earth) The Gaia Hypothesis, formulated by James Lovelock, states that all living matter on the Earth contributes to a single living macrocosmic organism. Retrospectively in the system of a living earth, the collective consciousness of humanity would be considered the central nervous system.

Governor

An unconscious pattern and function of the brain that binds a person's awareness to the physical world. It is a specific vibratory state which subsequently contributes to the rejection of all things that are not normal or that have yet to be discovered. (See: *Doe*)

Grid, The

An invisible planetary energy web that interconnects all living things. If one can plug into this grid, they will have access to planetary collective experiences existing in higher dimensional vibrations. (See: *Akashik Records*)

I's, The

The alternate personalities, roles, or egos within a person. A product of unconscious functioning, these I's unconsciously assist a person in coping with the environment.

In-Between, The

To be consciously shifted. There is a place between matter and energy where one can exist and be aware of both simultaneously. Not simply to be aware of yourself but to be in a special state of consciousness.

Intent

Something that is intended consciously or unconsciously; an aim or purpose. Intent precedes any choice or course of action.

Kundalini

The elemental energy of the human body which, like a serpent, rests coiled at the base of the spine. Everyone uses Kundalini energy or power to maintain consciousness, but it very seldom rises up the central spinal channel beyond the first chakra center (the groin chakra). The Foundation meditation practice can be used to ascend to and activate the higher chakra centers.

Lotus, Full

This traditional body position provides a solid base for the practice of meditation and Prana breathing exercises. The spine is erect; the legs are crossed over one another; and the flow of blood to the legs is constricted and redirected to the internal organs. Traditionally the posture is a reminder to emulate the lotus plant, with its roots in the earth and its face reaching towards the sunlight. It is also the basis of many other yogic postures.

Lotus, Half

This seated meditation posture is almost identical to the Full Lotus position stated above. However, with the half-lotus, one foot rests on top of the opposite thigh with the sole pointing upwards, while the other foot rests on the floor, as in the common Indian position. (see: *the meditation map provided with the Foundation Set in Meditation Within Eternity.*)

Magnetic Pill

A revolutionary supplement designed to "supercharge your neural network." It is a scientifically proven brain supplement designed to give you deeper meditations, expanded consciousness, and all the benefits of a body that is fine-tuned to greater levels of development. Its main ingredient, magnetite, develops psychic ability and enhances this sensory.

Mandala

A mandala is a concept that takes you on a path in a direction that ends up somewhere. It always leads down the same path no matter who thinks about it. You might start off with a different concept but after thinking about it for such a long time, it directs you like a dimensional map. As you think about it, you apply it to your other thoughts and it makes everything link together giving you an epiphany.

Matrix

The Matrix is a term or allegory that dramatically conveys the view that ordinary appearances do not depict true reality and that gaining the truth transforms one's life. The Matrix is the sensational world that traps one into believing that nothing outside the five senses even exists. The matrix is also a term for the apparent fabric of the reality in this dimension.

Metronome

A device used to mark time by using regularly recurring ticking sounds or flashes at adjustable intervals. An effective tool for inducing states of deep trance or hypnosis.

Micro-Macro

A term to reference zooming from micro (the very small) to macro (the very large).

Micro-verse

A micro version of the universe. A universe of the very small (micro).

Middle Pillar

A term in reference to the deepest core of one's consciousness that is completely interconnected with the Universe and all manifestations of life: It is the ultimate Self without a notion of ego separation.

Mindfulness

Discipline in which the mind reflects on a single point of reference. The state of attention or reflection of the mind's activities. The trait of staying aware. Using desired thought.

Navigator

The subtle urge everyone has in them that drives them to evolve and seek out the experiences of life to the fullest extent. It is an intuitive mechanism of the causal spirit used to perpetuate and direct the will of The Force.

Non-Thought

When masters suggested having non-thought, they meant to not have verbal words in one's head. It's thinking at a higher level without using the words. When you understand and internalize this concept, you can transcend the boundaries of everyday life.

Paranormal

Beyond normal. Beyond the range of normal experience or scientific explanation. Beyond or above normal human ability or senses. (See *E.S.P.*)

Pineal Gland

A small endocrine gland in the brain situated beneath the back part of the corpus callosum; secretes melatonin; realized by many to be 'the seat of the soul.'

Prana

This is originally a yogic term for cosmic energy or the evolving life force of the Universe. Prana is thought to flow through the body, enriching and aligning health and vitality. It is considered the vital link between spiritual dimensions and material dimensions. Harnessing this energy through meditation enables people to accelerate the development of psychic states and the ability to perform miracles.

Red Cell

A person who lives according to the natural purpose of Gaia and the vibration of the 'Doe' and is unconscious of the urge to pursue their full spiritual potential.

Scan

A technique of psychically receiving information from, but not limited to, a person, place, or thing.

Siddhartha

Siddhartha Gautama, known as the Buddha, was born in the sixth century B.C. as a son of a chief in what is now modern Nepal. Siddhartha left a life of wealth and submitted himself to rigorous ascetic practices. Not fully satisfied, he discovered a path of balance rather than extremism. He called this The Middle Way. Buddha attained enlightenment, thus earning the title Buddha, or "Enlightened One." Buddha preached the Dharma in an effort to help others reach enlightenment.

Sixth Sense

The Sixth Sense is the ordinary term for the faculties of Extra Sensory Perception. (See *E.S.P.*) The Sixth Sense is the ability to receive or send information beyond the realm of the five senses of sight, sound, taste, touch, or smell. The term was coined by German researcher Dr. Rudolf Tischner whose book *Telepathy and Clairvoyance* was written in German in 1920 and published in English in 1925. The first serious paranormal research was done by Dr. J.B. Rhine, Professor of Parapsychology at Duke University, North Carolina.

Sleeper

Someone who lies dormant. One who has yet to awaken their Sixth Sense but can feel the impulses of their Navigator.

Soul

A term for the life energy of an individual; an energy body of the non-physical self. That part of the individual which survives death and lives on into the hereafter, before being reincarnated.

Tones, The

The "Voice of God." A high pitched frequency usually heard on one side of the head – either the right or the left. Comes from within your consciousness. Focusing on it allows it to become louder and louder.

Tonal

This term refers to the vibratory degree of frequency that the energy of a person, place or thing exists at. (See: *Frequency; Vibration*)

Vibration

A particular frequency or resonation of a thing or event in existence. Not necessarily specific to that person or entity. (see: *Frequency; Tonal*)

White Cell

One who lives their life according to the divine will and direction of The Force or Universe.

About The Author

Eric Pepin, the Founder of Higher Balance Institute and author of 5 Amazon Bestsellers, is often referred to as "The Rebel Guru". He shies away from the structures of organized religion and believes that spirituality lies within the individual. Eric is truly dedicated to serving the Force and he is very passionate about sharing with others how to create a closer connection to God.

He has been involved in metaphysics, paranormal, psychic and spiritual phenomenon his entire life. He is self-taught and has evolved through his own personal experiences and this is why he believes that at the end of the day, your own experiences are the key to advancing your spirituality.

Diving deeper into consciousness than any teacher has ever gone, Eric provides quintessential lessons and techniques specifically designed to teach seekers how to tap into their own potential and experience spiritual, paranormal and psychic phenomenon for themselves.

Eric has been teaching for over 25 years, and in 2003 he founded the Higher Balance Institute with the mission to "Awaken the World One Mind at a Time". He has developed several advanced spiritual training courses and continues to teach at live events throughout the world. The knowledge that he shares is often described as "mind-blowing" and "what I have been searching for my whole life".